For Reference

Not to be taken

from this library

A Dictionary of Music Titles

A Dictionary of Music Titles

The Origins of the Names and Titles of 3,500 Musical Compositions

by
ADRIAN ROOM

McFarland & Company, Inc., Publishers
Jefferson, North Carolina, and London

Library of Congress Cataloguing-in-Publication Data

Room, Adrian.
A dictionary of music titles : the origins of the names and titles of
3,500 musical compositions / by Adrian Room
p.   cm.
Includes bibliographical references and index.
ISBN 0-7864-0771-9 (illustrated case binding : 50# alkaline paper ∞
1. Titles of musical compositions — Dictionaries.   I. Title.
ML102.T58R66   2000
780'.3 — dc21   99-57638

British Library Cataloguing-in-Publication data are available

Manufactured in the United States of America

*McFarland & Company, Inc., Publishers
Box 611, Jefferson, North Carolina 28640
www.mcfarlandpub.com*

TABLE OF CONTENTS

v

— But my riddle! he said. What opera is like a railway line?
— Opera? Mr. O'Madden Burke's sphinx face reriddled. Lenehan announced gladly:
— *The Rose of Castille*. See the wheeze? Rows of cast steel. Gee!

(James Joyce, *Ulysses*, 1922)

INTRODUCTION

This new dictionary aims to give the origins of the names and nicknames of almost 3,500 musical works, ranging from the familiar to the less well known or even obscure. Here are:

- *symphonies* such as Beethoven's *Eroica*, Mozart's *Jupiter*, Haydn's *Surprise*, Schubert's *Unfinished*, Prokofiev's *Classical*, and Shostakovich's *Leningrad*;
- *operas* such as Rossini's *William Tell*, Bellini's *Norma*, Weber's *Der Freischütz*, Gounod's *Faust,* and Mozart's *Così fan tutte*;
- *oratorios* such as Haydn's *Creation*, Handel's *Messiah*, Elgar's *Dream of Gerontius*, and Walton's *Belshazzar's Feast*;
- *ballets* such as Delibes's *Coppélia*, Adam's *Giselle*, and Stravinsky's *Firebird*;
- *orchestral works* such as Bach's *Brandenburg Concertos*, Handel's *Water Music*, Schubert's *Rosamunde*, Wagner's *Siegfried Idyll*, Elgar's *Enigma Variations,* Holst's *Planets*, and Honegger's *Pacific 231*;
- *choral works*, both sacred and secular, such as Nielsen's *Hymnus Amoris*, Elgar's *Sea Pictures*, Britten's *Cantata Academica*, Bliss's *Morning Heroes* and Tippett's *Songs for Dov*;
- *chamber music* such as Haydn's *Russian* quartets, Beethoven's *Kreutzer* sonata, Dvořák's *Dumky* trio, Ives's *Concord* sonata, and Messiaen's *Quatuor pour la fin du temps*;
- *keyboard compositions*, mostly for piano or organ, such as Bach's *Wedge Fugue*, Scarlatti's *Cat's Fugue*, Bizet's *Jeux d'enfants*, Ravel's *Jeux d'eau*, Chopin's *Raindrop* prelude, Mendelssohn's *Songs without Words*, and Grainger's *Handel in the Strand*.
- *songs* such as Schubert's *Dichterliebe*, Fauré's *L'Horizon chimérique*, Mahler's *Des Knaben Wunderhorn*, and Poulenc's *Tel jour telle nuit.*

Symphonies are among the best known orchestral works, and their names and nicknames are familiar to many. A composer's symphonies, if greater than one, are usually known by their number, such as Beethoven's 5th, Mozart's 39th, or Schumann's 4th. But in many cases the names have effectively and in some cases more or less officially ousted the ordinal number. Of Beethoven's nine symphonies, three (the *Eroica, Pastoral,* and *Choral*) have gained regular names, while of Mozart's 41 symphonies, five (the *Paris, Haffner, Linz, Prague,* and *Jupiter*) are as equally familiar by names as by numbers (both serial and in the Köchel catalog). Haydn's huge output of 104 symphonies has acquired a correspondingly higher proportion of titles, at least two dozen in all, among them the *Philosopher, Schoolmaster, Hunt, Bear, Oxford, Surprise, Miracle, Military, Drumroll,* and *London.* Some of the more common titles are shared by more than one composer. Thus Beethoven, Vaughan Williams, and Alan Rawsthorne, to name just three, wrote a *Pastoral* symphony, although in each case the application of the title was different. Other composers, such as Brahms, wrote several symphonies without any attracting a title. Symphony titles are thus the general giants of the classical music scene.

Operas, par excellence, are musical works that always bear a title, even if, as with Lucianio Berio, it is only *Opera.* The names of operas are familiar to many who have little

1

idea of the plot. They are mostly in a foreign language, often Italian but also French or German, and their very multiplicity and similarity make for confusion. The operatic genius has thus given the world *Alcina* and *Alzira*, *Il Barbiere di Siviglia* and *Der Barbier von Bagdad*, *Cendrillon* and *La Cenerentola*, *Don Carlos*, *Don Giovanni*, *Don Pasquale* and *Don Quichotte*, *Ermione* and *Ernani*, *Iphigénie en Aulide* and *Iphigénie en Tauride*, *Julien* and *Julietta*, *Katerina Ismailova* and *Kátya Kabanová*, *Manon* and *Mignon* (and for good measure *Manon Lescaut*), *Nerone* and *Norma*, *I Pagliacci* and *I Puritani*, *Le Roi l'a dit* and *Le Roi malgré lui*, *Il Segreto di Susanna* and *Il Matrimonio Segreto*, *La Traviata* and *Il Trovatore*, *Thaïs* and *Tosca*, *Werther* and *Wozzeck*, *Zaïde* and *Zampa*. What is one to make of all this? Who are all these characters? Are they fictional or historical? There is also the matter of translation. Operas are still mostly known by their foreign titles. Yet these must mean something in English. So how is one to translate *La Traviata* or *Il Trovatore*, let alone *Così fan tutte*?

Although most of the operas mentioned above are indeed normally known by their foreign titles, some are still better known by their English names. We thus generally think of *The Barber of Seville* rather than *Il Barbiere di Siviglia*, of *The Marriage of Figaro* rather than *Le Nozze di Figaro*, of *The Merry Widow* rather than *Die Lustige Witwe*, of *The Thieving Magpie* rather than *La Gazza Ladra*, and even of *The Magic Flute* rather than *Die Zauberflöte*. And when it comes to languages other than the reasonably familiar French, German, Italian, and Spanish, we certainly go for English: *The Cunning Little Vixen* not Czech *Příhody lišky Bystroušky* (which is actually not quite the same), *Duke Bluebeard's Castle* not Hungarian *A kékszakállú Herceg Vára*, *The Stone Guest* not Russian *Kamennyy gost'*. Again, some operas have what seems to be a title in an inappropriate language. Donizetti's *La Favorite*, known in Italy as *La Favorita*, has a French title. But this is because it has a French text, as it was based on a French play. Further, it is a good example of a musical work that has been performed under different titles, among

them *Dalila*, *Leonora di Guzman*, and *Riccardo e Matilda*. And its original planned title was *L'Ange de Nisida*!

This gives some idea of the complexities involved. And although we have paused specifically on opera titles here, this is perhaps the place to state the general principle regarding foreign language titles in this book:

French, German, Italian, and Spanish titles are usually given in their language of origin. Other foreign language titles are given in English.

In cases where a work is known by both English and foreign language title, the English title cross-refers to the foreign language one. Thus *The Fair Maid of Perth* refers to *La Jolie Fille de Perth*, *The Land of Smiles* to *Das Land des Lächelns*, and *The Silken Ladder* to *La Scala di Seta*. There are exceptions, as ever, but this is the general principle. It should be noted that it is the first word after the definite article (*The, La, Das,* etc.) that is alphabetized, so *The Fair Maid of Perth* (entered under *F*) refers to *La Jolie Fille de Perth* (entered under *J*).

An opera title regularly known to English speakers by its foreign title can be translated in different ways. A notorious example is Mozart's *Così fan tutte*, rendered in Kennedy (see Select Bibliography, pages 291–292, for this and the following references) as "Women are all the same," in Warrack and West as "Women are like that," in Arnold as "Women are all like that," in Nicholas as "Thus do all women," and in Staines and Buckley as "Thus do they all." Generally speaking, French, German, Italian, and Spanish speakers retain the original name in each others' languages, like English-speakers, while others directly translate it. Russians, for instance, know this opera as *Vse oni takovy*. But even this, like the English, does not fully reflect the original Italian feminine plural *tutte*.

Many operas have well known *arias*, and these are entered either in their language of origin, in quotes, or by their English name, usually as a duet or song. Again, there will be cross-referrals, but often from the former type of name to the latter. An example is Desdemona's aria "*Salce, salce*" in Verdi's *Otello*, which is cross-referred to *Willow Song*. Similarly Butterfly's and Suzuki's duet *"Scuoti quella fronda di ciliego"* in Puccini's *Madama Butterfly* is referred to *Flower Duet* (2).

The other types of musical composition listed at the start of this Introduction are also involved in cross-linguistic problems of this kind, while some further complicate the issue by consisting of several individual parts or items that each have their own title (subtitle). This can of course happen with a symphony. The four movements of Beethoven's *Pastoral*, mentioned above, each have an independent title or "heading." On the other hand, the individual acts, parts, or scenes of classical operas are usually untitled individually. But the compositions most often found to contain multiple titles are song cycles and piano works consisting of several individual pieces. Examples of both kinds are furnished by Schumann, whose *Liederkreis*, for instance, consists of two sets of songs, the first of nine, the second of 12. Again, his *Kinderszenen* for piano contains 13 individually titled pieces, his *Albumblätter* has 20, and his *Album für die Jugend* boasts a generous 43! The 18 pieces that make up his *Davidsbündlertänze*, however, do not have separate titles.

In such cases, and for example for those just cited, this book aims to give all of the individual subtitles and headings together with their translations, though for practical reasons this is not always possible.

Ballets have their own titling characteristics. Those based on existing compositions tend to have titles of two kinds. They either have a completely different title or one that evokes or even duplicates that of the original work. Rudi van Dantzig's *Four Last Songs*, for instance, retains the (English) title of the Richard Strauss work to which it is danced. On the other hand Kenneth MacMillan's *Olympiad*, set to Stravinsky's *Symphony in Three Movements*, has a different title. But George Balanchine's ballet, set to the same work, is named identically to it. Entirely original ballets, of course, usually have entirely original titles.

The names accompanying the ballet titles just mentioned are those of the choreographers, not the composers. This is a common convention, and rightly so, as the choreographer is the author or composer of the dance, and the equivalent of the composer of a musical work. For sake of conformity in this book, however, the name against ballet titles is that of the music's composer, whether an original work or not. This works well with a completely new work, but may seem incongruous in some instances. Thus the ballet entitled *Schumann Concerto*, choreographed by Bronislava Nijinska and staged in 1951, is entered with the composer's name and that date, whereas the work on which it is based, Schumann's Piano Concerto in A minor, Op. 54, is actually dated 1845. This should not result in any ambiguity, however, as in such cases entries give information (titles, names, and dates) for both works.

So where do we go from here? How do musical works come by their titles?

In many cases they are given by the composer, as one might expect. This is certainly true of most modern works. But they may equally have been given by a publisher, with the aim of "accessing" the work to the public, who are more likely to buy a named work than simply a numbered one. The German-born pianist, composer, and publisher, Johann Baptist Cramer (1771-1858), is credited with naming Beethoven's *Emperor Concerto* and perhaps even Mozart's *Jupiter Symphony*, but if he did, the reason for giving the latter name is uncertain. Again, the work may be named for its dedicatee. This is the case with Beethoven's *Archduke Trio*, for example, or his *Waldstein Sonata*. The dedicatee may be a patron or a player. Mozart's clarinet quintet in A, K 581, was written for the clarinetist Anton Stadler and thus is known as the *Stadler Quintet*. Yet again, a work may bear a title relating to its place of composition or first performance. Mozart's *Linz Symphony* was both composed and first performed in that Austrian city. (It was actually written for Count Thun, so might have been called the *Thun Symphony*.) The same composer's *Paris Symphony* is also named for its city of performance, as were

Haydn's *Paris Symphonies*. A placename title may mislead, however. Haydn's *Oxford Symphony* was not written for that city but was first performed in 1791, when the composer was there to receive an honorary doctorate in music. Oxford was far from Haydn's mind when he composed the work in 1789.

This last title strictly belongs to another category of name: that given for a particular occasion. This is generally the case for the various works named for a coronation, such as Purcell's *Coronation Anthem*, Mozart's *Coronation Concerto* and Elgar's *Coronation Ode*. The particular occasion need not necessarily be auspicious, and indeed may have been unforeseen at the time of writing. Chopin's *Cat Waltz* and Scarlatti's *Cat's Fugue* are said to be so named because their respective pet cats jumped or ran on the keyboard as their masters were composing. The names are a reminder that many musical titles are in fact nicknames. They are also a reminder that titles may arise from a pleasant story rather than a solidly documented incident. Anecdotes about particular occasions or spoken comments have led to such titles as those of Haydn's *Razor Quartet* and Chopin's *Raindrop Prelude*. And some of the more colorful anecdotes result in serious misinformation. Handel's *Harmonious Blacksmith* may have existed, but he almost certainly did not give the title of the popular harpsichord piece named for him.

Chopin's *Raindrop Prelude* runs down to a further category, this time a very broad one. If the raindrops led Chopin to represent their sound in repeated notes, the result is in a loosely descriptive name or nickname, in this case one deriving from a single passage. Familiar examples of descriptive titles of this type are those of Haydn's symphonies such as the *Bear* (with its "growling" passage), the *Hen* (with its "clucking"), and famously the *Surprise* (with its sudden and unexpected loud chord). In the majority of such cases it is at best uncertain who originated the name, or even to what extent the composer authorized it. More direct are the titles of Haydn's *Drumroll* symphony and *Paukenmesse* ("Kettledrum Mass"), referring to the use or prominence of particular instruments. But a work called "Kettledrum Mass" is close to one called "Clarinet Concerto," which although strictly speaking a title, is hardly distinctive enough to be categorized as such. In fact the "cutoff point" between a title and a direct designation is hard to define. It is after all just one small step from a "Clarinet Concerto" to a "Concerto," which even though lacking the name of the instrument, is specific enough as a genre to be regarded as a "title."

As such, it appears in this book in its own right (albeit combined with a particular work so titled), as do some of the more familiar generic terms frequently found in music titles proper. Examples of others are *Adagio, Andante, Bagatelle, Barcarolle, Cantata, Intermezzo, Prelude, Rhapsody, Scherzo, Sonata*, and *Toccata*. Other general titles with their own entries are those found in religious works, and in particular the Roman *Mass*, such as *Agnus Dei, Benedictus, Credo, De Profundis, Dies Irae, Gloria, Kyrie, Requiem*, and *Sanctus*.

The Content of the Entries

Each entry consists of two paragraphs. The first paragraph contains the following items: (1) title, (2) in parentheses, translation of title or foreign-language version of title, in the latter case with name of language; (3) name of composer(s); and (4) date(s) of composition or first performance.

The second paragraph basically consists of two pieces of information, although these usually run together. First comes a factual description of the work, with opus number if appropriate and in the case of works by Bach, Mozart, and Schubert, the BWV (*Bach-Werke Verzeichnis*, "Index to Bach's Works"), K (*Köchel*), or D (*Deutsch*) number. (Bach's cantatas are usually known by standard number, not BWV.) Following this comes an account of the origin of the work's title(s), as far as it is known. There may be quotations. If from one of the sources in the Select Bibliography (page 291–292), these are referred to author(s) and page. (Authors of more than one source have the publication year added.) If from any other source, they are followed by author(s), source title, and publication year. Accounts themselves are discursive, not in abbreviated or journalistic form.

In the case of operas, the general aim is to give the number of acts, the name(s) of the librettist(s), and the source(s), if the work is not original. The setting is also often given. There then follows enough account of the story or plot to explain the title, which as seen from the examples above is often that of the central character. The account of the plot is deliberately incomplete in most cases, and frequently includes a formula such as "The story centers on…" or "The story tells what happens when…," if this suffices to explain the title. For example, the information given for Spohr's opera *Jessonda* sets the scene but only takes the story far enough to say who Jessonda is. If the opera is based on a secondary source, then the primary source on which the latter is based is usually given as well. Thus Richard Strauss's opera *Elektra* is based on a play by Hugo von Hoffmansthal (secondary source) that is itself based on Sophocles's tragedy of the same name (primary source).

Works with an exactly identical title are usually dealt with in the same entry, even if they are of different types. Thus Malcolm Arnold's ballet *Elektra* is dealt with in the same entry as that of the Strauss opera just mentioned. As it happens it is based on the same primary source, but it might not have been. Entries with more than one work treat their titles in chronological order. So here Strauss's opera (1909) comes before Arnold's ballet (1963).

Ballet entries in many ways resemble those for operas. As mentioned, the composer of the music is named following the title, as also, if apppropriate, is its arranger. The entry proper will then normally name the librettist(s) and the choreographer(s) but not the set or costume designer. If the ballet is set to an earlier musical work, that is also named. Thus Ernest Chausson's ballet *Le Jardin aux lilas* (1936), with a libretto and choreography by Antony Tudor, is set to Chausson's own *Poème* (1896) for violin and orchestra. The style for summarizing the plot (if it exists) is on similar lines to that used for elucidating an opera title. (Some ballets are plotless, so require different treatment.)

Opera aria entries differ slightly in that the composer is not named and the year of composition or first performance not given. This is because the work of origin is cited in the entry itself and the necessary information will be found there. The entry itself is also generally briefer, since the objective here is to place the aria within the opera (by act or part), identify its singer(s), and relate its subject to the words of the title. Thus the aria "*Tacea la notte placida*" ("The calm night was still"), from Verdi's *Il Trovatore*, is in Act 1, is sung by Leonora, and consists of her musings on the troubadour with whom she has fallen in love. This information should be enough to enable the reader to place the title words in their correct context, without any further spelling out.

Adrian Room
Fall 1999

MUSIC TITLES

A

The Abduction from the Seraglio *see* Die **Entführung aus dem Serail**.

Abegg Variations   Robert Schumann, 1830.

The theme of the composer's Op. 1 for piano solo consists of the notes A-B-E-G-G, where B is the German equivalent of English B flat. The work is dedicated to his friend, Meta Abegg of Mannheim, whom he said to have met at a masked ball. The full original French title was *Thème sur le nom Abegg, varié pour le pianoforte, dédié à Mademoiselle Pauline, Comtesse d'Abegg* ("Theme on the name Abegg, varied for the pianoforte, dedicated to Miss Pauline, Countess of Abegg"). The title "Countess" was a whimsy. (The composer enjoyed verbal quips, and it is tempting to see the *Abegg* of his Op. 1 as a pun on *ab ovo*, "from the egg." Could this particular "egg" have produced his **Papillons**?)

L'Abeille ("The Bee")   Franz Schubert, *c.* 1861.

The once popular "busy, buzzing trifle" (Scholes, p. 932), No. 9 of the set of 12 bagatelles for violin, Op. 13, has a title of obvious origin (in the German equivalent, *Die Biene*). The composer (1808–78) should not be mistaken for his greater earlier namesake (1797–1828).

Les Abencérages   Luigi Cherubini, 1813.

The opera in three acts is set to a libretto by Victor Joseph Étienne de Jouy based on Jean-Pierre Florian's novel *Gonzalve de Cordove* ("Gonzalo de Córdoba") (1791), about the famous Spanish soldier of this name (1453–1515), nicknamed *El Gran Capitán* ("The Great Captain"), who distinguished himself in the wars against the Moors. The Abencerages (Abencerrajes) were Moorish warriors, their name coming from their family head, Yusuf ben-Siradj.

The story concerns the victories and final defeat at Granada in 1492 of Almansor (al-Mansur), the last of the Abencerages. The opera's subtitle is *L'Étendard de Granade* ("The Standard of Granada").

Die Abenteuer des Casanova ("The Adventures of Casanova")   Volkmar Andreae, 1924.

The opera, set to a libretto by Ferdinand Lion, is based on the *Memoirs* (1791–8) of the Italian adventurer Giovanni Giacomo Casanova, Chevalier de Seingalt (1725–1798).

Abesalom and Eteri (Russian, *Abesalom i Eteri*)   Zakhary Paliashvili, 1910–17.

The opera in four acts is set to a libretto by P. Mirianashvili based on the Georgian epic *Eteriani*, telling what happens when Prince Abesalom (Absalom) and his vizir, Murman, are out hunting one day and meet the beautiful Eteri, a peasant's daughter.

Abraham and Isaac   (1) Benjamin Britten, 1952; (2) Igor Stravinsky, 1962–3.

Britten's *Canticle II* for alto, tenor, and piano, Op. 51, is based on a text from the Chester miracle play. Stravinsky's sacred ballad for baritone and chamber orchestra comes from a Hebrew text. Both works ultimately retell the Old Testament story of God's command to Abraham to sacrifice his son, Isaac (Genesis 22).

Abraxas   Werner Egk, 1948.

The ballet in five scenes, with a libretto by the composer and choreography by Marcel Luipart, is based on Heinrich Heine's poem *Der Doktor Faust* ("Dr. Faust") (1847) and depicts what happens when the ageing Faust signs a pact with the she-devil, Bellastriga, to grant him his youth. The title, as the name of a supreme deity in Gnosticism, comprises seven Greek letters whose numerical values total 365, the number of days in the year.

Die Abreise ("The Departure") Eugen d'Albert, 1898.

The comic opera in one act is set to a libretto by Ferdinand von Sporck based on August von Steigentesch's drama of the same name. The story tells what happens when Trott tries to persuade Gilfen to set out on a journey so he can make advances to Gilfen's neglected wife, Luise.

Abschied ("Farewell").

A piece that represents or commemorates a departure of some kind. *See* (1) **Farewell Symphony**; (2) Das **Lied von der Erde**.

Abschiedsymphonie *see* **Farewell Symphony**.

Abu Hassan Carl Maria von Weber, 1811.

The one-act opera to a libretto by Franz Carl Hiemer is based on the tale in the *Thousand and One Nights* (added by Antoine Galland to the original collection in 1712) in which Abu Hassan and his wife Fatima both fake death to escape their creditors.

The Abyss Marga Richter, 1965.

The ballet in one act, with choreography by Stuart Hodes, is based on Leonid Andreyev's story of the same name (1902). "Alone together in the sunlight of late afternoon, a very young couple become lost and encounter strangers. Then fear, violence, madness … the abyss" (program note, quoted in Koegler, p. 1).

Academic Festival Overture (German, *Akademische Festouvertüre*) Johannes Brahms, 1881.

The composer dedicated his Op. 80 to Breslau University, where it was first performed, as a somewhat tongue-in-cheek acknowledgment of the honorary degree of doctor of philosophy conferred on him in 1879. It includes four German student songs.

Accompaniment to a Film Scene (German, *Begleitungsmusik zu einer Lichtspielszene*) Arnold Schoenberg, 1930.

The orchestral work, Op. 34, was not written for an actual movie but as a programmatic piece illustrating a sequence of emotions: impending danger, fear, and catastrophe.

Accordion Quartet Pyotr Tchaikovsky, 1871.

The String Quartet No. 1 in D major, Op. 11, is sometimes so known, because of the accordion-like rise and fall of the opening chords.

The Accursed Hunter *see* Le **Chasseur maudit**.

"Ach, ich fühl's" ("Oh, I feel it").

Pamina's aria in Act 2 of Mozart's Die **Zauberflöte**, when she can get no answer from her beloved Tamino. A fuller form is "*Ach, ich fühl's, es ist verschwunden*" ("Oh, I feel it, it has vanished"). "It" is human constancy.

Acis and Galatea George Frideric Handel, 1718

The masque (serenata) in two acts is set to a text by John Gay with additions by Alexander Pope, John Dryden, and others based ultimately on Ovid's *Metamorphoses*, Book 13, 750–897 (1st century AD). The plot tells what happens when Galatea mourns the absence of her husband, Acis, and he returns followed by the giant, Polyphemus, who also loves Galatea.

The Acrobats *see* Les **Saltimbanques**.

Acrobats of God Carlos Surinach, 1960.

The ballet in one act, with choreography by Martha Graham, aims to show that the dancer's world, with its pains and joys, is akin to that experienced in a religious vocation, for "the early Church Fathers who subjected themselves to the discipline of the desert were *athletae Dei*, the athletes of God" (program note, quoted in Koegler, p. 2).

Actaeon Transformed into a Stag Karl Ditters von Dittersdorf, *c.* 1784.

The symphony in G is No. 3 in a set of 12 based on Ovid's *Metamorphoses*. The others have similar titles.

Actus Tragicus ("Tragic Act") J.S. Bach, 1707.

The church cantata *Gottes Zeit ist die allerbeste Zeit* ("God's time is the best time"), BMV 106, was written for a funeral. Hence the title.

Adagietto.

A short **Adagio** composition, often at a tempo slightly faster than *adagio* itself. An example is the *Adagietto* for strings and harp, as the 4th movement of Mahler's Symphony No. 5 in C sharp minor (1901–2).

Adagio ("At ease").

The term indicates a tempo not as slow as **Largo** but slower than **Andante**. The word is frequently combined with another Italian term, as Edward Elgar's *Adagio cantabile* for wind quintet (1879), puckishly subtitled *Mrs. Winslow's Soothing Syrup*. (This presumably comes from an advertisement the composer had seen on the back of some sheet music.)

Adagio for Strings   Samuel Barber, 1938.

The composer orchestrated the work, Op. 11, from the slow movement of his String Quartet, Op. 11 (1936).

Adagio Hammerklavier   Ludwig van Beethoven, 1973.

The ballet in one act, with choreography by Hans van Manen, is based on the adagio movement of the **Hammerklavier Sonata**, and specifically its interpretation in the recording by Christoph Eschenbach.

Adam Zero   Arthur Bliss, 1946.

The ballet allegory in one act, with a libretto by Michael Benthall and choreography by Robert Helpmann, depicts the creation of a ballet, itself a process symbolizing the human path of life. Adam was the first man, and his path of life began from zero.

"Addio del passato" ("Farewell to the past").

Violetta's aria in Act 3 of Verdi's La **Traviata** when, having read Germont's letter, she bids farewell to her happy past with Alfredo.

Adelaïde   Ludwig van Beethoven, 1795–6.

The song, Op. 46, for high voice and piano, was written to words from a poem published in 1787 by the German poet Friedrich von Matthisson.

Adélaïde   Maurice Ravel, 1912.

The ballet in one act, with a libretto by the composer and choreography by Ivan Clustine, has as its music the orchestral version of the **Valses nobles et sentimentales**. It is set in the 1820 drawing room of a courtesan who expresses her changing moods through various flowers. Hence the subtitle, *Le Langage des fleurs* ("The Language of Flowers").

Adélaïde Concerto   Marius Casadesus, 1931.

The Violin Concerto in D major, K. Anh. 294a, was long wrongly attributed to the ten-year-old Mozart, *i.e.* supposedly written in 1766, and is so named because it bore a dedication to Princess Adélaïde (1732–1800), third daughter of King Louix XV of France. It was first performed in 1931, with Casadesus as soloist, and in 1977, at the age of 85, he admitted he had written it.

Adelson e Salvini   Vicenzo Bellini, 1825.

The opera in three acts, to a libretto by Andrea Leone Tottola, is set in Naples and tells of the courtship of the beautiful Countess Fanny by Lord Adelson and the painter, Salvini.

"Adieu, notre petite table" ("Goodbye, our little table").

Manon's aria in Act 2 of Massenet's **Manon**, bidding farewell to the little table in the room she has shared with Des Grieux.

Les Adieux   Ludwig van Beethoven, 1809–10.

The Piano Sonata No. 26 in E flat, Op. 81a, was given its French title by the publisher. The full form is *Sonate caractéristique; les adieux, l'absence et le retour*, "Characteristic Sonata; The farewell, the absence, and the return." The composer, who called it *Das Lebewohl*, "The farewell," dedicated it to Archduke Rudolph of Austria (1788–1831) on his departure from Vienna for nine months. *See also* The **Archduke Trio**.

Admeto, Rè di Tessaglia ("Admetus, King of Thessaly")   George Frideric Handel, 1727.

The opera in three acts is set to a libretto probably by Nicola Francesco Haym adapted from Aurelio Aureli's Italian libretto *L'Antigone delusa da Alceste* ("Antigone Disappointed by Alceste"). The plot is the same as that for Gluck's **Alceste**.

Adriana Lecouvreur   Francesco Cilea, 1902.

The opera in four acts is set to a libretto by Arturo Colautti based on Eugène Scribe and Ernest Legouvé's play *Adrienne Lecouvreur* (1849), telling of the doomed love of the famous tragic actress, Adrienne Lecouvreur (1692–1730), for Maurice Saxe, count of Saxony (1696–1750).

The Adventures of Mr. Brouček *see* The **Excursions of Mr. Brouček**.

Aeneid (Russian, *Eneida*)   Nikolai Lysenko, 1910.

The opera in three acts is set to a libretto by Nikolai Sadovsky based on Ivan Kotlyarevsky's poem of the same name (1842), itself drawing on Virgil's epic poem (29–19 BC) telling of the journeyings of Aeneas after the fall of Troy.

Africa Fantasy   Camille Saint-Saëns, 1891.

The Fantasy for Piano and Orchestra, is so named because it was written in Cairo, Egypt, where the composer spent some time on his way home from Ceylon. The work aims to evoke the sound of native African music, and includes an imitation of tomtoms.

L'Africaine ("The African Woman") Giacomo Meyerbeer, 1864.

The opera in five acts, to a libretto by Eugène Scribe, tells how Vasco da Gama sails to find a new land beyond Africa but is wrecked on the African coast. He returns to Portugal with two captives, the man Nelusko and the woman Selika ("l'Africaine" of the title), with whom he has fallen in love.

African Sanctus David Fanshawe, 1972.

The work, for two sopranos, piano, organ, chorus, percussion, amplified lead and rhythm guitars, is in an African idiom and incorporates tape recordings made in Africa.

After Eden Lee Hoiby, 1966.

The ballet in one act, with choreography by John Butler, depicts a "paradise lost" situation, in which two people explore an emotional landscape of danger and desperation.

The Afternoon of a Faun (1) *see* **Prélude à l'après-midi d'un faune**; (2) Claude Debussy, 1953.

The ballet in one act is based on (1), and shows an encounter between two dancers practicing in a studio with the proscenium (the front part of the stage) as an imaginary mirror.

Agathe's Prayer *see* **"Leise, leise."**

The Age of Anxiety Leonard Bernstein, 1947.

The Symphony No. 2 for piano and orchestra takes its theme and title from W.H. Auden's long poem of the same name, subtitled *A Baroque Eclogue* (1947). This is set in wartime New York and is a reflection on the spiritual and psychological conditions of its time. A ballet of the same name based on the work, with a libretto and choreography by Jerome Robbins, was produced in 1950.

The Age of Gold *see* The **Golden Age**.

The Age of Steel *see* Le **Pas d'acier**.

Agitation *see* **Lieder ohne Worte**.

Aglaë ("Aglaia") Johann Friedrich Keller, 1841.

The ballet divertissement in one act, with a libretto and choreography by Filippo Taglioni, has solo roles for the nymph, Aglaia, a pupil of Cupid, for Cupid himself, for a faun, and for a young man.

Agnes von Hohenstaufen Gasparo Spontini, 1829.

The opera in three acts, to a libretto by Ernst Raupach, is set in Mainz, Germany, and tells of the love of Agnes, daughter of the Countess Ermengard, for Henry of Brunswick, son of the rebel Duke of Saxony, and describes the political intrigues by the Emperor Henry VI of Hohenstaufen and the French king (disguised as the Duke of Burgundy) to prevent the lovers from marrying.

Agnese de Fitz-Henry Ferdinando Paer, 1809.

The opera, set to a libretto by Luigi Buonavoglia, is based on Amelia Opie's novel *The Father and Daughter* (1801), telling how Agnes Fitzhenry leaves her loving father to elope with Captain Clifford, who rapes and abandons her, an outcome that drives her father insane.

Agnus Dei (Latin, "Lamb of God").

The last main section of the Roman Catholic **Mass**, found in many settings by different composers. The opening words are: *"Agnus Dei, qui tollis peccata mundi, miserere nobis"* ("Lamb of God, who takest away the sins of the world, have mercy on us").

Agon Igor Stravinsky, 1957.

The plotless ballet for 12 dancers, choreographed by George Balanchine, has a Greek title meaning "Contest," referring to the rivalry of the dancers.

Agrionia Leonard Salzedo, 1964.

The ballet in one act, with a libretto and choreography by Leonard Salzedo, is set in World War I and depicts the feast of Agrionia, an annual festival of Bacchus celebrated in classical times. A young man, as a modern Dionysius (or Bacchus), taunts three sisters and incites them to madness, in which state they enact the ritual murder of the eldest sister's son. The feast name itself derives from Greek *agrion*, "wild," "savage."

Agrippina George Frideric Handel, 1709.

The opera in three acts to a libretto by Vincenzo Grimani has as its subject the intrigues of the Roman empress Agrippina (AD 16–59) to ensure the succession of her son Nero.

Die Ägyptische Helena ("The Egyptian Helen") Richard Strauss, 1928.

The opera in two acts to a libretto by Hugo von Hofmannsthal centers on the plans of King Menelaus of Sparta to murder his wife Helen, who caused the Trojan War. She is given a potion to erase her memory of this and Menelaus is told that she had been asleep in Egypt at the time when he and his warriors were engaged in the war.

"Ah! Belinda" ("Oh, Belinda").

Dido's grief-laden aria in Act 1 of Purcell's **Dido and Aeneas**, in which she confesses her anguish over her love for Aeneas to Belinda, her lady-in-waiting.

"Ah! fors' è lui" ("Oh, perchance 'tis he").

Violetta's aria in Act 1 of Verdi's La Traviata, in which she asks herself if she is really falling in love. She rejects the idea in "**Sempre libera**."

"Ah, fuggi il traditor" ("Oh, flee the traitor").

Donna Elvira's aria in Act 1 of Mozart's **Don Giovanni**, in which she urges Zerlina to flee Giovanni's advances.

"Ah, fuyez, douce image" ("Oh, flee, sweet image").

The aria sung by Manon's lover, Des Grieux, in Act 3 of Massenet's **Manon**, when he tries to drive her image from his mind.

"Ah, non giunge" ("Oh, joins not").

Amina's aria in Act 2 of Bellini's La **Sonnambula**, in which she awakens and sees her beloved Elvino ready to marry her.

"Ah sì, ben mio" ("Oh yes, my dear").

Manrico's aria to his beloved Leonora in Act 3 of Verdi's Il **Trovatore**, in which he consoles her as they shelter in a fortress.

"Ah taci, ingiusto core" ("Oh be still, unjust heart").

The trio in Act 2 of Mozart's **Don Giovanni** in which Don Giovanni pretends to woo Donna Elvira, while the disguised Leporello mocks the situation.

"Ai nostri monti" ("To our mountains").

The duet for Manrico and Azucena in Act 4 of Verdi's Il **Trovatore**, in which they console each other with memories of their homeland.

Aida   Giuseppe Verdi, 1871.

The opera in four acts, to a libretto by Antonio Ghislanzoni after a French text by Camille du Locle (1868), and with a plot by August Ma-

riette Bey, is set in Egypt and tells of the love of Radamès, captain of the guard, for the slave girl Aida.

L'Aiglon ("The Eaglet")   Jacques Ibert and Arthur Honegger, 1937.

The opera in five acts (Ibert wrote the first and last, Honegger the middle three) is set to a libretto by Henri Cain based on Edmond Rostand's drama of the same name (1900), centering on the Duke of Reichstadt, Napoleon's son, Napoleon II (1811–1832), nicknamed "The Eaglet" by Bonapartists as the successor to the throne (although he never reigned).

Aimez-vous Bach? ("Do You Like Bach?")   J.S. Bach, 1962.

The ballet in one act, choreographed by Brian Macdonald, is performed to a selection of Bach compositions and opens with a ballet-master correcting a female dancer. The title clearly puns on that of François Sagan's novel *Aimez-vous Brahms?* (1959).

Ainsi la nuit ("Thus the Night")   Henri Dutilleux, 1971–6.

The title of the string quartet perfectly describes its poetic dreamlike atmosphere. It is divided into seven parts, each bearing its own title as follows: (1) *Nocturne*, (2) *Miroir d'espace* ("Mirror of Space"), (3) *Litanies*, (4) *Litanies 2*, (5) *Constellation*, (6) *Nocturne 2*, (7) *Temps suspendu* ("Time Suspended").

Air des bijoux *see* **Jewel Song**.

Air on the G String   J.S. Bach, 1871

The title is that of the German violinist August Wilhelmj's arrangement for violin and piano of the second movement (Air) of Bach's Orchestral Suite No. 3 in D. The melody is transposed down a tone so it can be played on the lowest string (G) of the violin.

Airborne Symphony   Marc Blitzstein, 1946.

The symphony for narrator, tenor and bass soloists, chorus, and orchestra is set to the composer's own text on the evolution of flying. Hence its title.

L'Ajo nell'imbarazzo ("The Embarrassed Tutor")   Gaetano Donizetti, 1824.

The comic opera in two acts is set to a libretto by Jacopo Ferretti based on Giovanni Giraud's comedy of the same name (1807). The story tells what happens when Don Giulio's old housekeeper, Leonarda, discovers Gilda, wife of

Don Giulio's son, Enrico, in the room of Don Gregorio, Enrico's tutor, and assumes her to be Don Gregorio's mistress.

Akhnaten Philip Glass, 1984.

The opera in three acts, set to a libretto by the composer together with Shalom Goldman, Robert Israel, and Richard Riddell, is based on the life of the "heretic" pharaoh, Akhnaten (died *c*.1358 BC). The plot tells how he abandons polygamy in favor of his wife, Nefertiti, and builds a city in honor of his new god, Aten.

Ala and Lolly *see* **Scythian Suite**.

Aladdin Henry Bishop, 1826.

The fairy opera in three acts is set to a libretto by George Soane based on the oriental tale *Aladdin and his Wonderful Lamp*.

Alamein Ian Parrott, 1944.

The symphonic poem depicts the Eighth Army's offensive at El Alamein, Egypt, in 1942. The composer served in North Africa as a Royal Signals officer in World War II.

Alassio *see* **In the South**.

Albert Herring Benjamin Britten, 1947.

The comic chamber opera in three acts, Op. 39, is set to a libretto by Eric Crozier adapted from Guy de Maupassant's short story *Le Rosier de Madame Husson* ("Madame Husson's Rose Tree") (1888). In its English setting, the plot tells how a Suffolk town comes to elect a May King (Albert Herring) when a suitable May Queen cannot be found.

Alborada del gracioso *see* **Miroirs**.

Album for the Young *see* **Album für die Jugend**.

Album für die Jugend ("Album for the Young") Robert Schumann, 1848.

The set of 43 piano pieces, Op. 68, was designed for children to play. Hence the general title. Book I, entitled *Für Kleinere* ("For Little Ones"), contains 18 pieces, as follows: (1) *Melodie* ("Melody"), (2) *Soldatenmarsch* ("Soldiers' March"), (3) *Trällerliedchen* ("Trilling Song"), (4) *Ein Choral* ("A Chorale"), (5) *Stückchen* ("Little Piece"), (6) *Armes Waisenkind* ("Poor Orphan"), (7) *Jägerliedchen* ("Hunting Song"), (8) *Wilder Reiter* ("Wild Horseman"), (9) *Volksliedchen* ("Folksong"), (10) *Fröhlicher Landmann* ("Merry Peasant"), (11) *Sicilianisch* ("Siciliana"), (12) *Knecht Ruprecht* ("Knight Rupert"), (13) *Mai, lieber Mai* ("May, Sweet May"), (14) *Kleine*

Studie ("Little Study"), (15) *Frühlingsgesang* ("Spring Song"), (16) *Erster Verlust* ("First Loss"), (17) *Kleiner Morgenwanderer* ("Little Morning Wanderer"), (18) *Schnitterliedchen* ("Reaping Song"). Book II, entitled *Für Erwachsene* ("For Grown-Ups"), contains 25 pieces, as follows: (19) *Kleine Romanze* ("Little Romance"), (20) *Ländliches Lied* ("Country Song"), (21) ***, (22) *Rundgesang* ("Round"), (23) *Reiterstück* ("Horseman's Piece"), (24) *Ernteliedchen* ("Harvest Song"), (25) *Nachklänge aus dem Teater* ("Echoes from the Theater"), (26) ***, (27) *Kanonisches Liedchen* ("Canon Song"), (28) *Erinnerung* ("Memory"), (29) *Fremder Mann* ("Foreigner"), (30) ***, (31) *Kriegslied* ("War Song"), (32) *Sheherazade* ("Scheherazade"), (33) *Weinlesezeit—Fröhliche Zeit!* ("Vintage Time, Merry Time!"), (34) *Thema* ("Theme"), (35) *Mignon* ("Mignon"), (36) *Lied italienischer Marinari* ("Song of the Italian Seamen"), (37) *Matrosenlied* ("Sailors' Song"), (38) *Winterszeit I* ("Wintertime I"), (39) *Winterszeit II* ("Wintertime II"), (40) *Kleine Fuge* ("Little Fugue"), (41) *Nordisches Lied* ("Nordic Song"), (42) *Figurierter Choral* ("Figured Chorale"), (43) *Sylvesterlied* ("New Year's Eve Song"). Piece No. 28 is subtitled *4. November 1847. Todestag Mendelssohns* ("November 4, 1847. Day of Mendelssohn's Death"). Piece No. 41 is subtitled *Gruss an G.* ("Greetings to G."), meaning the Danish composer Niels Gade. The letters of his name (G, A, D, E) serve as notes for the theme.

Album Leaves (Czech, *Listecky do památníku*) Bedřich Smetana, 1851.

The five brief untitled pieces for piano are typical of those that the composer wrote at various times for his friends or to commemorate royal weddings. Earlier examples are the *Six Album Leaves* (1849), Op. 2, also untitled, and the three *Album Leaves* (1849), Op. 3, individually titled as follows: *To Robert Schumann, Wayfarer's Song* (Czech, *Písen pocestného*), and *There is Boiling and Foaming* (German, *Es siedet und braust*). This last is a corruption of *Es wallet und siedet und brauset und zischt* ("There is seething and boiling and foaming and hissing"), from Friedrich Schiller's ballad *Der Taucher* ("The Diver") (1797), about a page who dives into a whirlpool to retrieve a golden goblet. *Cf.* **Albumblätter**.

Albumblätter ("Album Leaves") Robert Schumann, 1832–45.

The 20 pieces for piano, Op. 124, are short and intimate, such as might have been written in a young lady's autograph album. The individual titles are: (1) *Impromptu*, (2) *Leides Ahnung* ("Sorry Premonition"), (3) *Scherzino*, (4) *Walzer* ("Waltz"), (5) *Fantasietanz* ("Fantasy Dance"), (6) *Wiegenliedchen* ("Lullaby"), (7) *Ländler* (a country dance), (8) *Leid ohne Ende* ("Sorrow Unending"), (9) *Impromptu*, (10) *Walzer*, (11) *Romanze* ("Romance"), (12) *Burla* ("Jest"), (13) *Larghetto*, (14) *Vision*, (15) *Walzer*, (16) *Schlummerlied* ("Cradlesong"), (17) *Elfe* ("Elf"), (18) *Botschaft* ("Message"), (19) *Fantasiestück* ("Fantasy Piece"), (20) *Canon*. *Cf.* **Album Leaves, Bunte Blätter, Feuilles d'album.**

Alceste   Christoph Gluck, 1767.

The opera in three acts is set to a text by Lebland du Rollet based on an Italian libretto by Ranieri de' Calzabigi that was itself based on Euripides' drama *Alcestis* (438 BC), about the wife of Admetus, king of Pherae, whom Apollo permitted not to die if someone else would agree to take his place. (*Cf.* **Alcestis.**)

Alcestis   Vivian Fine, 1960.

The ballet in one act, with choreography by Martha Graham, has as its theme the journey of Alcestis into the underworld to save her husband, Admetus, king of Pherae. (*Cf.* **Alceste.**)

Alcide (Russian, *Alkid*, "Alcides")   Dmitri Bortnyansky, 1778.

The opera in three acts was set to a libretto by Pietro Metastasio originally intended for the German composer, Johann Adolf Hasse. Its full title is *Alcide al bivio* ("Alcides at the Crossroads"), and its story is based on an allegory by the 5th-century Greek writer, Prodicus, telling what happened when Alcides (otherwise Heracles or Hercules) met two women at a crossroads, representing respectively Vice and Virtue, and had to choose his life's path according to the way one or the other indicated.

Alcina   George Frideric Handel, 1735.

The opera in three acts is set to a libretto by Antonio Marchi based on Ludovico Ariosto's *Orlando Furioso* (1516), in which the sorceress Alcina captures Ruggiero and makes him fall in love with her. *Cf.* La **Liberazione di Ruggiero dall'Isola d'Alcina.**

Aldona *see* I **Lituani.**

Aleko   Sergey Rachmaninov, 1892.

The opera in one act is set to a libretto by Vladimir Nemirovich-Danchenko based on Alexander Pushkin's poem *The Gypsies* (1824), telling what happens when Aleko abandons his quiet life to join a band of gypsies. The ballet of the same name in one act (four scenes), with a libretto and choreography by Léonide Massine based on the same source but set to an orchestrated version of Tchaikovsky's Piano Trio in A minor, Op. 50, was produced in 1942.

Alessandro   George Frideric Handel, 1726.

The opera in three acts is set to a libretto by Paolo Rolli adapted from Ortensio Mauro's *La Superbia d'Alessandro* ("The Pride of Alexander"), telling of Alexander the Great, king of Macedon, and his second wife Roxana. It was revived as *Rossane, ossia Alessandro nell'Indie* ("Roxana, or Alexander in India") (1743). (*Cf.* **Alessandro nell'Indie.**)

Alessandro nell'Indie ("Alexander in India")   J.C. Bach, 1762.

The opera in three acts is set to a libretto by Pietro Metastasio and tells the story of Alexander the Great, king of Macedon, and his second wife Roxana, who after a succcession of victories was finally forced to turn back when attempting to conquer India. (*Cf.* **Alessandro.**)

Alessandro Stradella   Friedrich Flotow, 1844.

The opera in three acts is set to a libretto by W. Friedrich (pen name of Friedrich Wilhelm Riese) based on Philippe Pittaud de Forges and Pierre Duport's play *Stradella* (1837). It is set in Venice and Rome in about 1670 and tells of (supposed) episodes in the life of the Italian composer Alessandro Stradella (1644–1682).

Alexander Balus   George Frideric Handel, 1748

The oratorio, compiled to a biblical text by the Rev. Thomas Morell, centers on Alexander Balas (died 145 BC), king of Syria, who appointed Jonathan Maccabeus as governor of Palestine. His story is told in the Apocrypha, where he is called "Alexander, the son of Antiochus surnamed Epiphanes" (1 Maccabees 10:1).

Alexander Nevsky (Russian, *Aleksandr Nevskiy*)   Sergey Prokofiev, 1938–9.

The cantata, Op. 78, to a text by the composer and Vladimir Lugovskoy, derives its music from Prokofiev's score for Sergey Eisenstein's film of the same name (1938). This tells of the exploits of the Russian hero Alexander Nevsky (1220–1263), who defeated the Swedes on the banks of the Neva (hence his name) in 1240 and the Teutonic Knights in 1242.

Alexander's Feast   George Frideric Handel, 1736.

The secular cantata is a setting of John Dryden's poem *Alexander's Feast; or, The Power of Musique. An Ode in Honour of St. Cecilia's Day* (1697), with additions and changes by Newburgh Hamilton. *Cf.* **Ode for St. Cecilia's Day**. The poem itself is based on the feast held by Alexander the Great to celebrate his victory over the Persians, his bride (mistress) Thais at his side.

Alfonso und Estrella ("Alfonso and Estrella")   Franz Schubert, 1821–2.

The opera in three acts, D 732, is set to a libretto by Franz von Schober telling how Alfonso, son of Troila, king of Leon, meets and falls in love with Estrella, daughter of Mauregato, usurper of Troila's throne. *See also* **Rosamunde**.

Alfred   Thomas Arne, 1740.

The masque (opera), to a libretto by James Thomson and David Mallet, centers on the life of King Alfred the Great (849–899). The work contains the song **Rule, Britannia!**

Alice in Wonderland   Joseph Horovitz, 1953.

The ballet in two acts, with a libretto by the composer, is based on Lewis Carroll's children's classic of the same title (1865).

Alkestis ("Alcestis")   Rutland Boughton, 1922.

The opera is set to a libretto based on Gilbert Murray's translation (1914) of Euripides' tragedy. *See* **Alceste**.

Alkmene ("Alcmena")   Giselher Klebe, 1961.

The opera in three acts is set to the composer's own libretto based on Heinrich von Kleist's play of the same name, telling how Jupiter (Zeus) assumes the form of the Theban general, Amphitryon, in order to pursue his conquest of Alcmena, Amphitryon's wife.

Alla Breve Fugue   J.S. Bach, *c.* 1708.

The Fugue in D major for organ, BWV 589, has been so called because it is marked *alla breve pro organo pleno*, "*alla breve* for full organ," *alla breve* meaning that the half-note must be taken as the beat unit, so that the tempo is twice as fast as the note values suggest. "A foolish title, as many other fugues have an equal claim to it" (Scholes, p. 677).

Allegretto on GEDGE   Edward Elgar, 1885.

The allegretto for violin and piano is based on the musical notes G, E, D, G, and E and ded-icated to the Gedge sisters of Malvern Wells, Worcestershire, to whom the composer was tutor.

Allegro Barbaro   Béla Bartók, 1911.

The work for solo piano has a title, literally "Barborous Allegro," alluding to its grotesque (some at the time thought cacophonous) style and content. *Allegro* literally means "lively."

Allegro Brillante   Pyotr Tchaikovsky, 1956.

The plotless ballet in one act, choreographed by George Balanchine, is set to the composer's so called Piano Concerto No. 3 in E flat, Op. 75, in fact largely the work of Sergey Taneyev.

Alleluia Symphony (German, *Alleluiasymphonie*)   Joseph Haydn, 1765.

The Symphony No. 30 in C major is so named because part of an Easter plainsong Alleluia is quoted in the first movement.

Allumez les étoiles ("Light Up the Stars") various (see below), 1972.

The ballet in 13 scenes, with a libretto by Roland Petit and Jean Ristat and choreography by Petit, is set to a selection of music by Sergey Prokofiev, Dmitri Shostakovich, and Modest Mussorgsky, with the addition of Georgian folksongs. The ballet itself is based on the life of the Russian revolutionary poet, Vladimir Mayakovsky (1893–1930), with the title from his lines: "Listen!— they are lighting up/the stars;/it is because someone needs them" (1913).

Alma   G. Costa, 1842.

The ballet in four acts, with a libretto by André Jean-Jacques Deshayes and choreography by Fanncy Cerrito and Jules Joseph Perrot, tells of the marble statue of a beautiful young woman that is brought alive by the hellish spirit, Belfagor, and starts seducing different men. The subtitle is *La Fille de feu* ("The Daughter of Fire").

Alma Mater   Kay Swift and Morton Gould, 1935.

The ballet in one act, with a libretto by Edward M. Warburg and choreography by George Balanchine, is set at an American football stadium entrance and tells of the antics of football-crazy college boys and their girlfriends. For them, their "alma mater" is football, rather than their college.

Almast   Alexander Spendiarov, 1930.

The (unfinished) opera in four acts is set to

a libretto by S. Parnok based on Ovanes Tumanyan's poem *The Capture of Tmuk Castle* (1902). The story tells how Almast, wife of the Armenian prince, Tatul, treacherously opened the gates of her husband's castle to the Persian enemy.

Almira   George Frideric Handel, 1705.

The opera in three acts is set to a libretto by Friedrich Feustking based on an Italian libretto by Giulio Pancieri (1691) for Giuseppe Boniventi. The title names the central character, a queen of Castile, who undergoes a change of fortune.

Der Alpenkönig und der Menschenfeind ("The Alpine King and the Misanthrope")   Leo Blech, 1903.

The opera, set to a libretto by Richard Batka, is based on Ferdinand Raimund's play of the same name (1828), telling how the "Alpenkönig" Astralagus undertakes to cure the misanthropy of the recluse Rappelkopf.

Eine Alpensinfonie ("An Alpine Symphony")   Richard Strauss, 1913.

The orchestral work, Op. 64, is a tone poem describing a day (and night) in the mountains. It is scored for a very large orchestra and includes parts for wind and thunder machines.

An Alpine Symphony *see* Eine **Alpensinfonie**.

Also sprach Zarathustra ("Thus Spake Zarathustra")   Richard Strauss, 1896.

The tone poem, Op. 30, is based on Friedrich Nietzsche's philosophical poem of the same name (1883–5), in which he used the Iranian religious reformer Zarathustra (Zoroaster) as his mouthpiece to explain his idea of a superhuman being (*Übermensch*).

Altenberglieder ("Songs by Altenberg") Alban Berg, 1912.

The five songs for voice and orchestra, Op. 4, are set to messages that the eccentric poet Peter Altenberg wrote on picture postcards and sent to friends and foes alike. Hence the work's full title: *Fünf Orchesterlieder nach Ansichtskartentexten von Peter Altenberg* ("Five Orchestral Songs on Viewcard Texts by Peter Altenberg"). Some of the messages are erotic.

Altitudes   Jean Martinon, 1964–6.

The Symphony No. 4, Op. 53, was inspired by Alpine mountain climbing, and mountain heights play a major part in the work's melodic construction. The composer wrote on the flyleaf of the score: "For what do they reach, these climbers of mountains? Like the pioneers of Cosmos, they seek the presence of God, God!" (quoted in Berkowitz, p. 5).

Alto Rhapsody (German, *Rhapsodie aus Goethes Harzreise im Winter*, "Rhapsody from Goethe's *Winter Journey in the Harz Mountains*")   Johannes Brahms, 1869.

The rhapsody for contralto solo, male chorus, and orchestra, Op. 53, is known by this title in English. Its German title refers to the poem by Goethe (1777) from which its text is taken.

"L'Altra notte" ("The other night").

Margherita's aria in Act 3 of Boito's **Mefistofele**, sung as she lies in prison and described the drowning of her child.

Alzira   Giuseppe Verdi, 1845.

The opera in a prologue and two acts is set to a libretto by Salvatore Cammarano based on Voltaire's play *Alzire, ou Les Américains* ("Alzira, or The Americans") (1736). The plot is set in 16th-century Peru and tells what happens when the Inca chief, Zamoro, returns to his tribe to find that his beloved, Alzira, has been abducted by the Christian governor, Gusmano.

Amadis   Jean-Baptiste Lully, 1684.

The opera in a prologue and five acts is set to a libretto by Philippe Quinault based on García Ordóñez de Montalvo's chivalric romance *Amadís de Gaula* ("Amadis of Gaul") (1508), telling of the handsome and valiant knight of this name, his incredible feats of arms, and his love for Oriana, daughter of Lisuarte, king of England. The work was the first French opera to be based on a subject other than classical mythology.

Amahl and the Night Visitors   Gian-Carlo Menotti, 1951.

The opera in one act is set to the composer's own libretto, itself inspired by Hieronymus Bosch's painting *The Adoration of the Magi* (*c.* 1500). The story tells how the crippled boy, Amahl, is visited by the Magi (the "night visitors" of the title) on their way to the infant Jesus.

Les Amants magnifiques ("The Magnificent Lovers")   Jean-Baptiste Lully, 1670.

The comedy ballet, choreographed by Pierre Beauchamp, has a libretto by Molière written specifically for it. The story concerns two rival princes who, while celebrating the Pythian games, entertain a young princess and her mother with great gallantry.

Amasis   Philip Michael Faraday, 1906.

The comic opera in two acts, to a libretto by Frederic Fenn, tells what happens when the young and wealthy Prince Amhotep of Philae, about to marry Princess Amasis, daughter of Amasis IX, pharaoh of Egypt, confesses that he has killed one of the Sacred Cats.

The Amber Witch   Vincent Wallace, 1861.

The opera is set to a libretto by Henry Fothergill Chorley based on Lady Duff-Gordon's translation (1844) of Johannes Wilhelm Meinhold's novel *Maria Schweidler, die Bernsteinhexe* ("Maria Schweidler, the Amber Witch") (1838). This tells what happens when the virtuous Maria Schweidler repulses the improper advances of an elder of the village and is accused of witchcraft.

Amelia al ballo ("Amelia Goes to the Ball") Gian-Carlo Menotti, 1937.

The comic opera in one act, to the composer's own libretto, tells what happens when Amelia, leaving to attend a ball, is detained by an argument between her husband and her lover.

Amelia Goes to the Ball *see* **Amelia al ballo**.

America   Ernest Bloch, 1926.

The symphonic ("epic") rhapsody in three parts resulted from the first years of the composer's life in the United States (from 1916). It is a study of America's history, destiny, and ideals, and quotes Native American songs, popular songs of the Civil War, and Negro melodies. At its climax the audience is asked to rise and sing an "anthem" in praise of the United States.

America the Beautiful   Samuel Augustus Ward, 1913.

The patriotic American hymn, with words by Katharine Lee Bates (1895), is set to music taken from Ward's hymn *Materna* (1882). Bates wrote her poem while standing on Pikes Peak, Colorado.

The American Flag (Czech, *Americký prapor*)   Antonín Dvořák, 1892.

The cantata for alto, tenor, and bass solo, chorus, and orchestra, Op. 102, is set to Joseph R. Drake's patriotic poem of the same name (1819). It was first performed in New York in 1893.

An American in Paris   George Gershwin, 1928.

The orchestral tone poem is a musical depiction of the title. The score includes parts for four taxi horns.

American Quartet   Antonín Dvořák, 1893.

The String Quartet in F major, Op. 96, was written at Spillville, Iowa, and is so called because it was partly inspired by Negro melodies. Hence its former alternate names of *Negro Quartet* and (even) *Nigger Quartet*.

Amériques ("Americas")   Edgard Varèse, 1926.

The work for large orchestra is the composer's musical depiction of the Americas, "evoking not so much his new homeland as new worlds of the imagination" (Griffiths, p. 17). Hence its alternate title, *New Worlds*. The score includes parts for cyclone whistle, fire siren, and crowcall.

L'Amfiparnaso ("Amphiparnassus")   Orazio Vecchi, 1594.

The madrigal comedy in prologue and three acts, to the composer's own libretto (possibly in collaboration with Giulio Cesare Croce), has a plot containing various episodes relating to love. In Greek mythology, Mt. Parnassus was sacred to Apollo and the Muses and hence a source of inspiration for poets. Vecchi held the view that the Parnassus of music was surmounted by a twofold summit representing tragedy and comedy. Hence the title, which literally means "Around Parnassus."

L'Amico Fritz ("Friend Fritz")   Pietro Mascagni, 1891.

The opera in three acts is set to a libretto by P. Suardon (pen name of Nicola Daspuro) based on the novel *L'Ami Fritz* (1864) by Émile Erckmann and Alexandre Chatrian (writing jointly as Erckmann-Chatrian). The plot is set in Alsace in the 19th century and tells what happens when Fritz, a wealthy middle-aged landowner, bets that he will always remain a bachelor.

Amid Nature *see* **Nature, Life, and Love**.

Amor   Romualdo Marenco, 1886.

The ballet in two parts (16 scenes), with a libretto and choreography by Luigi Manzotti, presents a number of spectacular scenes based on major historical events, but starts in the realm of mythology with Chaos and finishes there with the Temple of Love.

El Amor brujo ("Love, the Magician") Manuel de Falla, 1915.

The ballet in one act to a libretto by Martinez Sierra is based on an Andalusian gypsy tale. The work contains the famous **Ritual Fire**

Dance. Spanish *brujo* means "wizard," so the title might be better rendered as "Wed by Witchcraft."

L'Amore dei tre rè ("The Love of the Three Kings")   Italo Montemezzi, 1913.

The opera in three acts is set to a libretto by Sem Benelli based on his own verse tragedy of the same name (1910). The plot is set in 10th-century Italy and tells how King Archibaldo, suspecting the infidelity of his daughter-in-law, Fiora, to his son, Manfredo, murders her and poisons her lips so that her lover, Avito, dies when giving her a farewell kiss. He does, but so does Manfredo when he kisses her similarly. The three men are the "three kings" of the title.

L'Amore Medico   Ermanno Wolf-Ferrari, 1913.

The comic opera in two acts is set to a libretto by Enrico Golisciani based on Molière's comedy *L'Amour médecin* ("Doctor Love") (1665). The story tells how Arnolfo forbids his lovesick daughter, Lucinda, to marry, but her secret lover, Clitandro, disguises himself as a doctor and prescribes a mock marriage as the cure for her condition.

Amoroso ("Loving," "Affectionate")

A piece or composition intended to be played tenderly. The 4th movement of Gustav Mahler's Symphony No. 7 in B minor (1904–5) is marked *Andante amoroso*.

"L'Amour est un oiseau rebelle" ("Love is a rebel bird").

Carmen's sultry **Habanera** in Act 1 of Bizet's **Carmen**, telling of the capricious and dangerous nature of love.

L'Amour et son amour ("Love and His Love")   César Franck, 1948.

The ballet in two scenes, with a libretto and choreography by Jean Babilée, is set to the composer's symphonic poem **Psyché** and tells the classical story of the encounter between Eros, the god of love, and Psyche, the personification of the soul.

Amours d'Antoine et de Cléopâtre ("The Loves of Antony and Cleopatra")   Rodolphe Kreutzer, 1808.

The ballet, choreographed by Jean-Pierre Aumer, is based on Shakespeare's tragedy *Antony and Cleopatra* (1606), telling of the doomed love of the Roman triumvir Mark Antony (Marcus Antonius) (82 or 81–30 BC) for Queen Cleopatra of Egypt (69–30 BC). *Cf.* **Antony and Cleopatra**.

Amphion   Arthur Honegger, 1931.

The opera in one act, to a libretto by Paul Valéry, tells what happens when Apollo gives his lyre to Amphion, a favorite of the gods, and the music that he plays is so powerful that stones form shapes of their own accord.

Amy Robsart   Isidore de Lara, 1893.

The opera is set to a libretto by Augustus Henry Glossop Harris based on Sir Walter Scott's novel *Kenilworth* (1821), which tells what happens to Amy Robsart, the honorable wife of the Earl of Leicester, when, as Queen Elizabeth's favorite, he keeps the marriage secret.

An den Baum Daphne ("To the Daphne Tree")   Richard Strauss, 1943.

The title was originally that of the epilogue to the opera **Daphne** for unaccompanied nine-part mixed choir, set to words by the opera's librettist, Josef Gregor. The composer later discarded the choral finale in favor of an orchestral transformation scene, but set the words as this motet.

An der schönen blauen Donau *see* The **Blue Danube**.

An die ferne Geliebte ("To the Far Beloved")   Ludwig van Beethoven, 1816.

The six songs, Op. 98, for voice and piano, are settings of poems by Alois Jeitteles. The cycle should not be confused with the composer's songs *An die fernen Geliebten* ("To the Far Beloved Ones") (1809) and *An die Geliebte* ("To the Beloved") (1811).

An die Musik ("To Music")   Franz Schubert, 1817.

The song, D 547, takes its words from a poem by Ritter Franz von Schober, itself derived from a stanza of *Die bezauberte Rose* ("The Enchanted Rose") by Ernst Schulze.

Anacréon   Luigi Cherubini, 1803.

The opera-ballet in two acts, subtitled *L'Amour fugitif* ("Fleeting Love"), is set to a libretto by R. Mendouze about the mythical Greek of the name and his love for Agathocle.

Anastasia   Pyotr Tchaikovsky and Bohuslav Martinů, 1971.

The ballet in three acts, with a libretto and choreography by Kenneth MacMillan, centers on Anastasia Romanova (1901–1918), youngest daughter of the last Russian czar, Nicholas II, and on the woman who believed she was Anastasia following the royal family's execution in

1918. The first act is set to Tchaikovsky's Symphony No. 1 in G minor, Op. 13 (1866), the second to his Symphony No. 3 in D, Op. 29 (1875), and the third to electronic music (by Fritz Winkel and Rüdiger Rüfer) and Martinů's **Fantaisies symphoniques**.

The Anatomy Lesson (Dutch, *De anatomische les*)   Marcel Landowski, 1964.

The ballet in one act, choreographed by Glen Tetley, is based on Rembrandt's painting *The Anatomy Lesson of Dr. Tulp* (1631) and is set to the composer's Symphony No. 1, *Jean de la Peur*.

Ancient Voices of Children   George Crumb, 1975.

The ballet in one act, choreographed by Christopher Bruce, is set to the composer's song cycle based on poems by Federico García Lorca. "The ragged children arise in winding sheets, which serve also as cloaks, playthings, or protective wrappers, and act out their games, their loves, and their fantasies against the harshness of poverty and neglect" (David Dougill, quoted in Koegler, p. 15).

And Daddy Was a Fireman   Herbert Haufrecht, 1943.

The ballet in one act, with a libretto and choreography by Charles Weidman, is a sequel to Weidman's autobiographical *On My Mother's Side*, and depicts the rise of Fireman Weidman from the ranks to captain of the fire department of the Panama Canal.

And Suddenly It's Evening   Elisabeth Lutyens, 1967.

The work for tenor solo and instrumental ensemble is a setting of four symbolist poems of the same title, *Ed è subito sera* (1942), by the Italian poet Salvatore Quasimodo.

Andante ("Going").

The term, often found in titles, is used for music that is flowing and at a slowish tempo (but not too slow).

Andante cantabile   Pyotr Tchaikovsky, 1871.

This standard musical term for a "singing" **Andante**, meaning one with a prominent melody, has come to be associated with the second movement (which is so marked) of the String Quartet No. 1 in D major, Op. 11. *See* **Accordion Quartet**.

Andante favori ("Favorite Andante")   Ludwig van Beethoven, 1804.

This was the publisher's title for the Andante in F for piano solo that was intended for the **Waldstein Sonata** but that was discarded and published separately (1806).

Andante spianato   Fryderyk Chopin, 1834.

The standard musical term, meaning "smoothed" (literally "planed") **Andante**, has come to serve as the title of the work (which is so marked) for piano and orchestra, Op. 22.

Andantino.

The word properly implies a tempo rather slower than **Andante**, but in modern usage it is usually taken to mean a little quicker. An example is Edwin Lemare's *Andantino* in D flat for organ (1888), subsequently adapted by Charles Neil Daniels and Ben Black into the popular song "Moonlight and Roses" (1925).

Andrea Chénier   Umberto Giordano, 1896.

The opera in four acts to a libretto by Luigi Illica is based on the life of the French revolutionary poet André Chénier (1762–1794).

Andromaque ("Andromache")   André Grétry, 1780.

The opera, to a libretto by Louis Guillaume Pitra, is based on Racine's tragedy of the same name (1667), in turn based on the Greek legend telling what happens when Pyrrhus takes captive Andromache, Hector's faithful widow, and disdains the Greek princess Hermione, whom he is engaged to marry.

Angara   Andrei Eshpai, 1976.

The ballet in two acts, with a libretto and choreography by Yuri Grigorovich, is based on Alexei Arbuzov's play *The Irkutsk Story* (1959), about young Soviet construction workers engaged on a project on the Angara River in Siberia.

Angel of Light   Einojuhani Rautavaara, 1994.

The Symphony No. 7 is one of several works inspired by a flight when the composer looked out of the airplane window and saw a cloud formation shaped like an angel. Two earlier compositions resulting from this were the overture *Angels and Visitations* (1978) and a double bass concerto, *Angel of Dusk* (1980). The symphony's title is the composer's own.

Angelina *see* La **Cenerentola**.

Angélique   Jacques Ibert, 1927.

The opera in one act, set to a libretto by

Nino (presumably a pseudonym), tells what happens when Boniface, the owner of a Paris china shop, is persuaded by an old friend that the only way to be rid of his shrewish wife, Angélique, is to put her up for sale.

Angelo (Russian, *Andzhelo*)   César Cui, 1876.

The opera in four acts is set to a libretto by Viktor Burenin based on Victor Hugo's novel *Angelo, tyran de Padoue* ("Angelo, Tyrant of Padua") (1835). The story is set in Padua in 1549 and tells what happens when Caterina, Angelo's wife, and Thisbe, his mistress, both really love Rodolfo, while Homodei, an Inquisition spy, also loves Caterina.

Angelus   Edward Naylor, 1909.

The opera takes its title from the prayer to the Virgin Mary offered at morning, noon, and evening at the sound of the Angelus bell, and so called because it begins with the Latin words *"Angelus Domini nuntiavit Mariae,"* "The angel of the Lord brought tidings to Mary."

Angiolina   Antonio Salieri, 1800.

The opera, subtitled *Il matrimonio per susurro* ("The Marriage by Noise"), is set to a libretto by Carlo Prospero Defranceschi based on Ben Jonson's comedy *Epicene, or the Silent Woman* (1616). This tells what happens when the egotistic old bachelor, Morose, pathologically averse to noise, plans to disinherit his mocking nephew by marrying, so long as he can find a silent woman. Angiolina is (or rather is not) that woman.

Aniara   Karl-Birger Blomdahl, 1959.

The opera in two acts is set to a libretto by Eric Lindegren based on Harry Martinson's 102-poem saga of the same name (1956). The story tells what happens when a spaceship carries refugees from Earth, devastated in a nuclear war, to a settlement on Mars.

Les Animaux modèles ("The Model Animals")   Francis Poulenc, 1942.

The ballet in one act (a prologue, six scenes, and an epilogue), with a libretto and choreography by Serge Lifar, is based on six of Jean de la Fontaine's *Fables* (1668–94): *L'Ours et les deux compagnons* ("The Bear and the Two Companions"), *La Cigale et la Fourmi* ("The Grasshopper and the Ant"), *Le Lion amoureux* ("The Amorous Lion"), *L'Homme entre deux âges et ses deux maîtresses* ("The Man Between Two Ages and His Two Mistresses"), *La Mort et le Bûcheron* ("Death and the Woodcutter"), and *Les deux coqs* ("The Two Cocks").

Anna Bolena   Gaetano Donizetti, 1830.

The opera in two acts is set to a libretto by Felice Romani based, with a number of liberties, on the life of Anne Boleyn (1507–1536), second wife of Henry VIII, who had her executed for adultery.

Anna Karenina   Rodion Shchedrin, 1972.

The ballet in three acts, with a libretto by Boris Lvov-Anokhin and choreography by Maya Plisetskaya, Natalia Ryzhenko, and Victor Smirnov-Golovanov, is based fairly closely on Lev Tolstoy's novel of the same name (1873–6), about the doomed love of Anna Karenina for the handsome young officer, Alexei Vronski, although the subplot concerning the happy marriage of Konstantin Levin and his young wife, Kitty, is omitted.

Anna Magdalena Books   J.S. Bach, 1722, 1725.

The two collections of keyboard music, comprising two volumes of the composer's **Klavierbüchlein**, were written for the instruction of his second wife, Anna Magdalena.

Annabel Lee   Byron Schiffman, 1951.

The ballet in one act, choreographed by George Skibine, was inspired by Edgar Allan Poe's poem of the same name (1849), about the loss of a loved and beautiful woman, and is really an extended pas de deux for Annabel Lee and her lover, the poem being sung by a tenor.

Années de pèlerinage ("Years of Pilgrimage")   Franz Liszt, 1848–77.

The three volumes of piano pieces are based on the composer's travel impressions. Book 1 (1848–54), on Swiss subjects, is a revised version of *Album d'un voyageur* ("A Traveler's Album") (1835–6). Book 2 (1837–49) is on Italian subjects, and Book 3 (1867–77) a posthumous collection. *See also* **Dante Sonata**.

Anon in Love   William Walton, 1959.

The six songs for tenor and guitar are settings of anonymous 16th- and 17th-century love poems. Hence the title.

Antar   Nikolay Rimsky-Korsakov, 1869.

The Symphony No. 2, Op. 9, is based on an oriental tale by the Russian writer Osip Senkovsky, of which the hero was Antar, a 6th-century black Arab desert poet and warrior. The work was described as Symphony No. 2 when it first appeared, and on its second revision in 1897 was stated to be a "symphonic suite." The titles of the four movements are respectively *Introduction*, *Joy of Revenge*, *Joy of Power*, and *Joy of Love*.

Antarctic Symphony *see* **Sinfonia Antartica**.

Antechrist Peter Maxwell Davies, 1967.
The work for chamber ensemble is a musical religious "portrait" of the title character.

Antigone (1) Tommaso Traetta, 1772; (2) Arthur Honegger, 1927; (3) Carl Orff, 1947–8.
Traetta's opera, to a libretto by Marco Coltellini, and Honegger's opera, to a libretto by Jean Cocteau, are based on Sophocles' tragedy of the same name (442 BC), telling how Antigone, daughter of Oedipus and Jocasta, defies King Creon's ban on the burial of her brother, Polynices, and is condemned to be buried alive. Orff's opera is set to Friedrich Hölderlin's free translation of the original (1804).

Antonia Jean Sibelius, 1949.
The ballet in one act, with a libretto and choreography by Walter Gore, tells the story of a man who discovers the infidelity of his beloved, Antonia, and of his revenge. The ballet is set to The **Bard**, the incidental music to The **Tempest** (5), and **Scènes historiques**.

Antony and Cleopatra Samuel Barber, 1966.
The opera in three acts is set to a libretto by the composer and Franco Zeffirelli based on Shakespeare's play of the same name (1606) telling how Marc Antony, Julius Caesar's adopted son, sacrifices his honor for his love of Cleopatra, queen of Egypt. *Cf.* Les **Amours d'Antoine et Cléopâtre**.

Anush Armen Tigranyan, 1912.
The opera in four acts is set to Ovanes Tumanyan's poem of the same name (1890) telling of the tragic love between the Armenian peasant girl, Anush, and the young Saro.

Anvil Chorus Giuseppe Verdi, 1853.
The chorus of gypsies in Act 2 of Il **Trovatore**, which they sing as they swing their hammers in time to the music while working at their forging.

Apocalyptic Symphony Anton Bruckner, 1884–7.
The Symphony No. 8 in C minor is so named from the title of of its last movement, *An Apocalyptic Vision of the Cosmos at the Last Day.*

Apollo et Hyacinthus ("Apollo and Hyacinthus") W.A. Mozart, 1767.
The opera in one act, K 38, is set to a Latin libretto by Rufinus Widl based on the story in Ovid's *Metamorphoses* (1st century AD) telling how Apollo slays the beautiful boy, Hyacinthus, and turns him into a flower. The work was originally designed as an intermezzo for Widl's drama *Clementia Croesi* ("The Mercy of Croesus").

Apollon musagète ("Apollo Musagetes") Igor Stravinsky, 1928.
The ballet in two scenes, choreographed by Adolph Bolm, has a title of Greek origin translating as "Apollo, Leader of the Muses." It depicts the birth of Apollo, his education through the muses Terpsichore, Calliope, and Polyhymnia, and his ascent of Mt. Parnassus.

The Apostles Edward Elgar, 1903.
The oratorio, Op. 49, for six soloists, chorus, and orchestra, is set to a biblical text compiled by the composer. It was Part I of a planned trilogy. Part II was The **Kingdom**, but Part III was never completed.

Appalachia Frederick Delius, 1902.
The work for baritone solo, chorus, and orchestra, subtitled *Variations on an Old Slave Song*, is a musical depiction of North America, from the former Native American name for the present southeastern United States (not the mountains). The "old slave song" that is the theme of the variations is a Negro folksong.

Appalachian Spring Aaron Copland, 1944
The ballet in one act, choreographed by Martha Graham, was based on a poem by Hart Crane. It has the Puritan ethos of the American pioneers as its theme and tells the story of a newly wed couple who set up home in the Appalachian Mountains.

Apparitions Franz Liszt and Gordon Jacob, 1936.
The ballet in five scenes, including a prologue and epilogue, with a libretto by Constant Lambert and choreography by Frederick Ashton, was inspired by Hector Berlioz's **Symphonie fantastique** and depicts a romantic poet in his search for love. The music comprises Jacob's orchestration of various piano pieces by Liszt.

Appassionata *see* **Lieder ohne Worte**.

Appassionata Sonata   Ludwig van Beethoven, 1805.

The Piano Sonata No. 23 in F minor, Op. 57, was given its Italian title, meaning "Passionate," by its publisher, Cranz, of Hamburg. "It is justified by the eminently tragic tone of the whole work. ... The very beginning of the Finale is in itself a final stroke of fate, after which there is not a moment's doubt that the tragic passion is rushing deathwards" (Donald F. Tovey, *A Companion to Beethoven's Pianoforte Sonatas*, 1935).

L'Apprenti sorcier ("The Sorcerer's Apprentice")   Paul Dukas, 1897.

The symphonic scherzo is based on a poem by Goethe (*Der Zauberlehrling*) which is itself based on a dialogue by Lucian (2d century AD). The story is of an apprentice sorcerer who tries one of his master's spells in his absence and is unable to undo it.

L'Après-midi d'un faune   (1) *see* **Prélude à l'après-midi d'un faune**; (2) Claude Debussy, 1912.

The ballet in one act, with a libretto and choreography by Vaslav Nijinsky, is set to the music of (1) and depicts a faun surprised by nymphs on their way to bathe and his amorous entanglement with one of them.

Aquarelles ("Watercolors")   Eric Fenby, 1938.

The work is an arrangement for strings of Frederick Delius's two wordless choruses *To Be Sung of a Summer Night on the Water* (1917). The title echoes the original, but additionally implies that the music has a delicate texture, like that of a watercolor.

Arab Dance *see* **Nutcracker**.

Arabella   Richard Strauss, 1933.

The opera in three acts is set to a libretto by Hugo von Hofmannsthal based on a combination of the latter's short story *Lucidor* (1909), a comedy of misunderstanding set in Vienna in 1860, and his play *Der Fiaker als Graf* ("The Cabby as Count") (1925). It tells of the efforts of the impoverished Count Waldner to make a good marriage for his daughter, Arabella.

Arabesque ("In the Arabian style").

The term for a florid detail in Arabian architecture was adopted for a similarly colorful musical piece. In some cases it is hardly appropriate, as for Robert Schumann's *Arabeske* in C

for piano, Op. 18 (1839) or Claude Debussy's two *Arabesques* for piano (1888–91).

The Arcadians   Lionel Monckton and Howard Talbot, 1909.

The operetta in three acts, to a libretto by Mark Ambient, A.M. Thompson, and Robert Courtneidge, tells what happens when the inhabitants of the paradisical land of Arcady beg Father Time to show them a land they have heard of, peopled by ugly monsters called the English who live crowded together in a place called London.

Arcana   Edgard Varèse, 1925–7.

The work for large orchestra, a powerful collision of sound blocks, is inscribed with an arcane quotation from the German alchemist Paracelsus (1493–1541). Hence the title.

Archduke Trio   Ludwig van Beethoven, 1811.

The trio in B flat, Op.97, for piano, violin, and cello, is so called because it is dedicated to Archduke Rudolph of Austria (1788–1831), one of the composer's piano pupils. *See also* Les **Adieux**.

The Archers   Benjamin Carr, 1796.

The opera in three acts is set to a libretto by William Dunlap based on the legend of William Tell, the Swiss hero and crossbowman who famously shot an apple from his son's head.

Arden muss sterben ("Arden Must Die") Alexander Goehr, 1966.

The opera in three acts is set to a German libretto by Erich Fried based on the anonymous English play *Arden of Feversham* (1592), attributed by some to Shakespeare, telling of the attempts of Mistress Arden and her lover, Mosbie, to murder her husband. This was itself based on a true incident. (Feversham is modern Faversham, Kent.)

Ariadne auf Naxos ("Ariadne on Naxos") Richard Strauss, 1912.

The opera in one act is set to a libretto by Hugo von Hofmannsthal based on Molière's comedy *Le Bourgeois Gentilhomme* ("The Would-Be Gentleman") (1670), for which the composer had written incidental music. The work has a scenic prelude in which a wealthy gentleman (the *bourgeois gentilhomme*) has hired for his guests a *commedia dell'arte* troupe and an opera company who must perform simultaneously because of time limitations. The opera, enlivened by comments from the comedians, is

Ariadne, based on the classical legend telling how King Minos's daughter is abandoned by Theseus on the island of Naxos and as she awaits death is consoled by Bacchus. *Cf.* **Bacchus et Ariane.**

Ariadne's Lament (Italian, *Lamento d'Arianna*)   Claudio Monteverdi, 1608.

The lament of Ariadne when she is abandoned by Theseus (*see* **Ariadne auf Naxos**), beginning "*Lasciatemi morire*" ("Let me die"). It is the only surviving section of the composer's opera *Arianna*. He later transformed it into a five-part madrigal (1610).

Ariane et Barbe-bleue ("Ariadne and Bluebeard")   Paul Dukas, 1907.

The fantasy opera in three acts is set to a libretto by Maurice Maeterlinck based on his own drama of the same name (1902) written with the composer in mind. The story tells what happens when Bluebeard gives his sixth wife, Ariadne, six silver keys and one of gold but forbids her to use them.

Arianna *see* **Ariadne's Lament.**

Arianna a Naxos ("Ariadne on Naxos") Joseph Haydn, 1790.

The dramatic cantata for soprano or mezzosoprano soloists and haprsichord or piano is based on the classical legend telling how Ariadne, daughter of King Minos of Crete, is abandoned by Theseus on the island of Naxos. *Cf.* **Ariadne auf Naxos.**

Ariettes oubliées ("Forgotten Ariettas") Claude Debussy, 1885–8.

The six songs for voice and piano are set to poems by Paul Verlaine, who used the title for six of the poems in his *Romances sans paroles* ("Songs Without Words") (1874), written in prison. The individual songs (poems) are *C'est l'extase* ("It is ecstasy"), *Il pleure dans mon cœur* ("Tears fall in my heart"), *L'ombre des arbres* ("The shade of the trees"), *Chevaux de bois* ("Merry-go-round"), *Green*, and *Spleen*. An arietta is a shorter and simpler aria ("air").

Ariodant ("Ariodante")   Étienne-Nicolas Méhul, 1799.

The opera in three acts is set to a libretto by François Benoît Hoffmann based on Canti V and VI of Ludovico Ariosto's poem *Orlando furioso* (1516). The plot turns on the attempts of Othon to compromise Ina so as to force her to abandon her lover, Ariodant, and marry him instead. *Cf.* **Ariodante.**

Ariodante   George Frideric Handel, 1735.

The opera in three acts is set to an Italian libretto anonymously adopted from Antonio Salvi's *Ginevra, principessa di Scozia* ("Guinevere, Princess of Scotland") (1701) itself based on Canti V and VI of Ludovico Ariosto's poem *Orlando furioso* (1516). The plot tells how Ariodante is betrothed to Ginevra, daughter of the king of Scotland, but has a rival in Polinesso, Duke of Albany. (*Cf.* **Ariodant.**)

Arlecchino ("Harlequin")   Ferruccio Busoni, 1917.

The opera in one act, to the composer's own libretto, is a "theatrical caprice" centering on the traditional *commedia dell'arte* figures, including the zany and fool, Arlecchino (Harlequin), and the artful and coquettish servant girl that he loves, Columbina.

L'Arlesiana ("The Girl from Arles") Francesco Cilea, 1897.

The opera in three (originally four) acts is set to a libretto by Leopoldo Marenco based on Alphonse Daudet's play of the same name (1872), in turn based on a story from his *Lettres de mon moulin* ("Letters from my Mill") (1866). This tells what happens when Federico is in love with a girl from Arles but discovers she is the mistress of Metifio, a mule driver. (*Cf.* L'**Arlésienne.**)

L'Arlésienne ("The Girl from Arles") Georges Bizet, 1872.

The orchestral work comprises incidental music for Alphonse Daudet's play of the same name (1872), in turn based on a story from his *Lettres de mon moulin* ("Letters From My Mill") (1866), which tells what happens when Frédéri, a young peasant lad, falls for a heartless girl from Arles. (*Cf.* L'**Arlesiana.**)

Der Arme Heinrich ("Poor Henry")   Hans Pfitzner, 1895.

The opera in three acts is set to a libretto by James Grun based on a medieval legend. The story tells what happens when Heinrich, a knight and singer struck sick as a punishment for his arrogance towards God, is told he will recover only if a virgin sacrifices herself for him.

Armida   (1) Joseph Haydn, 1784; (2) Gioacchino Rossini, 1817; (3) Antonín Dvořák, 1902–3.

Haydn's opera in three acts, to a libretto by Jacopo Durandi, Rossini's opera in three acts, to a libretto by Giovanni Schmidt, and Dvořák's opera in four acts, Op. 115, to a libretto by Jaroslav Vrchlicky, are all based on Torquato Tasso's epic poem *Gerusalemme liberata* ("Jerusalem Liberated") (1574). The story tells what happens when the sorceress, Armida, unable to win the heart of Rinaldo, spirits him away to an enchanted island. (*Cf.* **Armide.**)

Armide   Christoph Gluck, 1777.

The opera in five acts is set to a libretto by Philippe Quinault based on Torquato Tasso's epic poem *Gerusalemme liberata* ("Jerusalem Liberated") (1574). The story is set in the First Crusade (1099) and tells how Hidraot, king of Damascus, and the sorceress, Armide, plan to kill Renaud, general of the victorious crusaders, but Armide falls in love with him. (*Cf.* **Armida.**) *See also* **Rinaldo.**

The Armourer of Nantes   Michael Balfe, 1863.

The opera is set to a libretto by John Vipon Bridgeman based on Victor Hugo's novel *Marie Tudor* (1833), itself a fictional historical drama telling what happens when Mary Tudor's Italian lover, Fabio Fabiani, seduces Jane, adopted daughter of the craftsman Gilbert.

Aroldo ("Harold")   Giuseppe Verdi, 1857.

The opera in four acts, to a libretto by Francesco Maria Piave, is a revised version of **Stiffelio**, this time set in late 12th-century Britain. The plot tells what happens when the Saxon warrior, Aroldo, returns from the Crusades to find that his wife, Mina, has been seduced by the knight, Godvino.

Arpeggione Sonata   Franz Schubert, 1824.

The Sonata for Cello and Piano in A minor, D 821, was originally written for the arpeggione, a type of guitar-shaped cello with a fretted fingerboard, played with a bow. It is now normally played on the standard cello.

The Arrival of the Queen of Sheba
George Frideric Handel, 1749.

A section of the opera **Solomon** portraying the grand arrival of the Queen of Sheba at the court of King Solomon in Jerusalem (1 Kings 10:2; 2 Chronicles 9:1).

Arsenal   Georgy Mayboroda, 1960.

The opera in three acts, to a libretto by A.S. Levada and Andrei Malyshko, is based on a historical event, the combat between workers at the *Arsenal* factory, Kiev, and counterrevolutionaries.

Arshin mal alan   Uzeir Hadjibekov, 1913.

The comic opera in four acts, set to the composer's own libretto, tells what happens when the cunning Suleyman advises his friend, Asker, how to surmount the Azerbaijani tradition that a groom must not see his bride before marriage. He can do this by disguising himself as an *arshin-malchi*, or peddler, and so penetrate all women's quarters and tempt them with his trinkets.

The Art of Fugue *see* Die **Kunst der Fuge**.

The Art of Touching the Keyboard   Judith Weir, 1983.

The piano composition aims to exploit the instrument's many different capabilities. It takes its title from François Couperin's famous book, *L'Art de toucher le clavecin* ("The Art of Playing the Harpsichord") (1716), containing instructions for fingering, methods of touch, and the execution of *agréments* (ornamentation) in harpsichord playing.

"Art thou troubled?" *see* **"Dove sei."**

Artaxerxes   Thomas Arne, 1762.

The opera in three acts is set to a libretto based on the composer's own translation of Pietro Metastasio's *Artaserse* (1730), telling of the attempts of Artabanus to gain the throne. He first kills King Xerxes, then attempts to poison his son, Artaxerxes.

An Artist's Life *see* **Künstlerleben**.

As Time Goes By   Joseph Haydn, 1973.

The ballet in three parts, choreographed by Twyla Tharp, begins with a silent introductory solo but continues with the last two movements of the **Farewell Symphony**. The title is that of Herman Hupfeld's song (1931), with its lines: "You must remember this, / A kiss is still a kiss, / A sigh is just a sigh —/ The fundamental things apply, / As time goes by."

Ascanio in Alba   W.A. Mozart, 1771.

The opera in two acts, K 111, is set to a libretto by Giuseppe Parini and tells how Ascanius is promised the nymph Silvia by his grandmother, Venus. The setting is in Alba Longa, a city said to have been built by Ascanius.

L'Ascension ("The Ascension")   Olivier Messiaen, 1933.

The orchestral work in four movements is a glorification of the Ascension of Christ. The composer arranged the work for organ in 1934. The titles of the movements are as follows:

(1) *Majesté du Christ demandant sa gloire à son Père* ("Majesty of Christ Asking His Glory of His Father"), (2) *Alléluias sereins d'une âme qui désire le ciel* ("Serene Alleluias of a Soul that Desires Heaven"), (3) *Alléluia sur la trompette, alléluia sur la cymbale* ("Alleluia on the Trumpet, Alleluia on the Cymbal"), (4) *Prière du Christ montant vers son Père* ("Prayer of Christ Ascending to His Father"). These titles also apply to the organ version, except that of the third movement, which is *Transports de joie d'une âme devant la gloire du Christ* ("Transports of Joy of a Soul Before the Glory of Christ").

Aschenbrödel ("Cinderella")   Johann Strauss II, 1901.

The ballet in three acts, partly orchestrated by Josef Bayer, with various choreographers, retells the familiar fairy tale. *See also* **Cinderella**.

Asel   Vladimir Vlasov, 1967.

The ballet in three acts, with a libretto by Boris Khaliulov and Nikolai Kharitonov and choreography by Oleg Vinogradov, is based on Chingis Aitmatov's romantic novel *My Little Poplar in the Red Kerchief* (1961) (known in English as *To Have and to Lose*). The story tells how a truck driver returns to Asel, the woman he had left in pursuit of a new love, but finds her married to a veteran soldier.

Askold's Tomb   Aleksei Verstovsky, 1835.

The opera in four acts is set to a libretto by Mikhail Zagoskin based on his novel of the same name (1833). The story is set in Kiev in the 10th century and tells what happens when the warrior, Neizvestny ("Unknown"), aiming to overthrow Prince Svyatoslav Igorevich with the aid of the princely youth, Vseslav, tells the latter that he is the grandson of the legendary Kievan prince, Askold.

Aspen Serenade   Darius Milhaud, 1957.

The work for nine instruments, Op. 361, was written for the music center at Aspen, Colorado, where the composer taught each summer.

Asrael   Josef Suk, 1905–6.

The Symphony No. 2 in C minor, Op. 27, takes its name from Asrael, the Islamic angel of death. The work was the composer's tribute to Antonín Dvořák, his father-in-law, who died in 1904, and to his own wife, who died a year later.

L'Assassinio nella cattedrale ("Murder in the Cathedral")   Ildebrando Pizzetti, 1958.

The opera in two acts is set to the composer's own libretto based on Alberto Caselli's translation of T.S. Eliot's play *Murder in the Cathedral* (1935), telling of the murder in 1170 of Thomas à Becket, archbishop of Canterbury, in his own cathedral.

L'Assedio de Calais ("The Siege of Calais")   Gaetano Donizetti, 1836.

The opera in three acts, to a libretto by Salvatore Cammarano, is set in 1347 in and outside the besieged city of Calais and tells how Edward III of England negotiates with the mayor and burghers to gain win control of the strategically sited town and port.

Assemble All Ye Maidens   Gustav Holst, 1927.

The song for female voices and strings, No. 7 of the *Seven Partsongs*, Op. 44, is set to words from Robert Bridges' poem so titled.

Assembly Ball   Georges Bizet, 1946.

The ballet in one act (four movements), with a libretto and choreography by Andrée Howard, is based on the composer's Symphony in C major (1855) and deals generally with the encounters and flirtations of various people at a ball.

"Assisa al piè d'un salice" *see* **Willow Song**.

Le Astuzie femminili ("Feminine Wiles")   Domenico Cimarosa, 1794.

The comic opera in two acts is set to a libretto by Giovanni Palomba telling what happens when Bellina, Rome's wealthiest heiress, is supposed under the terms of her father's will to marry the elderly merchant, Giampolo, is loved by her tutor, Romualdo (who is engaged to her governess, Leonora), and herself loves Filandro.

At Midnight   Gustav Mahler, 1967.

The ballet in one act, choreographed by Eliot Feld, is based on the composer's song cycle *Lieder nach Rückert* (1901), set to poems by Friedrich Rückert, the last being *Am Mitternacht* ("At Midnight").

At the Boar's Head   Gustav Holst, 1925.

The opera in one act to the composer's own libretto tells the story of Falstaff and is based on Shakespeare's *King Henry IV*, Parts 1 and 2 (1597), in which the London tavern of the name features. Much of the material is based on English folksong.

At the Tabard Inn *see* The **Canterbury Pilgrims** (3).

Atalanta   George Frideric Handel, 1736.

The opera in three acts is set to an anonymous libretto based on Belisario Valeriani's play *La caccia in Etolia* ("The Hunt in Aetolia"). The story tells of the love of Atlanta, the virgin athlete and huntress, for Meleager, the hunter and warrior. *Cf.* **Atalanta in Calydon**.

Atalanta in Calydon   Granville Bantock, 1912.

The "choral symphony" for voices only is based on A.C. Swinburne's poetic drama of the same title (1865) telling the story of the hunting of the wild boar sent by Artemis to ravage Calydon. It is slain by Meleager, who presents the spoils to the virgin athlete and huntress, Atalanta. *Cf.* **Atalanta**.

Athalia   George Frideric Handel, 1733.

The secular oratorio is set to a libretto by Samuel Humphreys based on Jean-Baptiste's Racine's tragedy *Athalie* (1691), telling how Athalia, daughter of Ahab and Jezebel, usurps the throne and massacres members of the royal house of Judah only to meet her own death. (*Cf.* **Athalie**.)

Athalie ("Athalia")   Felix Mendelssohn, 1843.

The orchestral work comprises incidental music to Jean-Baptiste Racine's tragedy *Athalie* (1691) (*see* **Athalia**).

La Atlántida ("Atlantis")   Manuel de Falla, 1962.

The "scenic oratorio" in a prologue and three parts is set to the composer's own adaptation of Mosén Jacinto Verdaguer's epic poem of the same name (1877) about the legendary island of Atlantis in the Atlantic Ocean.

L'Atlantide ("Atlantis")   Henri Tomasi, 1954.

The opera in four acts is set to a libretto by François Didelot based on Pierre Benoit's novel of the same name (1919). The story tells what happens when Antinea, who rules the land of Atlantis, lures two officers of the French Foreign Legion to her domain.

Atmosphères ("Atmospheres")   György Ligeti, 1961.

The orchestral work comprises shifting masses of sound that evoke "atmospheres" of different kinds. Hence the title.

L'Attaque du moulin ("The Attack on the Mill")   Alfred Bruneau, 1893.

The opera in four acts is set to a libretto by Louis Gallet based on the story in Émile Zola's *Les Soirées de Médan* ("Evenings at Médan") (1880). The work is an antiwar protest, based on an incident in the Franco-Prussian War (1870–1). The story tells what happens when Germans attack the mill where the betrothal of the young Flemish peasant, Dominique, and the miller's daughter, Françoise, is being celebrated and condemn Dominique to be shot.

Attila   Giuseppe Verdi, 1846.

The opera in a prologue and three acts is set to a libretto by Temistocle Solera based on Zacharias Werner's play *Attila, König der Hunnen* ("Attila, King of the Huns") (1808), itself telling how Odabella pretends loyalty to Attila but plans to murder him with the help of her lover, Foresto.

Aubade   Francis Poulenc, 1929.

The ballet in one act, with a libretto by the composer and choreography by Bronislava Nijinska, depicts the encounter of the virgin huntress, Diana, and the hunter, Actaeon, and his metamorphosis into a stag that is torn to pieces by Diana's dogs. Actaeon had risen early to pursue his quarry. Hence the title, as a term for a song or music at dawn.

Aubade Héroïque ("Heroic Dawn")   Constant Lambert, 1942.

The orchestral work was inspired by the composer's witnessing a dawn invasion of The Hague by German parachutists in 1940.

Aucassin et Nicolette   André Grétry, 1779.

The opera, subtitled *Les Mœurs du bon vieux temps* ("The Customs of the Good Old Time"), is set to a libretto by Michel-Jean Sedaine based on the 13th-century anonymous French tale which tells what happens when the slave girl Nicolette, raised as the daughter of a Christian count, runs away with her lover Aucassin.

Auf dem Anstand *see* **Horn Signal Symphony**.

Auf einer Gondel ("On a Gondola")   Felix Mendelssohn, 1834–43.

The composer gave this title to three of his **Lieder ohne Worte** for piano solo: No. 6 (Op. 19) in G minor (Book 1, 1830), No. 12 (Op. 30) in F minor (Book 2, 1835), and No. 29 (Op. 62) in A minor (Book 5, 1844), each having the individual title *Venezianisches Gondellied* ("Venetian Gondola Song").

Aufforderung zum Tanz ("Invitation to the Dance")   Carl Maria von Weber, 1819.

The Rondo Brillant in D flat major, Op. 65, for piano represents a ballroom scene. The English title is sometimes wrongly given as *Invitation to the Waltz*, partly because the piece is in a waltz form, partly either through confusion between German *Tanz* and *Walzer* or because *Deutscher Tanz* ("German dance") generally denotes some type of waltz. *See also* Le **Spectre de la Rose**.

Aufstieg und Fall der Stadt Mahagonny ("Rise and Fall of the City of Mahagonny") Kurt Weill, 1930.

The opera in three acts to a libretto by Bertolt Brecht is an expansion of the composer's earlier *Mahagonny Singspiel* (1927). It tells how three escaped convicts establish Mahagonny as a city of material pleasure that ultimately meets its destruction.

Das Augenlicht ("Eyesight")   Anton von Webern, 1935.

The work, Op. 26, for mixed chorus and orchestra, is a setting of a poem by Hildegard Jone.

Aureole   George Frideric Handel, 1962.

The ballet in one act, choreographed by Paul Taylor, is set to various pieces by the composer and progresses as a series of dances. The title is the general term for a halo of light.

Aurora's Wedding, Pyotr Tchaikovsky, 1890.

The divertissement is from the last act of the ballet The **Sleeping Beauty**, centering on the marriage of Aurora, the Princess's daughter. It is also known by the French title *Le Mariage de la Belle au bois dormant* ("The Marriage of the Sleeping Beauty"), misleadingly suggesting a reference to the Princess's marriage to the Prince, not that of her daughter.

Aus den sieben Tagen ("From the Seven Days")   Karlheinz Stockhausen, 1968.

The 15 compositions for varying ensembles are "text pieces" with no musical notation that are to be performed subjectively according to the instructions supplied for each. Their individual titles are: (1) *Richtige Dauern* ("Right Durations"), (2) *Unbegrenzt* ("Unlimited"), (3) *Verbindung* ("Union"), (4) *Treffpunkt* ("Rendezvous"), (5) *Nachtmusik* ("Night Music"), (6) *Abwärts* ("Downwards"), (7) *Aufwärts* ("Upwards"), (8) *Oben und Unten* ("High and Low"), (9) *Intensität* ("Intensity"), (10) *Setz die Segel zur Sonne* ("Set Sail for the Sun"), (11) *Kommunion* ("Communion"), (12) *Litanei* ("Litany"), (13) *Es* ("It"), (14) *Goldstaub* ("Gold Dust"), (15) *Ankunft* ("Arrival"). The overall title, with its suggestion of the biblical creation of the world, refers to the period planned for the work, seven days of meditative withdrawal, although in actual fact the compositions took five days (May 7–11, 1968).

Aus Italien ("From Italy")   Richard Strauss, 1886

The symphonic fantasy, Op. 16, is based on the composer's impressions during his first visit to Italy. The four movements have individual titles as follows: *The Campagna, The Ruins of Rome, On the Shore of Sorrento, Neapolitan Folk Life*.

Aus meinem Leben *see* **From My Life**.

Autumn Leaves   Fryderyk Chopin, 1918.

The ballet in one act, with a libretto and choreography by Anna Pavlova, is set to various pieces by the composer and tells how a chrysanthemum, lovingly tended by a poet in his garden, perishes in the cruel north wind.

"Avant de quitter ces lieux" ("Before I leave these places").

Valentin's aria in Act 2 of Gounod's **Faust**, in which he calls on God to protect his sister, Marguerite, as he prepares to leave for the wars.

Ave Maria ("Hail Mary")   Charles Gounod, 1853.

The piece for piano, violin or cello, and organ or cello known by this name originated as the *Méditation sur le premier prélude de J.S. Bach* ("Meditation on the First Prelude by J.S. Bach"), that is, on the Prelude No. 1 in C major from Das **Wohltemperierte Klavier**, with counterpoint melody by the composer. In 1859 this was arranged as a solo song with full title *Ave Maria: Mélodie religieuse adaptée au premier prélude de J.S. Bach* ("Ave Maria: Religious Melody Adapted from the First Prelude by J.S. Bach").

Ave verum corpus ("Hail True Body") W.A. Mozart, 1791.

The motet in D major, K 618, takes its title from the opening words of the anonymous eucharistic hymn of the same name: *Ave verum corpus, natum de Maria vergine* ("Hail true body, born of the Virgin Mary"). It may have been first performed on the feast of Corpus Christi in the year of its composition.

Aventures ("Adventures")   György Ligeti, 1962.

The work for three singers and seven instruments consists of short wordless dramatic scenes assembled in strip-cartoon fashion, as if recounting various adventures. A subsequent work, *Nouvelles aventures* ("New Adventures) (1962–5), was added to this to form a theater piece.

The Aviary (Italian, *L'uccelliera*)   Luigi Boccherini, 1771.

The String Quintet in D major, Op. 11 No. 6 (Gérard 276), contains many imitation bird calls and was apparently so titled by the composer himself. "It is clear that the inspiration for these musical scenes, typical of the taste of the period for 'les bergeries' [pastorals], came to the composer from the collection of birds which was brought together and beautifully cared for in the aviaries of the Infante Don Luis and from the tapestries of the hunt which decorated the royal apartments of his master" (Yves Gérard, *Thematic, Bibliographical and Critical Catalogue of the Works of Luigi Boccherini*, 1969, quoted in Berkowitz, p. 184).

B

Baal Shem   Ernest Bloch, 1923.

The suite for violin and piano, subtitled *Three Pictures of Hasidic Life*, centers on Baal Shem Tov (Master of the Good Name), founder of the Jewish sect of Hasidism in the 18th century. The three individual movements have respective titles *Vidui* ("Contrition"), *Nigun* ("Improvisation"), and *Simchas Torah* ("Rejoicing of the Law").

Babi-Yar   Dmitry Shostakovich, 1962.

The Symphony No. 13 in B flat minor, Op. 113, for solo bass, male chorus, and orchestra, is a setting of the five poems of the same title by Yevgeny Yevtushenko (1962) attacking anti-semitism in both Russia and Nazi Germany. Babi-Yar, a ravine on the outskirts of Kiev in Ukraine, was the site of a mass grave of Russian Jews killed by the Germans in 1943.

Bacchus et Ariane ("Bacchus and Ariadne") Albert Roussel, 1930.

The ballet in two acts, with a libretto by Abel Hernant and choreography by Serge Lifar,

retells the story of Bacchus's enchantment of Ariadne when she is abandoned by Theseus on the island of Naxos, and the bestowing of immortality on her by Bacchus's kiss. *Cf.* **Ariadne auf Naxos**.

Bachianas Brasileiras ("Brazilian Bachianas"): Heitor Villa-Lobos, 1930–45.

The nine works, for various groups of instruments and voices, combine elements of Brazilian folk music with the contrapuntal technique of J.S. Bach. Hence their overall title.

Bagatelle (French, "Trifle").

The word is used as the title of a short, unpretentious composition, often for a solo instrument. Examples are Antonín Dvořák's *Bagatelles* for two violins, cello, and harmonium, Op. 47 (1878), and William Walton's *Five Bagatelles* for solo guitar (1970–1).

Le Baiser de la fée ("The Fairy's Kiss") Igor Stravinsky, 1928.

The ballet in four scenes, with a libretto by the composer and choreography by Bronislava Nijinska, is based on Hans Christian Andersen's fairy tale *The Ice Maiden* (1835). "A fairy marks a young man with a mysterious kiss while he is still a child. ... She withdraws him from life on the day of his greatest happiness In order to possess him and preserve this happiness for ever" (from the composer's note prefacing the published score, quoted in Koegler, p. 29).

Die Bakchantinnen ("The Bacchantes") Egon Wellesz, 1931.

The opera is set to the composer's own libretto based on Euripides' play *Bacchae* (*c.*408 BC), about the priestesses or female votaries of Bacchus.

Le Bal ("The Ball")   Vittorio Rieti, 1929.

The ballet in one act (two scenes), with a libretto by Boris Kochno and choreography by George Balanchine, depicts a masked ball at which a young officer courts a beautiful woman.

Le Bal des blanchisseuses ("The Laundresses' Ball") Vernon Duke, 1946.

The ballet in one act, with a libretto by Boris Kochno and choreography by Roland Petit, depicts an improvised ball, in which a handsome young apprentice flirts with a laundress and her workmates.

Balance à trois ("Balance of Three")   Jean-Michel Damase, 1955.

The ballet in one act, with a libretto by

Constantin Nepo and choreography by Jean Ba-bilée, is set in a gymnasium, with two athletes parading in front of a girl.

"Il Balen" ("The flash").

The Count di Luna's aria in Act 2 of Verdi's Il **Trovatore**, in which he sings of his love for Leonora. A fuller form of the title is: "*Il balen del suo sorriso*" ("The flash of her smile").

A Ball in Old Vienna (German, *Ein Ball in Alt-Wien*) Joseph Lanner, 1932.

The ballet in one act, choreographed by Kurt Jooss, is set to the composer's *Hofballtänze* ("Court Ball Dances") and depicts "the gay and gallant life of the 1840s ... to the entrancing rhythm of the waltz" (program note, quoted in Koegler, p. 43).

The Ballad of Baby Doe Douglas Moore, 1956.

The opera in two acts, to a libretto by John Latouche, is set in the Colorado gold rush and centers on the life of the historical Elizabeth "Baby" Doe Tabor (1854–1935), second wife of the prospector, Horace Tabor (1830–1899), who ended her life freezing to death in the shack at the mouth of the mine that she was convinced would still yield more silver.

Ballade (French, "Ballad").

The term was given by Chopin to a long, dramatic type of piano piece, as a musical equivalent of a poetical ballad of the heroic type. He himself used it as a title of several of his works, as did Brahms, Liszt, Grieg, Fauré and later composers. A familiar example is Grieg's *Ballade* in G minor for piano, Op. 24 (1875–6).

Ballet Imperial Pyotr Tchaikovsky, 1941.

The plotless ballet in three movements, choreographed by George Balanchine, is set to the composer's Piano Concerto No. 2 in G major, Op. 44 (1879–80), and is a tribute to the French dancer, Marius Petipa (1818–1910), and the St.Petersburg ballet of his time. The ballet is now often billed as simply *Tchaikovsky Piano Concerto No. 2*.

Ballet mécanique ("Mechanical Ballet"), George Antheil, 1923–4.

The "abstract" ballet, originally designed as film music, is scored for eight pianos, a pianola, eight xylophones, two doorbells, and the sound of an aircraft propeller. For the première in 1927 the composer doubled the pianos, added car horns and anvils, and used a real propeller. This last alone justifies the title.

Ballet School various (see below), 1961.

The ballet in one act, choreographed by Asaf Messerer, is set to music by Anatol Lyadov, Alexander Glazunov, Anton Rubinstein, Sergey Lyapunov, and Dmitry Shostakovich, but now staged to Shostakovich's music only, depicts a display of the classic Moscow school style, with numbers of increasing difficulty. The original French title was *Leçon de danse* ("Dancing Class"). An alternate English title is *School of Ballet*.

Ballo della Regina ("The Queen's Ball") Giuseppe Verdi, 1977.

The ballet in one act, choreographed by George Balanchine, is set to music from the composer's **Don Carlos** and develops in the form of a divertissement, such as might have been staged at a royal ball.

Ballo delle ingrate ("Ball of the Ungrateful Ladies") Claudio Monteverdi, 1608.

The ballet, with a text by the poet, Ottavio Rinuccini, and choreography by Isacchino l'Ebreo, was first produced on June 4, 1608 at the court of Mantua. It centers on a dance of prudes, procured by Pluto from Hades at the request of Venus and Cupid, to demonstrate the consequences to young ladies who have vowed to abstain from love.

Un Ballo in Maschera ("A Masked Ball") Giuseppe Verdi, 1859.

The opera in three acts is set to a libretto by Antonio Somma based on Eugène Scribe's libretto for Daniel Auber's *Gustave III, ou Le Bal Masqué* ("Gustavus III, or The Masked Ball") (1833). The story is set in Stockholm in 1792 and deals with the supposed events surrounding the assassination of Gustavus III of Sweden (1746–1792) at a masked ball.

Balustrade Igor Stravinsky, 1941.

The plotless ballet in four movements, choreographed by George Balanchine, is set to the composer's Violin Concerto (1931) and derives its name from Pavel Tchelitchev's décor.

Bamboula Samuel Coleridge-Taylor, 1911.

The rhapsodic dance for orchestra is a form of bamboula, a dance taking its own name from the primitive tambourine used to accompany it. The instrument was formerly popular among black communities in Louisiana and is still found in the West Indies. The composer was himself the son of a native of Sierra Leone and an Englishwoman.

Banalités ("Banalities")   Francis Poulenc, 1940.

The song cycle is based on five poems by Guillaume Apollinaire. The individual titles are *Chansons d'Orkenise* ("Songs of the Orkneys"), *Hôtel* ("Hotel"), *Fagnes de Wallonies* ("Marshes of Wallonia"), *Voyage à Paris* ("Journey to Paris"), and *Sanglots* ("Sobs").

Banjuta   Alfrēds Kalniņs, 1920.

The opera in four acts, to a libretto by A. Krumiņš, is set in the 11th century and tells what happens when Daumant, son of Prince Valgud-is and husband of Banjuta, rapes and ruins the beautiful Jargala and is killed in revenge by her brother.

Bánk bán ("Ban Bánk") Ferenc Erkel, 1861.

The opera in three acts is set to a libretto by Béni Egressy based on József Katona's historical tragedy of the same name (1814). The story is set in 13th-century Hungary and tells what happens when Otto, brother of Queen Gertrud, tries to seduce Melinda, wife of Bánk bán, count of Hungary. (A *ban* was the governor of a *banat*, a military district on the borders of the Hungarian kingdom. The story is set in the fortress of Visegrád, north of Budapest.)

Bar aux Folies-Bergère ("Bar at the Folies-Bergère")   Emmanuel Chabrier, 1934.

The ballet in one act, with a libretto and choreography by Ninette de Valois, is based on the composer's *Dix pièces pittoresques* ("Ten Picturesque Pieces") for piano (1880) and starts and finishes with a group representing Edouard Manet's painting of the title (1881). The characters, however, seem to have been inspired by Toulouse-Lautrec, since one dance is a solo for La Goulue, the Moulin Rouge dancer depicted in that artist's first poster (1891), while another is a cancan.

Barabau   Vittorio Rieti, 1925.

The ballet in one act, with a libretto by the composer and choreography by George Balanchine, is a burlesque based on an Italian nursery song. It tells how Barabau, a cunning peasant, feigns death in oder to dupe some pillaging soldiers.

Barbe-bleue ("Bluebeard")   Jacques Offenbach, 1866.

The operetta in three acts, to a libretto by Henri Meilhac and Ludovic Halévy, is set in 15th-century Brittany and tells what happens when Bluebeard, the powerful vassal of Bobèche, king of Brittany, awaits the arrival of a sixth wife, having disposed of the previous five.

The Barber of Seville *see* Il **Barbiere di Siviglia**.

Der Barbier von Bagdad ("The Barber of Baghdad")   Peter Cornelius, 1858.

The comedy opera in two acts is set to the composer's own libretto based on *The Tale of the Tailor* from the *Thousand and One Nights* (*Arabian Nights*). The plot concerns the efforts of Nureddin, abetted by the barber, Abdul Hassan Ali ebn Bekar, to contrive a meeting with the caliph's daughter, Margiana.

Il Barbiere di Siviglia ("The Barber of Seville")   Gioacchino Rossini, 1816.

The opera in two acts is set to a libretto by Cesare Sterbini based on Pierre Augustin Caron de Beaumarchais' comedy *Le Barbier de Séville* (1775). The scene is set in 18th-century Seville, Spain, and concerns the wily barber Figaro's plan to help Count Almaviva woo and win Rosina. The opera's original title was *Almaviva, ossia L'inutile precauzione* ("Almaviva, or The Vain Precaution"). The characters reappear in Le **Nozze di Figaro**.

Barcarolle (French, "Boatman's Song").

The word is of Italian origin and alludes to songs sung by Venetian gondoliers. It is used as a title for a boat song or any composition with a steady rhythm like that of a gondolier's song. Examples are Chopin's *Barcarolle* in F sharp major, Op. 60 (1845–6), and the many *Barcarolles* for piano by Fauré, beginning with No. 1 in A minor, Op. 26 (1882).

The Bard (Finnish, *Barden*)   Jean Sibelius, 1913.

The tone poem for orchestra, Op. 64, is a musical portrait of an idealized Scandinavian poet and musician.

The Bartered Bride (Czech, *Prodaná nevesta*)   Bedřich Smetana, 1866.

The opera in three acts, to a libretto by Karel Sabina, concerns the endeavors of the peasant girl, Mařenka, to wed the poor man she loves despite her parents' plans for her to wed a rich man through the services of a marriage broker. She is thus the "bartered bride" of the title, which in the original Czech actually means "The Sold Bride." The definition of "bride" has also caused some comment. "The current English title is inaccurate: the heroine is not a bride, only betrothed. No doubt it is due to a literal but inexact translation of the German *Verkaufte Braut*" (Blom, p. 40). However, English "bride" can mean a woman before her marriage as well as after, so there may be some hair-splitting here. The Czech title was chosen by the composer himself, taking hints from the poets A. Wehl, who proposed *The Bridegroom Gives Away His Bride*, and Jan Neruda, who suggested *Sold Love*.

Basler Concerto   Igor Stravinsky, 1946.

The Concerto in D major for Strings was formerly known by this name. It was commissioned for the 20th anniversary of the Basel Chamber Orchestra, Switzerland, where it was first performed on January 21, 1947.

La Basoche ("The Basoche")   André Charles Messager, 1890.

The operetta in three acts, to a libretto by Albert Carré, tells of a student elected "King of the Basoche" who is mistaken for Louis XII. (The Basoche was the students' guild. The word itself is related to *basilica*.)

The Bassarids   Hans Werner Henze, 1966.

The opera in one act is set to a libretto by W.H. Auden and Chester Kallman based on Euripides' *The Bacchae* (*c.* 405 BC). The story concerns the attempts of Pentheus, king of Thebes, to ban the worship of the god Dionysus. He is lured to a Bacchic orgy where he is torn to pieces by the followers of Dionysus, the bassarids (bacchanals) of the title. (They are said to be so called from their dress of fox skins, from Greek *bassara*, "fox.")

Bastien und Bastienne ("Bastien and Bastienne")   W.A. Mozart, 1768.

The opera in one act, K 50, is set to a libretto by Friedrich Wilhelm Weiskern and J.A. Schachtner based on Charles-Simon Favart's comedy *Les Amours de Bastien et Bastienne* ("The Loves of Bastien and Bastienne"), itself a parody of Le **Devin du village**. The shepherdess Bastienne, believing that Bastien no longer loves her, asks the soothsayer Colas to help win him back.

The Bat *see* Die **Fledermaus**.

La Battaglia di Legnano ("The Battle of Legnano")   Giuseppe Verdi, 1849.

The opera in four acts is set to a libretto by Salvatore Cammarano based on Joseph Méry's play *La Bataille de Toulouse* (1828). It recounts the defeat of the Emperor Frederick Barbarossa by the Lombard League at Legnano, northern Italy, in 1176.

The Battle of Prague   Franz Kotzwara, 1788.

The piano piece with optional violin, cello, and drums is a musical description of the Battle of Prague (1757) in the Seven Years' War, in which the Prussians under Frederick the Great defeated the Austrians under Charles of Lorraine, each side losing thousands.

Battle of the Huns *see* **Hunnenschlacht**.

Battle Symphony   Ludwig van Beethoven, 1813.

The orchestral work (not an actual symphony as such) is intended to represent the English defeat of Napoleon's troops at Vitoria, Spain, in 1812. Its German title is *Wellingtons Sieg, oder Die Schlacht bei Vittoria* ("Wellington's Victory, or the Battle of Vitoria"), with *Vittoria* the composer's error for *Vitoria*.

La Bayadère (Russian, *Bayaderka*)   Léon Minkus, 1877.

The ballet in four acts, with a libretto by Sergei Khudekov and Marius Petipa and choreography by the latter, is based on two classical Indian plays, Kalidasa's *The Ring of Sakuntala* (5th century) and Sudraka's attributed *The Little Cart of Clay* (before the 7th century). The plot tells of the tragic life and love of the bayadère (dancing girl), Nikia. *Cf.* Le **Dieu et la Bayadère**.

Beach   Jean Françaix, 1933.

The ballet in one act, with a libretto by René Kerdyck and choreography by Léonide Massine, is set at a fashionable seaside resort where the gods of the sea appear as human bathers.

The Bear   William Walton, 1967.

The comic opera in one act is set to a libretto by Paul Dehn based on Anton Pavlovich Chekhov's play (vaudeville) of the same name (1888). The story tells what happens when the widow, Madame Popova, and the boorish Smirnov (the "bear" of the title), a creditor of her late husband, quarrel violently and decide to fight a duel.

Bear Symphony   Joseph Haydn, 1786.

The Symphony No. 82 in C major, the first of the **Paris Symphonies**, is so called either because the theme of the finale suggests the performance of a bear leader or because of a "growling" theme in this movement. It is also known as *L'Ours*, its equivalent French title.

Les Béatitudes ("The Beatitudes")   César Franck, 1879.

The oratorio, for soloists, chorus, and orchestra, is set to a text based on the biblical Sermon on the Mount (Matthew 5–7), which contains the Beatitudes (blessings) of Jesus.

The Beatitudes   Arthur Bliss, 1962.

The cantata for soprano and tenor soloists, chorus, organ, and orchestra, is based on a biblical text (not the New Testament Beatitudes) interspersed with poems.

Beatrice Cenci   Berthold Goldschmidt, 1988.

The opera in three acts is set to a libretto by Martin Esslin based on P. B. Shelley's verse drama *The Cenci* (1819), telling what happens when Count Francesco Cenci, a 16th-century Roman nobleman, rapes his daughter, Beatrice, and is murdered by hired assassins on the orders of Beatrice and her mother.

Beatrice di Tenda   Vicenzo Bellini, 1833.

The opera in two acts is set to a libretto by Felice Romani based on Carlo Tebaldi Fores's novel of the same title. The melodramatic plot, set in Milan in 1418, tells what happens when Beatrice, married to Filippo Visconti, duke of Milan, loves another, as does the duke himself.

Béatrice et Bénédict ("Beatrice and Benedict")   Hector Berlioz, 1862.

The opera in two acts is set to the composer's own libretto based on Shakespeare's *Much Ado About Nothing* (1598), in which Benedick and Beatrice are the young lovers in the subplot.

Beatrix   Adolphe Adam and Joseph Horovitz, 1966.

The ballet in three acts, choreographed by Jack Carter, is based on, and adapted from, La **Jolie Fille de Gand**, in which the central character is Beatrix.

Beau Brummel   Edward Elgar, 1928.

The work consists of incidental music to Bertram P. Matthews's play of the same name, dealing with the English dandy so known, otherwise George Bryan Brummell (1778–1840).

Beau Danube ("Beautiful Danube")   Johann Strauss II, Joseph Strauss, and Eduard Strauss I, 1924.

The ballet in one act, with a libretto and choreography by Léonide Massine, is set in the Vienna Prater of the 1860s and tells how a handsome hussar, engaged to the elder daughter of a noble family, is surprised by the appearance of his former mistress. The original title was *Le beau Danube bleu* ("The Beautiful Blue Danube"). *Cf.* The **Blue Danube**.

Beauty and the Beast   (1) Maurice Ravel, 1949; (2) Thea Musgrave, 1968.

Both ballets are based on the familiar fairy story telling how Beauty saves the life of her father by consenting to live with the Beast, who turns out to be a handsome prince. Ravel's music provides a ballet in one act choreographed by John Cranko. Musgrave's gives a ballet in two acts with a libretto by Colin Graham and choreography by Peter Darrell.

The Beauty Stone   Arthur Sullivan, 1898.

The operetta in three acts, to a libretto by Arthur W. Pinero and K. Comyns Carr, is set in the 15th century and tells what happens when Laine, a weaver's lame and uncomely daughter, hears of the Beauty Stone, a small pebble which if laid bare on the breast will change the ugliest person into a miracle of beauty.

Beckus the Dandipratt   Malcolm Arnold, 1948.

The concert overture is a musical portrait of the named "dandipratt" (urchin).

The Bee's Wedding   Felix Mendelssohn, 1845.

The name came to be popularly applied to piano piece Op. 67 No. 4 in C major in Book 6 of the **Lieder ohne Worte**. The reference is to the fancied "buzzing" effect of the rapid and closely set notes of the accompaniment, which can also be taken as "weaving." It was the latter evocation that must have prompted the Hungarian pianist, Stephen Heller, to name it *Spinning Song* (German, *Spinnerlied*).

Before Moscow (Russian, *Pod Moskvoy*)   Dmitry Kabalevsky, 1942.

The large-scale opera, with a libretto by Solodar, is a patriotic work about the Red Army's defense of Moscow against the Germans. The original title was *In the Fire* (Russian, *V ogne*), but this was altered as now in 1947. The composer subsequently withdrew the work, using the music for his next opera, The **Taras Family**.

Before the Cloister Gate (Norwegian, *Foran sydens kloster*, "Before a Southern Convent")   Edvard Grieg, 1871.

The dramatic cantata for soprano and contralto soloist, women's chorus, and orchestra, Op. 20, is based on a episode in Bjørnsterne

Bjørnson's epic poem *Arnljot Gelline* (1870), based on Norse saga lore, and tells what happens when an unknown girl knocks on a convent door for sanctuary.

The Beggar's Opera   Johann Christoph Pepusch, 1728.

The ballad opera in three acts, set to a libretto by John Gay, is introduced by a beggar (in a spoken role) who finally intervenes to prevent an execution and bring about a happy ending. *See also* **Polly**.

"Bel raggio lusinghier" ("Beautiful enticing ray").

Semiramide's aria in Act 1 of Rossini's **Semiramide**, in which she rejoices that a ray of love will shine into her heart now that Arsace has returned.

Belfagor   Ottorino Respighi, 1923.

The opera in a prologue, two acts, and an epilogue is set to a libretto by Claudio Guastalla based on Ercole Luigi Morselli's comedy of the same name (1920). The story tells what happens when Candida, an apothecary's daughter, is coerced into marrying Ipsilonne, who is really a devil, Belfagor.

Belisario ("Belisarius")   Gaetano Donizetti, 1836.

The opera in three acts is set to a libretto by Salvatore Cammarano based on Jean-François Marmontel's novel *Bélisaire* (1767), about the Roman general, Belisarius (*c.* 505–565).

Bell Anthem   Henry Purcell, 1685.

The verse anthem *Rejoice in the Lord Alway* is so called from the pealing scale passages of the instrumental introduction. The name dates from the composer's lifetime.

Bell Quartet *see* **Fifths Quartet**.

Bell Rondo (Italian, *Rondo alla campanella*)   Niccolò Paganini, 1826.

The finale of the Violin Concerto No. 2 in B minor is so named for its bell-like effect. *See also* La **Campanella**.

Bell Song   Léo Delibes, 1883.

The aria *"Ou va la jeune Hindoue?"* ("Where goes the young Hindu girl?") sung by Lakmé in Act 2 of **Lakmé**, so called because of its bell effects. The "young Hindu girl" is the daughter of the Brahmin priest Nilakantha.

Bell Symphony *see* **Symphony with a Bell**.

"Bella figlia dell'amore" ("Beautiful daughter of love").

The quartet in Act 3 of Verdi's **Rigoletto**, in which the Duke woos Maddalena while Rigolleto consoles the anguished Gilda with a promise of retribution.

La Belle Dame Sans Merci ("The Beautiful Lady Without Pity")   Alexander Goehr, 1958.

The ballet in one act, with a libretto and choreography by Andrée Howard, is based on John Keats's poem of the same title (1819), telling of a knight held in thrall by a beautiful lady.

La Belle Hélène ("Fair Helen")   Jacques Offenbach, 1864.

The opera in three acts to a libretto by Henri Meilhac and Ludovic Halévy is a parody of the classical legend of Helen of Troy, famous for her beauty. *See also* **Helen of Troy**.

The Bells   (1) (Russian, *Kolokola*) Sergey Rachmaninov, 1910; (2) (French, *Les Cloches*) Darius Milhaud, 1946.

Rachmaninov's choral symphony, Op. 35, is set to a text by Konstantin Balmont adapted from Edgar Allen Poe's poem of the same title (1849), itself depicting the different ways in which the sounds of bells can influence moods. Milhaud's ballet, Op. 256, with a libretto and choreography by Ruth Page, is also based on Poe's poem.

The Bells of Zlonice (Czech, *Zlonické zvony*)   Antonín Dvořák, 1865.

The Symphony No. 1 in C minor bases one of its themes on the pealing of the church bells in the small Czech town of Zlonice, northwest of Prague, where the composer was living at the time of its writing.

Belmonte und Constanze ("Belmont and Constance")   Johann André, 1781.

The opera is set to a libretto by Christoph Friedrich Bretzner based on Isaac Bickerstaffe's play *The Captive* (1769). This same libretto served as the basis for Mozart's much better known opera Die **Entführung aus dem Serail**, which is also the subtitle of André's work.

Belshazzar   George Frideric Handel, 1745.

The dramatic oratorio in three parts is set to a biblical text by Charles Jennens that tells the story of Belshazzar's feast (*see* **Belshazzar's Feast**).

Belshazzar's Feast   William Walton, 1931.

The cantata for baritone, chorus, and orchestra is set to a biblical text by Osbert Sitwell based on the story of Belshazzar, the king of Babylon whose feast was interrupted by a finger writing a message on a wall that he took to mean he had been weighed in the balance and found wanting (Daniel 5, 7, 8).

Benedictus (Latin, "Blessed").

The part of the Roman Catholic **Mass** that completes the **Sanctus** section. In musical performance it is usually sung separately. It is quite short, and its full words are: "*Benedictus qui venit in nomine Domini*" ("Blessed is he that cometh in the name of the Lord").

Beni Mora   Gustav Holst, 1909–10.

The oriental suite in E minor for orchestra, Op.29, No. 1, was written after a visit by the composer to Algeria.

Benvenuto Cellini   Hector Berlioz, 1838.

The opera in two acts, to a libretto by Léon de Wailly and Auguste Barbier, is loosely based on events in the life of the Italian goldsmith Benvenuto Cellini (1500–1571).

Berceuse (French, "Lullaby").

The term is used for a lullaby or a composition that in some way suggests one. A familiar example is Chopin's *Berceuse* in D flat for piano, Op. 57 (1844).

Berceuse élégiaque ("Elegiac Lullaby") Ferruccio Busoni, 1909.

The piano piece was rewritten in a version for orchestra (1909), Op. 42, subtitled *The Man's Lullaby at His Mother's Coffin*. This explains the source of the original.

Berenice   George Frideric Handel, 1737.

The opera in three acts to a libretto by Antonio Salvi is based on events in the life of the legendary Egyptian queen, Berenice.

Die Bergknappen ("The Miners")   Ignaz Umlauff, 1778.

The opera in one act, to a libretto by Paul Weidmann, tells what happens when Fritz and Sophie are prevented from marrying by Sophie's guardian, Walcher, a miner, who wants to marry her himself.

Bergliot   Edvard Grieg, 1871.

The work for reciter and piano, Op. 42, is based on Bjørnsterne Bjørnson's dramatic poem of the same name (1870), itself drawn from Norse legend, and tells what happens when Bergliot's husband, a peasant-proprietor, is treacherously slain by Harald Hårdråde (Harold III) (1015–1066). An orchestral version was published in 1885.

Die Bernauerin ("Bernauer's Wife")   Carl Orff, 1944.

The opera in two acts, subtitled *Ein bayrisches Stück* ("A Bavarian Tale"), is set to the composer's own libretto (in Bavarian dialect) based on a 17th-century ballad telling of the destruction of a marriage (Bernauer's) by demonic forces.

"Bess, you is my woman now."

The love duet between Porgy and Bess in Act 2 of Gershwin's **Porgy and Bess**.

Le Bestiaire, ou Cortège d'Orphée ("The Bestiary, or Procession of Orpheus")   Francis Poulenc, 1919.

The six songs for voice and seven instruments or piano are set to the six poems of Guillaume Apollinaire's poetic fantasy of the same name (1911).

Der Besuch der alten Dame ("The Visit of the Old Lady")   Gottfried von Einem, 1971.

The opera in three acts is set to a libretto by Friedrich Dürrenmatt based on his play of the same name (1955). The plot tells what happens when the once poor Clara Wäscher, now one of the richest women in the world, returns as Claire Zachanassian to her hometown of Güllen.

Betrothal in a Monastery *see* The **Duenna** (2).

Der Bettelstudent ("The Beggar Student") Karl Millöcker, 1882.

The operetta in three acts is set to a libretto by F. Zell (pen name of Camillo Walzel) and Richard Genée based on Victorien Sardou's play *Les Noces de Fernand* ("The Marriage of Fernand"). The story is set in Kraków, Poland, in 1704 and tells how Laura is tricked into marrying Symon, a penniless student, thinking he is a prince and a millionaire.

Bhakti   Jonathan Harvey, 1982.

The orchestral work for 15 instruments and quadraphonic tape takes its title from the Sanskrit word (meaning "portion," "share") for a Hindu movement directing worship to one single deity, usually Vishnu or Shiva. Each of the work's 12 movements quotes from one of the ancient *Rig Veda* hymns.

Bianca de'Rossi   Vittorio Trento, 1797.

The opera in three acts is set to a libretto attributed to Mattia Botturini based on Pierantonio Meneghelli's tragedy of the same name (c.1788). The story tells of the love of Ezzelino da Romano (1194–1259), magistrate of Verona, for Bianca de'Rossi, wife of Battista dalla Porta. "The horrifying tale stands out for the inhuman cruelty of Ezzelino and the extraordinary bravery of the object of his irrational love, a woman who managed to dislodge the prop holding up the lid of her husband's tomb which fell on her and killed her" (Marita Petzoldt McClymonds, "*Bianca de'Rossi* as Play, Ballet, Opera: Contours of 'Modern' Historical Tragedy in the 1790s," Luis Gámez, ed., *A Subtler Music: Essays on the Drama and Opera of Enlightenment Europe*, 1997).

Bianca e Fernando ("Bianca and Fernando") Vicenzo Bellini, 1826.

The opera in two acts is set to a libretto by Domenico Gilardoni based on Carlo Roti's play *Bianca e Fernando alla tomba di Carlo IV, duca di Agrigento* ("Bianca and Fernando at the Grave of Charles IV, Duke of Agrigento") (1820). The story tells how Fernando, son of the usurped Duke of Agrigento, overcomes the usurper, Filippo, first by pretending to support him and then by rescuing his father and preventing the marriage of his sister, Bianca, to Filippo. The original version of the opera was produced under the title *Bianca e Gernando*, as the Naples censorship forbade references to the royal name Fernando. Ferdinand (Fernando) (1751–1825) was both King of Naples (as Ferdinand IV) and King of the Two Sicilies (as Ferdinand I) at the time of his death.

Biblical Songs (Czech, *Biblické písně*) Antonín Dvořák, 1894.

The work for voice and piano, Op. 99, comprises ten settings from the Psalms.

Les Biches ("The Hinds")   Francis Poulenc, 1923.

The ballet in one act, choreographed by Bronislava Nijinska, depicts a privileged house party in the south of France at which young people flirt with one another. The French title is better interpreted as "The Little Darlings."

Big Bertha   various (see below), 1971.

The ballet, choreographed by Paul Taylor, is set to music from the collection of band machines in the St. Louis Melody Museum. It depicts the gradual disintegration of a typical American middle class family, who visit a fair and become increasingly fascinated by Big Bertha, a huge animated doll atop a music box that plays sentimental marches and waltzes.

The Big City   Aleksander Tansman, 1932.

The ballet in three scenes, with a libretto and choreography by Kurt Jooss, centers on the life of a young woman and her lover in a continental city, and depicts what happens when one day she is followed to her home by a libertine.

Billy Budd   Benjamin Britten, 1951.

The opera in four acts is set to a libretto by E.M. Forster and Eric Crozier based on Hermann Melville's (unfinished) novel of the same name (1891). In this, Billy Budd is a young sailor who has been impressed into the navy and falsely accused of treachery.

Billy the Kid   Aaron Copland, 1938.

The ballet in one act, with a libretto by Lincoln Kirstein and choreography by Eugene Loring, tells the story of the Wild West gunman originally named William Bonney (1859–1881).

Bird Quartet   Joseph Haydn, 1781.

The String Quartet in C major, Op. 33 No. 39, one of the **Russian Quartets**, is so named because the composer seems to have based some of its material on bird calls.

The Birds (Italian, *Gli uccelli*)   Ottorino Respighi, 1927.

The suite for small orchestra is based on bird pieces for lute and harpsichord by 17th- and 18th-century composers such as Jean-Philippe Rameau and Bernardo Pasquini. Its movements are entitled: *Prelude, Dove, Hen, Nightingale*, and *Cuckoo*.

The Birth of Arthur   Rutland Boughton, 1908–16.

The "choral drama" is devoted to the Arthurian cycle, and is a work that the composer envisaged on a scale to match Das **Ring des Nibelungen**. It was originally called *Uther and Igraine*, for Uther Pendragon, King Arthur's father, and Igraine, his mother, but was changed as now when parts of the complete work were first performed in 1916.

A Birthday Offering   Alexander Glazunov arr. Robert Irving, 1956.

The ballet in one act was choreographed by Frederick Ashton as a grand divertissement for the seven ballerinas of the Sadler's Wells

Royal Ballet on the occasion of that company's 25th anniversary.

Bist du mei mir ("With Thee Beside Me") Gottfried Heinrich Stölzel, *c.* 1725.

The aria was long attributed to J.S. Bach and thought to come from the **Anna Magdalena Books**.

Black Key Etude   Fryderyk Chopin, 1833.

The Étude in G flat major, Op. 10 No. 5 for piano (1830), is so named because the right hand plays nothing but the black keys. The composer approved the name.

The Black Knight   Edward Elgar, 1893.

The symphony for chorus and orchestra, Op. 25, is a setting of H.W. Longfellow's translation in *Hyperion* (1839) of Ludwig Uhland's ballad *Der schwarze Ritter*, which tells what happens when the Black Knight rides into the lists at the king's "Feast of Gladness."

Black Mass Sonata   Alexander Skryabin, 1913.

The Sonata No. 9 in F major for Piano is said to be so named because its theme develops "evilly" and bears the notation: "A sweetness gradually becoming more and more caressing and poisonous" (Faubion Bowers, *Scriabin*, vol. II, p. 244, 1969). *Cf.* **White Mass Sonata**.

Black Pentecost   Peter Maxwell Davies, 1979.

The work for mezzosoprano, tenor, and orchestra, essentially a symphony in four movements with voices, takes its title from a line in George Mackay Brown's poem *Dark Angels*: "Now, cold angels, keep the valley from the bedlam and cinders of a Black Pentecost," and the text is from the Orkney writer's novel *Greenvoe* (1972), set on the imaginary island of Hellya as it is slowly destroyed by commercial exploitation. The inspiration for the work was the threat of uranium mining in Orkney.

B-la-F Quartet   Nikolay Rimsky-Korsakov, 1886.

The string quartet was composed for the 50th birthday of the Russian music publisher Mitrofan Belyayev (1836–1904) and its title puns on his name (in its French form Bélaïeff), spelling out the notes B flat, A, and F, on which it is constructed.

Die Blaue Mazur ("The Blue Mazurka") Franz Lehár, 1920.

The operetta in two acts (three scenes), to a libretto by Leo Stein and Béla Jenbach, is set in Vienna in 1920 and tells the story of a young couple, Count Julian Olinski, a Polish aristocrat, and Blanka von Lossin, an Austrian girl, who first met dancing the "Blue Mazurka," the traditional last dance at every ball in Poland and one that a Pole will reserve for the girl whose heart he seeks to win.

The Blessed Damozel (French, *La Damoiselle élue*)   Claude Debussy, 1887-8.

The cantata (*poème lyrique*) for soprano solo, women's choir, and orchestra is set to Gabriel Sarrazin's translation of Dante Gabriel Rossetti's poem of the same name (1850) about the "blessed damozel" who leans out of the ramparts of Heaven to watch the world below and the souls ascending to God and who prays for union with her earthly lover.

The Blessed Virgin's Expostulation Henry Purcell, 1693.

The song for soprano or treble is set to a text by Nahum Tate beginning, "Tell me some pitying angel." "Expostulation" here means "request."

Blest Pair of Sirens   Hubert Parry, 1887.

The cantata for chorus and orchestra is set to lines from John Milton's poem *At a Solemn Music* (1645), whose opening words are: "Blest pair of Sirens, pledges of Heav'n's joy." The "blest pair of sirens" themselves are "voice and verse" or, more crudely, words and music.

Blind Man's Buff   Peter Maxwell Davies, 1972.

The masque to the composer's own libretto, scored for soprano, mezzosoprano, mime, and orchestra, is based on nursery rhymes and Georg Büchner's satire *Leonce und Lena* (1836).

Blind-Sight   Bob Downes, 1969.

The ballet in one act, choreographed by Norman Morrice, portrays blind and sighted characters who represent the contrast between closed and open minds.

Blond Eckbert   Judith Weir, 1994.

The opera in two acts is set to a libretto by the composer based on Ludwig Tieck's tale *Der blonde Eckbert* (1797). It tells how Eckbert and Bertha, together in a childless marriage, are visited by an old friend, Philipp Walther, to whom Bertha recounts the strange tale of her life.

Blood on the Floor   Mark-Anthony Turnage, 1996.

The jazz-style work in seven movements takes its title from a painting by Francis Bacon and was written in response to the death of the composer's brother from a heroin overdose. The final movement is entitled *Dispelling the Fears* and ends on a lyrical note.

Blood Wedding   Denis ApIvor, 1953.

The ballet in one act, with a libretto by the composer and Alfred Rodrigues, and choreography by the latter, is based on Federico García Lorca's tragedy *Bodas de Sangre* ("Blood Wedding") (1933), telling how a bride, on the eve of her marriage to a man she does not love, escapes with her lover into the woods, where the two men kill each other.

Blossom Time   Franz Schubert arr. Sigmund Romberg, 1921.

The operetta in one act is set to a libretto by Dorothy Donnelly loosely based on Heinrich Berté's opera *Das Dreimäderlhaus* ("The House of Three Maidens") (1916). This made liberal use of Schubert's melodies and was set to a libretto by A.M. Willner and Heinz Reichert based on Rudolf Hans Bartsch's novel *Schwammerl* (1912), a sentimental life of Schubert. (Its own title, meaning "Fungus," was Schubert's nickname.) An English version was produced in 1922 under the title *Lilac Time*, with music arranged by George Clutsam and a libretto by Adrian Ross.

The Blue Bird   (1) Charles Villiers Stanford, 1911; (2) *see* L'**Oiseau bleu**.

The partsong for mixed chorus with soprano solo, Op. 119 No. 4, is a setting of the poem of the same name by Mary Coleridge (1861–1907).

The Blue Danube   Johann Strauss II, 1867.

The concert waltz, Op. 314, has the full German title *An der schönen, blauen Donau* ("By the Beautiful Blue Danube"), and is essentially a lyrical tribute to that river. The composer had no precise descriptive intention in bestowing the name.

Bluebeard   Jacques Offenbach and Antal Dorati, 1941.

The ballet in two prologues, four acts, and three interludes, with a libretto and choreography by Michel Fokine, is based on Offenbach's comic opera **Barbe-bleue** and tells how Count Bluebeard kills his wives one by one when, out of curiosity, they enter a forbidden room.

Blues Suite   traditional, 1958.

The ballet was created by Alvin Ailey to traditional blues melodies arranged and sung by Brother John Sellers, the individual solo and ensemble numbers expressing different "blue" emotions such as grief, despair, and anger.

Blumenstück   ("Flower Piece")   Robert Schumann, 1839.

The piece for piano solo, Op. 19, is simply a "musical flower," or delicately fashioned piece.

The Boatswain's Mate   Ethel Smyth, 1916.

The comic opera in one act is set to the composer's own libretto based on W.W. Jacobs' story *Captains All*. The story tells how Harry Benn, a former boatswain, devises a plan to persuade the landlady of "The Beehive" inn, Mrs. Waters, to marry him.

Boccaccio   Franz von Suppé, 1879.

The opera in three acts is set to a libretto by F. Zell (pen name of Camillo Walzel) and Richard Genée based on the life of the Italian poet, Giovanni Boccaccio (1313–1375).

Böcklin Suite   *see* Vier Tondichtungen nach A. Böcklin.

Le Bœuf sur le toit   ("The Ox on the Roof")   Darius Milhaud, 1919.

The pantomimic divertissement, Op. 58, with a libretto by Jean Cocteau, is set in an American bar during Prohibition. The characters include a black dwarf, a red-headed woman dressed as a man, a boxer, and a barman with a face like that of Antinous. The title comes from a Brazilian popular song, "*O boi no telhado.*" Originally planned to accompany a Charlie Chaplin movie, the work was given its definitive title when first staged in 1920.

Bogdan Khmelnitsky   Konstantin Dankevich, 1951.

The opera in four acts, to a libretto by Vanda Vasilevskaya and Alexander Korneychuk, centers on the Cossack leader, Bogdan Khmelnitsky (*c*.1595–1657), organizer of a rebellion against Polish rule in Ukraine.

La Bohème   ("Bohemian Life")   Giacomo Puccini, 1896.

The opera in four acts is set to a libretto by Luigi Illica and Giuseppe Giacosa based on Henri Murger's novel *Scènes de la vie de Bohème* ("Scenes from Bohemian Life") (1847–9). The story is of four Bohemians sharing a Paris attic, one of whom falls in love with their neighbor, Mimi. The French title is sometimes translated in English as "The Bohemian Girl," as if referring to the opera's heroine, Mimi. This may have come about through titles such as L'**Arlésienne** or La **Navarraise**, or even by confusion with Balfe's The **Bohemian Girl**. Technically, *La Bohème* can mean either, so long as one appreciates that "Bohemia" here relates not to the nationality but to the colorful life led by artists, poets, and musicians in the Latin Quarter of Paris in the 1830s. A girl from Bohemia would be thus be *une Bohémienne* (and a gypsy girl, by extension, *une bohémienne*).

The Bohemian Girl   Michael Balfe, 1843.

The opera in three acts is set to a libretto by Alfred Bunn based on Jules-Henri Vernoy de Saint-Georges' ballet-pantomime *La Gipsy* (1839), itself based on Miguel Cervantes' *La Gitanilla* ("The Gypsy Girl") (1613). The story is set in 19th-century Hungary and tells of the love of the Polish refugee, Thaddeus, for Arline (the "Bohemian girl" of the title), who was kidnapped and raised by gypsies. *Cf.* **Preciosa**.

"Bois épais" ("Thick woods").

The aria of Amadis in Act 2 of Lully's **Amadis**, in which he declares that the somber woods can never be as dark as his despair, for he will never again see his beloved Oriane.

La Boîte à joujoux ("The Box of Toys") Claude Debussy, 1913.

The children's ballet in four scenes for piano, with a libretto and choreography by André Hellé, tells of a *ménage à trois* among the dolls in a toybox.

Boléro ("Bolero")   Maurice Ravel, 1928.

The one-act ballet, choreographed by Bronislava Nijinska, has the bolero for its music, as a lively Spanish dance with a castanet accompaniment and a distinctive repetitive rhythm. (The word may come from Spanish *bola*, "ball," in allusion to the dancer's whirling motion.) It was originally set in a Spanish tavern, where a gypsy dancing on a table gradually induced the onlookers into a state of ecstasy. But is the ballet title appropriate? "It is a bolero only in name. This was used simply as the title to the ballet. It is too slow in pace and the rhythm is all wrong. A bolero is exceedingly gay and dashing" (Norman Demuth, *Ravel*, 1947).

Bolivar   Darius Milhaud, 1943.

The opera in three acts, Op. 236, to a libretto by the composer's wife, Madeleine Milhaud, and Jules Supervielle, deals with events in the life of the South American liberator, Simón

Bolívar (1783–1830) (who gave the name of Bolivia).

The Bolt (Russian, *Bolt*)   Dmitry Shostakovich, 1930.

The choreographic spectacle (ballet) in three acts, with a libretto by Vladimir Smirnov and choreography by Fyodor Lopokov, was the Soviet Union's first industrial ballet. The story tells what happens when drunken petty bourgeois attempt to sabotage the socialist process by putting a bolt in a machine as a "spanner in the works" exercise.

Bomarzo   Alberto Ginastera, 1967.

The opera in two acts, a "gothic melodrama of sex and violence," is set to a libretto by Manuel Mujica Láinez based on his own novel of the same name (1962). The story is set in 16th-century Italy and tells what happens when an astrologer gives Pier Francesco Orsini, duke of Bomarzo, a potion that is meant to make him immortal.

Bonduca   Henry Purcell, 1695.

The work comprises incidental music to a play adapted from Francis Beaumont and John Fletcher's play *Boadicea* (1611) about the 1st-century AD queen of the Iceni (native Britons) of this name (otherwise Boudicca). The subtitle is *The British Heroine*.

Bonne-Bouche ("Tidbit")   Arthur Oldham, 1952.

The ballet in three scenes, with a libretto and choreography by John Cranko, is set in Edwardian times in fashionable Kensington, London, and in the African jungle, where a mother marries her daughter to a cannibal king. She is thus the "bonne-bouche" of the title.

La Bonne chanson ("The Good Song") Gabriel Fauré, 1894.

The nine songs that comprise the work, Op. 61, are settings of Paul Verlaine's poems of the same title (1890).

Les Boréades ("The Descendants of Boreas") Jean-Philippe Rameau, 1762–3.

The (unfinished) opera in five acts is set to a libretto possibly by Louis de Cahusac based on the classical story of the offspring of Boreas, god of the north wind, notably Abaris, the legendary devotee of Apollo from the far north. Hence the opera's subtitle, *Abaris*.

Boris Godunov   Modest Mussorgsky, 1874.

The opera in a prologue and four acts is set

to the composer's own libretto based on Alexander Pushkin's drama of the same name (1825) and Nikolai Karamzin's *History of the Russian Empire* (1829). Its central character is the Russian czar Boris Godunov (reigned 1598–1605). *See also* **Dimitrij**.

Boston Common *see* **Three Places in New England**.

Boulevard Solitude   Hans Werner Henze, 1952.

The opera in one act (seven scenes) is set to a libretto by the composer and Grete Weil based on Walter Jöckisch's version of Abbé Antoine-François Prévost's novel *Manon Lescaut* (1731) (*see* **Manon**). It is essentially an updating of the original story, set in Paris in the late 1940s. The title hints at the despair and tragedy to come.

Le Bourgeois gentilhomme ("The Would-Be Gentleman")   Jean-Baptiste Lully, 1670.

The comedy ballet in five acts is set to Molière's play of the name (1670), itself a satire on the aping of the aristocracy by the nouveaux riches. It is really more a play with songs and dances than either a proper opera or ballet.

Bourrée fantasque ("Fantastic Bourrée")   Emmanuel Chabrier, 1949.

Aside from the title piece, the plotless ballet in three parts, choreographed by George Balanchine, uses the intermezzo from the composer's opera **Gwendoline** and his *Fête polonaise* ("Polish Festival"). The bourrée originated as a French folk dance.

La Boutique fantasque ("The Fantastic Toyshop")   Ottorino Respighi, 1919.

The ballet in one act, with a libretto by André Derain and choreography by Léonide Massine, has music arranged from Gioacchino Rossini's **Soirées musicales** and other pieces and is a modernized and dramatically improved version of Josef Bayer's The **Fairy Doll**.

Boyhood's End   Michael Tippett, 1943.

The cantata, for tenor and piano, is based on texts by the naturalist W.H.Hudson, author of such studies of rural life as *A Little Boy Lost* (1907) and *The Land's End* (1908). A direct source was his autobiography, *Far Away and Long Ago: History of My Early Life* (1918).

Brahms Double *see* **Double Concerto**.

Brahms's Lullaby *see* **Wiegenlied**.

Brandenburg Concertos   J.S. Bach, 1711–20.

The six concerti grossi BWV 1046–51, for various combinations of instruments, are named for their dedication (1721) to Margrave Christian Ludwig of Brandenburg, although they were apparently never played for him. Bach's own title for the works was *Concerts avec plusieurs instruments* ("Concertos with several instruments").

The Brandenburgers in Bohemia (Czech, *Braniboři v Čechách*)   Bedřich Smetana, 1863.

The opera in three acts, to a libretto by Karel Sabina, is set in 13th-century Bohemia and tells what happens when the widow of Přemysl Otakar II, killed in battle against the hated Habsburgs, requests the aid of Otto V, Margrave of Brandenburg, against the Habsburgs.

Die Brautwahl ("The Choice of a Bride")   Ferruccio Busoni, 1912.

The opera in three acts is set to the composer's own libretto based on E.T.A. Hoffmann's story of the same name (1820) but set in a fantasy world in Berlin in about 1920. The "bridal choice" is the one that rival suitors make, by choosing the correct one of three caskets, for the hand of Albertine, daughter of the "Kommissionsrat" Voswinkel.

Il Bravo ("The Bravo")   Saverio Mercadante, 1839.

The opera in three acts is set to a libretto by Gaetano Rossi and M.M. Marcello based on James Fenimore Cooper's novel *The Bravo* (1831) and Anicet Bourgeois's play *La Vénitienne* ("The Venetian Girl"). The story is set in 18th-century Venice and tells what happens when Foscari, the nobleman who loves Violetta, kills her guardian and her mother, Teodora, pays the government assassin, the Bravo, to abduct her.

Brazilian Sinfonietta   Ernst Krenek, 1952.

The work for string orchestra is so named because the composer wrote it in the first three months of 1952, when he was in Brazil.

La Brebis égarée ("The Lost Sheep")   Darius Milhaud, 1910–15.

The opera in three acts, Op. 4, is based on Francis Jammes's play of the same name (1910), telling what happens when Paul's wife, Françoise, becomes bored with her mundane life and elopes (as a "lost sheep") with the sensitive composer Pierre, Paul's friend since childhood. The title has a biblical ring. (The French *brebis* properly means "ewe" but is used in the Bible where English has "sheep," *e.g.* in Psalm 119:176, where English "I have gone astray like a lost sheep" corresponds to French *"J'ai été égaré comme une brebis perdue."*)

Bridal Chorus *see* **Wedding March** (1).

The Bride of Messina (Czech, *Nevěsta mesinská*)   Zdeněk Fibich, 1884.

The opera is set to a libretto by Otakar Hostinsky based on Friedrich Schiller's tragedy *Die Braut von Messina* (1803) telling what happens when two princes of Messina, Don Manuel and Don Cesar, unwittingly love the same girl, Beatrice, the bride in question.

Bridesmaids' Chorus   Carl Maria von Weber, 1821.

The chorus is that in Act 2 of Die **Freischütz**, in which the village girls bring a wreath to Agathe and prepare her for her wedding.

I Briganti ("The Brigands")   Saverio Mercadante, 1836.

The opera is set to a libretto by Jacopo Crescini based on Friedrich Schiller's drama *Die Räuber* (1781), telling what happens when a robber band under the command of the son of a Franconian nobleman, Herr von Moor, terrorizes the region of the Bohemian Forest.

Brigg Fair   Frederick Delius, 1907.

The orchestral work, subtitled *An English Rhapsody*, is a set of variations based on the arrangement of a folksong by Percy Grainger, who collected it at the North Lincolnshire Music Competition Festival at Brigg in 1905. *Cf.* **Lincolnshire Posy**.

The Bright Stream (Russian, *Svetlyy ruchey*)   Dmitry Shostakovich, 1934.

The ballet in three acts (four scenes), with a libretto and choreography by Fyodor Lopokov, takes its name from that of a collective farm in the Kuban region of the former Soviet Union, where a group of artists arrives.

Broken Strings   Param Vir, 1992.

The opera in one act, to a libretto by David Rudkin, is based on a traditional Buddist story, *Guttil Jatak*. It tells what happens when the king asks for a play to be performed and Guttil, a forgotten old musician, plays him a magical song on an instrument whose strings break one by one until the instrument itself no longer exists.

The Bronze Horse *see* Le **Cheval de bronze**.

The Bronze Horseman (Russian, *Mednyy vsadnik*)   Reinhold Glière, 1949.

The ballet in a prologue and four acts (nine scenes), with a libretto by P. Abolimov and choreography by Rostislav Zakharov, is based on Alexander Pushkin's poem of the same title (1833), telling of the tragic love affair between Yevgeny and Parasha, set against the historic flood of St. Petersburg in 1824, in which Yevgeny stands before the statue of the Bronze Horseman, depicting Peter the Great, and accuses it of pursuing him.

Brotherhood Symphony *see* A **Symphony of Brotherhood**

Brouillards ("Mists")   Claude Debussy, 1970.

The ballet in one act, choreographed by John Cranko, takes its title from piano piece No. 1 of Book II of the composer's **Préludes** and is based on nine of the pieces. It evokes a series of moods and meetings that are negative and transitory, like a mist, and that end in uncertainty.

Brünnhilde's Immolation   Richard Wagner, 1876.

The name usually given to the final scene of *Götterdämmerung* in Das **Ring des Nibelungen**, in which Brünnhilde bids farewell to life and rides into the flames.

Das Buch der hängenden Gärten ("The Book of the Hanging Gardens")   Arnold Schoenberg, 1903.

The songs for voice and piano, Op. 15, are settings of 15 poems of the same title by Stefan George, themselves part of the trilogy, *Die Bücher der Hirten- und Preisgedichte, der Sagen und Sänge und der hangenden Gärten* ("The Books of Pastorals and Praises, of Legends and Songs, and of the Hanging Gardens") (1895).

The Buffoon (Russian, *Skazka pro shuta*, "Tale of a Buffoon")   Sergey Prokofiev, 1921.

The ballet in six scenes, with a libretto by the composer and choreography by Tadeusz Slavinsky and Mikhail Larionov, is based on Alexander Afanasyev's collection of Russian folk tales (1855–64), one of which is about a buffoon who fools seven of his colleagues. The ballet is also known as *Chout*, a French spelling of Russian *shut*, "fool," "buffoon."

Bunte Blätter ("Colored Leaves")   Robert Schumann, 1852.

The 14 pieces for piano solo, Op. 99, are colorfully intimate, like drawings in an autograph album. The titles are as follows: (1)–(3)

Drei Stücklein ("Three Little Pieces"), (4)–(8) *Fünf Albumblätter* ("Five Album Leaves"), (9) *Novellette* (*see* **Novelletten**), (10) *Präludium*, (11) *Marsch*, (12) *Abendmusik* ("Evening Music"), (13) *Scherzo*, (14) *Geschwindmarsch* ("Quick March"). The original plan was to publish each piece separately in a different color.

La Buona figliuola ("The Good Daughter") Niccolò Piccinni, 1760.

The comic opera in three acts is set to a libretto by Carlo Goldini based on Samuel Richardson's novel *Pamela, or Virtue Rewarded* (1740), in which Pamela Andrews is the virtuous servant girl who repels numerous assaults on her virtue by the young squire, Mr. B——, but finally gets him to marry her. The opera's full title is *La Cecchina, ossia La buona figliuola* ("La Cecchina, or The Good Daughter"). The story tells of the love and eventual marriage of Cecchina, apparently a servant and orphan but in reality the long-lost daughter of a German baron, and the Marquis Conchiglia.

Burlesque (French, "Mockery").

The term is used for a composition that contains elements of parody or exaggeration, and in the 18th century one that alternated comic and serious elements. A familiar example is Richard Strauss's *Burleske* in D minor for piano and orchestra (1885–6).

The Burning Fiery Furnace Benjamin Britten, 1966.

The church parable, Op. 77, is set to a text by William Plomer based on the apocryphal story telling how King Nebuchadnezzar casts Shadrach, Meshach, and Abednego into a "burning fiery furnace" (Daniel 3).

The Burrow Frank Martin, 1958.

The ballet in one act, with a libretto and choreography by Kenneth MacMillan, is set to the composer's Concerto for Seven Wind Instruments, Timpani, Percussion, and Strings (1949) and deals with the relationships of a group of people living together in a small room, their "burrow," where they are clearly hiding from something.

Búsqueda ("Search") James MacMillan, 1988.

The music theater piece for narrator, eight actors, three sopranos, and instrumental ensemble takes its text from poems written by the mothers of those who "disappeared" during the Argentinian junta (1976–83), interwoven with fragments of the Latin **Mass**.

Butterfly Etude Fryderyk Chopin, 1836.

The Étude for Piano, Op. 25 No. 6 in G flat major, was so named by its publisher. The description is apt enough for a piece that is "light, fluttery, and when well performed, gives the impression of the whirr of a butterfly" (Berkowitz, p. 16).

C

Le Cadi dupé ("The Cadi Duped") Christoph Gluck, 1761.

The comic opera in one act tells how Zelmire, who loves Nuradin, uses her skill and cunning to rebuff the advances of the Cadi and make him return to his wife, Fatime. (A cadi is a magistrate in Muslim countries.)

The Cage Igor Stravinsky, 1951.

The ballet in one act, with a libretto and choreography by Jerome Robbins, is set to the composer's Concerto in D for strings (1946) and tells the story of two male intruders into a female society, where they are to be regarded as prey and dealt with accordingly.

Cain and Abel Andrzej Panufnik, 1968.

The ballet in one act, choreographed by Kenneth Macmillan, is set to the composer's *Sinfonia Sacra* (1963) and *Tragic Overture* (1942) as a contemporary version of the biblical story telling how Cain murders his brother Abel (Genesis 4:1–8), although here it is the snake (Genesis 3:13) that is the agent provocateur.

Cakewalk Louis Moreau Gottschalk, arr. Hershy Kay, 1951.

The ballet in three parts, with a libretto and choreography by Ruthanna Boris, is a parody of an oldtime minstrel show, ending with the whole company strutting across the stage in a cakewalk (the syncopated dance of the North American Negro said to be so named from the custom of giving a piece of cake to the dancer that executed it best).

Le Calife de Bagdad ("The Caliph of Baghdad") François Boieldieu, 1800.

The opera in one act is set to a libretto by Claude Godard d'Aucour de Saint-Just based on the *Thousand and One Nights* (*Arabian Nights*). The story tells how Harun al Raschid, the (historical) Caliph of the title who figures in many of the tales, rescues Zubaydah from robbers and comes to marry her.

La Calinda   Frederick Delius, 1896–7.

The orchestral dance interlude in the opera **Koanga** is named after a Negro dance imported to America by African slaves. The word itself is apparently of Spanish-American origin.

La Calisto ("Callisto")   Francesco Cavalli, 1651.

The opera in three acts is set to a text by Giovanni Faustini based on Ovid's *Metamorphoses* Book 2, 401–507 (1st century BC). It tells the story of the nymph Callisto, who is turned into a little bear by Juno and placed in the heavens by Jupiter as the constellation of Ursa Minor.

Calligrammes ("Calligrams")   Francis Poulenc, 1948.

The song cycle is set to seven poems from Guillaume Apollinaire's collection of the same name (1918). A calligram, literally "beautiful writing," is an arrangement of letters or words so as to form a design. Many of Apollinaire's shorter poems are typographically arranged to represent the subject of the poem. Thus *Il pleut* ("It is raining") has the letters trickling down the page. Musical pieces can equally have a shape or form that evokes their subject. The titles are: (1) *L'Espionne* ("The lady spy"), (2) *Mutation* ("Alteration"), (3) *Vers le Sud* ("Toward the south"), (4) *Il pleut* ("It is raining"), (5) *La Gâce exilée* ("La Gâce exiled"), (6) *Aussi bien que les cigales* ("As well as the grasshoppers"), (7) *Voyage* ("Journey").

Calm Sea and Prosperous Voyage *see* **Meeresstille und glückliche Fahrt**.

"La Calumnia" ("Slander").

Don Basilio's aria in Act 1 of Rossini's Il **Barbiere di Siviglia**, in which he describes the growth of slander from a little breeze into a gale that can damage a person's reputation.

Camberwell Green *see* **Spring Song**.

La Cambiale di matrimonio ("The Marriage Contract")   Gioacchino Rossini, 1810.

The comic opera in one act is set to a libretto by Gaetano Rossi based on Camillo Federici's comedy of the same title (1790). The story tells what happens when the Canadian merchant, Slook, offers the English businessman, Sir Tobias Mill, a large sum of money if he will find him a wife and Mill suggests his daughter, Fanny, although she loves Edoardo Milfort.

Cambridge Symphony   Hubert Parry, 1882–3.

The Symphony No. 2 in F major was written for the Cambridge Musical Society and has a "program" of Cambridge student life as its background. Hence its name.

The Camp Meeting   Charles Ives, 1904–11.

The Symphony No. 3 was inspired by New England and incorporates hymn tunes such as *What a Friend We Have in Jesus* and *O for a Thousand Tongues* to portray the camp meetings held in Danbury, Connecticut, when the composer was a boy.

La Campana sommersa ("The Sunken Bell")   Ottorini Respighi, 1927.

The opera in four acts is set to a libretto by Claudio Gaustalla based on Gerhart Hauptmann's "fairy drama" *Die versunkene Glocke* ("The Sunken Bell") (1896). The story tells what happens when the bellfounder, Heinrich, falls under the spell of the fairy, Rautendelein, and follows her into the mountains.

La Campanella ("The Little Bell")   Franz Liszt, 1831–2.

The piece is a transcription for piano of Paganini's **Bell Rondo**.

Il Campanello di notte ("The Night Bell")   Gaetano Donizetti, 1836.

The comic opera in one act is set to the composer's own libretto based on the vaudeville *La Sonnette de nuit* ("The Night Bell") by Léon Lévy Brunswick, Mathieu-Barthélemy Troin, and Victor Lhérie. The story tells what happens when the elderly apothecary, Don Annibale, and his young wife, Serafina, retire to bed on their wedding night and Serafina's rejected lover, Enrico, repeatedly rings the apothecary's bell to demand outlandish prescriptions. The plot gave the opera's alternate title, *La campanello dello speziale* ("The Apothecary's Bell").

Il Campiello ("The Little Square")   Ermanno Wolf-Ferrari, 1936.

The opera in three acts is set to a libretto by Mario Ghisalberti based on Carlo Goldoni's comedy of the same name (1756). The plot is set in Venice and tells of the lives and loves (and quarrels and confusions) of four families who live around a little square.

Le Candélabre à sept branches ("The Seven-Branched Candelabrum")   Darius Milhaud, 1951.

The piano work, Op. 315, is a musical evocation of the menorah, the candelabrum with seven branches that is a symbol of Judaism. The seven pieces represent the principal festivals of the Hebrew calendar with titles (and identities) translating as follows: (1) *First Day of the New Year* (Rosh Hashana), (2) *Day of Repentance* (Yom Kippur), (3) *Festival of the Booths* (Succoth), (4) *Resistance of the Maccabees* (Hanukkah), (5) *The Festival of Queen Esther* (Purim), (6) *Passover* (Pesach), (7) *Pentecost* (Shavuoth).

Candide   Leonard Bernstein, 1956.

The comic operetta in two acts is set to a libretto by Lilliam Hellman, Richard Wilbur, Dorothy Parker, and John Latouche based on Voltaire's philosophical novel of the same name title (1759), in which Candide is a gentle and innocent young man (hence his name) who believes Dr. Pangloss's teaching that this is "the best of all possible worlds."

Canfield   Pauline Oliveros, 1969.

The plotless ballet by Merce Cunningham has 12 dancers performing their individual movements and actions in a remote and detached fashion and hence derives its name from the game of canfield, or solitaire (patience). The game itself gets its name from the American gambler, R.A. Canfield (1855–1914).

Canon X   Conlon Nancarrow, *c*.1951.

The title is that of Study No. 21 in the composer's *Studies for Player Piano*. The piece is a canon, with one voice starting slowly in the bass and the other fast in the treble. The two voices speed up and slow down respectively until they eventually cross (hence the title), so that by the end the fast voice has slowed down and the slow voice become fast.

Cantata   Igor Stravinsky, 1951–2.

The work is a setting for soprano, tenor soloists, female chorus, and instrumental ensemble of anonymous 15th- and 16th-century English poems, among them the *Lyke Wake Dirge* and *Westron Wind*. The title (Italian for "sung") alludes to the work's basic character.

Cantata Academica   Benjamin Britten, 1959.

The choral work, Op. 62, for soloists and orchestra, was composed for the quincentennial of Basel University, Switzerland. Hence the title, Latin for "Academic Cantata." Its Latin subtitle is *Carmen Basiliense*, "Song of Basel." The work as a whole is a setting of a Latin text by Bernhard Wyss, compiled from the university charter and from eulogies of Basel.

Cantata Profana   Béla Bartók, 1930.

The choral work for tenor and baritone soloists with double chorus and orchestra has a Latin title meaning "Profane Cantata." The text is the composer's own translation and arrangement of an old Romanian folk ballad. Its Hungarian subtitle is *A kilenc csodaszarvas*, "The Nine Enchanted Stags." The cantata is "profane" in the sense that it is not sacred, as most are. ("Sacred" and "profane" are traditionally contrasted. *Cf.* Benjamin Britten's **Sacred and Profane**.) The theme of the work is the union of man with nature, and the story concerns an old man's nine sons who go hunting and are changed into stags.

The Canterbury Pilgrims   (1) Charles Villiers Stanford, 1884; (2) Reginald de Koven, 1917; (3) George Dyson, 1931.

Stanford's opera in three acts, to a libretto by Gilbert Arthur A'Beckett, and De Koven's opera, to a libretto by Percy MacKaye, are both based on Geoffrey Chaucer's famous poem *The Canterbury Tales* (*c.* 1387), recounting the tales told by pilgrims on the road to Canterbury. Dyson's cantata is also based on this, but with a modernized text. Its overture is titled *At the Tabard Inn*, after the Southwark inn where the pilgrims met before setting out.

Canti di prigionia   ("Songs of Imprisonment")   Luigi Dallapiccola, 1938–41.

The work for chorus, two pianos, two harps, and percussion is set to texts by Queen Mary Stuart (Mary Queen of Scots) (1542–1587), the Roman scholar Boethius (480–525), and the Italian preacher Savonarola (1452–1498), all of whom were imprisoned and executed (at the same age of 45). The titles of the movements are: (1) *Preghiera di Maria Stuarda* ("Prayer of Mary Stuart"), (2) *Invocazione di Boezio* ("Appeal of Boethius"), (3) *Congedo di Girolamo Savonarola* ("Envoi of Girolamo Savonarola"). The work was a protest against Mussolini's adoption of Hitler's racial policies, which threatened the composer's Jewish wife.

Canticle for Innocent Comedians   Thomas Ribbink, 1952.

The ballet in one act, choreographed by Martha Graham, is a "dance of joy, in praise of the world as it turns" (program notes, quoted in Koegler, p. 83). The title thus alludes to the pure pleasure expressed by the dancers.

Canticles   Benjamin Britten, 1947–54.

The composer gave this linking name to five compositions: (1) **My Beloved Is Mine**, (2) **Abraham and Isaac**, (3) **Still Falls the Rain**, (4) **Journey of the Magi**, and (5) The **Death of St. Narcissus**. A canticle often (but not exclusively) has a religious text.

Canticum Sacrum   Igor Stravinsky, 1955.

The choral work in five movements, for tenor and baritone soloists, chorus, and orchestra, is set to the composer's version of a biblical text. Its full Latin title is *Cantium sacrum ad honorem Sancti Marci nominis*, "Sacred Song in Honor of the Name of St. Mark." The work was first performed at St. Mark's, Venice.

Cantiones sacrae ("Sacred Songs") William Byrd, 1589–91.

The name is that of two books of motets on sacred subjects. Book I (1589) contains 29 motets for five voices, and Book II (1591) 20 motets for five voices and 12 for six.

Il Canto sospeso ("The Song Suspended") Luigi Nono, 1956.

The work for chorus and orchestra, based on the final messages of Resistance fighters before their execution, creates the effect of time standing still, or of a frozen moment in time. Hence the title.

Cantus Arcticus ("Arctic Song")   Einojuhani Rautavaara, 1972.

The work is described by the Finnish composer as a "concerto for birds and orchestra" and juxtaposes his own recordings of arctic birds with orchestral music. The song of the title is thus birdsong.

Capital Capitals   Virgil Thomson, 1927.

The work for four male voices and piano, with a text by Gertrude Stein, is an evocation of Provence imagined as a conversation among the four cities of Aix, Arles, Avignon, and Les Baux, all historic capitals.

Capriccio   Richard Strauss, 1942.

The opera in one act (but usually performed in a two-act version) is set to a libretto by the composer and Clemens Krauss based loosely on Giovanni Battista Casti's libretto for Antonio Salieri's opera **Prima la musica e poi le parole**. The work is described as a "conversation piece with music" and discusses the relative importance of words and music in opera. A capriccio is literally a caprice, *i.e.* a "whim" or "fancy."

Capriccio Burlesco   William Walton, 1968.

The orchestral work, commissioned for the 125th anniversary of the New York Philharmonic Orchestra, who gave its first performance, has a title that points to its lively and (for Walton) unconventional nature, with its "sly musical gesticulations and saucy ideas" (Neil Tierney, *Dictionary of National Biography*, 1990).

Capriccio espagnol (Russian, *Ispanskoye kaprichchio*, "Spanish Caprice")   Nikolay Rimsky-Korsakov, 1887.

The orchestral work, Op. 34, is in the Italian idiom and was originally intended to be for violin and orchestra as a companion piece to the *Fantasia on Russian Themes* (1886). The title of this Spanish-oriented work by a Russian composer is a hybrid of Italian and French, just like Tchaikovsky's **Capriccio italien**.

Capriccio italien (Russian, *Ital'yanskoye kaprichchio*, "Italian Caprice")   Pyotr Tchaikovsky, 1880.

The orchestral work, Op. 45, is in the Italian idiom. Its hybrid title is half Italian, half French, on the same lines as Rimsky-Korsakov's **Capriccio espagnol**.

Capriol Suite   Peter Warlock, 1926.

The suite for string orchestra (or piano duet) bases its six movements on old French dances from Thoinot Arbeau's *Orchésographie* ("Orchesography") (1589), a dancing manual in which "Capriol" is a character. (His name means "capriole," "caper," literally "goat's leap," ultimately from Latin *caper*, "goat.")

The Captain's Daughter (Russian, *Kapitanskaya dochka*)   César Cui, 1911.

The opera in four acts is set to the composer's own libretto based on Alexander Pushkin's novel of the same name (1836). The story is set in the 18th century and tells of the love of Andrei Grinyov for Maria Ivanovna, the "captain's daughter."

The Captive of the Caucasus (Russian, *Kavkazsky plennik*)   César Cui, 1883.

The opera is set to a libretto by Viktor Krylov based on Alexander Pushkin's romantic narrative poem of the same name (1822).

I Capuleti e i Montecchi ("The Capulets and the Montagues")   Vicenzo Bellini, 1830.

The opera in four parts (two acts) is set to a libretto by Felice Romani modified from his libretto for Nicola Vaccai's opera **Giulietta e Romeo**. The story is thus that of Romeo and Juliet, as in Shakespeare's play (1594), and tells of the love of Romeo, a Montague, for Giulietta, daughter of Capellio, head of the Capulets. *See also* **Romeo and Juliet**.

Caractacus   Edward Elgar, 1898.

The dramatic cantata, Op. 35, is set to a libretto by Harry Acworth based on the life of the 1st-century AD British king, Caractacus (Caratacus), who led the resistance against the Romans.

Cardillac   Paul Hindemith, 1926.

The opera in three acts is set to a libretto by Ferdinand Lion after E.T.A. Hoffmann's story *Das Fräulein von Scuderi* ("The Young Woman of Scutari") from his collection *Die Serapionsbrüder* ("The Serapion Brethren") (1819–21). The action is set in 17th-century Paris and concerns a master jeweler, Cardillac, and his (unnamed) daughter, the "young woman" of Hoffmann's tale.

"Care selve" ("Dear woods").

Meleagro's opening arioso in Handel's **Atalanta**, when (as "Tirsi") he is seeking his love in the forests.

Carignane   Jacques Ibert, 1953.

The Arabesque for Bassoon and Piano was so named by the composer for the small town of Carignan in northeastern France, partly for its wine and partly for the euphony of the name.

Carillon   Edward Elgar, 1914.

The recitation with orchestra, Op. 75, is set to the Belgian poet Émile Cammaerts's poem so titled and was composed as a tribute to Belgium, whose neutrality had been violated by the German army in the opening months of World War I. A carillon is a set of bells in a church steeple played by a keyboard below, as often found in Belgian churches.

Carmen   Georges Bizet, 1875.

The opera in four acts is set to a libretto by Henri Meilhac and Ludovic Halévy based on Prosper Mérimée's novel of the same name (1845). This is set in Seville, Spain, in 1820 and tells the story of the Spanish gypsy Carmen, who falls for the toreador Escamillo. The ballet of the same name in five scenes (1949), with a libretto and choreography by Roland Petit, follows the plot of Mérimée's story and Bizet's opera fairly closely.

Carmina Burana ("Songs of Beuron")   Carl Orff, 1935.

The secular oratorio for soprano, tenor, and baritone soloists, boys' choir, chorus, and organ is a setting of a Latin text based on poems in Latin, Old German, and Old French manuscripts dated 1280 and found in the Benedictine monastery of Beuron, western Germany. Hence the Latin title, in full *Carmina Burana* (*cantiones profanae*) ("Songs of Beuron, Profane Songs"). The songs themselves are student songs about wine, women, and love, and the three parts have the respective titles (in translation) *Spring*, *In the Tavern*, and *Love*. The work is the first part of the trilogy **Trionfi** and was followed by **Catulli Carmina**.

Carnaval ("Carnival")   Robert Schumann, 1833–5.

The set of 22 pieces for piano solo, Op. 9, is subtitled *Scènes mignonnes sur quatre notes* ("Dainty Scenes on Four Notes"), these being A, S, C, and H (the German equivalent of A flat, E flat, C, and B), spelling out Asch, the home town of Ernestine von Fricken, to whom the composer was engaged for a time. The four letters are also the only musical ones in his own name. (See No. 11 below.) The individual titles, all French, are as follows (translated only where the English is different): (1) *Préambule* ("Preamble"), (2) *Pierrot*, (3) *Arlequin* ("Harlequin"), (4) *Valse noble* ("Noble Waltz"), (5) *Eusebius*, (6) *Florestan*, (7) *Coquette*, (8) *Réplique* ("Reply"), (9) *Sphinxes*, (10) *Papillons* ("Butterflies"), (11) *A.S.C.H.–S.C.H.A.* (*Lettres dansantes*) ("A.S.C.H.–S.C.H.A (Dancing Letters)"), (12) *Chiarina*, (13) *Chopin*, (14) *Estrella*, (15) *Reconnaissance* ("Gratitude"), (16) *Pantalon et Colombine* ("Pantaloon and Columbine"), (17) *Valse allemande* ("German Waltz"), (18) *Paganini*, (19) *Aveu* ("Avowal"), (20) *Promenade* ("Walk"), (21) *Pause*, (22) *Marche des "Davidsbündler" contre les Philistines* ("March of the 'Davidsbündler' against the Philistines"). In piece No. 14, Estrella is Ernestine herself. For the names of Nos. 5, 6, and 12, and for the reference in No. 22, *see* **Davidsbündlertänze**. The other names are either the composer's musician friends and contemporaries (Chopin, Paganini) or characters in the Italian *commedia dell'arte* (Pierrot, Harlequin, Pantaloon, Columbine).

Le Carnaval ("The Carnival")   Robert Schumann, 1910.

The ballet in one act, with a libretto and choreography by Michel Fokine, is based on the music of the composer's **Carnaval**, orchestrated by Alexander Glazunov and others, and was first produced in St.Petersburg on the occasion of a ball for the magazine *Satyricon*.

Carnaval à Paris ("Carnival in Paris") Johan Svendsen, 1879.

The "episode for orchestra," Op. 9, is a musical depiction of the scene stated in the title.

Le Carnaval d'Aix ("The Carnival at Aix") Darius Milhaud, 1926.

The work for piano and orchestra, Op. 83b, is based on music from the composer's ballet **Salade**. Milhaud was born in Aix-en-Provence, France.

Carnaval de Venise ("Carnival in Venice") Niccolò Paganini, 1829.

The set of variations for unaccompanied violin, Op. 10, is based on the popular Venetian song of the same name, better known as *O mamma mia* ("O Mother Mine").

Le Carnaval des animaux ("The Carnival of the Animals") Camille Saint-Saëns, 1886.

The "grand zoological fantasy" for two pianos and orchestra is in 14 movements, each representing a different animal. Hence the general title, referring to the "carnival" or colorful display of each. Movement No. 13 is the famous *Le Cygne* ("The Swan"). (*See* **The Dying Swan.**) The others are: *Marche royale du lion* ("Royal March of the Lion"), *Poules et coqs* ("Hens and Cocks"), *Ânes* ("Donkeys"), *Tortues* ("Tortoises"), *Éléphant* ("Elephant"), *Kangourou* ("Kangaroo"), *Aquarium* ("Aquarium"), *Personnages aux longues oreilles* ("Personages with Long Ears"), *Le Coucou au fond des bois* ("The Cuckoo in the Depth of the Woods"), *Volière* ("Aviary"), *Pianistes* ("Pianists"), *Fossiles* ("Fossils"), *Finale*.

Le Carnaval romain ("Roman Carnival") Hector Berlioz, 1844.

The orchestral overture, Op. 9, representing a public holiday in Rome, used material from the opera **Benvenuto Cellini**.

Carneval *see* **Nature, Life, and Love.**

Carnival (Russian, *Karneval*) Alexander Glazunov, 1894.

The overture, Op. 45, is a musical depiction of the title.

The Carnival of the Animals *see* Le **Carnaval des animaux.**

"Caro nome" ("Dear name").

Gilda's aria in Act 1 of Verdi's **Rigoletto**, expressing her love for the "student" Gualtier Maldé, who is really the Duke of Mantua.

Le Carrosse du Saint-Sacrement ("The Carriage of the Holy Sacrament") Lord Berners, 1924.

The one-act opera is set to the composer's own libretto based on Prosper Mérimée's comedy of the same name (1830). *See* La **Périchole.**

Cartridge Music John Cage, 1960.

The composition is so named because the performers use phonograph cartridges to pick up and amplify the sounds they can make with objects to hand.

La Casa del diavolo ("The House of the Devil") Luigi Boccherini, 1771.

The Symphony in D minor, Op. 12 No. 4 (Gérard 506), has a generally "infernal" theme with a last movement based on the "Dance of the Furies" in Gluck's opera **Orfeo ed Euridice**. The title is said to have been found in the composer's autograph catalog.

Cassation (German *Kassation*, "Serenade").

A type of 18th-century composition similar to a **Divertimento** or **Serenade** and often designed to be performed outdoors. An example is Mozart's *Cassation* in B flat, K99 (1769).

Casse-noisette *see* **Nutcracker.**

"Casta diva" ("Chaste goddess").

Norma's aria with chorus in Act 1 of Bellini's **Norma**, in which she prays to the moon for peace between Gaul and Rome.

Castor et Pollux ("Castor and Pollux") Jean-Philippe Rameau, 1737.

The opera in a prologue and five acts is set to a libretto by Pierre-Joseph Bernard based on the classical story about the love of the heavenly twins, Castor and Pollux, for Hilaria (Hiläeira), here called Thélaïre.

Cat Fugue *see* **Cat's Fugue.**

Cat Waltz Fryderyk Chopin, 1838.

The Valse in F for Piano, Op. 34 No. 3, is so nicknamed because of a story that "the composer's cat jumped on the keyboard as he was composing and, running up and down, suggested to him the appoggiatura passage in the fourth section" (Scholes, p. 679). *Cf.* **Cat's Fugue, Minute Waltz.**

Catalogue Aria W.A. Mozart, 1787.

Leporello's aria in Act 1, Scene 2 of **Don**

Giovanni, in which he itemizes to Donna Elvira a tally of Don Giovanni's amorous conquests in different countries, ending each with the words "but in Spain, a thousand and three."

Catalogue d'oiseaux ("Catalogue of Birds")
Olivier Messiaen, 1959.

The work for solo piano contains 13 pieces, each including the notated song of a different bird. The individual titles are: (1) *Le Chocard des Alpes* ("The Alpine Chough"), (2) *Le Loriot* ("The Golden Oriole"), (3) *Le Merle bleu* ("The Blue Song Thrush"), (4) *Le Traquet strapazin* ("The Black-Eared Wheatear"), (5) *La Chouette hulotte* ("The Tawny Owl"), (6) *L'Alouette lulu* ("The Woodlark"), (7) *La Rousserolle effarvatte* ("The Reed Warbler"), (8) *L'Alouette calandrelle* ("The Short-Toed Lark"), (9) *La Bouscarle* ("Cetti's Warbler"), (10) *Le Merle de roche* ("The Rock Thrush"), (11) *La Buse variable* ("The Buzzard"), (12) *Le Traquet rieur* ("The Black Wheatear"), (13) *Le Courlis cendré* ("The Curlew"). *Cf.* **Oiseaux exotiques**, **Réveil des oiseaux**.

Catarina   Cesare Pugni, 1846.

The ballet in three acts (five scenes), with a libretto and choreography by Jules Joseph Perrot, tells the story of the Italian painter Salvator Rosa (1615–1673), who falls in love with Catarina, chief of the bandits, also loved by her lieutenant, Diavolino. Hence the subtitle, *La Fille du bandit* ("The Bandit's Daughter").

Caterina Cornaro   Gaetano Donizetti, 1844.

The opera in a prologue and two acts is set to a libretto by Giacomo Sacchero based on Jules-Henri Vernoy de Saint-Georges's libretto for Ludovic Halévy's play *La Reine de Chypre* ("The Queen of Cyprus") (1841). The story tells what happens when Caterina, daughter of Andreas, although set to marry the young Frenchman, Gerardo, has her marriage postponed because Lusignano, king of Cyprus, wishes to marry her instead.

La Cathédrale engloutie ("The Submerged Cathedral")   Claude Debussy, 1910.

The piano piece, No. 10 in Book I of the **Préludes**, based its music on the story of the legendary city of Ys, submerged off the Breton coast, with the tolling bells and chanting that can be heard from its cathedral. The legend also inspired Lalo's opera Le **Roi d'Ys**.

Cathleen ni Houlihan   Arnold Bax, 1903.

The orchestral tone poem was inspired by W.B. Yeats's play of the same name (1902) about the struggle for Irish independence. Cathleen ni Houlihan herself is a mysterious aged figure whose four fields, representing the four provinces of Ireland, have been seized by strangers.

The Catiline Conspiracy   Iain Hamilton, 1972–3.

The opera in two acts is set to the composer's own libretto based on Ben Jonson's tragedy *Catiline* (1611), about the dissolute Roman aristocrat Lucius Sergius Catilina (*c.*108–62 BC) who led an unsuccessful conspiracy to overthrow the Roman republic.

Cat's Fugue   Domenico Scarlatti, *c.* 1738.

The Sonata in G minor for Harpsichord, L 499, is said to be so named because the composer's cat walked over the keyboard, so providing the notes that form the subject of the fugue, rising from below middle C as G, B flat, E, F sharp, B flat, C sharp. These are curious intervals, of the kind that a cat on a keyboard could well pick out. But as the harpsichordist Ralph Kirkpatrick comments: "It might be remarked that only a light-footed and accurate cat, possibly a kitten, could refrain from [involuntarily stepping on] neighboring tones on the flats and sharps of the Fugue subject" (quoted in Berkowitz, p. 19). The piece is also known as the *Cat Fugue*. *Cf.* **Cat Waltz**.

Catulli Carmina ("Songs of Catullus")
Carl Orff, 1943.

The scenic cantata for soloists, chorus, four pianos, four timpani, and up to 12 percussionists, is a setting of 12 Latin poems by Catullus. Hence its title. The work is the successor to **Carmina Burana** and the second part of the trilogy **Trionfi**.

Caucasian Sketches (Russian, *Kavkazskiye eskizy*)   Mikhail Ippolitov-Ivanov, 1895.

The symphonic suite for orchestra, Op. 10, is a musical depiction of the Caucasus and its people, as detailed in the titles of the four movements: (1) *In the Mountain Pass*, (2) *In the Village*, (3) *In the Mosque*, (4) *March of the Sirdar*.

The Cauldron of Annwn   Joseph Holbrooke, 1912–29.

The operatic trilogy, Opp. 53, 56, and 75, is a setting of Lord Howard de Walden's dramatic poem of the same name (1922) based on *Pedair Cainc y Mabinogi* ("The Four Branches of the Mabinogi"), four medieval Welsh tales. The three operas are: *The Children of Don* (1912),

Dylan, Son of the Wave (1913), and *Bronwen* (1929). Don (more properly, Dôn) is the Welsh name of the Celtic goddess, Danu, related to the name of the Danube. Dylan, or Dylan Ail Ton ("Dylan, son of the wave"), evolved from a sea god. Bronwen is the "fair breasted one." Annwn, perhaps from Welsh *dwfn*, "world," prefixed by *an*, "in," is a name for the Celtic Otherworld, regarded either as an island in the west or as a place underground.

I Cavalieri di Ekebù ("The Knights of Ekebù")   Riccardo Zandonai, 1925.

The opera in four acts is set to a libretto by Arturo Rossato based on Selma Lagerlöf's novel *Gösta Berlings Saga* (1891), telling the story of the 12 knights of Ekebù led by the renegade priest, Gösta Berling.

Cavalleria rusticana ("Rustic Chivalry")
Pietro Mascagni, 1890.

The opera in one act is set to a libretto by Giovanni Targioni-Tozzetti and Guido Menasci based on Giovanni Verga's drama of the same name (1884), in turn taken from his own story (1880). The story tells what happens when the soldier Turiddù finds that his love, Lola, has married the village carter, Alfio, following his earlier fling with Santuzza, who is pregnant by him. It all ends in tears, and the "chivalry" of the title is thus ironic. The opera is traditionally coupled with Leoncavallo's I **Pagliacci**, and the combined bill nicknamed "Cav. and Pag." (pronounced "Kav 'n' Padge").

Cave of the Heart   Samuel Barber, 1946.

The ballet in one act, Op. 23, choreographed by Martha Graham, is based on the classical legend telling how the magician and enchantress, Medea, helped Jason win the Golden Fleece and bore him two children, whom she later killed. The work's original title was *Serpent Heart*, but this was changed as now for its New York performance in 1947. That same year the composer arranged an orchestral suite from the score as *Medea*.

Ce que l'amour me dit ("What Love Tells Me")   Gustav Mahler, 1974.

The ballet in three scenes, with a libretto and choreography by Maurice Béjart, is set to the fourth, fifth, and sixth movements of the composer's Symphony No. 3 in D minor (1895–6) and takes its title from the last of these. The plot concerns a young man's quest for love and happiness, which he eventually finds with a boy. *Cf.* **Mahler, Third Symphony by Gustav Mahler.**

Ce qu'on entend sur la montagne ("What Is Heard on the Mountain")   Franz Liszt, 1848–9.

The symphonic poem for piano, orchestrated by Joachim Raff, is based on No. 5 of Victor Hugo's collection of lyric poems *Feuilles d'automne* ("Autumn Leaves") (1831). Its German title is simply *Bergsymphonie*, "Mountain Symphony."

Cecilia   Licinio Refice, 1934.

The opera in three acts is set to a libretto by E. Mucci based on the legend of St. Cecilia, the patron saint of music, and St. Valerian, and of the former's martyrdom.

Cello Symphony   Benjamin Britten, 1963.

This is the short title of the Symphony for Cello and Orchestra, Op. 68, composed for (and dedicated to) the Russian cellist, Mstislav Rostropovich, who gave its first performance.

Celos aun del aire matan ("Jealousy even of the air is deadly")   Juan Hidalgo, 1660.

The opera, to a libretto by Calderón de la Barca, is based on the mythological story of Cephalus and Procris. The handsome prince Cephalus married Procris but was stolen by Aurora. The goddess returned him in a new form to his wife, whom he seduced, but when he was given back his original shape Procris felt so guilty that she ran away. Although later reconciled, she jealously spied on him but he mistook her in the woods and accidentally killed her.

Celtic Requiem   John Tavener, 1969.

The work for soprano, children's chorus, chorus, and orchestra is set to a text compiled from the **Requiem** Mass, poems by Henry Vaughan, John Henry Newman, and the Irish poet Blathmac, and children's singing games. The title reflects the Celtic input, although the work overall expresses the composer's Russian Orthodox beliefs.

A Celtic Song Cycle   Arnold Bax, 1904.

The five songs for voice and piano are settings of poems by the Scottish writer "Fiona Macleod" (real name, William Sharp), with individual titles: *Eilidh my Fawn, Closing Doors, Thy Dark eyes to mine, A Celtic Lullaby*, and *At the last*.

La Cena delle Beffe ("The Mocking Supper")   Umberto Giordano, 1924.

The opera in four acts is set to a libretto by Sem Benelli based on his own play of the same name. The story is set in 15th-century Florence and tells what happens when Giannetto is brutally treated by the brothers Neri and Gabriello because he is in love with the former's mistress, Ginevra.

Cendrillon ("Cinderella") Jules Massenet, 1899.

The opera in four acts to a libretto by Henri Cain is based on Charles Perrault's story of Cinderella in his *Contes de ma mère l'Oye* ("Mother Goose Tales") (1697). (*Cf.* La **Cenerentola**.)

La Cenerentola ("Cinderella") Gioacchino Rossini, 1817.

The opera in two acts is set to a libretto by Jacopo Ferretti based on Charles-Guillaume's text for Nicolò Isouard's opera *Cendrillon* (1810), and itself derived from Charles Perrault's story of Cinderella in his *Contes de ma mère l'Oye* ("Mother Goose Tales") (1697). The subtitle is *La bontà in trionfo* ("Goodness Triumphant"). An alternate title sometime found for the opera, especially in German use, is *Angelina*, this being the proper name of Cinderella. (*Cf.* **Cendrillon**.)

Les Cent Baisers ("The Hundred Kisses") Frédéric d'Erlanger, 1935.

The ballet in one act, with a libretto by Boris Kochno and choreography by Bronislava Nijinska, is based on Hans Christian Andersen's fairy tale *The Swineherd* (1842), telling how a prince who fails to win a princess disguises himself as a swineherd and offers her toys which she agrees to pay for with a hundred kisses.

Les Cent Vierges ("The Hundred Virgins") Charles Lecocq, 1972.

The operetta in three acts, to a libretto by Louis François Clairville, Henri Chivot, and Alfred Duru, tells what happens when the government advertises for "a hundred virgins" to volunteer to go out to the Île Verte ("Green Island") as prospective wives for the men who have just colonized this new French possession.

Central Park in the Dark Charles Ives, 1906.

The work for small orchestra has the full title *Central Park in the Dark in the Good Old Summertime*, the subtitle being *A Contemplation of Nothing Serious*. *Cf.* The **Unanswered Question**. The subject of contemplation, serious or not, is New York's Central Park.

A Ceremony of Carols Benjamin Britten, 1942.

The work in 11 movements, Op. 28, for tre-

ble voices and harp, comprises settings of medieval carols, their plainsong arranged in a modern idiom. The "ceremony" of the title relates to the celebratory nature of the carols and the spiritual joy they express.

Chaconne.

A French word from Spanish *chacona*, originally a type of dance in a three-in-a-measure rhythm (from Basque *chocuna*, "pretty"), but now similar to a **Passacaglia**. One of the best known examples is the *Chaconne* at the end of J.S. Bach's **Partita** No.2 in A minor for solo violin, BWV 1004 (*c.*1720). A further example is Purcell's *Chacony* in G minor (1680), and his **Dido's Lament** is also a chaconne.

The Chagall Windows John McCabe, 1974.

The orchestral work was inspired by Marc Chagall's stained glass windows in the synagogue of the Hadassah Hospital at the Hebrew University, Jerusalem. The windows themselves represent the 12 tribes of Israel.

Chain Witold Lutoslawski, 1983–6.

The three orchestral pieces that comprise the work, *Chain I* (1983), *Chain II* (1985), and *Chain III* (1986), are constructed so that each, while being a self-contained unit, connects with the other two like links in a chain. Hence the title.

Chamber Concerto (German, *Kammerkonzert*) Alban Berg, 1927.

The concerto is for solo piano and violin and a small "chamber" orchestra of 13 instruments. The title was subsequently adopted by Györgi Ligeti for his own "chamber concerto" (1970) for 13 instruments, each having a part of equal importance to play.

Chamber Symphony (German, *Kammersymphonie*) Arnold Schoenberg, 1906, 1906–39.

The title of the two orchestral works, No. 1 (Op. 9) and No. 2 (Op. 38), alludes to the relatively small number of instruments required for each, fewer than for a full orchestra.

Champagne Aria W.A. Mozart, 1787.

Don Giovanni's aria "*Finch' han dal vino*" ("While there is wine") in Act 1 of **Don Giovanni**, in which he bids Leporello prepare for the party. The performer traditionally sings it with a glass of champagne in his hand.

Chandos Anthems George Frideric Handel, 1717–18

Handel composed the 12 anthems on religious texts when he was resident composer for James Brydges, Earl of Carnarvon (1673–1744), later the Duke of Chandos, at his palace, Cannons, near Edgware, north of London.

Chanson bohémienne *see* "Les **Tringles des sistres tintaient.**"

Chanson de Matin ("Morning Song") Edward Elgar, 1899.

The work for violin and piano, Op. 15 No. 2, was intended to complement the **Chanson de Nuit** and was giving a matching title accordingly. The composer described it as "cheerful" by comparison with the earlier piece.

Chanson de Nuit ("Night Song") Edward Elgar, 1897.

The work for violin and piano, Op. 15 No. 1, was originally called *Evensong*. The composer then proposed *Vesper*, but it was eventually published under the present title, which probably best indicates its lyrical nature.

Chanson triste ("Sad Song") Pyotr Tchaikovsky, 1878.

No. 2 of the *Twelve Pieces* for piano, Op. 40, is so named for its melancholy melody.

Chansons de Bilitis ("Songs of Bilitis") Claude Debussy, 1897–8.

The three songs for voice and piano are set to prose poems by Pierre Louÿs, who wrote under the supposedly Greek name of Bilitis. Their individual titles are *La Flûte de Pan* ("The Pipes of Pan"), *La Chevelure* ("The Head of Hair"), and *Le Tombeau des naïades* ("The Tomb of the Naiads").

Chansons madécasses ("Songs of Madagascar") Maurice Ravel, 1926.

The three songs for voice, flute, cello, and piano are settings of the prose poems of the same name (1787) by the Réunion-born French poet Évariste Parny, themselves supposedly based on native songs. Their individual titles are *Nahandove*, *Aoua!* (a screech of rage), and *Il est doux* ("It is sweet").

Chansons sans paroles *see* **Lieder ohne Worte.**

Le Chant du rossignol ("The Song of the Nightingale") Igor Stravinsky, 1920.

The ballet in one act, choreographed by Léonide Massine, is based on Hans Christian Andersen's fairy tale *The Nightingale* (1845), telling the story of the emperor of China who

bans a real nightingale and replaces it with a mechanical one.

Chants d'Auvergne ("Songs of the Auvergne") Joseph Canteloube, 1923–30.

The work is based on traditional dialect songs of the Auvergne collected by the composer and published in four volumes over the dates given. Best known is the suite of nine for soprano and orchestra drawn from series 1 through 4, with individual titles as follows: (1) *Baïlèro*, (2) *L'Aio dè rotso* ("Spring Water"), (3) *Ound 'onorèn gorda?* ("Where shall we go to graze?"), (4) *Obal din lou Limouzi* ("Down there in Limousin"), (5) *La delaïssádo* ("The Forsaken Girl"), (6) *Lo Fiolairé* ("The Spinning Girl"), (7) *Passo pel prat* ("Come through the meadow"), (8) *Brezairola* ("Cradle Song"), (9) *Chut, chut* ("Hush, hush").

Chants populaires ("Popular Songs") Maurice Ravel, 1910–7.

The seven songs for voice and piano are settings of traditional airs of different nationalities, with individual titles *Chanson espagnole* ("Spanish Song"), *Chanson française* ("French Song"), *Chanson italienne* ("Italian Song"), *Chanson hébraïque* ("Hebraic Song"), *Chanson écossaise* ("Scottish Song"), *Chanson flamande* ("Flemish Song"), and *Chanson russe* ("Russian Song"). The first four of these were subsequently orchestrated.

A Charm of Lullabies Benjamin Britten, 1947.

The songs for mezzosoprano and piano, Op. 41, are set to poems that are lullabies by William Blake, Robert Burns, Matthew Green, Thomas Randolph, and Ambrose Philips. "Charm" can mean both "attraction" and "collection" (as in a charm of goldfinches), and the word was probably intended to play on both senses here.

La Chartreuse de Parme ("The Carthusian Monastery of Parma") Henri Sauguet, 1927–36.

The opera is set to a libretto by Armand Lunel based on Stendhal's novel of the same name (1839). This is itself based on on a 17th-century chronicle of a Renaissance story, but is set in contemporary Italy and recounts the amorous and other adventures of the hero, Fabrice del Dongo, before he finally retired to the monastery of the title.

La Chasse ("The Hunt") (1) Joseph Haydn, (i) 1760, (ii) 1781; (2) Ludwig van Beethoven, 1802; (3) Niccolò Paganini, *c.* 1805.

Haydn's String Quartet in B flat major, Op. 1 No. 1, is so nicknamed because of the suggestion of a horn call in the opening phrase. His Symphony No. 73 in D major is so named because of the "hunting" motif in the last movement. Beethoven's Sonata for Piano in E flat major, Op. 31 No. 3, is named for the presto "hunting" opening theme of the Finale. Paganini's Caprice for Violin No. 9 in E major produces its "hunting" theme in double stops.

La Chasse du jeune Henri *see* Le **Jeune Henri**.

Le Chasseur Maudit ("The Accursed Hunter") César Franck, 1881–2.

The symphonic poem is based on Gottfried August Bürger's ballad *Der Wilde Jäger* ("The Wild Hunter") (1786) about a hunter doomed to ride to his death.

La Chatte ("The Cat") Henri Sauguet, 1927.

The ballet in one act, with a libretto by Sobeka (pen name of Boris Kochno) and choreography by George Balanchine, is based on the fable by Aesop in which a young man asks Aphrodite to change the cat, with whom he has fallen in love, into a young girl.

"Che farò senza Euridice" ("What shall I do without Euridice").

Orfeo's lament at the loss of his wife Euridice in Act 3 of Gluck's **Orfeo ed Euridice**. The aria is well known in English as "What is life without thee."

"Che gelida manina" ("How frozen thy little hand").

Rodolfo's aria to Mimi in Act 1 of Puccini's La **Bohème** as he makes his first approach to her. The usual English title is "Your tiny hand is frozen" (or, irreverently, "You're tiny — and it's frozen").

"Che puro ciel" ("What pure heaven").

Orfeo's arioso as he gazes on the beauties of the Elysian Fields in Act 2 of Gluck's **Orfeo ed Euridice**.

Cheap Imitation John Cage, 1969.

The piano piece is a tribute to Erik Satie and consists simply of a repetition of a melodic line from that composer's **Socrate** using the I Ching to determine the mode and transposition of each bar or half-bar. It is thus a "cheap imitation" of the original.

Checkmate Arthur Bliss, 1937.

The ballet in one act, with a libretto by the composer and choreography by Ninette de Valois, depicts a game of love and death, acted out to the rules of chess. It is finally won by the Black Queen. The composer himself was a keen chess player.

Le Chemin de fer ("The Railroad") Alkan, 1844.

The piece for piano, Op. 27, aims to represent the sound and speed of a steam train.

La Cheminée du roi René ("King René's Chimney") Darius Milhaud, 1939.

The suite for flute, oboe, clarinet, bassoon, and horn, Op. 205, takes its title from the street in Aix-en-Provence that commemorates René I, duke of Anjou (1409–1480), titular king of Naples.

Cherevichki *see* **Vakula the Smith**.

Cherry Duet Pietro Mascagni, 1891.

The duet between Suzel and Fritz in Act 2 of L'**Amico Fritz**, set in an orchard near a farm. As Suzel picks cherries, singing happily, Fritz enters and greets her with "*Suzel, buon dì*" ("Good morning, Suzel"). She tells him the cherries are ripe and throws them down to him.

"Cherry Ripe" Charles Edward Horn, *c.* 1825.

The song is a setting of Robert Herrick's poem of the same name from his *Hesperides* (1648). The words are supposedly those of a cherry seller but are really those of a lover about his loved one's lips: "Cherry ripe, ripe, ripe, I cry, / Full and fair ones; come and buy!"

Chérubin ("Cherubino") Jules Massenet, 1905.

The opera in three acts is set to a libretto by Henri Cain and Francis de Croisset based on the latter's play of the same name, which tells of the subsequent doing of Cherubino, the amorous pageboy in Beaumarchais' comedy *Le Mariage de Figaro* (1784) (and so in Mozart's opera Le **Nozze di Figaro**).

Le Cheval de bronze ("The Bronze Horse") Daniel Auber, 1835.

The opera in three acts, to a libretto by Eugène Scribe, is set in China and tells what happens when Peki, wife of the mandarin, Tsing Sing, flies on the magic bronze horse to seek the help of the fairy princess, Stella, when her husband is turned to stone by another of his wives.

Le Chevalier et la Damoiselle ("The Knight and the Young Lady")   Philippe Gaubert, 1941.

The ballet in two acts, with a libretto and choreography by Serge Lifar, is based on a medieval Burgundian legend telling how a knight errant meets a white-antlered hind which changes into a young girl when he stabs it.

"Chi mi frena" ("Who checks me?").

The sextet in Act 2 of Donizetti's **Lucia di Lammermoor**, in which Eduardo finds his anger checked by the sight of Lucia's distress. The full opening words are: "*Chi me frena in tal momento?*" ("Who checks me at such a moment?").

Chichester Psalms   Leonard Bernstein, 1965.

The choral work for countertenor, chorus, and orchestra, to a Hebrew text, was written for Chichester cathedral, England, where it was first performed.

The Chieftain   Arthur Sullivan, 1894.

The operetta in two acts, to a libretto by F.C. Burnand, is an extended version of *The Contrabandista* (1867), set in northern Spain. The story tells what happens when the British tourist, Peter Adolphus Grigg, while taking a photograph, is captured by a band of brigands led by Ferdinand de Roxas, the Chieftain of the Ladrones ("Brigands").

A Child of Our Time   Michael Tippett, 1939–41.

The oratorio for soprano, alto, tenor, and bass soloists, chorus, and orchestra is a setting of the composer's own text suggested by the *Kristallnacht* ("night of crystal"), the night of violence against Jews and subsequent pogroms that followed the assassination in Paris of the Nazi diplomat Ernst vom Rath by Herschel Grynszpan, a 17-year-old Polish-Jewish student, on November 9, 1938. He is thus the "child of our time" of the title.

The Childhood of Christ *see* **L'Enfance du Christ**.

Children's Corner   Claude Debussy, 1908.

The suite of piano pieces was dedicated by the composer to his young daughter, Claude-Emma, nicknamed Chouchou (1905–1919). All of the titles, including the main one, are English, probably because the little girl had an English governess. They are: *Doctor Gradus ad Parnassum* (*see* **Gradus ad Parnassum**), *Jimbo's Lullaby* ("Jimbo" being an error for "Jumbo"), *Serenade for the Doll*, *The Snow Is Dancing*, *The Little Shepherd*, and *Golliwogg's Cakewalk*. *Jimbo's Lullaby* pays "homage" to Chouchou's toy elephant, as *Serenade for the Doll* does to her doll. The rather strange use of "corner" in the title probably arose because French *coin* has a wider sense than the English, meaning not only "corner" but also "locality," "place where one lives." A "children's corner" is thus that part of a house, such as a nursery, that is given over to young children. Debussy wrote the suite in the year that he married his second wife, Emma Bardac. (*See* **Dolly**.)

The Children's Crusade   Benjamin Britten, 1968.

The "ballad for children's voices and orchestra," Op. 82, written to mark the 50th anniversary of the Save the Children Fund, is based on Hans Keller's translation of Bertolt Brecht's poem *Der Kinderkreuzzug* ("The Children's Crusade"), about children forced by the ravages of war to assume adult responsibilities in order to survive.

A Children's Overture   Roger Quilter, 1914.

The orchestral work, based on the traditional tunes for nursery rhymes, was intended to be the overture to Clifford Mills and John Ramsey's play *Where the Rainbow Ends* (1911), for which the composer wrote the incidental music, but in the end was not used.

Chinese Dance *see* **Nutcracker**.

The Chinese Orphan Boy (Italian, *L'orfano della China*)   Gaspero Angiolini, 1774.

The ballet, long ascribed to Christoph Gluck, is based on Voltaire's tragedy *L'Orphelin de la Chine* ("The Chinese Orphan Boy") (1755), telling how a faithful mandarin sacrifices his own son to save the heir of the throne when Genghis Khan and his Tartars conquer Peking.

The Chocolate Soldier (German, *Der tapfere Soldat*, "The Valiant Soldier")   Oscar Straus, 1908.

The operetta in three acts is set to a libretto by Rudolf Bernauer and Leopold Jacobson based on George Bernard Shaw's play *Arms and the Man* (1894), a light-hearted treatment of love and war. Captain Bluntschli in Shaw's play is nicknamed "the chocolate soldier" because he carries chocolate into battle instead of cartridges. (Hence the use of the phrase for a soldier who will not fight.) The German title is thus ironic.

Les Choëphores ("The Choephori")   Darius Milhaud, 1919.

The opera in one act, Op. 24, is set to a libretto by Paul Claudel based on the second part of Aeschylus's trilogy *Oresteia* (458 BC), dealing with the relationship between Agamemnon's daughter, Electra, and his son, Orestes. The title means "The Libation Bearers."

Chopin Concerto   Fryderyk Chopin, 1937.

The ballet in three movements, choreographed by Bronislava Nijinska, is based on the composer's Concerto for Piano and Orchestra No. 1 in E minor, Op. 11 (1830). There is no plot, but the dancers aim to reflect the different moods of the music.

Choral Fantasia   (1) Ludwig van Beethoven, 1808; (2) Gustav Holst, 1930.

Beethoven's Op. 80 in C minor for piano, chorus, and orchestra is set to a poem by Christoph Kuffner. Holst's Op. 51 for soprano, chorus, organ, strings, brass, and percussion is set to words by the poet Robert Bridges. The title of each relates both to work's the choral content and to its poetic inspiration.

Choral Symphony   Ludwig van Beethoven, 1824.

The Symphony No. 9 in D minor, Op. 125, is so called because it has a setting of Friedrich von Schiller's *Ode to Joy* (German, *An die Freude*) (1785) for chorus and soloists in the last movement. The name does not exist for the work in German. *See also* **Ninth Symphony**.

Choreartium   Johannes Brahms, 1933.

The ballet in four movements, choreographed by Léonide Massine, is set to the composer's Symphony No. 4 in E minor, Op.98 (1884–5), and represents an abstract interpretation of the music. The classically-based title is presumably is means to mean "Art of the Dance."

Chorus of the Hebrew Slaves   Giuseppe Verdi, 1841.

The chorus of exiled Hebrew slaves in Act 3 of **Nabucco**, sending winged thoughts to their homeland. It is also known by its leading words, "*Va, pensiero*" ("Go, thought").

Chota Roustaveli   various (see below), 1946.

The ballet or choreographic epic in four acts, with a libretto and choreography by Serge Lifar, is set to music by Arthur Honegger, Nicolai Tcherepnin, and Tibor Harsányi and is based on the long epic poem *The Knight in the Panther's Skin* by the Georgian poet Shota Rustaveli (*c.*1172–*c.*1216). The ballet recounts the adventures of the poet and Queen Tamara, his inspiration and his love. The title spells the poet's name in the French fashion.

Chout *see* The **Buffoon**.

Das Christelflein ("The Christmas Elf")   Hans Pfitzner, 1917.

The opera in two acts, Op. 20, is set to the composer's own libretto based on Ilse von Stach's play of the same name.

A Christmas Carol   Thea Musgrave, 1979.

The opera in two acts is set to the composer's own libretto based on Charles Dickens's novel of the same name (1843), telling what happens when the old curmudgeon, Scrooge, receives a visit from the ghost of Marley, his late business partner.

Christmas Concerto   Arcangelo Corelli, 1714.

The **Concerto Grosso** in G minor, Op. 6 No.8, for strings and continuo, was intended for church use and was inscribed "*fatto per la notte di Natale*" ("done for Christmas night"). Hence the title.

Christmas Eve (Russian, *Noch' pered Rozhdestvom*)   Nikolay Rimsky-Korsakov, 1895.

The opera in four acts is set to the composer's own libretto based on Nikolai Gogol's tale of this name in *Evenings on a Farm near Dikanka* (1832). The story tells what happens on Christmas Eve when the Devil and the witch, Solokha, decide to steal the moon. This hinders the blacksmith, Vakula, who has come to court Oxana. The same story gave the plot of Tchaikovsky's opera **Vakula the Smith**.

Christmas Oratorio (German, *Weinachtsoratorium*)   J.S. Bach, 1734.

The oratorio for soloists, chorus, and orchestra, BWV 248, is set to texts relating the biblical story of the Nativity. It comprises six cantatas intended for performance in Leipzig on the three days of the Christmas festival, on New Year's Day (the Circumcision), on the Sunday following, and on the Epiphany. It thus merits its title for its content and the occasion of its first performance. Its Latin title is *Oratorium tempore Nativitatis Christi* ("Oratorio of the Time of Christ's Nativity").

Christmas Symphony   (1) Krzysztof Penderecki, 1980; (2) *see* **Lamentation Symphony**.

The Symphony No. 2 is so named because it includes the Christmas carol *Silent Night*.

Christophe Colomb ("Christopher Columbus")   Darius Milhaud, 1930.

The opera in two acts, Op. 102, to a libretto by Paul Claudel is in 27 scenes (incorporating film) and recounts the events of Columbus's life.

Christopher Columbus   William Walton, 1942.

The work comprises incidental music for a BBC radio program written by Louis MacNeice and broadcast in 1942 to mark the 450th anniversary of Columbus's first voyage to America.

Christus   Franz Liszt, 1867.

The oratorio for soprano, alto, tenor, baritone and bass soloists, chorus, organ, and orchestra is set to a biblical and liturgical text. Hence its title, the Latin name of Christ.

Christus am Ölberge ("Christ on the Mount of Olives")   Ludwig van Beethoven, 1803.

The oratorio, Op. 85, for soprano, tenor, bass, chorus, and orchestra, is set to a text by Franz Xaver Huber based on the biblical texts describing the events in the life of Christ that are associated with the Mount of Olives. (He enters Jerusalem from it and goes there for prayer when in or around Jerusalem. Acts 1:12 also implies that the Ascension took place there.) An English adapation changes the subject to the Old Testament story of David under the title *En Gedi*, the city of Judah where David lived (1 Samuel 23:29).

Chromatic Fantasia and Fugue (German, *Chromatische Fantasie und Fuge*)   J.S. Bach, 1720.

The work in D minor for harpsichord, BWV 903, has several passages that are chromatic, that is, they ascend or descend by semitones. (A chromatic scale is a regular major or minor scale to which semitones have been added to give it "color.") Hence the title.

Chronica   Berthold Goldschmidt, 1939.

The ballet in three acts, with a libretto and choreography by Kurt Jooss, is set against an Italian renaissance background and tells of the condottiere (mercenary leader), Fortunato.

Chronochromie ("Chronochromy")   Olivier Messiaen, 1960.

The orchestral work, whose Greek-based title means literally "time color," is abstract in nature and comprises seven sections: (1) *Introduction*, (2) *Strophe I*, (3) *Antistrophe I*, (4) *Strophe II*, (5) *Antistrophe II*, (6) *Epode*, (7) *Coda*. In classical Greek drama, a strophe (literally "turning") was the first part of a choral ode chanted by the chorus as they moved from one side of the stage to the other. It was followed by the antistrophe ("counterturning"), a reverse movement. The strophe and antistrophe were completed by the epode ("additional song"), in a different metrical form. Messaien thus follows the classical pattern. His *Epode* is written for 18 strings, each playing a different birdsong.

Ciboulette   Reynaldo Hahn, 1923.

The operetta in three acts, to a libretto by Robert de Flers and Francis de Croisset, is set in and around Paris in the 1860s and tells of the adventures of a country girl, Ciboulette ("Chives"), when she becomes involved with a Paris aristocrat, Antonin de Mourmelon.

Le Cid ("The Cid")   Jules Massenet, 1885.

The opera in four acts is set to a libretto by Adolphe Philippe d'Ennery, Louis Gallet, and Édouard Blau based on Pierre Corneille's tragicomedy of the same title (1636), itself inspired by medieval tales about the Castilian military leader and national hero Rodrigo Díaz de Vivar (*c*.1043–1099), known as "El Cid" ("The Lord").

"Cielo e mar!" ("Sky and sea!").

Enzo's aria praising the sky and sea in Act 2 of Ponchielli's La **Gioconda**.

La Cigale et la Fourmi ("The Grasshopper and the Ant")   Edmond Audran, 1886.

The comic opera in three acts (six scenes), is set to a libretto by Henri Charles Chivot and Alfred Duru based on Jean de La Fontaine's fable of the same name (1668). The story is set in the 17th century and centers on two orphan sisters who share a Flemish farmhouse home. One, Charlotte, steadfast and industrious, is nicknamed "The Ant," while the other, Marton, bright and vivacious, and with an ambition to become an opera singer, is "The Grasshopper."

Cinderella   (1) (Russian, *Zolushka*) Sergey Prokofiev, 1945; (2) *see* **Aschenbrödel**; **Cendrillon**; La **Cenerentola**.

The ballet in three acts (seven scenes), with a libretto by Nikolai Volkov and choreography by Rostislav Zakharov, is based on Charles Perrault's famous story in his *Contes de ma mère l'Oye* ("Mother Goose Tales") (1697) about the pretty girl who is forced to do all of the housework by her stepmother and ugly sisters but who finally meets and marries a prince.

Le Cinesi ("The Chinese Ladies")
Christoph Gluck, 1754.

The opera serenade in one act is set to a text expanded from a libretto written by Pietro Metastasio for Antonio Caldara. The plot concerns three young Chinese women who amuse themselves by acting out dramatic scenes.

Cinq Mélodies populaires grecques
("Five Popular Greek Tunes") Maurice Ravel, 1904–6.

The work consists of five pieces for voice and orchestra based on traditional Greek folksongs, translated from the Greek by the French-born music critic of Greek parentage, Michel-Dimitri Calvocoressi. Their individual titles are: (1) *Le Réveil de la mariée* ("The Bride's Awakening"), (2) *Là-bas vers l'église* ("Down There by the Church"), (3) *Quel galant!* ("How Gallant!"), (4) *Chanson des cueilleuses de lentisques* ("Song of the Women Collecting Mastic"), (5) *Tout gai!* ("All happy!").

Circe Alan Hovhaness, 1963.

The ballet in one act, with a libretto and choreography by Martha Graham, is based on the classical myth of the sorceress, Circe, who was exiled to an island where she turned all the men of Odysseus into swine.

Circles Luciano Berio, 1960.

The work for female voice, harp, and two percussionists is a setting of texts by E.E. Cummings from his *Poems 1923–54*. It is so named because the singer "circles" or moves to different positions between movements to identify with different instrumentalists, and so to a greater or lesser extent to identify verbal with musical sound. "A circling on the platform thus coincides with a circling from comprehensible language to disjointed vocal sound and back again" (Griffiths, p. 50).

Circus Polka Igor Stravinsky, 1942.

The ballet, choreographed by George Balanchine as an "original choreographical tour de force", was composed for Barnum and Bailey's circus to be danced by a troupe of 50 young elephants and 50 beautiful girls. Hence its full title, *Circus Polka for a Young Elephant*.

Ciro in Babilonia ("Cyrus in Babylon")
Gioacchino Rossini, 1812.

The opera in two acts, to a libretto by Francesco Aventi, centers historically on Cyrus (died 529 BC), the Persian king who conquered Babylon, killed its ruler, Balthasar (Belshazzar), and became king himself. The subtitle is *La caduta di Baldassare* ("The Fall of Balthasar").

Clair de lune ("Moonlight") (1) Gabriel Fauré, 1887; (2) Claude Debussy, 1890.

Fauré's song, Op. 46 No. 2, is set to Paul Verlaine's poem of the same title, the third of his *Fêtes galantes* ("Courtly Celebrations") (1869). The title is also that of the third movement of Debussy's **Suite bergamasque** (1890) for piano, and of his song to the same poem (1891). *See also* **Fêtes galantes**, **Masques et Bergamasques**.

Clarissa Robin Holloway, 1968–76.

The opera in two acts, Op. 30, is set to the composer's own libretto based on Samuel Richardson's novel *Clarissa Harlowe* (1747), about the delicate and modest girl of this name who becomes fascinated by the nobleman Lovelace.

Classical Symphony (Russian, *Klassicheskaya simfoniya*) Sergey Prokofiev, 1916.

The Symphony No. 1 in D major, Op. 25, was deliberately written in the classical style typical of Haydn and Mozart. Hence the title.

La Clemenza di Tito ("The Clemency of Titus) W.A. Mozart, 1791.

The opera in two acts, K 621, is set to a libretto by Pietro Metastasio that was adapted by Caterino Mazzolà. It centers on the Roman emperor Titus (AD 39–81) and tells how he comes to forgive Sextus and Vitellia, who respectively campaign and conspire against him.

Cléopâtre ("Cleopatra") Anton Arensky, 1908.

The ballet in one act, with a libretto and choreography by Michel Fokine, represents an Egyptian romance between Queen Cleopatra and the slave, Amoûn. The original French and Russian titles were respectively *Une nuit d'Égypte* ("An Egyptian Night") and *Yegipetskiye nochi* ("Egyptian Nights").

Clo-Clo Franz Lehár, 1924.

The operetta in three acts is set to a libretto by Béla Jenbach based on Julius Horst and Alexander Engel's farce *Der Schrei nach dem Kinde* ("The Urge for a Child"). The story is set in Paris in 1924 and centers on the young revue star, Clo-Clo Mustache.

Les Cloches de Corneville ("The Bells of Corneville")   Robert Planquette, 1877.

The opera in three acts, to a libretto by Charles Gabet and Louis François Clairville, is set in Normandy in the 17th century and tells how Henri, descendant of the duke of Corneville, hopes he can prove his claim to the vacant dukedom by fulfilling a local legend that the bells of the castle of Corneville will ring of their own accord when the rightful heir approaches.

Clock Symphony (German, Uhr-Sinfonie)   Joseph Haydn, 1794.

The Symphony No.101 in D major is so nicknamed because of the measured "tick-tock" accompaniment to the first subject of the second movement. The minuet of the third movement is also a variant of one of four that the composer wrote for a mechanical clock.

Clocks and Clouds   György Ligeti, 1973.

The work for 12 voice female chorus and orchestra takes its title from the essay Of Clouds and Clocks (1966) by the Austrian-born British philosopher Karl Popper.

The Cloud Messenger   Gustav Holst, 1910.

The ode for chorus and orchestra, Op. 30, is set to the composer's own text based on the Sanskrit lyric Meghaduta ("The Cloud Messenger") by the 5th-century Indian poet Kalidasa. The poem is a message from a lover to his absent beloved interspersed with descriptions of the landscape of northern India.

The Clowns   Hershy Kay, 1968.

The ballet in one act, choreographed by Gerald Arpino, aims to show how clowns act out the duality of humankind, which both destroys itself yet struggles fiercely to survive.

Club Anthem   John Blow, Pelham Humfrey, William Turner, 1664.

The anthem, a setting of "I will always give thanks" for three or four voices, strings, and organ, was written while the composers were choirboys at the Chapel Royal "as a memorial of their fraternal esteem and friendship." Hence the title.

Clytemnestra   Halim El-Dabh, 1958.

The ballet in two acts, with a prologue and epilogue, has a libretto and choreography by Martha Graham and is based on Aeschylus's trilogy Oresteia (458 BC), telling how Clytemnestra, during the absence in the Trojan War of her husband, Agamemnon, takes his cousin, Aegisthus, as a lover and together with him murders Agamemnon on his return, for which she is killed in revenge by her son, Orestes. The ballet re-enacts the main events and depicts Clytemnestra awaiting the decision of the gods about her eternal fate.

Coast of Happiness (Russian, Bereg schast'ya)   Antonio Spadavecchia, 1948.

The ballet in three acts, with a libretto by P. Abolimov and choreography by Vladimir Burmeyster and I V Kurilov, tells of the growing up of Natasha and the three Pioneers, Petya, Kostya, and Tolya, and their heroism in the Great Patriotic War (1941–5). The ballet is also known in English as Shore of Happiness or The Happy Coast.

Coast of Hope (Russian, Bereg nadezhdy)   Andrei Petrov, 1959.

The ballet in three acts, with a libretto by Yuri Slonimsky and choreography by Igor Belsky, tells the story of two fishing villages, one on the Soviet side of the sea, friendly and happy, the other on the other side, unfriendly and dreary. An alternate English title is Shore of Hope.

Cocardes ("Cockades")   Francis Poulenc, 1919.

The three songs for voice and piano are set to texts by Jean Cocteau respectively titled Miel de Narbonne ("Honey of Narbonne"), Bonne d'enfants ("Nursemaid"), and Enfant de troupe ("Army-Raised Child").

Cockaigne   Edward Elgar, 1901.

The concert overture, Op. 40, subtitled In London Town, is named for the imaginary land of idleness and luxury that because of a punning association with "Cockney" came to be associated with London, itself musically portrayed here as a busy, self-important city.

Cockcrow Sonata   Ludwig van Beethoven, 1812.

The Sonata for Violin and Piano in G major, Op. 96, was formerly so named, perhaps with some sarcastic reference to the declining skills of the violinist, Pierre Rode, for whom it was specifically composed.

Le Cœur et la Main ("With Heart and Mind")   Charles Lecocq, 1883.

The comic opera in three acts, to a libretto by Charles Nuittier and Alexandre Beaumont, is set in and around the royal palace of Aragon and tells what happens when the Infanta, Micaela, marries Don Gaeton, duke of Madeira, and an edict goes out that all girls marrying on the same day may do so at the crown's expense.

Coffee Cantata (German, *Kaffeecantate*) J.S. Bach, 1732.

The humorous cantata *Schweigt stille, plaudert nicht* ("Keep silent, do not talk"), BWV 211, to a libretto by Picander (Christian Friedrich Henrici), was composed at a time when there was a growing fondness for drinking coffee. Hence the name. The work is sometimes performed as an opera. "*Coffee Cantata* is Bach's only known opera about sex, a frothy tale of an alcoholic father's desperate attempts to stop his hot-headed and lascivious daughter's addiction to coffee. For coffee, read sex" (Joanna Pitman, *The Times*, August 9, 1997).

Colas Breugnon (Russian, *Master iz Klamesi*, "The Craftsman of Clamecy") Dmitry Kabalevsky, 1938.

The opera in three acts is set to a libretto by the composer and V.A. Bragin based on Romand Rolland's novel of the same name (1919). The plot is set in 17th-century Burgundy and centers on the love of the sculptor, Colas Breugnon, for Selina. The opera's popular English title, from the name of the hero, is strictly that of the overture only. The Russian title describes the hero and names the town where he lives (and where Rolland was himself born).

Colonel Bogey Kenneth Alford, 1914.

The military march derives its title from the imaginary player in golf whose score of one stroke above par must be beaten by his opponent(s). ("Bogey" is a nickname of the devil.)

A Colour Symphony Arthur Bliss, 1921

The composer had come across a book of heraldry giving the symbolic meanings associated with different colors. He therefore aimed to represent four of the main colors musically by devoting a movement to each. The first movement, a ceremonial march with ominous undertones, is titled *Purple: the colour of Amethysts, Royalty, Pageantry and Death*. The second movement, a vigorous scherzo, is *Red: the colour of Rubies, Wine, Revelry, Furnaces, Courage and Magic*. The third movement, slow and pastoral in character, is *Blue: the colour of Sapphires, Deep Water, Skies, Loyalty and Melancholy*. The final movement, a double fugue culminating in a festive march, is *Green: the Colour of Emeralds,* *Hope, Youth, Joy, Spring and Victory*. Each movement is thus a "mood piece."

Le Combat ("The Combat") R. de Banfield, 1949.

The ballet in one act, with a libretto and choreography by William Dollar, is based on Torquato Tasso's *Gerusalemme liberata* ("Jerusalem Liberated") (1580) and tells of the Christian warrior, Tancred, and the Saracen girl, Clorinda, that he loves. *Cf.* Il **Combattimento di Tancredi e Clorinda**.

Il Combattimento di Tancredi e Clorinda ("The Combat of Tancred and Clorinda") Claudio Monteverdi, 1624.

The scenic cantata is set to a text from Canto XII (verses 52–68) of Torquato Tasso's *Gerusalemme liberata* ("Jerusalem Liberated") (1580), in which the Christian warrior Tancred, in love with Clorinda, fights a duel with a Saracen. *Cf.* Le **Combat**.

"Com'è gentil" ("How lovely it is").

Ernesto's serenade in Act 3 of Donizetti's **Don Pasquale**.

Come Out Steve Reich, 1966.

The work for tape was produced for a benefit concert in support of six black youths who had been beaten while in police custody. One of them told how he squeezed his bruises "to let some of the bruise blood come out to show them" so he could leave jail and go to hospital. Reich subjected the five words "come out to show them" to a simple phasing process.

"Come scoglio" ("Like a rock").

Fiordiligi's aria in Act 1 of Mozart's **Così fan tutte**, in which she declares that she will remain as firm as a rock against any attempt to seduce her.

Come Ye Sons of Art Henry Purcell, 1694.

The ode for soprano, two altos, and bass, chorus, and orchestra, was composed for the 32d birthday of Queen Mary, wife of William III. (She died the same year.) The "sons of art" of the title are the musicians, exhorted to play in celebration.

The Comedians (1) (Russian, *Komedianty*) Dmitry Kabalevsky, 1940; (2) *see* A **Daughter of Castile**.

The suite for small orchestra was written as incidental music for M. Daniel's play *The Inventor and the Comedians* (1946).

Comedy on the Bridge (Czech, *Komedie na mostě*) Bohuslav Martinů, 1937.

The comic opera in one act is set to a libretto by Václav Kliment Klicpera telling of events on a bridge between two feuding villages.

Commotio Carl Nielsen, 1931.

The work for organ, Op. 58, is in four section, respectively a fantasia, a fugue, a slow movement, and a second fugue. The Latin title means "movement," symbolizing the importance the composer attached to "current" in music. In a letter to the organist Emilius Bangert he explained: "The Latin word *Commotio* really applies to all music, but is here especially used as an expression for self-objectivization (*Selbst-Objektivierung*)" (quoted in Robert Simpson, *Carl Nielsen*, 1952).

Compliments Quartet (German, *Kompliment-Quartett*) Ludwig van Beethoven, 1798.

The String Quartet in G major, Op. 18 No. 2, is said to be so named because its opening four bars and their response are said to suggest "bowing and scraping," or even an elaborate reception at court. The name is used among German speakers rather than in English.

Le Comte Ory ("Count Ory") Gioacchino Rossini, 1828.

The comic opera in two acts is to a libretto by Eugène Scribe and C.G. Delestre-Poirson is based on an alleged old Picard legend set down by Pierre-Antoine de la Place in 1785. It tells of the amorous Count Ory, who during the Crusades tricked his way into the favors of the Countess Adèle.

Comus (1) Henry Lawes, 1634; (2) Thomas Arne, 1738; (3) Henry Purcell, arr. Constant Lambert, 1942.

The name is that of the pagan god who was invented by John Milton as the central character of his masque (1634), a mimed play with incidental dances. It was written at the suggestion of Lawes, who wrote the music and himself took part. Arne composed new music for John Dalton's adaptation of the work. The ballet based on Purcell's music was choreographed by Robert Helpmann and based on Milton's masque.

Con Amore ("With Love") Gioacchino Rossini, 1953.

The ballet in one act (three scenes), with a libretto by James Graham Luján and choreography by Lew Christensen, is set to three of the composer's overtures and tells of a bandit who is captured by Amazons and has problems resisting their amorous advances. The title can be taken literally but also alludes to the musical direction, "indicating an enthusiastic manner of performance" (Blom, p. 111).

The Concert Fryderyk Chopin, 1956.

The ballet in one act, choreographed by Jerome Robbins, depicts a series of humorous sketches in which concertgoers live out their flights of fancy while listening to a recital of piano pieces by the composer.

Concertino Pastorale John Ireland, 1939.

The work for string orchestra is in three movements respectively titled *Eclogue*, *Threnody*, and *Toccata*. The allusion is thus at least partly to Greek pastoral poetry, in which an eclogue (literally "selection") is a pastoral dialogue or soliloquy. A threnody (literally "wailing song") was originally a Greek choral ode but is now any kind of lamentation.

Concerto Dmitry Shostakovich, 1966.

The plotless ballet in three movements, choreographed by Kenneth MacMillan, reflects the various moods of the composer's Piano Concerto No. 2 in F major, Op.102 (1957). *Concerto* itself is Italian for "concert," originally (in the 16th century) by a group of instruments but later (18th century) by a solo instrument.

Concerto Accademico ("Academic Concerto") Ralph Vaughan Williams, 1925.

The concerto in D minor for violin and strings bears an Italian title that the composer later rejected.

Concerto Barocco ("Baroque Concerto") J.S. Bach, 1941.

The plotless ballet in three movements, choreographed by George Balanchine, is set to the composer's Concerto in D minor for Two Violins, BWV 1043, and progresses as a visual comment on the music, as ornamented by the dancers.

Concerto for Orchestra Béla Bartók, 1942–3.

A **Concerto** is traditionally a work for one or more solo instruments and orchestra. The "concerto for orchestra" is a 20th-century development. The composer explained that he so named his work, in five movements, because of "its tendency to treat the single instrument or instrument groups in concertante or soloistic manner" (quoted in Nicholas, p. 66). The second movement is subtitled *Gioco delle coppie* ("Game of the Couples"), and presents the instruments in pairs.

Concerto for the Left Hand (French, *Concerto pour la main gauche*)   Maurice Ravel, 1931.

The Piano Concerto in D was commissioned and first performed by the Austrian pianist Paul Wittgenstein (1887–1961), whose right arm had been injured and amputated in World War I. In 1939 the pianist Alfred Cortot published an edition which laid the solo part out for two hands, but most musicians agree that it should properly be played by the left hand alone.

Concerto Grosso (Italian, "Great Concerto").

An early form of the **Concerto**, usually with a small body of strings alternating or contrasting with a larger group. An example is Corelli's **Christmas Concerto**. Bach's **Brandenburg Concertos** Nos. 2, 4, 5, and 6 are also traditional concerti grossi.

Concerto Italiano ("Italian Concerto") Mario Castelnuovo-Tedesco, 1926.

The composer so named his Violin Concerto No. 1 for its specifically "Italian" inspiration and content. *See* The **Prophets**.

Conchita   Riccardo Zandonai, 1911.

The opera in four acts (six scenes) is set to a libretto by Maurizio Vaucaire and Carlo Zangarini based on Pierre Louÿs's novel *La Femme et le Pantin* ("The Woman and the Puppet") (1898). The story is set in Seville in the early 20th century and tells of the attempts of Matteo, an elderly rake, to convince Conchita, a flamenco dancer, that he loves her.

Concierto de Aranjuez ("Aranjuez Concerto")   Joaquín Rodrigo, 1939.

The concerto for guitar and orchestra evokes old Spain and is named for the little town of Aranjuez, outside Madrid, where the composer and his wife moved in the year of its composition.

Concord Sonata   Charles Ives, 1911–15.

The work for piano with solos for viola and flute has the full title *Sonata No. 2 (Concord, Massachusetts, 1840–60)*. It was written in honor of the Concord group of writers that the composer admired, their names forming the titles of the individual movements: *Emerson, Hawthorne, The Alcotts*, and *Thoreau*. These were leading members of the Transcendentalist philosophical and literary movement active in Concord during the given dates.

La Concurrence ("Competition")   Georges Auric, 1932.

The ballet in one act, with a libretto by André Derain and choreography by George Balanchine, tells of the competition between two tailors, who bicker in the street to draw custom.

Confession of Isobel Gowdie   James MacMillan, 1990.

The orchestral work takes its title from the Scotswoman Isobel Gowdie, who in 1662 was tortured into confessing she was a witch. The composer used the incident as a metaphor for his fears regarding the rise of fascism in Europe.

Confessional   Jean Sibelius, 1941.

The ballet in one act, choreographed by Walter Gore, is based on Robert Browning's poem *The Confessional* (1845) and on the composer's incidental music to Maurice Maeterlinck's play *Pelléas et Mélisande*, Op.46 (1905). The story tells of the despair of a girl who betrays her lover in the confessional.

Confessions of a Justified Sinner Thomas Wilson, 1976.

The opera in three acts is set to a libretto by John Currie based on James Hogg's novel *The Private Memoirs and Confessions of a Justified Sinner* (1824), a macabre tale in which the central character, Colwan, commits a series of horrifying murders under the influence of a malign stranger.

Confetti   Gioacchino Rossini, 1970.

The ballet in one act, choreographed by Gerald Arpino, is a bravura performance by six dancers, using confetti, to the overture to the composer's opera **Semiramide**.

Confidence *see* Lieder ohne Worte.

"Connais-tu le pays?" ("Knowest thou the land?").

Mignon's aria in Act 1 of Thomas' **Mignon**, as the famous "*Kennst du das Land?*" of Goethe's *Wilhelm Meisters Lehrjahre*, in which she tries to answer Wilhelm's questions about her origins.

The Consecration of Sound (German, *Die Weihe der Töne*)   Ludwig Spohr, 1835.

The Symphony No. 4, Op. 86, was inspired by Karl Pfeiffer's poem of the same name, the composer requesting that it be either read aloud before the work was performed or else printed on the program. The symphony is alternately known in English as *The Power of Sound*, or formally as *A Characteristic Tone Painting in the Form of a Symphony After a Poem by Karl Pfeiffer.*

The Consecration of the House (German, *Die Weihe des Hauses*)   Ludwig van Beethoven, 1822.

The overture in C major, Op. 124, was written for the opening of the Josefstadt Theatre, Vienna and first performed there, conducted by the composer, on October 3, 1822. The title is appropriate for such an occasion but in fact is that of a play by the Austrian playwright Karl Meisl, for which Beethoven intended to compose incidental music, although only one item was completed. Since the play was an adaptation of Kotzebue's play *Die Ruinen von Athen,* for which Beethoven had composed incidental music (*see* Die **Ruinen von Athen**), he rearranged his music for that for *Die Weihe des Hauses,* but wrote a new overture.

Conservatory (Danish, *Konservatoriet*) Holger Simon Paulli, 1849.

The vaudeville ballet in two acts, choreographed by August Bournonville, depicts a dancing class of the Paris Conservatoire, originally set against a background of amorous intrigues. The subtitle is *Proposal of Marriage Through a Newspaper* (Danish, *Et Avisfrieri*).

Consolation *see* **Lieder ohne Worte**.

Consolations   Franz Liszt, 1849–50.

The six pieces (nocturnes) for solo piano are so named for their consoling or comforting effect.

Constantia   Fryderyk Chopin, 1944.

The ballet in three movements, choreographed by William Dollar, is set to the composer's Piano Concerto No. 2 in F minor, Op. 21 (1829–30), and was inspired by his love for the popular young singer, Constantia Gladkowska, to whom he dedicated the slow movement.

Construction in Metal   John Cage, 1939–41.

The three works for six and four percussion players respectively are so named for their metallic instruments. The impressive battery of the first *Construction* (1939) thus included orchestral bells, thundersheets, sleigh bells, ox bells, brake drums, anvils, water gongs, and tamtams.

The Consul   Gian-Carlo Menotti, 1950.

The opera in three acts, to the composer's own libretto, is set in an anonymous police state

in Europe and describes the efforts of Magda Sorel to obtain a visa for herself and her husband, John, a revolutionary wanted by the seret police. The consul's secretary, however, frustrates all her attempts to see the consul himself.

Contemplation *see* **Lieder ohne Worte**.

Les Contes d'Hoffmann ("The Tales of Hoffmann")   Jacques Offenbach, 1881.

The opera in three acts, with a prologue and epilogue, is set to a libretto by Jules Barbier and Michel Carré based on E.T.A. Hoffmann's stories *Der Sandmann* ("The Sandman") (1816), *Geschichte vom Verlorenen Spiegelbilde* ("Tale of the Lost Reflection," usually known in English as "The New Year's Eve Adventure") (1816), and *Rat Krespel* ("Councillor Krespel") (1818). These interconnected stories provide the subjects of the three acts, with Hoffmann himself the overall central figure. *See also* **Tales of Hoffmann**.

Contes Russes ("Russian Tales")   Anatol Lyadov, 1917.

The ballet in a prologue and four scenes, choreographed by Léonide Massine, unfolds as a series of episodes from Russian fairy tales and folklore.

The Contrabandista *see* **The Chieftain**.

Contrasts   Béla Bartók, 1938.

The work in two movements for violin, clarinet, and piano is so named because the violinist plays on two instruments, one being tuned unconventionally for 30 bars to G sharp, D, A, and E flat, instead of the usual G, D, A, and E.

Le Convenienze e inconvenienze teatrali ("The Theatrical Conveniences and Inconveniences")   Gaetano Donizetti, 1827.

The opera in two acts (originally one), subtitled *Viva la Mamma* ("Long Live Mother"), is set to a libretto by the composer based on two plays by Antonio Sografi. It tells of a series of operatic backstage intrigues centering on Mamma Agata ("Mother Agatha"), a "drag" role. The "conveniences" were the rules of etiquette governing the rank of singers in 19th-century Italian opera, so that the principal soprano, for example, was the *prima donna* ("first lady"), and the principal tenor the *primo uomo* ("first man").

Conversations   Arthur Bliss, 1920.

The work in five movements for chamber orchestra aims to represent different types of conversations at different locations, as indicated by the titles of the movements: (1) *The Committee Meeting*, (2) *In the Wood*, (3) *In the Ball Room*, (4) *Soliloquy* (a "conversation" with oneself), and (5) *In the Tube at Oxford Circus* (meaning the Underground or subway in London).

Coppélia   Léo Delibes, 1870.

The ballet in three acts, subtitled *La Fille aux yeux d'émail* ("The Girl with Enamel Eyes"), is set to a libretto by Charles Nuittier and Arthur Saint-Léon, with choreography by the latter, based on E.T.A. Hoffmann's story *Der Sandmann* ("The Sandman") (1816), telling how the dollmaker Coppelius seeks to make a doll (Coppelia) with a soul. *See also* La **Poupée**.

Le Coq d'or *see* The **Golden Cockerel**.

Corelli Fugue   J.S. Bach, *c.* 1710.

The Fugue in B minor for organ, BWV 579, is so named because it is based on two subjects from Arcangelo Corelli's Op. 3 No. 4 in his *Sonatas a tre* (1689).

Coriolan ("Coriolanus")   Ludwig van Beethoven, 1807.

The overture, Op. 62, was composed for a revival of Heinrich Joseph von Collin's (not Shakespeare's) play *Coriolan* (1804), about the legendary Roman hero Gaius Coriolanus (so named for the courage he showed at the capture of the Volscian town of Corioli in 439 BC).

Coro ("Chorus")   Luciano Berio, 1974–6.

The work is for a chorus of 40 singers, each placed beside an instrumentalist of corresponding range. Hence the title, which thus alludes to both types of performer.

Coronation Anthem   Henry Purcell, 1685.

The anthem *My Heart is Inditing* was composed for the coronation of James II in Westminster Abbey on April 23, 1685 and was performed on that occasion. The anthem's title is of biblical origin: "My heart is inditing a good matter" (Psalm 45:1). *Cf.* **Coronation Anthems**.

Coronation Anthems   George Frideric Handel, 1727.

The four anthems *The King Shall Rejoice*, *Let Thy Hand Be Strengthened*, *My Heart Is Inditing*, and **Zadok the Priest** were composed for the coronation of George II on October 11, 1727.

Coronation Concerto   W.A. Mozart, 1788

The Piano Concerto No. 26 in D major, K 537, is so named as it was performed in Frankfurt on the occasion of the coronation of Leopold II as emperor of Germany (1790).

Coronation Mass   (1) W.A. Mozart, 1779; (2) *see* **Nelson Mass**.

The Mass in C major, K 317, is said to be so named because Antonio Salieri (*see* **Mozart and Salieri**) directed a performance of it at the coronation of Leopold II in Prague as emperor of Germany (1790). This origin has had other explanations: "It has been conjectured that Mozart dedicated the work to an image of the Virgin Mary, crowned in 1751, or wrote it for a commemoration of that crowning" (Blom, p. 117).

Coronation Ode   Edward Elgar, 1902.

The choral work, Op. 44, for four soloists, chorus, and orchestra, to texts by A.C. Benson, was commissioned for the coronation of Edward VII (1902). The seven parts are as follows: (1) *Crown the King with Life*, (2) *Daughter of Ancient Kings*, (3) *Britain, Ask of Thyself*, (4) *Hark upon the Hallowed Air*, (5) *Only Let the Heart Be Pure*, (6) *Peace, Gentle Peace*, (7) (Finale) **Land of Hope and Glory**.

The Coronation of Poppea *see* L'**Incoronazione di Poppea**.

Les Corps glorieux ("The Glorious Hosts") Olivier Messiaen, 1939.

The work for organ is religiomystical in nature, as indicated by the titles of its seven movements: (1) *Subtilité des corps glorieux* ("Subtlety of the Glorious Hosts"), (2) *Les Eaux de la grâce* ("The Waters of Grace"), (3) *L'Ange aux parfums* ("The Angel of Perfumes"), (4) *Combat de la mort et de la vie* ("Struggle of Life and Death"), (5) *Force et agilité des corps glorieux* ("Strength and Agility of the Glorious Hosts"), (6) *Joie et clarté des corps glorieux* ("Joy and Light of the Glorious Hosts"), (7) *Mystère de la Sainte Trinité* ("Mystery of the Holy Trinity").

Der Corregidor ("The Mayor")   Hugo Wolf, 1896.

The opera in four acts is set to a libretto by Rosa Mayreder based on the story by Pedro Antonio de Alarcón (1874) that later gave Falla's ballet El **Sombrero de tres picos**.

Le Corsaire ("The Corsair")   (1) Hector Berlioz, 1844; (2) Adolphe Adam, 1856.

Both Berlioz's overture, Op. 21, and Adam's ballet in three acts and five scenes, with a libretto by Jules-Henri Vernoy de Saint-Georges and Joseph Mazilier, are based on Byron's poem *The*

Corsair (1814), telling of a Greek girl, Medora, who is sold into slavery and miraculously saved by the pirate (corsair) Conrad, who becomes her lover. *Cf.* Il **Corsaro**.

Il Corsaro ("The Corsair")   Giuseppe Verdi, 1848.
The opera in three acts is set to a libretto by Francesco Maria Piave based on Byron's poem *The Corsair* (1814). *See* Le **Corsaire**.

"Cortigiani, vil razza" ("Courtiers, vile rabble").
Rigoletto's aria in Act 2 of Verdi's **Rigoletto**, in which he denounces the courtiers who have abducted his daughter. The title is sometimes shortened to just "*Cortigiani*".

Una Cosa rara ("A Rare Thing")   Vicente Martín y Soler, 1786.
The comic opera in two acts is set to a libretto by Lorenzo da Ponte based on Luis Vélez de Guevara's story *La luna della sierra* ("The Moon of the Mountains"). The story is set in a Spanish village in the 18th century and tells what happens when the peasant girl, Lilla, promised by her brother, Tita, as a bride for the magistrate, Don Lisargo, is herself in love with Lubino, to whom she remains faithful when pursued by Prince Giovanni and his chamberlain, Corrado. The subtitle is *Bellezza ed onestà* ("Beauty and Honesty").

Così fan tutte ("Thus Do All Women")   W.A. Mozart, 1790.
The opera in two acts, K 588, is set to a libretto by Lorenzo da Ponte probably based on Canto 43 of Ludovico Ariosto's *Orlando furioso* (1516). The plot centers on the the wager by two officers that their respective lovers will be faithful in their absence. That they are not is because "all women are like that." The opera, subtitled *La scuola degli amanti* ("The School for Lovers"), is thus a cynical comedy on love and sexual relationships. "There has always been a difficulty in translating this title, the English language lacking a means of indicating the gender of 'tutte'. 'Thus do all [women]' would be literal. 'That's what women are!' might do" (Scholes, p. 259, footnote). Another solution might be "That's Women For You" or even just "Women!" (to counterbalance the female "Men!"). *Cf.* "La **Donna è mobile**." Pronunciation of the Italian title is equally variable: an American-style "Cozy Van Toody" is a frequent outcome.

Le Coucou ("The Cuckoo")   Louis Claude Daquin, 1735.

The piece for harpsichord is so named because it imitates the call of the cuckoo. (The second theme has the repeated phrase G, E in the treble to do this.)

The Count of Luxembourg *see* Der **Graf von Luxemburg**.

Count Ory *see* Le **Comte Ory**.

The Countess Maritza *see* Die **Gräfin Mariza**.

Country Gardens   Percy Grainger, 1908–18.
The piano piece is an arrangement of an English country dance tune first published in 1728 and itself a close variant of the tune to which *The Vicar of Bray* is traditionally sung. A modern version of the tune with words by Robert Jordan became familiar from the 1962 hit *English Country Garden* by the American pop singer Jimmie Rodgers.

The Covetous Knight *see* The **Miserly Knight**.

Cox and Box   Arthur Sullivan, 1867.
The operetta in one act is set to a libretto by Francis Cowley Burnand based on John Addison Morton's farce *Box and Cox* (1847), a rewriting of his *The Double Bedded-Room* (1843), in which a room is rented to two people at once, the journeyman hatter Cox, who works all day, and the journeyman printer Box, who works all night. The story tells what happens when Cox is given the day off. A good clue is given in the opera's subtitle, *The Long-Lost Brothers*.

The Cradle Will Rock   Marc Blitzstein, 1936.
The opera-musical in one act, to the composer's own libretto, tells of the conflict between a steel magnate and the trade unions. The title comes from the familiar nursery rhyme *Hush-a-bye, baby*.

The Creation (German, *Die Schöpfung*)   Joseph Haydn, 1797–8.
The oratorio for soprano, tenor, and bass soloists, chorus, and orchestra is set to a translation by Baron Gottfried van Swieten of an unknown English author's text based on John Milton's *Paradise Lost* (1667). The focus of the narrative is the biblical creation of the world.

La Création du monde ("The Creation of the World")   Darius Milhaud, 1922.

The ballet in one act, Op. 81, with a libretto by Blaise Cendrars and choreography by Jean Börlin, is based on the story of the biblical creation as seen through the eyes of a black African.

Creation Mass (German, *Schöpfungsmesse*) Joseph Haydn, 1801.

The Mass No. 13 in B flat major is so called because the *Qui tollis* (*see* **Agnus Dei**) contains a quotation from the oratorio The **Creation**.

The Creatures of Prometheus (German, *Die Geschöpfe des Prometheus*) Ludwig van Beethoven, 1801.

The ballet in an overture, introduction, and 16 numbers, to a lost libretto, with choreography by Salvatore Viganò, originally had the Italian title *Gli uomini di Prometeo*, "The Men of Prometheus." The story centers on the Titan of Greek mythology who created men from clay.

Credo (Latin, "I believe").

The Creed in the Roman Catholic **Mass**, as a statement of the worshiper's Christian belief. The opening words are: "*Credo in unum Deum, Patrem omnipotentem, factorem coeli et terrae*" ("I believe in one God, the Father almighty, maker of heaven and earth").

"Credo in un Dio crudel" ("I believe in a cruel God").

Iago's aria in Act 2 of Verdi's **Otello**, in which he declares his belief in a cruel god, who has fashioned him in his own likeness. The words are not in Shakespeare's original. The aria is also known as *Iago's Creed*.

Credo Mass W.A. Mozart, 1776.

The Mass in C major, K 257, is so named because its **Credo** is regarded as having the most distinctive and appropriate music of all of the credos in the composer's masses.

Crimson Sails (Russian, *Alyye parusa*) V.M. Yurovsky, 1942.

The ballet in a prologue and three acts, choreographed by Alexander Radunsky, Nikolai Popko, and Lev Pospekhin, is based on Alexander Grin's story of the same name (1923) about a little girl, Assol, who dreams of the day when a ship with red sails will appear, bringing a strong sailor to take her off to a faraway happy land. An alternate English title is *Red Sails*, although the original Russian translates better as *Scarlet Sails*.

Crispino e la comare ("Crispin and the Fairy") Luigi and Federico Ricci, 1850.

The comic opera in four acts, to a libretto by Francesco Maria Piave, tells what happens when the poor cobbler, Crispino, enlists the help of a fairy to become a wealthy physician.

The Critic Charles Villiers Stanford, 1916.

The opera in two acts, Op. 144, is set to a libretto by Lewis Cairns James based on Richard Brinsley Sheridan's comedy of the same name (1779), in which the critics, Dangle and Sneer, attend a disastrous rehearsal of the parodic tragedy *The Spanish Armada*. The opera is subtitled *An Opera Rehearsed*. Sheridan's play is subtitled *A Tragedy Rehearsed*, and was itself based on George Villiers Buckingham's farcical comedy *The Rehearsal* (1672).

Il Crociato in Egitto ("The Crusader in Egypt") Giacomo Meyerbeer, 1824.

The opera in two acts, to a libretto by Gaetano Rossi, is set in 13th-century Egypt during the Sixth Crusade and tells what happens when Armando d'Orville, a knight of Rhodes believed dead, assumes the false name Elmireno and becomes an adviser to the Sultan Aladino.

La Croqueuse de diamants ("The Fortune Hunter") Jean-Michel Damase, 1950.

The ballet in four scenes, with a libretto by Roland Petit and Alfred Adam, choreography by Petit, and couplets by Raymond Queneau, tells of the member of a gang of girls at Les Halles, the Paris market, who steals diamonds only to eat them with relish.

Crown Imperial William Walton, 1937.

The march for orchestra was composed for the coronation of George VI (1937). The score is headed by a line from the poem *In Honour of the City* by William Dunbar (1465–1513): "In beautie beryng the crone imperiall." The title is appropriate for a king who was crowned with the Imperial State Crown and who (until 1947) was *Indiae Imperator* (Emperor of India). *Cf.* **Orb and Sceptre**.

The Crown of India Edward Elgar, 1912.

The masque, Op. 66, for contralto and bass soloists, choir, and orchestra, is set to words by Henry Hamilton and was written to celebrate the Coronation Durbar (viceroy's levee) of December 11, 1911, when Delhi became the official capital of India and the foundation stone of New Delhi was laid. Its 12 sections have titles: (1) (a) *Introduction*, (b) *Sacred Measure*, (2) *Dance of Nautch Girls*, (3) *Hail, Immemorial Ind*, (4) *March of Mogul Emperors*, (5) *Entrance of John*

Company, (6) *Rule of England*, (7) *Interlude*, (8) *Warriors' Dance*, (9) *Cities of India*, (10) *Crown of India March*, (11) *Crowning of Delhi*, (12) *Ave Imperator*.

The Crucible   Robert Ward, 1961.

The opera in four acts is set to a libretto by Bernard Stambler based on Arthur Miller's play of the same name (1952) about the 1692 witchcraft trials in Salem, Massachusetts.

The Crucifixion   John Stainer, 1887

The oratorio, for tenor and bass soloists, chorus, organ, and orchestra, is set to a text by J. Sparrow-Simpson with extracts from the New Testament relating to Christ's crucifixion.

"Cruda sorte" ("Cruel fate").

Isabella's aria in Act 1 of Rossini's **L'Italiana in Algeri**, in which she laments her separation from her lover, Lindoro, when she is captured by pirates, but then realizes she can use her feminine charms to handle the situation.

The Cuckoo *see* **Le Coucou**.

Cuckoo Sonata   Ludwig van Beethoven, 1809.

The Sonata (or Sonatina) No. 25, Op. 79, in G major is sometimes so named for the recurring two-note phrase in the left hand of the first movement, which suggest the call of the cuckoo.

The Cunning Little Vixen (Czech, *Příhody lišky Bystroušky*, "Adventures of the Little Vixen Bystrouška")   Leoš Janáček, 1924.

The opera in three acts to a libretto by the composer is based on Rudolf Tesnohlídek's verses for drawings by Stanislav Lolek, published in the Brno newspaper *Lidové noviny* ("People's News") (1920). The story, a parable that alternates between people and animals, concerns a young vixen, Bystrouška ("Sharpears"), who is caught and raised as a pet by a gamekeeper.

The Cunning Peasant (Czech, *Selma sedlák*)   Antonín Dvořák, 1877.

The comic opera in two acts, set to a libretto by Josef Vesely based to some extent on Mozart's The **Marriage of Figaro**, tells how the peasant, Martin, uses his cunning to secure a rich husband for his daughter.

The Curlew   Peter Warlock, 1920–2.

The song cycle for tenor, flute, English horn, and string quartet is a setting of four poems by W.B. Yeats, one being *He Reproves the Curlew* ("O curlew, cry no more in the air, / Or only to the water in the West") (1899).

Curlew River   Benjamin Britten, 1964.

The church parable, Op. 71, is set to a text by William Plomer based on the Japanese *no*-play *Sumidagawa* ("Sumida River") by Juro Motomasa (1395–1431). The story was transposed from Japan to the English Fenlands, and tells of a madwoman searching for her lost son.

Le Cygne *see* The **Dying Swan**.

The Cypresses (Czech, *Cypřise*)   Antonín Dvořák, 1865.

The cycle of 18 love songs, based on poems by G. Pfleger-Moravsky, was unpublished in its original form but published as *Six Songs*, Op. 2 (1881–2), *Love Songs* (Czech, *Písně milostné*), Op. 83 (1888), and *Cypresses* for string quartet (1887).

Cyrano de Bergerac   (1) Leopold Damrosch, 1913; (2) Franco Alfano, 1936; (3) Marius Constant, 1959.

Damrosch's opera in four acts, to a libretto by William James Henderson, Alfano's opera in four acts, to a libretto by Henri Cain, and Constant's ballet in three acts, with a libretto and choreography by Roland Petit, are all based on Edmond Rostand's play of the same name (1897). This is set in Paris in 1640 and tells what happens when Cyrano, a noble knight with a large nose, falls in love with his cousin, Roxane.

Czar Saltan *see* The **Tale of Czar Saltan**.

Die Czardasfürstin ("The Gypsy Princess")   Emmerich Kálmán, 1915.

The operetta in three acts, to a libretto by Leo Stein and Béla Jenbach, is set in Budapest and Vienna and centers on the actress and singer Sylva Varescu, known as "The Gypsy Princess."

The Czarina's Shoes *see* **Vakul the Smith**.

The Czar's Bride (Russian, *Tsarskaya nevesta*)   Nikolay Rimsky-Korsakov, 1899.

The opera in four acts is set to a libretto adopted by the composer from Lev Alexandrovich Mey's play of the same name (1849), with additions by I.F. Tyumenev. The story is set in Russia in 1572 and centers on Marfa, chosen by Ivan the Terrible as his bride, who is loved by both Ivan Lykov, whom she loves, and the *oprichnik* (member of the *oprichnina*, the élite administration) Ivan Gryaznoy, who tries to win her with a love potion.

Czech Dances   Bedřich Smetana, 1877–9.

The work for piano consists of a set of four polkas, without titles, written in 1877, and a second set of 10 dances, composed in 1879, with individual titles as follows: (1) *Furiant*, (2) *Slepička* ("Little Hen"), (3) *Oves* ("Oats"), (4) *Medvěd* ("Bear"), (5) *Cibulička* ("Little Onion"), (6) *Dupák*, (7) *Hulán* ("The Lancer"), (8) *Obkročák*, (9) *Sousedská*, (10) *Skočná*. Dances (3), (5), and (7) take their names from the first line of the folksongs to which they are set. Dance (4) is a dance known as the *bavorák*. Dance (6) is a stamping dance.

Czech Suite (Czech, *Česká suita*)   Antonín Dvořák, 1879.

The Suite for Orchestra, Op. 39, in D major is so named for its markedly national flavor.

D

Dafne ("Daphne")   Jacopo Peri, 1597.

The opera in a prologue and six scenes to a libretto by Ottavio Rinuccini is based on Ovid's *Metamorphoses*, Book 1, 453–567 (1st century AD), which tells how the Greek virgin huntress Daphne changed into a bay tree when pursued by Apollo. *See also* **Daphne**.

Daisi ("Twilight")   Zakhary Paliashvili, 1923.

The opera in three acts, to a libretto by Valerian Gunia, is set in 18th-century Georgia and tells what happens when Maro, engaged to Malkhaz, who has been long abroad and of whom there is no news, yields to her mother's wishes and instead marries the dour soldier, Kiazo.

Dalibor   Bedřich Smetana, 1868.

The opera in three acts is set to a libretto by Josef Wenzig translated from the German into Czech by Ervín Spindler. The story is set in Prague in the late 15th century and tells how Dalibor, imprisoned for assassinating the Burgrave, is pitied by the Burgrave's daughter, Milada, who attempts to rescue him.

"Dalla sua pace" ("On thy peace").

Ottavio's aria in Act 1 of Mozart's **Don Giovanni**, declaring that his joy or sorrow depends on that of Donna Anna.

La Dame blanche ("The White Lady")   François Boieldieu, 1825.

The opera in three acts is set to a libretto by Eugène Scribe based on Sir Walter Scott's novels *The Monastery* (1820) and *Guy Mannering* (1815). The "white lady" of the title, an apparent ghost in Count Avenel's castle, turns out to be Anna, ward of the Count's steward, Gaveston.

La Dame de Pique ("The Queen of Spades")   Pyotr Tchaikovsky, 1978.

The ballet in six scenes, with a libretto and choreography by Roland Petit, uses a selection of music from the composer's opera The **Queen of Spades** while closely following the plot of Alexander Pushkin's original story.

La Damnation de Faust ("The Damnation of Faust")   Hector Berlioz, 1845–6.

The cantata, Op. 24, is set to a text by Gérard de Nerval based on Goethe's poem *Faust* (1808, 1832), in which Faust trades his soul with Mephistopheles in exchange for youth. *See also* **Doktor Faust**, **Faust**.

La Damoiselle élue *see* The **Blessed Damozel**.

"D'amor sull'ali rosee" ("Of love on rosy wings").

Leonora's aria in Act 4 of Verdi's Il **Trovatore**, in which she sings of her love for Manrico while standing beneath the tower in which he is imprisoned.

Les Danaïdes ("The Danaïdes")   Antonio Salieri, 1784.

The opera in three acts is set to a libretto by François Louis Lebland du Roullet and Louis Théodore Tschudi partly based on and translated from Ranieri de' Calzabigi's libretto for *Ipermestra* ("Hypermnestra"), intended for Christoph Willibald Gluck (to whom it was originally ascribed). The story is set in Greece in mythological times and tells what happens when all but one of the 50 Danaïdes, the daughters of Danaus, obey their father and kill their husbands, the sons of Aegyptus, Danaus's brother. The exception is Hypermnestra.

Dance Before the Golden Calf   Arnold Schoenberg, 1932.

The title is that of the (mainly orchestral) climax of Act 2 of the **Moses und Aron**, when

Moses descends from Mount Sinai and finds the people worshipping the Golden Calf. An alternate form of the title is *Dance around the Golden Calf.*

Dance Duet   Engelbert Humperdinck, 1893.

The long duet between Hänsel and Gretel in Act 1 of **Hänsel und Gretel**. It opens with Gretel's invitation, "Brother, come and dance with me," and culminates in a dance.

Dance of Death   *see* (1) **Danse macabre**; (2) **Totentanz**.

Dance of the Apprentices   Richard Wagner, 1868.

The dance is that of the Nuremberg apprentices and the girls from Fürth in Act 3 of Die **Meistersinger von Nürnberg**.

Dance of the Blessed Spirits, Christoph Gluck, 1762.

The slow dance in Act 2 of **Orfeo ed Euridice** is that of the "blessed spirits" among whom Orfeo (Orpheus) finds Euridice (Eurydice).

Dance of the Buffoons   *see* **Dance of the Tumblers**.

Dance of the Comedians, Bedřich Smetana, 1866.

The dance is that of the clowns and acrobats of the traveling circus when they are put through their paces in Act 3 of The **Bartered Bride**.

Dance of the Elves   Antonio Bazzini, 1852.

The lively violin solo, evoking a puckish prancing, is known in French as *Ronde des lutins* and alternately in English as *Dance of the Goblins*, as French *lutins* can mean both.

Dance of the Flutes   *see* **Nutcracker**.

Dance of the Goblins   *see* **Dance of the Elves**.

Dance of the Hours   Amilcare Ponchielli, 1876

The ballet music in Act 3 of La **Gioconda** is an entertainment staged by Alvise Badoero for his guests. It symbolizes the conflict between darkness and light. (The "Hours" are not the 60-minute divisions of the day but the *Horae*, the classical goddesses of the seasons.)

Dance of the Seven Veils   Richard Strauss, 1905.

The name is that of Salome's dance before Herod in the opera **Salome**. She removes her seven veils one by one, in a sort of oriental striptease. (Maria Ewing went the distance in a 1988 Covent Garden performance.) Her dancing is mentioned only generally in the biblical original (Matthew 14) but the particular dance of this kind is specified in Oscar Wilde's play *Salomé* (1893), on which the opera is based.

Dance of the Sugar Plum Fairy   *see* **Nutcracker**.

Dance of the Sylphs   Hector Berlioz, 1845–6.

The orchestral episode in La **Damnation de Faust** forms part of Faust's dream on the banks of the Elbe River.

Dance of the Tumblers   Nikolay Rimsky-Korsakov, 1880–1.

The episode in Act 3 of **The Snow Maiden** is a dance by acrobats for the Czar Berendey. An alternate title is *Dance of the Buffoons*.

Dance Rhapsody   Frederick Delius, 1908, 1916.

The composer gave this name to two orchestral works, No. 1 (1908) and No. 2 (1923). *See also* **Rhapsody**.

Dance Suite (Hungarian, *Táncszvit*)   Béla Bartók, 1923.

The orchestral work, properly Suite for Orchestra, No. 3, comprises individual dance melodies but is not actually danced (although the music has been adopted for a ballet). It was commissioned to celebrate the 50th anniversary of the merging of Buda and Pest to form Budapest, where it was first performed.

Dance Symphony (Russian, *Tantssimfoniya*)   Ludwig van Beethoven, 1923.

The ballet in four movements, choreographed by Fyodor Lopokov, is set to the composer's Symphony No. 4 in B flat major, Op. 60 (1806), and has 18 dancers depicting its four movements as *Birth of Light, Triumph of Life over Death, Awakening of Nature in the Sun of Spring,* and *The Cosmogonic Spiral.* The subtitle is *The Magnificence of the Universe* (Russian, *Velichiye mirozdaniya*).

A Dance Symphony   Aaron Copland, 1930.

The symphony is based on the composer's ballet *Grogh* (1922–5).

Dances at a Gathering   Fryderyk Chopin, 1969.

The plotless ballet in one act, choreographed by Jerome Robbins, is set to a number of the composer's études, waltzes, and mazurkas, as well as a nocturne and a scherzo, and is generally about "togetherness," as expressed by five male and five female dancers.

Dances of Galánta (Hungarian, *Galántai táncok*)   Zoltán Kodály, 1933.

The orchestral suite is based on gypsy tunes collected in the market town of Galánta.

Dances of Love and Death   Carl Davis and Conlon Nancarrow, 1981.

The ballet in two acts, choreographed by Robert Cohan, depicts Love and Death in symbolic contention over well-known lovers, including Pluto and Persephone, Tristan and Iseult, the Sleeping Beauty and her Prince, Cathy and Heathcliff from *Wuthering Heights*, and Marilyn Monroe from real life.

Danina   Peter von Lindpaintner, 1826.

The ballet in four acts, with a libretto and choreography by Filippo Taglioni, is based on a French melodrama telling of the beautiful Brazilian girl, Danina, who one day saves the ape, Jocko, from being bitten by a snake. The subtitle is thus *Jocko, the Brazilian Ape*.

Danse macabre ("Dance of Death")   Camille Saint-Saëns, 1874.

The symphonic poem, Op. 40, is based on a poem by Henri Cazalis in which Death the Fiddler summons skeletons from their graves at midnight to dance. The phrase itself dates back in French to at least the 14th century. *See also* **Totentanz**.

Danses Concertantes   Igor Stravinsky, 1944.

The ballet in five movements, choreographed by George Balanchine, is set to music by the composer written in 1942 that was originally intended for concert performance only. The title, however, seems to imply that a stage performance for dancers is a logical development.

Dante Sonata   Franz Liszt, 1839.

The work for solo piano is the seventh piece in Book 2 of the **Années de pèlerinage**. Its full French title is *Après une lecture de Dante, fantasia quasi sonata* ("After Reading Dante, Fantasia in the Style of a Sonata"). A ballet based on the music, inspired by John Flaxman's illustrations (1802) for Dante's *Divina Commedia*, was choreographed by Frederick Ashton (1940) and depicts the fight of the Children of Light against the Children of Darkness.

Dante Symphony   Franz Liszt, 1855–6.

The work for female choir and orchestral, in two movements, has the full German title *Eine Symphonie zu Dantes Divina commedia* ("A Symphony to Dante's *Divine Comedy*"). The two movements are named respectively *Inferno* and *Purgatorio*.

Dantons Tod ("Danton's Death")   Gottfried von Einem, 1944–6.

The opera in two parts, Op. 6, is set to a libretto by the composer and Boris Blacher based on Georg Büchner's drama of the same name (1835), telling of the arrest, trial, and execution of the French revolutionary, Georges Jacques Danton (1759–1794).

The Danube Cossacks (Russian, *Zaporozhets za Dunayem*)   Semyon Gulak-Artemovsky, 1863.

The opera in three acts, with choruses and dances, is set to the composer's own libretto and is based on the fate of the Zaporozhian Cossacks, many of whom fled to the region around the mouth of the Danube in Turkish territory following the Russian government's destruction of their homeland in 1755 west of the Dnieper in Ukraine, and who were able to return only after the Russo-Turkish War (1828–9). The opera's Russian title literally means "The Zaporozhian Cossack beyond the Danube."

Daphne   Richard Strauss, 1936–7.

The opera in one act is set to a libretto by Josef Gregor based on the classical story that tells how the virgin huntress, Daphne, was changed into a bay tree when pursued by Apollo. *See also* **An den Baum Daphne**.

Daphnis et Chloé ("Daphnis and Chloe")   Maurice Ravel, 1912.

The ballet in three scenes, with a libretto and choreography by Michel Fokine, is based on Longus's *The Pastoral Story of Daphnis and Chloe* (2d century AD), telling of the love of the young shepherd Daphnis for the beautiful Chloe.

Dardanus   Jean-Philippe Rameau, 1739.

The opera in a prologue and five acts is set to a libretto by Leclerc de la Bruyère based on the classical story of the love of Iphise for Dardanus, son of Jupiter.

Dark Elegies   Gustav Mahler, 1937.

The ballet in one act, with a libretto and choreography by Antony Tudor, is based on the composer's **Kindertotenlieder**, sung by a baritone on stage while a group of villagers dance their grief and ultimate resignation about the disaster that has struck them.

Dark Meadow   Carlos Chávez, 1946.

The ballet in four sections, choreographed by Martha Graham, is "a re-enactment of the Mysteries which attend the eternal adventure of seeking" (Martha Graham, quoted in Koegler, p. 117). A dark meadow is clearly one with a mystery.

Das (German, "The").

For titles beginning with this word, see the next word, *e.g.* Das **Veilchen**.

A Daughter of Castile (Russian, *Doch' Kastilii*)   Reinhold Glière, 1955.

The ballet in four acts (six scenes), with a libretto and choreography by A.V. Tchitchinadze, is based on Felix Lope de Vega's play *Fuente ovejuna* ("The Sheep Well") (1618) and tells of the rising of the peasants in a Castilian village, led by Laurencia, the "daughter of Castile" of the title, and her betrothed, Frondoso. *Cf.* **Laurencia**.

The Daughter of the Regiment *see* La **Fille du régiment**.

David   Darius Milhaud, 1952.

The opera in five acts (12 scenes), Op. 320, is set to a libretto by Armand Lunel based on the Old Testament account of David, the great king of Israel, as told in 1 and 2 Samuel. The work was commissioned to mark the 3,000th anniversary of the founding of Jerusalem.

David triomphant ("David Triumphant")   Vittorio Rieti, 1936.

The ballet in two acts (three scenes), choreographed by Serge Lifar, tells the biblical story (1 and 2 Samuel) of David and Goliath and of King Saul and his jealousy of David's deeds.

Davidde penitente ("David the Penitent")   W.A. Mozart, 1785.

The oratorio, K 469, for two sopranos and tenor soloist, chorus, and orchestra, is set to a text probably by Lorenzo da Ponte that is based on the Old Testament story of King David, who repented after killing Uriah the Hittite and seducing his wife, Bathsheba (2 Samuel 12).

Davidsbündlertänze ("Dances of the Davidites")   Robert Schumann, 1837.

The 18 pieces for solo piano, Op. 6, take their overall title from the *Davidsbund* ("League of David"), the imaginary society of musicians invented by the composer to oppose the established philistines in the pages of his magazine *Neue Zeitschrift für Musik* ("New Music Journal"). (The reference is to the biblical David, who killed the Philistine giant Goliath.) Some members appear in the journal under fanciful names   Friedrich Wieck, Schumann's father-in-law, is Master Raro, his wife, Clara, is Chiara or Chiarina, and he himself is either Florestan or Eusebius, representing the two sides of his nature, active and fiery or passive and gentle. (The names are those of characters in an unrealized novel.) Other names come from the writings of Jean Paul Richter. The pieces do not have individual titles.

"De' miei bollenti spiriti" ("Of my fiery spirits").

Alfredo's aria opening Act 2 of Verdi's La **Traviata**, in which he sings of his happiness with Violetta.

De Profundis ("Out of the depths").

The opening words of Psalm 129 in the Vulgate (Latin version of the Bible) (Psalm 130 in the Authorized Version), set by many composers. It is one of the so called "Seven Penitential Psalms" and has a place in the Roman Catholic Office of the Dead.

Dead March in Saul   George Frideric Handel, 1739.

The name is popularly applied to the funeral march in **Saul**. It is still traditionally played at state funerals.

Dead Souls (Russian, *Myortvyye dushi*)   Rodion Shchedrin, 1977.

The opera in three acts is set to the composer's own libretto based on Nikolai Gogol's novel of the same name (1842) about a petty landowner, Chichikov, who travels Russia buying up cheaply peasants who have died since the last census, but whose deaths have not been registered, so he can point to his ownership of these "dead souls" to back his claim for a loan.

Death and the Maiden *see* Der **Tod und das Mädchen**.

Death and Transfiguration *see* **Tod und Verklärung**.

Death in Venice Benjamin Britten, 1973.

The opera in two acts is set to a libretto by Myfanwy Piper based on Thomas Mann's novella *Der Tod in Venedig* ("Death in Venice") (1911), the death being that of the central character, the writer, Gustav von Aschenbach.

Death of a Squadron (Russian, *Gibel' eskadry*) Vitaly Gubarenko, 1967.

The musical drama (opera) in two acts is set to a libretto by the composer and V.V. Bychko based on Alexander Korneychuk's revolutionary play of the same name (1933). The story is set in Ukraine at the start of the Russian Civil War (1918) and tells how crew members of the Black Sea Fleet manage to save the ships of their squadron from the Germans.

The Death of Klinghoffer John Adams, 1990–1.

The opera in two acts is set to a libretto by Alice Goodman based on the events following the hijacking by four Palestinian terrorists of the Italian cruise liner *Achille Lauro* in Alexandria (1985), when the disabled American passenger, Leon Klinghoffer, was shot and thrown overboard in his wheelchair.

The Death of Moses Alexander Goehr, 1991–2.

The choral work is set to a text by John Hollander based on the Old Testament story of Moses, leader of the Jews, who was forbidden by God from entering the Promised Land and who died after seeing Israel from a distance.

Deaths and Entrances Hunter Johnson, 1943.

The ballet in one act, choreographed by Martha Graham, is based on the life of the Brontë sisters, Charlotte (1816–1855), Emily (1818–1848), and Anne (1820–1849), who all died young. The title predates that of Dylan Thomas's poems *Deaths and Entrances* (1946).

Deborah George Frideric Handel, 1733.

The oratorio is set to a text by Samuel Humphreys based on the biblical story of Deborah, the prophetess and judge who led the Israelites against Sisera (Judges 4,5).

The Decembrists (Russian, *Dekabristy*) Yury Shaporin, 1953.

The opera in four acts is set to a libretto by Vsevolod Rozhdestvensky based on verses by Alexei Tolstoy. The story is set in Russian in 1825 and centers on the uprising in December that

year of young aristocrats with military backgrounds who were discontented with the system of ownership and serfdom and who refused to take an oath of loyalty to the new czar, Nicholas I.

Decoration Day Charles Ives, 1912.

The orchestral work became the second movement of the symphony **New England Holidays**.

"Deh, vieni alla finestra" ("Oh, come to the window").

Don Giovanni's serenade to Elvira's maid in Act 2 of Mozart's **Don Giovanni**, in which he sings to his own mandolin accompaniment.

Deidamia George Frideric Handel, 1741.

The opera in three acts to a libretto by Paolo Rolli tells the classical story of the marriage between Achilles and Lycomedes's daughter, Deidamia.

Deliciae basiliensis ("Delights of Basel") Arthur Honegger, 1946.

The Symphony No. 4 is so named because its second movement is based on an old popular song of Basel, Switzerland, while the Finale quotes the tune *Basler Morgenstreich* ("Morning Prank of Basel"). The composer commented: "Because of the quotations of these characteristic songs, and even more for personal reasons, I have employed the subtitle 'Deliciae basiliensis'" (quoted in Berkowitz, p. 31).

Demetrio ("Demetrius") Johann Adolf Hasse, 1732.

The opera in three acts is set to a libretto by Pietro Metastasio telling of the love between Demetrio, son of the exiled king of Syria, and Cleonice, daughter of the usurper, Alessandro.

Demetrio e Polibio ("Demetrius and Polybius") Gioacchino Rossini, 1806.

The opera in two acts is set to a libretto by Vincenza Vigarnò-Mombelli based on Pietro Metastasio's libretto for Johann Adolf Hasse's opera **Demetrio**.

Demofoonte ("Demophon") Niccolò Jommelli, 1764.

The opera in three acts, to a libretto by Pietro Metastasio, tells what happens when Demophon, king of Chersonesus, seeks to put an end to the annual sacrifice of a virgin that the gods require of him.

Les Demoiselles de la nuit ("The Young Ladies of the Night") Jean Françaix, 1948.

The ballet in one act (three scenes), with a libretto by Jean Anouilh and choreography by Roland Petit, tells of a young musician who falls in love with a cat, Agathe. She tries very hard to be his wife but cannot resist the nocturnal wailing of the tomcats, for she is one of the "young ladies of the night."

The Demon (1) (Russian, *Demon*) Anton Rubinstein, 1875; (2) (German, *Der Dämon*) Paul Hindemith, 1923.

Rubinstein's opera in three acts is set to a libretto by Pavel Viskovatov based on Mikhail Lermontov's poem of the same name (1841). The story is set in the Caucasus in legendary times and tells what happens when the Demon, a human with satanic traits, falls in love with Tamara, betrothed to Prince Sinidal. Hindemith's ballet, in two scenes, directed by Albrecht Joseph and with a libretto by Max Krell, tells how a demon subjugates two sisters in succession and then turns to his next victim.

Density 21.5 Edgard Varèse, 1936.

The piece for solo flute was composed for the flutist Georges Barrère to play when inaugurating his platinum flute. Platinum has a relative density of 21.5 (or more exactly 21.45). Hence the title.

The Departure *see* **Lieder ohne Worte**.

"Depuis le jour" ("Since the day").

Louise's aria in Act 3 of Charpentier's **Louise**, recalling the day when she first succumbed to Julien.

Der (German, "The" or "of the").

For titles beginning with this word, see the next word, *e.g.* Der **Freischütz**.

Des (German, "of the").

For German titles beginning with this word, see the next word, *e.g.* Des **Knaben Wunderhorn**.

Des canyons aux étoiles ("From the Canyons to the Stars") Olivier Messiaen, 1970–4.

The work for piano, horn, and orchestra was inspired by the landscape in Utah, where Mt. Messiaen is named in the composer's honor.

Deserts Edgard Varèse, 1967.

The ballet in one act, choreographed by Anna Sokolow and set to the composer's **Déserts**, is a work, as the name implies, about barrenness, timelessness, and loneliness.

Déserts ("Deserts") Edgard Varèse, 1950–4.

The work alternates orchestral music with taped sections of "organized sound," the aim being to make the tapes sound like the orchestra, and vice versa. The result is a portrait of an urban desert. Hence the title.

Designs with Strings Pyotr Tchaikovsky, 1948.

The ballet in one act, choreographed by John Taras, is set to the second movement of the composer's Trio in A major. It has no definite plot but reflects the uncertainties of young love. The title puns on the instruments of the trio.

Desperation *see* **Twenty-Four Preludes**.

Dettingen Te Deum and Anthem George Frideric Handel, 1743.

The two choral works were composed to celebrate the British victory over the French at Dettingen, near Frankfurt, in 1743. The anthem is set to the biblical text "The king shall rejoice" (Psalm 63:11).

Deuce Coupe Beach Boys, 1973.

The ballet in one act, choreographed by Twyla Tharp, comprises a set of dances with classical steps in alphabetical order set to spunky pop music. The title comes from the Beach Boys' hit *Little Deuce Coupe* (1963), a deuce coupe being a "hot rod" (a powerful, specially prepared car).

Deuil en 24 heures ("Twenty-Four Hours' Mourning") M. Thiriet, 1953.

The ballet in one act (five scenes), with a libretto and choreography by Roland Petit, is a music hall farce in the style of an early silent movie. The story concerns a beautiful blonde lady who, when her husband dies of fright at the prospect of a duel, enjoys celebrating her widowhood at Maxim's in an elegant black dress.

Deutsche Sinfonie ("German Symphony") Hanns Eisler, 1935–9.

The work, at first provisionally entitled *Konzentrationslager-Sinfonie* ("Concentration Camp Symphony"), is an "antifascist cantata" (more precisely, series of cantatas with orchestral interludes) set to words by Bertolt Brecht.

Ein Deutsches Requiem *see* A **German Requiem**.

Les Deux journées ("The Two Days") Luigi Cherubini, 1800

The opera in three acts, to a libretto by Jean Nicolas Bouilly, is set in Paris in 1647 and tells the story of the escape and pardon of Count Armand, who has fallen into disfavor with Cardinal Mazarin. The events unfold over two days. The former English title was *The Water Carrier*, alluding to the water seller who allows the Count to escape in his barrel.

Les Deux pigeons ("The Two Pigeons") André Charles Messager, 1886.

The ballet in three acts, with a libretto by Henry Régnier and Louis Mérante and choreography by the latter, is based on Jean de Lafontaine's story of the two pigeons in his *Fables* (1688). The story tells what happens when Pepino dreams of a life of adventure with the gypsies and leaves his betrothed, Gourouli. These two are thus the "two pigeons" of the title.

The Devil and Daniel Webster Douglas Moore, 1939.

The opera in one act is set to the a libretto by the composer's and Stephen Vincent Benét based on the latter's story *Thirteen O'Clock* (1937). The plot tells how a New Hampshire farmer, Jabez Stone, sells his soul to the Devil for ten years of prosperity. When the Devil comes to his wedding to collect his debt, Daniel Webster comes to Stone's aid.

The Devil and Kate (Czech, *Čert a Káča*) Antonín Dvořák, 1899.

The comic opera is set to a libretto by Adolf Wenig based on Božena Němcová's *Fairy Tales* (1845). The story tells what happens when nobody wants to partner the unattractive and talkative Káča at a country fair and she offers to "dance with the Devil" instead.

The Devil in the Village (Serbo-Croat, *Davo u selu*) F. Lhotka, 1935.

The ballet in three acts (eight scenes), with a libretto and choreography by Pino and Pia Mlakar, tells of the young peasant, Mirko, who loves Jela but who is seduced by the Devil.

Devil's Holiday Vincenzo Tommasini, 1939.

The ballet in a prologue and three scenes (and two entr'actes), with a libretto by the composer and choreography by Frederick Ashton, is arranged to themes from Paganini. The story tells how the love affair between the daughter of an impoverished lord and a poor young man is opposed by her father, who wants her to marry a rich man, so the Devil has to play some tricks during the carnival to sort things out.

The Devils of Loudun (Polish, *Diabły z Loudun*) Krzysztof Penderecki, 1969.

The opera in three acts is set to a libretto by the composer based on John Whiting's play *The Devils* (1961), itself based on Aldous Huxley's *The Devils of Loudun* (1952), a study of the alleged demonic possession of a group of Ursuline nuns in the French town of Loudun in 1734.

The Devil's Opera George Macfarren, 1838.

The opera, to a libretto by George Macfarren, Sr., the composer's father, is a satire on the diabolic elements in works such as Weber's Der **Freischütz**, Meyerbeer's **Robert le Diable**, Marschner's Der **Vampyr**, etc. Hence the title.

Devil's Trill Sonata (Italian, *Il trillo del diavolo*) Giuseppe Tartini, 1714.

The Violin Sonata in G minor is so nicknamed because of the long trill in the last bar of its four movements. The legend is that the composer dreamed he had made a deal with the Devil, to whom he gave his violin. The Devil played such a beautiful solo that when Tartini awoke he tried to play it. He failed, but composed the "Devil's trill" instead.

The Devil's Wall (Czech, *Čertova stěna*) Bedřich Smetana, 1879–82.

The opera in three acts, to a libretto by Eliska Krásnohorská, is set in 13th-century Bohemia and tells what happens when the Devil builds a dam (the "wall" of the title) across the Vltava River in order to engulf a monastery and drown the ruler, Petr Vok, Lord of Rozmberk, who had taken refuge there.

Le Devin du village ("The Village Soothsayer") Jean-Jacques Rousseau, 1752.

The opera in one act to the composer's own libretto tells how a soothsayer resolves the misunderstandings between the young rustic lovers Colin and Colette. Mozart's **Bastien und Bastienne** is a parody.

"Di quella pira" ("From that pyre").

Manrico's aria in Act 3 of Verdi's Il **Trovatore**, urging his followers to join him in saving his mother, Azucena, from being burned alive.

"Di scrivermi ogni giorno" ("To write to me every day").

The quintet in Act 1 of Mozart's **Così fan tutte**, in which the sisters Dorabella and Fiordiligi exchange promises with their lovers, Ferrando and Guglielmo, that they will write to one another every day dring their absence.

"Di tanti palpiti" ("Of so many beats").

Tancredi's song declaring his worthiness of

Amenaide in Act 1 of Rossini's **Tancredi**. In Venice it was known as the the *Rice Aria* (*Aria dei risi*), as the composer was said to have written it in four minutes while waiting for the rice to cook. (Such a time would have been unlikely for either event.) *Cf.* I **Palpiti**.

Di tre re ("Of Three Ds")   Arthur Honegger, 1951.

The Symphony No. 5 is so named because each of its three movements ends with a simultaneous pizzicato and kettledrum stroke on the note D.

Diabelli Variations (German, *Veränderungen über einen Walzer von Anton Diabelli*, "Variations on a Waltz by Anton Diabelli") Ludwig van Beethoven, 1819–23.

The variations for piano, Op.120, take their name from the publisher, Anton Diabelli (1781–1858), who commissioned 50 composers to write one variation each on his theme. Beethoven's contribution developed into the 33 variations of the present work.

Le Diable à quatre ("The Devil to Pay") Adolphe Adam, 1845.

The ballet in three acts, with a libretto by Adolphe de Leuven and choreography by Joseph Mazilier, is set in Poland and tells the story of two couples: the Count and Countess, and the basketmaker, Mazurki, and his wife, Mazurka. The entanglements that follow are reflected in the French title, literally meaning "The Devil of Four" but conventionally translated as above, with the subtitle *The Wives Metamorphosed*.

Le Diable amoureux ("The Amorous Devil")   François Benoist and Napoléon-Henri Reber, 1840.

The ballet in three acts (eight scenes), with a libretto by Jules-Henri Vernoy de Saint-Georges and choreography by Joseph Mazilier, tells how the female demon, Urielle (the "amorous devil" of the title), disguises herself as a pageboy in an attempt to win the soul of the impoverished count Frédéric.

Le Diable boîteux ("The Devil on Two Sticks")   Casimir Gide, 1836.

The pantomimic ballet in three acts, with a libretto by Butat de Burguy and A. Nourrit and choreography by Jean Coralli, is based on Alain René Lesage's novel of the same title (1707). The story tells what happens when the student, Cléophas, helps the demon, Asmodée, to escape from the bottle in which he is imprisoned. The French title literally means "The Lame Devil," but is conventionally translated as above.

Dialogues des Carmélites ("Dialogues of the Carmelites")   Francis Poulenc, 1957.

The opera in three acts is set to the composer's own libretto based on Georges Bernanos's play of the same name, itself based on Gertrude von Le Fort's novel *Die Letzte am Schafott* ("The Last on the Scaffold") (1931) and a film scenario by Fr. Raymond Brückberger and Philippe Agostini that in turn drew on the recollections of one of the original nuns of Compiègne, Sister Marie of the Incarnation. The story tells of the martyrdom of a group of Carmelite nuns during the French Revolution.

Les Diamants de la couronne ("The Crown Diamonds")   Daniel Auber, 1841.

The opera in three acts, to a libretto by Eugène Scribe and Jules-Henri Vernoy de Saint Georges, is set in Portugal in 1777 and tells what happens when the heiress to the throne plans to replenish the nation's depleted treasury by selling the crown jewels and replacing them with fakes.

Diary of One Who Disappeared (Czech, *Zápisník zmizelého*)   Leoš Janáček, 1917–19.

The song cycle for tenor, contralto, three women's voices, and piano comprises settings of 22 anonymous poems on the linking theme of unrequited love. The work was prompted by some poems in the Brno newspaper *Lidové noviny* about a young man who became infatuated with a gypsy girl and forsook his family. He was thus "the one who disappeared."

Il Dibuk *see* The **Dybbuk**.

"Dich, teure Halle" ("Thee, dear hall").

Elisabeth's aria opening Act 2 of Wagner's **Tannhäuser**, in which she greets the Hall of Song in the Wartburg where the song contest is to be held.

Dichterliebe ("Poet's Love")   Robert Schumann, 1840.

The song cycle for voice and piano, Op. 48, comprises settings of 16 poems by Heinrich Heine drawn from the section *Lyrisches Intermezzo* ("Lyrical Intermezzo") in his *Buch der Lieder* ("Songbook") (1827). Heine himself, of course, is the "poet," and most of the poems in his collection treat of dreams and love.

Dido and Aeneas   Henry Purcell, 1689.

The opera in a prologue and three acts is

set to a text by Nahum Tate based on Book 4 of Virgil's *Aeneid* (29–19 BC), telling the story of the love of Dido, Queen of Carthage, for the great warrior, Aeneas. *See also* **Dido's Lament**.

Dido's Lament   Henry Purcell, 1689.

The title is that of the aria in which Dido looks forward to death at the end of Act 3 of **Dido and Aeneas**. It opens with Nahum Tate's lines: "When I am laid in earth / May my wrongs create / No trouble in thy breast; / Remember me, but ah! forget my fate."

Die (German, "The").

For titles beginning with this word, see the next word, *e.g.* Die **Gräfin Mariza**.

"Dies Bildnis ist bezaubernd schön" ("This picture is enchantingly lovely").

Tamino's aria in Act 1 of Mozart's Die **Zauberflöte**, declaring his love for Pamina on first seeing her portrait. It is also known in English as the *Portrait Aria*.

Dies Irae (Latin, "Day of Wrath").

A section of the **Requiem Mass**, with words by Thomas Celano (*c.*1190–1260): "*Dies irae, dies illa, / Solvet saeclum in favilla, / teste David cum Sibylla*" ("The day of wrath, that day, will turn the universe to ashes, as David foretells with the Sibyl"). Settings of the *Requiem* often contain vivid versions, as that by Verdi (1873–4).

Dies Natalis ("Birthday") Gerald Finzi, 1926–39

The cantata for soprano or tenor and strings, Op. 8, is in five movements. The first is instrumental, the second a setting of a prose passage from *Centuries of Meditation* by Thomas Traherne (1638–1674), and the last three settings of Traherne's poems.

Le Dieu bleu ("The Blue God")   Reynaldo Hahn, 1912.

The ballet in one act, with a libretto by Jean Cocteau and Frédéric de Madrazo and choreography by Michel Fokine, depicts a Hindu legend of the love of a young couple, set against a background of temple rituals.

Le Dieu et la Bayadère ("The God and the Bayadère")   Daniel Auber, 1830.

The ballet divertissement, choreographed by Filippo Taglioni, is based on the composer's opera of the same name, in turn drawing on Goethe's ballad *Der Gott und die Bajadere* ("The God and the Bayadère") (1797). This is the story of an Indian prostitute, the bayadère of the title,

who is visited by the god, Siva, unrecognized in human form. *Cf.* La **Bayadère**.

Different Trains   Steve Reich, 1988.

The work for string quartet and tape is autobiographical in inspiration. As a child, the composer traveled from coast to coast visiting his divorced parents. He later realized that, as a Jew, he would have ridden on very different trains if he had lived in occupied Europe. He thus took fragments from the taped reminiscences of his governess, a Pullman porter, and Holocaust survivors, and notated the speech rhythms and pitches for the quartet to play, combining it with train sounds and the speech fragments.

Dim Lustre   Richard Strauss, 1943.

The ballet in one act, with a libretto and choreography by Antony Tudor, is set to the composer's *Burleske* in D minor for piano and orchestra (1885–6) and centers on "a whiff of perfume, the touch of a hand, a stolen kiss, releasing whirls of memories" (program note, quoted in Koegler, p. 126).

Dimitrij   Antonín Dvořák, 1882.

The opera in four acts is set to a libretto by Marie Červinková-Riegrová based on writings by Ferdinand Mikovec and Friedrich von Schiller's unfinished play *Demetrius* (1805), about the False Dmitry (1580–1606), the pretender to the Russian throne who claimed to be the son of Ivan the Terrible. The story begins at the point where Modest Mussorgsky's opera **Boris Godunov** ends.

A Dinner Engagement   Lennox Berkeley, 1954.

The comic opera in one act is set to a libretto by Paul Dehn telling what happens when the newly impoverished Lord and Lady Dunmow attempt to marry their daughter, Susan, to Philippe, a prince.

Dinorah   Giacomo Meyerbeer, 1859.

The opera in three acts, to a libretto by Jules Barbier and Michel Carré, is set in Brittany and tells what happens when the goatherd, Hoël, postpones his wedding to his betrothed, Dinorah, and goes in search of treasure. The subtitle is *Le Pardon de Ploërmel* ("The Pardon of Ploërmel"). A pardon is a religious festival at which indulgences are granted. Ploërmel is a town in Brittany.

Dioclesian   Henry Purcell, 1690.

The semiopera is set to a libretto by

Thomas Betterton based on a play by John Fletcher and Philip Massinger. Its full title is *The Prophetess, or The History of Dioclesian*. The plot centers on the Roman emperor Diocletian (245–313).

Dirge for Two Veterans   (1) Gustav Holst, 1914; (2) Ralph Vaughan Williams, 1911.

Holst's work for male voices, brass, and percussion is a setting of Walt Whitman's poem of this name (1865–6) about the funeral of two battle veterans, father and son, from his cycle of poems about the Civil War, *Drum Taps*. Vaughan Williams set the same text for chorus and orchestra and later used it as the fourth movement of his cantata *Dona nobis pacem* ("Give Us Peace") (1936).

Dissonance Quartet (German, *Dissonanzen-Quartett*)   W.A. Mozart, 1785.

The String Quartet No. 19 in C major, K 465, one of the **Haydn Quartets**, is so named because the slow introduction contains a striking example of dissonance.

Il Distratto ("The Absent-Minded Man") Joseph Haydn, 1776.

The Symphony No. 60 in C major is so called because it includes the composer's incidental music for the revival (1774) of Jean-François Regnard's comedy *Le Distrait* ("The Absent-Minded Man") (1697). The symphony also itself contains a number of unorthodox or "distraught" devices, such as a sudden loud tutti after a lengthy diminuendo in the first movement and an unexpected fanfare in the slow movement.

Diversion of Angels   Norman Dello Joio, 1948.

The plotless ballet in one act, choreographed by Martha Graham, is "a lyric ballet about the loveliness of youth, the pleasure and playfulness, quick joy and quick sadness of being in love for the first time" (program note, quoted in Koegler, p. 126). The title, originally *Wilderness Stair*, comes from a poem by Ben Bellitt.

Diversions   Arthur Bliss, 1961.

The plotless ballet in one act, choreographed by Kenneth MacMillan, is set to the composer's *Music for Strings* (1935). Its two contrasting solo dancers and eight female dancers present the "diversions" of the title.

Divertimento   Alexei Haieff, 1947.

The plotless ballet in five parts, choreographed by George Balanchine, centers on a girl going from one party to another, and so presenting a "divertimento," or diversion (in the sense of an entertainment). The proper meaning of the Italian word is "Amusement," and the term applied in the 18th century to a suite of movements of light, recreational music, often for outdoor performance. Mozart wrote 25. *Cf.* **Divertissement**.

Divertimento No. 15   W.A. Mozart, 1956.

The plotless ballet in five movements, choreographed by George Balanchine, is set to the composer's Divertimento in B flat major, K 287 (1777), and danced in a way that reflects the serene mood of the individual movements.

Divertissement (French, "Amusement").

The same as a **Divertimento**, but with the additional meaning of an entertainment of songs and dances inserted in an 18th-century stage spectacle or sometimes in a ballet or opera. In later usage the name came to apply to a suite of dances without a linking plot. A well known example is Jacques Ibert's *Divertissement* (1928), an adaptation of his music for Eugène Labiche's play *Un chapeau de paille d'Italie* ("An Italian Straw Hat") (1851).

The Divine Poem (Russian, *Bozhestvennaya poema*)   Alexander Skryabin, 1902–4.

The Symphony No. 3 in C minor, Op. 43, illustrates the composer's theosophical ideas. Its three movements are called *Struggles*, *Delights*, and *Divine Play*.

Djamileh   Georges Bizet, 1872.

The opera in one act is set to a libretto by Louis Gallet based on Alfred de Musset's poem *Namouna* (1832). The story is set in a palace in Cairo and tells how the slave girl, Djamileh, falls in love with Haroun at the end of her time on his monthly rota of mistresses and plans to reintroduce herself in disguise.

Les Djinns ("The Genii")   César Franck, 1884.

The symphonic poem for piano and orchestra is based on verses from Victor Hugo's poem *Les Orientales* (1829), one of which has this title and all of which vividly convey the author's conception of the East, with its heat, languor, and savagery.

Dobrynya Nikitich   Alexander Grechaninov, 1903.

The folk-epic opera in three acts, to the composer's own libretto, is based on various *byliny* (traditional Russian heroic poems), but mainly that of the legendary warrior, Dobrynya Nikitich.

Le Docteur Miracle ("Doctor Miracle") (1) Georges Bizet, 1857; (2) Charles Lecocq, 1857.

Bizet's operetta in one act is set to a libretto by Léon Battu and Ludovic Halévy and tells how Captain Pasquin disguises himself as a charlatan doctor in order to make contact with his beloved, Laurette, whose father has forbidden her to consort with soldiers. Lecocq's opera has the same plot, from the same librettists. The two composers won joint first prize in a contest organized by Jacques Offenbach for a one-act comic opera with four characters that lasted 45 minutes. The first performance of Lecocq's opera took place one day before Bizet's.

Dr. Gradus ad Parnassum *see* **Children's Corner.**

Dog Waltz *see* **Minute Waltz.**

Doktor Faust ("Doctor Faust") Ferruccio Busoni, 1925.

The opera in eight scenes is set to the composer's own libretto based on Christopher Marlowe's *The Tragical History of Dr. Faustus* (1588). Having made his pact with Mephistopheles (*see* La **Damnation de Faust**), Faust seduces the Duchess of Parma following her marriage to the Duke and elopes with her. *See also* **Faust.**

Doktor und Apotheker ("Doctor and Apothecary") Carl Ditters von Dittersdorf, 1786.

The comic opera in two acts is set to a libretto by Gottlieb Stephanie based on the play *L'Apothicaire de Murcie* ("The Apothecary of Murcia") by "le Comte N." The story is set in a small town in Germany and tells what happens when Gotthold and Leonore are forbidden to marry because of the enmity between their fathers, the doctor, Krautmann, and the apothecary, Stössel.

"Dolce notte" ("Sweet night").

The love duet between Cio-Cio-San and Lieutenant Pinkerton at the end of Act 1 of Puccini's **Madama Butterfly.**

Doll Song Jacques Offenbach, 1881.

The aria sung by the mechanical doll, Olympia, in Act 1 of Les **Contes d'Hoffmann,** in which she is "wound up." The opening words are: "*Les oiseaux dans la charmille*" ("The birds in the arbor").

Die Dollarprinzessin ("The Dollar Princess") Leo Fall, 1907.

The operetta in three acts is set to a libretto by Alfred Maria Willner and Fritz Grünbaum based on the comedy by Gatti-Trotha. The story is set in New York and Canada in 1907 and tells of the love of Alice Couder, a millionaire's daughter and the "Dollar Princess" of the title, for Freddy Wehrburg, a German employee of her father.

Dolly Gabriel Fauré, 1897.

The suite for piano duet, Op. 56, is a composition for (or about) young children in six movements, with individual titles as follows: (1) *Berceuse* ("Cradle Song"), (2) *Mi-a-ou* ("Meeow"), (3) *Le Jardin de Dolly* ("Dolly's Garden"), (4) *Kitty-valse* ("Kitty Waltz"), (5) *Tendresse* ("Tenderness"), (6) *Le Pas espagnol* ("The Spanish Step"). It was dedicated to Hélène Bardac, nicknamed Dolly, the young daughter of Emma Bardac, later Debussy's second wife, and as for Debussy's **Children's Corner** suite, written for his own daughter by that wife, the titles seem to suggest some English connection.

Dom Sébastien, Roi de Portugal ("Dom Sebastian, King of Portugal") Gaetano Donizetti, 1843.

The opera in five acts is set to a libretto by Eugène Scribe based on Paul-Henri Foucher's play *Dom Sébastien de Portugal* (1838). It is set in Lisbon and the Moroccan coast in 1577 and tells what happens when Don Sebastien, king of Portugal, leads a crusade to Africa.

Domaines ("Domains") Pierre Boulez, 1968.

The work is for clarinet and six instrumental groups: (1) four trombones, (2) string sextet, (3) marimba and double bass, (4) flute, trumpet, alto saxophone, bassoon, and harp, (5) oboe, horn, and electric guitar, (6) bass clarinet. It is so named because the clarinetist chooses the order in which he or she will play six passages of "original material," and then play each of these in the "domain" of one of the instrumental groups. The group whose domain the soloist is occupying, then plays its own commentary on the "original." The underlying symmetry of the work relates it to **Pli selon pli.**

"Dôme épais de jasmin" *see* **Flower Duet** (1).

Domestic Symphony *see* **Symphonia Domestica.**

Dominicus Mass   W.A. Mozart, 1769.

The Mass in C major, K 66, was written for the first celebration of mass at St. Peter's, Salzburg, by a young priest, Cajetan Hagenauer, who had taken the religious name Fr. Dominicus. Hence the work's alternate title, *Pater Dominicus Mass.*

Le Domino noir ("The Black Domino") Daniel Auber, 1837.

The opera in three acts, to a libretto by Eugène Scribe, tells what happens when two friends, Horatio and Juliano, attend the Queen's annual Christmas ball in the hope they will again see a beautiful woman who comes dressed in a black domino (a loose cloak with a mask to cover the upper part of the face).

Don Carlos   Giuseppe Verdi, 1867.

The opera in five acts to a libretto by François Joseph Méry and Camille du Locle is based on Friedrich von Schiller's drama of the same name (1787). The action is set in France and Spain in 1560 and opens with the betrothal of Don Carlos, the Spanish infante, to Elisabeth de Valois. However, Carlos's father, King Philip, has decided to marry her himself.

Don Giovanni   W.A. Mozart, 1787.

The opera in two acts, K 527, is set to a libretto by Lorenzo da Ponte that is partly based on Giovanni Bertati's libretto for Giuseppe Gazzaniga's opera *Don Giovanni Tenorio, ossia Il convitato di pietra* ("Don Giovanni Tenorio, or The Stone Guest") (1787). The plot, a version of the **Don Juan** legend, involves the attempts of Don Giovanni to seduce Donna Anna, betrothed to Don Ottavio. The original title was *Il dissoluto punito* ("The Rake Punished").

Don Juan   (1) Christoph Gluck, 1761; (2) Richard Strauss, 1888.

Gluck's ballet, with a libretto and choreography by Gaspero Angiolini, is a simplified version of the legend of the notorious seducer Don Juan. Its subtitle is *Le Festin de pierre* ("The Stone Guest"), referring to the statue that comes to life and condemns Don Juan to Hell. Strauss's tone poem, Op. 20, is based on Nikolaus Lenau's version of the story in his dramatic poem of the same name (1844). *See also* The **Return of Don Juan.**

Don Pasquale   Gaetano Donizetti, 1843.

The opera in three acts is set to a libretto by the composer and Giovanni Ruffini based on Angelo Anelli's libretto for Stefano Pavesi's opera *Ser Marc' Antonio* (1810). The plot concerns the decision of the elderly bachelor Don Pasquale to marry in order to disinherit his nephew, Ernesto, who refuses to marry the woman his uncle has chosen for him.

Don Procopio   Georges Bizet, 1859.

The opera in two acts is set to a libretto by Paul Collin and Paul de Choudens translated from an original text by Carlo Cambiaggio. The story is set in a country house in Spain at the turn of the 17th century and tells what happens when Don Andronico, to general disapproval, agreees to marry his niece, Bettina, to Don Procopio, a rich old miser.

Don Quichotte ("Don Quixote")   Jules Massenet, 1910.

The opera in five acts is set to a libretto by Henri Cain based on Jacques Le Lorrain's play *Le Chevalier de la longue figure* ("The Thin-Faced Knight") (1906), itself based on Miguel Cervantes's novel (*see* **Don Quixote**).

Don Quichotte à Dulcinée ("Don Quixote to Dulcinea")   Maurice Ravel, 1933.

The three songs for voice and orchestra are settings of poems by Paul Morand with individual titles *Chanson romantique* ("Romantic Song"), *Chanson épique* ("Epic Song"), and *Chanson à boire* ("Drinking Song"). Dulcinea is the peasant girl whom Don Quixote (*see* **Don Quixote**) visualizes as his ideal lady and to whom he dedicates all his knightly exploits.

Don Quixote   (1) Léon Minkus, 1869; (2) Richard Strauss, 1896.

Minkus's ballet in a prologue and four acts (eight scenes), with a libretto and choreography by Marius Petipa, is based on Miguel Cervantes's novel of the same name (1605, 1615) about the Spaniard who reads so many chivalric romances that he believes he is a medieval knight and embarks in search of adventure with his squire, Sancho Panza. Strauss's tone poem, with an introduction, theme and ten variations, and finale, derives from the same source and is subtitled *Fantastische Variationen über ein Thema ritterlichen Charakters* ("Fantastic Variations on a Theme of Knightly Character").

Don Rodrigo   Alberto Ginastera, 1964.

The opera in the three acts, to a libretto by Alejandro Casona, tells of the brief reign of Don Rodrigo (died 711), the last Visigoth king of Spain.

Don Sanche   Franz Liszt, 1825.

The opera in one act is set to a libretto by

Emmanuel Guillaume Théaulon de Lambert and De Rancé based on a tale by Jean-Pierre Claris de Florian (1792). The story tells what happens when Don Sanche wishes to enter a moated castle owned by the magician, Alidor, but is told that only those who love and are loved may be admitted.

Doña Francisquita   Amadeo Vives, 1923.

The opera in three acts is set to a text by Frederico Romero and Guillermo Fernández Shaw based on Lope de Vega's play *La discreta enamorada* ("The Secret Lover"). The story is set in Madrid and centers on the love of Doña Francisquita for Fernando Soler, a student, himself in love with the actress Beltrana.

Doña Ines de Castro   Joaquín Serra, 1952.

The ballet in one act (five scenes), with a libretto and choreography by Ana Ricarda, tells of the tragic love of the Portuguese heir to the throne, Don Pedro, for Doña Inês de Castro (*c*.1323–1355), whose assassination made her a national Spanish heroine.

Das Donauweibchen ("The Danube Sprite")   Ferdinand Kauer, 1798.

The opera in three acts is set to the text of Karl Friedrich Hensler's play with full title *Das Donauweibchen: Ein romantisch-komisches Volksmärchen mit Gesang nach einer Sage der Vorzeit* ("The Danube Sprite: A Romantic-Comic Folk Tale with Song after a Saga of Olden Times") (1798). This play influenced Alexander Pushkin's *Rusalka* (1832) and therefore Alexander Dargomyzhsky's opera **Rusalka** (1856).

Donkey Quartet *see* **Fifths Quartet**.

La Donna del lago ("The Lady of the Lake")   Gioacchino Rossini, 1819.

The opera in two acts is set to a libretto by Andrea Leone Tottola based on Sir Walter Scott's poem of the same name (1810). The story is set in 16th-century Scotland and tells what happens when Elena, the "lady of the lake," is in love with Malcolm despite being promised by her father to Rodrigo. (In the poem she is Ellen and promised to Roderick.)

Donna Diana   Emil Reznicek, 1894.

The opera in three acts is set to the composer's own libretto based on Agustín Moreto y Cavaña's comedy *El lindo Don Diego* ("The Handsome Don Diego") (1654), about a foppish young man whose arrival in Madrid threatens the happiness of two young lovers.

"La Donna è mobile" ("Woman is fickle").

The Duke of Mantua's aria in Act 3 of Verdi's **Rigoletto**, declaring his views on the nature of women. *Cf.* **Così fan tutte**.

Donna Juanita   Franz von Suppé, 1880.

The operetta in three acts, to a libretto by F. Zell (pen name of Camillo Walzel) and Richard Genée, is set in Spain during the British occupation of 1796 and tells of a French army cadet who disguises himself as a flirtatious girl (Donna Juanita) to help the French capture San Sebastián.

"Donna non vidi mai" ("I never saw a woman").

Des Grieux's aria in Act 1 of Puccini's **Manon Lescaut**, in which he expresses his feelings on first seeing Manon.

Le Donne curiose ("The Inquisitive Women")   Ermanno Wolf-Ferrari, 1903.

The comic opera in three acts is set to a libretto by Luigi Sugana based on Carlo Goldoni's play of the same name. The story is set in 18th-century Venice and tells what happens when two wives and their friend decide to spy on their husbands and lover at their all-male club, where they suspect they are indulging in orgies.

Donnerstag aus Licht *see* **Licht**.

Dorabella   Edward Elgar, 1899.

The tenth (Intermezzo) of the **Enigma Variations** is a musical portrait of the composer's friend Dora Penny (Mrs. Richard Powell), the nickname deriving from Dorabella in **Così fan tutte**.

Das Dorf ohne Glocke ("The Village Without a Bell")   Eduard Künneke, 1919.

The operetta in three acts is set to a libretto by Arpad Pasztor based on a Hungarian legend. The story tells how villagers get a new bell for their church when the old one was removed by the Turks in the Turko-Hungarian War.

Der Dorfbarbier ("The Village Barber") Johann Baptist Schenk, 1796.

The opera in one act, to a libretto by Joseph and Paul Weidmann, tells what happens when a village barber, Lux, wishes to marry his ward, Suschen, although she loves Josef.

Dorian Toccata and Fugue   J.S. Bach, *c.* 1710.

The Toccata and Fugue in D minor for organ, BWV 538, is so named because the original copy omitted the B flat key signature, thus suggesting the so called Dorian mode or scale (represented by the white notes of the piano beginning on D).

Double Concerto   Johannes Brahms, 1887.

Any concerto for two instruments may be called by this title, but unless another composer is specified, it is usually taken to apply to Brahms's Concerto for Violin and Cello in A minor, Op. 102, also known colloquially as the *Brahms Double*.

Double Symphony   Ludwig Spohr, 1842.

The Symphony No. 7 in C major, Op. 121, is so named because it is performed by two orchestras, one large, one small. The composer's own title for the work was *Irdisches und Göttliches im Menschenleben* ("Worldly and Godly in the Lives of Men"). The larger orchestra thus represents the first of these, as worldly sophistication, or evil, while the smaller one represents the second, as childish innocence, or good. The latter overcomes the former. The idea of using two orchestras is said to have come from the composer's wife.

"Dove sei" ("Where'er thou art").

Grimoaldo's aria in Act 1 of Handel's **Rodelinda**, expressing his longing for his beloved Rodelinda. The song was formerly familiar as *"Art thou troubled?"*, but has also been given biblical words and sung as "Holy, Holy, Holy, Lord God Almighty."

"Dove sono" ("Where'er I am").

The Countess's aria in Act 3 of Mozart's Le **Nozze di Figaro**, mourning the loss of her husband's love.

Dover Beach   Samuel Barber, 1931.

The work, Op. 3, for baritone or tenor and string quartet (or string orchestra) is a setting of Matthew Arnold's poem of the same name (1867), a meditation on the sound and motion of the sea tide on the beach at Dover, England.

Down by the Greenwood Side   Harrison Birtwistle, 1969.

The work is a dramatic pastoral to a libretto by Michael Nyman for soprano, mime and speech, and chamber ensemble. The "greenwood side" is the edge of the forest, as in Gray's *Elegy*: "Him have we seen the greenwood side along."

Down in the Valley   Kurt Weill, 1948.

The opera in one act, to a libretto by Arnold Sundgaard, is based on an American folksong and, in a series of flashbacks, tells the story of a man awaiting execution for having killed his rival in love in self-defense. The title is that of the anonymous song, with its well-known lines: "Down in the valley, the valley so low, / Hang your head over, hear the wind blow."

Dramatic Symphony   Anton Rubinstein, 1874.

The Symphony No. 4 in D minor, Op. 95, is so named because the various instruments are introduced separately, like the characters in a play. The work also contains several "monologues" and "dialogues," which enhances the dramatic concept.

Le Drapeau belge ("The Belgian Flag")   Edward Elgar, 1917.

The work for reciter and orchestra, Op. 79, is set to the Belgian poet Émile Cammaerts's patriotic poem of the same name.

The Draughtsman's Contract   Michael Nyman, 1993.

The work for chamber orchestra is based on a plot by the movie director Peter Greenaway originally given the composer in 1981. It was set in 1684 and concerned the commissioning of a young draughtsman by a gentlewoman to create 12 drawings of an English country house. Nyman wrote the music, and Greenaway then shot the film around it (1982). The composer later recast the work as the present suite.

The Dream   Felix Mendelssohn, 1964.

The ballet in one act, with a libretto and choreography by Frederick Ashton, is set to the composer's incidental music (1843) to Shakespeare's play *A Midsummer Night's Dream* (1595), which the plot itself broadly follows.

Dream Aria   Jules Massenet, 1884.

Des Grieux's aria in Act 2 of **Manon Lescaut**, in which he describes how he saw Manon in a dream. The song is also known by its opening words, *"En fermant les yeux"* ("Closing my eyes").

Dream Children   Edward Elgar, 1902.

The two pieces for small orchestra, Op. 43, take their title from Charles Lamb's essay of the same name in *Essays of Elia* (1820–3). The composer quoted a passage from this in the score: "And while I stood gazing, both the children gradually grew fainter to my view, receding, and still receding till nothing at last but two mournful features were seen in the uppermost distance which, without speech, strangely impressed upon me the effects of speech; 'We are not of Alice, nor of thee, nor are we children at all ... We are nothing; less than nothing, and dreams. We are only what might have been...'."

The Dream of Gerontius   Edward Elgar, 1900.

The choral work, Op. 38, is a setting of Cardinal John Henry Newman's poem (dramatic monologue) of the same title (1866), about the vision of a just soul on the point of death. Gerontius is a name of Greek origin personifying an old man.

Dream Quartet   Joseph Haydn, c. 1787.

The String Quartet in F major, Op. 50 No. 48, is so named for its slow movement, which has some elaborate "dreamlike" solo passages for the violin.

Dreaming About Thérèse (Swedish, *Drömmem om Thérèse*)   Lars Johan Werle, 1964.

The chamber opera in two acts is set to a libretto by Lars Runsten based on Émile Zola's story *Pour une nuit d'amour* ("For a Night of Love"). The story tells what happens when Thérèse accidentally kills Colombel and promises Julien a night of love if he will dispose of the body.

Dreams (Czech, *Sny*)   Bedřich Smetana, 1875.

The suite of six pieces for piano are musical evocations with individual titles (in translation) as follows: (1) *Bygone Happiness*, (2) *Consolation*, (3) *In the Salon*, (4) *In Bohemia*, (5) *Before the Castle*, (6) *Harvest Home*.

Die Drei Pintos ("The Three Pintos") Carl Maria von Weber, 1888.

The comic opera in three acts is set to a libretto by Theodor Hell based on Carl Ludwig Seidl's story *Der Brautkampf* ("The Bridal Contest"). The story is set in Spain and tells how Don Pinto is planning to marry Clarissa when a rival deceives him and masquerades as him. Clarissa actually loves Don Gomez, however, and he masquerades as Don Pinto in turn.

Die Dreigroschenoper ("The Threepenny Opera")   Kurt Weill, 1928.

The opera in a prologue and eight scenes has a libretto by the composer based fairly closely on John Gay's The **Beggar's Opera.**

Das Dreimäderlhaus   *see* **Blossom Time.**

Drinking Song   Giuseppe Verdi, 1853.

The spirited song sung by Alfredo and Violetta in Act 1 of La **Traviata,** its key words being "*Libiamo, libiamo*" ("Let us drink, let us drink"). There are other drinking songs, such as "**Viva il vino,**" but this is probably the best known.

The Drowned Woman (Russian, *Utoplennitsa*)   Nikolai Lysenko, 1885.

The opera in three acts is set to a libretto by Mikhail Staritsky based on Nikolai Gogol's story *May Night, or the Drowned Woman,* in *Evenings on a Farm near Dikanka* (1831–2). (*See* **May Night.**) The story tells what happens when Levko, who loves Hanna, recounts to her the legend of Pannochka, who drowned herself to escape from her wicked stepmother and who became a water sprite. The stepmother also drowned, but was unable to be distinguished from the good water sprites. *Cf.* **Rusalka.**

Drum Mass   *see* **Paukenmesse.**

Drumming   Steve Reich, 1971.

The work for four pairs of tuned bongos, three marimbas, three glockenspiels, two female voices, whistle, and piccolo was written after the composer had paid a visit to Ghana to study the music of the Ewe people. The title encapsulates its essence.

Drumroll Symphony (German, *Paukenwirbel*)   Joseph Haydn, 1795.

The Symphony No. 103 in E flat major is so nicknamed because its slow introduction opens with a roll on the kettledrums. *See also* **Surprise Symphony.**

Dubrovsky   Eduard Nápravník, 1895.

The opera in four acts is set to a libretto by Modest Tchaikovsky (brother of the composer) based on Alexander Pushkin's unfinished story of the same name (1832) about a nobleman turned robber and the girl he loves, Masha.

Il Duca di Alba ("The Duke of Alba") Gaetano Donizetti, 1882.

The opera in four acts, to a libretto by Eugène Scribe and Charles Duveyrier, is set in 16th-century Flanders and tells how Egmont's daughter, Amelia, is in love with Marcello, who turns out to be the missing son of the Duke of Alba, the Spanish ruler of Flanders.

I Due Foscari ("The Two Foscari") Giuseppe Verdi, 1844.

The opera in three acts is set to a libretto by Francesco Maria Piave based on Byron's drama *The Two Foscari* (1821). The story is set in Venice in 1457 and tells what happens when Francesco Foscari, Doge of Venice, accepts the decision of the Council of Ten to extend the exile of his son, Jacopo, falsely accused of murder.

The Duenna (1) Thomas Linley, Sr. and Jr., 1775; (2) (Russian, *Obrucheniye v monastyre*, "Betrothal in a Monastery") Sergey Prokofiev, 1940–1; (3) Roberto Gerhard, 1945–7.

The opera in three acts by Thomas Linley and his identically named son is set to the text of the play written for them by Richard Brinsley Sheridan, who was Linley Senior's son-in-law. The story is set in 18th-century Seville and tells how Louisa, daughter of Don Jerome, although promised to old Mendoza, wants to marry Antonio, and disguises herself as her duenna (chaperone), Margaret, to run away. She meets her brother, Fernando, eloping with Clara d'Almanzo. Margaret, with Clara's help, disguises herself as Louisa in order to marry Mendoza. Hence the opera's subtitle, *The Double Elopement*. Prokofiev's opera in four acts, increasingly known in English as *Betrothal in a Monastery*, is set to his own libretto based on the same play. The Russian title refers to the monastery where Clara hides so that Louisa can take her place and where all the parties eventually meet. Gerhard's opera in three acts is also set to his own libretto and based on Sheridan's play.

Duetto ("Duet")   Felix Mendelssohn, 1837.

The piano piece Op. 38 No. 6 in A flat major in Book 3 of **Lieder ohne Worte** was so named by the composer for its two prominent "songs," first a treble melody, then a tenor, and finally the two together in unison. The obvious imagery is of the accord of a happy couple.

Du fond de l'abîme ("From the depths of the abyss")   Lili Boulanger, 1914–17.

The symphonic poem for alto and tenor soloists, chorus, organ, and orchestra is a setting of the **De Profundis**. The work reflects not only the despair of World War I but the composer's own illness. She died of cancer in 1918 at the age of 24.

Duke Bluebeard's Castle (Hungarian, *A kékszakállú herceg vára*)   Béla Bartók, 1918.

The one-act opera, Op. 11, to a libretto by Béla Balázs, tells how Bluebeard (not the Gilles de Rais monster of the fairy tale) takes his newest bride, Judith, to his gloomy castle, where she makes him unlock his secret doors one by one.

Dumbarton Oaks Concerto   Igor Stravinsky, 1938.

The concerto in E flat for chamber orchestra was commissioned by Mr. and Mrs. Robert Woods Bliss and first performed at Dumbarton Oaks, their mansion in Washington, DC.

Dumky Trio   Antonín Dvořák, 1890.

The Piano Trio in E minor, Op. 90, has six movements with music like that of the *dumka*, a Slavonic folk ballad that alternates between moods of joy and despair. The word itself, here in the plural form, comes from a Slavic root meaning "to think," "to ponder" (as for the Russian *Duma*, the legislative body of the general assembly).

Dunkirk   Walter Damrosch, 1943.

The work for baritone, male chorus, and orchestra is a setting of Robert Nathan's poem of the same title (1942) about the 1940 evacuation of British and some Allied troops from Dunkirk, northern France.

"Dunque io son" ("Then I am").

The duet between Rosina and Figaro in Act 1 of Rossini's Il **Barbiere di Siviglia**, in which Figaro invents the story that his cousin, a poor student, is in love with a certain girl. The words are those of the letter that Rosina has already written for the disguised Count Almaviva: *"Dunque io son, tu non m'inganni?"* ("Then I am, dost thou not deceive me?")

Duo Concertant   Igor Stravinsky, 1972.

The plotless ballet in one act (five movements), choreographed by George Balanchine, is a piece for two dancers who relate to the musicians at one side of the stage. Hence the title.

"Durch die Wälder" ("Through the woods").

Max's aria in Act 1 of Weber's Der **Freischütz**, in which he reflects how he used to wander happily through the countryside before misfortune befell him.

"Durch Zärtlichkeit und Schmeicheln" ("Though tenderness and flattery").

Blonde's aria in Act 2 of Mozart's Die **Entführung aus dem Serail**, in which she declares that a young woman's heart may be won by tenderness and flattery, never by force.

The Dybbuk (1) (Italian, *Il dibuk*) Lodovico Rocca, 1934; (2) David Tamkin, 1951.

Rocca's opera in a prologue and three acts

is set to a libretto by Renato Simoni based on the play of the same name (1926) by S. An-ski (pen name of Solomon Zanvel Rappoport), drawing on Jewish mystical folklore. (A dybbuk is the soul of a person pursued by demons that has found temporary refuge in the body of a living person.) The story tells how Chanon studies the Kabala and tries to discover a way of winning riches so he can marry Leah. He dies, however, and his soul enters Leah's body. David Tamkin's opera in three acts, with a libretto by Alex Tamkin, is based on the same source.

Dybbuk Variations Leonard Bernstein, 1974.

The ballet in one act, choreographed by Jerome Robbins, takes the play by S. An-ski (*see* The **Dybbuk**) as its starting point and develops a series of dances reflecting its mood and relationships.

The Dying Swan (Russian, *Umirayushchiy lebed'*) Camille Saint-Saëns, 1907.

The solo dance, choreographed by Michel Fokine for Anna Pavlova (1881–1931), is set to *Le Cygne* from the composer's Le **Carnaval des animaux**. The dance itself is a poignant visual poem about the final struggle for life of a dying bird, and in this case its "swan song." Pavlova became intimately associated with the dance, and in many ways she was thought of in terms of it, especially when her technique as a dancer faltered towards the end of her life.

E

"È amore un ladroncello" ("Love is a petty thief").

Dorabella's aria in Act 2 of Mozart's **Così fan tutte**, in which she reflects on how love gives both imprisonment and release.

"È il sol dell'anima" ("It is the sun of the soul").

The Duke's aria in Act 1 of Verdi's **Rigoletto**, in which he declares his love for Gilda. The full line runs: "*È il sol dell'anima, la vita è amore*" ("Love is the sun of the soul, it is life").

"E lucevan le stelle" ("And the stars were shining").

Cavaradossi's aria in Act 3 of Puccini's **Tosca**, in which he recalls his meetings with Tosca on starlit nights.

"È scherzo" ("It's a joke").

The quintet in Act 1 of Verdi's Un **Ballo in Maschera**, in which Oscar, Mam'zelle Arvidson, Gustavus, Ribbing, and Horn, all in disguise, react in various ways to the prophecy that Gustavus will die at the hand of a friend. A fuller version of the words is "*È scherzo, od è follia*" ("It's a joke, or it's madness").

Eagles Ned Rorem, 1958.

The orchestral work was inspired by Walt Whitman's poem *The Dalliance of the Eagles* (1880) in his collection *By the Roadside*, a description of the mating ritual of a pair of eagles.

Earth Dances Harrison Birtwistle, 1985–6.

The orchestral work aims to represent the "dance" or perpetual imperceptible motion of the Earth's continents which, according to plate tectonics, results from the interaction of rigid plates moving slowly over the underlying mantle.

Easter Symphony Josef Förster, 1905.

The Symphony No. 4 in C minor is based on the rite of Easter, as indicated by the individual titles of the work's four movements: (1) *The Road to Calvary*, (2) *A Child's Good Friday*, (3) *The Charm of Solitude*, (4) *Holy Sabbath Victorious*.

Eaters of Darkness Benjamin Britten, 1958.

The ballet in one act, with a libretto and choreography by Walter Gore, is set to the composer's **Variations on a Theme of Frank Bridge** and tells how a young bride, although mentally normal, is committed by her husband to an asylum, where she is driven mad by the inmates. The ballet was originally produced in Frankfurt under the German title *Die im Schatten leben*, "Those Who Live in Shadow."

Ebony Concerto Igor Stravinsky, 1946.

The concerto for clarinet and orchestra, composed for Woody Herman, its first performer, is named for the "ebony stick" (clarinet) that is its solo instrument.

"Ecco l'orrido campo" ("Behold the fearful field").

Amelia's aria opening Act 2 of Verdi's Un **Ballo in maschera**, expressing her fear and horror as she comes to the deserted spot where she is to pick the herb that will repress her love for the King.

"Ecco ridente" ("Behold laughing").

Count Almaviva's aria in Act 1 of Rossini's Il **Barbiere di Siviglia**, in which, disguised as Lindoro, he serenades Rosina. A longer version of the title is *"Ecco ridente in cielo"* ("Behold laughing in heaven").

Echoing of Trumpets Bohuslav Martinů, 1963.

The ballet in one act, with a libretto and choreography by Antony Tudor, is set to the composer's Symphony No. 6 (*Fantaisies Symphoniques*) (1951–3) and tells of a partisan who returns to his war-ravaged village only to be discovered by the occupants and executed. The work was originally produced in Stockholm under the equivalent Swedish title, *Ekon av Trumpeter*. An alternate English title is *Echo of Trumpets*. The title itself appears to hint at the words from John Bunyan's *The Pilgrim's Progress*: "So he passed over, and all the trumpets sounded for him on the other side."

Éclairs sur l'au-delà ("Flashes on the Beyond") Olivier Messiaen, 1988–91.

The composer completed the vast orchestral cycle of 11 movements shortly before his death. It was inspired by the Revelation of St. John the Divine and was a summation of his lifetime's deep faith and his life's work, his vision of the life to come.

Éclat ("Fragment") Pierre Boulez, 1965.

The work for chamber orchestra (15 instruments) has a title that indicates it is (or was) "work in progress" and that there was more to come. In fact it was revised and expanded in 1970 as *Éclat/Multiples* ("Fragment/Multiples"), the second half of the title alluding to the many instruments required. "Tuned percussion are ultimately joined by winds and no fewer than ten violas for the 'multiple reflections' implied in the title" (*The Times*, February 3, 1999). (The reviewer has apparently taken *"Éclat"* in its secondary sense of "brightness," "glare." It is possible Boulez intended both meanings, although "fragment" seems more appropriate, at least for the original work. The reviewer notes that the revised and expanded version "goes on a little too long.")

Ecstatic Orange Michael Torke, 1985–7.

The composer expresses his interest in synesthesia (the ability to perceive one sensory stimulus in terms of another) in his many "color" pieces, in which he aims to create an aural equivalent of a specific color sensation. This was his first orchestral work of the type. Other titles name other colors, such as *The Yellow Pages* (1984), *Bright Blue Music* (1985), *Green* (1986), *Verdant Music* (1986), *Purple* (1987), and *Red* (1991).

Ecuatorial ("Equatorial") Edgard Varèse, 1933–4.

The work for bass voice (or chorus) and orchestra is a setting of a Maya prayer in Spanish translation. Hence the Spanish title.

Edgar Giacomo Puccini, 1889.

The opera in four acts is set to a libretto by Ferdinando Fontana based on Alfred de Musset's verse drama *La Coupe et les Lèvres* ("The Cup and the Lips") (1832). (The title alludes to the proverb, *Il y a loin de la coupe aux lèvres*, "There's many a slip 'twixt cup and lip.") The story is set in Flanders in 1302 and tells how Edgar deserts his love, Fidelia, for the Moorish girl, Tigrana.

The Edge of the Storm (Estonian, *Iormide rand*) Gustav Ernesaks, 1949.

The opera in five acts, to a libretto by Juhan Smuul, is set in the early 19th century and tells what happens when Count Ungru (von Unger-Sternberg) extinguishes a lighthouse beacon and sets up a false light to lure ships onto the rocks, where he robs them of their booty.

Une Éducation manquée ("A Defective Education") Emanuel Chabrier, 1879.

The comic opera in one act, to a libretto by Eugène Leterrier and Albert Vanloo, is set in 18th-century France and tells what happens when Count Gontran de Boismassif arrives home with his new bride, Hélène, totally uninstructed by his tutor, Pausanias, on the facts of life.

Education of the Girlchild Meredith Monk, 1972.

The ballet in two parts was originally danced by the composer and choreographer herself. Its first part "consists of detailed episodes, literary in their associations, in which she and six female 'companions,' who may represent either a family or a composite of the heroine, take a walk through life" (Anna Kisselgoff, quoted in Koegler, p. 139). In the second part, Monk traces her life backwards, beginning as an old woman. (In reality she was 30 at the time.)

Egdon Heath Gustav Holst, 1928.

The orchestral work, Op. 47, subtitled

Homage to Hardy, was inspired by a passage describing Egdon Heath (a fictionalized Salisbury Plain) in Thomas Hardy's novel *The Return of the Native* (1878) as "a place perfectly accordant with man's nature — neither ghastly, hateful, nor ugly; neither commonplace, unmeaning, nor tame; but like man, slighted and enduring; and withal singularly colossal and mysterious in its swarthy monotony" (Chapter 1).

L'Egisto ("Egisto")   Francesco Cavalli, 1643.

The opera in three acts, to a libretto by Giovanni Battista Faustini, is set on the island of Zakynthos in mythological times and tells what happens when Egisto relates to Climene how he and Clori were captured by Corsican bandits.

Egmont   Ludwig van Beethoven, 1809–10.

The overture and incidental music, Op. 84, was written for Goethe's historical drama of the same name (1787) about the Flemish statesman and soldier, Lamoral, Count of Egmont (1522–1568), who defied Philip II of Spain and was beheaded.

Egyptian Concerto   Camille Saint-Saëns, 1896.

The Piano Concerto No. 5 in F major, Op. 103, is so sometimes nicknamed because it was influenced by a visit the composer had made to Luxor on the Nile.

The Egyptian Helen *see* **Die Ägyptische Helena**.

Eight Songs for a Mad King   Peter Maxwell Davies, 1969.

The theater piece in eight movements for male actor-singer and chamber ensemble is set to a text by Randolph Stow and George III, the latter being the "mad king" of the title.

1812 (Russian, *1812 god*)   Pyotr Tchaikovsky, 1880.

The concert overture, Op. 49, commemorates Napoleon's retreat from Moscow in 1812. Hence the name. The work quotes the French and Russian national anthems.

Ein (German, "A").

For titles beginning with this word, see the next word, *e.g.* Ein **Heldenleben**.

Eine (German, "A").

For titles beginning with this word, see the next word, *e.g.* Eine **Kleine Nachtmusik**.

"Einsam in trüben Tagen" *see* **Elsa's Dream**.

Einstein on the Beach   Philip Glass and Robert Wilson, 1976.

The opera in four acts and five "knee plays" (intermezzos) is set to a libretto ("spoken texts") by Christopher Knowles, Lucinda Childs, and Samuel M. Johnson. It was inspired by Wilson's drawings and performance art and although the title refers to the historical physicist Albert Einstein (1879–1955), his relation to the opera is, one might say, relative. A violinist on stage is dressed as Einstein, but so are the other performers. There is no actual beach.

El Greco   Désiré Inghelbrecht, 1920.

The ballet in one act, with a libretto and choreography by Jean Börlin, was inspired by El Greco's paintings and evolves as a series of mimed scenes, culminating in *The Entombment of Count Orgaz* (1586).

The Electrification of the Soviet Union   Nigel Osborne, 1987.

The opera in two acts is set to a libretto by Craig Raine based on Boris Pasternak's story *Povest'* ("A Tale") (1929), translated as *The Last Summer* (1959), and his unfinished autobiographical novel in verse *Spektorsky* (1924–30), both set against the background of the early years of the Soviet Union. The title is based on a famous quotation from Lenin: "Communism is Soviet power plus the electrification of the whole country" (1920).

Elegiaca Symphony   Gian Francesco Malipiero, 1936.

The composer has explained why his Symphony No. 2 is so named: "In regard to my Second Symphony I want to avoid confusion and misunderstanding. I wish to refer at once to the subtitle 'Elegiaca.' This qualificative is an explanation how music that I wrote in the anxious and tragic month of the year 1936, a year full of sadness, yet remains outside of the events and has elegiac character. This Symphony is just music.... I wish to emphasize that in the term elegiaca there is no intention of program music" (program note, quoted in Berkowitz, pp. 39–40).

Elegy *see* **Lieder ohne Worte**.

Elegy for Young Lovers (German, *Elegie für junge Liebende*)   Hans Werner Henze, 1961.

The opera in three acts, to a libretto by W.H. Auden and Chester Kallman, tells how the ageing poet Gregor Mittenhofer goes to the Alps to seek inspiration and there finds Toni and Elisabeth, the young lovers of the title. Their death while collecting edelweiss inspires his greatest poem, *Elegy for Young Lovers*.

Elektra ("Electra") (1) Richard Strauss, 1909; (2) Malcolm Arnold, 1963.

The opera in one act is set to a libretto by Hugo von Hoffmansthal after his drama of the same name (1903), itself based on Sophocles's tragedy (*c.*410 BC). This tells how Electra and her brother, Orestes, avenge their father, Agamemnon, when he is murdered by their mother, Clytemnestra. Arnold's ballet in one act, choreographed by Robert Helpmann, is a melodramatic retelling of the same work.

Les Elfes ("The Elves") (1) Nicolo Gabrielli, 1856; (2) Felix Mendelssohn, 1924.

Gabrielli's ballet in three acts, to a libretto by Jules-Henri Vernoy de Saint-Georges and choreography by Joseph Mazilier, tells of a count who falls in love with a statue of Sylvia, which the Queen of the Elves brings to life. Mendelssohn's plotless ballet in one act, choreographed by Michel Fokine, is set to the composer's overture from **A Midsummer Night's Dream** and attempts to portray the atmosphere of the music.

Elijah   Felix Mendelssohn, 1846.

The oratorio, Op. 70, for soprano, contralto, tenor, bass, and treble soloists, boys' chorus, chorus, and orchestra, is set to a text by Julius Schubring based on the Old Testament story of the prophet Elijah in 1 Kings 17–19.

Elisabetta, regina d'Inghilterra ("Elizabeth, Queen of England")   Gioacchino Rossini, 1815.

The opera in two acts is set to a libretto by Giovanni Schmidt based on Carlo Federici's play of the same title (1814) itself based on Sophie Lee's novel *The Recess* (1783–5). The plot centers on Queen Elizabeth I of England (1533–1603) and tells what happens when she learns from the Duke of Norfolk that her favorite, the Earl of Leicester, has secretly married Mathilde.

L'Elisir d'amore ("The Love Potion")   Gaetano Donizetti, 1832.

The comic opera in two acts is set to a libretto by Felice Romani based on Eugène Scribe's libretto for Daniel Auber's opera *Le Philtre* ("The Philter") (1831). This tells what happens when Nemorino obtains a love potion from the quack Dulcamara to help him win the heart of the capricious Adina.

"Ella giammai m'amo" ("She never loved me").

Philip II's aria in Act 4 of Verdi's **Don Carlos**, in which he grieves over his loneliness as a man who has never been loved by his wife, as well as his isolation as a king.

"Elle a fui" ("She has fled").

Antonio's aria at the piano in Act 2 (Antonia's act) of Offenbach's Les **Contes d'Hoffmann**. A fuller form is: "*Elle a fui, la tourterelle*" ("She has fled, the turtledove").

Elsa's Dream   Richard Wagner, 1850.

Elsa's aria in Act 1 of **Lohengrin**, in which she recounts her dream of rescuing a hero. Her song is also known by its leading words: "*Einsam in trüben Tagen*" ("Alone in dull days").

Elvira Madigan Concerto   W.A. Mozart, 1785.

The Piano Concerto No. 21 in C major, K 467, is sometimes known so nicknamed, since its slow movement served as background music in the 1967 movie of this name.

Embattled Garden   Carlos Surinach, 1958.

The ballet in one act, choreographed by Martha Graham, has "the Garden of Love" as its subject, a garden that "seems always to be threatened by the Stranger's knowledge of the world outside and by the old knowledge of those like Lilith (according to legend, Adam's wife before Eve) who lived there first" (program note, quoted by Koegler, p. 143).

Embrace Tiger and Return to Mountain   Morton Subotnick, 1968.

The ballet in one act, choreographed by Glen Tetley, is set to the composer's *Silver Apples of the Moon* (1967) and was inspired by the Chinese system of shadow boxing known as t'ai chi. The title is that of one of the sport's prescribed exercise forms, all named for the image created by their execution. (Others are "White stork displays its wings" and "Fall back and twist like monkey.") An early form of the sport involved emulations of the five creatures: bear, bird, deer, monkey, and tiger.

The Emerald Isle   Arthur Sullivan, 1901.

The posthumous comic opera in two acts, to a libretto by Basil Hood, is subtitled *The Caves of Carig-Cleena* and, as the title indicates, is set in Ireland. The opera was completed by Edward German.

Emperor Concerto   Ludwig van Beethoven, 1809.

The Piano Concerto No. 5 in E flat major,

Op. 73, has a name of uncertain origin. It would not have been for the Emperor Napoleon, whom Beethoven formerly admired but now derided. It is not even certain who gave the name. It may have been the publisher, J.B. Cramer. The nickname is not inappropriate for the work, the composer's last piano concerto.

The Emperor Jones (1) Louis Gruenberg, 1933; (2) Heitor Villa-Lobos, 1956.

The opera in two acts is set to a libretto by Kathleen de Jaffa based on Eugene O'Neill's play of the same title (1921). The story centers on Brutus "Emperor" Jones, an ex–Pullman porter and escaped convict, who rules his island in the Caribbean as a royal despot. Villa-Lobos's ballet in one act, choreographed by José Limón, was inspired by the same play.

Emperor Quartet (German, *Kaiserquartett*) Joseph Haydn, 1797.

The String Quartet in C major, Op. 76 No. 3, is so named because the slow movement is a set of variations the composer wrote for the *Emperor's Hymn*, the Austrian national anthem.

Emperor Waltz *see* **Kaiser-Walzer.**

"En fermant les yeux" *see* **Dream Aria.**

En Gedi *see* **Christus am Ölberge.**

En Saga *see* **En Saga.**

The Enchanted Lake (Russian, *Volshebnoye ozero*): Anatol Lyadov, 1909.

The symphonic tone poem is a musical description of the lake of the title, set among dark trees and inhabited by water nymphs.

Enchanted Summer Arnold Bax, 1910.

The work is a setting for two sopranos, chorus, and orchestra of words from Act 2, scene 2 of P.B. Shelley's lyrical drama *Prometheus Unbound* (1820), in which two young forest fauns listen to choruses of spirits singing of the magic charms of summer.

The Enchantress (1) (Russian, *Charodeyka*) Pyotr Tchaikovsky, 1887; (2) Arthur Bliss, 1952.

Tchaikovsky's opera in four acts is set to a libretto by Ippolit Shpazhinsky based on his melodrama of the same name (1884). The story centers on Nastasya, nicknamed Gossip, the owner of a wayside inn, and the influence for good or ill that she has on the men who love her or hate her. Bliss's work for contralto and orchestra is a setting of a poem ("idyll") by the 3d-

century BC Greek poet Theocritus, in which a young woman evolves a spell that can charm back a roving lover or destroy him.

Endless Parade Harrison Birtwistle, 1987.

The work for solo trumpet, vibraphone, and strings is effectively a trumpet concerto designed to represent the parade of the title.

L'Enfance du Christ ("The Childhood of Christ") Hector Berlioz, 1854.

The oratorio, Op. 25, for seven soloists, chorus, and orchestra, is set to the composer's own text based on the Gospel accounts of the birth and boyhood of Jesus.

L'Enfant et les Sortilèges ("The Child and the Charms") Maurice Ravel, 1917–25.

The opera (*"fantaisie lyrique"*) in two parts is set to a libretto by Colette and tells what happens when the young Child misbehaves and is upbraided by pets and domestic objects. In 1916 Colette had written a libretto for a divertimento called *Ballet pour ma fille* ("Ballet for My Daughter"). In 1917 this was offered to the composer who "at first declined the invitation because he had not got a daughter [although Colette had, born 1913] and the title seemed to him inappropriate. However, with a certain amount of pressure he eventually consented, and the work was renamed *L'Enfant et les sortilèges*" (Norman Demuth, *Ravel*, 1947).

L'Enfant prodigue ("The Prodigal Son") Claude Debussy, 1884.

The cantata, for soprano, tenor, and baritone soloists, chorus, and orchestra, is set to a text by Ernest Guinand based on the New Testament parable. *See* The **Prodigal Son.**

The English Cat (German, *Die englische Katze*) Hans Werner Henze, 1983.

The "story for singers and instrumentalists" in two acts is set to a libretto by Edward Bond based on Honoré de Balzac's *Peines de cœur d'une chatte anglaise* ("Heartaches of an English Cat") (1840), a satirical tale, in which all of the characters are cats, contrasting the English and French ways of making amorous advances.

English Lyrics Hubert Parry, 1874–1920.

The title is that of 12 sets of songs (74 in all) for voice and piano that are all settings of English poetry.

An English Suite Hubert Parry, 1890–1916.

The (unfinished) Suite in G major in seven

movements for string orchestra has English themes and melodies as its basis.

English Suites   J.S. Bach, 1715.

The six keyboard suites are said to be so named from a manuscript comment by the composer's youngest son, Johann Christian Bach, that the work was "*fait pour les Anglais*" ("made for the English"). "So called probably because they have long preludes for first movements, which seems to have been considered an English fashion, perhaps because Purcell's suites have preludes" (Blom, p. 157). *Cf.* **French Suites**, **German Suites**.

Enigma Variations   Edward Elgar, 1899.

The orchestral work, Op. 36, formally titled *Variations on an Original Theme* (*Enigma*), consists of a theme and 14 variations, the "enigma" apparently being the theme itself and perhaps representing the composer, who wrote in the program note for the first performance: "The enigma I will not explain – its 'dark saying' must be left unguessed, and I warn you that the apparent connection between the Variations and the Theme is often of the slightest texture; further, through and over the whole set another and larger theme 'goes', but is not played" (quoted in Michael Kennedy, *Portrait of Elgar*, 1982). This means that there are actually two enigmas: the original theme and the unheard one. This second melody has never been conclusively detected.

The work as a whole is dedicated "to my friends pictured within," so that each variation is a musical portrait. Two of the best known are No. 9, **Nimrod**, and No. 10, **Dorabella**. The others are as follows (identity in brackets): No. 1, C.A.E. (Caroline Alice Elgar, née Roberts, the composer's wife), No. 2, H.D.S.-P. (Hew David Steuart-Powell), No. 3, R.B.T. (Richard Baxter Townshend), No. 4, W.M.B. (William Meath Baker), No. 5, R.P.A. (Richard P. Arnold), No. 6, Ysobel (Isabel Fitton), No. 7, Troyte (Arthur Troyte Griffith), No. 8, W.N. (Winifred Norbury), No. 11, G.R.S. (Dr. G.R. Sinclair, although the piece itself portrays his bulldog, Dan), No. 12, B.G.N. (Basil G. Nevinson), No. 13, *** (Lady Mary Lygon) (the composer may have been wary of entering a person's initials as the 13th variation), No. 14, E.D.U. (Edward William Elgar, the composer himself, the letters representing "Edoo," his wife's name for him, as if from *Eduard*, the German equivalent of his first name). A ballet choreographed by Frederick

Ashton was set to the work and produced in 1968.

Die Entführung aus dem Serail ("The Abduction from the Seraglio")   W.A. Mozart, 1782.

The opera in three acts, K 384, is set to a libretto by Gottlieb Stephanie based on Christoph Friedrich Bretzner's libretto for Johann André's opera **Belmonte und Constanze**. The plot is set in 16th-century Turkey and opens as the Spanish nobleman Belmonte arrives at the Pasha's palace seeking his betrothed, Constanze, who has been enslaved together with her English maid, Blonde, and his servant, Pedrillo. The story tells how they escape.

Entr'acte   Franz Schubert, 1823.

The title, a term for a piece of music "between the acts," was in this case written to be played between the acts of **Rosamunde**.

Les Éolides ("The Breezes")   César Franck, 1876.

The symphonic poem is based on a poem by Charles-Marie Leconte de Lisle of the same title, one of his *Poèmes antiques* ("Ancient Poems") (1852), describing the flight of the breezes, the daughters of Aeolus, god of the winds, over the southern lands.

Éoline   Cesare Pugni, 1845.

The ballet in six scenes, with a libretto and choreography by Jules Joseph Perrot, is based on Johann Karl August Musäus's fairy tale *Libussa* (1782), telling how the wood nymph, Éoline, dies on her wedding day because the gnome, Rübezahl, sets fire to the fir tree that is her home. The ballet's full title is *Éoline, ou la Dryade* ("Eoline, or the Dryad").

Episodes   Anton von Webern, 1959.

The ballet was originally in two parts. The first was choreographed by Martha Graham and set to the composer's *Passacaglia*, Op. 1 (1908), and *Sechs Stücke* ("Six Pieces") for orchestra, Op. 6 (1909–10). It recalled some moments in the life of Mary, Queen of Scots (Maria Stuart) (1542–1587), on her way to the scaffold. The plotless second part was choreographed by George Balanchine and set to the composer's Symphony, Op. 21 (1928), *Fünf Stücke* ("Five Pieces") for orchestra, Op. 10 (1911–13), *Concerto for Nine Instruments*, Op. 24 (1931–4), *Variations* for orchestra, Op. 30 (1940), and *Ricercare* for six voices from Bach's Das **Musikalische Opfer**. The first part was soon dropped from the repertory, as were the *Variations*, so that today the work comprises just the four Balanchine numbers. The title remains, however, as a reminder of the episodes portrayed in the first part.

Epitaffio per Federico García Lorca ("Epitaph for Federico García Lorca") Luigi Nono, 1951–3.

The work, for various combinations of singers and players, is in three parts: (1) *España en la corazón* ("Spain in the Heart"), (2) *Y su sangre ya viene cantando* ("And His Blood Now Comes Singing"), (3) *Memento: romance de la guardia civil española* ("Memento: Romance of the Spanish Civil Guard"). As the title indicates, the work is dedicated to the Spanish poet and dramatist Federico García Lorca (1899–1936), assassinated in the Spanish Civil War.

Epitaph György Ligeti, 1969.

The ballet in one act, choreographed by Rudi van Dantzig and set to the composer's **Atmosphères** and *Volumina* (1961), is a personal statement about the difficulties of communication in a modern society. The title implies that the statement is final.

L'Épreuve de l'amour ("The Test of Love") attrib. W.A. Mozart, 1936.

The ballet in one act, with a libretto and choreography by Michel Fokine, is based on a Korean fairy tale and tells the story of the daughter of a mandarin who is supposed to marry a rich ambassador but who loves a poor young man. The music for the ballet was discovered in 1928 and originally attributed to Mozart. In fact it is probably by various composers.

Equivoci, Gli ("The Doubles") Stephen Storace, 1786.

The opera is set to a libretto by Lorenzo da Ponte based on Shakespeare's comedy *The Comedy of Errors* (1592), which involves confusion of identity between two sons called Antipholus and two slaves called Dromio.

Ercole amante ("Hercules in Love") Francesco Cavalli, 1662.

The opera in a prologue and five acts, to a libretto by Francesco Buti, tells of the love of Ercole and his son, Hyllo, for Iole. The opera was written to celebrate the marriage in 1660 of Louis XIV of France (Ercole) to Marie-Thérèse of Austria.

"Eri tu" ("It was thou").

Anckarstroem's aria in Act 3 of Verdi's Un **Ballo in maschera**, in which he resolves not to punish his supposedly unfaithful wife but his friend and king, Gustavus. A fuller version of the words is: "*Eri tu che macchiavi quell'anima*" ("It was thou who stained that soul").

Der Erlkönig ("The Erl-King") Franz Schubert, 1815.

The song, D 328, takes its words from Goethe's ballad opera *Die Fischerin* ("The Fisherwoman") (1782), in which the song is sung by the title character, Dortchen. In German folklore the Erl-King is a king of the elves who appears to children in the Black Forest and lures them to their deaths. Although "Erl-King" is now understood to mean "elf-king," German *Erlkönig* actually means "king of the alders." The name arose as a mistranslation by Goethe's fellow poet, Gottfried von Herder, of Danish *ellerkonge*, "elf-king," which he confused with *elverkonge*, "alder-king." "The English title, though meaningless, is so generally accepted that it must be retained" (Blom, p. 159).

Erminie Edward Jacobowski, 1885.

The comic opera in three acts is set to a libretto by Harry and Edward Paulton based on Benjamin Antier and Jean-Armand Saint-Armand's play *L'Auberge des Edrets* ("The Inn of the Edrets") (1823), in which the villain is Robert Macaire. The story tells of the love of the Marquis's daughter, Erminie, and Eugène, brother of Erminie's companion, Cerise Marcel.

Ermione Gioacchino Rossini, 1819.

The opera in two acts is set to a libretto by Andrea Leone Tottola based on Pierre Racine's tragedy *Andromaque* (1667), telling how Hermione, daughter of Helen and Menelaus in Greek legend, plays Orestes, to whom she is promised, against Pyrrhus, to whom she is given in marriage, and commits suicide when the latter is murdered by the former at her instigation.

Ernani Giuseppe Verdi, 1844.

The opera in four acts is set to a libretto by Francesco Maria Piave based on Victor Hugo's tragedy *Hernani* (1830). The story is set in 16th-century Spain and concerns the love of Elvira, betrothed to the grandee Silva, for the outlaw known as Ernani, who is really the banished nobleman Don Juan of Aragon.

"Ernani, involami" ("Ernani, take me away").

Elvira's aria in Act 1 of Verdi's **Ernani**, in which she hopes that Ernani will flee with her.

Ero the Joker (Serbo-Croat, *Ero s onoga svijeta*, "Ero from the Other World") Jakov Gotovac, 1935.

The opera in three acts is set to a libretto by Milan Begović based on a Dalmatian fairy tale. The story tells what happens when Mischa appears from a hayloft to land among a group of girls. He claims to be Ero, and to have fallen from Heaven because it was boring there.

Eroica Sonata   Edward MacDowell, 1895.

The Piano Sonata No. 2 in G minor, Op. 50, was inspired by the Arthurian legend and is headed "Flos regum Arthuris" ("Flower of the Reign of Arthur"). Its name generally accords with a character regarded as heroic: "ARTHUR (6th century) semi-legendary king of the Britons — and national hero" (*Chambers Biographical Dictionary*, 1990).

Eroica Symphony   Ludwig van Beethoven, 1804.

The Symphony No. 3 in E flat major, Op. 55, was published under the title *Sinfonia eroica, composta per festiggiare il Sovvenire di un grand Uomo* ("Heroic symphony, composed to celebrate the memory of a great man"), the man in question being Napoleon. The composer had planned to call the symphony simply *Bonaparte*, in honor of the Revolutionary hero, but was disillusioned on learning that Napoleon had declared himself Emperor in May 1804. Hence the change of title, its dedicatee remaining unnamed.

Eroica Variations   Ludwig van Beethoven, 1802.

The Piano Variations in E flat major, Op. 35, are based on a theme from the composer's ballet The **Creatures of Prometheus** that he later used in his **Eroica Symphony**. Hence the name, which was not given by Beethoven himself.

Errand into the Maze   Gian-Carlo Menotti, 1947.

The ballet in one act, choreographed by Martha Graham, is based on the classical legend of Theseus and the Minotaur. Hence the title, referring literally to the mission of Theseus that took him into the labyrinth to kill the Minotaur, and figuratively to our own victory over the fears that lie at the heart of our own mental maze.

Errante   Franz Schubert, arr. Franz Liszt, 1933.

The ballet in one act, with a libretto by George Balanchine and Pavel Tchelitchev and choreography also by Balanchine, centers on an enigmatic woman and her fight against obscure emotional problems. The work is set to Liszt's transcription (1851) of Schubert's **Wanderer Fantasy**. Hence the title, as the Italian for "wandering." (An alternate English title is actually *The Wanderer*.)

Die Erste Walpurgisnacht ("The First Walpurgis Night")   Felix Mendelssohn, 1832.

The cantata, Op. 60, for solo voices, chorus, and orchestra, is a setting of Goethe's ballad of the same name describing the annual festival on the eve of May 1 (St. Walburga's night) when witches ride to the Brocken in the Harz Mountains

Ertmannsonate I   Johann Friedrich Reichardt, 1813.

The Grande Sonate in F minor for Piano, Denn 57a, is named for its dedicatee, Frau von Ertmann. *Cf.* **Ertmannsonate II.**

Ertmannsonate II   Johann Friedrich Reichardt, 1813.

The Sonata in E minor for Piano, Denn 57B, is dedicated to "Mad. la Bar. de Ertmann." *Cf.* **Ertmannsonate I.**

Erwartung ("Expectation")   Arnold Schoenberg, 1924.

The opera in one act is set to a libretto by Marie Pappenheim and tells how a woman awaiting her lover at night in the woods stumbles on his corpse.

"Es gibt ein Land" ("There is a land").

Ariadne's aria in Richard Strauss's **Ariadne auf Naxos**, in which she dreams of a land where everything is pure. The land is death.

Es war einmal ("Once Upon a Time")   Alexander Zemlinsky, 1897–9.

The opera, based on Hans Christian Andersen's fairy tale *The Swineherd* (1842), itself a reworking of a Danish folktale, tells what happens when a Prince comes with his companion, Kaspar, as the latest in a long line of suitors for the hand of a Princess. The title is the stock fairy tale opening.

Escales *see* **Ports of Call.**

Esclarmonde   Jules Massenet, 1889.

The opera in a prologue, four acts, and an epilogue is set to a libretto by Alfred Blau and Louis de Gramont based on the medieval romance *Partenopoeus de Bloix* ("Parthenopeus of Blois") (before 1188). The story tells what happens when the sorceress, Esclarmonde, wins the knight, Roland de Blois, through her powers of enchantment.

La Esmeralda ("Esmeralda") Cesare Pugni, 1933.

The ballet in three acts (five scenes), with a libretto and choreography by Jules Joseph Perrot, is based on Victor Hugo's novel *Notre-Dame de Paris*, usually known in English as *The Hunchback of Notre-Dame* (1831), telling of the hopeless love of the deaf and hunchbacked bellringer, Quasimodo, for the gypsy girl, Esmeralda. *Cf.* **Notre Dame.**

Les Espaces acoustiques ("Acoustic Spaces") Gérard Grisey, 1974–85.

The composition for electro-acoustic instruments began as a single work that eventually became six separate pieces designed to be played either separately or in association with those adjacent to it. In their proper sequence they are: *Prologue* (1976), *Périodes* (1974), *Partiels* (1975), *Modulations* (1978), *Transitoires* (1981), *Épilogue* (1985). "The overall title points to Grisey's guiding interest in the innate qualities of sound and its context" (*The Times*, December 4, 1998). The composer himself explained: "Sound only exists in relation to its individuality, and this individuality only become manifest in a context that illuminates it and gives it meaning. I therefore consider it essential for a composer to act not only on the material, but also on its 'space' on the 'defense' that separates the sounds" (*ibid.*).

España ("Spain") Emanuel Chabrier, 1883.

The orchestral rhapsody quotes tunes and rhythms collected by the composer during a visit to Spain in 1882–3. Hence its name.

Espansiva *see* **Sinfonia espansiva.**

Estampes ("Engravings") Claude Debussy, 1903.

The three piano pieces are "pictures" entitled *Pagodes* ("Pagodas"), *Soirée dans Grenade* ("Evening in Granada"), and *Jardins sous la pluie* ("Gardens in the Rain").

Esther George Frideric Handel, 1732.

The first English oratorio is set to a text by Samuel Humphreys based on Jean Racine's tragedy of the same name (1689), telling of the Jewish woman taken as queen by the Persian king Ahasuerus. Her story is told in the biblical book named for her. The work was first performed in 1720 as the masque *Haman and Mordecai* but then expanded into the present concert oratorio.

Esther de Carpentras ("Esther of Carpentras") Darius Milhaud, 1925.

The opera buffa, Op. 89, with a libretto by Armand Lunel, is set in the town of Carpentras in the south of France and concerns the reaction of the Catholic authorities when the Jews in the ghetto there stage their play *The Tragedy of Esther* in the public square. The play itself centers on the age-old story of Esther, heroine of the Old Testament book bearing her name.

L'Estro armonico ("The Harmonious Inspiration") Antonio Vivaldi, 1712.

The twelve concertos for various instruments, Op. 3, have a general title indicating their musical genesis.

"Esultate!" ("Exult!").

Otello's announcement of victory over the Turks in Act 1 of Verdi's **Otello.**

Et exspecto resurrectionem mortuorum ("And I Look for the Resurrection of the Dead") Olivier Messiaen, 1964.

The work for woodwind, brass, and percussion was commissioned by the French government and dedicated to the memory of the dead of both world wars. The title is from a sentence in the **Credo.**

L'Étoile ("The Star") Emmanuel Chabrier, 1877.

The comic opera in three acts, to a libretto by Eugène Leterrier and Albert Vanloo, tells how King Ouf seeks a victim for execution and finds one in the pedlar, Lazuli. However, the court astrologer reveals that the king will die 24 hours after Lazuli and the execution is cancelled. Lazuli goes on to survive other fates, and is thus the "lucky star" of the title.

L'Étoile du nord ("The Northern Star") Giacomo Meyerbeer, 1854.

The comic opera in three acts is set to a libretto by Eugène Scribe based on the libretto that Ludwig Rellstab wrote for the original version, entitled *Ein Feldlager in Schlesien* ("A Camp in Silesia") (1844), about an incident in the life of Frederick the Great. The action was transferred to Russia for the later opera, and Peter the Great (the "Northern Star") substituted for Frederick. The story tells of Peter's love for a village girl, Katherine, who takes the place of her brother, Georges, in the Russian army. Peter disguises himself as a carpenter to woo her and makes her his wife (the czarina).

L'Étrange farandole ("The Strange Farandole")   Dmitry Shostakovich, 1939.

The ballet in four movements, choreographed by Léonide Massine, is set to the composer's Symphony No. 1 in F minor, Op. 10 (1924–5), with the four movements respectively representing *Aggression*, *City and Country*, *Loneliness*, and *Fate*. The ballet's original title was *Le Rouge et le Noir* ("Red and Black"), presumably after Stendhal's novel (1830). A farandole is a lively Provençal dance.

Etruscan Concerto   Peggy Glanville-Hicks, 1955.

The Concerto for Piano and Chamber Orchestra is so titled because it aims to reflect the atmosphere of the Etruscan tombs of Tarquinia.

Étude   J.S. Bach, 1925.

The plotless ballet in six movements, choreographed by Bronislava Nijinska, was originally entitled *Holy Etudes*, while a 1926 version was *Un estudio religioso* ("A Religious Study"). The ballet attempts to translate the composer's music into visual terms. An *étude* ("study") is basically a composition intended to provide a basis for the improvement of the performer's technique, but in piano music is usually restricted to the exploitation of one type of passage.

Étude aux chemins de fer ("Railway Study")   Pierre Schaeffer, 1948.

The first piece of *musique concrète* (a term coined by the composer) was an assemblage of recorded sounds of railway trains.

Études ("Studies")   (1) Claude Debussy, 1915; (2) Knudåge Riisage, 1948.

Debussy's work comprises 12 piano pieces designed to give the player practice in various techniques and musical forms while exploring whole musical worlds in miniature. The titles are simply indications of the technique involved, such as *Pour les cinq doigts* ("For the five fingers") or *Pour les tierces* ("For thirds") or *Pour les notes répétées* ("For repeated notes"). Riisage's ballet in one act, choreographed by Harald Lander, is set to music based on that of Karl Czerny, famous for his instructive studies for the piano. The ballet mirrors this theme, and progresses through a range of dance exercises of increasing technical difficulty.

Études d'exécution transcendante ("Transcendental Studies")   Franz Liszt, 1851.

The 12 pieces for solo piano are based on the *24 Grandes Études* ("24 Great Studies") (1837) and *Mazeppa* (1840) (*see* **Mazeppa**). They are "transcendental" in that they are based on earlier pieces but transformed into virtuoso works. Their individual titles (two lack one) are as follows: (1) *Preludio*, (2) (in A minor), (3) *Paysage* ("Landscape"), (4) *Mazeppa*, (5) *Feux follets* ("Will-o'-the-Wisps"), (6) *Vision*, (7) *Eroica*, (8) *Wilde Jagd* ("Wild Chase"), (9) *Ricordanza* ("Memory"), (10) (in F minor), (11) *Harmonies du soir* ("Evening Harmonies"), (12) *Chasse-neige* ("Snowplow").

Études d'exécution transcendante d'après Paganini ("Transcendental Studies after Paganini")   Franz Liszt, 1838.

The work for solo piano consists of transcriptions of six of Paganini's violin caprices. They are "transcendental" in that they transform the original pieces into virtuoso compositions.

Études symphoniques ("Symphonic Studies")   Robert Schumann, 1834–7.

The work for solo piano, Op. 13, was originally entitled *Etuden im Orchester-Charakter für Pianoforte von Florestan und Eusebius* ("Studies in the Orchestral Style for Pianoforte by Florestan and Eusebius") (*see* **Davidsbündlertänze**), but the second version (1852) was called *Études en formes de variations* ("Studies in the Form of Variations").

Eugene Onegin (Russian, *Yevgeny Onegin*)   Pyotr Tchaikovsky, 1879.

The opera in three acts is set to a libretto by the composer and Konstantin Shilovsky based on Alexander Pushkin's poem of the same title (1831). This centers on the love of Tatyana for the aristocrat, Onegin. She first falls for him when, together with the poet, Lensky, he pays a visit to her mother, Madame Larina. Her elder sister, Olga, is Lensky's betrothed. The opera is irreverently known to those in the business as "Eugene One Gin."

Euphrosine   Étienne-Nicolas Méhul, 1790.

The opera in five (later three, then finally four) acts, to a libretto by Franz Benoît Hoffman, tells of the eventually successful endeavors of Euphrosine to win the misogynist, Coradin, in spite of the efforts of the bitter, rejected Countess.

Euridice ("Eurydice")   Jacopo Peri, 1600.

The opera in a prologue and six scenes,

with contributions from Giulio Caccini (who soon after wrote a similar opera on the same subject), is set to a libretto by Ottavio Rinuccini based on the familiar classical legend of Eurydice, wife of Orpheus. *See* **Orfeo ed Euridice**.

L'Europe galante ("Gallantries of Europe") André Campra, 1697.

The opera-ballet, to a libretto by Antoine Houdar de la Motte, has four entrées (acts) depicting the respective romantic attitudes of France, Spain, Italy, and Turkey.

Euryanthe Carl Maria von Weber, 1823.

The opera in three acts is set to a libretto by Helmina von Chézy based on a 13th-century French romance which tells of Lysiart's wager with Adolar that he can seduce Euryanthe, whom Adolar loves.

Eva Josef Bohuslav Förster, 1899.

The opera in three acts is set to the composer's own libretto based on Gabriela Preissová's play *Gazdina roba* ("The Gaffer's Woman") (1890). The story tells of the doomed love between Mánek, a wealthy farmer's son, and Eva, a poor seamstress.

Der Evangelimann ("The Evangelist") Wilhelm Kienzl, 1895.

The opera in two acts is set to the composer's own libretto based on Leopold Florian Meissner's story of the same name (1894). The plot is set in St. Othmar, Austria, in the first half of the 19th century and tells how jealousy leads Johannes to commit acts which ruin the love of Matthias, his brother, and Martha, send him innocent to prison, and result in his becoming an evangelical preacher.

Evening Hymn Henry Purcell, 1688.

The sacred song is set to lines by William Fuller beginning "Now that the sun hath veil'd his light." The full title is *An Evening Hymn on a Ground Bass*, and as such it is a good example of the composer's treatment of a ground bass (a recurring melody in the bass).

The Evening Star *see* **Lieder ohne Worte**.

L'Éventail de Jeanne ("Jeanne's Fan") various (see below), 1927.

The ballet in ten numbers, with choreography by Yvonne Franck and Alice Bourgat, was commissioned by Jeanne Dubost (the Jeanne of the title) for her Paris ballet school. She gave the ten leaves of her fan to ten composers, asking each to compose a number. Those who participated (their contribution in parentheses) were: Maurice Ravel (*Fanfare*), Pierre-Octave Ferroud (*March*), Jacques Ibert (*Valse*), Roland Manuel (*Canarie*), Marcel Delannoy (*Bourrée*), Albert Roussel (*Sarabande*), Darius Milhaud (*Polka*), Francis Poulenc (*Pastourelle*), and Florent Schmitt (*Finale*). The identity of the tenth composer was long unknown but he is now believed to be Georges Auric.

Events Robert Prince, 1961.

The ballet in one act, choreographed by Jerome Robbins, is about the different methods used to deal with the numerous threats imposed by modern society.

Eventyr ("Once Upon a Time") Frederick Delius, 1917.

The ballad for orchestra is based on the fairy tales of the Norwegian writer and folklorist Peter Christen Asbjørnsen (1812–1885).

Every Soul Is a Circus Paul Nordhoff, 1939.

The ballet in one act, choreographed by Martha Graham, is based on Vachel Lindsay's poem of the same name (1929), telling of the split personality of a woman who watches the reactions of her partners as she flirts with a ringmaster and an acrobat.

Everyman (1) Walford Davies, 1904, (2) Jean Sibelius, 1916; (3) Frank Martin, 1943.

Davies's oratorio is based on the 15th-century morality play *Everyman*, an allegory of death and the fate of the human soul, Everyman's soul. Sibelius's incidental music for small orchestra was composed for Hugo von Hofmannsthal's version of the play, *Jedermann* (1912), while Martin's six monologues for baritone or contralto and piano or orchestra are set to the latter.

Évocations ("Evocations") Albert Roussel, 1910–11.

The work consists of three symphonic poems titled respectively *Les Dieux dans l'ombre des cavernes* ("The Gods in the Shade of the Caves"), *La Ville rose* ("The Pink Town"), and *Aux bords du fleuve sacré* ("On the Banks of the Sacred River").

Excelsior Romualdo Marenco, 1881.

The ballet in six parts (12 scenes), with a libretto and choreography by Luigi Manzotti, depicts the rise of human civilization and progress of technology as a vigorous struggle between the

Spirit of Darkness and the Spirit of Light. Eventually, as the title implies, the Spirit of Darkness admits defeat, and the rise culminates in an apotheosis of light and peace.

The Excursions of Mr. Brouček (Czech, *Vylety páně Broučkovy*)   Leoš Janáček, 1915–17.

The opera in two parts is set to a text by the composer, with contributions from others, based on Svatopluk Čech's two satirical novels *Vylet pana Broučka do měsíce* ("Mr. Brouček's Excursion to the Moon") (1888) and *Vylet pana Broučka do XV. století* ("Mr. Brouček's Excursion to the 15th Century") (1889). In these, the Prague landlord Mr. Brouček first goes to the moon, where he encounters a world of outlandish aesthetes, then goes back in time to the 15th century, where he behaves in a cowardly manner during the Hussite revolt.

The Execution of Stepan Razin (Russian, *Kazn' Stepana Razina*)   Dmitry Shostakovich, 1964.

The cantata for bass solo, chorus, and orchestra, Op. 119, is set to a text by Yevgeny Evtushenko telling of the capture, torture, and execution of the Cossack rebel leader Stepan Razin (usually known as Stenka Razin) (c.1630–1671).

Exsultate, jubilate ("Rejoice, Be Glad") W.A. Mozart, 1773.

The motet for soprano, organ, and orchestra, K 165, is set to words by an unknown librettist apparently based on the Psalms. Free renderings of the Psalms such as this were popular in Italy at this time, and the Psalms themselves contain many exhortations to rejoice and be glad. The first three lines of the text are: "*Exsultate, jubilate / o vos animae beatae, / dulcia cantica canendo* ("Exult, rejoice / O ye blessed souls, / singing sweet songs").

Ezio   George Frideric Handel, 1732.

The opera in three acts is set to a libretto by Pietro Metastasio for Nicola Porpora (1725) adapted and abridged by the composer. It is set in Rome in the mid–5th century BC and tells what happens when Ezio, returning from defeating Rome's enemy, Attila the Hun, learns that Fulvia, whom he loves, is wanted by the Roman emperor, Valentiniano, for himself.

F

Fables for Our Time   Freda Miller, 1947.

The ballet in four parts, choreographed by Charles Weidman, retells four of the 28 fables in James Furber's collection of the same name (1940): *The Unicorn in the Garden, The Shrike and the Chipmunk, The Owl Who Was God,* and *The Courtship of Al and Arthur.*

Façade   William Walton, 1920–1.

The "entertainment" for reciter and chamber ensemble is based on 21 poems from Edith Sitwell's collection of the same name declaimed in notated rhythm to the instrumental accompaniment composed for them. The fantastic images of the poems themselves present a "façade" of reality, as well as of conventional poetry. A ballet based on the work, choreographed by Frederick Ashton, was produced in 1931.

Les Fâcheux ("The Annoyers")   (1) Pierre Beauchamp, 1661; (2) Georges Auric, 1924.

Beauchamp's ballet was set to Molière's comedy written for it. The story tells how a lover, Eraste, awaiting a tryst with his mistress, Orphise, is frustratingly delayed by a variety of annoying people who oblige him to take part in their whimsies. Auric's ballet in one act, choreographed by Bronislava Nijinska, is based on the same comedy.

Facsimile   Leonard Bernstein, 1946.

The ballet in one scene, choreographed by Jerome Robbins, depicts a triangular affair between a woman and two men on a beach.

Fadetta   Léo Delibes, 1934.

The ballet in three acts (four scenes), with a libretto by Yuri Slonimsky and choreography by Leonid Lavrovsky, is set to the music of the composer's **Sylvia** and based on George Sand's novel *La Petite Fadette* ("Little Fadette") (1849), telling of the love between the son of rich peasants and Fadette, the granddaughter of an old woman who has been ostracized as a witch.

The Faery Queen *see* The **Fairy Queen**.

The Fair Maid of Perth *see* La **Jolie Fille de Perth**.

The Fair Melusina (German, *Märchen von die schönen Melusine,* "Tale of the Fair Melusine")   Felix Mendelssohn, 1833.

The overture in C major, Op. 32, was prompted by Conradin Kreutzer's opera *Melu-*

sine (1833) set to Franz Grillparzer's libretto *Melusina* (1823), itself a variant of the *Schöne Melusine* ("Fair Melusine"). This is a German version of the French legend about a beautiful mermaid who marries Raimund, Count of Poitiers, on condition that he does not seek her out on a Saturday. He does so, however, finds her in her bath, and discovers that the lower half of her body ends in a fish's tail. Grillparzer originally wrote his libretto for Beethoven, but he did not take it up.

The Fairies   John Christopher Smith, 1755.

The opera is set to the composer's own libretto based on Shakespeare's comedy *A Midsummer Night's Dream* (1595), in which fairies play a prominent part. (Two of the main characters are the fairy king and queen, Oberon and Titania.)

The Fairy Doll   Josef Bayer, 1888.

The pantomimic divertissement in one act, with a libretto by Joseph Hassreiter and F. Gaul and choreography by Hassreiter, is set in a toy shop and tells what happens when the dolls there come to life, led by the Fairy Doll.

The Fairy Queen   Henry Purcell, 1692.

The semiopera in a prologue and five acts is set to a libretto, possibly by Elkanah Settle, based on (but not quoting) Shakespeare's play *A Midsummer Night's Dream* (1595), in which Titania is the "fairy queen" of the title. *Cf.* The **Fairies**.

The Fairy's Kiss *see* Le **Baiser de la fée**.

Faith *see* **Lieder ohne Worte**.

Fall River Legend   Morton Gould, 1947.

The ballet in one act (eight scenes), with a libretto and choreography by Agnes de Mille, was suggested by the case of Lizzie Borden, accused of murdering her father and stepmother with an ax. The murders took place on August 4, 1892, at the Borden family home in Fall River, Massachusetts.

The Fallen Woman *see* La **Traviata**.

Falstaff   Giuseppe Verdi, 1893.

The opera in three acts to a libretto by Arrigo Boito is based on Shakespeare's plays *The Merry Wives of Windsor* (1599) and *Henry IV* (1597), in which Falstaff is a prominent character. The plot concerns Falstaff's amorous involvements with Alice Ford and Meg Page.

La Fanciulla del West ("The Girl of the Golden West")   Giacomo Puccini, 1910.

The opera in three acts is set to a libretto by Carlo Zangarini and Guelfo Civinini based on David Belasco's play *The Girl of the Golden West* (1905). The plot, set in California at the time of the gold rush, concerns the love of saloon keeper Minnie, the "girl" of the title, for the stranger Dick Johnson, who is actually a bandit.

Fancy Free   Leonard Bernstein, 1944.

The ballet in one act, with a libretto and choreography by Jerome Robbins, tells what happens when three sailors visit a Manhattan bar and take up with some girls. The phrase of the title, which dates back to Shakespeare's day, originally meant "free from the power of love" but now means almost the opposite, i.e. not free *from* love but free *to* love.

Fanfare   Benjamin Britten, 1953.

The ballet in one act, choreographed by Jerome Robbins, is based on the composer's **Young Person's Guide to the Orchestra** and sets out to depict the characters of the different instruments in dancing terms.

Fanfare for the Common Man, Aaron Copland, 1942.

The work for brass and percussion was commissioned as one of a series of wartime fanfares. Its title indicates its general appeal as a musical morale booster at a time of common resolve.

"Fanget an!" ("Begin!").

Walther's trial song in Act 1 of Wagner's **Die Meistersinger von Nürnberg**, in which he takes the marker Beckmesser's instruction to begin as words describing how everything begins anew in spring.

Fanny Robin   Edward Harper, 1975.

The opera in one act is set to the composer's own libretto based on Thomas Hardy's *Wessex Poems* (1898) and his novel *Far from the Madding Crowd* (1874). Fanny Robin is the servant betrayed by Sergeant Troy in the latter.

Fantaisies symphoniques ("Symphonic Fantasies")   Bohuslav Martinů, 1951–3.

The Symphony No. 6 was originally titled *Nouvelle Symphonie fantastique* ("New Fantastic Symphony"), for its somewhat extravagant nature. But the composer later changed this to the present title, apparently in order to avoid confusion with similarly named works, notably Berlioz's **Symphonie fantastique**.

Fantasia (Italian, "Fantasy").

The term originated in the 16th century as

an instrumental composition imitating a vocal motet. In England such a piece was usually known as a "fancy." The word then came to apply to music suggesting an improvisational character, with a "free fancy" on the part of the composer. Examples of the various applications of the word can be seen in the titles below.

Fantasía Bética ("Baetican Fantasy") Manuel de Falla, 1919.

The work for piano is named for Baetica, the Roman name of Andalusia, in the composer's native Spain.

Fantasia Concertante on a Theme of Corelli   Michael Tippett, 1953.

The work for strings takes its theme from Arcangelo Corelli's *Concerto Grosso* Op. 6 No. 2 (1714).

Fantasia Contrappuntistica   Ferruccio Busoni, 1910.

The work for solo piano, subtitled *Preludio al corale "Gloria al Signori nei Cieli" e fuga a quattro soggetti obbligati sopra un frumento di Bach* ("Prelude to the Chorale 'Glory to the Lord in the Heavens' and Fugue for Four Obbligato Subjects on a Fragment by Bach"), is based on the Contrapunctus XVIII from *Die Kunst der Fugue*, the aim being to complete Bach's unfinished fugue.

Fantasia on a Theme by Thomas Tallis Ralph Vaughan Williams, 1910.

The work for double string orchestra and string quartet takes its theme from the third ("Why fumeth in fight") of the nine psalm tunes composed by Thomas Tallis in 1567.

Fantasia on British Sea Songs   Henry Wood, 1905.

The work is an orchestral arrangement of traditional and other songs made to celebrate the centennial of Nelson's victory at Trafalgar in 1805. The nine sections, with original composers in brackets, are: (1) *Naval Bugle Calls*, (2) *The Anchor's Weighed*, (3) *The Saucy Arethusa*, (4) *Tom Bowling*, (5) *Hornpipe: Jack's the Lad*, (6) *Farewell and Adieu, Ye Spanish Ladies*, (7) *Home, Sweet Home* (Henry Bishop), (8) *See, the Conquering Hero Comes* (George Frideric Handel), (9) *Rule! Britannia* (Thomas Arne).

Fantasia on Christmas Carols   Ralph Vaughan Williams, 1912.

The work for baritone, chorus, and orchestra is based on four traditional carols: *The Truth sent From Above*, *Come All You Worthy Gentlemen*, *On Christmas Night*, and *There Is A Fountain*. There are also fragments of others.

Fantasia on "Greensleeves"   Ralph Vaughan Williams arr. Ralph Greaves, 1934.

The work is an arrangement for one or two flutes, harp, and strings of an interlude from Vaughan Williams's opera **Sir John in Love**, which quotes *Greensleeves*, an Elizabethan melody of unknown authorship (but mentioned by Shakespeare in *The Merry Wives of Windsor*, on which the opera is based).

Fantasias on an In Nomine by John Taverner   Peter Maxwell Davies, (1) 1962, (2) 1964.

The two orchestral works were composed as studies for the composer's opera **Taverner**. An "In nomine" (from Latin *In nomine Domini*, "In the name of the Lord") is a type of contrapuntal instrumental composition introduced by Taverner in the 16th century.

Fantasiestücke ("Fantasy Pieces")   Robert Schumann, 1837–8.

The eight pieces for solo piano, Op. 12, are flights of fancy, as the title indicates. The individual titles are as follows: (1) *Des Abends* ("In the Evening"), (2) *Aufschwung* ("Uplift"), (3) *Warum?* ("Why?"), (4) *Grillen* ("Crickets"), (5) *In der Nacht* ("In the Night"), (6) *Fabel* ("Fable"), (7) *Traumes Wirren* ("Disturbing Dreams"), (8) *Ende vom Lied* ("End of the Song"). The title was formerly also spelled *Phantasiestücke*.

Fantasio   Ethel Smyth, 1898.

The opera is set to the composer's own libretto based on Alfred de Musset's comedy of the same name (1834), which tells what happens when Fantasio, a young gentlemen of Munich, disguises himself as the king of Bavaria's jester to escape his creditors and secure a free lodging at court.

Fantastic Symphony *see* **Symphonie fantastique**.

Far from Denmark (Danish, *Fjernt fra Danmark*)   Josef Glaeser, 1860.

The vaudeville ballet in two acts, with a libretto and choreography by August Bournonville, tells what happens when a Danish frigate anchors in an Argentine harbor.

A Farewell *see* **Lieder ohne Worte**.

The Farewell   Gustav Mahler, 1962.

The solo dance, choreographed by Pauline

Koner to the last movement of the composer's Das **Lied von der Erde**, which bears this title, was the dancer's tribute to the memory of Doris Humphrey (1895–1958), long her friend, teacher, and collaborator.

Farewell Symphony (German, *Abschiedsymphonie*) Joseph Haydn, 1772.

The Symphony No. 45 in F minor is so named because in the finale the orchestra is gradually reduced until only two violins are left. Haydn composed it as a way of persuading his employer, Prince Nikolaus, not to prolong the musicians' stay at the prince's castle but to let them return to their families. At the first performance, the players crept out when their music finished, leaving only Haydn himself and Luigi Tomasini.

Faschingsschwank aus Wien ("Carnival Jest from Vienna") Robert Schumann, 1839–40.

The work for solo piano in five movements, Op. 26, subtitled *Fantasiebilder* ("Fantasy Pieces"), is a musical depiction of carnival merriment. There is an actual "jest from Vienna" in the first movement, where in one episode the composer introduces the French national anthem, the *Marseillaise*, a tune then forbidden in Vienna for political reasons.

Fastes ("Fasti") Henri Sauguet, 1933.

The ballet in one act, with a libretto by André Derain and choreography by George Balanchine, depicts a pagan ritual in an Italian market square. Ovid's *Fasti* (1st century AD) is a poetic calendar of the Roman year, with its various observances and festivals.

Fate (Czech, *Osud*) Leoš Janáček, 1934.

The opera in three acts is set to the composer's own libretto adapted by Fedora Bartošová. The plot tells what happens when Míla, discouraged by her mother from meeting the composer, Živný, decides to live with him.

The Fate of a Man (Russian, *Sud'ba cheloveka*) Ivan Dzerzhinsky, 1961.

The opera in three acts is set to the composer's own libretto based on Mikhail Sholokhov's story of the same name (1956–7), telling of the tragic events in the life of the central character, Andrei Sokolov.

Fate Symphony Ludwig van Beethoven, 1804–8.

The Symphony No. 5 in C minor, Op. 67, has been so called, mainly because the composer

is said to have described its four opening notes as "Fate knocking on the door." These same four notes suggest the letter V in Morse code (dot-dot-dot-dash), and since V came to symbolize Victory in World War II, the symphony gained (among the Allies) the nickname *Victory Symphony* during that period.

Fauré's Requiem *see* **Requiem** (2).

Faust Charles Gounod, 1859.

The opera in five acts is set to a libretto by Jules Barbier and Michel Carré based on Part I (1808) of Goethe's verse tragedy of the same name. It tells how the legendary ageing philosopher Faust (based on a 16th-century itinerant conjuror so named) sells his soul to Mephistopheles in return for eternal youth and the beautiful Marguerite. *See also* **Walpurgis Night**.

A Faust Overture (German, *Eine Faust-Ouvertüre*) Richard Wagner, 1839–40.

The concert overture was originally intended as the first movement of a *Faust Symphony*.

A Faust Symphony (German, *Eine Faust-Symphonie*) Franz Liszt, 1854–7.

The symphony for tenor, male voices, and orchestra is based on Goethe's dramatic poem (*see* **Faust**). Its three *Charakterbildern* ("character studies") are entitled *Faust*, *Gretchen*, and *Mephistopheles*.

La Favola d'Orfeo ("The Legend of Orpheus") Claudio Monteverdi, 1607.

The opera in a prologue and five acts is set to a libretto by Alessandro Striggio based on the classical story of the poet and musician, Orpheus, who after the death of his beloved wife, Eurydice, followed her to Hades to get her back.

La Favorite ("The Favorite") Gaetano Donizetti, 1840.

The opera in four acts is set to a libretto by Alphonse Royer and Gustave Vaëz based on F.T. de Baculard d'Arnaud's play *Le Comte de Comminges* ("The Count of Comminges") (1764) and other material. The plot is set in Castile in 1340 and tells what happens when the novice, Fernand, abandons the monastic life to win the mysterious Léonore, who is actually the mistress ("favorite") of King Alfonso. The opera was originally to be titled *L'Ange de Nisida* ("The Angel of Nisida"), and has also been performed in Italian as *Dalila* ("Delilah"), *Leonora di Guzman*, and *La Favorita*, and in German (changing the names) as *Richard und Mathilda*.

Feast in Albano (Danish, *Festen i Albano*)
J.F. Frölich, 1839.

The idyllic ballet in one act, choreographed by August Bournonville, was created to celebrate the return from Rome of the Danish neoclassical sculptor Bertel Thorvaldsen (1768–1844) to his native Copenhagen, and is modeled on several of his statues. Albano is the region near Rome (today's Lake Albano and the Alban Hills) famed for its classical remains.

Feast of Ashes   Carlos Surinach, 1962.

The ballet in one act, choreographed by Alvin Ailey, is set to the composer's *Doppio Concertino* and part of his *Ritmo Jondo*, and is based on Federico García Lorca's play *La casa de Bernarda Alba* ("The House of Bernarda Alba") (1936). The story tells of the tragedy that ensues when the son of a wealthy family is supposed to marry the eldest daughter of the widowed Bernarda Alba but loves her youngest sister. *Cf.* Las **Hermanas**.

The Feast of Love   Virgil Thomson, 1964.

The work for baritone and orchestra is set to the composer's own translation of the Latin poem *Pervigilium Veneris* ("Eve of Venus"), ascribed to Tiberianus (4th century AD). This is set in Sicily on the eve of the spring festival of Venus and celebrates the procreative power of the goddess in nature.

La Fedeltà premiata ("Fidelity Rewarded")
Joseph Haydn, 1780.

The comic opera in three acts is set to a libretto based on Giovanni Battista Lorenzini's play *L'infidelità fedele* ("Faithful Infidelity"). The story is set in classical times and tells how a pair of faithful lovers must be sacrificed to a monster until one such lover offers his own life.

Fedora   Umberto Giordano, 1898.

The opera in three acts is set to a libretto by Arturo Calautti based on Victorien Sardou's play *Fédora* (1882), telling what happens when Princess Fedora Romanov sets out to take her revenge on the Russian nihilist, Loris Ipanov, who has killed her intended husband.

Fedra ("Phaedra")   Ildebrando Pizzetti, 1915.

The opera in three acts is set to a libretto by Gabriele d'Annunzio based on Euripides' tragedy *Hippolytus* (428 BC), which also inspired Jean Racine's tragedy *Phèdre* (1677). The story tells what happens when Phaedra, the wife of Theseus, falls in love with her stepson, Hippolytus.

La Fée Urgèle ("The Fairy Urgele")   Egidio Romualdo Duni, 1765.

The opera, subtitled *Ce qui plaît aux dames* ("What Pleases the Ladies"), is set to a libretto by Charles Simon Favart based on a story by Voltaire in turn based on Chaucer's *Wife of Bath's Tale* in *The Canterbury Tales* (*c.*1397), in which a knight is asked to answer the question, "What do women most desire?"

Die Feen ("The Fairies")   Richard Wagner, 1888.

The opera in three acts is set to the composer's libretto based on Carlo Gozzi's comedy *La donna serpente* ("The Snake Woman") (1762), telling what happens when King Arindel of Tramond puts a curse on his fairy wife, Ada.

Feldeinsamkeit ("Solitude in the Fields")
Johannes Brahms, 1877–9.

The song for voice and piano, the second of a set of six, Op. 86, is based on a poem of the same name by Hermann Allmers (1821–1902). It tells of the poet's sense of loneliness and longing in the fields of summer.

Ein Feldlager in Schlesien *see* L'**Étoile du nord**.

Fennimore and Gerda   Frederick Delius, 1919.

The opera in 11 scenes is set to the composer's own libretto based on Jens Peter Jacobsen's novel *Niels Lyhne* (1880). The story tells how Fennimore makes an unhappy marriage to the painter, Erik, while being loved by Erik's friend, Niels, who himself finally marries Gerda.

Fernand Cortez   Gasparo Spontini, 1809.

The opera in three acts is set to a libretto by Victor Joseph Étienne de Jouy and Joseph Alphonse Esménard based on Alexis Piron's historical tragedy of the same name (1744). The story centers on the Spanish conquistador Hernán Cortés (1485–1547), who overthrew the Aztec empire and won Mexico for the crown of Spain. The opera's subtitle is thus *La Conquête de Mexique* ("The Conquest of Mexico").

Der Ferne Klang ("The Distant Sound")
Franz Schreker, 1912.

The opera in three acts is set to the composer's own libretto telling what happens when the composer, Fritz, leaves his beloved, Grete, to go in search of a "lost chord."

Fervaal   Vincent d'Indy, 1897.

The opera in a prologue and three acts, to

the composer's own libretto, is set in southern France at the time of the Saracen invasions and tells how the Celtic chief, Fervaal, is nursed back to health by the Saracen sorceress, Guilhen, after being wounded in battle.

Feste Romane ("Romans Festivals")
Ottorino Respighi, 1928.

The symphonic poem musically depicts four Roman festivals, one per movement, respectively entitled *Circus Maximus*, *The Jubilee*, *The October Festival*, and *Epiphany*.

Festgesang ("Festive Hymn")   Felix Mendelssohn, 1840.

The work for male voices and orchestra, to words by Professor A.E. Prölss of Freiburg, was composed for the festival in Leipzig in 1840 to celebrate the quatercentennial of Gutenberg's invention of the printing press.

Le Festin de l'araignée ("The Spider's Feast")   Albert Roussel, 1913.

The ballet pantomime, with a libretto by Gilbert de Voisins and choreography by Léo Staats, tells what happens when a spider catches a number of insects in her web and begins to feast.

Festival March (Czech, *Slavnostní pochod*)
Antonín Dvořák, 1879.

The orchestral march, Op. 54, was written to celebrate the silver wedding of Franz Joseph and Elizabeth of Austria (married 1854).

Festive Symphony *see* **Triumph Symphony**.

La Fête étrange ("The Strange Celebration")
Gabriel Fauré, 1940.

The ballet in two scenes, with a libretto by Ronald Crichton and choreography by Andrée Howard, was inspired by Alain-Fournier's novel *Le Grand Meaulnes*, usually known in English as *The Lost Domain* (1913). "Wandering in the forest at the break of a winter's day, a country boy meets some children, who lead him to a château where the approaching marriage of the Châtelaine is being celebrated" (program note, quoted in Koegler, p. 153). The title alludes to the unwitting estrangement that ensues.

Fêtes galantes ("Courtly Celebrations")
Claude Debussy, 1903, 1904.

The two sets of songs for voice and piano are set to Paul Verlaine's poems of the same name (1869). The first version (1882) comprised *Pantomime*, *En sourdine* ("In Secret"), *Mandoline*,

Clair de lune (*see* **Clair de lune**), and *Fantoches* ("Puppets"), but three of the songs were revised and were published (1903) as Set I: *En sourdine*, *Fantoches*, and *Clair de lune*. Set II (1904) comprises *Les Ingénus* ("The Innocents"), *Le Faune* ("The Faun"), and *Colloque sentimental* ("Sentimental Conversation"). A *fête galante* was an 18th-century rural entertainment at which members of the court dressed up as shepherds and shepherdesses.

Fetonte ("Phaeton")   Niccolò Jommelli, 1768.

The opera in three acts is set to a libretto by Mattia Verazi based on Ovid's *Metamorphoses*, Book 2 (1st century AD). The story tells what happens when Fetonte, son of Il Sole (The Sun), to prove his divine parentage, asks if he may drive the chariot of the sun for a day.

Feuersnot ("Fire Famine")   Richard Strauss, 1901.

The opera in one act is set to a libretto by Ernst von Wolzogen based on *The Quenched Fires of Oudenaarde* in J.W. Wolf's *Sagas of the Netherlands* (1843). The plot, set in 12th-century Munich, tells how Kunrad causes all of the fires in the city to be extinguished and allows them to rekindle only when the girl he loves, Diemut, reciprocates his feelings.

Feuersymphonie ("Fire Symphony")
Joseph Haydn, 1776–8.

The Symphony No. 59 in A major is said to be so named because it was intended as an overture to a (possibly spurious) opera *Die Feuerbrunst* ("The Conflagration"). (A symphony or *sinfonia* was effectively an overture in 18th-century usage.)

Feuilles d'album ("Album Leaves")
Georges Bizet, 1866.

The title of the set of six songs is the French equivalent of Schumann's **Albumblätter** and has much the same romantic ring. One song, for example, is *Adieux à Suzon* ("Farewell to Suzon"), set to a love poem by Alfred de Musset.

Feux d'artifice ("Fireworks")   Claude Debussy, 1913.

No. 12 (and last) of Book II of the **Préludes** is a brilliant display piece. Hence its name.

La Fiamma ("The Flame")   Ottorino Respighi, 1931–3.

The opera in three acts is set to a libretto by Claudio Guastalla based on Hans Wiessner Jenssen's play *The Witch*. The story is set in 17th-century Ravenna and tells what happens when

Silvana, second wife of Basilio, hides Agnes de Carvia, accused of sorcery, but is unable to prevent her being hanged.

Fiddle Fugue   J.S. Bach, *c.* 1720.

The **Fugue** in D minor for Organ, BWV 539, is so named because it was adapted from an earlier version for solo violin (1720).

Fidelio   Ludwig van Beethoven, 1805.

The opera in two acts, subtitled *Die eheliche Liebe* ("Married Love"), and originally intended by the composer to be called *Leonore*, is set to a libretto by Josef Sonnleithner based on Jean-Nicolas Bouilly's libretto for Pierre Gaveaux's opera **Léonore**. The plot is set in 18th-century Seville and tells how the imprisoned nobleman, Florestan, is rescued by his wife, Leonora, disguised as a boy named Fidelio ("Faithful"). The opera has four overtures, all named for the heroine: *Leonora No. 1*, composed for a planned Prague performance, *Leonora No. 2*, played at the première, *Leonora No. 3*, sometimes played before the final scene, and *Leonora No. 4*, which now begins the work.

Field Figures   Karlheinz Stockhausen, 1970.

The ballet in one act, choreographed by Glen Tetley, is set to the pieces *Setz die Segel zur Sonne* and *Verbindung* from the composer's **Aus den sieben Tagen** and is a free-form pas de deux (dance for two), interrupted by the five accompanying dancers. The title refers to the figures formed against the "field" that is the background.

Fierrabras   Franz Schubert, 1823.

The opera in three acts is set to a libretto by Josef Kupelwieser based on the story of this name by J.G.G. Büsching and F.H. von der Hagen in the *Buch der Liebe* ("Book of Love") (1809) and Friedrich de la Motte Fouqué's play *Eginhard und Emma* ("Eginhard and Emma") (1811). The story is set in the time of Charlemagne and centers on the Saracen giant Fierrabras (Fier-à-Bras, Sir Ferumbras, "Iron Arm").

The Fiery Angel (Russian, *Ognennyy angel*) Sergey Prokofiev, 1919–23.

The opera in five acts is set to the composer's own libretto based Valery Bryusov's historical novel of the same name (1908). The plot is set in 16th-century Germany and tells how the knight Ruprecht meets Renata in a state of possession in which she takes him to be Heinrich, a former lover whom she believed to be the rein-carnation of her guardian angel. An alternate English title for the opera is *The Flaming Angel*.

Fiesta   Darius Milhaud, 1958.

The one-act opera, Op. 370, to a libretto by Boris Vian, is set in a fishing village somewhere in the American tropics and tells what happens when a half-drowned man is rescued from a crippled ship, nursed back to life, and becomes rather too lively for comfort, especially in his amorous intentions. The title is thus semi-ironic.

Fifine at the Fair   Granville Bantock, 1901.

The Tone Poem No. 3 is based on Robert Browning's poem of the same name (1872), telling how Don Juan, strolling by a fair with his wife, Elvire, is attracted by the gypsy dancer, Fifine.

Fifths Quartet (German, *Quintenquartett*) Joseph Haydn, 1797–8.

The String Quartet in D minor, Op. 76 No. 76, is so named because the opening theme begins with melodic leaps of a fifth down (A to D in the first bar, E to A in the second). This same phrase has given the alternate nicknames of *Bell Quartet* and *Donkey Quartet*, the descending fifth suggesting a bell peal to some and a "hee-haw" to others. The unusual minuet in the third movement is sometimes known as the *Witch Minuet* (German, *Hexenmenuett*).

La Figlia di Jorio ("Jorio's Daughter") Ildebrando Pizzetti, 1954.

The opera in three acts is a virtual verbatim setting of Gabriele d'Annunzio's tragedy of the same name (1903) telling what happens when Mila, daughter of the sorcerer, Jolio, flees from the peasants who think she is a witch and is saved by Aligi, who falls in love with her.

La Fille aux cheveux de lin ("The Girl with the Flaxen Hair")   Claude Debussy, 1910.

The piano piece, No. 8 in Book I of the **Préludes**, was inspired by Charles-Marie Leconte de Lisle's poem of this name, itself based on a Scottish song.

La Fille de Madame Angot ("Madame Angot's Daughter")   Charles Lecocq, 1872.

The operetta in three acts is set to a libretto by Paul Siraudin, Louis François Clairville, and Victor Koning based on Antoine François Eve Maillot's vaudeville *Madame Angot, ou La Poissarde parvenue* ("Madame Angot, or the Upstart Fishwife") (1796). The story centers on Clairette, daughter of the late Madame Angot, who loves the satirist, Ange Pitou, although she is engaged to the hairdresser, Pomponnet. *See also* **Mam'zelle Angot**.

La Fille de marbre ("The Marble Girl") Cesare Pugni, 1847.

The ballet in two acts (three scenes), with a libretto and choreography by Arthur Saint-Léon, tells of a statue (the "marble girl" of the title) with whom the sculptor falls in love. *See also* The **Marble Maiden**.

La Fille du Danube ("Daughter of the Danube") Adolphe Adam, 1836.

The ballet in two acts (four scenes), with a libretto and choreography by Filippo Taglioni, tells of an orphan girl, found as a child by the Danube, who falls in love with a baron's son.

La Fille du pharaon ("Pharaoh's Daughter") Cesare Pugni, 1862.

The ballet in a prologue, three acts (nine scenes), and an epilogue, with a libretto by Jules-Henri Vernoy de Saint-Georges and Marius Petipa, and choreography by the latter, was inspired by Théophile Gautier's novel *Le Roman de la momie* ("The Romance of the Mummy") (1858), telling of an English lord and his servant who become involved in opium dreams in a pyramid. The ballet was originally produced in St. Petersburg under the equivalent Russian title, *Doch' faraona*.

La Fille du régiment ("The Daughter of the Regiment") Gaetano Donizetti, 1840.

The opera in two acts to a libretto by Jules-Henri Vernoy de Saint-Georges and Jean François Alfred Bayard is set in the Swiss Tyrol in *c*.1815 and tells of the love of Marie, an orphan raised as a "daughter" by the 21st Regiment, for the young Tyrolean, Tonie. An Italian version, *La figlia del reggimento*, was first performed later the same year. *See also* La **Fille du tambour-maor**.

La Fille du tambour-major ("The Drum Major's Daughter) Jacques Offenbach, 1879.

The comic opera in three acts (four scenes), to a libretto by Alfred Duru and Henri Chivot, is a thinly disguised adaptation of the plot of Donizetti's opera La **Fille du régiment**, although this time the lovers are Stella, supposedly a duke's daughter but actually the daughter of the elderly drum major, Monthabor, and Robert, an army lieutenant.

La Fille mal gardée ("The Unchaperoned Daughter") various (see below), 1789.

The ballet in two acts (three scenes), with a libretto and choreography by Jean Dauberval, is set to a medley of popular French songs and airs and tells of the rural romance between Lise, the "unchaperoned daughter" of Widow Simone, and Colas. An alternate English title for the ballet is *Vain Precautions*.

La Filleule des fées ("The Fairies' Goddaughter") Adolphe Adam and H.F. de Saint-Julien, 1849.

The ballet in a prologue and three acts (seven scenes), with a libretto by Jules-Henri Vernoy de Saint-Georges and choreography by Jules Joseph Perrot, tells of Ysaure, the "fairies' goddaughter" of the title, who is at the mercy of both friendly and wicked fairies.

Filling Station Virgil Thomson, 1938.

The ballet in one act, with a libretto by Lincoln Kirstein and choreography by Lew Christensen, centers on the filling station attendant, Mac, with all the characters drawn as cartoon figures.

Il Filosofo di campagna ("The Country Philosopher") Baldassare Galuppi, 1754.

The opera in three acts is set to a libretto by Carlo Goldoni and tells what happens when Don Tritemio, the "country philosopher" of the title, succumbs to the charms of Lesbina, companion of his daughter, Eugenia.

La Fin du jour ("The End of the Day") Maurice Ravel, 1979.

The ballet in one act, choreographed by Kenneth MacMillan, is set to the composer's Piano Concerto in G major (1929–31) and interprets its music in a dance idiom of the 1930s. The end of the day is the time for enjoying oneself and "having a fling."

"Finch'han dal vino" *see* Champagne Aria.

Fingal's Cave (German, *Fingals-Höhle*) Felix Mendelssohn, 1832.

The overture, Op. 26, based on an earlier version called *Die einsame Insel* ("The Solitary Island") (1829), is effectively a tone poem describing Fingal's Cave, a cave of basalt rocks on the island of Staffa in the Inner Hebrides, Scotland. The composer visited both the Hebrides and Staffa in 1829. Hence the overture's alternate name, *The Hebrides* (German, *Die Hebriden*).

Fingal is the Scottish name of the legendary hero known to the Irish as Finn mac Cool (Fionn mac Cumhail), or simply Finn, who came from Scotland to help the Irish drive out Scandinavian invaders.

Finlandia   Jean Sibelius, 1899.

The orchestral work, Op. 26, was written as the final tableau of a patriotic pageant to raise contributions for a press pension fund in Helsinki. Its title is the Late Latin name of Finland. The material sounds as if it is based on folk music but it is all the composer's own invention.

La Finta giardiniera ("The Fake Lady Gardener")   W.A. Mozart, 1775.

The opera in three acts, K 196, is set to a libretto by Marco Coltellini based on Ranieri de' Calzabigi's libretto for Pasquale Anfossi's opera of the same name (1774). The story tells how the Countess Violante disguises herself as a gardener, Sandrina, to search for her lost lover, Belfiore. Her name gave the opera's alternate English title, *Sandrina's Secret.*

La Finta semplice ("The Fake Simpleton")   W.A. Mozart, 1769.

The opera in three acts, K 51, is set to a libretto by Marco Coltellini based on a libretto by Carlo Goldoni originally written for Salvatore Perillo's opera of the same title (1764). The plot tells how the Hungarian baroness, Rosina, persuades the infatuated brothers, Cassandro and Polidor, to let her own brother, Fracasso, marry their sister, Giacinta. She does this by pretending to be a simpleton, so that the brothers both fall for her. Hence the title.

Fire Symphony *see* **Feuersymphonie**.

The Firebird (Russian, *Zhar-ptitsa*)   Igor Stravinsky, 1909–10.

The ballet in two acts, with a libretto and choreography by Michel Fokine, is based on motifs from various Russian fairy tales. The main one tells how Prince Ivan captures the mysterious Firebird who obtains her release by giving him a feather with which he can call on her when in danger. The ballet is also known by its French title, *L'Oiseau de feu*. (The word *zhar* in the Russian title does not actually mean "fire" but "heat." The Firebird is thus not a sort of Slavic phoenix.)

Fires of Vengeance (Estonian, *Tasuleegid*)   Eugen Kapp, 1945.

The opera in three acts, to a libretto by Paul Rummo, is set in 1343 and tells of the struggle of the Estonian people against the Teutonic Knights. The "fires of vengeance" were those lit as the signal for the St. George's Night Uprising (in the early hours of April 23).

Fireworks (Russian, *Feyerverk*)   Igor Stravinsky, 1908.

The fantasy for large orchestra, Op. 4, includes some brilliant passages. Hence the name.

Fireworks Music   George Frideric Handel, 1749.

The instrumental suite of eight movements, formally known as *Music for the Royal Fireworks*, was written for and played at the fireworks display at Green Park, London, to mark the Peace of Aix-la-Chapelle in 1748.

The First of May (Russian, *Pervomayskaya simfoniya*)   Dmitry Shostakovich, 1929.

The Symphony No. 3 in E flat major for Chorus and Orchestra, with a text by Semyon Kirsanov, was written to commemorate the annual May Day Celebrations in the former Soviet Union. The work's actual première was not on May Day, however, but on November 6, the eve of the annual October Revolution celebrations in 1930.

Five   David Bedford, 1967.

The title of the String Quintet simply refers to the number of players: two violins, a viola, and two cellos.

Five Kings   Aaron Copland, 1939.

The work was composed as incidental music to Orson Welles's play of this name, based on the five Shakespeare plays in which Falstaff appears or is mentioned (*1 Henry IV*, *2 Henry IV*, *The Merry Wives of Windsor*, *Henry V*, *1 Henry VI*). Welles himself played Falstaff.

Five Poems by J.P. Jacobsen (Danish, *Fem digte af J.P. Jacobsen*)   Carl Nielsen, 1891.

The composer's Op. 4 for voice and piano, as the title indicates, is a setting of five poems by Jens Peter Jacobsen (*see* **Gurrelieder**). The poems themselves are *Sundown* (Danish, *Solnedgang*), *In the Garden of the Harem* (Danish, *I Seraillets have*), *To Asali* (Danish, *Til Asali*), *Irmelin Rose* (Danish, *Irmelin rose*), and *The Day Has Gone* (Danish, *Dagen sænket*).

Five Tudor Portraits   Ralph Vaughan Williams, 1935.

The choral suite for mezzosoprano, baritone, chorus, and orchestra is in five movements, each set to a poem by John Skelton (1460–1529) as follows: (1) (Ballad) *The Tunning of Elinor Rumming*, (2) (Intermezzo) *My Pretty Bess*, (3) (Burlesca) *Epitaph on John Jayberd of Diss*, (4) (Romanza) *Jane Scroop: Her Lament for Philip Sparrow*, (5) (Scherzo) *Jolly Rutterkin*. The characters in the poems are thus the subjects of the "five Tudor portraits."

Five Wesendonck Songs (German, *Fünf Gedichte von Mathilde Wesendonck*)   Richard Wagner, 1857–8.

The five songs for voice and piano were set to poems written by the composer's mistress, Mathilde Wesendonck, née Luckemeyer (1828–1902). Their titles are: (1) *Der Engel* ("The Angel"), (2) *Stehe still!* ("Stand Still!"), (3) *Im Treibhaus* ("In the Greenhouse"), (4) *Schmerzen* ("Agonies"), (5) *Träume* ("Dreams"). They are often called the *Wesendonck-Lieder* ("Wesendonck Songs"). The Wesendoncks befriended the composer and put their house in Zürich at his disposal. (He wrote part of **Tristan und Isolde** there, as well as the five songs, so that she was Isolde to his Tristan.)

The Flames of Paris (Russian, *Plamya Parizha*)   Boris Asafiev, 1932.

The ballet in four acts (five scenes), with a libretto by N. Volkov and V. Dmitriev and choreography by Vasily Vainonen, is set in postrevolutionary France in 1792 and depicts the march of the rebellious people of Marseilles and the storming of the Tuileries in Paris.

The Flaming Angel *see* The **Fiery Angel**.

Flammen ("Flames")   Ervín Schulhoff, 1927–9.

The opera in two acts, to a libretto by Karel Benes and Max Brod, is a reworking of the story of **Don Juan** and opens with a series of scenes in which Juan encounters and lusts after women pursued by a chorus of shadows and Death in the form of a woman. The shadowy women later symbolically appear in flames to signify both lust and death. Hence the title.

The Fledermaus ("The Bat")   Johann Strauss II, 1874.

The operetta in three acts is set to a libretto by Carl Haffner and Richard Genée based on Henri Meilhac and Ludovic Halévy's play *Le Réveillon* ("The Midnight Supper") (1872), itself based on Roderich Bendix's comedy *Das Gefängnis* ("The Prison") (1851). The story is set in Vienna, and tells what happens when Eisenstein, about to go to prison, instead goes with his friend, Dr. Falke, to a ball given by Prince Orlovsky, at which all the guests are in disguise. Eisenstein and Falke tell the Prince how they both attended a fancy dress party in their youth at which Eisenstein was disguised as a butterfly and Falke as a bat. Falke had got drunk and had to walk home in his costume, which earned him the nickname "Dr. Bat."

The Fleecy Cloud *see* **Lieder ohne Worte**.

"La Fleur que tu m'avais jetée" *see* **Flower Song**.

Flick und Flocks Abenteuer ("Flick and Flock's Adventure")   Peter Ludwig Hertel, 1858.

The comedy ballet in three acts (six scenes), with a libretto and choreography by Paul Taglioni, is an adventure story of two friends, Flick and Flock, who undergo a number of improbable magical experiences. The work's usual English title is simply *Flik and Flok*.

Der Fliegende Holländer ("The Flying Dutchman")   Richard Wagner, 1843.

The opera in three acts (originally one) is set to a libretto by the composer based on the legend told in Chapter 7 of Heinrich Heine's *Aus den Memoiren des Herren von Schnabelewopski* ("From the Memoirs of Herr von Schnabelewopski") (1831), which tells how the Dutchman has been condemned for blasphemy to sail his ship forever unless redeemed by a woman who will love him. The woman he meets is a Norwegian sea captain's daughter, Senta, who though loved by another has long been obsessed with the legend of the Dutchman and falls for him immediately.

Flight   Jonathan Dove, 1998.

The opera in three acts, with a libretto by April de Angelis, is set in an airport and centers on the efforts of the characters to escape ("take flight") from their personal predicaments. They cannot do so literally for at the end of the first act all the aircraft are grounded.

The Flight *see* **Lieder ohne Worte**.

The Flight of the Bumble Bee (Russian, *Polët shmelya*)   Nikolay Rimsky-Korsakov, 1900.

The orchestral interlude occurs in Act 3 of the opera The **Tale of Czar Saltan** in which Prince Gvidon becomes a bee and stings his evil relatives. The music evokes the bee's buzzing flight.

The Flood   Igor Stravinsky, 1962.

The opera or musical play for three speakers, tenor, and two basses, chorus, orchestra, and actors is set to a libretto by Robert Craft based on the biblical story of the Flood as told in Genesis and in the York and Chester mystery plays.

Flore et Zéphire ("Flora and Zephyr") Cesare Bossi, 1796.

The ballet divertissement in one act, with a libretto and choreography by Charles-Louis Didelot, is a pastoral comedy telling how Zéphire loves Chloris but is punished for his fickleness until he vows eternal fidelity to Flore. *See also* **Zéphire et Flore**.

Eine Florentinische Tragödie ("A Florentine Tragedy") Alexander Zemlinsky, 1917.

The opera in one act is set to a libretto by Max Meyerfeld based on Oscar Wilde's play *A Florentine Tragedy* (1908), telling how the jealous merchant, Simone, married to Bianca, murders her lover, Giudo Bardi.

Flos Campi ("Flower of the Field") Ralph Vaughan Williams, 1925.

The suite in six movements for solo viola, mixed chorus, and small orchestra is based on images from the Old Testament (in which a human being is described as "a flower of the field") with each movement prefaced by a Latin quotation from the Song of Solomon.

Das Floss der "Medusa" ("The Raft of the 'Medusa'") Hans Werner Henze, 1971.

The cantata is set to a text by Ernst Schnabel based on the story behind Théodore Géricault's painting of the same title (1819), depicting a historical event. The *Medusa* was one of four government ships that set sail from France for Senegal on June 17, 1816, following the treaty of 1815 which proclaimed that country a French colony. The shipwreck occurred on July 2 on a sandbank some 135 miles off the African coast. An improvised raft picked up 149 survivors who existed together for 12 days. Only 15 remained alive when they were rescued by the brig *Argus*, the others having either been thrown overboard or eaten by their fellows.

Flower Duet   (1) Léo Delibes, 1883; (2) Giacomo Puccini, 1904.

In Act 1 of Delibes' **Lakmé**, the duet sung in the temple garden by Lakmé and Mallika as they prepare to bathe in the stream. It is also known by its leading words: "*Dôme épais de jasmin*" ("Thick dome of jasmin"). Puccini's duet so named is that sung by Butterfly and Suzuki in Act 2 of **Madama Butterfly** as they strew the house with flowers in readiness for Pinkerton's return. It is alternately known by its leading words: "*Scuoti quella fronda di ciliego*" ("Shake that branch of cherry blossom").

Flower Festival in Genzano (Danish, *Blomsterfesten i Genzano*) E. Helsted and Holger Simon Paulli, 1858.

The ballet in one act, choreographed by August Bournonville, is based on a real event from the early 19th century. It tells of the love between Rosa and the young sniper, Paolo, and is set in Genzano, Italy.

Flower Song   Georges Bizet, 1875.

Don José's aria in Act 2 of **Carmen**, telling Carmen how has treasured the flower that she threw him, and with it the hope of her love. The song is also known by its leading words: "*La fleur que tu m'avais jetée*" ("The flower that thou hadst thrown me").

The Flying Dutchman *see* Der **Fliegende Holländer**.

A Folk Tale (Danish, *Et Folkesagn*) Niels Gade and J.P.E. Hartmann, 1854.

The ballet in three acts (14 scenes), with a libretto and choreography by August Bournonville, is a Danish fairy tale, set in Jutland in the early 16th century. The story centers on Hilda, a girl who lives in the mountain with the witch, Muri, and her trolls.

Folksong *see* **Volkslied**.

Folksong Symphony   Roy Harris, 1940.

The Symphony No. 4 for Chorus and Orchestra in seven movements contains several examples of folksong material, such as cowboy songs in the second movement, *Jump Up, My Lady* and *The Blackbird and the Crow* in the fifth, and *When Johnny Comes Marching Home* in the Finale.

Fontane di Roma ("Fountains of Rome") Ottorino Respighi, 1914–16.

The symphonic poem in four sections depicts the emotions of the composer when viewing four of Rome's most famous fountains: the Vale Giulia at dawn, the Tritone in mid-morning, the Trevi at noon, and the Villa Medici at sunset.

The Footballer (Russian, *Futbolist*)   V.A. Oransky, 1930.

The ballet in three acts, with a libretto by V. Kurdyumov and choreography by Lev Lashchilin and Igor Moiseyev, depicts the conflicts between a middle-class dandy and a lady on the one hand and a working-class female scavenger and a footballer on the other when each falls in love with a member of the wrong class.

For the Fallen   Edward Elgar, 1916.

The choral work commemorating those who lost their lives in World War I later formed the third movement of The **Spirit of England**.

Les Forains ("The Entertainers")   Henri Sauguet, 1945.

The ballet in one act, with a libretto by Boris Kochno and choreography by Roland Petit, depicts a troupe of strolling comedians giving a performance on a street square.

The Force of Destiny *see* La **Forza del Destino**.

Die Forelle ("The Trout")   Franz Schubert, 1817.

The song for voice and piano, D 550, is set to the 1783 poem of the same title by Christian Friedrich Daniel Schubart. The poem itself is a didactic one with a moral: do not be like the trout, which allows itself to be caught because it lacks intelligence. *See also* **Trout Quintet**.

A Forest Song (Ukrainian, *Lisova pisnya*)   Vitaly Kireyko, 1958.

The folk opera in three acts is set to the composer's own libretto based on the dramatic poem of the same name (1912) by Lesya Ukrainka (pen name of Larisa Kosach), itself drawing on Ukrainian folk motifs.

Forest Murmurs (German, *Waldweben*)   Richard Wagner, 1876.

The scene in Act 2 of *Siegfried* in Der **Ring des Nibelungen** in which Siegfried lies under a lime tree and listens to the rustling of the leaves and the song of the Woodbird just before his encounter with Fafner.

The Forgotten Rite   John Ireland, 1913.

The orchestral work is a musical depiction of an unspecified rite associated with the Channel Islands, and more precisely with the prehistoric remains there.

The Forty-eight *see* Das **Wohltemperirte Klavier**.

La Forza del destino ("The Force of Destiny")   Giuseppe Verdi, 1862.

The opera in four acts is set to a libretto by Francesco Maria Piave based on Ángel de Saavedra Ramírez de Baquedano, Duke of Rivas's drama *Don Álvaro, o la fuerzo del sino* ("Don Alvaro, or the Force of Destiny") (1835) and a scene from Friedrich von Schiller's drama *Wallensteins Lager* ("Wallenstein's Camp") (1799). The plot tells how Don Carlo pursues Don Alvaro in revenge for the latter's (accidental) killing of his brother, the Marquis of Calatrava, father of Don Alvaro's beloved, Leonora. Don Carlo and Leonora also die, but Don Alvaro lives on, a victim of destiny.

Le Fosse Ardeatine ("The Ardeatine Caves")   William Schuman, 1968.

The Symphony No. 9 was written following the composer's visit to the Ardeatine Caves in Rome. The caves are the place where on March 24, 1944, German forces under the command of Major H. Kappler killed 335 Italian hostages as a reprisal for an attack by Italian partisans on German troops in the Via Rasella, killing 35 SS soldiers. Schuman notes: "Although the work does not attempt to depict the horror of what I saw realistically, I chose the subtitle for philosophical reasons" (quoted in Berkowitz, p. 9).

The Fountain of Bakhchisaray (Russian, *Bakhchisarayskiy fontan*)   Boris Asafiev, 1934.

The ballet in four acts, with a libretto by N. Volkov and choreography by Rostislav Zakharov, is based on Alexander Pushkin's poem of the same name (1822), telling of a Polish princess, Maria, who is abducted by the khan Mengli Giray. (It was he who founded the town of Bakhchisaray, now in Ukraine, as capital of the Crimean khanate in the early 16th century.)

Fountains of Rome *see* **Fontane di Roma**

Four Last Songs, (1) Ralph Vaughan Williams, 1954–8; (2) *see* **Vier letzte Lieder**.

Vaughan Williams's songs for voice and piano are set to words by his wife, Ursula. Their individual titles are: (1) *Procris*, (2) *Tired*, (3) *Hands, Eyes, and Heart*, and (4) *Menelaus*. The title was given by their publisher. (The composer died in 1958.)

4' 33"   John Cage, 1952.

The famous (or infamous) piano piece has a title that gains meaning from a description of its score, which "bears the numbers I, II, III, each marked 'TACET' and each given a duration in minutes and seconds which together add up to four minutes, thirty-three seconds. A secondary part of the notation tells the performer that the piece may be done on any instrument, for any length of time. Since 'tacet' is the notation which informs a player that he should play nothing during a movement, the performer of *4'33"* is asked to make no sounds in the three timed sections" (Michael Nyman, *Experimental Music*, 1974). In other words, the "music" is whatever sound comes from elsewhere, whether inside or outside the location where the piece is performed. A later work, *0'00"* (1962), also known as *4'33"* No. 2, is similarly "to be performed in any way by anyone."

Four Saints in Three Acts   Virgil Thomson, 1933.

The opera in a prologue and four (*sic*) acts, to a libretto by Gertrude Stein, is a surreal allegory telling how St. Teresa (in two roles), surrounded by men, and St. Ignatius Loyola, surrounded by women, work together and help each other to become saints. Stein had been discussing a possible opera with Thomson in 1927: "'I think it should be late eighteenth-century or early nineteenth-century saints. Four saints in three acts. And others'" (quoted in Virgil Thomson, *Virgil Thomson*, 1967). Thomson commented: "*Four Saints in Three Acts* is merely a title; actually there are thirty or more saints and four acts" (*ibid.*). In the work itself, characters constantly ask: "How many saints are there in it? How many acts are there in it?" The prologue and acts each have their own somewhat cryptic heading or title as the only indication that the libretto has any sort of "story": (Prologue) *A narrative of Prepare for Saints*, (1) *Saint Teresa half indoors and half out of doors*, (2) *Might it be mountains if it were not Barcelona*, (3) *Saint Ignatius and one of two literally*, (4) *The sisters and saints reassembled and re-enacting why they went away to stay.*

The Four Seasons   (1) (Italian, *Le quattro stagioni*) Antonio Vivaldi, 1725; (2) Henry Hadley, 1902; (3) Giuseppe Verdi, 1975; (3) Giuseppe Verdi, 1979.

Vivaldi's four violin concertos are the first four of his *Il cimento dell' armonia e dell' inventione* ("The Contest between Harmony and Invention"), a set of 12. They are *Spring* in E major, with musical representations of birdsong, *Summer* in G minor, with thunderstorms, *Autumn* in F major, with harvesting, and *Winter* in F

minor, with shivering and skating. The four movements of Hadley's Symphony No. 2 in F minor, Op. 30, present the seasons in the order *Winter, Spring, Summer,* and *Autumn*. The ballet in four parts set to Verdi's music for Les **Vêpres siciliennes** and other works was choreographed by Kenneth MacMillan as a "gay and frolicsome divertissement, with some distinctly Italian accents" (Koegler, p. 162), while a later ballet, also in four parts, choreographed by Jerome Robbins, was set to the same work plus excerpts from I **Lombardi** and Il **Trovatore**. It developed as a suite of classical dances celebrating the four seasons. Hence the title. *See also* Les **Quatre Saisons**.

Four Serious Songs   *see* **Vier ernste Gesänge**.

The Four Temperaments   (1) (Danish, *De fire temperamenter*) Carl Nielsen, 1902; (2) Paul Hindemith, 1940.

Nielsen's Symphony No. 2 in C minor, Op. 16, was inspired by a series of paintings the composer had seen in a country inn, each of the four movements describing one of the medieval "temperaments" of human character: choleric, phlegmatic, melancholic, and sanguine. These are reflected in their tempo markings, respectively *Allegro collerico, Allegro commodo e flemmatico, Andante malincolico* (Nielsen's error for *malinconico*), and *Allegro sanguineo*. Hindemith's Theme and Variations for piano and strings is devoted to the same "temperaments," but in the order melancholic, sanguine, phlegmatic, and choleric. Hindemith's music was adopted for the ballet of the same title, choreographed by George Balanchine, that was first produced as "a dance ballet without plot" in 1946. It deals in an almost abstract way with the four temperaments mentioned.

Four Tone Poems after Böcklin   *see* **Vier Tondichtungen nach A. Böcklin**.

The Fourth Symphony   Gustav Mahler, 1977.

The ballet in four movements, choreographed by John Neumeier, is set to the composer's Symphony No. 4 in G major (1899–1900), as the title indicates. The four individual movements have titles corresponding to those of the movements of the symphony: (1) *Beginning*, (2) *Shadows*, (3) *Evening*, (4) *Epilogue: The Lost Paradise*. The ballet depicts the growing-up pains of a boy who finally decides to leave his parents and set out on his own.

Fra Diavolo ("Brother Devil")   Daniel Auber, 1830.

The comic opera in three acts, to a libretto by Eugène Scribe, is based on the life of the notorious Italian bandit and renegade monk known as Fra Diavolo, real name Michele Pezza (1771–1806). The opera's subtitle, *L'Hôtellerie de Terracine* ("The Terracina Inn"), refers to Zerlina, the innkeeper's daughter who is compromised by Fra Diavolo when passing himself off as the Marquis of San Marco in a plot to rob an Englishman and his wife. Scribe probably took some of his material from Washington Irving's story *The Italian Banditti* in *Tales of a Traveler* (1824).

Fra Gherardo   Ildebrando Pizzetti, 1928.

The opera in three acts is set to the composer's own libretto based on the 13th-century Chronicles of Salimbene da Parma. The story is set in 12th-century Parma and tells what happens when the wealthy weaver, Gherardo, leaves the city after an affair with the orphan girl, Mariola, and joins an order of friars.

Fragmente-Stille, an Diotima ("Fragments-Silence, To Diotima")   Luigi Nono, 1979–80.

The work for string quartet was inspired by the poetry of the German writer Friedrich Hölderlin (1770–1843), who dedicated his poems to "Diotima," the name he used for his lover, Susette Gontard. It was originally the name of the priestess in Plato's *Symposium*.

Francesca da Rimini   (1) (Russian, *Francheska da Rimini*) Pyotr Tchaikovsky, 1876; (2) (Russian, *Francheska da Rimini*) Sergey Rachmaninov, 1906; (3) Riccardo Zandonai, 1914.

Tchaikovsky's symphonic fantasia, Op. 32, is based on a picture by Gustave Doré of Francesca da Rimini, the adulterous lover of her brother-in-law Paolo in Canto V of Dante's *Inferno* in his *Divina Commedia* (*c.*1307–21). (Francesca da Rimini was Francesca da Polenta, who died *c.*1283. She was married to Gianciotto Malatesta *c.*1275 to unite the Polenta and Malatesta families, but following her adulterous affair with Paolo she and her lover were slain by her husband. She was "da Rimini" because that was the home town of the Malatestas.) Rachmaninov's opera, in a prologue, two scenes, and an epilogue, is set to a libretto by Modest Tchaikovsky, the composer's brother, based on the same source. Zandonai's opera, in four acts, is set to a libretto by Tito Ricordi based on Gabriele

d'Annunzio's tragedy of the same title (1902), itself also from Dante.

Les Francs-juges ("The Judges of the Secret Court")   Hector Berlioz, 1826.

The overture, Op. 3, was written for an opera the composer later abandoned. It would have been about the *Vehmgericht*, the secret tribunal that flourished in medieval Westphalia.

Frankie and Johnny   Jerome Moross, 1938.

The ballet in one act, with a libretto by Michael Blandford and the composer and choreography by Ruth Page and Bentley Stone, is based on the popular ballad about Frankie, a prostitute in the Chicago of the 1890s, and her faithless pimp, Johnny, whom she eventually guns down: "Frankie and Johnny were lovers, my gawd, how they could love, / Swore to be true to each other, true as the stars above; / He was her man, but he done her wrong."

Frasquita   Franz Lehár, 1922.

The operetta in three acts, to a libretto by Alfred Maria Willner and Heinz Reichert, tells of the love of Armand Mireau, nephew of the industrialist, Aristide Girot, for the Spanish gypsy girl, Frasquita.

Lo Frate 'nnamorato ("The Brother in Love")   Giovanni Pergolesi, 1732.

The opera, to a text by Gennaro Antonio Federico, tells of the entanglements that ensue when twin sisters, Nina and Nena, love Ascanio rather than their intended husbands but eventually discover that he is their brother, much to the delight of the girl he himself loves, Lucrezia.

Die Frau ohne Schatten ("The Woman Without a Shadow")   Richard Strauss, 1919.

The opera in three acts is set to a libretto by Hugo von Hofmannsthal based on his own story of the same title (1919). It tells of a supernatural princess who has married an emperor but who is childless, a condition symbolized by her inability to cast a shadow.

Frauenliebe und -leben ("Woman's Love and Life")   Robert Schumann, 1840.

The song cycle for female voice and piano, Op. 42, comprises eight settings of Adalbert von Chamisso's poems of the same title (1830). The individual titles are: (1) *Seit ich ihn gesehen* ("Since I saw him"), (2) *Er, der Herrlichste von allen* ("He, the finest of all"), (3) *Ich kann's nicht fassen* ("I cannot understand it"), (4) *Du Ring an meinem Finger* ("Thou ring on my finger"), (5) *Helft mir, ihr Schwestern* ("Help me, ye sisters"),

(6) *Süsser Freund, du blickest* ("Sweet friend, thou seest"), (7) *An meinem Herzen* ("In my arms"), (8) *Nun hast du mir den ersten Schmerz getan* ("Now hast thou caused me the first pain").

Fredigundis   Franz Schmidt, 1916–21.

The opera in three acts is set to a libretto by B. Warden and I.M. Welleminsky based on Felix Dahn's historical romance about Fredegund (*c.*545–597), queen of Neustria, who got her lover, Chilperic I, king of Soissons, to murder his wife, Galswintha (568), and married him.

Freefall   Max Schubel, 1967.

The ballet in one act, choreographed by Glen Tetley, is set to the composer's Concerto for Five Instruments (*Insected Surfaces*) and explores the mind in limbo as it attempts to adjust to changes in the environment.

Frei aber Einsam ("Free but Lonely") Johannes Brahms, Robert Schumann, Albert Dietrich, 1853.

Each of the three composers contributed a movement to the sonata for violin and piano, whose title suggests that each felt isolated without the others. Brahms's own personal motto was "*Frei aber Froh*" ("Free but happy").

Der Freischütz ("The Freeshooter")   Carl Maria von Weber, 1821.

The opera in three acts is set to a libretto by Johann Friedrich Kind based on Johann Apel and Friedrich Laun's *Gespensterbuch* ("Ghost Book") (1811). The plot is set in 17th-century Bohemia and centers on the shooting contest held by the head forester, Cuno, to decide who shall marry his daughter, Agathe. Max, who loves her, loses in a trial and in desperation obtains magic bullets from Kaspar, who has sold his soul to the devil.

French Suites   J.S. Bach, 1722.

The set of six suites for keyboard is so named, possibly without authorization, because many of the pieces are in the style of French dances, such as the allemande, courante, gigue, minuet, and gavotte. The airs, too, suggest French songs. *Cf.* **English Suites, German Suites.**

Die Freunde von Salamanka ("The Friends from Salamanca")   Franz Schubert, 1815.

The opera, to a libretto by Johann Mayrhofer, has sometimes appeared under the German title *Die beiden Freunde von Salamanka* ("The Two Friends from Salamanca"), but *bei-*

den ("both") is a later addition and is misleading, as there are three friends, not two.

Friedenstag ("Day of Peace")   Richard Strauss, 1938.

The opera in one act is set to a libretto by Josef Gregor based on Pedro Calderón's play *La redención de Breda* ("The Surrender of Breda") (1625) and Diego Velázquez's painting of this historical event, *The Surrender of Breda* (1634–5). The plot tells what happens when, on the day that the Peace of Westphalia is signed at the end of the Thirty Years' War (October 24, 1648), the commandant of Breda refuses to surrender to the commandant of the besieging army.

Friederike   Franz Lehár, 1928.

The operetta in three acts is set to a libretto by Ludwig Herzer and Fritz Löhner dealing with the German poet Goethe's early love for Friederike Brion, a pastor's daughter from Sesenheim, and the lyrics she inspired in him.

Frog Quartet (German, *Froschquartett*) Joseph Haydn, 1878.

The String Quartet in D, Op. 50 No. 6, is so named for the "croaking" theme in the finale.

Froissart   Edward Elgar, 1890.

The concert overture, Op. 19, has a title that refers to a passage in Sir Walter Scott's novel *Old Mortality* (1816) in which Colonel John Grahame of Claverhouse praises the historical romances and *Chronicles* of the French writer Jean Froissart (1333–1400). The score is headed with a line from Keats: "When chivalry lifted up her lance on high."

From Bohemia's Meadows and Forests *see* **Má Vlast.**

From Fjeld and Fjord (Norwegian, *Rejseminder fra fjeld og fjord*, "Travel Memories from Mountain and Fjord")   Edvard Grieg, 1886.

The four songs, Op. 44, are based on Holger Drachmann's verses of the same title, itself something of a misnomer, since they are portraits of girls and women that had caught the poet's eye when he and the composer toured the Jotunheim mountains in the summer of 1886. In between a Prologue and an Epilogue, the titles of the individual songs are the names of the subjects: *Johanne, Ragnhild, Ingebjørg,* and *Ragna.* Johanne was the wife of the sculptor Nils Bergslien (musically represented as the giant in The **Mountain Thrall**), while Ragna was her daughter. Ingebjørg was a peasant girl with a fund of traditional songs. Drachmann himself had originally proposed the title *From Troldhaugen to Tvindehaugen.* (*See* **Wedding Day at Troldhaugen.**) A Norwegian *fjeld,* related to English *fell,* is more a rocky plateau than an actual mountain.

From me flows what you call Time
Toru Takemitsu, 1990.

The work for five percussion instruments and orchestra has a title that refers to New York's Carnegie Hall, with the composer imagining 100 years of time flowing through its space. The work consists of a fluid sequence of 11 episodes, from *A Breath of Air* to *A Prayer.*

From My Life (Czech, *Z mého života*)
Bedřich Smetana, 1876.

The String Quartet No. 1 in E minor is a musical self-portrait, culminating in a sustained high E in the finale to represent the whistling in the composer's ear that foretold his deafness. The first movement represents Smetana's youthful love of art, the second his enjoyment of dancing, the third his first love for the young woman who became his wife, and the fourth his appreciation of national music and the realization of his growing deafness. The work is also known by the equivalent German title, *Aus meinem Leben.*

From Olden Times (Hungarian, *Elmúlt időkböl*)
Béla Bartók, 1935.

The choral work in three movements for male voices is inscribed on the first page: "Based on the texts of old songs and folksongs." Hence the title, more literally "From Past Times."

From the Bavarian Highlands
Edward Elgar, 1895.

The six choral songs, Op. 27, are adapted from Bavarian folksongs. The composer later arranged three of them for orchestra alone as *Three Bavarian Dances* (1897).

From the Diary of Virginia Woolf
Dominick Argento, 1974.

The song cycle for medium voice and piano comprises settings of eight texts from the writings of Virginia Woolf, as follows: (1) *The Diary,* (2) *Anxiety,* (3) *Fancy,* (4) *Hardy's Funeral,* (5) *Rome,* (6) *War,* (7) *Parents,* (8) *Last Entry.*

From the House of the Dead (Czech, *Z mrtvého domu*)
Leoš Janáček, 1930.

The opera in three acts is set to the composer's own libretto based on Fyodor Dostoyevsky's *Notes from the House of the Dead* (1862) about his experiences in a Siberian prison camp.

From the New World *see* New World Symphony.

Frühlingslied *see* Spring Song.

Frühlingsrauschen *see* Rustle of Spring.

Frühlingstimmen ("Voices of Spring")
Johann Strauss II, 1881.

The waltzes, Op. 410, are designed to evoke the freshness and gaiety of spring, the "voices" being the inner ones of nature and love.

Fugue ("Flight").
A composition for a number of instruments or voices in which the "voices" enter successively in imitation of one another. There are many examples in the works of Bach, notably in Die **Kunst der Fuge**, and Beethoven has a fine fugue in his **Grosse Fuge**. In more modern times there is the fugue that closes Britten's The **Young Person's Guide to the Orchestra**.

Funeral March *see* (1) Lieder ohne Worte; (2) Twenty-Four Preludes.

Funeral March of a Marionette (French, *Convoi funèbre d'une marionette*)
Charles Gounod, 1872.

The work for piano is a light-hearted musical depiction of the funeral procession of a marionette who has been killed in a duel. It was originally one of the movements for a planned *Suite burlesque* for piano that never materialized.

Funiculì, funiculà
Luigi Denza, 1880.

The song was composed to mark the opening of the Naples funicular railway. Hence the seminonsensical words of the chorus.

"Fuor del mar" ("Away from the sea").
Idomeneno's aria in Act 2 of Mozart's **Idomeneo**, in which he expresses his despair that although he is now free from the dangers of the sea, he faces a more serious threat from Neptune as a result of his rash vow that he will sacrifice the first living creature he meets in return for deliverance from death. A fuller form of the title is: "*Fuor del mar ho un mar in seno*" ("Away from the sea I have a sea in my breast").

Für Elise ("For Elise")
Ludwig van Beethoven, 1808 or 1810.

The autograph score of the Bagatelle in A minor for piano is inscribed "*Für Elise am 27 April zur Erinnerung von L. v. Bthvn*" ("For Elise in memory of April 27 from Ludwig van Beethoven"). It is uncertain who Elise is. According to the musicologist Max Unger, the name may have been a copyist's misreading of "*Therese*," for Therese Malfatti (1792–1851), to whom the composer is said to have proposed marriage (1810), especially as the score was discovered among her papers.

G

The Gadfly (Russian, *Ovod*)   Antonio Spadavecchia, 1957.

The opera in four acts, to a libretto by I. Keller, is based on Ethel Voynich's anticlerical novel of the same name (1896), set in Italy, which tells of the love between the young revolutionary, Gemma, and Arthur, a naively pious Catholic. Gemma is the "gadfly" who denounces Arthur as a traitor when he reveals the names of freedom fighters in the confessional (the priest informs the police) and who slaps his face by way of a "sting."

Gaelic Symphony   Amy Marcy Beach, 1896.

The Symphony in E minor, Op. 32, is so named for the marked Gaelic character of the third movement, which has a characteristic Celtic closing cadence.

Gaîté parisienne ("Parisian Gaiety") Jacques Offenbach arr. Manuel Rosenthal, 1938.

The ballet in one act, with a libretto by Comte Étienne de Beaumont and choreography by Léonide Massine, takes some of the characters from the composer's opera La **Vie parisienne** and shows their flirtations in a Paris nightclub.

Gala Performance   Sergey Prokofiev, 1938.

The ballet in one act (two scenes), with a libretto and choreography by Antony Tudor, depicts the preparations for a ballet gala set to the first movement of the composer's Piano Concerto No. 3 in C major, Op. 26 (1917–21). The gala itself then follows to the **Classical Symphony**.

The Gambler (Russian, *Igrok*)   Sergey Prokofiev, 1929.

The opera in four acts is set to the com-poser's own libretto based on Fyodor Dostoyevsky's short story of the same name (1866) about a general who has gambled away all his money and who keenly awaits the death of his wealthy old aunt so that he can inherit her fortune.

The Gamblers (Russian, *Igroki*)   Dmitry Shostakovich, 1942.

The (unfinished) opera, planned as the composer's Op. 63, is set to his own libretto based on Nikolay Gogol's comedy of the same name (1832) about gambling scoundrels.

Gamelan   Lou Harrison, 1963.

The ballet in one act, choreographed by Robert Joffrey, was inspired by the Japanese haiku and is presented in a succession of eight vignettes. A gamelan is a type of orchestra found in South-East Asia notable for its range of percussion instruments, such as gongs, drums, chimes, and marimbas.

Games   various (see below), 1951.

The ballet in one act, choreographed by Donald McKayle, is set to a number of traditional songs and depicts children in a city's slum district playing their games while keeping one eye open for "the cops."

The Garden   Joseph Tal, 1988.

The chamber opera, set to a libretto by Israel Eliraz, is loosely based on the biblical story of the Garden of Eden and tells what happens when Adam and Eve return in middle age to Eden and ponder what has been achieved with the Knowledge that occasioned their expulsion.

The Garden of Fand   Arnold Bax, 1913–16.

The symphonic poem tells of Fand, the "Pearl of Beauty," a heroine of Irish legend, whose "garden" was the sea. *See also* **Picnic at Tintagel**.

Gaspard de la nuit ("Caspar of the Night") Maurice Ravel, 1908.

The three piano pieces take their title from a collection of prose ballads on medieval themes by Aloysius (Louis) Bertrand subtitled *Fantaisies à la manière de Rembrandt et de Callot* ("Fantasies in the Manner of Rembrandt and Callot") (1842). Their individual titles are *Ondine*, *Le Gibet* ("The Gibbet"), and *Scarbo*. Gaspard (Caspar) is a name for the Devil. Ondine is a water sprite (*see* **Ondine**). Scarbo is a goblin.

Gasparone   Karl Millöcker, 1884.

The operetta in three acts, to a libretto by

F. Zell (pen name of Camillo Walzel) and Richard Genée, is set in and around Syracuse, Sicily, at the turn of the 19th century. The story tells what happens when a band of smugglers invent a fictitious brigand named Gasparone as the one responsible for all the crimes of the neighborhood.

Gaspésienne Symphony   Claude Champagne, 1945.

The Canadian composer's symphony was inspired by the scenery of the Gaspésie region of eastern Quebec province.

Gawain   Harrison Birtwistle, 1987–90.

The opera in two acts is set to a libretto by David Harsent based on the anonymous 14th-century poem *Sir Gawayne and the Grene Knight* about the famous hero of Arthurian legend.

Gayané (Russian, *Gayane*)   Aram Khachaturian, 1942.

The ballet in four acts, with a libretto by Konstantin Derzhavin and choreography by Nina Anisimova, is set in an Armenian cotton cooperative, where Gayaneh, a cotton picker, is married to the drunkard, Giko, but loves the cooperative chairman, Kasakov. The ballet was originally planned under the title *Happiness* (Russian, *Schast'ye*).

La Gazza ladra ("The Thieving Magpie") Gioacchino Rossini, 1817.

The opera in two acts is set to a libretto by Giovanni Gerhardini based on Jean Marie Théodore Baudouin d'Aubigny and Louis Charles Caigniez's comedy *La Pie voleuse* ("The The Thieving Magpie") (1815). The plot tells how the maid Ninetta is suspected of stealing and selling some of her master's silverware. The real thief, however, is found to be a magpie.

Der Geburtstag der Infantin *see* Der Zwerg.

Geister Trio ("Ghost Trio")   Ludwig van Beethoven, 1808.

The Piano Trio in D major, Op. 70 No. 1, is so named because of the mysterious atmosphere of the slow movement, which includes a theme planned for an opera on Shakespeare's *Macbeth*, in which the ghost of Hamlet's father plays a significant part. In the event the opera was never realized. "You have only to hear the mysterious opening bars of the slow movement of this Beethoven trio to know why it is known as the *Ghost*. Rather like the equally famous

Moonlight Sonata the music immediately suggests its title" (*The Times*, November 17, 1998).

Gemini   Hans Werner Henze, 1973.

The plotless ballet in three movements, choreographed by Glen Tetley, is set to the composer's Symphony No. 3 (1949–50) and deals with the relationships of two couples of dancers. Hence the title, implying "twins."

General William Booth Enters into Heaven   Charles Ives, 1914.

The song for voice and piano is set to words from Vachel Lindsay's poem of the same title (1913) about General William Booth (1829–1912), founder of the Salvation Army.

Genoveva ("Genevieve")   Robert Schumann, 1847–9.

The opera in four acts, Op. 81, is set to the composer's own libretto based on the second draft of Robert Reinick's adaptation of Johann Ludwig Tieck's tragedy *Leben und Tod der Heiligen Genoveva* ("Life and Death of St. Genevieve") (1799) and Christian Friedrich Hebbel's tragedy *Genoveva* (1843). The plot is set in 8th-century Strasbourg and tells what happens when Genoveva, during the absence of her husband, Count Siegfried, rebuffs the advances made to her by Golo. (The Genevieve involved here is not the 5th-century patron saint of Paris but the legendary Genevieve of Brabant, victim of the machinations of her absent husband's seneschal, Golo.)

The Gentle Shepherd   traditional, 1729.

The Scottish ballad opera in five acts is set to a libretto by Allan Ramsay who selected traditional airs for what was originally, as the title hints, a pastoral comedy without songs.

A German Requiem (German, *Ein deutsches Requiem*)   Johannes Brahms, 1857–68.

The choral work in seven movements, Op. 45, for soprano and baritone soloists, chorus, and orchestra is so called because the religious text comes not from the Roman Catholic liturgy, as prayers for the dead, but from passages selected by the composer from Luther's translation of the Bible, as extracts offering consolation to the mourners. The title thus means that the text is in German, not Latin, as it is for most requiems. "The exact meaning is 'a Requiem in German,' and it becomes misleading when translated into any other language. A proper title for the work in English would be 'A Protestant Requiem'" (Blom, p. 198).

German Suites   J.S. Bach, 1731.

The six **Partitas** for keyboard are so named to emphasize their specific German character by comparison with the earlier **English Suites** and **French Suites**. The title was unauthorized.

Germania ("Germany")   Alberto Franchetti, 1902.

The opera in a prologue, two acts, and an epilogue, to a libretto by Luigi Illica, is set during the Napleonic wars and tells of the activities of a group of patriotic German students.

Gesang der Jünglinge ("Song of the Young Boys")   Karlheinz Stockhausen, 1955–6.

The work is a piece of electronic music in which a boy's treble voice, speaking and singing the Benedicite in German translation, is transformed, multiplied, and combined with electronic sounds, as if originating from several voices.

Gesang der Parzen ("Song of the Fates")   Johannes Brahms, 1882.

The ballad, Op. 89, for six-part chorus and orchestra is set to a text from Goethe's tragedy *Iphigenie auf Tauris* ("Iphigenia in Tauris") (1787), in which the Fates (Parcae) sing their song of destiny.

Gesangszene ("Sung Scena")   Ludwig Spohr, 1816.

The Violin Concerto No. 8 in A minor was marked by the composer as *in modo d'una scena cantante* ("in the form of a sung scena"), a scena being a concert aria for voice and orchestra. The work imitates a three-part operatic aria, although written in a single movement.

Die Geschöpfe des Prometheus *see* The **Creatures of Prometheus**.

Die Gespenstersonate ("The Ghost Sonata")   Aribert Reimann, 1983.

The opera in three scenes is set to a libretto by the composer and Uwe Schendel based on August Strindberg's play *Spöksonaten* ("The Ghost Sonata") (1907), about hidden murders and hovering death.

Gettysburg Address Symphony   Roy Harris, 1944.

The Symphony No. 6 pays homage to Abraham Lincoln and was directly inspired by his Gettysburg Address. The composer shared Lincoln's birthday (February 12).

Der Gewaltige Hahnrei ("The Magnificent Cuckold")   Berthold Goldschmidt, 1932.

The opera in three acts, based on Fernand Crommelynck's play *Le Cocu magnifique* (1920), tells what happens when Bruno, devoted husband of Stella, suspects that his wife has a lover. It is he, therefore, who is the "magnificent cuckold" of the title.

Die Gezeichneten ("The Stigmatized Ones")   Franz Schreker, 1918.

The opera in three acts, to the composer's own libretto, is set in 16th-century Genoa on an island pleasure garden created by a hunchbacked nobleman, Alviano Salvago, where young nobles, among them Vitelozzo Tamare, hold orgies with women abducted from the city. One of them is Carlotta, the mayor's consumptive daughter. The plot centers on a love triangle between these three, who are the "stigmatized ones" of the title. Salvago kills Tamare but is rejected by Carlotta, who dies of her disease. He then goes mad.

The Ghost Sonata *see* **Die Gespenstersonate**.

The Ghost Trio *see* **Geister Trio**.

The Ghosts of Versailles   John Corigliano, 1980–91.

The opera buffa in two acts is set to a libretto by William M. Hoffman loosely based on Pierre Beaumarchais's play *La mère coupable* ("The Guilty Mother") (1792), about the difficulties of Figaro's married life (*see* Le **Nozze di Figaro**). The plot involves a series of overlaps between two central groups of characters: the ghosts of Marie-Antoinette and her court, and the characters of an "opera-within-an-opera" in which Figaro retells his life story. The latter are also "ghosts," as is Beaumarchais himself, forever prompting his characters.

Gianni Schicci   Giacomo Puccini, 1918.

The comic opera in one act is set to a libretto by Giovacchino Forzano based on Canto XXX of Dante's *Inferno* in his *Divina Commedia* (c.1307–21). It is set in Florence in 1299 and tells how the wily Gianni Schicci alters the will of Buoso, who has left his fortune to a monastery, to his own advantage and that of his daughter, Lauretta, who loves Buoso's nephew, Rinuccio. The opera is the third panel (part) of Il **Trittico**.

Giant Fugue   J.S. Bach, 1739.

The organ fugue in D minor in Part 3 of the **Klavierübung** is so nicknamed because of the giant-like strides of the pedal part. The name was apparently given by the London organist George Cooper (1820–1876), who did much to popularize Bach's organ music in England.

Giasone ("Jason")   Francesco Cavalli, 1649.

The opera in a prologue and three acts, to a libretto by Giacinto Andrea Cicognini, tells the classical story of Jason and the Argonauts, with romantic attention focusing on the love of Jason and Medea.

The Gingerbread Heart (Serbo-Croat, *Licitarsko srce*)   Kresimir Baranović, 1924.

The ballet in three acts, choreographed by Margarita Froman, tells what happens when a young man presents a gingerbread heart to his sweetheart.

La Gioconda ("The Joyful Girl")   Amilcare Ponchielli, 1876.

The opera in four acts is set to a libretto by Arrigo Boito based on Victor Hugo's play *Angelo, tyran de Padoue* ("Angelo, Tyrant of Padua") (1835), in which La Gioconda is a street singer in love with the banished nobleman, Enzo Grimaldo.

I Gioielli della Madonna ("The Jewels of the Madonna")   Ermanno Wolf-Ferrari, 1911.

The opera in three acts, to a libretto by Enrico Golisciani and Carlo Zangarini, centers on a theft of jewels from a statue of the Madonna in Naples. The opera opened in Berlin under the equivalent German title, *Der Schmuck der Madonna*.

Un Giorno di regno ("King for a Day")   Giuseppe Verdi, 1840.

The comic opera in two acts is set to a libretto by Felice Romani originally written for Adalbert Gyrowetz's opera *Il finto Stanislao* ("The Fake Stanislas") (1818) and based on Alexandre Vincent Pineu-Duval's play *Le Faux Stanislas* ("The False Stanislas") (1808). The story ultimately evolves from an incident in the War of the Polish Succession and tells how a French officer, Belfiore, poses as Stanislas, king of Poland, in order to act as a decoy while the real Stanislas tries to secure the throne.

Giovanna d'Arco ("Joan of Arc")   Giuseppe Verdi, 1845.

The opera in a prologue and three acts is set to a libretto by Temistocle Solera based on Friedrich Schiller's play *Die Jungfrau von Orleans* ("The Maid of Orleans") (1801), itself based on events in the life of Joan of Arc (*c*.1412–1431), the

French national heroine. *Cf.* **Joan of Arc**, The **Maid of Orleans**.

Gipsy (as first word of title)   *see* **Gypsy**.

The Girl from the Woodlands   Yevgeny Tikotsky, 1953.

The opera in four acts, to a libretto by Petrus Brovka and Ye.S. Romanovich, is the third version of an opera originally titled *Alesya* (1944). The action takes place in Belorussia in 1941 and centers on the love of two collective farm leaders, Alesya and Sergei. As the Germans advance, Sergei joins the army and Alesya becomes a partisan, her activities making her known to the enemy as simply "the girl from the woodlands." (The "woodlands" here are those of the Pripet Marshes.)

The Girl of the Golden West *see* La **Fanciulla del West**.

The Girl with the Flaxen Hair *see* La **Fille aux cheveux de lin**.

Giroflé-Girofla   Charles Lecocq, 1874.

The operetta in three acts, to a libretto by Albert van Loo and Eugène Letterier, is set in the house of the governor of an African colony, Don Boléro d'Alcarazas, and centers on the forthcoming marriage of his twin daughters, Giroflé and Girofla, who are so alike that it is almost impossible to tell them apart. (In performance they are usually played by the same actress.) The names themselves are based on French *giroflée*, "gillyflower."

Giselle   Adolphe Adam, 1841.

The ballet in two acts, with a libretto by Jules-Henri Vernoy de Saint-Georges, Théophile Gautier, and Jean Coralli and choreography by Coralli and Jules Joseph Perrot, is based on a legend from Heinrich Heine's *Zur Geschichte der neueren schönen Literatur in Deutschland* ("On the History of Current Belles-Lettres in Germany") (1833). This tells how the peasant girl, Giselle, loves Albert, unaware that he is a count and betrothed to another. The ballet's subtitle is *Les Wilis* ("The Wilis"), these being the embodied spirits of brides who died before their wedding day. (*Cf.* Le **Villi**.)

La Gitana ("The Gypsy Girl")   Gustav Schmidt and Daniel Auber, 1838.

The ballet in a prologue and three acts (five scenes), with a libretto and choreography by Filippo Taglioni, tells the story of Lauretta, a duke's daughter abducted and raised by gypsies, and

Ivan, son of the governor of Nizhny Novgorod, who falls in love with her. *Cf.* La **Gypsy.**

Giuditta ("Judith")   Franz Lehár, 1934.

The opera in three acts is set to a libretto by Paul Knepler and Fritz Löhner and tells what happens when Giuditta deserts her husband to accompany Octavio, an army officer who has seduced her, to Africa.

Giulietta e Romeo ("Romeo and Juliet")
(1) Niccolò Zingarelli, 1796; (2) Nicola Vaccai, 1825; (3) Riccardo Zandonai, 1922.

Zingarelli's opera, to a libretto by Giuseppe Maria Foppa, Vaccai's opera in two acts, to a libretto by Felice Romani, and Zandonai's opera, to a libretto by Arturo Rossato, are all based on Shakespeare's play *Romeo and Juliet* (1594). *See* **Romeo and Juliet.**

Giulio Cesare in Egitto ("Julius Caesar in Egypt")   George Frideric Handel, 1724.

The opera in three acts is set to a libretto by Nicolà Francesco Haym based on Giacomo Bussani's libretto for Antonio Sartorio's opera of the same title (1876) and ultimately deriving from classical sources. The story is set in Alexandra and centers on the courtship of the Roman emperor Julius Caesar and the Egyptian queen Cleopatra.

Il Giuramento ("The Oath")   Saverio Mercadante, 1837.

The opera in three acts is set to a libretto by Gaetano Rossi based on Victor Hugo's play *Angelo, tyran de Padoue* ("Angelo, Tyrant of Padua") (1835). The story is set in 14th-century Syracuse and centers on the oath of eternal friendship sworn by Elaisa with an unknown benefactress who once saved her father's life.

Giustino   George Frideric Handel, 1737.

The opera in three acts is set to a libretto based on a three-act version of Nicolò Beregani's libretto for Giovanni Legrenzi (1683) originally made for Antonio Vivaldi (1724). The story is set in the Byzantine empire in the 6th century AD and tells how the plowboy Giustino comes to succeed Anastasio as emperor of Byzantium and marry his sister, Leocasta.

Glagolitic Mass (Czech, *Glagolská mše*)
Leoš Janáček, 1926.

The cantata for soprano, alto, tenor, and bass soloists, chorus, orchestra, and organ is set to an adaptation of the Ordinary of the Mass by Miloš Weingart. The vernacular version of the Old Slavonic Ordinary was taken by the composer from a church magazine. He mistakenly called Old Slavonic (the Slavic language found in texts from the 9th century) "Glagolitic," a term properly referring to one form of that language's script and alphabet, the other being Cyrillic, which eventually superseded it.

Gli (Italian, "The").

For titles beginning with this word, see the next word, *e.g.* Gli **Equivoci.**

Gloria   Francis Poulenc, 1980.

The ballet in one act, choreographed by Kenneth MacMillan, is set to the composer's *Gloria* in G major for soprano, chorus, and orchestra (1959) (hence the title) and was inspired by Vera Brittain's autobiographical *Testament of Youth* (1933), mourning the wasted lives of those who died young in World War I. In the liturgical sense, a *Gloria* (short for *Gloria in excelsis Deo*, "Glory to God in the highest") is a song of the angels announcing the birth of Christ, as in the Roman Catholic **Mass** and in the Communion service of the Anglican Church. An example is the *Gloria* in Bach's **St. Matthew Passion.**

Gloriana   Benjamin Britten, 1952–3.

The opera in three acts, Op. 53, is set to a libretto by William Plomer based on Lytton Strachey's historical biography *Elizabeth and Essex* (1928), which tells of the relationship between Queen Elizabeth I and the Earl of Essex. Gloriana was Elizabeth's poetic nickname. The opera was commissioned to celebrate the coronation of Queen Elizabeth II (1953), who attended its first performance.

Die Glückliche Hand ("The Knack")
Arnold Schoenberg, 1924.

The opera in one act, to the composer's own libretto, tells of the artist's quest for happiness, beset as he is by difficulties, temptations, and frustrations. What is "the knack" of finding it?

The Gods Go a-Begging   George Frideric Handel arr. Thomas Beecham, 1928.

The ballet in one act, with a libretto by Sobeka (the pen name of Boris Kochno) and choreography by George Balanchine, tells of a young shepherd who joins a party of young aristocrats and falls in love with a pretty girl. When the other guests make fun of the young lovers, he suddenly reveals that they are both gods. The ballet has an equivalent French subtitle, *Les Dieux mendiants.*

Goin' Home *see* **New World Symphony**.

Gold and Silver (German, *Gold und Silber*) Franz Lehár, 1902.

The waltz so named was composed for a gold and silver ball given by Prince Metternich of Austria in January 1902.

Gold Coast Customs Humphrey Searle, 1947–9.

The work for speakers, men's chorus, wind instruments, two pianos, and orchestra is a setting of the poem of this name by Edith Sitwell (1929), attacking the disparity in the world between rich and poor, sated and starving. (Slaves and gold were exported to the West from the Gold Coast, now Ghana.)

Goldberg Variations (German, *Goldberg-variationen*) J.S. Bach, 1742.

The 30 variations on an original theme for harpsichord, BWV 988, were presented by the composer to Johann Goldberg (1727–1756), harpsichordist to Count Keyserlingk, although it seems he did not commission them. *See also* **Klavierübung**.

The Golden Age (Russian, *Zolotoy vek*) Dmitry Shostakovich, 1927–30.

The ballet in three acts and five scenes, with a libretto by A. Ivanovsky and choreography by E. Kaplan and Vasily Vainonen, takes its title from an exhibition in a capitalist city, where a fight takes place between some Fascists and a Soviet football team. The "golden age" is the age of work.

The Golden Cockerel (Russian, *Zolotoy petushok*) Nikolai Rimsky-Korsakov, 1909.

The opera in three acts is set to a libretto by Vladimir Ivanovich Belsky based on Alexander Pushkin's poem of the same title (1834). The fairy tale plot tells what happens when an astrologer gives King Dodon a golden cockerel that will crow if he is threatened with danger. The opera is also known by the French title, *Le Coq d'or*.

The Golden Legend Arthur Sullivan, 1886.

The cantata for soloists, chorus, and orchestra is set to text based on H.W. Longfellow's dramatic poem of the same name (1851) based on *Der arme Heinrich* ("Poor Henry"), by the 12th-century German minnesinger, Hartmann von der Aue. The story tells what happens when Prince Henry of Hoheneck, a student of alchemy, falls sick and Lucifer, disguised as a physician, pretends to cure him.

Golden Sonata Henry Purcell, 1697.

The Sonata in F major for two violins, viola da gamba, and organ or harpsichord continuo, No. 9 of the set of ten published, is apparently so named for its brilliance. The name is not the composer's and dates from 1704.

The Golden Spinning Wheel (Czech, *Zlatý kolovrat*) Antonín Dvořák, 1896.

The symphonic poem, Op. 109, is based on a ballad by K.J. Erben telling how a stepmother's guilty secret is revealed by a spinning wheel.

The Golden Vanity Benjamin Britten, 1966.

The work for boys' voices and piano, Op. 78, is set to a libretto by Colin Graham based on an anonymous shanty, beginning: "There was a ship came from the north country, / And the name of the ship was the *Golden Vanity*." The story tells how a cabin boy saves the lives of the entire ship's crew by swimming to a pirate ship and drilling a hole beneath its waterline.

The Golem John Casken, 1989.

The opera in two parts (Prelude and Legend) is set to a libretto by the composer and Pierre Audi based on the Jewish legend of the golem, a figure of clay brought to life by Cabbalistic magic.

Golestan various (see below), 1973.

The ballet in four scenes, choreographed by Maurice Béjart, is set to traditional Iranian music and was inspired by the poems of the same name by the 13th-century Persian poet Sa'adi. The name itself means "Rose Garden." Hence the ballet's alternate French title, *Le Jardin des roses* ("The Garden of Roses"). Its individual scenes have French titles as follows: (1) *Chant des hommes dans le désert* ("Song of the Men in the Desert"), (2) *Vision du jardin* ("Vision of the Garden"), (3) *Apparition de la lumière: La Rose mystique* ("Apparition of Light: The Mystic Rose"), (4) *Ritual: Le Voile et le Miroir* ("Ritual: The Veil and the Mirror").

Golgotha Frank Martin, 1945–8.

The oratorio for solo voices, choir, and orchestra is set to a text from the Bible and the writings of St. Augustine. It is divided into seven pictures, with biblical words, separated by passages from St. Augustine's meditations, and was suggested by Rembrandt's etching *The Three*

Crosses (1653). Golgotha was the place outside Jerusalem where Christ was crucified.

Golliwogg's Cakewalk *see* **Children's Corner**.

Gondola Song *see* **Venezianisches Gondellied**.

The Gondoliers Arthur Sullivan, 1889.

The operetta in two acts, subtitled *The King of Barataria*, is set to a libretto by W.S. Gilbert and tells what happens when two Venetian gondoliers are made joint kings of Barataria.

Good Friday Music (German, *Karfreitagzauber*) Richard Wagner, 1882.

The music in Act 3, Scene 1 of **Parsifal** as Parsifal, returning from his wanderings, is anointed in preparation for his entry into the Castle of the Grail.

The Good-Humored Ladies Domenico Scarlatti arr. Vincenzo Tommasini, 1917.

The orchestral ballet suite in one act, choreographed by Léonide Massine, is based on Carlo Goldoni's comedy *Le donne di buon umore* ("The Good-Humored Ladies"), telling of the complicated love affair between Costanza and Rinaldo. The work's original French title was *Les Femmes de bonne humeur*.

Gorda D.A. Toradze, 1949.

The Georgian ballet in four acts (ten scenes), choreographed by Vakhtang Chaboukiani, tells of a young sculptor, Gorda, who loves the Czarevna and becomes a keen warrior to defend his native land against the Arabs.

Gorianka ("The Mountain Girl") Murad Kashlaev, 1968.

The ballet in three acts, choreographed by Oleg Vinogradov, tells what happens when a girl from the country leaves her family and fiancé to lead a life of her own in the city.

Gothic Symphony Havergal Brian, 1919–27.

The Symphony No. 1 in D minor is indirectly named for its grandiose content and composition, requiring soprano, alto, tenor, and bass soloists, quadruple chorus, children's chorus, four brass bands, and a huge orchestra. The title's direct reference is to the inspiration of the work, a dream in which the composer saw a towered and turreted city.

"Gott! welch' Dunkel hier" ("God! what darkness here").

Florestan's aria opening Act 2 of Beethoven's **Fidelio**, in which he laments the silence and darkness of his imprisonment.

Götterdämmerung *see* Der **Ring des Nibelungen**.

Les Goûts-Réunis ("The Combined Styles") François Couperin, 1722.

The set of ten *concerts* for various instruments is intended as a harmonious whole, despite the differing styles, and includes the "grand trio sonata" Le **Parnasse**.

Goyescas ("Scenes from Goya") Enrique Granados, 1911, 1916.

The seven piano pieces (1911) were inspired by the paintings of Francisco de Goya. Hence the name, with an alternate title *Los majos enamorados* ("Youth in Love"). The individual titles are: (1) *Los requiebros* ("Flirting Words"), (2) *Coloquio en la reja* ("Conversation through the Grating"), (3) *El fandango del candil* ("The Kitchen Fandango"), (4) *Quejas, o la maja y el ruiseñor* ("Lament, or the Maja and the Nightingale"), (5) *El amor y la muerte* ("Love and Death"), (6) *Epílogo: la serenada del espectro* ("Epilogue: The Ghost's Serenade"), (7) *El pelele* ("The Simpleton"). The opera, to a libretto by Fernando Periquet y Zuaznabar (1916), is an amplified and scored version (made at the suggestion of the American pianist Ernest Schelling) of the piano pieces. It tells how Rosario arouses the jealousy of her lover, Fernando, by accepting the attentions of the bullfighter, Paquiro.

Grabstein für Stefan ("Gravestone for Stefan") György Kurtág, 1989.

The work for guitar and instrumental ensemble, Op. 15c, was written as a memorial to the husband of the Hungarian psychologist Marianne Stein, who encouraged Kurtág to go back to first principles as a composer.

Graduation Ball Johann Strauss II arr. Antal Dorati, 1940.

The ballet in one act, with a libretto and choreography by David Lichine, is set in a Viennese boarding school and tells how the girls stage a ball with the cadets from the city's military academy.

Gradus ad Parnassum ("Steps to Parnassus") Muzio Clementi, 1817.

The collection of 100 piano studies takes its title from earlier dictionaries of Latin prosody. The use of such works enables the student to ascend Mt. Parnassus, the abode of Apollo and the

Muses in classical mythology. The first piece in Debussy's **Children's Corner**, *Dr. Gradus ad Parnassum*, parodies a child's hesitant efforts to play a Clementi study.

Der Graf von Luxemburg ("The Count of Luxembourg") Franz Lehár, 1909.

The operetta in three acts is set to a libretto by Robert Bodansky and Alfred Maria Willner telling what happens when the profligate René, Count of Luxembourg, agrees for a sum of money to marry the singer, Angèle Didier, a commoner, thus raising her to noble rank.

Die Gräfin Mariza ("The Countess Maritza") Emmerich Kálmán, 1924.

The operetta in three acts, to a libretto by Julius Brammer and Alfred Grünwald, is set in Hungary and centers on the love between the young heiress, Countess Maritza, and Count Tassilo, who manages her estate disguised as a bailiff named Bela Török.

The Grammar Fairies J. More Smieton, c.1897.

The work, with words by T.M. Davidson, is a "Cantata upon English Grammar" designed to teach children the basic principles of that subject. "A careful perusal ... of the cantata compels us to admit that it is not only of very superior merit, but it is certain to give much pleasure and delight as an evening's entertainment, as well as to permanently and graphically impress the uses of the parts of speech upon the minds of the young. We like the music, as it is appropriately and attractively wedded to the words" (*The Schoolmistress*).

The Grand Duke Arthur Sullivan, 1895–6.

The comic opera in two acts, to a libretto by W.S. Gilbert, tells what happens when the miserly Grand Duke Rudolph is challenged to a duel and wins, the duel being decided not with swords but by the drawing of the lowest card. The opera is subtitled *The Statutory Duel.*

Grand Duo Franz Schubert, 1824.

The Sonata in C major for piano duet, D 813, was so named by the publisher (in 1838). The name itself means simply "Great Duet."

Le Grand Macabre ("The Great Macabre") György Ligeti, 1978.

The opera in two acts is set to a libretto by Michael Meschke and the composer based on Michel de Ghelderode's play *La Ballade du Grand Macabre*. The work is a satirical fantasy about the end of the world.

Grand' Messe des Morts ("High Mass for the Dead") Hector Berlioz, 1837.

The name is that of the Requiem, Op. 5, for tenor solo, boys' chorus, chorus, and orchestra.

Grand Trio Franz Schubert, 1979.

The ballet in four movements, choreographed by Hans van Manen, is set to the composer's Piano Trio No. 1 in B flat major, D 898 (1827), and deals with an affair between a society lady and a young man. The title was presumably suggested by the composer's **Grand Duo**.

La Grande-Duchesse de Gérolstein ("The Grand Duchess of Gerolstein") Jacques Offenbach, 1867.

The operetta in three acts is set to a libretto by Henri Meilhac and Ludovic Halévy telling what happens when the Prime Minister, Baron Puck, wishes his Grand Duchess to marry Prince Paul. The work is a satire on petty German princedoms.

Grande sonate pathétique *see* **Pathétique Sonata**.

Grande Symphonie funèbre et triomphale *see* **Symphonie funèbre et triomphale**.

The Great Fugue (German, *Grosse Fuge*) J.S. Bach, c.1720.

The Fantasia and Fugue in G minor for Organ, BWV 542, is probably so named for its unusual expressiveness, rather than for its length. *Cf.* **Little Fugue**.

Great Symphony Franz Schubert, 1825.

The Symphony No. 9 in C major, D 944, came to be so named both for its impressive dimensions and for its deeply expressive passages. According to Schumann, "it transports us into a world where we cannot recall ever having been before" (quoted in Berkowitz, p. 63). According to others, however, it is so named not from any intrinsic "greatness" but simply for distinction from the **Little Symphony**.

the greatest happiness principle David Sawer, 1997.

The orchestral work takes its (lowercase) title from the words of the English philosopher, Jeremy Bentham: "The greatest happiness of the greatest number is the foundation of morals and legislation" (*The Commonplace Book*, 1843). The work is a comment on Bentham's design of a circular "panoptic" penitentiary that aimed to improve prison conditions but that placed the inmates under perpetual surveillance. Here the "penitentiary" is the orchestra, under the constant surveillance of its conductor.

Greek   Mark-Anthony Turnage, 1987–8.

The opera in two acts is set to a libretto by the composer and Jonathan Moore based on Steven Berkoff's play of the same name (1979), a reworking of the Oedipus myth (*see* **Oedipe**) transferred to the East End of modern London. The Greek is thus Oedipus, here renamed Eddy.

The Greek Passion (Czech, *Řecké pašije*) Bohuslav Martinů, 1956–9.

The opera in four acts is set to a libretto by the composer and Nikos Kazantzakis based on the latter's novel *Christ Recrucified* (1948). The story is set in a Greek village and tells what happens when the various actors in a passion play begin to take on the characteristics of the individuals they are portraying.

The Green Table   Frederic Cohen, 1932.

The ballet, a dance of death in eight scenes, with a libretto and choreography by Kurt Jooss, depicts the horrors of war as they affect ordinary people, and begins with the pointless discussions of diplomats around a green table.

Greening   Arne Nordheim, 1975.

The ballet in one act, choreographed by Glen Tetley, deals with people waiting on the edge of something they are unable to define, or encountering an emotional upset they do not understand. They are thus "greening," in the sense of longing or yearning.

Gretchen am Spinnrade ("Gretchen at the Spinning Wheel")   Franz Schubert, 1814.

The song for voice and piano, D 118, is set to words from Goethe's dramatic poem *Faust* (1808). In this, Gretchen is a pure young maiden eventually seduced by Faust. Her song at the spinning wheel, in Part 1, begins: "*Meine Ruh' ist hin, / Mein Herz ist schwer*" ("My peace is gone, / My heart is heavy").

Grisélidis ("Griselda")   Jules Massenet, 1901.

The opera in a prologue and three acts is set to a libretto by Armand Silvestre and Eugène Morand based on their play of the same name (1891), in turn based on the story of "patient Griselda" in Giovanni Boccaccio's *Decameron* (1349–51).

Grosse Fuge ("Great Fugue")   Ludwig van Beethoven, 1825.

The **Fugue** in B flat major for string quartet, Op. 133, was originally intended as the last movement of the String Quartet No. 13 in B flat major, Op. 130 (1825). Although usually referred to by its German title, the composer himself gave it the French title, *Grande Fugue tantôt libre tantôt recherché* ("Great Fugue Now Free Now Deliberate"). The fugue is "great" by virtue of its length and its complexity.

Grosse Orgelmesse ("Great Organ Mass") Joseph Haydn, 1768.

The Mass No. 4 in E flat major has the full Latin title, *Missa in honorem Beata Vergine Maria* ("Mass in Honor of the Blessed Virgin Mary"), or *Missa Sancti Josephi* ("Mass of St. Joseph"). *Cf.* **Kleine Orgelmesse**.

The Growing Castle   Malcolm Williamson, 1968.

The chamber opera in two acts is set to the composer's own libretto based on August Strindberg's mystically surreal drama *A Dream Play* (1902).

Gruppen ("Groups")   Karlheinz Stockhausen, 1955–7.

The work is for three orchestras, respectively of 36, 37, and 36 instruments, each placed in a different part of the hall and each playing different music. The "groups" of orchestras thus produce disparate "groups" of music. The title refers not only to this division, however, but to the writing principle that the composer calls *Gruppenform* ("group form"). This form does not take the note as the basic element but rather the group of sounds that must be defined well enough to be distinguishable. Each group is determined by its dimension, its shape, and its density, but mostly by its sound quality. A group may be simply a brief isolated note.

Il Guarany ("The Guarani")   Carlos Gomes, 1879.

The opera in four acts is set to a libretto by Tomaso Scalvini and Carlo d'Ormeville based on José Martiniano de Alencar's novel *O Guarani* ("The Guarani") (1857). The story tells what happens when the Guarani prince, Pery, rescues his beloved, Cecilia, from three Spaniards who had planned to hand her over to the enemy Aymara tribe.

Guglielmo Ratcliff ("William Ratcliff")
Pietro Mascagni, 1895.

The opera in four acts is set to a libretto by Count Andrea Maffei based on Heinrich Heine's tragedy *Wilhelm Ratcliff* (1822). The story is set in Scotland in the 17th century and tells what happens when William Ratcliff falls in love with Maria, daughter of MacGregor, and vows to kill anyone who tries to marry her. *See also* **William Ratcliff**.

Guillaume Tell ("William Tell")
Gioacchino Rossini, 1829.

The opera in four acts is set to a libretto by Étienne de Jouy, Florent Bis, and Armand Marast based on Friedrich von Schiller's drama *Wilhelm Tell* (1804). It tells the familiar story of the legendary Swiss hero who rallied the Swiss against the Austrians and who famously shot an apple from his son's head.

Guns and Castanets Georges Bizet, 1939.

The ballet in one act, with a libretto by Ruth Page and choreography by Page and Bentley Stone, is an updated version of the composer's **Carmen**, using poems by Federico García Lorca. It is set against the background of the Spanish Civil War (1936–9), in progress at the time of the original production.

Guntram Richard Strauss, 1887–93.

The opera in three acts, to the composer's own libretto, is set in 13th-century Germany and tells what happens when Guntram kills the tyrannical Duke Robert in a duel.

Gurrelieder ("Songs of Gurra") Arnold Schoenberg, 1900–13.

The work for five solo voices, speaker, three male choruses, mixed chorus, and orchestra is set to a German text translated by R.F. Arnold from Jens Peter Jacobsen's Danish poems (1886). The story is set in the 14th century and tells of the love between King Waldemar and the heroine, Tove, who lives in Gurra Castle, Denmark.

Gwendoline Emmanuel Chabrier, 1885.

The opera in three acts, to a libretto by Catulle Mendès, is set in 8th-century Britain and tells of the Viking king, Harald, who falls in love with Gwendoline, the daughter of his Saxon prisoner, Armel.

Gymnopédies ("Gymnopedias") Erik Satie, 1888.

The three piano pieces have a title based on the Gymnopaidia (from Greek *gymnos*, "naked," and *paidia*, "youth"), an annual festival held in Sparta in honor of those who fell at Thyrea in the "battle of the champions" between the Spartans and the Argives. At the festival, choral dances were performed by naked men and boys divided by age into choruses. The inspiration for the composition may have been the painting on a Greek vase.

La Gypsy ("The Gypsy Girl") François Benoist, Ambroise Thomas, and T. Marliani, 1839.

The ballet in three acts (five scenes), with a libretto by Jules-Henri Vernoy de Saint-Georges and Joseph Mazilier and choreography by the latter, is based on Miguel de Cervantes's *Novelas exemplares* ("Exemplary Novels") (1613), and tells the story of Sarah, the daughter of a Scottish lord, who is abducted from her parents' castle and raised among gypsies. *Cf.* La **Gitana**.

The Gypsy Baron *see* Der **Zigeunerbaron**.

Gypsy Love *see* **Zigeunerliebe**.

Gypsy Melodies (Czech, *Cigánské melodie*) Antonín Dvořák, 1880.

The cycle of seven songs for tenor and piano, Op. 55, set to poems by Adolf Heyduk, comprises the following: (1) *My Song of Love Rings Through the Dusk* (Czech, *Má píseň zas mi láskou zní*), (2) *Hey! Ring Out My Triangle* (Czech, *Aj! Kterak trojhranec můj přerozkošně zvoní*), (3) *All Round About the Woods Are Still* (Czech, *A les je tichý kolem kol*), (4) **Songs My Mother Taught Me**, (5) *Tune Thy Strings, O Gypsy* (Czech, *Struna naladěna, hochu toč se v kole*), (6) *Wide the Sleeves and Trousers* (Czech, *Široké rukávy, a široké gatě*), (7) *Give the Hawk a Fine Cage* (also known as *Cloudy Heights of Tatra*) (Czech, *Dejte klec jestřábu ze zlata ryzého*). The cycle is also known as *Gypsy Songs*.

The Gypsy Princess *see* Die **Czardasfürstin**.

Gypsy Songs *see* **Gypsy Melodies**.

H

"Ha! welch' ein Augenblick!" ("Ah! what a moment!").

Pizarro's aria in Act 1 of Beethoven's **Fidelio**, in which he resolves to murder his prisoner, Florestan.

Haakon Jarl   Bedřich Smetana, 1861.

The symphonic poem takes its subject from the historical tragedy *Hakon Jarl hin Rige* ("Earl Haakon the Great") (1807) by the Danish poet Adam Oehlenschläger, telling how Haakon, Jarl of Jade, seized power in Norway in 970 and ruled tyrannically until his defeat in 995 by **Olav Trygvason**.

Habanera (Spanish, "Havanan").

The name is that of a Cuban dance in slow duple time, so called after the Cuban capital, Havana. A famous example is the *habanera* "L'**Amour est un oiseau rebelle**" in Bizet's **Carmen**, and Ravel's *Habanera* for two pianos (1895) was later incorporated in his **Rapsodie espagnole**. *See also* **Vocalise en forme d'habanera**.

Haffner Serenade   W.A. Mozart, 1776.

The Serenade in D major, K 250, was commissioned by Siegmund Haffner (1756–1787), the son of a respected Salzburg businessman, to celebrate the marriage of his sister, Marie Elizabeth Haffner (1753–1784), to Franz Xaver Späth (1750–1808). *Cf.* **Haffner Symphony**.

Haffner Symphony   W.A. Mozart, 1782.

The Symphony No. 35 in D major, K 385, was originally intended as a serenade (not the **Haffner Serenade**) to mark the ennoblement of Siegmund Haffner on July 29, 1782. Salzburg was Mozart's native city.

Halka ("Helen")   Stanisław Moniuszko, 1848.

The opera in four (originally two) acts is set to a libretto by Włodzimierz Wolski based on Kazimierz Władysław Wójcicki's story *Góralka* ("The Mountain Maid"). The plot is set in the Carpathians around 1840 and tells of the doomed love of Halka for Janusz, who is in love with Zofia.

Hallelujah Chorus   George Frideric Handel, 1742.

The chorus that closes Part 2 of **Messiah** is so called because of the repetition of the word "Hallelujah," meaning "praise ye the Lord." This phrase prefaces 11 Psalms in the Bible and the word itself occurs four times (in the King James Version as "Alleluia") in Revelation 19. *Cf.* **Hallelujah Concerto**.

Hallelujah Concerto   George Frideric Handel, 1760.

The Concerto in B flat major for Organ and Strings, Op 7 No. 3, is sometimes so known as its first movement makes repeated use of the opening phrase of the **Hallelujah Chorus**.

Halte de Cavalerie ("Cavalry Halt") Johann Arnsheimer, 1896.

The ballet in one act, with a libretto and choreography by Marius Petipa, centers on Marie, daughter of the most important man in an Austrian village, and on the peasant, Pierre, that she loves. The story tells what happens when a troop of hussars and lancers appears.

Hamburger Ebb und Fluht ("Hamburg Ebb and Flow")   Georg Telemann, 1723.

The suite in C major is a musical depiction of life on and beside Hamburg's Alster River.

Hamlet   (1) Franz Liszt, 1859; (2) Ambroise Thomas, 1868; (3) (Russian, *Gamlet*) Pyotr Tchaikovsky, 1888, 1891; (4) Humphrey Searle, 1968.

Liszt's symphonic poem, Thomas's opera in five acts, to a libretto by Jules Barbier and Michel Carré, Tchaikovsky's fantasy overture, Op. 67a (1888), and incidental music, Op. 67b (1891), and Searle's opera in three acts, to his own libretto, are all based on Shakespeare's play of the same name (1600) about the prince of Denmark who sees the ghost of his father, learns that he was murdered by his brother, Claudius, now king and husband of Hamlet's mother, Gertrude, and is demanded by the ghost to seek revenge. Liszt's work was written as a prelude to the play. The ballet in one scene of the same name, based on Shakespeare's play and set to Tchaikovsky's music, was first produced in 1942 with a libretto and choreography by Robert Helpmann.

Hammerklavier Sonata   Ludwig van Beethoven, 1817–18.

The Piano Sonata No. 29 in B flat, Op.106, is so named because it was composed for the pianoforte, for which the German word is *Hammerklavier* (literally "hammer keyboard"). Beethoven said he had decided to use the word on all his piano music with German titles, and "this is to be clearly understood once and for all."

Handel in the Strand   Percy Grainger, 1911–12.

The piece for piano, No. 2 of *Room Music Tit-Bits*, "to be played to, or without, clog dancing," includes the following in the composer's program note: "My title was originally 'Clog Dance.' But my dear friend William Gair

Rathbone (to whom the piece is dedicated) suggested the title 'Handel in the Strand,' because the music seemed to reflect both Handel and English musical comedy (the 'Strand' is the home of London musical comedy)."

Handel's Largo   George Frideric Handel, 1738.

The name is popularly given to any arrangement of the aria **"Ombra mai fù"** from **Serse**. In the original, the aria is actually marked larghetto. It was also meant to be satirical, but under its new name is usually taken somberly.

Hans Heiling   Heinrich Marschner, 1833.

The opera in a prologue and three acts is set to a libretto by Eduard Devrient based on an old folk tale telling how Hans Heiling, son of the Spirit Queen and a mortal father, assumes human shape and falls in love with Anna.

Hansel and Gretel *see* **Hänsel und Gretel**.

Hänsel und Gretel ("Hansel and Gretel") Engelbert Humperdinck, 1893.

The opera in three acts is set to a libretto by Adelheid Wette based on the story in the Grimm brothers' *Fairy Tales* (1812–14). This tells how the children Hänsel and Gretel, brother and sister, are sent into the woods by their angry mother, lost there, sent to sleep by the Sandman, captured by a witch, and finally reunited with their parents.

Happy End   Kurt Weill, 1928–9.

The comedy with music in three acts is set to a libretto by D. Lane (pen name of Elisabeth Hauptmann) with lyrics by the composer. The story leads to the satisfactory conclusion expressed by the title. The work itself contains the songs *Bilbao Song* and *Surabaya Johnny*.

The Happy Prince   Malcolm Williamson, 1965.

The opera in one act, for children's and women's voices, piano duet, percussion, and optional string quartet, is set to the composer's own libretto based on Oscar Wilde's fairy tale of the same name (1888). This tells how the statue of a pleasure-loving prince, looking down on human misery, brings relief to those in trouble with the help of a late-returning swallow.

Harawi, chant d'amour et de mort ("Harawi, Song of Love and Death")   Olivier Messiaen, 1945.

The song cycle for soprano and piano, set to the composer's own text, was inspired by the legend of Tristan and Isolde as well as by Peruvian mythology. The *harawi* is a form of lament.

Harbinger   Sergey Prokofiev, 1967.

The ballet in five movements, choreographed by Eliot Feld, is set to the composer's Piano Concerto No. 5 in G major, Op. 55 (1932), and reflects the generally carefree atmosphere of the music. It was Feld's first ballet, so the title was perhaps a promise of things to come. If so, the promise has been abundantly fulfilled.

Hark, Hark the Lark (German, *Horch, horche, die Lerche*)   Franz Schubert, 1827.

The well known song, D 291, officially entitled **Ständchen**, is set to Franz Grillparzer's translation of the song from Shakespeare's *Cymbeline* (1609), II, iii, beginning: "Hark! hark! the lark at heaven's gate sings, / And Phoebus 'gins arise."

Harlequin in April   Richard Arnell, 1951.

The ballet in two acts, with a libretto and choreography by John Cranko, shows how Harlequin is born out of chaos and devastation to a new life. April is the month when all springs anew.

Harlequinade   Riccardo Drigo, 1965.

The ballet in two acts, choreographed by George Balanchine, is set to the music of the composer's Les **Millions d'Arlequin** and shows how the Good Fairy provided Harlequin with enough gold to impress Cassandre, the father of his beloved Columbine.

Die Harmonie der Welt ("The Harmony of the World")   Paul Hindemith, 1957.

The opera in five acts to the composer's own libretto is based on the life of the astronomer Johannes Kepler (1571–1630), author of *Harmonice mundi* ("Harmonics of the World") (1619), in which he expounded his third theory of planetary motion.

Harmonielehre ("Treatise on Harmony") John Adams, 1984–5.

The composer took the title of his orchestral work from Schoenberg's treatise on harmony (1911), thus declaring his faith in tonality as a still living tradition.

Harmoniemesse ("Windband Mass") Joseph Haydn, 1802.

The Mass No. 14 in B flat major is so named because it makes fuller use of wind instruments than the composer's other masses.

The Harmonious Blacksmith　George Frideric Handel, 1720.

The air and variations in the Harpsichord Suite No. 5 in E from the first set of eight suites is so popularly named because Handel is said to have heard its melody sung by a blacksmith at Edgware, north of London. However, the title arose some time after the composer's death and has no proven connection with the circumstances of the work's composition. The blacksmith in question is said to have been one William Powell (*c*.1702–1780), whose grave at Little Stanmore, west of Edgware, was originally surrounded by a wooden rail on one side of which was painted "Sacred to the memory of William Powell, the HARMONIOUS BLACKSMITH, died Feb. 27, 1780, aged about 78," and on the other: "He was Parish Clerk at this Church many years, and during the Time the Immortal Handel resided much at Cannons with the Duke of Chandos [*see* **Chandos Anthems**]." But then, "this humble rail was in 1868 displaced by a substantial stone bearing, in a sunk medallion, hammer, anvil, laurel-leaf, and a bar of music, and a somewhat modified inscription to the effect that 'He was parish clerk during the time the immortal Handel was organist of this church.' This is the Powell whose rhythmical beating on his forge ... suggested to Handel his charming melody of the Harmonious Blacksmith" (James Thorne, *Handbook to the Environs of London*, 1876). The link with Powell came suspiciously late, however, when the anvil was mysteriously "discovered" and sold by auction. Blom points out that the title was already current at the end of the 18th century for quite another reason. One of the publishers J. and W. Lintern, who brought out an edition of the work under that name, had been a blacksmith in his youth, "and this is the only origin of the title that should be accepted as authenticated" (p. 231).

Harnasie ("Hetmen")　Karol Szymanowski, 1926.

The ballet in three scenes, with a libretto by the composer, deals with the Polish Highlanders and the legendary robbers of the Tatra region.

Harold en Italie ("Harold in Italy")　Hector Berlioz, 1834.

The symphony, Op. 16, for viola and orchestra, was inspired by Byron's poem *Childe Harold's Pilgrimage* (1812, 1816, 1818), in which the hero makes a long pilgrimage across Europe and the poet himself describes a literary and historical tour of Italy.

The Harp of the Poet　*see* **Lieder ohne Worte**.

Harp Quartet　Ludwig van Beethoven, 1809.

The String Quartet in E flat major, Op. 74, is so named because of the pizzicato arpeggios in the first movement, "which however do not sound in the least like a harp" (Blom, p. 232). The title could be regarded as misleading, "as uninformed concertgoers naturally expect to see on the platform, if not four harps, at least one" (Scholes, p. 678).

The Harvest According　Virgil Thomson, 1952.

The ballet in three parts, choreographed by Agnes de Mille, is one woman's overview of life. The inspiration for the ballet, and thus its title, came from Walt Whitman's poem *As I Watch'd the Plowman Plowing* (1871), with its final line: "(Life, life is the tillage, and Death is the harvest according.)"

Háry János ("John Háry")　Zoltán Kodály, 1926.

The opera in a prologue, five scenes, and an epilogue is set to a libretto by Béla Paulini and Zsolt Harsányi based on János Garay's poem *Az Obsitos* ("The Veteran") (1843), the hero of which is the great liar Háry János, who falls in love with Napoleon's second wife, Archduchess Maria Louisa of Austria.

Hassan　Frederick Delius, 1920–3.

The incidental music to James Elroy Flecker's (posthumous) play of the same name (1922) includes songs, dances, and choral episodes. The play tells what happens when Hassan, a middle-aged confectioner in old Baghdad, becomes embroiled in the cruel court of the caliph as a result of his love for the courtesan, Yasmin. The subtitle, *The Golden Journey to Samarkand*, refers to the road along which Hassan eventually escapes.

Haugtussa ("The Mountain Maid")　Edvard Grieg, 1895.

The song cycle for soprano and piano, Op. 67, comprises settings of eight poems by Arne Garborg written in archaic Norwegian (1895). Their titles are: (1) *Det syng* ("The Singing"), (2) *Veslemøy* ("Little Maid"), (3) *Blaabærli* ("Bilberry Slopes"), (4) *Møte* ("Meeting"), (5) *Elsk* ("Love"), (6) *Killingsdans* ("Kidlings' Dance"), (7) *Vond dag* ("Evil Day"), (8) *Ved Gjætlebekken* ("By the Brook"). The poems themselves were inspired by the desolate farming country south of Stavanger and tell the story of a young girl who has the gift of insight into the supernatural world.

The Haunted Ballroom   Geoffrey Toye, 1934.

The ballet in one act (two scenes), with a libretto by the composer and choreography by Ninette de Valois, tells how the Masters of Tregennis are condemned to dance themselves to death in the gloomy room where the faded portraits of the family's ancestors hang.

The Haunted Manor (Polish, *Straszny dwór*)   Stanisław Moniuszko, 1865.

The opera in four acts, to a libretto by Jan Chęciński, tells the story of two young soldiers who vow not to marry so they can go to war at a moment's notice. Their aunt finds brides for them, but is alarmed when they say they are visiting a manor where two young single ladies live. She tries to frighten them off with tales of ghosts, but this only strengthens their resolve to make the visit. The opera makes the most of the spooky scenes that ensue.

Der Häusliche Krieg ("Domestic War") Franz Schubert, 1861.

The opera in one act, D 787, is set to a libretto by Ignaz Franz Castelli based on Aristophanes' comedy *Lysistrata* (411 BC). The story tells how the Crusaders' wives go on sexual strike until their husbands agree to forswear war. The original title, now the subtitle, was *Die Verschworenen* ("The Conspirators"), but the Viennese political censor objected to this and the present title was adopted instead.

Haut Voltage ("High Voltage")   Marius Constant and Pierre Henry, 1956.

The ballet in one act, with a libretto by P. Rhallys and choreography by Maurice Béjart, tells what happens when a woman with supernatural powers causes the electrocution of two lovers.

Haydn Quartets   W.A. Mozart, 1782–5.

The six string quartets, No. 14 in G major, K 387, No. 15 in D minor, K 421, No. 16 in E flat major, K 428, No. 17 in B flat minor, K 458 (the **Hunt Quartet**), No. 18 in A major, K 464, and No. 19 in C major, K 465 (the **Dissonance Quartet**), are so named because the composer dedicated them to Haydn, who played the first violin in Mozart's house (while the latter played the viola).

Hear My Prayer (German, *Hör mein Bitten*) Felix Mendelssohn, 1844.

The hymn for soprano solo, choir, and organ has a text based on passages from the Psalms, such as: "Let my prayer come before me: incline thine ear unto my cry" (Psalm 88:2). It contains the section "O for the wings of a dove," sometimes sung separately, based on: "Oh that I had wings like a dove! for then would I fly away, and be at rest" (Psalm 55:6).

Hear Ye! Hear Ye!   Aaron Copland, 1934.

The ballet in one act, with a libretto by Ruth Page and N. Remisoff and choreography by Page, depicts a courtroom scene in which, following a murder in a night club, witnesses give their contrasting evidence of what happened. The title represents the call of the court official to pay heed to the words spoken.

The Heart of the Hills (Russian, *Serdtse gor*)   Andrei Balanchivadze, 1938.

The ballet in three acts (five scenes), with a libretto by Georgi Leonidze and N. Volkov and choreography by Vakhtang Chaboukiani, is based on an episode of Georgian history and tells how rebels, led by Djardje, rise up against their overlord.

The Heart's Assurance   Michael Tippett, 1950–1.

The song cycle for high voice and piano is set to poems by Sidney Keyes (1922–1943) and Alun Lewis (1915–1944), their premature deaths giving a general theme of love under the shadow of death. The composer dedicated the songs to Francesca Allison, a young woman he had loved who committed suicide in 1945.

Hebridean Symphony   Granville Bantock, 1915.

The composer wrote this work after hearing folk tunes from the Hebrides, Scotland.

The Hebrides   *see* **Fingal's Cave.**

Heidenröslein ("Little Moorland Rose") Franz Schubert, 1815.

The song for voice and piano, D 257, is set to words from a poem by Goethe written in 1771 and published in 1789. It concerns a young boy who plucks a wild red rose, despite its reluctance, and is pricked by it.

Heiligmesse ("Holy Mass")   Joseph Haydn, 1796.

The Mass No. 10 in B flat is so called because of the special treatment of the words "Holy, holy" in the Sanctus.

The Heirs of the White Mountain
(Czech, *Dědicové bílé hory*)   Antonín Dvořák, 1872.
The work for mixed chorus and orchestra, Op. 30, frequently referred to as *Hymnus* ("Hymn"), is set to the patriotic ode of the same name by Vítezslav Hálek, an assertion of the undying love of the Czechs for their country following Bohemia's humiliating defeat and loss of independence in the 1620 Battle of White Mountain (Czech, *Bílá hora*).

Ein Heldenleben ("A Hero's Life")
Richard Strauss, 1897–8.
The "hero" of the orchestral tone poem, Op. 40, is the composer himself, and in the fifth of the six sections, the *Hero's Works of Peace*, he quotes from several of his own compositions.

Helen of Troy   Jacques Offenbach arr. Antal Dorati, 1942.
The comic ballet in a prologue and three scenes, with a libretto by David Lichine and Antal Dorati, is based on the music and plot of the composer's opera La **Belle Hélène**.

Helena Variations   Granville Bantock, 1898.
The orchestral variations are named for the composer's wife, Helen Francesca Maude, née von Schweitzer, whom he married in the year of their composition.

Helicopter Quartet   Karlheinz Stockhausen, 1995.
The composition for string quartet and four helicopters was inspired by the composer's dream of helicopters flying in the sky. The work was originally performed by the Arditti String Quartet at the 1995 Holland Festival in Amsterdam. Each player flew in a separate helicopter which was then linked with the others by remote cameras and microphones. The roar of the rotorblades was an integral part of the performance, which was relayed to a concert hall where the composer mixed and matched the sound.

Héliogabale ("Heliogabalus")   various (see below), 1976.
The ballet (spectacle) in two parts based on a text by Antonin Artaud and choreographed by Maurice Béjart, is set to music from various sources including Giuseppe Verdi, J.S. Bach, and ritual African music. The plot deals with the ambiguous mysteries of the Middle Eastern cult of the sun which celebrates the union of man and woman in the figure of a hermaphrodite. The

work's subtitle is *L'Anarchiste couronné* ("The Anarchist Crowned"). Heliogabalus (Elagabalus) was the name of the sun god assumed by the Roman emperor Aurelius Antoninus (204–222), the "anarchist" of the subtitle, whose flouting of convention and orgiastic practices led to his assassination.

Heliogabalus Imperator ("Emperor Heliogabalus")   Hans Werner Henze, 1971–2.
The tone poem ("allegory for music") for orchestra is based on Hans Magnus Enzensberger's writings on the Roman emperor, Heliogabalus (204–222).

Helios   Carl Nielsen, 1903.
The overture, Op. 17, is a descriptive work depicting the sun's journey across the sky. It was composed while the composer and his wife were staying in Greece in a room overlooking the Aegean. Hence the classical inspiration. Helios, god of the sun in Greek mythology, was sacred to the island of Rhodes in the Aegean.

Hen Symphony   Joseph Haydn, 1785.
The Symphony No. 83 in G minor, the second of the **Paris Symphonies**, is so called for the "clucking" second subject of the first movement. The name dates no earlier than the 19th century. The symphony is also known as *La Poule*, its equivalent French title.

Henri VIII ("Henry VIII")   Camille Saint-Saëns, 1883.
The opera in four acts is set to a libretto by Léonce Détroyat and Armand Silvestre telling of the love of the English king, Henry VIII (1491–1547), for Anne Boleyn (1507–1536), his second wife, despite her own love for the Spanish ambassador, Gomez.

Here Comes the Bride *see* Wedding March (1).

Las Hermanas ("The Sisters")   Frank Martin, 1963.
The ballet in one act, with a libretto and choreography by Kenneth MacMillan, is based on Federico García Lorca's play *La casa de Bernarda Alba* ("The House of Bernarda Alba") (1936), telling what happens when the widowed Bernarda Alba confines her five daughters to the family home although they desperately seek love and freedom. *Cf.* **Feast of Ashes**.

Hermione   Max Bruch, 1872.
The opera is set to a libretto by Emil Hopffer based on Shakespeare's tragedy *The*

Winter's Tale (1610), in which Hermione is the noble wife of Leontes, who is wrongly charged with adultery.

Hero Quartet   Ludwig van Beethoven, 1805–6.

The String Quartet in C major, Op. 59 No. 3, the third of the **Razumovsky Quartets**, is sometimes known by this name for its intense dramatic qualities. Some claim it expresses the composer's triumph in overcoming his suicidal feelings.

Herodiade   Paul Hindemith, 1944.

The ballet in one act, choreographed by Martha Graham, follows Stéphane Mallarmé's dramatic poem *Hérodiade* ("Herodias") (1876–87) fairly closely: Herodias is confronted in a mirror with her past and her future and so led to accept her fate. *Cf.* **Hérodiade**.

Hérodiade ("Herodias")   Jules Massenet, 1881.

The opera in four (originally three) acts is set to a libretto by Paul Milliet and Henri Grémont (pen name of Georges Hartmann) based on Gustave Flaubert's story *Hérodias* (1877) about Herodias, the Jewish princess who in the biblical account (Matthew 14) was the granddaughter of Herod, mother of Salome, and wife of Herod Antipas. *Cf.* **Herodiade**.

Heroic Poem (The Geologists) (Russian, *Geroicheskaya poema (Geologi)*)   Nikolai Karetnikov, 1964.

The ballet in one act, with a libretto and choreography by Natalia Kasatkina and Vladimir Vasiliov, tells the story of three geologists, two men and a woman, who undertake an exploration of the taiga and experience extreme conditions.

Heroic Song (Czech, *Píseň bohatýrská*) Antonín Dvořák, 1897.

The symphonic poem, Op. 111, was not based on any historic or literary hero but took the artist as champion of the spirit as its theme. There is no evidence, however, that the composer had himself in mind, unlike Strauss in Ein **Heldenleben**.

Héroïque Polonaise ("Heroic Polonaise") Frédéric Chopin, 1836.

The Polonaise for Piano in A flat major, Op. 53, is so named for the "heroic" nature of its principal theme, which is solemn and almost declamatory. It is uncertain to what extent the composer intended the work to be a heroic poem inspired by nostalgia when he was in exile.

L'Heure espagnole ("Spanish Time") Maurice Ravel, 1907–9.

The opera ("*comédie musicale*") in one act is set to a libretto by Franc-Nohain (pen name of Maurice Legrand) based on his own comedy of the same name (1904). The story is set in 18th-century Toledo and tells how Concepción, wife of the clockmaker, Torquemada, uses the absence of her husband servicing the town's clocks to pursue her love affairs.

Hexaméron ("Hexameron")   various (see below), 1837.

Hexameron implies "six parts," and the work comprises six variations for piano on a march from Vincenzo Bellini's opera I **Puritani**, each written by a different composer: Franz Liszt, Sigismond Thalberg, Johann Peter Pixis, Joachim Herz, Karl Czerny, and Fryderyk Chopin. The first performance took place at a Paris charity concert in 1837, the composers sitting at a piano each and each playing his own variation. (*Hexameron* literally means "six days," the word originally referring to the biblical account of the creation of the world in this time.)

Hiawatha   Samuel Coleridge-Taylor, 1898–1900.

The cantata in three parts is based on H.W. Longfellow's poem *The Song of Hiawatha* (1855) about an American Indian brave who marries Minnehaha. The titles of the three parts are *Hiawatha's Wedding Feast*, *The Death of Minnehaha*, and *Hiawatha's Departure*. (The first and last of these correspond to those of Parts XV and XXI of Longfellow's original.)

Higglety Pigglety Pop!   Oliver Knussen, 1984–90.

The fantasy opera in one act is set to a libretto by the composer and Maurice Sendak based on the latter's children's book of the same title (1967) about a dog named Jennie who leaves home in search of excitement and becomes a theater performer.

Hiller Variations   Max Reger, 1907.

Although usually known by this title, the orchestral work has the full formal title *Variations and Fugue on a Theme of J.H. Hiller*, referring to the German composer Johann Adam Hiller (1728–1804). (It was once billed for a London Promenade Concert as the *Hitler Variations*.)

Hin und Zurück ("There and Back")   Paul Hindemith, 1927.

The opera in one act is set to a libretto by

Marcellus Schiffer based on an English revue sketch. The story reaches its climax with a pistol shot, at which point supernatural forces intervene to re-enact the plot in reverse. Hence the title.

Hippolyte et Aricie ("Hippolytus and Aricia")   Jean-Philippe Rameau, 1733.

The opera in a prologue and five acts is set to a libretto by Abbé Simon Joseph de Pellegrin based on Euripides's tragedy *Hippolytus* (428 BC) and Jean-Baptiste Racine's tragedy *Phèdre* ("Phaedra") (1677). The story is based on the classical myth telling of the adulterous love of Phaedra, second wife of Theseus, for his son, Hippolytus, who in turn loves Aricia.

Hiroshima   W. Bukovy, 1962.

The ballet in five scenes, with a libretto by Vladimír Vašut and choreography by Imre Eck, depicts the conflict of the American pilot who dropped the first atom bomb (on Hiroshima in 1945).

Der Hirt auf dem Felsen ("The Shepherd on the Rock")   Franz Schubert, 1828.

The song for soprano and piano, D 965, is based on Wilhelm Müller and Helmine von Chézy's poem *Der Berghirt* ("The Mountain Shepherd").

L'Histoire de Babar le petit éléphant ("The Story of Babar the Little Elephant")   Francis Poulenc, 1940–5.

The work for piano and narrator is set to Jean de Brunhoff's children's story of the same name (1931), itself the first of many such tales.

L'Histoire d'un soldat ("A Soldier's Tale")   Igor Stravinsky, 1918.

The balletic pantomime in two parts for two speakers, two dancers, and small orchestra, with a libretto by Charles Ferdinand Ramuz, is based on a Russian tale in which a soldier and a devil try to outsmart each other. (The devil wins.) The full title is *The Story of a Soldier: The Tale of a Renegade Soldier and the Devil.*

Histoires naturelles ("Natural Histories")   Maurice Ravel, 1906.

The song cycle for voice and piano is based on five of Jules Renard's miniature descriptions of animal life of the same title (1894). The five are: *Le Paon* ("The Peacock"), *Le Grillon* ("The Cricket"), *Le Cygne* ("The Swan"), *Le Martin-pêcheur* ("The Kingfisher"), and *La Pintade* ("The Guinea Fowl").

Historical Symphony   Ludwig Spohr, 1840.

The Symphony No. 6 in G major, Op. 116, was written to evoke four different periods of history. The first period (1720) is that of Bach and Handel, the second (1780) is that of Haydn and Mozart, the third (1820) is that of Beethoven, and the last (1840) is contemporary.

H.M.S. Pinafore, Arthur Sullivan, 1878.

The comic opera in two acts, to a libretto by W.S. Gilbert, tells how the sailors on board H.M.S. *Pinafore* are visited by the First Lord of the Admiralty, Sir Joseph Porter, who seeks the hand of Captain Corcoran's daughter, Josephine, herself in love with a common sailor, Ralph Rackstraw. The latter circumstance gave the subtitle, *The Lass That Loved a Sailor.*

Die Hochzeit des Camacho ("Camacho's Wedding")   Felix Mendelssohn, 1827.

The comic opera in two acts, Op. 10, is set to a libretto probably by Franz Voight (but earlier believed to be by Carl August Ludwig von Lichtenstein) based on the episode in Part 2, Book 2, Chapters 3 and 4 of Cervantes' *Don Quixote* (1605–15) in which the rich man, Camacho, is cheated out of his bride, Quiteria, just as he has provided a great feast for his wedding. ("It is like Camacho's wedding in Don Quixote, where Sancho ladled out whole pullets and fat geese from the soup-kettles at a pull." William Hazlitt, *On the English Poets*, 1818.)

Hodie ("Today")   Ralph Vaughan Williams, 1953–4.

The Christmas cantata is set to a text selected by the composer from the Bible and a range of writers including John Milton, George Herbert, Thomas Hardy, and Vaughan Williams's wife, Ursula. The reference is to the birth of Jesus. The original title was in Latin and English, *Hodie* (*On This Day*), but the composer preferred the one-word title, which has now been generally adopted.

Hoffmeister Quartet   W.A. Mozart, 1786.

The String Quartet in D major, K 499, is so named as it was published in Vienna by Franz Anton Hoffmeister.

"Ho-jo-to-ho!"

The war cry of Brünnhilde in Act 2, and of the other Valkyries in Act 3, of Wagner's *Die Walküre* in Der **Ring des Nibelungen**.

Holberg Suite (Norwegian, *Fra Holbergs tid*, "From Holberg's Time")   Edvard Grieg, 1884.

The suite for piano (later, strings) in five movements, Op. 40, was written to celebrate the bicentennial of the birth of the Norwegian dramatist Ludvig Holberg (1684–1754). The subtitle is *Suite in Olden Style for Pianoforte* (Norwegian, *Suite i gammel stil for Pianoforte*).

Holidays Symphony *see* **New England Holidays**.

"Der Hölle Rache" ("Hell's revenge").

The Queen of the Night's aria in Act 2 of Mozart's Die **Zauberflöte**, in which she swears revenge on Sarastro. A fuller version is: *"Der Hölle Rache kocht in meinem Herzen"* ("Hell's revenge boils in my heart").

The Holy Sonnets of John Donne Benjamin Britten, 1945.

The song cycle, Op.35, for soprano or tenor and piano, consists of settings of nine of the 19 sonnets in John Donne's *Holy Sonnets* (1609).

Homage to the Queen   Malcolm Arnold, 1953.

The ballet in one act, choreographed by Frederick Ashton, was produced in London on the night of the coronation of Queen Elizabeth II (June 2, 1953).

"Home, Sweet Home"   Henry Bishop, 1821.

The melody of this name was originally composed by Bishop for an album of national airs described as "Sicilian." In 1823 it was incorporated, with words by J.H. Payne, into Bishop's opera *Clari, or the Maid of Milan*. An altered version of the tune occurs in Donizetti's **Anna Bolena**, leading to a legal action by Bishop on a charge of "piracy and breach of copyright." Payne's text has the well-known words: "Be it ever so humble, there's no place like home."

Homelessness *see* **Lieder ohne Worte**.

Les Hommages ("Homages")   Nicolai Nabokov, 1951–2.

The composer explained the title of his cello concerto as follows: "I have called it 'Les Hommages' because it is dedicated to the memory or rather to reminiscences of melodies by Tchaikovsky ('Serenata di Pietro'), by Dargomijsky ('Ballata d'Alessandro') and Glinka ('Corale di Michele'). Within the musical texture of both the first and second movement are concealed bits of melodies by Tchaikovsky and Dargomijsky.... The last movement is a chorale on a famous theme by Glinka" (quoted in Berkowitz, p. 71).

L'Homme et son désir ("Man and His Desire"): Darius Milhaud, 1918.

The ballet in three scenes, Op. 48, with a libretto by Paul Claudel and choreography by Jean Börlin, depicts, according to Claudel, man's "eternal dance of longing, of desire and of exile, of his prisoners and of his abandoned lovers" (quoted in Koegler, p. 205).

Hope *see* **Lieder ohne Worte**.

L'Horizon chimérique ("The Fanciful Horizon")   Gabriel Fauré, 1921.

The song cycle, Op. 118, comprises four songs set to poems by J. de la Ville de Mirmont.

Horn Signal Symphony (German, *Mit dem Hörnersignal*, "With the Horn Call")   Joseph Haydn, 1765.

The Symphony No. 31 in D major is so called because the slow movement includes calls for four horns. An alternate German title is *Auf dem Anstand* ("At the Lookout"). An *Anstand* is a raised hide where the hunter lies in wait to sight his quarry.

Hornpipe Concerto   George Frideric Handel, 1739.

The Concerto Grosso in B minor, Op. 6 No. 12, is so named for the dancelike rhythm of the finale.

Horoscope   Constant Lambert, 1937.

The ballet in one act, with a libretto by the composer and choreography by Frederick Ashton, tells how the signs of the zodiac govern the lives of two young lovers.

The Horseman (Finnish *Ratsumies*)   Aulis Sallinen, 1975.

The opera in three acts, to a libretto by Paavo Haavikko, is set in Russia and Finland at the time of the union with Sweden and tells the story of Antti, the horseman of the title, and his wife Anna. As the words of the Prologue put it, "If you want to hear a tale that tells of a man and a woman, of war, horses, women, luck, death, then listen."

The Housatonic at Stockbridge *see* **Three Places in New England**.

House of Birds   Federico Mompou, 1955.

The ballet in one act, with a libretto and choreography by Kenneth MacMillan, is based on the Grimm brothers' fairy tale *Jorinda and Joringel* and tells of a birdwoman who catches young boys and girls and turns them into birds.

How Do You Do? Joseph Haydn, 1781.

The String Quartet in G major, Op. 33 No. 42, one of the **Russian Quartets,** is so nicknamed "because the words fit the first motif of the music" (Scholes, p. 681).

How Long, Brethren? Genevieve Pitôt, 1937.

The ballet in seven episodes, choreographed by Helen Tamiris, is based on the *Negro Songs of Protest* in the Siegmeister-Gellert collection. It is preceded by some solo spirituals, "the plaintive songs of slavery, songs of resignation and hope only in Heaven" (Margaret Lloyd, quoted in Koegler, p. 207).

HPSCHD John Cage, 1967–9.

The work is scored for seven harpsichord soloists (as the title suggests) and 51 or any number of computer-generated tapes.

Hugh the Drover Ralph Vaughan Williams, 1910–14.

The romantic ballad opera in two acts is set to a libretto by Harold Child based on folk material. It is set in the Cotswold Hills, England, during the Napoleonic Wars and tells how Hugh is accused of spying for the French and put in the village stocks, from which he is rescued by his betrothed, Mary. Hence the work's subtitle, *Love in the Stocks.*

Les Huguenots ("The Huguenots") Giacomo Meyerbeer, 1836.

The opera in five acts is set to a libretto by Eugène Scribe and Émile Deschamps and centers on the events surrounding the St. Batholomew's Day massacre (1572), when thousands of Huguenots (Protestants) were murdered in Paris by Roman Catholics.

Huldigungsmarsch ("Homage March") Richard Wagner, 1864.

The composer wrote the march for military band in honor of his patron, King Ludwig II of Bavaria, and it was first performed at the laying of the foundation stone of his long-planned festival theater at Bayreuth (1872).

Humming Chorus Giacomo Puccini, 1904.

This is the name usually given to the hidden chorus that ends Act 2 of **Madama Butterfly,** as Butterfly, Suzuki, and the baby, Dolore, watch and wait until Pinkerton arrives.

Humoresque (German *Humor,* "humor").

The word is used by some composers as a title for a lively and perhaps also rather sad piece. Examples are Dvořák's eight *Humoresques* for piano, Op. 101 (1894) and Schumann's *Humoreske* in B flat major for piano, Op. 20 (1839).

The Humpbacked Horse (Russian, *Konyok-gorbunok*) Cesare Pugni, 1864.

The ballet in five acts (ten scenes), with a libretto and choreography by Arthur Saint-Léon, is based on Pyotr Petrovich Yershov's fairy tale of the same name (1834), telling of the spectacular deeds of Ivanushka with the help of the Humpbacked Horse, through which he finally wins the Czar Maiden.

Hungarian Dances (German, *Ungarische Tänze*) Johannes Brahms, 1852–69.

The 21 piano duets are so named because they are largely based on Hungarian Gypsy tunes the composer had collected.

Hungarian Rhapsodies Franz Liszt, 1846–85.

The 19 works for piano are so called because many of them are based on or suggested by the Gypsy melodies the composer heard during his visit to Hungary in 1839–40.

Die Hunnenschlacht ("The Battle of the Huns") Franz Liszt, 1856–7.

The symphonic poem was inspired by Wilhelm von Kaulbach's mural of the same title (1834–7) depicting the legendary battle in the air between the ghosts of slain Huns and Romans after the Battle of the Catalaunian Plains near present Châlons-sur-Marne in 451.

Hunt Quartet W.A. Mozart, 1784.

The String Quartet No. 17 in B flat major, K 458, one of the **Haydn Quartets,** is so named because of the "hunting" motifs that introduce the first subject of the first movement.

Hunt Symphony *see* La **Chasse.**

Hunting Song *see* **Lieder ohne Worte.**

Le Huron ("The Huron") André Grétry, 1768.

The comic opera in two acts is set to a libretto by Jean François Marmontel based on Voltaire's satirical tale *L'Ingénu* ("The Innocent") (1767). The story is set in a coastal village in Brittany and tells what happens when the daughter of Saint-Yves does not wish to marry Gilotin, as their parents have arranged, because she has fallen in love with a Huron Indian.

The Hussite (Czech, *Husitská*) Antonín Dvořák, 1883.

The dramatic overture, Op. 67, was planned as the prelude to a patriotic trilogy dealing with the origins of the Hussite movement that the Czech theatrical director F.A. Šubert intended to write. In the event, he abandoned the trilogy after the first act.

Hymn of Jesus　Gustav Holst, 1917.

The choral work, Op. 37, for two choruses, female semichorus, and orchestra is set to a text translated by the composer from the apocryphal Acts of St. John, which contain a Hymn of Christ.

Hymn of Praise *see* **Lobgesang**.

Hymn of the Sun　Pietro Mascagni, 1898.

The chorus in Act 1, repeated in Act 3, of **Iris**. The opera opens at the home of Iris before dawn, and the music depicts the passage from night into day. It rises to a crashing climax while voices reiterate "*Calore! Luce! Amor!*" ("Warmth! Light! Love!"). *Cf.* **Hymn to the Sun**.

Hymn to St. Cecilia　Benjamin Britten, 1942.

The work for unaccompanied five-part choir, Op. 27, is a setting of W.H. Auden's poem *Anthem for St. Cecilia's Day* (1941), which was dedicated to the composer. St. Cecilia is the patron saint of music.

Hymn to St. Magnus　Peter Maxwell Davies, 1972.

The work for soprano and chamber orchestra is set to a Latin text based on the 12th-century Orcadian hymn known by this title. St. Magnus (*c.* 1075–1116) is the principal saint of Orkney, Scotland, which the composer has made his home since 1970. *Cf.* The **Martyrdom of St. Magnus**.

Hymn to the Sun　Nikolai Rimsky-Korsakov, 1909.

The aria with which the Queen of Shemakha introduces herself in Act 2 of The **Golden Cockerel**. *Cf.* **Hymn of the Sun**.

Hymnen ("Anthems")　Karlheinz Stockhausen, 1966–7.

The composition exists in three versions, including one for electronic instruments and *musique concrète* and one with added soloists. The anthems of the title are national anthems from around the world.

Hymnus (Dvořák) *see* The **Heirs of the White Mountain**.

Hymnus ambrosianus ("Ambrosian Hymn")　Darius Milhaud, 1946.

The Symphony No. 3, Op. 271, is so named because the fourth movement is for chorus and orchestra and evokes the type of plainsong known as Ambrosian chant, itself so named for St. Ambrose, the 4th-century bishop of Milan who reorganized singing and tonality in the Christian church.

Hymnus amoris ("Hymn of Love")　Carl Nielsen, 1896.

The cantata for soprano, tenor, baritone, and bass soloists, three-part children's chorus, five-part mixed chorus, and orchestra, Op. 12, is set to a Danish text by Johan Ludvig Heiberg and a Latin text by Axel Olrik, in which the successive ages of life (childhood, youth, the prime, old age) praise the power of love. Thus children sing "Love gives me life," ardent youth sings "Love is my aspiration and desire," men in their prime sing "Love is my spring, and deeds flower on its banks," and old men sing "Love is my peace, my sunset."

Hymnus Paradisi ("Hymn of Paradise")　Herbert Howells, 1950.

The requiem, for soprano, tenor, choir, and orchestra, is set to texts the composer collected from the Latin Mass for the Dead, Psalm 23, Psalm 121, the Burial Service, and a translation of the Salisbury Diurnal. He composed it in 1938 in memory of his young son, who died of poliomyelitis in 1935, but did not release it until 1950.

Hyperprism　Edgard Varèse, 1923.

The title of the four-minute work for small orchestra and percussion has no regular dictionary definition and "presumably means 'intensifying a prismatic function,' and therefore implies a basic unity strongly refracted by surface contrasts" (Whittall, p. 199). Put another way, the suggestion is of a geometrical object in four dimensions, an apt image for music of clashing sound objects.

I

I (Italian, "The").

For titles beginning with this word, see the next word, *e.g.* I **Masnadieri**.

I Was Glad   Hubert Parry, 1902.

The anthem with processional music was composed for the coronation of Edward VII in 1902. It is a setting of Psalm 122, whose first verse runs: "I was glad when they said unto me, Let us go into the house of the Lord."

"I trionfi" di Petrarcha ("The *Triumphs* of Petrarch")   Luciano Berio, 1974.

The ballet in six "triumphs" (scenes) was choreographed by Maurice Béjart, who took his inspiration from Petrarch's allegorical poem *Trionfi* ("Triumphs") (1374), describing the progress of the human soul from earthly passion to fulfillment in God. The six are: (1) *The Triumph of Love*, (2) *The Triumph of Chastity*, (3) *The Triumph of Death*, (4) *The Triumph of Fame*, (5) *The Triumph of Time*, and (6) *The Triumph of Eternity*.

Iberia   Isaac Albéniz, 1909.

The work contains four books of three pieces each for piano evoking the composer's native Spain. *Cf.* **Ibéria**.

Ibéria ("Iberia") Claude Debussy, 1905–8.

The orchestral work, the second of the **Images**, is an evocation of Spain, as the title implies. Its three parts are *Par les rues et par les chemins* ("By Highways and Byways"), *Les Parfums de la nuit* ("Night Scents"), and *Le Matin d'un jour de fête* ("Morning of a Festival Day"). The composer went to Spain for just one day in his life, and that to see a bullfight.

The Ice Break   Michael Tippett, 1977.

The opera in three acts, to the composer's own libretto, deals with the submerging of personality and the need for rebirth. The plot is set in an American airport where Lev, after 20 years in prison camps, arrives to join his wife, Nadia, and son, Yuri. Following a series of tense situations, Yuri is seriously injured in a race riot. He is operated on and finally released from his cracking plaster to be reconciled with his father. His release and reconciliation are the symbolic "ice break" of the title.

The Ice Maiden (Russian, *Ledyanaya deva*) Edvard Grieg, arr. Boris Asafiev, 1927.

The ballet in a prologue, three acts (five scenes), and an epilogue, choreographed by Fyodor Lopokov, tells the story of the Ice Maiden, who disguises herself as a beautiful girl to attract young men and bring them death. The music is mainly from the composer's **Peer Gynt**.

"Ich baue ganz auf deine Stärke" ("I am entirely based on thy power").

Belmonte's aria in Act 3 of Mozart's Die **Entführung aus dem Serail**, which Pedrillo instructs him to sing so as to conceal the placing of the escape ladders to the seraglio windows.

Die Ideale ("The Ideals")   Franz Liszt, 1857

The symphonic poem is based on Friedrich Schiller's poem of the same title (1796), a lament for the losses imposed on the human mind by the passage of time.

Idomeneo, rè di Creta ("Idomeneo, King of Crete") W.A. Mozart, 1781.

The opera in three acts, K 366, is set to a libretto by Giambattista Varesco based on Antoine Danchet's libretto for André Campra's opera *Idoménée* ("Idomeneo") (1712). The plot tells what happens when King Idomeneo, returning home from the Trojan War, runs into a sudden storm and vows to Neptune that in return for his safety he will sacrifice the first person he meets on landing. The subtitle is *Ilia ed Idamante* ("Ilia and Idamantes"), referring to the Trojan captive, Ilia, and the man who loves her, Idamantes, Idomeneo's son.

Idyll.

A term sometimes used for music of a peaceful pastoral character. A well-known example is Wagner's **Siegfried Idyll**.

Idyll: Once I Passed through a Populous City   Frederick Delius, 1930–2.

The work for soprano, baritone, and orchestra is set to Walt Whitman's seven-line poem *Once I Pass'd Through A Populous City* (1860), telling of the woman the poet met and loved in the city through which he passed.

Idylle ("Idyll")   François Serette, 1954.

The ballet in one act (three scenes), with a libretto and choreography by Alwyn Camble, tells of a white mare that lives quite happily with a black stallion until a gray circus horse appears.

Il (Italian, "The").

For titles beginning with this word, see the next word, *e.g.* Il **Maestro di capella**.

L'Île joyeuse ("The Island of Joy")   Claude Debussy, 1904.

The piano piece was inspired by Antoine Watteau's painting *L'Embarquement pour Cythère* ("The Embarkation for Cythera") (1717), depicting pairs of lovers departing from (rather than embarking for) the island of Cythera, the haven of love sacred to Venus.

Les Illuminations ("The Illuminations")
Benjamin Britten, 1940.

The song cycle, Op. 18, for high voice and string orchestra is a setting of nine of Arthur Rimbaud's prose poems in *Les Illuminations* and *Poèmes en prose* (1872–3). The movements are: (1) *Fanfare*, (2) *Villes* ("Towns"), (3) (a) *Phrase*, (b) *Antique*, (4) *Royauté* ("Royalty"), (5) *Marine*, (6) *Interlude*, (7) *Being beauteous*, (8) *Parade*, (9) *Départ* ("Departure"). The "illuminations" are the poet's insights into the poetic creative process and the world of the imagination. The dramatic ballet in one act of the same name, choreographed by Frederick Ashton and based on the composer's work, was produced in 1950.

Ilya Murometz (Russian, *Il'ya Muromets*)
Reinhold Glière, 1911.

The Symphony No. 3, Op. 42, is a musical portrait of the named Russian folk hero, a legendary warrior and defender of Russia.

Im Walde ("In the Forest")   Joachim Raff, 1869.

The Symphony No. 3 in F major, Op. 153, was inspired by woodland scenes. Hence the title.

Images ("Pictures")   Claude Debussy
1905–7, 1905–12.

The title is that of two distinct works. The first comprises two sets of piano pieces, the first (1905) having individual titles *Reflets dans l'eau* ("Reflections in the Water"), *Hommage à Rameau* ("Homage to Rameau"), and *Mouvement* ("Movement"), the second (1907) having *Cloches à travers les feuilles* ("Bells through the Leaves"), *Et la lune descend sur le temple qui fut* ("And the moon descends on the temple that used to be"), and *Poissons d'or* ("Goldfish"). The second work comprises three orchestral pieces: *Gigues* ("Jigs") (1909–12), **Ibéria**, and *Rondes de printemps* ("Rounds of Spring") (1905–9).

Images of Love   Peter Tranchell, 1964.

The ballet in nine parts, choreographed by Kenneth MacMillan, has its individual episodes based on speeches from Shakespeare's plays and his Sonnet CXLIV ("Two loves I have of comfort and despair"). The ballet was part of the triple bill premiered on the occasion of the Shakespeare Quatercentenary. (The others were **Hamlet** and The **Dream**.)

Imaginary Landscape   John Cage, 1939–52.

The title is that of five works. No. 1 (1939) is for two variable-speed phonograph turntables, frequency recordings, muted piano, and cymbal. No. 2, subtitled *March No. 1* (1942), is for percussion quintet. No. 3 (1942) is for percussion sextet. No. 4, subtitled *March No. 2* (1951), is for 12 radios with two players each, one operating the volume control, the other altering the wavelength. No. 5 (1952) is electronic and was prepared by recording sounds from 42 phonograph records, cutting the tape, and reassembling it at random. Hence the five "imaginary landscapes."

An Imaginary Trip to the Faroe Islands
(Danish, *En fantasirejse til Færøerne*)   Carl Nielsen, 1927.

The rhapsodic overture was written to order to welcome some Faroese visitors to Denmark. It incorporates the Faroese folksong popular in Denmark, *Easter Bells Chime Softly* (Faroese, *Paaskeklokken kimed' mildt*).

The Immortal Hour   Rutland Boughton, 1914.

The music drama in two acts is set to the composer's own libretto based on the Celtic-inspired drama of the same name (1900) by Fiona McLeod (pen name of William Sharp). It tells how Dalua, the Lord of Shadow, allows the mortal, King Eochaidh, to marry the fairy princess, Etain. The marriage lasts a year (the "immortal hour" of the title) and ends when Dalua reclaims Etain.

Imperial Mass *see* **Nelson Mass**.

Imperial Symphony (French, *L'Impériale*)
Joseph Haydn, 1774.

The Symphony No. 53 in D major was so first named in a 19th-century Paris catalog. The reason for the name is unknown, but there may have been some connection with a visit of the Empress Maria Theresa to the palace of Eszterháza while the composer was there.

The Importance of Being Earnest
Mario Castelnuovo-Tedesco, 1961–2.

The opera in three acts is set to the composer's own libretto based on Oscar Wilde's play of the same title (1895), telling of the courtships and betrothals of two young men-about-town, John (Jack) Worthing, known in town as Earnest, and Algernon (Algy) Moncrieff.

The Impresario *see* Der **Schauspieldirektor**.

Impromptu (French, "Improvised").

The term is used for a short piece of

instrumental music, often in song-like form, that gives the impression of having been composed or played on the spur of the moment. Well known examples are Schubert's 11 *Impromptus* for piano (1828) and Schumann's six *Impromptus* for piano duet, Op. 66 (1848).

Improvviso ("Impromptu").

The name usually given to the aria "*Un dì, all'azzurro spazio*" ("One day, in the open blue") in Act 1 of Giordano's **Andrea Chénier**, in which Chénier composes a poem on the beauty of the world and man's inhumanity to man. A fuller form is *Improvviso di Chénier*. *Cf.* **Impromptu**.

In a Summer Garden   Frederick Delius, 1908.

The rhapsody for orchestra was inspired by the composer's own "summer garden" at his home at Grez-sur-Loing, near Fontainebleau, France.

In a Well (Czech, *V studni*)   Vilém Blodek, 1867

The comic opera in one act is set to a libretto by Karel Sabina and tells what happens when Lidunka, wondering who she will marry, consults a local witch, Veruna, and is told she will see the face of her lover in a nearby well on St. John's Eve.

In Autumn (Norwegian, *I Höst*)   Edvard Grieg, 1866.

The concert overture, Op. 11, was based on a song that the composer had written earlier to a poem by Christian Richardt, "Autumn Storm." When reorchestrated in 1887 the overture was published under its equivalent German title, *Im Herbst*.

In Honour of the City   George Dyson, 1928.

The cantata is set to William Dunbar's poem *To the City of London* (*c.*1501), beginning "London, thou art of townes A *per se.*" *Cf.* **In Honour of the City of London**.

In Honour of the City of London
William Walton, 1937.

The cantata for chorus and orchestra is a setting of William Dunbar's poem *To the City of London* (*c.*1501). *Cf.* **In Honour of the City**.

In London Town *see* **Cockaigne**.

In Memoriam   (1) Arnold Bax, 1916; (2) Gian Francesco Malipiero, 1946.

Bax's funeral elegy for cor anglais and string quartet was written in memory of the Irish nationalist leader Patrick Pearse (1879–1916), executed following the 1916 Easter Uprising and a personal friend of the composer. The work was originally entitled *An Irish Elegy*. Malipiero's Symphony No. 4 was commissioned by the Russian-born conductor Serge Koussevitzky and was dedicated to the memory of his first wife, Natalie, who died in 1942.

In Memoriam Dylan   Daniel Jones, 1954.

The Symphony No. 4 was dedicated to the memory of the Welsh writer Dylan Thomas, who died in 1953. Thomas had been a friend of the composer since schooldays. *Cf.* **In Memoriam Dylan Thomas**.

In Memoriam Dylan Thomas   Igor Stravinsky, 1954.

The work for tenor, string quartet, and four trombones is a setting of Dylan Thomas's poem "Do not go gentle into that good night." It was composed soon after the poet's death in 1953 and was realized because Thomas had undertaken to write an opera libretto for Stravinsky.

In Nature's Realm *see* **Nature, Life, and Love**.

"In quelle trine morbide" ("In that soft lace").

Manon's aria in Act 2 of Puccini's **Manon Lescaut**, in which she tells of the chill in the splendor in which she lives and wishes she were back in the humble dwelling she once shared with Des Grieux.

In the Faery Hills (Irish, *An sluagh sidhe*) Arnold Bax, 1909.

The symphonic poem is the second of three with the overall title *Eire* (*i.e.* Ireland). The Faery Hills are in County Kerry.

In the Fen Country   Ralph Vaughan Williams, 1907.

The orchestral work is a symphonic impression of the region of eastern England (especially Cambridgeshire) known as the Fen Country or Fenland (or simply the Fens), so named for its reedy marshes and drainage channels.

In the Night   Fryderyk Chopin, 1970.

The ballet in four movements, choreographed by Jerome Robbins, is set to the composer's Nocturnes Op. 27 No. 1 (1835), Op. 55 Nos. 1 and 2 (1843), and Op. 9 No. 2 (1830), and shows three couples establishing different relationships as night draws on. The work is essentially Robbins's afterthought to his **Dances at a Gathering**. *See also* **Nocturne**.

In the South   Edward Elgar, 1903–4.

The concert overture, Op. 50, subtitled *Alassio*, was sketched at this Italian resort (in northwestern Italy, but "in the south" from England) and is an impression of Italy, its landscape, and its history.

In the Steppes of Central Asia (Russian, *V Sredney Azii*, "In Central Asia")   Alexander Borodin, 1880.

The "orchestral picture," a musical depiction of the approach and passing of a caravan, was composed to accompany a *tableau vivant* at the exhibition marking the silver jubilee of Alexander II's reign (1880). At some point the wording of the original Russian title was expanded in other languages to add the "steppes," presumably to lend a little local color.

In Windsor Forest   Ralph Vaughan Williams, 1930.

The cantata chorus and orchestra contains five items adapted from the opera **Sir John in Love**, itself based on Shakespeare's comedy *The Merry Wives of Windsor* (1599), in which an assignation is arranged for Falstaff in Windsor Forest.

L'Incontro improvviso ("The Unexpected Encounter")   Joseph Haydn, 1775.

The opera in three acts, to a libretto by Karl Friberth based on L.H. Dancourt's libretto for Gluck, *La Rencontre imprévue* (1764), is set in Cairo and tells how prince Ali and his beloved princess, Rezia, who has become the sultan's favorite following the couple's separation by pirates, are brought together again through an arranged "chance" meeting.

L'Incoronazione di Poppea ("The Coronation of Poppaea")   Claudio Monteverdi, 1642.

The opera in a prologue and three acts is set to a libretto by Gian Francesco Busenello based on Tacitus's *Annals*, XIII–XV (*c*.115). The story is set in Rome in AD 62 and tells what happens when Otho returns home to his mistress Poppaea to find that she has been appropriated by the emperor Nero.

Les Indes galantes ("Gallantry in the Indies")   Jean-Philippe Rameau, 1735.

The opera-ballet in a prologue, three entrées (acts), and an epilogue, with a libretto by Louis Fuzelier, tells four love stories from different parts of the world: *Le Turc généreux* ("The Generous Turk"), *Les Incas du Pérou* ("The Incas of Peru"), *Les Fleurs: Feste persane* ("The Flowers: Persian Festival"), and *Les Sauvages* ("The Savages"), this last from America, and involving a Native American girl. The name Indies formerly applied to both present-day India and adjacent lands and islands in the Far East (the East Indies) as well as to those lands of the Western Hemisphere that were discovered by Europeans in the 15th and 16th century, otherwise North and South America, with their American Indian inhabitants, and the present West Indies.

The Indian Queen   Henry Purcell, 1695.

The semiopera in five acts is set to a libretto based on the play of the same title by John Dryden and Robert Howard (1664) about rivalry between Mexicans and Peruvians. The "Indian queen" of the title is Orazia, daughter of the Inca king (who turns out to be king of the Mexicans), loved by the Aztec emperor, Montezuma.

Indian Suite   Edward MacDowell, 1891–5.

The Suite for Orchestra No. 2 in E minor, Op. 48, bases its themes on Indian (Native American) melodies, such as a harvest song, a war song, a women's dance, and a love song. Hence the title.

Indianische Fantasie ("Indian Fantasy")   Ferruccio Busoni, 1913.

The work for piano and orchestra, Op. 44, is based on American Indian themes. Hence the name.

Inès de Castro   James MacMillan, 1996.

The opera is based on the life of Inês de Castro (*c*.1323–1355), mistress (before his accession) of Peter I of Portugal and famous for her tragic death at the hands of assassins.

Inextinguishable Symphony (Danish, *Det uudslukkelige*)   Carl Nielsen, 1915–16.

The Symphony No. 4 was composed in World War I and its title indicates its intention to express the inextinguishable lifeforce that can somehow survive any disaster or tragedy. As Nielsen wrote in the foreword to the published score: "The composer has sought to indicate in one word what only music has the power to express in full: the elemental Will of Life. Music is Life and, like it, inextinguishable" (quoted in Staines and Buckley, p. 283).

L'Infedeltà delusa ("Deceit Outwitted")   Joseph Haydn, 1773.

The opera in two acts is set to a libretto by

Marco Coltellini telling how Vespina, sister of the peasant, Nanni, adopts various disguises to try and prevent the marriage for social advantage of the wealthy young Nencio to Filippo's daughter, Sandrina, who herself loves Nanni, while Vespina in turn loves (and is loved by) Nencio.

Initials R.B.M.E.   Johannes Brahms, 1972.

The ballet in four movements was choreographed by John Cranko and dedicated by him to the four top soloists of the Stuttgart Ballet, who danced the leads at the première. The initials are of their first names: Richard Cragun, Birgit Keil, Marcia Haydée, and Egon Madsen.

Inno delle Nazioni ("Hymn of the Nations")   Giuseppe Verdi, 1862.

The cantata for tenor, chorus, and orchestra was written for the International Exhibition in London and introduces different national airs.

Inori ("Adorations")   Karlheinz Stockhausen, 1973–4.

The work is for orchestra with one or two mimes who go through gestures of prayer in synchrony with the music's elaboration of a melody. Hence the Japanese title.

Inquest   N. Lloyd, 1944

The ballet in one act, with a libretto and choreography by Doris Humphrey, is based on a chapter in John Ruskin's essays on the respective duties of men and women, *Sesame and Lilies* (1865, 1871), and on a coroner's report on the death of starvation of a poor cobbler in the England of 1865.

Intégrales ("Integrals")   Edgard Varèse, 1924–5.

The work for small orchestra and percussion contains elements that were radical for its time, so that the title appears to be "a reference to the retreat from the exclusive, well-tempered scale into the integral world of instruments capable of a pitch continuum, filling the spaces between the semitones" (Whittall, p. 201). However, one could say more simply that the reference is to the way in which conventional (melodic) material and innovative (radical) material are truly "integral" to each other.

Intermezzo   (1) Richard Strauss, 1917–23; (2) Johannes Brahms, 1969.

Strauss's opera in two acts, Op. 72, to his own libretto, is based on a marital incident in his life, when his marriage was threatened by his receiving, through error, a love letter from an unknown admirer. The two main characters, the composer, Robert Storch, and his wife, Christine, thus represent Richard Strauss and his wife, Pauline. (Their names are sufficiently similar to suggest this identity, and their surnames are both bird names: *Strauß* is "ostrich" and *Storch* is "stork.") Brahms's romantic ballet in one act, choreographed by Eliot Feld, is set to his Op. 39 (waltzes for solo piano), and his *Intermezzi* Op. 117 No. 3, and Op. 118 No. 3, performed by three couples in a ballroom, the pianist being part of the setting. An "intermezzo" (Italian, "in the middle") is an interpolation in a longer event.

Les Intermittances du cœur ("The Vagaries of the Human Heart")   various (see below), 1974.

The ballet in two parts, choreographed by Roland Petit, is set to music by César Franck, Camille Saint-Saëns, Claude Debussy, Ludwig van Beethoven, Gabriel Fauré, Richard Wagner, and Reynaldo Hahn, and is a free treatment of some of the main episodes in Marcel Proust's series of autobiographical novels *À la recherche du temps perdu* ("In Remembrance of Times Past") (1913–27). The ballet was renamed *Marcel Proust Remembered* for its 1980 production in New York.

Interplay   Morton Gould, 1945

The ballet in four movements, choreographed by Jerome Robbins, is set to the composer's *American Concertette* (1943), with the four movements, arranged for four plus four dancers, having individual titles: *Free Play*, *Horseplay*, *Byplay* and *Teamplay*. Hence the overall title.

Intimate Letters (Czech, *Listy duvěrné*) Leoš Janáček, 1928.

The String Quartet No. 2 is so named because it is autobiographical. The "intimate letters" are those sent by the composer to Kamilla Stoesslová between 1917 and 1928. He originally planned to call the work *Love Letters*.

Into the Storm (Russian, *V buryu*)   Tikhon Khrennikov, 1939.

The opera in four acts is set to a libretto by Aleksei Fayko and Nikolai Virta based on the latter's novel *Loneliness* (1935). This centers on the so called Antonov Uprising during the Russian Civil War, as the anticommunist peasant rebellion in the Tambov province led by the Socialist Revolutionary, A.S. Antonov (killed 1922).

Intolleranza ("Intolerance") Luigi Nono, 1961.

The opera in two acts for five singers, mime, chorus, and orchestra is set to the composer's own libretto based on an idea by A.M. Ripellino. The work was originally entitled *Intolleranza 1960* and is a (left-wing) condemnation of the indifference and intolerance of the modern world. The plot itself concerns the plight of an immigrant caught in the machine of police surveillance and bourgeois capitalism.

"Invano, Alvaro" ("In vain, Alvaro").

The duet between Carlo and Alvaro in Act 4 of Verdi's La **Forza del destino**, in which Alvaro, now Padre Raffaello, tries to dissuade Carlo from challenging him to a duel.

The Invisible City of Kitezh (Russian, *Skazaniye o nevidimom grade Kitezhe i deve Fevronii*, "The Legend of the Invisible City of Kitezh and of the Maiden Fevronia") Nikolai Rimsky-Korsakov, 1903–5.

The opera in four acts is set to a libretto by Vladimir Ivanovich Belsky based on two Russian legends: that of St. Fevronia and that of the rescue of Kitezh from the Tatars. The story tells how the city is saved by becoming miraculously invisible, but Fevronia, wife of Vsevolod, prince of Kitezh, is captured. An alternate English title is *The Legend of the City of Kitezh*.

Invitation Mátyás Seiber, 1960.

The ballet in one act, with a libretto and choreography by Kenneth MacMillan, was inspired by Beatriz Guido's novel *The House of the Angel* (1954) and Colette's novel *Le Blé en herbe* ("Ripening Seed") (1923), and shows what happens to a young and innocent girl and her boy cousin when they encounter a quarrelling husband and wife at a house party.

Invitation to the Dance *see* **Aufforderung zum Tanz**.

Invocation Jan Ladislav Dušek, 1809.

The Piano Sonata No. 35 in F minor is one in which the composer aims to invoke the aid of benevolent powers in his stuggle with fate. Hence the title.

Iolanta Pyotr Tchaikovsky, 1891.

The opera in one act (nine scenes) is set to a libretto by the composer's brother, Modest Tchaikovsky, based on a Russian translation of Henrik Hertz's story *Kong Renés Datter* ("King René's Daughter") (1845), itself based on a tale by Hans Christian Andersen. The story is set in Provence in medieval times and tells what happens when Iolanta, daughter of King René of Provence, unaware that she has been blind from birth, has the truth revealed to her. The opera is sometimes billed in English as *Yolanta*.

Iolanthe Arthur Sullivan, 1882.

The comic opera in two acts, to a libretto by W.S. Gilbert, tells how Strephon, son of the fairy, Iolanthe, and a mortal, is in love with the shepherdess, Phyllis, who is courted by all of the peers of the House of Lords. Hence the subtitle, *The Peer and the Peri*.

Ionisation ("Ionization") Edgard Varèse, 1929–31.

The work for percussion instruments has a title that is the scientific term for the process whereby an atom liberates an electron and assumes a positive electric charge. In the composition, the rhythmic units or "sound masses" are similarly liberated and "charged."

Iphigénie en Aulide ("Iphigenia in Aulis") Christoph Gluck, 1774.

The opera in three acts is set to a libretto by Bailli Leblanc du Roullet based on Jean Racine's play *Iphigénie* (1674) itself based on Euripides's tragedy (*c*.405 BC) telling how Iphigenia, daughter of Agamemnon and Clytemnestra, is tricked into appearing at her sacrifice in Aulis by a promise of marriage to Achilles. *Cf.* **Iphigénie en Tauride**.

Iphigénie en Tauride ("Iphigenia in Tauris") Christoph Gluck, 1779.

The opera in four acts is set to a libretto by Nicolas François Guillard based on Euripides's tragedy (*c*.414 BC) telling how Iphigenia, who has been transported to Tauris as the priestess of Artemis, must sacrifice to the goddess all who come to the island. *Cf.* **Iphigénie en Aulide**.

Irdisches und Göttliches im Menschenleben *see* **Double Symphony**.

Iris Pietro Mascagni, 1898.

The opera in three acts, to a libretto by Luigi Illica, is set in Japan and tells how the pure girl, Iris, is loved by Osaka but is abducted and held in a brothel on his orders because she does not reciprocate his love.

Irische Legende ("Irish Legend") Werner Egk, 1955.

The opera in five acts is set to the composer's own libretto based on W.B. Yeats's verse play *The Countess Cathleen* (1892), which tells how the poet, Aleen, is abducted by demons, so that his lover, Countess Cathleen, offers to sell her soul to the Devil to redeem him.

An Irish Elegy *see* **In Memoriam** (1).

Irish Rhapsodies Charles Villiers Stanford, 1902–14.

The six orchestral pieces are based on Irish folktunes and legends. The composer's own favorite was said to be No. 4, *The Fishermen of Lough Neagh and What They Saw*.

Irish Symphony (1) Charles Villiers Stanford, 1887; (2) Hamilton Harty, 1904.

Stanford's Symphony No. 3 in F minor, Op. 28, pays tribute to his native land, as do many of his works. Harty's symphony in four movements is based on Irish folksongs. The first movement portrays the shores of a lough, the second a fair day, and the third the Antrim Hills. The fourth, titled *The Twelfth of July*, commemorates the Battle of the Boyne (July 1, 1690, or in modern calendars, July 12), in which the Protestant forces of William III of England defeated the Catholic supporters of the former James II.

Irmelin Frederick Delius, 1890–2.

The opera in three acts is set to the composer's own libretto telling how the Princess Irmelin, seeking true love, finds it (or him) at the end of the silver stream.

Isabeau Pietro Mascagni, 1911.

The opera in three acts, to a libretto by Luigi Illica, is a version of the Lady Godiva story, telling how Princess Isabeau, daughter of King Raimondo, is ordered by her father to ride naked through the streets at noon as a punishment for being unwilling to choose a husband.

Isadora Richard Rodney Bennett, 1981.

The ballet in two acts, with a libretto by Gillian Freeman and choreography by Kenneth MacMillan, tells of the stormy life and loves of the American dancer and teacher, Isadora Duncan (1877–1927). Her role is divided between an actress, who quotes from Duncan's memoirs and other sources, and a dancer.

Islamey Mily Balakirev, 1869.

The oriental fantasy for piano is based on the Caucasian folk dance known as the *islamey*, a type of lezginka.

The Island Spell John Ireland, 1913.

The piano piece is one of three in *Decorations*. Its inspiration came while the composer was swimming off Jersey, in the Channel Islands. (The other two are *Moonglade* and *Scarlet Ceremonies*.) *Cf.* **Sarnia**.

The Isle of the Dead (Russian, *Ostrov mërtvykh*) Sergey Rachmaninov, 1909.

The symphonic poem, Op. 29 was inspired by Arnold Böcklin's painting *Toteninsel* ("Island of the Dead") (1880), depicting a sinister-looking island with a fortress and a shrouded figure in a boat about to land. *See also* **Vier Tondichtungen nach A. Böcklin**.

L'Isola disabitata ("The Desert Island") Joseph Haydn, 1779.

The opera in two acts to a libretto by Pietro Metastasio tells how Gernando, his wife, Costanza, and her sister, Silvia, are shipwrecked on an island, where Gernando is captured by pirates.

Israel in Egypt George Frideric Handel, 1739.

The oratorio is set to a biblical text that the composer probably compiled himself. It tells the story of the captivity of the Hebrews (Israelites) in Egypt and of their departure from it, as recounted in Exodus. *See also* **Mosè in Egitto**.

Israel Symphony Ernest Bloch, 1912–16.

The work for two sopranos, two contraltos, bass, and orchestra is one of several of Jewish inspiration, and so is dedicated to the Jewish homeland. *Cf.* **Baal Shem**.

Istar ("Ishtar") Vincent d'Indy, 1896

The symphonic variations for orchestra are based on the legend of the descent into limbo of the Babylonian goddess, Ishtar (Astarte), the equivalent of the Greek Persephone. The work depicts her gradual disrobing at each of the seven stages of her descent by presenting the variations first, in decreasing complexity, and by stating the theme at the end, when she removes her final garment, in bare octave unison.

"It ain't necessarily so."

Sporting Life's cynical song in Act 2 of Gershwin's **Porgy and Bess**, in which he casts doubt on the truths set forth in the Bible.

Italian Caprice *see* **Capriccio italien**.

Italian Concerto J.S. Bach, 1735.

The work for harpsichord, BWV 971, published in the second section of the **Klavierübung**, is probably so called because it is in three movements, like the Italian **Concerto Grosso**, and because there are passages of alternation and contrast.

The Italian Girl in Algiers *see* **L'Italiana in Algeri**.

Italian Quartets   W.A. Mozart, 1772–3.

The seven string quartets, No. 1 in G major, K 80, No. 2 in D major, K 155, No. 3 in G major, K 156, No. 4 in C major, K 157, No. 5 in F major, K 158, No. 6 in B flat major, K 159, and No. 7 in E flat major, K 160, are sometimes so called because they were written while the composer was traveling in Italy. All but the first two were probably written in Milan, and all are in the Italian style, with three movements, not four.

Italian Serenade (German, *Italienische Serenade*)   Hugo Wolf, 1887.

The string quartet is so named because it is composed in the Italian style.

The Italian Straw Hat (Italian, *Il cappello di paglia di Firenze*, "The Florentine Straw Hat")   Nino Rota, 1946.

The comic opera in four acts is set to a libretto by the composer and Ernesta Rota based on Eugène Labiche's comedy *Un chapeau de paille d'Italie* ("An Italian Straw Hat") (1851). The story tells what happens when the horse of Fadinard, engaged to Hélène, eats an expensive Florentine straw hat belonging to Annaïs, who demands a replacement.

Italian Symphony   Felix Mendelssohn, 1833.

The Symphony No. 4 in A major, Op. 90, was so named by the composer because he began to write it in Italy. The Italian influence is particularly marked in the last movement, the Saltarello.

L'Italiana in Algeri ("The Italian Girl in Algiers")   Gioacchino Rossini, 1813.

The comic opera in two acts, to a libretto by Angelo Anelli, tells how Mustafà, the Bey of Algiers, is bored with his wife, Elvira, and seeks a European wife instead. The solution appears to be in Isabella, an Italian girl who comes ashore following a shipwreck off the Algerian coast, and who is brought to him.

Italienisches Liederbuch ("Italian Songbook")   Hugo Wolf, 1890–1, 1896.

The 46 songs for voice and piano are all settings of poems translated from the Italian by Paul von Heyse (1830–1914) and published in 1860.

"Ite sull'colle" ("Go upon the hills").

Oroveso's aria opening Act 1 of Bellini's **Norma**, urging the Druids to go upon the hills to see when the new moon appears.

Ivan IV   Georges Bizet, 1865.

The opera in five acts, to a libretto by François-Hippolyte Leroy and Henri Trianon, tells of events in the reign of the Russian czar, Ivan the Terrible (1547–84). The work was originally withdrawn by the composer, but the score is in the Paris Conservatoire library, where the Nazis during their occupation of Paris in 1944 are said to have prepared it for production at Dresden under the title of *König Turpin* ("King Turpin"), laying the scene in France at the Merovingian court of the 6th century. The actual first performance took place at Mühringen (Württemberg) in 1946 under the original title.

Ivan Susanin   *see* A **Life for the Czar**.

Ivan the Terrible   (1) (Russian, *Ivan Groznyy*) Sergey Prokofiev, 1975; (2) *see* The **Maid of Pskov**.

The ballet in two acts, with a libretto and choreography by Yuri Grigorovich, is based on the composer's music for Eisenstein's film of the same title (1942–5), together with excerpts from his Symphony No. 3 in C minor, Op. 44 (1928), and music for the film *Alexander Nevsky* (1938). The story is thus that of the Russian czar, Ivan IV (Ivan the Terrible) (1530–1584), but told from the perspective of his love for his wife, Anastasia. (It was after she was poisoned in 1560 that he set out on his reign of terror.)

Ivanhoe   Arthur Sullivan, 1890.

The opera in four acts is set to a libretto by Julian Russell Sturgis based on Sir Walter Scott's identically titled novel (1819). This is set in 12th-century England and centers on the brave knight of the name who loves Rowena, daughter of the Saxon, Cedric, and who returns with Richard I in disguise from the Third Crusade to rescue England from misrule.

Ivesiana   Charles Ives, 1954.

The ballet in six episodes, choreographed by George Balanchine, is set to the composer's six works: (1) **Central Park in the Dark**, (2) *Hallowe'en* (1911), (3) The **Unanswered Question**, (4) *Over the Pavements* (1906), (5) *In the Inn* (1906), (6) *In the Night* (1906). Episodes (2) and (4) have been dropped since the 1961 première of the revised version.

L'Ivrogne corrigé ("The Drunkard Reformed")   Christoph Gluck, 1760.

The opera in two acts is set to a libretto by Louis Anseaume based on Jean de La Fontaine's fable *L'Ivrogne en Enfer* ("The Drunkard in

Hell") (1668). The story tells what happens when Colette and her lover, Cléon, devise a scheme to balk the plan of her uncle, Mathurin, to marry her off to his old friend, Lucas, by simulating a scene in hell one evening when Mathurin and Lucas are drunk. The subtitle is *Le Mariage du diable* ("The Devil's Marriage").

J

Jack Pudding   Hans Werner Henze, 1949.
The ballet in three parts, with a libretto by the composer and choreography by Edgar von Pelchrzin, is based on Molière's comedy *George Dandin* (1668), depicting the miseries of a constantly deceived and cuckolded husband. The ballet has the alternate French title *Jacques Pudding*.

Jack-in-the-Box   Erik Satie, 1926.
The ballet in three dances, choreographed by George Balanchine, centers on a mischievous jumping jack like a rubber ball who is pushed about and played with by three ballerinas.

The Jacobin (Czech, *Jakobín*)   Antonín Dvořák, 1887–8.
The opera in three acts, Op. 84, to a libretto by Marie Červinková-Riegrová, tells how the Jacobin, Bohuš, back in Bohemia incognito from political exile, reestablishes his position in the community with the help of his musician friend, Benda.

Die Jagd ("The Chase")   Johann Adam Hiller, 1770.
The opera is set to a libretto by Christian Felix Weisse based on Michel-Jean Sedaine's libretto for Pierre-Alexandre Monsigny's opera *Le Roy et le Fermier* ("The King and the Farmer") (1762), in turn based on Robert Dodsley's farce *The King and the Miller of Mansfield* (1737).

Der Jahreslauf ("The Course of the Year")   Karlheinz Stockhausen, 1977.
The work, a scene from *Dienstag aus Licht* (*see* **Licht**), is a ballet of the years, decades, centuries, and millennia, scored for gagaku ensemble or western equivalent, with tape.

Die Jahreszeiten *see* The **Seasons** (1).

Die Jakobsleiter ("Jacob's Ladder")   Arnold Schoenberg, 1917–22.

The (unfinished) oratorio for six soloists, speaking chorus, chorus, and orchestra, is a setting of the composer's own text dealing with the Swedenborgian journey of the soul towards perfection. The allusion is to the ladder that Jacob dreamed of, which was "set up on the earth, and the top of it reached to heaven: and behold the angels of God ascending and descending on it" (Genesis 28:12).

Jamaican Rumba   Arthur Benjamin, 1938.
The piece for two pianos, the first of two *Jamaican Pieces*, has a descriptive title relating to its West Indian dance motif.

Le Jardin aux lilas ("The Lilac Garden")   Ernest Chausson, 1936.
The ballet in one act, with a libretto and choreography by Antony Tudor, is set to the composer's *Poème* for violin and orchestra, Op. 25 (1896), and centers on a farewell party held in a lilac garden before a marriage of convenience.

Le Jardin clos ("The Enclosed Garden")   Gabriel Fauré, 1915–18.
The song cycle for high or medium voice and piano, Op. 106, comprises settings of eight poems from Charles van Lerberghe's poetic cycle *Chansons d'Ève* ("Songs of Eve") (1904), an evocation of the awakening of Eve in the Garden of Eden.

La Jarre ("The Jar")   Alfredo Casella, 1924.
The ballet in one act, with a libretto by Luigi Pirandello and choreography by Jean Börlin, is a comedy telling how a broken jar is repaired by a village tinker only for him to find that he is trapped inside. The work is also known by the alternate Italian title, *La giara*.

Der Jasager ("The Yesman")   Kurt Weill, 1930.
The opera in two acts is set to a libretto by Bertolt Brecht based on a 15th-century Japanese *no*-play. The story tells what happens when a boy (the "yesman" of the title) plans to accompany his teacher and three older students on an arduous expedition to search for a wise man who can cure his sick mother.

Jazz Calendar   Richard Rodney Bennett, 1963–4.
The ballet in seven parts, choreographed by Frederick Ashton, is based on the children's rhyme: "Monday's child is fair of face, / Tuesday's child is full of grace, / Wednesday's child is full of woe, / Thursday's child has far to go, /

Friday's child is loving and giving, / Saturday's child works hard for his living, / And the child that is born on the Sabbath day / Is bonny and blithe, and good and gay."

"Je crois entendre encore" ("I seem to hear still").

Nadir's aria in Act 1 of Bizet's Les **Pêcheurs de perles**, in which he sings of his love for Leila.

"Je dis que rien ne m'épouvante" ("I say that nothing affrights me").

Micaëla's aria in Act 3 of Bizet's **Carmen**, in which she prays to God to deliver her from the fear which despite herself has overcome her as she seeks Don José in the mountains.

"Je suis Titania" ("I am Titania").

Philine's aria in Act 2 of Thomas's **Mignon**, which she sings as she remembers her role in the performance the strolling players have been giving of *A Midsummer Night's Dream*.

Jean de Paris ("John of Paris")   François Boieldieu, 1812.

The opera in two acts, to a libretto by Claude Godard d'Aucour de Saint-Just, is set in a Pyrenean village in the 17th century. The story tells what happens when the young widowed Princess of Navarre, destined to marry the Crown Prince of France, is about to arrive at an inn when preparations for her reception are interrupted by the appearance of the Prince himself, disguised as Jean de Paris.

Jeanie Deans   Hamish MacCunn, 1894.

The opera is set to a libretto by Joseph Bennett based on Sir Walter Scott's novel *The Heart of Midlothian* (1818), in which Jeanie Deans, a Presbyterian farmer's daughter, successfully pleads for the life of her sister, Effie, charged with murdering her illegitimate child.

Jeanne d'Arc au bûcher ("Joan of Arc at the Stake")   Arthur Honegger, 1934–5.

Honegger's dramatic oratorio, for four speakers, three sopranos, tenor, bass, ondes Martinot, choir, and orchestra, is set to a text written specifically for it by Paul Claudel, recounting the final hours of Joan of Arc, burned at the stake for heresy in 1431.

Jena Symphony   Friedrich Witt, c.1797.

The symphony in C major, originally attributed to Beethoven because it bore the inscription "par L. van Beethoven," is so named because it was found by the musicologist Fritz Stein at Jena, Germany, in 1909. The critic H.C.

Robbins Landon established in 1957 that it was actually by Friedrich Witt (1770–1836).

Jenůfa   Leoš Janáček, 1904.

The opera in three acts is set to the composer's own libretto based on Gabriela Preissová's drama *Její pastorkyňa* ("Her Foster Daughter") (1891), telling how the orphan Jenůfa is raised by her aunt and loved by two stepbrothers but disfigured by one of them out of jealousy when she prefers the other. In Czech-speaking countries the opera is known by the title of the originating play.

Jephtha   George Frideric Handel, 1751.

The oratorio is set to a biblical text compiled by the Revd. Thomas Morell and based on the story of Jephtha, one of the great judges of Israel, as told in Judges 11–12.

Jeremiah   Leonard Bernstein, 1941.

The Symphony No.1 has a mezzosoprano soloist in the last movement singing words from the biblical Book of Jeremiah. Hence the overall name.

"Jerum! jerum!"

Hans Sachs's cobbling song in Act 2 of Wagner's Die **Meistersinger von Nürnberg**. The words are simply imitative.

Jerusalem   Hubert Parry, 1916.

The work for unison chorus is a setting of the Preface to William Blake's long poem *Milton* (1804–8), in which the poet says he "will not cease from mental fight" "Till we have built Jerusalem / In England's green and pleasant land." It is thus not set to his *Jerusalem* (1815).

Jérusalem ("Jerusalem")   Giuseppe Verdi, 1847.

The opera in four acts is set to a libretto by Alphonse Reyer and Gustave Vaëz as a French version of the earlier opera I **Lombardi alla Prima Crociata**, which is partly set in the Holy Land.

Jessonda   Louis Spohr, 1822–3.

The opera in three acts is set to a libretto by Eduard Heinrich Gehe based on Antoine-Marin Lemierre's tragedy *La Veuve de Malabar* ("The Widow of Malabar") (1770). The story is set in India in the early 16th century and tells what happens when custom decrees that Jessonda, the Rajah's widow, must die on her husband's funeral pyre.

Jesu, Joy of Man's Desiring   J.S. Bach, 1723.

This is the English title of the chorale *Jesu, bleibet meine Freude* ("Jesu, Remain My Joy") in the church cantata No. 147, *Herz und Mund und Tat und Leben* ("Heart and Mind and Deed and Life").

Jeu de cartes ("Game of Cards")   Igor Stravinsky, 1937.

The ballet "in three deals" has a libretto by the composer and choreography by George Balanchine, who explained: "In *Card Game*, Stravinsky and I attempted to show that the highest cards — the kings, queens, and jacks — in reality have nothing on the other side. They are big people, but they can easily be beaten by small cards" (quoted in Koegler, p. 220). The central figure is the Joker.

Le Jeune Henri ("The Young Henry") Étienne-Nicolas Méhul, 1797.

The opera is set to a libretto by Jean-Nicolas Bouilly that was originally intended for Grétry and called *La Jeunesse de Henri IV* ("The Youth of Henry IV"). The subject of the work is thus the Protestant king Henry IV of France (1553–1610), otherwise Henry of Navarre, who in his teens led punitive expeditions against the Catholics. Long after the opera was forgotten, its overture continued to be performed as a concert piece under the title *La Chasse du jeune Henri* ("Young Henry's Hunt"), meaning his pursuit of the Catholics.

Le Jeune homme à marier (Danish, *Den unge mand skal gifts*, "The Young Man Must Marry")   Per Nørgård, 1965.

The television ballet, with a libretto by Eugène Ionesco and choreography by Flemming Flindt, is based on Ionesco's nonsense play *Jacques, ou la Soumission* ("Jacques, or Submission") (1955), telling of a young man who reluctantly agrees to marry but refuses all the brides his family presents to him until he meets one with three faces.

Le Jeune homme et la mort ("The Young Man and Death")   J.S.Bach, 1946.

The ballet in two scenes, choreographed by Roland Petit, is set to an orchestrated version of the composer's Passacaglia in C minor, BWV 582 (but without the Fugue), repeated three times. The story concerns a young Parisian painter who is driven by his girl to hang himself.

La Jeunesse d'Hercule ("The Youth of Hercules")   Camille Saint-Saëns, 1877.

The symphonic poem, Op. 50, is a musical depiction of the youth of the famous hero of classical mythology.

Jeunehomme Concerto   W.A. Mozart, 1777.

The Piano Concerto No. 9 in E flat major, K 271, was written for the French pianist, Mlle Jeunehomme, about whom little is known. Hence the name.

Jeux ("Games")   Claude Debussy, 1912–13.

The *poème dansée* (ballet) in one act, choreographed by Vaslav Nijinsky, tells how three tennis players, a man and two women, meet by chance in a garden. The "games" of the title are more of titillation than of tennis.

Jeux d'eau ("Fountains")   Maurice Ravel, 1901.

The work for piano is essentially a musical representation of playing fountains. The composer himself wrote that it was "inspired by the noise of water, and the musical sounds which fountains of water, cascades and streams make" (quoted in Norman Demuth, *Ravel*, 1947). The original score was headed by a quotation from the contemporary French poet Henri de Régnier: "*Dieu fluvial riant de l'eau qui le chatouille*" ("River god laughing from the water that tickles him").

Jeux d'enfants ("Children's Games") Georges Bizet, 1871.

The suite of 12 pieces for piano duet, Op.22, is designed to evoke memories of childhood, as the titles indicate: (1) *L'Escarpolette. Rêverie* ("The Swing: Daydream"), (2) *La Toupie: Impromptu* ("The Top: Impromptu"), (3) *La Poupée: Berceuse* ("The Doll: Lullaby"), (4) *Les Chevaux de bois: Scherzo* ("Wooden Horses: Scherzo"), (5) *Le Volant: Fantaisie* ("Shuttlecock: Fantasy"), (6) *Trompette et tambour: Marche* ("Trumpet and Drum: March"), (7) *Les Bulles de savon: Rondino* ("Soap Bubbles: Rondino"), (8) *Les Quatre Coins: Esquisse* ("Puss in the Corner: Sketch"), (9) *Colin-maillard: Nocturne* ("Blind Man's Buff: Nocturne"), (10) *Saute-mouton: Caprice* ("Leapfrog: Capriccio"), (11) *Petit Mari, petite femme: Duo* ("Little Husband, Little Wife: Duet"), (12) *Le Bal: Galop* ("The Ball: Gallop").

Jewel Song (French, *Air des bijoux*)   Charles Gounod, 1859.

Marguerite's aria in Act 3 of **Faust**, in which she admires the jewels in the casket brought to her by Faust and Méphistophélès. Its leading words are: "*Ah! je ris de me voir*" ("Oh, I laugh to see myself").

Jewels   various (see below), 1967.

The ballet in three parts, choreographed by George Balanchine, comprises three plotless divertissements each named for a jewel and set to music by a different composer, as follows: (1) *Emeralds*, to Gabriel Fauré's incidental music to *Pelléas et Mélisande*, Op. 80 (1901), and *Shylock*, Op. 57 (1889), (2) *Rubies*, to Igor Stravinsky's *Capriccio* for piano and orchestra (1928–9), (3) *Diamonds*, to Pyotr Tchaikovsky's **Polish Symphony** (but without the first movement).

The Jewels of the Madonna *see* **I Gioielli della Madonna**.

Jinx   Benjamin Britten, 1942.

The ballet in one act, choreographed by Lew Christensen, deals with superstition, as the title implies, and centers on a clown who is shunned by everybody for causing mishaps.

Joan of Arc   N. Peiko, 1957.

The ballet in three acts, with a libretto by V. Pletneva and choreography by Vladimir Burmeyster, tells the story of the life of Joan of Arc (*c.*1412–1431). *Cf.* **Giovanna d'Arco**, The **Maid of Orleans**.

Joan von Zarissa   Werner Egk, 1940.

The ballet in a prologue, four scenes, and an epilogue, with a libretto by the composer, recounts the amorous adventures of a 15th-century Burgundian knight. Egk took his inspiration from a painting by the 15th-century French artist, Jean Fouquet.

Job   (1) Ralph Vaughan Williams, 1930; (2) Luigi Dallapiccola, 1949–50.

Vaughan Williams's "masque for dancing" in eight scenes, choreographed by Ninette de Valois, has a libretto by Geoffrey Keynes and Gwen Raverat based on William Blake's 21 watercolor illustrations for the biblical book of Job (1825). Dallapiccola's opera in one act is set to the composer's libretto based on this same book.

Jocelyn   Benjamin Godard, 1888.

The opera is set to a libretto by Paul Armand Silvestre and Victor Capoul based on Alphonse de Lamartine's narrative poem of the same name (1836). This purports to be the diary of a young seminarist, Jocelyn, who flees from the Revolution to a hiding place in the mountains.

Johannesburg Festival Overture
William Walton, 1956.

The concert overture was composed to mark the 70th anniversary of the city of Johannesburg, South Africa, where it was first performed.

Joke Quartet   Joseph Haydn, 1781.

The string quartet in E flat major, Op. 33 No. 38, one of the **Russian Quartets**, is so named for the unusual repetition of the main theme in the finale, with a two-bar rest afer each phrase.

La Jolie Fille de Gand ("The Fair Maid of Ghent")   Adolphe Adam, 1839.

The pantomime ballet in three acts (nine scenes), with a libretto by Jules-Henri Vernoy de Saint-Georges and François Albert and choreography by the latter, tells of Beatrix, the "fair maid of Ghent" of the title, who is about to marry Benedict but who is also courted by the Marquis de San Lucar.

La Jolie Fille de Perth ("The Fair Maid of Perth")   Georges Bizet, 1867.

The opera in four acts is set to a libretto by Jules-Henri Vernoy de Saint-Georges and Jules Adenis loosely based on Sir Walter Scott's novel *The Fair Maid of Perth* (1823), set in Scotland around the turn of the 15th century and telling the story of Catherine Glover, "the fair maid of Perth," loved by the armorer, Henry Smith.

Jones Beach   Jurriaan Andriessen, 1950.

The ballet in four parts, choreographed by George Balanchine, depicts episodes from a typical summer's day at New York's famous beach named in the title.

Le Jongleur de Notre Dame ("Our Lady's Juggler")   (1) Jules Massenet, 1902; (2) Peter Maxwell Davies, 1978.

Massenet's opera in three acts is set to a libretto by Maurice Léna based on Anatole France's story *L'Étui de nacre* ("The Mother-of-Pearl Case") (1892), itself based on a medieval miracle play. The plot centers on the juggler, Jean, who is a novice in an order of monks. Davies's masque in one act, for baritone, mime, chamber ensemble, and children's band, is set to his own libretto and based on the same story.

Jonny spielt auf ("Johnny Strikes Up")
Ernst Krenek, 1927.

The opera in two parts, to the composer's own libretto, tells how the black jazz musician,

Johnny, becomes the world's greatest living player.

Joseph   (1) George Frideric Handel, 1744; (2) Étienne-Nicolas Méhul, 1807.

Handel's oratorio, with full title *Joseph and His Brethren*, is based on James Miller's play of the same (full) title (1744) centering on the son of Jacob and Rachel whose story is told in Genesis 30–50. Méhul's opera in three acts is set to a libretto by Alexandre Duval based on the same source.

Joseph the Beautiful   (Russian, *Iosif prekrasnyy*)   Sergei Vasilenko, 1925.

The ballet in two acts (five scenes), choreographed by Kasyan Goleizovsky, tells how the biblical boy Joseph is sold into Egyptian slavery and becomes the object of the amorous pursuits of Pharaoh's wife.

Die Josephslegende   ("The Legend of Joseph")   Richard Strauss, 1913–14.

The ballet in one act, with a libretto by Harry Graf Kessler and Hugo von Hofmannsthal, and choreography by Mikhail Fokine, tells the biblical story of the shepherd, Joseph, and his rejection of the wife of Potiphar, but sets it in 16th-century Venice.

Joshua   George Frideric Handel, 1748.

The oratorio is set to a text probably by the Revd. Thomas Morell based on the biblical story of Joshua, leader of the Israelites after Moses, as told in Exodus and the book named for him.

Jota Aragonesa   (Russian, *Aragonskaya khota*, "The Aragon Jota")   Mikhail Glinka, 1845.

The ballet in one act, choreographed by Michel Fokine, is a somewhat sinister representation of Spanish life. The jota is a traditional dance of northern Spain performed by couples in rapid triple time.

Une Journée   ("A Day")   Darius Milhaud, 1946.

The suite of easy piano pieces, Op. 269, is a musical evocation of a child's responses to the world around him from dawn to dusk.

The Journey   Pierre Henry, 1962.

The ballet, with a libretto and choreography by Maurice Béjart, is based on the Tibetan *Book of the Dead* and shows the way of life, which is the journey to death, from which man is reborn. The ballet was originally produced in Cologne under the equivalent German title, *Die Reise*. It is also known by its French title, *Le Voyage*.

Jovita   Théodore Labarre, 1853.

The pantomime ballet in three scenes, with a libretto and choreography by Joseph Mazilier, tells the story of Jovita, a rich farmer's daughter, who loves the naval officer, Don Altamirano. The subtitle is *Les Boucaniers* ("The Buccaneers"), referring to the camp of buccaneers where her lover is held captive and which she enters dressed as a gypsy to free him.

The Joyous Peasant *see* **Lieder ohne Worte**.

Jubel-Ouvertüre   ("Jubilee Overture")   Carl Maria Weber, 1818.

The concert overture, Op. 59, was composed as a companion piece to the *Jubel-Kantate* ("Jubilee Cantata") (1818) for the 50th anniversary of the accession of the king of Saxony, Frederick Augustus I (1750–1827).

Jubilate   ("O Be Joyful").

The opening word of Psalm 100 (Psalm 99 in the Latin Psalter), as the title of a setting of this. A fuller form is *Jubilate Deo* ("O Be Joyful to God"), the actual words of the English Psalter being "Make a joyful noise unto the Lord." Examples of the setting are Purcell's *Jubilate Deo* in D (1694) and Britten's *Jubilate Deo* (1961). *Cf.* **Exsultate, Jubilate**.

Judas Maccabaeus   George Frideric Handel, 1746.

The oratorio is set to a text by the Revd. Thomas Morell based on the exploits of the Jewish warrior Judas Maccabaeus who won victories over the Syrians and purified the Temple. His story is told in the Apocrypha in 1 Maccabees 36–61.

The Judgment of Paris   Kurt Weill, 1938.

The ballet in one act, with a libretto by Hugh Laing and choreography by Antony Tudor, is set to the composer's suite from Die **Dreigroschenoper** and parallels the classical story of Paris's selection of Aphrodite as the most beautiful goddess by a modern equivalent in a sordid night bar. *Cf.* Le **Jugement de Pâris**.

Judith   (1) Thomas Arne, 1761; (2) (Russian, *Yudif*) Alexander Serov, 1863; (3) Hubert Parry, 1888; (4) Arthur Honegger, 1926.

Arne's oratorio is set to a text by Isaac Bickerstaffe based on the Book of Judith in the Apocrypha, which tells of the young widow so named who cut off the head of the Babylonian general Holofernes to save her city. Serov's opera in five acts, to a libretto by K. Zvantsev and D. Lobanov with the assistance of Apollon Maykov, Parry's oratorio, for soprano, alto, tenor, and bass soloists, chorus, and orchestra, and Honegger's opera in three acts, to a libretto by René Morax, are all based on the same source.

Le Jugement de Pâris ("The Judgment of Paris")   Cesare Pugni, 1846.

The ballet divertissement in one act, choreographed by Jules Joseph Perrot, re-enacts the classical story of Paris's selection of Aphrodite (Venus) as the most beautiful of three goddesses, the others being Hera (Juno) and Athena.

Le Juif polonais ("The Polish Jew") Camille Erlanger, 1900.

The opera is set to a libretto by Henri Cain and Pierre Barthélemy Gheusi based on Erckmann-Chatrian's novel of the same name (1869), familiar in Leopold Lewis's dramatization titled *The Bells* (1871), in which the central character is the guilt-ridden burgomaster Mathias, the "Polish Jew" of the original title.

La Juive ("The Jewess")   Fromental Halévy, 1835.

The opera in five acts to a libretto by Eugène Scribe is set in 15th-century Constance and tells what happens when the Jewess of the title, Rachel, discovers that her lover, whom she knows as Samuel, is actually Prince Léopold.

Julien ("Julian")   Gustave Charpentier, 1913.

The opera in a prologue and four acts is set to the composer's own libretto telling of the love of the poet, Julien, for the heroine of the earlier opera **Louise**, of which it is thus the sequel. The subtitle is *La Vie du poète* ("The Poet's Life").

Julietta   Bohuslav Martinů, 1938.

The opera in three acts is set to the composer's own libretto based on Georges Neveux's novel *Juliette, ou La Clé des songes* ("Juliet, or The Key of Dreams") (1930). It tells how Michel, a traveling bookseller, returns to the small coastal town where he has haunting memories of Juliette, a girl singing at a window. The subtitle is *The Dream Book* (Czech, *Snár*).

The Jumping Frog of Calaveras County Lukas Foss, 1950.

The opera in one act is set to a libretto by J. Karsavina based on Mark Twain's story *The Celebrated Jumping Frog of Calaveras County* (1865), itself based on an old folk tale. It tells how the jumping frog, Dan'l Webster, is defeated in a contest when its gullet is filled with quail shot while its gambler owner, Jim Smiley, has his attention distracted.

Der Junge Lord ("The Young Lord")   Hans Werner Henze, 1965.

The opera in two acts is set to a libretto by Ingeborg Bachmann based on a parable in Wilhelm Schauff's *Der Scheik von Alexandria und seine Sklaven* ("The Sheik of Alexandria and his Slaves") (1827). The plot tells what happens when Sir Edgar introduces his nephew, Lord Barrett, the "young lord" of the title, to the inhabitants of the small German provincial town of Grünwiesel.

Die Junge Magd ("The Young Servant Girl")   Paul Hindemith, 1922.

The six songs for alto, flute, clarinet, and string quartet are set to lyric poems by the Austrian poet Georg Trakl (1887–1914).

Jungfernquartette *see* **Russian Quartets**.

Jungle   Henk Badings, 1961.

The ballet in four scenes, choreographed by Rudi van Dantzig, is a parable that depicts man's cruelty to man through the social attitudes of animals in a jungle.

Jupiter Symphony   W.A. Mozart, 1788.

The Symphony No. 41 in C major, K 551, has a name that has still not been satisfactorily explained. It is even uncertain when or by whom it was introduced, but it may have first appeared in a program for a performance by the Philharmonic Society of London in 1821. The composer's son, Franz Xaver Wolfgang Mozart, claimed that it was invented by the violinist and impresario, Johann Peter Salomon (*see* **London Symphonies**). "It is not well suited to any but the last movement and to the first at a pinch" (Blom, p. 275).

K

Kaddish Symphony   Leonard Bernstein, 1963.

The Symphony No. 3, for orchestra, mixed chorus, boys' chorus, speaker, and soprano solo, is a setting of the Kaddish, the Jewish mourners' prayer.

Der Kaiser von Atlantis ("The Emperor of Atlantis")   Viktor Ullmann, 1944.

The opera (legend) in four scenes, Op. 49, to a libretto by Peter Kien, was composed in the concentration camp of Theresienstadt (Terezín) and is a vigorous defiance of Nazism. The opera was rehearsed at the camp and had reached dress rehearsal stage when the Nazi guards realized that the central character, Kaiser Überall ("Emperor Everywhere"), was a satirical portrait of Hitler. Both composer and librettist were sent to Auschwitz, where they died. The subtitle is *Die Tod-Verweigerung* ("The Denial of Death").

Kaiser-Walzer ("Emperor Waltz")   Johann Strauss II, 1888.

The waltz, Op. 437, was composed to mark the 40th anniversary of the accession of the Austrian emperor, Franz Josef (1848).

Kaisermarsch ("Emperor March")   Richard Wagner, 1871.

The work for unison male voices and orchestra was composed to mark the German victory in the Franco-Prussian War (1870) and the election of Wilhelm I as emperor of Prussia (1871).

Kakadu Variations   Ludwig van Beethoven, 1798.

The Variations for piano trio, Op. 121a, take their name from their theme, Wenzel Müller's song *Ich bin der Schneider Kakadu* ("I am the Tailor Cockatoo") from the musical play *Die Schwestern von Prag* ("The Sisters from Prague") (1794).

Kalkabrino   Léon Minkus, 1891.

The fantastic ballet in three acts, with a libretto by Modest Tchaikovsky and choreography by Marius Petipa, is set in Provence and tells the story of a smuggler captain, Kalkabrino, who is captivated by a peasant girl but falls prey to evil spirits.

Kamarinskaya ("Wedding Song")   Mikhail Glinka, 1848.

The orchestral fantasia on two Russian folksongs takes its title from the dance of the name (itself said to come from the village of Kamarichi).

Kammermusik No. 2 ("Chamber Music No. 2")   Paul Hindemith, 1978.

The ballet in four movements, choreographed by George Balanchine, is set to the composer's work of the title, Op. 36 No.1 (1924), for piano and 12 solo instruments, and depicts encounters between two couples of soloists and an all-male corps of eight dancers. Hindemith himself composed seven instrumental works so titled between 1922 and 1927. They are not themselves chamber music (the first is a suite for 12 instruments, the other six are concertos), but they were written for a festival of contemporary chamber music.

Kanon Pokajanen ("Canon of Repentance") Arvo Pärt, 1998.

The choral work is a setting of an 8th-century text by St. Andrew of Crete dealing with the symbolism of transformation: night into day, prophecy into fulfillment, sin into redemption, this last coming through repentance.

Karelia   Jean Sibelius, 1895.

The overture and suite for orchestra, Opp. 10 and 11, take their name from the province of Karelia in southern Finland.

Kashchey the Immortal (Russian, *Kashchey Bessmertnyy*)   Nikolai Rimsky-Korsakov, 1902.

The opera in one act is set to a libretto by the composer based on Ye.M. Petrovsky's account of the wicked magician whose death is concealed in various animals and objects inside one another. The traditional tale tells of an distant island on which an oak tree grows. Under the oak is buried a chest. In the chest is a hare, in the hare is a duck, in the duck is an egg, and in the egg is the death of Kashchey the Immortal. His name literally means "captive."

Kát'a Kabanová   Leoš Janáček, 1921.

The opera in three acts is set to the composer's own libretto based on Alexander Ostrovsky's drama *The Storm* (Russian, *Groza*) (1859), in which Katya, married to Tikhon, has a secret passion for Boris.

Katalyse ("Catalyst")   Dmitry Shostakovich, 1961.

The ballet in three movements, choreographed by John Cranko, is set to the composer's Piano Concerto No. 1 in C minor, Op. 35 (1933), and shows the effect of the catalyst, a male dancer, on two contrasting groups of dancers dressed in black and white.

Katarina ("Catherine")   Arthur Rubinstein and Adolphe Adam, 1935.

The ballet in three acts (seven scenes), with a libretto and choreography by Leonid Lavrovsky, is based on a story from the history of the Russian serf theater telling how the serf ballerina, Katarina, commits suicide to escape the pursuits of the governor.

Katerina Nikolai Arkas, 1899.

The opera in three acts is set to the composer's own libretto based on Taras Shevchenko's poem of the same name (1840), telling the tragic tale of Katerina, a young Ukrainian girl abandoned with her baby by the army officer who had made her pregnant.

Katerina Izmaylova *see* **Lady Macbeth of the Mtsensk District**.

Kegelstatt Trio ("Skittle Alley Trio") W.A. Mozart, 1786.

The Trio in E flat for piano, clarinet, and viola, K 498, is said to be so named because the composer planned it mentally during a game of skittles.

Keltic Sonata Edward MacDowell, 1900.

The Piano Sonata No. 4 in E minor, Op. 59, was inspired by the Irish legend about the beautiful Deirdre ("of the Sorrows"), who killed herself to escape her unhappy marriage to Conchobhar, the ageing king of Ulster. The work was dedicated to Grieg, and above the dedication the following quatrain was printed: "Who minds now Keltic days of Yore / Dark Druid rhymes that thrall / Deirdre's Song and wizard lore / or Great Cuchulin's fall" (quoted in Berkowitz, p. 83).

Kermesse in Bruges (Danish, *Kermessen i Brügge*) Holger Simon Paulli, 1851.

The romantic ballet in three acts, choreographed by August Bournonville, was inspired by the paintings of Jan Steen and David Teniers and is set at the kermesse (holy fair) in Bruges, where three brothers experience fantastic adventures. Hence the subtitle, *The Three Gifts* (Danish, *De tre Gaver*).

Keto and Kote (Russian, *Keto i Kote*) Viktor Dolidze, 1919.

The comic opera in four acts is set to the composer's own libretto based on Avksenty Tsagareli's comedy *Khanuma* (1882). The story tells of the love intrigue between Keto, a rich Georgian merchant's daughter, and Kote, a prince's nephew.

Kettentanz ("Chain Dance") Johann Strauss I and Johann Simon Mayer, 1971.

The ballet in nine dances, choreographed by Gerald Arpino, progresses in an unbroken chain of dances for six couples as a virtuoso display of energy.

Kettledrum Mass *see* **Paukenmesse**.

Khadra Jean Sibelius, 1946.

The ballet in one act, choreographed by Celia Franca, is based on the composer's incidental music to *Belshazzar's Feast*, Op. 51 (1906). The story unfolds as a series of Persian miniatures around Khadra, a young girl who is full of wondering astonishment at what life has in store for her.

Khovanshchina ("The Khovansky Affair") Modest Mussorgsky, 1886.

The opera in five acts is set to a libretto by the composer and Vladimir Stasov based on the complex political situation that existed at the time of the accession of Peter the Great in 1682. (The opera was unfinished and was completed by Rimsky-Korsakov.) It concerns the rivalry between the different factions, and notably that of the Streltsy (Guards), led by Prince Ivan Khovansky (executed 1682), against that of Peter's adherents, led by Prince Galitsin (Golitsyn) (1643–1714).

Kikimora Anatol Lyadov, 1910.

The symphonic poem portrays the kikimora, the ugly hobgoblin in female form of Russian fairy tales. (Its name is related to the *mare* of "nightmare.")

Kinderszenen ("Scenes from Childhood"), Robert Schumann, 1838.

The suite of 13 piano pieces, Op. 15, was intended to evoke happy memories of childhood for the elderly. Hence the general title (which some mistakenly take to imply that the pieces were intended for children to play). The individual titles are as follows: (1) *Von fremden Ländern und Menschen* ("From Foreign Countries and Peoples"), (2) *Kuriose Geschichte* ("Strange Story"), (3) *Haschemann* ("Catch Me If You Can"), (4) *Bittendes Kind* ("Suppliant Child"), (5) *Glückes genug* ("Perfect Happiness"), (6) *Wichtige Begebenheit* ("An Important Event"), (7) *Träumerei* ("Dreaming"), (8) *Am Kamin* ("By the Fireside"), (9) *Ritter vom Steckenpferd* ("Knight of the Hobbyhorse"), (10) *Fast zu ernst* ("Almost Too Serious"), (11) *Fürchtenmachen* ("Frightening"), (12) *Kind im Einschlummern* ("Child Falling Asleep"), and *Der Dichter spricht* ("The Poet Speaks").

Kindertotenlieder ("Songs of the Death of Children") Gustav Mahler, 1901–4.

The song cycle consists of five songs set to Friedrich Rückert's poems of the same title (written 1834, published 1872) on the death of his two children, presumably from diphtheria.

Kinetic Molpai   Jess Meeker, 1935.

The ballet in 11 sections, choreographed by Ted Shawn, comprises a succession of individual dances about the human power of self-assertion, realized through a display of drive and male energy. The sections are: (1) *Strife*, (2) *Oppositions*, (3) *Solvent*, (4) *Dynamic Contrasts*, (5) *Resilience*, (6) *Successions*, (7) *Unfolding and Folding*, (8) *Dirge*, (9) *Limbo*, (10) *Surge*, and (11) *Apotheosis*. The first word of the title derives from Greek *kinēsis*, "movement"; the second represents Greek *molpē*, "dancing to music."

King and Charcoal Burner (Czech, *Král a uhlíř*)   Antonín Dvořák, 1871.

The comic opera in three acts is set to a libretto by B.J. Lobesky (pseudonym of Bernard Guldener) based on an old puppet play. Lobesky originally called his play *Make Yourself At Home, Mr. Matthew* (Czech, *Pane Matej, jako doma*), but this was then changed as above.

King Arthur   Henry Purcell, 1691.

The semiopera in a prologue, five acts, and an epilogue, subtitled *The British Worthy*, is set to a libretto by John Dryden based on the life of the legendary King Arthur.

King Charles II   George Macfarren, 1849.

The opera is set to a libretto by Michael Desmond Ryan based on John Howard Payne's play *Charles the Second; or, The Merry Monarch* (1824), itself adapted from a French play with the anonymous assistance of Washington Irving. It tells what happens when the Earl of Rochester attempts to reform Charles II and takes the king in disguise to a sailors' tavern.

The King Goes Forth to France (Finnish, *Kuningas lähtee Ranskaan*)   Aulis Sallinen, 1984.

The opera in three acts, to a libretto by Paavo Haavikko, is set at a time in the future when England is being overwhelmed by a new Ice Age. The story tells how the King, urged to marry, decides to abandon England and lead his people across the English Channel to France.

King Harald's Saga   Judith Weir, 1979.

The work for solo soprano in three acts is set to the composer's own libretto based on the 13th-century Icelandic saga *Heimskringla*, and centers on Harald Haardrade (Harold III) (1015–1066), king of Norway, who sailed to England in 1066 and lost his life in the Battle of Hastings.

King Lear   (1) Hector Berlioz, 1831; (2) Mily Balakirev, 1859–61; (3) Dmitry Shostakovich, 1971.

Berlioz's overture, Op. 4, Balakirev's overture and incidental music, and Shostakovich's film music are all based on Shakespeare's play of the same name (1606) about the old king who decides to divide his kingdom among his three daughters. Shostakovich's music, Op. 137, was for the Russian film of the play (1971) in Boris Pasternak's translation. *See also* **Lear**.

King of Prussia Quartets   W.A. Mozart, 1789–90.

The three string quartets, No. 21 in D major, K 575, No. 22 in B flat major, K 589, and No. 23 in F major, K 590, are so called because they were commissioned by Friedrich Wilhelm II of Prussia. (He requested six quartets, but only three were composed.)

King Olaf *see* **Scenes from the Saga of King Olaf**.

King Priam   Michael Tippett, 1958–61.

The opera in three acts is set to a libretto by the composer based on Homer's *Iliad*, which centers on the Trojan War and tells how King Priam of Troy chooses the death of his baby son Paris because he believes he will cause his father's death.

King Roger (Polish, *Król Roger*)   Karol Szymanowski, 1918–24.

The opera in three acts, to a libretto by the composer and Jaroslaw Iwaszkiewicz, deals with the supposed events in the reign of Roger II of Sicily (*c*.1095–1154).

King Stag *see* **König Hirsch**.

The Kingdom   Edward Elgar, 1901–6.

The oratorio, Op. 51, for four soloists, chorus, and orchestra, is set to a biblical text compiled by the composer, who conceived it as a sequel to The **Apostles**.

The King's Henchman   Deems Taylor, 1927.

The opera in three acts, Op. 19, to a libretto by Edna St. Vincent Millay, is set in 10th-century Britain and tells what happens when King Eadgar hears of the beauty of Princess Aelfrida of Devon and sends his closest associate (henchman), Aethelwold, to Devon to woo her on his behalf.

The Kiss (Czech, *Hubička*)   Bedřich Smetana, 1876.

The comic opera in two acts is set to a libretto by Eliška Krásnohorská based on a story (1871) by Karolína Svetlá (pen name of Johanna Mužáková). It tells how the widower, Lukás, wishes to marry his old love, Vendulka, but she refuses to let him kiss her because of the superstition that a kiss given a widower before his remarriage causes grief to the late wife. The work was a great success. "Miss Krásnohorská found it embarrassing that the deaf composer always shouted when he spoke, without being conscious that he was doing so. When they met in the street one day he bellowed out that he was so pleased she had given him that *Kiss*" (John Clapham, *Smetana*, 1972).

Das Klagende Lied (The Song of Sorrow") Gustav Mahler, 1880.

The cantata for soprano, contralto, tenor, and bass soloists, chorus, and orchestra, is set to the composer's own text based on a fairy tale by Ludwig Bechstein, in turn derived from an old German legend. It tells what happens when two brothers love the same proud queen and the elder murders the younger out of jealousy. It is in three parts: *Waldmärchen* ("Forest Legend"), *Der Spielmann* ("The Minstrel"), and *Hochzeitstück* ("Wedding Piece").

Klavierbüchlein ("Little Keyboard Book") J.S. Bach, 1720–5.

The composer gave this title to three of his collections of keyboard music: pieces for the instruction of his eldest son, Wilhelm Friedemann Bach (1720), a similar but smaller collection for his second wife, Anna Magdalena (1722), and a larger collection for her (1725). *See also* **Anna Magdalena Books**.

Klavierübung ("Keyboard Exercises") J.S. Bach, 1731–42.

The composer adopted this title from Johann Kuhnau's *Neue Clavier-Übung* ("New Keyboard Exercises") (1689, 1692) for four sets of his keyboard works. The first (1731) contains the six **Partitas**, the second (1735) contains the **Italian Concerto** and the Partita in B minor, the third (1739) is a book of organ works, including the **St. Anne Fugue**, and the fourth (1742) is the **Goldberg Variations**.

Eine Kleine Nachtmusik ("A Little Night Music") W.A. Mozart, 1787.

The Serenade No. 13 in G major, K 525, for small string orchestra, has a vernacular name to emphasize its character as either a serenade or a nocturne, both being compositions that cen-

ter on the romantic associations of night. It may have been composed for a particular such occasion, although it is not known what this was. "The title must not be taken as indicating a work noticeably smaller than Mozart's other serenades; but it is unique among his compositions, and may perhaps refer to the German or rather Austrian character of the music, which is especially striking in the finale" (Blom, p. 286).

Kleine Orgelmesse ("Little Organ Mass") Joseph Haydn, 1775.

The Mass No. 7 in B flat major has the full Latin title, *Missa brevis Sancti Joannis de Deo* ("Short Mass of St. John of God"). *Cf.* **Grosse Orgelmesse**.

Die Kluge ("The Clever Girl") Carl Orff, 1941–2.

The comic opera in six scenes is set to the composer's own libretto which combines different versions of the folktale recorded by the Grimm brothers in their *Fairy Tales* (1812). The story tells what happens when the king, bored with the wise sayings of the clever girl he has married, sends her packing, saying she can have anything in the palace she wants.

Des Knaben Wunderhorn ("The Boy's Magic Horn") Gustav Mahler, 1888–91.

Books II and III of **Lieder und Gesänge aus der Jugendzeit** contain nine settings from the anthology of German folk poems so named (published 1805–8), which the composer also drew on for 12 further settings in *Lieder aus Des Knaben Wunderhorn* (1888–99). The title refers to the picture of a boy on a horse brandishing a horn, which illustrated the first poem.

Knight Errant Richard Strauss, 1968.

The ballet in one act, with a libretto and choreography by Antony Tudor, is set to the composer's incidental music for *Der Bürger als Edelmann* (*i.e. Le Bourgeois Gentilhomme*), Op. 60 (1912–17), and the prelude to **Ariadne auf Naxos**, and is based on an episode from the 79th letter in Pierre Choderlos de Laclos's epistolary novel *Les Liaisons dangereuses* ("Dangerous Acquaintances") (1782). The knight errant of the title seduces three women in one night and betrays them to their husbands, after which he in turn is betrayed.

The Knot Garden Michael Tippett, 1970.

The opera in three acts, to the composer's own libretto, is a complex metaphysical drama of human relationships. The symbolic knot garden of the title revolves on stage to represent the scene of the loves and hates of the seven characters. (A "knot garden" is one laid out in an intricate way.) The characters themselves are Faber, a civil engineer, Thea, his wife, Flora, their adolescent ward, Mangus, a psychoanalyst, Denise, Thea's freedom-fighter sister, Dov, a homosexual musician, and Mel, the latter's black lover. *See also* **Songs for Dov.**

Knoxville: Summer of 1915   Samuel Barber, 1947.

The scena (ballet suite) for soprano and orchestra, Op. 24, is set to a prose text by James Agee that is a nostalgic evocation of American small-town life in the town and year stated.

Koanga   Frederick Delius, 1904.

The opera in a prologue, three acts, and an epilogue is set to a libretto by Charles Francis Keary based on George Washington Cable's novel *The Grandissimes* (1880). The story is set on a Mississippi river plantation in the late 18th century and tells what happens when the mulatto, Palmyra, repulses the plantation overseer, Pérez, and falls in love with a newly arrived slave, the former African chieftain, Koanga.

Kol Nidrei ("All Vows")   (1) Max Bruch, 1881; (2) Arnold Schoenberg, 1938.

Bruch's work for cello and orchestra is an Adagio on Hebrew melodies. Schoenberg's work, Op. 39, for speaker, chorus, and orchestra, is a setting of the *Kol Nidre*, the opening prayer of the Jewish service on the evening of the Day of Atonement (Yom Kippur). (The prayer declares that all of the vows that will be uttered in the coming year are null and void.)

König Hirsch ("King Stag")   Hans Werner Henze, 1952.

The opera in three acts is set to a libretto by Heinz von Cramer based on Carlo Gozzi's fairy-tale play *Rè Cervo* ("King Stag") (1762). The story tells what happens when King Leandro, raised in the forest by wild animals, returns to claim his crown and choose his bride but is obliged to renounce the throne and return to the forest, where he enters the body of a stag.

König Stephan   Ludwig van Beethoven, 1811.

The overture and incidental music, Op. 117, were composed for August von Kotzebue's play of this name written for the opening night of the German theater in Budapest (1812). The king in question is Stephen I (St. Stephen) (977–1038), first king of Hungary, regarded as the founder of the Hungarian state. *See also* Die **Ruinen von Aten.**

Die Königin von Saba ("The Queen of Sheba")   Karl Goldmark, 1875.

The opera in four acts is set to a libretto by Salomon Hermann Mosenthal based on the biblical account of the visit of the opulent Queen of Sheba to King Solomon (1 Kings 10). *Cf.* La **Reine de Saba.**

Die Königskinder ("The King's Children")   Engelbert Humperdinck, 1910.

The opera in three acts is set to a libretto by Ernst Rosmer (pen name of Elsa Bernstein-Porges) based on her own play of the same name (1894) for which the composer had written incidental music. The story tells what happens when the Prince falls in love with the beautiful Goose Girl but a Wicked Witch refuses to release her.

Kontakte ("Contacts")   Karlheinz Stockhausen, 1959–60.

The work for four-track tape has a title that suggests the contacts it establishes with its hearers or with its own disparate strands.

Kontra-Punkte ("Counter-Points")   Karlheinz Stockhausen, 1952–3.

The work is for piano and nine other instruments which drop out one by one as the piece moves through different harmonic regions. These "dropout" points are those alluded to in the title, which at the same time refers back to *Punkte* ("Points") (1952), the orchestral work of which this is a revised version.

La Korrigane ("The Korrigan")   Charles-Marie Widor, 1880.

The fantastic ballet in two acts, with a libretto by François Coppé and Louis Mérante and choreography by the latter, is set in 17th-century Brittany and tells of a poor girl who is bewitched by a korrigan (a malevolent Breton fairy sorceress) but sought out and rescued by her lover.

Kossuth   Béla Bartók, 1903.

The symphonic poem in ten tableaux is based on the life of Lajos Kossuth (1802–1894), leader of an unsuccessful Hungarian uprising against Austria (1848–9).

Koyaanisqatsi   Philip Glass, 1982.

The work is a score for the movie of the same name (1983), filmed entirely in North

America as a portrait of the USA seen in terms of an imbalance of technology. The title is a Hopi word meaning "life out of balance."

Krämerspiegel ("Shopkeeper's Mirror") Richard Strauss, 1918.

The song cycle for voice and piano, Op. 66, comprises 12 songs set to poems by Alfred Kerr (1867–1948) that contain satirical and punning references to many of the German music publishers with whom the composer was in dispute regarding copyright.

Krazy-Kat John Alden Carpenter, 1921.

The ballet, using jazz idioms, is based on George Herriman's *Krazy Kat* comic strip.

Der Kreidekreis ("The Chalk Circle") Alexander Zemlinsky, 1933.

The opera in three acts is set to the composer's own libretto based on the play of the same name (1925) by Klabund (pen name of Alfred Henschke), in turn adapted from a 13th-century Chinese parable by Li Tsing Hao. The story centers on two women who both claim to be a child's mother. To resolve the dispute, a judge decides that the child must be placed in the middle of a chalk circle and each woman instructed to take him by an arm. Whoever pulls the child out of the circle is the child's true mother. The same story lies behind Bertolt Brecht's play *The Caucasian Chalk Circle* (German, *Der kaukasische Kreidekreis*) (1943).

Kreisleriana Robert Schumann, 1838.

The work for solo piano, Op. 16, comprising eight fantasies, has a title referring to the half-crazed musician Johannes Kreisler in E.T.A. Hoffmann's stories. These appeared at various dates between 1812 and 1820 but the main group was published under the title *Kreisleriana* in *Phantasiestücke in Callots Manier* ("Fantasy Pieces in the Style of Callot") (1814). Schumann believed Kreisler was based on the eccentric genius Ludwig Böhner (1787–1860), but he is really a caricature of Hoffmann himself. The pieces do not have individual titles.

Kreutzer Sonata (1) Ludwig van Beethoven, 1802–3; (2) Leoš Janáček, 1923.

Beethoven's Violin Sonata in A, Op. 47, is so called because it was dedicated to the French violinist Rodolphe Kreutzer (1766–1831), who is believed never to have played it. Janáček's String Quartet No. 1 had written on the score, "Inspired by L.N. Tolstoy's *Kreutzer-sonata*," referring to Leo Tolstoy's story *The Kreutzer Sonata* (Russian, *Kreytserova sonata*) (1891), in which Beethoven's work has a disastrous effect on the characters.

Kullervo Jean Sibelius, 1892.

The symphonic poem, Op. 7, for soprano, baritone, male chorus, and orchestra, is based on the collection of Finnish legends known as the *Kalevala*, in which the tragic hero, Kullervo, is forced by fate to be a slave from childhood.

Die Kunst der Fuge ("The Art of Fugue") J.S. Bach, 1748–9.

The (unfinished) work for unspecified instruments aims to show the various ways of treating a simple subject in different types of fugues and canons.

Künstlerleben ("An Artist's Life") Johann Strauss II, 1867.

The waltzes, Op. 316, represent the colorful life of the Viennese artist.

Kuolema *see* **Valse triste**.

Kurzwellen ("Short Waves") Karlheinz Stockhausen, 1968.

The work is for a live electronic ensemble of four musicians, each of whom is also equipped with a shortwave radio. Hence the title. It is also realized with tapes of Beethoven instead of shortwave signals under the pleasant crossover title *Kurzwellen mit Beethoven* (*Stockhoven-Beethausen Opus 1970*).

Kyrie (Greek, "Lord").

The section of the Roman Catholic **Mass** that follows the Introit (initial chant). It has three parts: *Kyrie eleison, Christe eleison, Kyrie eleison* ("Lord have mercy, Christ have mercy, Lord have mercy"). Raymond Leppard has a *Kyrie* in the movie *Lord of the Flies* (1963) and the *Kyrie* from Ligeti's **Requiem** (1963–5) was used in *2001: A Space Odyssey* (1968).

L

L' (French, Italian, "The").

For titles beginning with this word, see the next word, *e.g.* L'**Elisir d'amore**.

La (French, Italian, Spanish, "The").

For titles beginning with this word, see the next word, *e.g.* La **Belle Hélène**.

"Là ci darem la mano" ("Give me your hand").

The duet in Act 1 of Mozart's **Don Giovanni** in which Don Giovanni woos the initially reluctant Zerlina.

Laborintus   Luciano Berio, 1972.

The ballet in one act, choreographed by Glen Tetley, is set to the composer's *Laborintus II* for voices and orchestra (1965), and is "a commentary on life, trapped in a labyrinth from which the only way out leads to death" (John Percival, quoted in Koegler, p. 242).

Labyrinth   Franz Schubert, 1941.

The ballet in four scenes, with a libretto by Salvador Dalí and choreography by Léonide Massine, is set to the composer's Symphony No. 7 in E major (1821). It is based on the "thread of Ariadne," the ball of yarn that Ariadne gave Theseus to guide him out of the Labyrinth, here symbolizing "the thread of continuity of classicism" (program note, quoted in Koegler, p. 242).

Le Lac des Cygnes *see* **Swan Lake**.

"Il Lacerato spirito" ("The torn soul").

Fiesco's aria in the prologue to Verdi's **Simon Boccanegra**, in which he sings of his tortured soul.

Der Lächerliche Prinz Jodelet ("The Comical Prince Jodelet")   Reinhard Keiser, 1726.

The opera is set to a libretto by Johann Philipp Praetorius based on Paul Scarron's comedy *Jodelet ou le Maître-Valet* ("Jodelet or the Master Valet") (1643), inspired by the French actor Jodelet (real name Julien Bedeau) (c.1595–1660), famous for his floured face and nasal delivery. Jodelet took his pseudonym from Scarron's play, in which he acted the name part.

Lachrimae ("Tears")   John Dowland, 1604.

The collection of 21 pieces for five viols and flute has the full title *Lachrimae, or Seaven Teares*, the "seaven teares" being seven pavans, each beginning with the theme of the composer's song *Flow my Tears*, followed by variations. The other 14 pieces are dances.

Lachrymae   Benjamin Britten, 1950.

The work for viola and piano, Op. 48, consists of "reflections on a song of John Dowland," that is, the one that features in Dowland's **Lachrimae**.

The Lady and the Fool   Giuseppe Verdi, arr. Charles Mackerras, 1954.

The ballet in one act (three scenes), with a libretto and choreography by John Cranko, is set to a medley of melodies from the composer's lesser known operas and tells of a beauty, La Capricciosa ("The Capricious"), who is courted by some socially smart suitors but who prefers two dowdy clowns.

The Lady and the Hooligan (Russian, *Baryshnya i khuligan*)   Dmitry Shostakovich, 1962.

The ballet (choreographic short story) in seven episodes, with a libretto by A.A. Belinsky and choreography by K. Boyarsky, was inspired by Vladimir Mayakovsky's film scenario of the same title (1918), itself based on Edmondo de Amicis's story *The Schoolmistress of the Workers*, and set to the composer's *Suite for Orchestra* (1934). The story tells of a teenage gang member (the hooligan) who falls in love with a teacher (the lady) but is rejected by her.

The Lady and the Unicorn (French, *La Dame et la Licorne*)   J. Chailley, 1953.

The ballet in one act, with a libretto by Jean Cocteau and choreography by Heinz Rosen, was inspired by the 15th-century tapestries at the Musée de Cluny, Paris, and tells of a unicorn which must eat only from the hands of a virgin, and which will die when she yields to the amorous advances of a knight.

Lady from the Sea   Knudåge Riisager, 1960.

The ballet in one act (five scenes), with a libretto and choreography by Birgit Cullberg, is based on Henrik Ibsen's play of the same name (1888). The story tells of Ellida, torn between her love for a sailor, who has left her and returned to sea, and the security of her life with an unloved husband.

Lady in the Dark   Kurt Weill, 1939–40.

The musical play in two acts is set to the book of the same name by Moss Hart and lyrics by Ira Gershwin. The story tells of a fashion magazine editor who because of her insecurity (as a "lady in the dark") jilts her lover, falls in love with a movie star, and finally marries her advertising manager.

Lady into Fox   Arthur Honegger, arr. Charles Lynch, 1939.

The ballet in one act (three scenes), with a libretto and choreography by Andrée Howard, is based on David Garnett's novel of the same name (1922) and set to a collection of orchestral pieces by the composer. The story tells of a gracious hostess who is really a vixen and who is torn between her love for a husband and her natural instincts as an animal.

Lady Macbeth of the Mtsensk District

(Russian, *Ledi Makbet Mtsenskogo uyezda*) Dmitry Shostakovich, 1930–2.

The opera in four acts, Op. 29, is set to a libretto by the composer and Alexander Preys based on the story of the same title by Nikolay Leskov (1865), which tells what happens when Katerina Izmaylova, the "Lady Macbeth" of the title, tires of her life in the provincial district of Mtsensk and has an affair with a young estate employee while her wealthy but dull merchant husband is away. The opera's subtitle, and subsequently regular title of the revised version, Op. 114 (1955–63), is thus *Katerina Izmaylova*.

The Lady of Shalott   Phyllis Tate, 1956.

The cantata for tenor, viola, percussion, two pianos, and celesta is a setting of Lord Alfred Tennyson's poem of the same name (1832), telling of the princess who falls in love with Lancelot and dies of unrequited love.

Lady of the Camellias (German, *Die Kameliendame*)   Fryderyk Chopin, 1978.

The ballet in a prologue and three acts, with a libretto and choreography by John Neumeier, is closely based on Alexandre Dumas's novel *La Dame aux camélias* (1848), centering on the beautiful courtesan, Marguerite Gautier, who escapes from the fashionable world of Paris to the country with her penniless lover, Armand Duval. The ballet uses only the composer's original and unarranged music, including the whole of the Piano Concerto No. 2 in F minor, Op. 21 (1829–30), the Romanze from the Piano Concerto No. 1 in E minor, Op. 11 (1830), the *Grande Fantaisie on Polish Airs*, Op. 13 (1828), the *Grande Polonaise Brillante* in E flat, Op. 22 (1830–1), and some individual piano pieces. *See also* **Marguerite and Armand**.

The Lady of the Lake   Franz Schubert, 1826.

An English name for the songs for voice and piano that the composer set to D.A. Storck's German translations (1825) from Sir Walter Scott's poem so titled (1810), published as Op. 52. They are: *Ellens Gesang I: Raste, Krieger, Krieg ist aus* ("Ellen's Song I: Soldier, rest! thy warfare's o'er") (D 837), *Ellens Gesang II: Jäger, ruhe von der Jagd!* ("Ellen's Song II: Huntsman, rest! thy chase is done") (D 838), *Ellens Gesang III (Hymne an die Jungfrau): Ave Maria! Jungfrau mild!* ("Ellen's Song III [Hymn to the Virgin]: *Ave Maria!* maiden mild!") (D 839), *Lied des gefangenen Jägers: Mein Ross so müd' in dem Stalle* ("Lay of the Imprisoned Huntsman: My horse is weary of his stall") (D 843), and *Normans Gesang: Die Nacht bricht bald herein* ("Norman's Song: The heath this night must be my bed") (D 846). The "Lady of the Lake" herself is Ellen Douglas, daughter of the outlawed Lord James of Douglas. The lake is Loch Katrine.

Lady Radnor's Suite   Hubert Parry, 1894.

The suite for string orchestra in six movements was composed for an orchestra conducted by Lady Radnor, an amateur musician. Hence the name.

Lady Rohesia   Antony Hopkins, 1948.

The "operatic frolic" is set to the composer's own libretto based on Richard Barham's *Ingoldsby Legends* (1840–7), in which Lady Rohesia Ingoldsby rallies from her deathbed just as her husband, Sir Guy de Montgomeri, is kissing the pretty young maid Beatrice Grey as his chosen new wife.

Lagertha   Claus Schall, 1801.

The ballet in three acts, choreographed by Vincenzo Galeotti, has a libretto based on Book IX of the *Gesta Danorum* ("Story of the Danes") (*c.*1200) by Saxo Grammaticus, in which Lagertha is a woman warrior.

Laiderette ("Ugly Little Girl") Frank Martin, 1954.

The ballet in one act, with a libretto and choreography by Kenneth MacMillan, is set to the composer's *Petite Symphonie Concertante* (1944–5) and tells of a bald and ugly little girl who is abandoned by her parents on a rich man's doorstep.

Lakmé   Léo Delibes, 1883.

The opera in three acts is set to a libretto by Philippe Gille and Edmond Gondinet based on Pierre Loti's novel *Rarahu* (1880), later retitled *Le Mariage de Loti* (1882). The plot is set in mid–19th-century India and tells what ensues from the love between Gérard, a British officer, and Lakmé, daughter of a Brahmin priest, Nilakantha.

Lalla Rookh   Cesare Pugni, 1846.

The ballet in four scenes, with a libretto and choreography by Jules Joseph Perrot, is based on Thomas Moore's oriental romance of the same name (1817) about the beautiful daughter of the

Emperor of Hindustan. (According to Moore himself, her name means "Tulip Cheek.")

The Lambton Worm Robert Sherlaw Johnson, 1977.

The opera in two acts is set to a libretto by Anne Ridler based on a medieval legend about Lambton Castle, Co. Durham, England, whose feudal lord was Robert de Lambton, and which remained in the hands of the Lambton family until the 20th century. The story goes that the Lambton Worm "was caught by the heir of Lambton when fishing on a Sunday, and thrown into a well; the worm grew too large for its habitation and betook itself to the Wear [River], and grew and grew, levying toll until it became the terror of the county. The worm, which had the power of self-union, was killed by Lambton after his return from the Crusades; he had several fierce combats with it, and finally conquered by following the advice of a wise woman" (*Cassell's Gazetteer of Great Britain and Ireland*, 1895).

Lament of the Waves Gerard Masson, 1970.

The ballet in one act, with a libretto and choreography by Frederick Ashton, is set to the composer's *Dans le deuil des vagues II* ("In the Mourning of the Waves II") and is an extended duo for two lovers, who relive their moment of happiness as they drown in the sea.

Lamentation Zoltán Kodály, 1930.

The solo dance, choreographed by Martha Graham, is set to the composer's Piano Piece Op. 3 No. 2 and is "a portrait of an isolated, solitary sufferer" (Don McDonagh, quoted in Koegler, p. 245).

Lamentation Symphony Joseph Haydn, 1765.

The Symphony No. 26 in D minor is so named because some of its themes suggest the plainsong melodies sung in Roman Catholic churches in Holy Week. It is also known as the *Weihnachtssymphonie* ("Christmas Symphony"), but the reason for this name is unknown.

Lamento d'Arianna *see* **Ariadne's Lament**.

Das Land des Lächelns ("The Land of Smiles") Franz Lehár, 1929.

The operetta in three acts is set to a libretto by Ludwig Herzer and Fritz Löhner based on an earlier unsuccessful operetta, *Die gelbe Jacke* ("The Yellow Jacket") (1923). The story takes place in Vienna and Peking in 1912 and tells how

Lisa, daughter of Count Ferdinand Lichtenfels, marries Prince Souchong, a Chinese diplomat, and goes with him to live in China, the "Land of Smiles." Soon, however, it becomes the "Land of Tears."

Land of Hope and Glory Edward Elgar, 1902.

The title is that of the finale of the **Coronation Ode**, set to words by A.C.Benson. The land so described is England. The tune is to a melody adapted from the trio section of the first **Pomp and Circumstance** march.

The Land of Lost Content John Ireland, 1921.

The song cycle for high voice and piano comprises settings of six poems from the 63 in A.E. Housman's book of verse *A Shropshire Lad* (1896). The individual titles are: (1) *The Lent Lily*, (2) *Ladslove*, (3) *Goal and Wicket*, (4) *The Vain Desire*, (5) *The Encounter*, (6) *Epilogue*. Most of the poems are untitled, and only the first song's title is that of the original. The overall title comes from poem No. 40, the second of whose two verses begins, "That is the land of lost content."

The Land of Smiles *see* **Das Land des Lächelns**.

Landrover various (see below), 1972.

The ballet in four parts, choreographed by Merce Cunningham, is set to a sound arrangement by John Cage, Gordon Mumma, and David Tudor and is a dance that "radiates friendliness and good humor" with "pauses which convey a sense of alert calm" (Jack Anderson, quoted in Koegler, p. 246). The title does not relate to the British vehicle of the name.

Das Lange Weihnachtsmahl ("The Long Christmas Dinner") Paul Hindemith, 1960.

The opera in one act is set to a libretto by Thornton Wilder based on his one-act play of the same title (1931). The story encapsulates, in a single hour, 90 Christmas dinners in the Bayard family. Characters exit and enter through different doors representing birth and death.

Largo *see* **Handel's Largo**.

"Largo al factotum" ("Room for the factotum").

Figaro's aria introducing himself in all his versatility in Act 1 of Rossini's Il **Barbiere di Siviglia**. A fuller version is "*Largo al factotum della città*" ("Room for the city's factotum").

Largo Quartet   Joseph Haydn, *c.* 1797.

The String Quartet in D major, Op. 76 No. 79, is so named for its eloquent slow movement, marked Largo.

The Lark Ascending   Ralph Vaughan Williams, 1914.

The romance for violin and orchestra was inspired by George Meredith's poem of the same title (1881) about the bird and its soaring flight and song. The score was prefaced with four lines from this: "He rises and begins to round, / He drops the silver chain of sound / Of many links without a break, / In chirrup, whistle, slur and shake."

Lark Quartet   (German, *Lerchenquartett*) Joseph Haydn, 1790.

The String Quartet in D major, Op. 64 No. 67, is so named because of the soaring violin theme of its opening. "From the earth-bound accompaniment of the lower parts, the first violin soars up to heavenly heights" (Karl Geiringer, *Haydn: A Creative Life in Music*, 1946).

Las   (Spanish, "The").

For titles beginning with this word, see the next word, *e.g.* Las **Hermanas**.

"Lasciatemi morire"   *see* **Ariadne's Lament**.

The Last Rose of Summer   Friedrich von Flotow, 1847.

The song sung by Lady Harriet in Act 2 of **Martha** originated as an old Irish air, *Castle Hyde*. This became *The Groves of Blarney* in *c.* 1790 with words by R.A. Millikin. Thomas Moore included it, with new words, in his *Irish Melodies* (1813), and it is this version that is included in Flotow's opera. Beethoven meantime set the air (1810), and Mendelssohn wrote a piano fantasia on it as Op. 15 (1827).

The Last Savage   Gian-Carlo Menotti, 1963.

The opera in three acts, to the composer's own libretto, is set in India and Chicago and tells how the father of the American college girl, Kitty, wanting to marry her off to the Indian prince, Kodanda, arranges for her to capture and tame a "prehistoric man" to bring this about. The man he hires to play the part is thus the "last savage" of the title. The opera was first performed under its equivalent Italian title, *L'ultimo selvaggio*.

The Last Sleep of the Virgin   (French, *Le Dernier Sommeil de la Vierge*)   Jules Massenet, 1880.

The orchestral interlude comes from the oratorio La **Vierge**.

The Last Temptations   (Finnish, *Viimeiset kiusaukset*)   Joonas Kokkonen, 1973–5.

The opera in two acts is based on Lauri Kokkonen's play of the same name (1959) about the temptations and final redemption of the Finnish evangelist Paavo Ruotsalainen (1777–1852).

The Last Waltz   *see* Der **Letzte Walzer**.

Late Swallows   Frederick Delius, 1916.

The third movement of the Second String Quartet is so named for its evocation of the title.

Laudate Dominum   ("Praise the Lord") W.A. Mozart, 1780.

The work for soprano solo and orchestra is a setting of Psalm 116 from the **Vesperae solennes de confessore**. (In the Prayer Book it is Psalm 117.)

Laudon Symphony   Joseph Haydn, 1779.

The Symphony No. 69 in C major is so named for its dedication to the Austrian field-marshal, Gideon Ernst Freiherr von Laudon (or Loudon) (1717–1790).

Laurencia   A.A. Krein, 1939.

The ballet in three acts (five scenes), with a libretto by Eugen Mandelberg and choreography by Vakhtang Chaboukiani, is based on Felix Lope de Vega's play *Fuente ovejuna* ("The Sheep Well") (1618) and tells of the rising of the peasants in a Castilian village, led by Laurencia and her betrothed, Frondoso. *Cf.* A **Daughter of Castile**.

Le   (French, Italian, "The").

For titles beginning with this word, see the next word, *e.g.* Le **Rêve**.

Lear   Aribert Reimann, 1976–8.

The opera in two parts is set to a libretto by Claus Henneberg based on Shakespeare's play *King Lear* (1606) about the old king who decides to divide his kingdom among his three daughters. *See also* **King Lear**.

The Leaves Are Fading   Antonín Dvořák, 1975.

The ballet in one act, choreographed by Antony Tudor, is set to a selection of little known pieces by the composer to the music of which "young people meet and flirt and part" (Alexander Bland, quoted in Koegler, p. 250). The title implies a transient pleasure.

Das Lebewohl *see* Les **Adieux**.

The Legend of Czar Saltan *see* The **Tale of Czar Saltan**.

The Legend of Joseph *see* Die **Josephslegende**.

Legend of Judith Mordecai Seter, 1962.

The ballet in one act, choreographed by Martha Graham, has an action that "takes place entirely within the 'unknown landscape of the mind' of a woman, a kind of Judith," whose soul "confronts the past in its true, mythic dimensions and accepts the consequences of love and brutality and violence" (program note, quoted in Koegler, p. 251). The reference is thus to the biblical Judith (*see* **Judith**).

Legend of Love (Russian, *Legenda o lyubvi*) Arif Melikov, 1961.

The ballet in three acts (seven scenes), with a libretto by Nazim Hikmet and choreography by Yuri Grigorovich, is based on Hikmet's play of the same name, telling of Queen Mekhmeneh Bahnu, who sacrifices her beauty to save the life of her sick sister, Princess Shyrin, and of Ferkhad, the young painter who is Shyrin's lover.

Legend of Ochrid (Serbo-Croat, *Ohridska legenda*) Stevan Hristić, 1947.

The ballet in four acts (five scenes), with a libretto by the composer and choreography by Margarita Froman, is based on a Macedonian fairy tale telling of the love of Marco and Biljana and the nymphs from Lake Ochrid who come to their aid.

The Legend of the City of Kitezh *see* The **Invisible City of Kitezh**.

Legend of the Invisible City of Kitezh *see* The **Invisible City of Kitezh**.

Die Legende von der Heiligen Elisabeth ("The Legend of St. Elizabeth") Franz Liszt, 1857–62.

The oratorio, for soprano, alto, three baritones, bass, chorus, organ, and orchestra, is set to a text by the German writer Otto Roquette based on the life of St. Elizabeth of Hungary (1207–1231).

Leicester Daniel Auber, 1823.

The opera, subtitled *Le Château de Kenilworth* ("Kenilworth Castle"), is set to a libretto by Eugène Scribe and Anne Honoré Joseph Mélesville based on Sir Walter Scott's historical novel *Kenilworth* (1821), in which the Earl of Leicester, favorite of Queen Elizabeth, is one of the key characters.

Leili and Mejnun (Russian, *Leyli i Medzhnun*) Uzeir Hadjibekov, 1908.

The opera in four acts, to the composer's own libretto, is based on the Azerbaijani poet Mukhammed Fizuli's epic poem of the same name (1536–7), itself a reworking of the romantic poem by the 12th-century Persian poet Nizami telling the Romeo-and-Juliet-style tale of the semilegendary 7th-century Bedouin poet, Kais, nicknamed Mejnun ("Madman"), and the daughter, Leili, of the cruel ruler of the town.

"Leise, leise" ("Gentle, gentle").

Agathe's aria in Act 2 of Weber's Der **Freischütz**, in which she prays for protection for her beloved Max. A fuller version of the words is "*Leise, leise, fromme Weise*" ("Gentle, gentle, good way"), often rendered in English as "Gently gently lift my song." The aria is also known as *Agathe's Prayer*.

Lélio Hector Berlioz, 1831–2.

The monodrama, Op. 14 *bis*, is set to the composer's own text and is a sequel to the **Symphonie fantastique**, which ends with the death of the hero, Lélio. Its subtitle (and original title) is *Le Retour à la vie* ("The Return to Life").

Lemminkäinen Legends (Finnish, *Lemminkäis-sarja*) Jean Sibelius, 1894–5.

The suite for orchestra, Op. 22, is based on legends from the *Kalevala*, the Finnish national epic, and is in four movements, as follows: (1) *Lemminkäinen and the Maidens of the Island* (Finnish, *Lemminkäinen ja saaren neidot*), (2) *Lemminkäinen in Tuonela* (Finnish, *Lemminkäinen Tuonelassa*), (3) The **Swan of Tuonela**, (4) *Lemminkäinen's Return* (Finnish, *Lemminkäisen paluu*). One of the main strands of the epic tells how Lemminkäinen, a carefree adventurer and "ladykiller," goes to Pohjola to woo the beautiful daughter of Louhi. *See also* **Pohjola's Daughter**.

Leningrad Symphony (Russian, *Leningradskaya simfoniya*) Dmitry Shostakovich, 1941.

The Symphony No. 7 in C major, Op. 60, was composed during the German siege of Leningrad (now again St. Petersburg) and expresses the months of sacrifice endured. But the composer commented: "I have nothing against calling the *Seventh* the *Leningrad* ... but it's not about the Leningrad under siege, it's about the

Leningrad that Stalin destroyed and Hitler finished off" (quoted in Staines and Buckley, p. 386).

Lenore Symphony   Joachim Raff, 1873.

The Symphony No. 5 in E major, Op. 177, was inspired by Gottfried August Bürger's ballad *Lenore*, published in 1774. It is in turn based on the Scottish ballad *Sweet William's Ghost* and tells of Lenore's grief at the death of her lover in the Seven Years War, of Wilhelm's appearance on horseback beneath her window, and of her night ride as his pillion companion, until the lover reveals himself as a grisly skeleton and she sinks down dead.

Leonora *see* **Fidelio**.

Leonore *see* **Fidelio**.

Léonore ("Leonora")   Pierre Gaveaux, 1798.

The opera in two acts is set to a libretto by Jean-Nicolas Bouilly telling the story that gave the basic plot of Beethoven's **Fidelio**. Its subtitle is *L'Amour conjugal* ("Married Love").

Leonore 40/45   Rolf Liebermann, 1952.

The opera in two acts, to a libretto by Heinrich Strobel, is set in Paris in the 1940s and tells of the love between the French girl, Huguette, and the German soldier, Alfred, who meet during the Nazi occupation. The title alludes to the love story that gave the basic plot of Beethoven's **Fidelio**, with the figures indicating its transfer to the war years 1940–45.

Les (French, "The").

For titles beginning with this word, see the next word, *e.g.* Les **Sylphides**.

The Lesson, Georges Delerue, 1963.

The television ballet, choreographed by Flemming Flindt, is based on Eugène Ionesco's play of the same name (1958), telling of a professor who is so carried away by his work that he eventually murders his pupil. As Flindt's first work, the ballet originally had the equivalent Danish title, *En Etime*. It is also known by the French title *La Leçon*.

Let Us Garlands Bring   Gerald Finzi, 1929–42.

The song cycle for baritone and piano (or orchestra) comprises five songs from Shakespeare, as follows: (1) *Come Away, Death* (from *Twelfth Night*), (2) *Who Is Sylvia?* (from *The Two Gentlemen of Verona*), (3) *Fear No More the Heat o' the Sun* (from *Cymbeline*), (4) *O Mistress Mine* (from *Twelfth Night*), (5) *It Was a Lover and His Lass* (from *As You Like It*). The overall title comes from the last line of *Who Is Sylvia?*: "To her let us garlands bring."

Let's Make an Opera   Benjamin Britten, 1949.

The "entertainment for young people," Op. 45, set to a libretto by Eric Crozier, is in two parts. The first involves the preparations by children and adults to stage an opera, the second is the opera itself. This is *The Little Sweep*, a loose adaptation of part of Charles Kingsley's children's novel *The Water Babies* (1863), telling how a family rescues an eight-year-old apprentice sweep, Sammy, from his master, Black Bob.

Letter Duet   W.A. Mozart, 1786.

The duet between the Countess and Susanna in Act 3 of Le **Nozze di Figaro**, in which the Countess dictates to Susanna the letter to be sent to the Count arranging an assignation that evening in the garden.

Letter Scene   (1) Pyotr Tchaikovsky, 1879; (2) Jules Massenet, 1885–7.

The title is usually taken to refer to the scene in Act 1 of Tchaikovsky's **Eugene Onegin** in which Tatyana sits up all night writing a letter to Onegin declaring her love. It is also used for the scene in Act 3 of Massenet's **Werther** in which Charlotte rereads letters from Werther.

Letter Song   Jacques Offenbach, 1868.

The name is sometimes used for the scene in Act 1 of La **Périchole** in which La Périchole writes a letter to say goodbye to her beloved Piquillo.

Letter to the World   Hunter Johnson, 1940.

The ballet in one act, choreographed by Martha Graham, deals with the inner life of the American poet, Emily Dickinson (1830–1886), who is represented by two dancers, One Who Dances and One Who Speaks.

Letters of Love (Russian, *Pis'ma lyubvi*) Vitaly Gubarenko, 1975.

The monodrama in four parts is set to the composer's own libretto based on Henri Barbusse's story *Tendresse* ("Tenderness") (1921), telling how a young woman writes four letters to her lover to be delivered on predetermined dates: the following day, a year later, ten years later, and 25 years later. The final letter reveals that she committed suicide before writing the first.

Die Letzte Walzer ("The Last Waltz") Oscar Straus, 1920.

The operetta in three acts, to a libretto by Julius Brammer and Alfred Grünwald, is set in Warsaw in 1910 and tells of the last waltz danced by Count Dimitri, under sentence of death for his well-intentioned rescue of two ladies from the drunken importunities of Prince Paul, and Vera Lisaveta, one of the two so rescued, now betrothed to the older General Krasinski.

Leutgeb Quintet (German, *Leutgebisches Quintett*)   W.A. Mozart, 1782.

The Quintet in E flat major, K 407, for violin, two violas, cello, and horn, was probably written for the hornplayer Joseph Leutgeb, and is still occasionally known by his name (sometimes misspelled *Leitgeb*).

La Liberazione di Ruggiero dall'Isola d'Alcina ("The Release of Ruggiero from the Island of Alcina")   Francesca Caccini, 1625.

The opera is set to a libretto by Ferdinando Saracinelli based on Ludovico Ariosto's *Orlando Furioso* (1516). The story tells what happens when the benevolent sorceress, Melissa, arrives on Alcina's enchanted island and declares her intention of rescuing Ruggiero from Alcina's wiles and recalling him to martial duty. *Cf.* **Alcina**.

"Libiamo, libiamo" *see* **Drinking Song**.

Libuše   Bedřich Smetana, 1881.

The opera in three acts, to a German libretto by Josef Wenzig translated into Czech by Ervín Špindler, is based on Czech historical legend and tells how the princess, Libuše ("Little Love"), chooses the wise and strong peasant, Přemysl, as her husband and abdicates her power to him, whereupon he becomes the founder of the Přemysl dynasty, the first Czech ruling house. Legend ascribes the founding of Prague, the Czech capital, to the princess and her husband.

Licht: Die sieben Tage der Woche ("Light: The Seven Days of the Week")   Karlheinz Stockhausen, 1977–91.

The title is that of a cycle of seven operas, one for each day of the week. The following were the first to be completed: *Dienstag aus Licht* ("Tuesday from Light") (1977–91), *Donnerstag aus Licht* ("Thursday from Light") (1978–80), *Samstag aus Licht* ("Saturday from Light") (1981–4), and *Montag aus Licht* ("Monday from Light") (1984–8). A fifth instalment, *Freitag aus Licht* ("Friday from Light") was premiered in 1996 and the cycle is planned to be completed in 2002 with *Sonntag aus Licht* ("Sunday from Light"). The work is steeped in mysticism and spirituality. *Donnerstag aus Licht*, the first to be completed, is in three separately performable acts: *Michaels Jugend* ("Michael's Youth"), about the artistic and sexual awakening of the hero, the Archangel Michael, *Michaels Reise um die Erde* ("Michael's Journey Around the Earth"), a trumpet concerto in which Michael encounters different cultures, and *Michaels Heimkehr* ("Michael's Homecoming"), as Michael's celestial triumph and visionary account of himself. *Samstag aus Licht*, the next to be completed, is in four such scenes: *Luzifers Traum, oder Klavierstück XIII* ("Lucifer's Dream, or Piano Piece XVIII"), a fantastic sequence of pianism dreamed by the solo bass, Lucifer, *Kathinkas Gesang als Luzifers Requiem* ("Kathinka's Song as Lucifer's Requiem"), a long mimed and played solo by the flutist Kathinka, a cat, *Luzifers Tanz* ("Lucifer's Dance"), a ballet for windband, interrupted by Michael's entrance as trumpeter, and *Luzifers Abschied* ("Lucifer's Farewell"), a slow ceremonial for chanting male chorus, organ, and trombones.

Lie Strewn the White Flocks *see* **Pastoral**.

Die Liebe der Danae ("The Love of Danae")   Richard Strauss, 1938–40.

The opera in three acts is set to a libretto by Josef Gregor based on a draft text by Hugo von Hofmannsthal. The plot is classical in origin and tells what happens when Jupiter, in love with Danae, assumes the form of Midas, who also loves her.

Liebesgruß *see* **Salut d'amour**.

Liebesliederwalzer ("Love Song Waltzes")   Johannes Brahms, 1868–9.

The 18 walzes, Op. 52, for two pianos with soprano, alto, tenor, and bass soloists, are set to texts from Georg Friedrich Daumer's *Polydora*. The 1960 ballet of the same name was set to the work and choreographed by George Balanchine.

Das Liebesmahl der Apostel ("The Love Feast of the Apostles")   Richard Wagner, 1843.

The "biblical scene" for male chorus and orchestra is set to the composer's own text based on the New Testament account of the *agape* or shared meal that became the Lord's Supper or Eucharist.

Liebestod ("Love Death")   Richard Wagner, 1865.

The title is that of Isolde's final aria at the end of Act 3 of **Tristan und Isolde**, where Isolde joins Tristan in a mutual embrace of death.

Liebesträume ("Love Dreams")   Franz Liszt, 1850.

The three nocturnes for solo piano are transcriptions of the composer's songs *Hohe Liebe* ("Great Love"), *Gestorben war ich* ("Dead Was I"), and *O Liebe, so lang du lieben kannst* ("O Love, So Long Canst Thou Love").

Das Liebesverbot ("The Ban on Love") Richard Wagner, 1836.

The opera in two acts is set to the composer's own libretto based on Shakespeare's play *Measure for Measure* (1604), and tells how the governor of Sicily, Friedrich, has issued a ban on love-making under pain of death. The subtitle is *Die Novize von Palermo* ("The Novice of Palermo"), referring to Isabella, who intercedes for her brother, Claudio, when he is falsely condemned under the charge.

Das Lied von der Erde ("The Song of the Earth")   Gustav Mahler, 1907–9.

The symphony for contralto (or baritone), tenor, and orchestra comprises settings of six poems from Hans Bethge's *Die chinesische Flöte* ("The Chinese Flute") (1907), themselves versions of the Chinese originals. The individual titles are: (1) *Das Trinklied vom Jammer der Erde* ("The Drinking Song of Earth's Sorrow"), (2) *Der Einsame im Herbst* ("The Lonely One in Autumn"), (3) *Von der Jugend* ("Of Youth"), (4) *Von der Schönheit* ("Of Beauty"), (5) *Der Trunkene im Frühling* ("The Drunkard in Spring"), (6) *Der Abschied* ("The Farewell"). *See also* **Song of the Earth**.

Lieder eines fahrenden Gesellen ("Songs of a Wayfaring Man")   Gustav Mahler, 1883–5.

The song cycle of four songs for baritone or mezzosoprano and orchestra is set to the composer's own poems based on Des **Knaben Wunderhorn**. *See also* **Song of a Wayfarer**.

Lieder ohne Worte ("Songs Without Words")   Felix Mendelssohn, 1834–43.

The name is that of eight books of pieces for piano solo, each containing six pieces: Book 1, Op. 19 (1830), Book 2, Op. 30, (1835), Book 3, Op. 38 (1837), Book 4, Op. 53 (1841), Book 5, Op. 62 (1844), Book 6, Op. 67 (1845), Book 7, Op. 85 (1850), Book 8, Op. 102 (*c*.1845). The term *Lied ohne Worte* was introduced by Mendelssohn to describe a piece in which a song-like melody progresses against an accompaniment. It should be noted that the last word of the title is spelled as above, not *Wörte* or *Worter* or *Wörter*, although all three are frequently found, the first even in Arnold (p. 1742). (German *Wort*, "word," has two plurals. When it means "vocabulary word" it is *Wörter*. Hence *Wörterbuch*, "dictionary." When it means "utterance" it is *Worte*, as here.) The 1977 ballet of the same name, choreographed by Hans van Manen, was set to a selection of these pieces.

Mendelssohn gave titles to only five of the 48 pieces: one as **Duetto**, three as **Venezianisches Gondellied**, and one as **Volkslied**. (*See also* **Spring Song**.) The Hungarian pianist, Stephen Heller, however, gave French titles to the remainder. These were translated into English in an edition of the work published in Philadelphia in 1898 and are as follows (with respective opus numbers as above): Book 1: *Sweet Remembrance* (No. 1 in E major), *Regrets* (No. 2 in A minor), *Hunting Song* (No. 3 in A major), *Confidence* (No. 4 in A major), *Restlessness* (No. 5 in F sharp minor); Book 2: *Contemplation* (No. 1 in E flat major), *Without Repose* (No. 2 in B flat minor), *Consolation* (No. 3 in E major), *The Wanderer* (No. 4 in B minor), *A Rivulet* (No. 5 in D major); Book 3: *The Evening Star* (No. 1 in E flat major), *Lost Happiness* (No. 2 in C minor), *The Harp of the Poet* (No. 3 in E major), *Hope* (No. 4 in A major), *Appassionata* (No. 5 in A minor); Book 4: *On the Shore* (No. 1 in A flat major), *The Vision* (No. 2 in E flat major), *Agitation* (No. 3 in G minor), *The Sorrowful Soul* (No. 4 in F major), *The Flight* (No. 6 in A major); Book 5: *May Breezes* (No. 1 in G major), *The Departure* (No. 2 in B flat major), *Funeral March* (No. 3 in E minor), *Morning Song* (No. 4 in G major); Book 6: *Meditation* (No. 1 in E flat major), *Lost Illusion* (No. 2 in F minor), *The Pilgrims* (No. 3 in B flat major), *Spinning Song* (see The **Bee's Wedding**), *The Shepherd's Complaint* (No. 5 in B minor), *Serenade* (No. 6 in E major); Book 7: *Reverie* (No. 1 in F major), *A Farewell* (No. 2 in A minor), *Passion* (No. 3 in E flat major), *Elegy* (No. 4 in E major), *The Return* (No. 5 in A major), *Song of the Traveler* (No. 6 in B flat major); Book 8: *Homelessness* (No. 1 in E minor), *Retrospection* (No. 2 in D major), *Tarantella* (No. 3 in C major), *The Sighing Wind* (No. 4 in G minor), *The Joyous Peasant* (No. 5 in A major), *Faith* (No. 6 in C major). *The Vision* (Op. 53 No. 2) is also known as *The Fleecy Cloud*. Most of the names are reasonably apt, if sentimentally so in many cases.

Lieder und Gesänge aus der Jugendzeit

("Songs of Youth")   Gustav Mahler, 1880–91.

The title is that of 14 songs for voice and piano in three books. Book I (1880–3) contains five songs: *Frühlingsmorgen* ("Spring Morning"), *Erinnerung* ("Memory"), *Hans und Grete* ("Hans and Grete"), *Serenade aus Don Juan* ("Serenade from Don Juan"), and *Fantasie aus Don Juan* ("Fantasy from Don Juan"). Books II and III (1888–91) contain nine settings from Des **Knaben Wunderhorn**. Book II: *Um schlimme Kinder artig zu machen* ("To Make Bad Children Good"), *Ich ging mit Lust durch einen grünen Wald* ("I Walked with Joy through a Green Wood"), *Aus! Aus!* ("Over! Over!"), *Starke Einbildungskraft* ("Strong Imagination"). Book III: *Zu Straßburg auf der Schanz'* ("On the Ramparts of Strasbourg"), *Ablösung im Sommer* ("Changing of the Guard in Summer"), *Scheiden und Meiden* ("Farewell and Forgo"), *Nicht Wiedersehen* ("Never to Meet Again"), *Selbstgefühl* ("Self-esteem").

Liederkreis

("Song Cycle")   Robert Schumann, 1840.

The title is that of two sets of songs. The first, Op. 24, comprises nine settings from Heinrich Heine: (1) *Morgens steh' ich auf* ("I Arise in the Morning"), (2) *Es treibt mich hin* ("It Drives Me Back"), (3) *Ich wandelte unter den Bäumen* ("I Walked Beneath the Trees"), (4) *Lieb' Liebchen* ("Love, Sweetheart"), (5) *Schöne Wiege meiner Leiden* ("Lovely Cradle of my Sorrows"), (6) *Warte, warte, wilder Schiffsmann* ("Wait, Wait, Wild Sailor"), (7) *Berg' und Burgen schau'n herunter* ("Hills and Castles Look Down"), (8) *Anfangs wollt' ich fast verzagen* ("At First I Near Lost Heart"), (9) *Mit Myrthen und Rosen* ("With Myrtle and Roses"). The second, Op. 39, has 12 settings from Joseph von Eichendorff: (1) *In der Fremde* ("In Foreign Lands"), (2) *Intermezzo* ("Intermezzo"), (3) *Waldesgespräch* ("Forest Talks"), (4) *Die Stille* ("Peace"), (5) *Mondnacht* ("Moonlit Night"), (6) *Schöne Fremde* ("Beautiful Foreign Land"), (7) *Auf einer Burg* ("On a Castle"), (8) *In der Fremde* ("In Foreign Lands"), (9) *Wehmut* ("Melancholy"), (10) *Zwielicht* ("Twilight"), (11) *Im Walde* ("In the Forest"), (12) *Frühlingsnacht* ("Spring Night").

Lieutenant Kijé

(Russian, *Poruchik Kizhe*) Sergei Prokofiev, 1934.

The orchestral suite in five movements, Op. 60, derives from the music for the film of the same name (1934), a comedy centering on the nonexistent Lieutenant Kijé, who got into the list by accident and enjoyed a fabulous career at the court of Czar Paul. The 1963 ballet of the same name, with a libretto by A L. Veitsler and choreography by O. Tarasova and Alexander Lapauri, was set to the work.

A Life for the Czar

(Russian, *Zhizn' za tsarya*)   Mikhail Glinka, 1836.

The opera in four acts and an epilogue is set to a libretto by Baron Georgy Rosen based on a subject suggested by the poet Vasily Zhukovsky. It tells of the Russian peasant, Ivan Susanin, who by misleading Polish troops in 1613 saved the life of Czar Mikhail, founder of the Romanov dynasty, at the cost of his own life. The original title was *Ivan Susanin*, but this was changed to the present name when Czar Nicholas I took an interest in the opera and it was dedicated to him before its first performance. The new title did not please the Soviet authorities, however, and the original was accordingly readopted after the Revolution.

The Life Guards on Amager

(Danish, *Livjaegerne på Amager*)   W. Holm, 1871.

The ballet in two acts, choreographed by August Bournonville, is set at carnival time in 1808 on the island of Amager, near Copenhagen, and tells what happens while the voluntary corps are awaiting an attack by the English. An alternate English title is *The King's Voluntary Corps on Amager*.

The Life Guardsman *see* The Oprichnik.

Life of the Bee

Paul Hindemith, 1929.

The ballet in one act, choreographed by Doris Humphrey and accompanied by offstage humming and only later by the composer's *Kammermusik* No. 1, Op. 24 (1922), falls into four continuously linked sections: "the nurturing and birth of the new queen; the queen's coming to life; the battle between the new queen and the old, with the challenger victorious; and a dance of celebration presided over by the new queen" (Marcia B. Siegel, quoted in Koegler, p. 256).

Life with an Idiot

(Russian, *Zhizn's idiotom*)   Alfred Schnittke, 1991–2.

The opera in two acts, to a libretto by Viktor Yerofeyev, involves three main characters: I (the narrator), Wife, and Vova. The plot tells what happens when for some unspecified misdemeanor I has to take an Idiot into his apartment and chooses Vova, who can only utter the word "Ekh!" The whole work is a comment on the collapse of the Soviet system and on the ir-rationalities of life in general.

Life's Dance Frederick Delius, 1899.

The tone poem for orchestra is based on Helge Rode's play *Dansen Gaar* ("A Dance Goes On"). The first version was titled with the French near equivalent, *La Danse se déroule* ("The Dance Goes On"). The present English title was adopted for the revised version (1901).

Ligatura–Message to Frances-Marie György Kurtág, 1989.

The work for cello with two bows, strings, and organ or celesta, Op. 31b, subtitled *The Answered Unanswered Question*, was written in response to the musical interrogation of Charles Ives's The **Unanswered Question**. It was composed for Frances-Marie Uitti, a cellist who had developed a technique of playing with two bows. A ligature is both a slur and a tie, here not just in the strict musical sense but more generally and allusively.

Light Fantastic Emmanuel Chabrier, 1953.

The ballet in one act, choreographed by Walter Gore, shows how a Go-Getter, a Moon-Gazer, and Three Hopefuls ruminate on what young men's fancy turns to in the spring. The title quotes the familiar phrase from John Milton's *L'Allegro* (1631): "Come and trip it as ye go / On the light fantastic toe."

The Light of Life Edward Elgar, 1895–6.

The oratorio, Op. 29, is set to a biblical text by Edward Capel Cure. The work is also known by the Latin title originally proposed for it, *Lux Christi* ("The Light of Christ"), but this was thought to be too Catholic for the (Anglican) Worcester Festival where it was first performed. The English title quotes Christ's words: "I am the light of the world: he that followeth me shall not walk in darkness, but shall have the light of life" (John 8:12). (At one point Elgar had favored the title *The Light that Shineth*, believing that *The Light of Life* had been used by another composer.)

The Lighthouse Peter Maxwell Davies, 1979.

The opera in a prologue and one act, to the composer's own libretto, is set in the Hebrides in 1900 and tells the story of three lighthouse keepers who are driven mad by claustrophobia and isolation, only to be replaced by a fresh trio who will inevitably meet the same fate. The plot is based on an actual event in 1900 when the three keepers of the Flannan lighthouse in the Outer Hebrides mysteriously disappeared.

Lights Out Ivor Gurney, 1918–25.

The song cycle comprises settings of six poems by Edward Thomas, including the one of the title, beginning "I have come to the borders of sleep" (1917).

Lilac Time *see* **Blossom Time**.

The Lily of Killarney Julius Benedict, 1862.

The opera in three acts is set to a libretto by John Oxenford and Dion Boucicault based on the latter's play *The Colleen Bawn* (1860). The story tells what happens when Hardress Cregan is encouraged to marry the heiress, Ann Chute, to solve his family's financial problems, although he is already married in secret to the peasant, Eily O'Connor, the "lily of Killarney" of the title. (The play's title represents Irish *cailín bán*, "fair-haired girl.")

A Lincoln Portrait Aaron Copland, 1942.

The work for speaker and orchestra is a study of the personality and career of Abraham Lincoln (1809–1865) and its text is made up of extracts from Lincoln's letters and speeches.

A Lincoln Symphony Daniel Gregory Mason, 1935–6.

The four movements of the Symphony No. 3, Op. 35, depict various stages in the life of Abraham Lincoln (1809–1865). The movements are: (1) *The Candidate from Springfield*, describing Lincoln's early manhood; (2) *Massa Linkum*, patterned after a spiritual, to reflect Lincoln's popularity among blacks; (3) *Old Abe's Yarns*, representing his broad sense of humor; (4) *1865 — marcia funebre*, a lament for his assassination. The first movement includes the *Quaboag Quickstep*, a popular song of the 1860s.

Lincolnshire Posy Percy Grainger, 1937–8.

The suite for two pianos comprises settings of Lincolnshire folksongs that the composer had himself collected some 30 years earlier. *Cf.* **Brigg Fair**.

Linda di Chamounix ("Linda of Chamonix") Gaetano Donizetti, 1842.

The opera in three acts is set to a libretto by Gaetano Rossi based on the vaudeville *La Grâce de Dieu* ("The Grace of God") (1841) by Adolphe Philippe d'Ennery and Gustave Lemoine. The plot is set in France in the 1760s and tells what happens when Antonio and Maddalena, of Chamonix in Haute-Savoie, send their daughter, Linda, to Paris in order to avoid the attentions of the Marchese de Boisfleury, who had offered to educate her at his château.

Linz Symphony   W.A. Mozart, 1783.

The Symphony No. 36 in C major, K 425, is so named because it was composed in the Austrian town of Linz at the house of Count Thun, where Mozart and his wife stayed on their return from Salzburg to Vienna, and because it was first performed in that town.

Litanies à la Vierge Noire de Rocamadour ("Litanies to the Black Virgin of Rocamadour")   Francis Poulenc, 1936.

The work for women's or children's chorus and organ was written when the composer recovered his religious faith following the death of a close friend in an automobile crash. The revival of his Roman Catholicism involved a visit to the shrine of the Black Virgin of the title. Rocamadour is a village in central France.

The Little Fugue (German, *Kleine Fuge*) J.S. Bach, c. 1717.

The Fugue in G minor for Organ, BWV 578, is so named to distinguish it from the **Great Fugue** in the same key.

The Little Mermaid (Danish, *Den lille Havfrue*)   Fini Henriques, 1909.

The fairy ballet in three acts, with a libretto by John Lehmann and choreography by Hans Beck, is based on Hans Christian Andersen's fairy tale of the same name (1836), telling how the youngest daughter of a merking rescues a young prince from a shipwreck and falls in love with him.

Little Russian Symphony (Russian, *Malorossiyskaya simfoniya*)   Pyotr Tchaikovsky, 1872.

The Symphony No. 2 in C minor, Op. 17, is so called not for its brevity but because it incorporates folksongs from "Little Russia" (modern Ukraine). Hence the work's alternate title of *Ukrainian Symphony*.

The Little Stork (Russian, *Aistyonok*) Dmitry Klebanov, 1937.

The ballet in three acts, choreographed by Alexander Radunsky, Lev Pospekhin, and Nikolai Popko, tells how a lost baby stork is rescued and raised by some pioneers.

The Little Sweep *see* **Let's Make an Opera**.

Little Symphony   Franz Schubert, 1818.

The Symphony No. 6 in C major, D 589, is sometimes so known, either by contrast with the the longer Symphony No. 7 in E major (1821) or for distinction from the **Great Symphony** in the same key.

Liturgical Symphony (French, *Symphonie liturgique*)   Arthur Honegger, 1946.

The composer commented on the name of his Symphony No. 3: "Each of the three sections endeavors to express an idea, a thought which I should presume to call philosophical, but which is my own personal feeling. I have therefore called upon liturgical subtitles and given the work the name of 'Liturgical Symphony.'" (quoted in Berkowitz, p. 93). The three movements themselves have individual titles: *Dies Irae* ("Day of Wrath"), *De Profundis Clamavi* ("Out of the Depths Have I Cried"), and *Dona Nobis Pacem* ("Give Us Peace").

Liverpool Overture   Alan Bush, 1972.

The orchestral overture was composed to mark the 125th anniversary of the Liverpool Trades Council. It includes maritime themes, as appropriate for one of England's leading seaports.

Livre du Saint Sacrament ("Book of the Holy Sacrament")   Olivier Messiaen, 1982.

The organ work in 18 sections celebrates the transubstantiation of Christ during the Eucharist (the conversion of the bread and wine into his body and blood), and this is thus the Holy Sacrament of the title.

Livre pour quatuor (French, "Book for Quartet")   Pierre Boulez, 1949.

The work is a string quartet in six movements. It is a "book" since it can be opened and read (played) at random and each movement performed separately or in permutation with any or all of the others, according to the wish of the players. An orchestrated version of the work was entitled *Livre pour cordes* ("Book for Strings") (1960).

Lo (Italian, "The").

For titles beginning with this word, see the next word, *e.g.* Lo **Speziale**.

Lobgesang ("Hymn of Praise")   Felix Mendelssohn, 1840.

The symphony-cantata in B flat, Op. 52, otherwise Symphony No. 2, is in four movements of which only the last is choral as a "hymn of praise."

The Lodger   Phyllis Tate, 1959–60.

The opera in two acts is set to a libretto by David Franklin based on the novel of the same name by Marie Belloc-Lowndes (1913) about the "Jack the Ripper" murders in London.

Lodoïska   Luigi Cherubini, 1791.

The opera in three acts is set to a libretto by Claude François Fillette-Loraux based on an episode in Jean-Baptiste Louvet de Couvray's long novel *Les Amours du chevalier de Faublas* ("The Loves of the Chevalier de Faublas") (1787–9). The story tells what happens when Count Floreski goes in search of Lodoïska, whom he wishes to marry, and learns that Dourlinksi, who also plans to wed her, is holding her prisoner in his castle.

Lodoletta   Pietro Mascagni, 1917.

The opera in three acts is set to a libretto by Giovacchino Forzano based on Ouida's novel *Two Little Wooden Shoes* (1874). The story is set in 19th-century Holland and tells what happens when Antonio loves Lodoletta and gives her a pair of new red shoes.

Lohengrin   Richard Wagner, 1850.

The opera in three acts is set to a libretto by the composer based on an anonymous German epic. The story takes place in 10th-century Antwerp and centers on the mysterious knight, Lohengrin, who suddenly appears to champion the duke's daughter, Elsa, and who agrees to marry her if she never asks his name. *See also* **Wedding March**.

I Lombardi alla prima crociata ("The Lombards at the First Crusade")   Giuseppe Verdi, 1842–3.

The opera in four acts is set to a libretto by Temistocle Solera based on Tommaso Grossi's poem of the same title (1826). The plot is set in Milan and the Holy Land in the 11th century and tells what happens when Pagano returns from an exile imposed for trying to kill his brother, Arvino, on the day of his marriage to Viclinda, whom both brothers love. *See also* **Jérusalem**.

A London Overture   John Ireland, 1936.

The orchestral work was originally written for brass band (1934) under the title *Comedy Overture*. It is based on the sights and sounds of London, and one of the themes is said to have been suggested by a bus conductor's call of "Dilly! Piccadilly!".

London Symphonies   Joseph Haydn, 1791–5.

The name is that of the last 12 symphonies, Nos. 93 through 104. They were composed for the impresario Johann Peter Salomon (hence their alternate name of *Salomon Symphonies*) and were first performed in London during the composer's visits in 1791–2 and 1794–5. They include the **Clock**, **Drumroll**, **Miracle**, **Military**, and **Surprise** symphonies, and the last of the group, No. 104, is usually known, perhaps as it completes the series, as the *London Symphony*, or less often as the *Salomon Symphony*.

London Symphony *see* **London Symphonies**.

A London Symphony   Ralph Vaughan Williams, 1912–13.

The Symphony No. 2 contains musical evocations of early 20th-century London, such as Westminster chimes, a lavender seller's cry, the jingle of hansom cabs, and the sounds of street musicians. The composer himself felt that a better title might be *Symphony by a Londoner*.

Londonderry Air *see* **Irish Tune from County Derry**

The Long Christmas Dinner *see* **Das Lange Weihnachtsmahl**.

Lord Byron   Virgil Thomson, 1972.

The opera in three acts, to a libretto by Jack Larson, is set in London and restropectively recounts key events in the life of the named romantic poet (1788–1824).

Die Lorelei ("The Lorelei")   Felix Mendelssohn, 1847.

The (unfinished) opera in three acts is set to a libretto by Emmanuel von Giebel based on the German legend of the Lorelei, a siren (beautiful woman) who sings on a mountain by the Rhine and lures sailors to their death on the rocks below. *Cf.* **Loreley**.

Loreley ("Lorelei")   Alfredo Catalani, 1890.

The opera in three acts is set to a libretto by Carlo d'Ormeville based on the German legend of the Lorelei, a siren who sings on a mountain by the Rhine and lures sailors to their death on the rocks below. *Cf.* Die **Lorelei**.

The Lost Chord   Arthur Sullivan, 1877.

The song is set to Adelaide Anne Procter's poem *A Lost Chord* (1858) about a woman who is "weary and ill at ease" as she sits at the organ but who who finally strikes "one chord of music / Like the sound of a great Amen." Sullivan composed the song when grieving for his brother.

Lost Happiness *see* **Lieder ohne Worte.**

Lost Illusion *see* **Lieder ohne Worte.**

Lost Illusions (Russian, *Utrachennye illyuzii*) Boris Asafiev, 1935.

The ballet in three acts (13 scenes), with a libretto by V. Dmitriev and choreography by Rostislav Zakharov, is based on Honoré de Balzac's novel cycle *Splendeurs et misères des courtisanes* ("Splendors and Miseries of the Courtesans") (1838–47), and centers on the poor composer, Lucien, who loves a ballerina but leaves her for a rival in order to get his ballet performed.

Louise   Gustave Charpentier, 1896.

The opera in four acts, to the composer's own libretto, tells what happens when the working-class girl, Louise, loves the painter, Julien, but their parents refuse to allow them to marry. The composer's mistress was named Louise at the time he wrote the work. *See also* **Julien.**

Le Loup ("The Wolf")   Henri Dutilleux, 1953.

The ballet in one act, with a libretto by Jean Anouilh and G. Neveux and choreography by Roland Petit, tells what happens when a bride is tricked by her bridegroom into marrying a wolf.

The Love for Three Oranges (Russian, *Lyubov' k trëm apel'sinam*)   Sergey Prokofiev, 1921.

The opera in a prologue and four acts, Op. 33, is set to the composer's own libretto based on Carlo Gozzi's play *L'amore delle tre melarance* ("The Love for Three Oranges") (1761). The story is set in a mythical land and tells what happens when the witch, Fata Morgana, prophesies that the Prince finds will fall in love with three oranges and so be cured of his melancholy. The English title sometimes appears in the somewhat ambiguous form *The Love of Three Oranges.*

Love in a Village   Thomas Arne, 1762

The ballad opera ("*pasticcio*") in three acts, with music collected and arranged by the composer and 16 others, has rustic love as its overall theme.

The Love of Three Oranges *see* **The Love for Three Oranges.**

The Love Potion *see* **L'Elisir d'amore**

"Love, too frequently betrayed."

Tom Rakewell's aria in Act 1 of Stravinsky's The **Rake's Progress**, in which he calls on love to remain with him even as he betrays it in Mother Goose's brothel.

"The Lover and the nightingale" *see* "La Maja y el ruiseñor."

Lovers, Learners and Libations   Judith Weir, 1987.

The work for singers and early music consort, subtitled *Scenes from 13th-Century Parisian Life*, is based on the music of the French liturgical composer Pérotin (*c.*1160–*c.*1236). The title alludes alliteratively to three preoccupations of the day, a sort of medieval equivalent of "wine, women, and song."

The Loves of Mars and Venus   Henry Symonds, 1717.

The *ballet d'action* in six scenes, with a libretto and choreography by John Weaver, first introduces the two gods and lovers, Mars and Venus, then shows how Vulcan forges the net in which the Cyclops eventually ensnares them.

"La Luce langue" ("The light fades").

Lady Macbeth's aria in Act 2 of Verdi's **Macbeth**, welcoming the darkness of night that will mask the murder of Duncan.

Lucia di Lammermoor   Gaetano Donizetti, 1835.

The opera in three acts is set to a libretto by Salvatore Cammarano based on Sir Walter Scott's novel *The Bride of Lammermoor* (1819), in which Lucy Ashton is a young woman who goes mad and dies on her wedding night when forced to marry a man she does not love.

Lucifer   Halim El-Dabh, 1975.

The ballet in one act, with a libretto and choreography by Martha Graham, centers on the biblical Lucifer, but presents him as a bringer of light (the literal meaning of his name), not as Satan: "When Lucifer fell from the heavens, he became half god, half man, and he came to know man's fear and challenge" (Martha Graham, quoted in Koegler, p. 263).

Lucio Silla   W.A. Mozart, 1772.

The opera in three acts, K 135, to a libretto by Giovanni da Gamerra (altered by Pietro Metastasio), tells of an incident in the life of the Roman dictator Lucius Silla (138–78 BC).

Lucky Peter's Journey   Malcolm Williamson, 1969.

The opera in three acts is set to a libretto

by Edmund Tracey based on August Strindberg's play *Lycko-Pers resa* ("Lucky Peter's Journey") (1881). The story is that of the quest-hero of the title who finds both himself and true love after rejecting the false lures of worldly success.

Lucrezia Borgia Gaetano Donizetti, 1833.

The opera in a prologue and two acts is set to a libretto by Felice Romani based on Victor Hugo's tragedy *Lucrèce Borgia* (1833) centering on the historical Lucrezia Borgia (1480–1519), daughter of the future pope, Alexander VI, and telling of the fate of the young captain, Gennaro, who is drawn to her and whom she alone knows to be her son.

Ludus tonalis ("The Play of Tones") Paul Hindemith, 1942.

The piano pieces, consisting of a prelude, 12 fugues with 11 interludes, and a postlude, are subtitled *Studies in Counterpoint, Tonal Organization, and Piano Playing*. The Latin title could equally be translated, however, as "The Play of Notes."

Luisa Miller Giuseppe Verdi, 1849.

The opera in three acts is set to a libretto by Salvatore Cammarano based on Friedrich von Schiller's tragedy *Kabale und Liebe* ("Intrigue and Love") (1784). The story is set in the Tyrol in the early 18th century and tells of the love of Luisa, daughter of the old soldier Miller, for Rodolfo, whom she believes to be a commoner but who is really a count's son.

Lulu Alban Berg, 1937.

The (unfinished) opera in three acts is set to the composer's own libretto based on Frank Wedekind's dramas *Erdgeist* ("Earth Spirit") (1895) and *Die Büchse der Pandora* ("Pandora's Box") (1901). The story recounts the fate of the *femme fatale*, Lulu, and of her various husbands.

Luonnotar Jean Sibelius, 1910–13.

The tone poem for soprano and orchestra, Op. 70, is set to words from the Finnish epic *Kalevala* telling of the creation of the world.

Lurline Vincent Wallace, 1860.

The opera is set to a libretto by Edward Fitzball based on the German legend of the Lorelei. (*See* **Loreley**.) Lurline is the bewitching woman who is the central character. (Her name is based on *Lurlei*, an older German form of *Lorelei*.)

Der Lustige Krieg ("The Merry War") Johann Strauss II, 1881.

The operetta in three acts, to a libretto by F. Zell (pen name of Camillo Walzell) and Richard Genée, is set in and around Massa, Italy, in the early 18th century. The story tells of the "merry war" between the Prince of Massa-Carrara and the Doge of Genoa, "merry" because it arose as dispute over a ballerina, and also because the Prince's army is entirely officered by ladies of his court, with Countess Violetta Lomellini as commander-in-chief.

Die Lustige Witwe ("The Merry Widow") Franz Lehár, 1905.

The operetta in three acts is set to a libretto by Viktor Léon and Leo Stein based on Henri Meilhac's comedy *L'Attaché d'ambassade* ("The Embassy Attaché"). The plot centers on the attempts of Baron Mirko Zeta to obtain the fortune of Hanna Glawari (the "merry widow" of the title) for his impoverished country of Pontevedria.

Die Lustigen Weiber von Windsor ("The Merry Wives of Windsor") Otto Nicolai, 1849.

The opera in three acts is set to a libretto by Salomon Hermann Mosenthal based on Shakespeare's comedy of the same name (1599).

Lux Christi *see* The **Light of Life**.

Lyric Pieces *see* **Lyric Suite** (1).

Lyric Suite (1) Edvard Grieg, 1904; (2) Alban Berg, 1925–6.

Grieg's work is an orchestral arrangement of four of the six piano pieces in Book 5, Op. 54 (1891), of his *Lyric Pieces* (Norwegian, *Lyriske stykker*), Op. 54 (1891), with individual titles: *Shepherd Boy* (Norwegian, *Gjætergut*; German, *Hirtenknabe*), *Norwegian March* (Norwegian, *Gangar*; German, *Norwegischer Bauernmarsch*), *March of the Trolls* (Norwegian, *Troltog*; German, *Zug der Zwerge*), *Nocturne* (*Notturno*). The title reflects the overall work in ten books (1867–1901) from which the suite derives. (*See also* **Wedding Day at Troldhaugen**.) Berg's string quartet in six movements was inspired by his love affair with Hanna Fuchs-Robettin, whose initials, combined with his own, provide the German note row H-F-A-B (the equivalent of B-F-A-B flat). The work's title relates to its romantic origin and is reflected in the musical directions of the movements: *Allegretto giovale*, *Andante amoroso*, *Allegro misterioso-Trio estatico*, *Adagio appassionato*, *Presto delirando-Tenebroso*, and *Largo desolato*. It also quotes from Alexander Zemlinsky's **Lyrische Symphonie**.

Lyrische Symphonie ("Lyric Symphony")
Alexander Zemlinsky, 1922–3.

The work for soprano, baritone, and orchestra comprises seven songs based on poems by Rabindranath Tagore (1861–1941) in the composer's own German translation. The individual titles are: (1) *Ich bin friedlos* ("I am restless"), (2) *Mutter, der junge Prinz muß an unsere Türe vorbeikommen* ("Mother, the young prince will pass our door"), (3) *Du bist die Abendwolke* ("Thou art the evening cloud"), (4) *Sprich zu mir, Geliebter!* ("Speak to me, beloved"), (5) *Befrei mich von den Banden deiner süße Lieb!* ("Free me from the bonds of thy sweet love"), (6) *Vollende denn das letzte Lied und laß uns auseinandergehn* ("Then finish the last song and let us leave"), (7) *Friede, mein Herz* ("Peace, my heart"). In the fourth movement of his **Lyric Suite**, which is dedicated to Zemlinsky, Alban Berg quotes the principal theme from No. 3, heard at the words *"Du bist mein Eigen"* ("Thou art my own").

M

Ma mère l'Oye ("Mother Goose")   Maurice Ravel, 1908–10.

The suite in five movements for piano duet was inspired by illustrations to Charles Perrault's fairy tales of the same title (1697). The movements are: *Pavane de la Belle au bois dormant* ("Sleeping Beauty's Pavan"), *Petit poucet* ("Tom Thumb"), *Laideronnette, impératrice des pagodes* ("Ugly Duckling, Empress of the Pagodas"), *Les Entretiens de la Belle et la Bête* ("Conversations of Beauty and the Beast"), and *Le Jardin féerique* ("The Fairy Garden").

Má Vlast ("My Fatherland")   Bedřich Smetana, 1872–9.

The six symphonic poems relate to the composer's native Bohemia (now the western half of the Czech Republic) and have titles as follows: (1) *Vyšehrad* ("High Citadel") (the 9th-century castle around which Prague arose), (2) *Vltava* (the river, also known as the Moldau), (3) *Šárka* (leader of the Bohemian Amazons), (4) *Z českých luhů a hájů* ("From Bohemia's Meadows and Forests"), (5) *Tábor* (the town that was the stronghold of the Hussites), (6) *Blaník* (the mountain in southern Bohemia that is the Valhalla of the Hussite heroes).

Macbeth   (1) Giuseppe Verdi, 1846–7;
(2) Richard Strauss, 1887–8.

Verdi's opera in four acts is set to a text by Francesco Maria Pieve based on Shakespeare's tragedy of the same name (1605), centering on the Scottish noble, Macbeth, whose rise to the throne is predicted by three witches. Strauss's tone poem, Op. 23, was inspired by the same source.

Mad Scene   Gaetano Donizetti, 1835.

The scene in Act 3 of **Lucia di Lammermoor** in which Lucia loses her reason after killing her husband on her wedding night. There are mad scenes in other operas (*cf.* **"Qui la voce"**), but this is the best known.

Mad Tristan   Richard Wagner, 1944.

The ballet in two scenes, with a libretto by Salvador Dalí and choreography by Léonide Massine, is a surrealist portrayal of the feverish dreams of Tristan, with Isolde turning into a praying mantis. *Cf.* **Tristan und Isolde**.

Madam Noy   Arthur Bliss, 1918.

The "Witchery Song" for soprano, flute, clarinet, bassoon, harp, viola, and double bass is set to a text by Edward Meyerstein based on the nursery rhyme *Old Mother Hubbard*.

Madama Butterfly   Giacomo Puccini, 1904.

The opera in two acts is set to a libretto by Giuseppe Giacosa and Luigi Illica based on David Belasco's drama *Madame Butterfly* (1900). This was in turn taken from John Luther Long's short story of the same name (1898) based on a real event. The plot concerns a Japanese geisha who falls in love with an American naval officer, Pinkerton. The geisha's name is Cio-Cio-San, and this gives the opera's title in some countries. *Cf.* **Madame Chrysanthème**.

Madame Chrysanthème ("Madame Chrysanthemum")   André Charles Messager, 1893.

The operetta in a prologue, four acts, and an epilogue is set to a libretto by Georges Hartmann and André Alexandre based on Pierre Loti's novel of the same name (1888). The story is set on a French warship in the late 19th century and tells of the brief marriage of the French naval officer, Pierre, to a Japanese geisha, Madame Chrysanthème. *Cf.* **Madama Butterfly**.

Madame Sans-Gêne ("Madame Carefree")
Umberto Giordano, 1915.

The opera in three acts is set to a libretto by Renato Simoni based on Émile Moreau and Victorien Sardou's play of the same name (1893). The story is set in France in the late 18th and early 19th century and tells how a laundress, Catherine Huebscher ("Madame Carefree" of the title), rises to become a duchess and marry a Napoleonic marshal.

"Ein Mädchen oder Weibchen" ("A girl or a woman").

Papageno's aria in Act 2 of Mozart's Die Zauberflöte, in which he sings of his longing for a wife.

Mademoiselle Fifi (Russian, *Mademuazel' Fifi*)   César Cui, 1903.

The opera is set to a libretto based on Guy de Maupassant's tale of the same name (1882) recounting an episode of the Franco-Prussian war. It tells what happens when a French prostitute shoots a Prussian officer (nicknamed "Mademoiselle Fifi" for his effeminate appearance) who has insulted the French flag.

"Madre, pietosa vergine" ("Mother, merciful Virgin").

Leonora's aria in Act 2 of Verdi's La **Forza del destino**, in which she begs the Virgin Mary for forgiveness as she arrives at the Monastery of Hornachuelos.

Il Maestro di Capella ("The Chorus Master")   Domenico Cimarosa, 1786–93.

The intermezzo for baritone and orchestra is a monodrama about a pompous maestro who rehearses an orchestra and imitates the sounds of the instruments.

The Magelone Romances *see* Die Schöne Magelone.

Magic Fire Music   Richard Wagner, 1876.

The name generally given to the music accompanying the final scene of *Die Walküre* in Der **Ring des Nibelungen**, as Wotan conjures up the fire that will protect Brünnhilde as she sleeps on her rock.

The Magic Flute (1) (Russian, *Volshebnaya fleyta*)   Riccardo Drigo, 1893; (2) *see* Die Zauberflöte.

The ballet in one act, with a libretto and choreography by Lev Ivanov, has nothing to do with Mozart's opera Die Zauberflöte. It centers on Lise, the daughter of a wealthy countrywoman, who loves Luc, a poor peasant boy, and tells what happens when a hermit gives Luc a flute that makes everyone dance.

The Magic Fountain   Frederick Delius, 1893–5.

The opera in three acts, set to the composer's own libretto, tells what happens when a 16th-century Spanish explorer, Solano, is shipwrecked off the coast of Florida while searching for the fountain of youth, the "magic fountain" of the title.

Magnificat ("Magnifieth").

The first word of the Latin Canticle of the Virgin Mary, more fully "*Magnificat anima mea Dominum*," "My soul doth magnify the Lord" (Luke 1:46). There are many settings for both church and concert performance, among them C.P.E. Bach's *Magnificat* (1749) and Vaughan Williams's *Magnificat* (1932). *See also* **Nunc Dimittis**.

Mahler   Gustav Mahler, 1978.

The ballet in three parts, choreographed by Maurice Béjart, is set to the composer's music for the three individual parts titled as follows: (1) *Ce que la mort me dit* ("What Death Tells Me"), from the *Lieder nach Rückert* ("Rückert Lieder") (1901–2) and Des **Knaben Wunderhorn**, (2) *Chant du compagnon errant* ("Song of the Wayfarer"), from **Lieder eines fahrenden Gesellen**, and (3) *Ce que l'amour me dit* ("What Love Tells Me"), from the last three movements of the Symphony No. 3 in D minor (1895–6) (*see* **Ce que l'amour me dit**). The titles of (1) and (3) are punningly similar in French.

Mai-Dun   John Ireland, 1921.

The symphonic rhapsody for orchestra was inspired by Maiden Castle, a prehistoric fortification in Dorset, England, and the title represents the version of its name used by Thomas Hardy in his novels.

Maid Marian   Henry Bishop, 1822.

The opera, subtitled *The Huntress of Arlingford*, is set to a libretto by James Robinson Planché based on Thomas Love Peacock's novel of the same title (1822), a medieval romance featuring Maid Marian (Robin Hood's sweetheart), Friar Tuck, and Prince John and lampooning institutions such as the monarchy and the church. Many of the novel's scenes are essentially cast as duets or quartets, and this, together with its subject, facilitated its rapid reworking as an operetta.

The Maid of Honour   Michael Balfe, 1847.

The opera, set to a libretto by Edward

Fitzball, is based on the same subject as Flotow's **Martha**, so that the "maid of honor" of the title is Lady Harriet Durham.

The Maid of Orleans (Russian, *Orleanskaya deva*) Pyotr Tchaikovsky, 1878–9.

The opera in four acts is set to the composer's own libretto based on Vasily Andreyevich Zhukovsky's translation of Friedrich Schiller's verse play *Die Jungfrau von Orleans* ("The Maid of Orleans") (1801) about Joan of Arc. *Cf.* **Giovanna d'Arco, Joan of Arc.**

The Maid of Pskov (Russian, *Pskovityanka*) Nikolai Rimsky-Korsakov, 1868–72.

The opera in four acts is set to the composer's own libretto based on Lev Alexandrovich Mey's verse play of the same title (1860). The story is set in 16th-century Russia and tells how Ivan the Terrible, having destroyed Novgorod, enters Pskov and there meets the governor's niece, Olga (the "maid" of the title), in love with Tucha. The opera is thus sometimes known by the alternate title *Ivan the Terrible*.

The Maid of the Mill (1) Samuel Arnold, 1765; (2) *see* Die **Schöne Müllerin.**

The opera, a pasticcio, is set to a libretto by Isaac Bickerstaffe based on Samuel Richardson's novel *Pamela* (1740–1). Pamela Andrews is thus the "maid of the mill" of the title.

The Maiden's Prayer (Polish, *Modlitwa dziewicy*) Tekla Badarczewska-Baranowska, 1856.

The song with piano accompaniment, "the most popular of tasteless and sentimental ... drawing-room pieces ever written" (Blom, p. 341), tells of a young woman's yearning for a handsome lover. A French version was published in 1859 as *La Prière d'une vierge*.

The Maids Darius Milhaud, 1957.

The ballet in one act, choreographed by Herbert Ross, is based on Jean Genet's play *Les Bonnes* ("The Maids") (1947) and set to the composer's Concerto for Percussion and Small Orchestra, Op. 109 (1929). The story tells of two maids, played by men, who enact a sinister charade, each trying to impersonate their mistress until one eventually suffocates the other.

Die Mainacht ("The May Night") Johannes Brahms, 1868.

The song for voice and piano, the second of his set of four, Op. 43, is a setting of one of Ludwig Hölty's *Gedichte* ("Poems") (1783).

Maisara's Tricks (Russian, *Prodelki Maysary*) Suleiman Yudakov, 1959.

The comic opera in a prologue and three acts is set to a libretto by Sabir Abdulla and M. Mukhamedov based on Khakimzade Khamza's play of the same name (1926). The story tells how the cunning Uzbek widow, Maisara, helps her young nephew outsmart his rivals for the hand of the beautiful Aikhon.

Le Maître de chapelle ("The Music Master") Ferdinando Paer, 1821.

The comic opera in two acts is set to a libretto by Sophie Gay based on Alexandre Duval's comedy *Le Souper imprévu* ("The Unforeseen Supper") (1796). The story tells how Barnabé, a fashionable opera composer, tries to enlist the help of his French cook, Gertrude, in a performance of his opera *Cléopâtre* ("Cleopatra").

"La Maja y el ruiseñor" ("The lover and the nightingale").

Rosario's aria in Tableau 3 of Granados's **Goyescas,** sung as she waits for her lover and reflects on the nature of love. Its English title, as above, is commonly used.

Makrokosmos George Crumb, 1972.

The 12 fantasy pieces for amplified piano are depictions of the 12 signs of the Zodiac and portraits of 12 of the composer's friends, each born under a different sign. The overall title represents the Greek word meaning "macrocosm," "universe" (literally "great world").

The Makropulos Affair (Czech, *Věc Makropulos*) Leoš Janáček, 1926.

The opera in three acts is set to a libretto by the composer based on Karel Čapek's drama of the same name (1922). The plot centers on Elena Makropulos, a 300-year-old woman who seeks the formula of the elixir that she was forced to take and that made her the age she is. The Czech title literally translates as "The Makropulos Thing," hence variations in the English title, which is also found as *The Makropulos Case* or *The Makropulos Secret*.

Les Malheurs d'Orphée ("The Sorrows of Orpheus") Darius Milhaud, 1924.

The opera in three acts, Op. 85, to a libretto by Armand Lunel, is a modern retelling of the story about the poet and musician, Orpheus, who followed his wife, Eurydice, to the underworld after her death to get her back. In this version, the magic that Orpheus uses to heal animals is unable to cure his gypsy lover, Eurydice, when she develops a serious illness.

La Malinche ("Malinche")   N. Lloyd, 1949.

The ballet in one act, with a libretto and choreography by José Limón, deals with Hernán Cortés's conquest of Mexico (1519–21). The title is the name of the Indian princess (*c*.1501–1550) who served Cortés as an interpreter.

The Mamelles de Tirésias ("The Breasts of Tiresias")   Francis Poulenc, 1947.

The opera in two acts is set to a libretto based on Guillaume Apollinaire's surrealist play of the same name (1917). This tells how Thérèse is converted to feminism and to demonstrate her liberation does away with her sinful breasts (by symbolically bursting balloons) and adopts the male name Tirésias. In classical mythology Tiresias was the blind prophet who was transformed from a man into a woman. *See also* **Tiresias**.

"La Mamma morta" ("My mother dead").

Madeleine de Coigny's aria in Act 3 of Giordano's **Andrea Chénier**, in which she tells Gérard of the terrible death of her mother when their house was burned by the revolutionary mob.

Mam'zelle Angot   Charles Lecocq, 1943.

The ballet in three scenes, with a librettoand choreography by Léonide Massine, is based on the composer's operetta La **Fille de Madame Angot**, and depicts a relay of characters who are each in love with somebody who unfortunately loves someone else.

Mam'zelle Nitouche   Hervé (pen name of Florimond Ronger), 1883.

The operetta in three acts, to a libretto by Henri Meilhac and Albert Millaud, is set in Paris in 1883 and tells of a convent girl, Denise de Flavigny, who visits a theater under the alias of "Mam'zelle Nitouche" and steps into the breach when the leading actress suddenly leaves. *Sainte nitouche* is a French nickname for a pious hypocrite (from *sainte*, "holy" and *n'y touche pas*, "don't touch").

The Man Who Mistook His Wife for a Hat   Michael Nyman, 1985–6.

The opera is set to a libretto by Christopher Rawlence based on Oliver Sacks's neurological case-study of the same name (1985). The plot recounts what happens when Dr. P, prone to making absurd visual errors, grabs his wife's head instead of his hat on leaving his surgery.

The Man Without a Country   Leopold Damrosch, 1937.

The opera in two acts is set to a libretto by Arthur Guiterman based on Edward Everett Hale's tale of the same name (1863), written to inspire greater patriotism in the Civil War. The story tells what happens when Philip Nolan, a young US Army officer, is deported for his impulsive shouts of treason in a courtroom and travels without a country for 50 years.

La Mandragola ("The Mandrake")   Mario Castelnuovo-Tedesco, 1920.

The opera is set to a libretto based on Machiavelli's *Commedia di Callimaco e di Lucrezia* ("Comedy of Callimachus and Lucretia"), later retitled *La Mandragora* (1518), satirizing the wickedness and corruption of men, and especially the clergy. The forked root of the mandrake, resembling a male human figure, was long believed to possess an evil power.

Manfred   (1) Robert Schumann, 1848–9; (2) Pyotr Tchaikovsky, 1885.

Schumann's overture and 15 items of incidental music, Op. 115, were written for K.A. Suckow's translation of Byron's verse drama of the same title (1817), in which Manfred is a man haunted by the demons of guilt for an unexplained crime. Tchaikovsky's (unnumbered) Symphony, Op. 58, is based on the same source.

Il Maniatico ("The Manic")   Gaetano Brunetti, 1786.

The Symphony No. 33 in C minor has a prominent solo cello part which at times displays excessive enthusiasm and has to be calmed by the orchestra. The allusion is believed to be to Brunetti's rival composer, Luigi Boccherini, a noted cellist.

Manon   Jules Massenet, 1884.

The opera in five acts is set to a libretto by Henri Meilhac and Philippe Gille based on Abbé Antoine-François Prévost's novel *Manon Lescaut* (in full, *Histoire du chevalier des Grieux et de Manon Lescaut*) (1731), in which the Chevalier des Grieux falls in love with Manon when he meets her at an inn with her cousin Lescaut on her way to a convent. The 1974 ballet of the same name, with a libretto and choreography by Kenneth MacMillan, is set to the music for this work and also roughly follows Abbé Prévost's novel. *See also* **Boulevard Solitude, Manon Lescaut**.

Manon Lescaut   Giacomo Puccini, 1893.

The opera in four acts is set to a libretto by

Luigi Illica, Giuseppe Giacosa, Giulio Ricordi, Marco Praga, and Domenica Oliva based on Abbé Antoine-François Prévost's novel of the same name (1731) (*see* **Manon**).

Manru   Ignacy Paderewski, 1901.

The opera in three acts is set to a libretto by Alfred Nossig based on Josef Ignacy Kraszewski's novel *The Cabin Behind the Wood* (1843). The story tells what happens when Ulana marries the gypsy, Manru, against her mother's wishes but he proves inconstant.

Mantra   Karlheinz Stockhausen, 1969–70.

The work for two amplified, ring-modulated pianos and percussion (woodblocks and little bells, also played by the pianists) is based on a single melodic formula. Hence its title, from the Indian word for a mystical repetition (literally, "instrument of thought").

Manzoni Requiem. *see* **Requiem** (1).

Maometto II ("Mahomet II")   Gioacchino Rossini, 1820.

The opera in two acts is set to a libretto by Cesare della Valle based on his own play *Anna Erizo* and Voltaire's tragedy *Mahomet* (1741). The story is set in the 15th century and tells what happens when Anna, daughter of the governor of a Venetian colony in Greece, falls in love with the Turkish monarch, Maometto. The revised version of the opera was Le **Siège de Corinthe**.

The Marble Maiden   Adolphe Adam, 1845.

The ballet by Jules-Henri Vernoy de Saint-Georges, choreographed by François Albert, is an English version of La **Fille de marbre**.

March of the Women   Ethel Smyth, 1911.

The work for chorus and orchestra was written as the battle song of the Women's Social and Political Union, a women's rights organization. The composer was in Holloway Jail at the time as a result of her militant campaign for women's suffrage, and she conducted the work's maiden performance out of her cell window with a toothbrush while women in the yard below sang the words (by Cicely Hamilton).

Marche militaire ("Military March")   Franz Schubert, 1822.

The popular March No. 1 in D major for Two Pianos, D 733, the first of a set of three, is a piece such as a military band might play, and has indeed been arranged for such.

Marche slave   *see* **Slavonic March**.

Marco Spada   Daniel Auber, 1857.

The ballet in three acts (six scenes), with a libretto by Eugène Scribe and choreography by Joseph Mazilier, tells what happens when Count Federici, who is betrothed to the Marchesa Sampietri, loves Angela without realizing that she is the daughter of the bandit chief, Marco Spada. The subtitle is thus *La Fille du bandit* ("The Bandit's Daughter").

Marguerite and Armand   Franz Liszt, arr. Humphrey Searle, 1963.

The ballet in one act, with a libretto and choreography by Frederick Ashton, is set to an orchestral version of the composer's Piano Sonata in B minor (1852–3) and *La Lugubre Gondole* ("The Lugubrious Gondola") (1882). The story tells the story of Marguerite Gautier and her lover, Armand, from Alexandre Dumas's novel *La Dame aux camélias* (1848) (*see* The **Lady of the Camellias**), with events shown in a series of flashbacks from her deathbed.

Maria di Rohan   Gaetano Donizetti, 1843.

The opera in three acts is set to a libretto by Salvatore Cammarano based on the play *Un duel sous le Cardinal de Richelieu* ("A Duel Under Cardinal Richelieu") (1832) by Édouard Lockroy (pen name of Joseph-Philippe Simon). Maria is secretly married to Enrico, duc de Chevreuse, who is arrested when he kills Cardinal Richelieu's nephew in a duel. The story tells what happens when she fall in love with Riccardo, comte de Chalais, and begs him to intercede for Enrico.

Maria Golovin   Gian-Carlo Menotti, 1958.

The opera in three acts, to the composer's own libretto, tells how Maria, awaiting the return of her husband from a prisoner-of-war camp, becomes the mistress of a jealous young blind man.

Maria Stuarda ("Mary Stuart")   Gaetano Donizetti, 1834.

The opera in three acts is set to a libretto by Giuseppe Bardari based on Friedrich von Schiller's play *Maria Stuart* (1800). This is set in England in 1567 and centers on the love of Queen Elizabeth I for the Earl of Leicester, who himself loves Mary, Queen of Scots (Mary Stuart), imprisoned at Fortheringhay Castle. When censorship caused the first performance to be banned, the music was used for an opera with a different plot, *Buondelmonte*. The first performance of *Maria Stuarda* was thus in 1835.

Maria Theresia Symphony   Joseph Haydn, 1768–9.

The Symphony No. 48 in C major was written for visit by the Austrian empress, Maria Theresa (Marie-Thérèse), to Prince Paul Esterházy at the palace of Eszterháza, where the composer was then residing and employed. The title is often rendered in English as the *Maria Theresa Symphony*.

Le Mariage aux lanternes ("Marriage by Lamplight")   Jacques Offenbach, 1853.

The operetta in one act, to a libretto by Jules Dubois (pen name of Léon Battu and Michel Carré), is set outside a country farmhouse and tells of the love of the farmer, Guillot, for his cousin, Denise, and of their eventual marriage by the light of the villagers' lanterns.

Mariazellermesse ("Mariazell Mass") Joseph Haydn, 1782.

The Mass No. 6 in C major was commissioned as a votive offering for the Benedictine monastery at Mariazell, southwest of Vienna. Hence the title.

Das Marienleben ("The Life of Mary") Paul Hindemith, 1922–3.

The song cycle for soprano and piano is set to Rainer Maria Rilke's short poetry cycle of the same title (1913) on the life of the Virgin Mary.

Les Mariés de la tour Eiffel ("The Couples on the Eiffel Tower")   various (see below), 1921.

The ballet in one act, with a libretto by Jean Cocteau and choreography by Jean Börlin, is set to music by Georges Auric, Darius Milhaud, Germaine Tailleferre, Arthur Honegger, and Francis Poulenc, five members of the group of young "progressive" French composers known as Les Six. The action takes place on July 14, the French national holiday, on the first platform of the Eiffel Tower, Paris, where the attempts of a hunchbacked photographer to take shots of a wedding party are constantly frustrated.

Marino Faliero   Gaetano Donizetti, 1835.

The opera in three acts is set to a libretto by Emanuele Bidera based on Casimir Delavigne's tragedy of the same name (1829), itself based on Byron's tragedy *Marino Faliero, Doge of Venice* (1821). The story, founded on historical fact, is set in Venice in 1355 and tells of the love of Elena, wife of the Doge of Venice, Marino Faliero (1274–1355), for the Doge's nephew, Fernando.

Maritana   Vincent Wallace, 1845.

The opera in three acts is set to a libretto by Edward Fitzball (with interpolated lyrics by Alfred Bunn) based on Adolphe Philippe d'Ennery and Philippe François Dumanoir's play *Don César de Bazan* ("Don Caesar of Bazan") (1844). The story tells how the young wealthy courtier, Don José, attempts to win the love of the queen of Spain by hatching a devious plot which involves his persuading the gypsy street singer, Maritana, to marry an impecunious nobleman, Don Caesar de Bazan.

Mârouf, savetier du Caire ("Mârouf, Cobbler of Cairo")   Henri Rabaud, 1914.

The opera in four acts is set to a libretto by Lucien Népoty based on the *Thousand and One Nights* (*Arabian Nights*) telling what happens when the cobbler, Mârouf, goes to sea to escape his shrewish wife, Fatoumah.

La Marquise de Brinvilliers ("The Marquise de Brinvilliers")   various (see below), 1831.

The opera in three acts, collectively composed by Daniel Auber, Désiré Batton, Henri-Montan Berton, Felice Blangini, François Boieldieu, Michele Carafa, Luigi Cherubini, Ferdinand Hérold, and Ferdinando Paer, is set to a libretto by Eugène Scribe and François Castil-Blaze treating the life and loves of the famous (or infamous) poisoner, Marie-Madeleine d'Aubray, marquise de Brinvilliers (1630–1676).

The Marriage (Russian, *Zhenit'ba*)   Modest Mussorgsky, 1868.

The (unfinished) opera in four acts is set to the composer's own libretto based on Nikolai Gogol's comedy of the same name (1842). The story centers on the clerk, Podkolesin, who is undecided about marrying Agafya, a merchant's daughter, but who is urged by the marriage broker, Fyokla, not to delay.

The Marriage of Figaro *see* Le **Nozze di Figaro**.

Le Marteau sans maître ("The Hammer Without a Master")   Pierre Boulez, 1952–4.

The work in nine interlocking movements for contralto, alto flute, guitar, vibraphone, xylorimba, percussion, and viola, comprises settings of and commentaries on three surrealist poems by René Char of this title (1934).

"Martern aller Arten" ("Torments of all kinds").

Constanze's aria in Act 2 of Mozart's Die **Entführung aus dem Serail**, in which she declares that neither torture nor even death will make her yield to the Pasha.

Martha   Friedrich von Flotow, 1847.

The opera in four acts is set to a libretto by Friedrich Wilhelm Riese based on Jules-Henri Vernoy de Saint-Georges's ballet pantomime *Lady Henriette, ou La Servante de Greenwich* ("Lady Harriet, or the Servant Girl of Greenwich") (1844), for which Flotow had written some music. The opera is subtitled *Der Markt von Richmond* ("Richmond Fair") and is set in Richmond, near London, around 1710. The story tells what happens when Lady Harriet Durham, a maid of honor to Queen Anne, together with her waiting maid, Nancy, go to Richmond Fair disguised as country girls under the names of Martha and Julia. *See also* The **Maid of Honour**.

The Martyrdom of St. Magnus   Peter Maxwell Davies, 1976–7.

The chamber opera in one act is set to the composer's own libretto based on George Mackay Brown's poem *Magnus* (1973), a lyrical account of the martyrdom of St. Magnus (*c.*1075–1116), the principal saint of Orkney, Scotland, which the composer has made his home since 1970. (The work was given its first performance in St. Magnus Cathedral, Kirkwall, Orkney.) *Cf.* **Hymn to St. Magnus**.

Le Martyre de Saint Sébastien ("The Martyrdom of St. Sebastian")   Claude Debussy, 1911.

The incidental music was composed for Gabriele d'Annunzio's five-act mystery play of the same name (1911), based on the life and martyrdom of St. Sebastian.

Les Martyrs *see* **Poliuto**.

Mary of Egypt   John Tavener, 1990–1.

The opera in five acts, to a libretto by Mother Thekla, is described by the composer as an "Ikon in Music and Dance" and centers on Mary of Egypt, a prostitute in Alexandria, and Zossima, a holy man in a monastery in Palestine. Mother Thekla, abbess of a Greek Orthodox monastery in England, is the spiritual adviser of the composer, who joined the Russian Orthodox Church in 1977.

Mary, Queen of Scots   (1) John McCabe, 1975; (2) Thea Musgrave, 1977.

McCabe's ballet in two acts, with a libretto by Noël Goodwin and choreography by Peter Darrell, presents the life of Mary, Queen of Scots (Mary I Stuart) (1542–1587) from queen of France at age 17 to execution at Fotheringhay Castle at age 45, taking in the men she attracted and married and her relationship with Queen Elizabeth I. Musgrave's opera in three acts is set to a libretto by the composer based on Amalia Elguera's play *Moray*, centering on Mary's time in Scotland.

Masaniello *see* La **Muette de Portici**.

Le Maschere ("The Masks")   Pietro Mascagni, 1901.

The opera in a prologue and three acts, to a libretto by Luigi Illica, has a plot of *commedia dell'arte* characters telling how Florindo and Rosaura, aided by Columbina and Arlecchino, attempt to prevent the marriage which Rosaura's father, Pantalone, has planned for her. The characters wore masks. Hence the title.

La Mascotte ("The Mascot")   Edmond Audran, 1880.

The operetta in three acts, to a libretto by Alfred Duru and Henri Charles Chivot, is set in Piombino, Italy, in the 17th century and tells what happens when the farmer, Rocco, is plagued by misfortune and his brother sends him a goose girl, Bettina, as a lucky mascot.

The Mask of Orpheus   Harrison Birtwistle, 1973–5, 1981–4.

The opera in three acts is set to a libretto by Peter Zinovieff based on the classical legend of the poet and musician, Orpheus, and his wife, Eurydice, who died when she trod on a snake while being pursued by Aristaeus and whom Orpheus sought in Hades after her death. Each of the three roles is taken by three performers to represents three aspects of each (person, hero, and myth), and each of the three acts treats a different aspect of the legend.

Maskarade ("Masquerade")   Carl Nielsen, 1904–6.

The comic opera in three acts is set to a libretto by Vilhelm Andersen based on a play by Ludvig Holberg (1684–1754). The story is set in Copenhagen in 1723 and tells what happens when Leander rejects the bride chosen for him by his parents when he falls in love with Leonora, whom he meets at a masked ball.

A Masked Ball *see* Un **Ballo in Maschera**.

I Masnadieri ("The Robbers"), Giuseppe Verdi, 1847.

The opera in four acts is set to a libretto by

Count Andrea Maffei based on Friedrich von Schiller's play *Die Räuber* ("The Robbers") (1781), telling how Carlo is banished from his father's home and driven to become the leader of a robber band.

Masonic Funeral Music *see* **Maurerische Trauermusik**.

Les Masques ("The Masks")   Francis Poulenc, 1933.

The ballet in one act, with a libretto and choreography by Frederick Ashton, tells how a husband and wife meet at a masked ball and fail to recognize each other.

Masques et bergamasques ("Masks and Bergomasks")   Gabriel Fauré, 1919.

The divertissement, Op. 112, is set to a Watteau scenario by René Fauchois and was inspired by the poetry of Paul Verlaine. The work includes an orchestral version of Verlaine's poem *Clair de lune* ("Moonlight") in which the words of the title occur. *See* **Clair de lune** (1).

Mass.

The word is used for an elaborate choral setting of the principal ritual of the Roman Catholic Church, originally for unaccompanied chorus but later for soloists, chorus, and orchestra. The five sections that are most frequently set are: (1) **Kyrie**, (2) **Gloria**, (3) **Credo**, (4) **Sanctus** (with **Benedictus** properly part of it but usually separated), and (5) **Agnus Dei**. An example of the original type of Mass is Palestrina's **Missa Papae Marcelli**.

Mass for Our Time (French, *Messe pour le temps présent*)   Pierre Henry, 1967.

The work in nine episodes by Maurice Béjart was dedicated to the memory of the French dancer Patrick Belda (1943–1967), killed in am auto accident. The texts were taken from the writings of the Buddha, the biblical Song of Songs, Friedrich Nietzsche's *Also sprach Zarathustra* (*see* **Also sprach Zarathustra**), and nursery rhymes. The sound effects were produced by Béjart himself, while Venugopal Mukunda played the vina (an Indian stringed instrument with a fretted fingerboard over two gourds) and Pierre Henry composed the rock music. The nine episodes are: (1) *The Breath*, (2) *The Body*, (3) *The World*, (4) *The Dance*, (5) *The Couple*, (6) *"Mein Kampf"*, (7) *The Night*, (8) *The Silence*, and (9) *The Waiting*.

A Mass of Life (German, *Eine Messe des Lebens*)   Frederick Delius, 1904–5.

The work for soprano, alto, tenor, and bass soloists, chorus, and orchestra is set to a German text selected by Fritz Cassirer from Friedrich Nietzsche's philosophical poem *Also sprach Zarathustra* ("Thus Spake Zarathustra") (1883–5).

Master Peter's Puppet Show *see* El **Retablo de Maese Pedro**.

The Mastersingers of Nuremberg *see* Die **Meistersinger von Nürnberg**.

Match   Siegfried Matthus, 1970.

The dance duo, choreographed by Tom Schilling, is a pas de deux (dance for two) in the form of a tennis match.

Les Matelots ("The Sailors")   Georges Auric, 1925.

The ballet in five scenes, with a libretto by Boris Kochno and choreography by Léonide Massine, tells how a sailor becomes engaged to his girl before returning to sea, then comes back in disguise with three shipmates to test her fidelity.

Mathilde   Richard Wagner, 1965.

The ballet in one act, with a libretto and choreography by Maurice Béjart, is set to the composer's Prélude and Liebestod from **Tristan und Isolde** and the **Five Wesendonck Songs**. The title refers to his mistress, Mathilde Wesendonck, née Luckemeyer (1828–1902).

Mathis der Maler ("Matthias the Painter")   Paul Hindemith, 1938.

The opera in seven scenes is set to the composer's own libretto based on the life of the German artist Matthias Grünewald (c.1460–1530) and his altarpiece at Isenheim (1512–15). The composer's symphony of the same title (1934) based on the opera has three movements, each representing a panel of the altarpiece: *Engelkonzert* ("Angels' Concert"), *Grablegung* ("Burial"), and *Versuchung des heiligen Antonius* ("Temptation of St. Anthony").

Le Matin ("Morning")   Joseph Haydn, 1761.

The Symphony No. 6 in D major is the first of three regarded as representing a day, the others being Le **Midi** and Le **Soir**.

Il Matrimonio segreto ("The Secret Marriage")   Domenico Cimarosa, 1792.

The opera in two acts is set to a libretto by Giovanni Bertati based on George Colman and David Garrick's comedy *The Clandestine*

Marriage (1766). The plot is set in 18th-century Bologna and concerns the secret marriage between Paolino and Geronimo's daughter, Carolina. (In the original, Lovewell secretly marries Fanny.)

Maurerische Trauermusik ("Masonic Funeral Music")   W.A. Mozart, 1785.

The work in C minor for wind instruments and strings, K 477, was written for the installation of a master freemason (which includes funerary imagery) and was performed again the same year at a memorial service for two of the composer's lodge brothers.

Mavra   Igor Stravinsky, 1921–2.

The opera in one act is set to a libretto by Boris Kochno based on Alexander Pushkin's poem *The Little House at Kolomna* (1830), in which Parasha disguises her soldier boyfriend, Vasily, as a maid named Mavra to get him into her mother's house.

Maximilien ("Maximilian")   Darius Milhaud, 1930.

The opera in three acts, Op. 110, is set to a libretto by Armand Luel based on Rudolf Stephen Hoffmann's play of the same name, itself based on Franz Werfel's play *Juarez und Maximilian* ("Juarez and Maximilian") (1924), dealing with the conflict between the deposed Mexican president, Benito Juárez (1806–1872), and his successor, Maximilian, and of the capture and execution of the latter by Mexican forces in 1867.

May Breezes   *see* Lieder ohne Worte.

May Night (Russian, *Mayskaya noch'*)   Nikolai Rimsky-Korsakov, 1878–9.

The opera in three acts is set to the composer's own libretto based on Nikolai Gogol's story of the same name in *Evenings on a Farm near Dikanka* (1831–2). The fairy-tale plot tells how Levko, who loves Hanna, uses the aid of the water sprite, Pannochka, to teach his father a lesson for trying to seduce her. *See also* The **Drowned Woman.**

Mayerling   Franz Liszt arr. by John Lanchbery, 1978.

The ballet in a prologue, three acts, and an epilogue, choreographed by Kenneth MacMillan, centers on Crown Prince Rudolf of Austria-Hungary (1858–1889) and follows events from his marriage in 1881 to Princess Stephanie of Belgium through his gradual moral and physical decline to his suicide, together with that of his 17-year-old mistress, Baroness Marie Vetsera, at his hunting lodge of Mayerling, near Vienna.

Mazeppa   (1) Franz Liszt, 1840, 1851; (2) Pyotr Tchaikovsky, 1884.

Liszt use the title for three works: a piano piece (1840), No. 4 of **Études d'exécution transcendante** (1851), and a symphonic poem for orchestra (1851) based on Victor Hugo's story about the Cossack hetman (chief) Ivan Stepanovich Mazeppa (*c*.1644–1709). Tchaikovsky's opera in three acts is set to a libretto by Viktor Burenin based on Alexander Pushkin's poem *Poltava* (1829). This centers on the battle of Poltava (1709), at which Mazeppa fought Charles XII of Sweden, and tells of the love between Maria, daughter of Kochubey, and Mazeppa.

Meadowlark   attrib. Joseph Haydn, 1968.

The ballet in one act, choreographed by Eliot Feld, is set to individual movements from the composer's attributed Flute Quartets, Op. 5, and the Finale from his String Quartet, Op. 74 No. 1 (1793), and depictds a *fête champêtre* for six couples. The title alludes both to the setting for this and, punningly, to the fun and games enjoyed.

Medea (1) Béla Bartók, arr. H. Sandberg, 1950; (2) *see* **Cave of the Heart**; (3) *see* **Médée.**

The ballet in one act (five scenes), with a libretto and choreography by Birgit Cullberg, is set to selected pieces from the composer's **Mikrokosmos** and deals with Medea's revenge when her husband, Jason, deserts her for his new wife, Creusa (Glauce).

Le Médecin malgré lui ("The Doctor Despite Himself")   Charles Gounod, 1858.

The comic opera in three acts is set to a libretto by Jules Barbier and Michel Carré based on Molière's comedy of the same name (1666), telling how the peasant, Sganarelle, obliged by circumstances to pretend to be a doctor, succeeds where the other doctors have failed.

Médée ("Medea")   Luigi Cherubini, 1797.

The opera in three acts is set to a French libretto by François Benoît Hoffman based on Pierre Corneille's tragedy of the same name (1635), itself deriving from Euripides's play (431 BC) about the magician and enchantress of Greek legend who helped Jason win the Golden Fleece and who bore him two children but killed them when he planned to desert her.

Meditation (1) Pyotr Tchaikovsky, 1963; (2) *see* **Lieder ohne Worte**..

The dance for two people, choreographed by George Balanchine, is set to the composer's Op. 42 No. 1 for violin and piano and is a dramatic pas de deux (dance for two) in a contemplative mood, as the title implies.

The Meditation from "Thaïs" Jules Massenet, 1892–3.

The violin solo over harp and eventually full orchestra and chorus that comes as an interlude between the first two scenes of Act 2 of **Thaïs**. It represents Thaïs's mood of introspection and returns to haunt the monk Athanaël at the end of the opera.

The Medium Gian-Carlo Menotti, 1946.

The opera in two acts is set to the composer's own libretto telling how the fake medium, Madame Flora, assisted by her daughter, Monica, and the dumb boy who loves her, Toby, puts gullible clients in touch with their dead children.

Meeresstille und glückliche Fahrt ("Calm Sea and Prosperous Voyage") (1) Ludwig van Beethoven, 1815; (2) Felix Mendelssohn, 1832.

Beethoven's cantata for chorus and orchestra, Op. 112, and Mendelssohn's concert overture, Op. 27, are based on Goethe's two poems *Meeresstille* and *Glückliche Fahrt* (both 1796), referring respectively to a ship becalmed and one sailing before a favorable wind.

Meet My Folks! Gordon Crosse, 1964.

The "theme and relations" (as distinct from variations), Op. 10, for speaker, children's chorus, percussion and wind instruments, cello, and piano, comprises settings of Ted Hughes's verses for children of the same title (1961), a set of comic family portraits.

Mefistofele ("Mephistopheles") Arrigo Boito, 1866–7.

The opera in a prologue, five acts, and an epilogue is set to the composer's own libretto based on both parts of Goethe's dramatic poem *Faust* (1808, 1832), telling how the devil, Mephistopheles, offers Faust a life of power in return for his soul.

"Mein Herr Marquis" ("My Lord Marquis").

Adele's laughing song in Act 2 of Johann Strauss's Die **Fledermaus**, in which, disguised at Prince Orlovsky's party, she flirts with her employer, Herr von Eisenstein, who has been introduced as Marquis Renard.

Die Meistersinger von Nürnberg ("The Mastersingers of Nuremberg") Richard Wagner, 1868.

The opera in three acts, to a libretto by the composer, is set in 16th-century Nuremberg and tells how the goldsmith's daughter, Eva, is betrothed to the winner of a singing contest held by the Guild of Mastersingers.

Mêlée Fantasque ("Fantastic Medley") Arthur Bliss, 1921.

The orchestral work aims to depict the color and movement of the theater and was dedicated to the memory of the artist and stage designer, Claude Lovat Fraser (1890–1921).

Melody (Greek *melos*, "song").

As a title, the word is sometimes used for small, simple piece with a more or less memorable tune. A familiar example is Rubinstein's *Melody in F*, Op. 3 No. 1, for piano. The composition may be weightier when the word is qualified, as in Walford Davies's *Solemn Melody* for organ and strings (1908).

Melusine *see* The **Fair Melusina**.

Memento Vitae ("Memory of Life") Thea Musgrave, 1969–70.

The concerto for orchestra was written in homage to Beethoven, so his is the life that the Latin title remembers.

Memorial to Lidice Bohuslav Martinů, 1943.

The symphonic poem for orchestra was composed in memory of the Czech village of Lidice, annihilated in a reprisal attack by the Germans on June 10, 1942 following the murder by Czech underground fighters of Reinhard Heydrich, deputy leader of the Nazi SS.

Menuet sur le nom d'Haydn ("Minuet on the Name of Haydn") Maurice Ravel, 1909.

The piano piece is based on the letters of Haydn's name taken as musical notes: "An explanation of the method of writing a piece on the letters of Haydn's name may perhaps make plain a problem which French composers have often set the world. It is accomplished simply by renaming the notes of the theme or the scale in rising octaves. There is, of course, no reason save custom for calling the note C by this letter ... If one chooses to call a note 'N' and provided due notice is given, who shall gainsay it?" (Norman

Demuth, *Ravel*, 1947). *Cf.* **Variations on the name of Gabriel Fauré.**

Mephisto Valse ("Mephisto Waltz")   Franz Liszt, 1934.

The ballet in one act, with a libretto and choreography by Frederick Ashton, centers on Marguerite (Gretchen), Faust, and Mephistopheles as the central characters in the legend of Faust. *See* **Faust.**

Mephisto Waltzes *see* **Mephistowalzer.**

Mephistowalzer ("Mephisto Waltzes")   Franz Liszt, 1881–5.

The collective name is that of four different waltzes: No. 1, originally for orchestra as No. 2 (*Der Tanz in der Dorfschenke,* "The Dance in the Village Inn") of *Two Episodes from Lenau's Faust* (before 1861), is a transcription for piano solo and duet (1881). No. 2, also originally for orchestra, is a similar transcription (1881). No. 3 is for piano (1883), as is No. 4 (1885). "Mephisto," as the short form of "Mephistopheles," relates to the "devilish" or virtuoso nature of the waltzes.

La Mer ("The Sea")   Claude Debussy, 1903–5.

The three symphonic sketches depict different aspects of the sea and have titles as follows: *De l'aube à midi sur la mer* ("From Dawn to Noon on the Sea"), *Jeux de vagues* ("Play of the Waves"), and *Dialogue du vent et de la mer* ("Dialogue of the Wind and the Sea"). The 1968 ballet of the same name, with a libretto and choreography by Tom Schilling and set to this work, tells how two young lovers on the beach are trapped by the rising tide.

Mercure ("Mercury")   Erik Satie, 1924.

The tableaux in three scenes, with a libretto and choreography by Léonide Massine, aims to depict various aspects of Mercury's mythological personality.

Mercury Symphony   Joseph Haydn, 1772.

The Symphony No. 43 in E flat major is perhaps so nicknamed with reference to the work's general fleetness of pace, with many passages of 16th notes. Mercury was the Roman messenger of the gods.

Meridian   Pierre Boulez, 1960.

The ballet in one act, choreographed by Paul Taylor, is set to the composer's Le **Marteau sans maître** and is a trio of one female dancer and two men, their movements presumably seen as describing a circle like that of the meridian, or as following the pathway through the body along which life energy flows, or as simply being a dance performed at noon. The title could allude to any or all of these.

Merrie England   Edward German, 1902.

The comic opera in two acts, to a libretto by Basil Hood, is set in 16th-century England and tells how Sir Walter Raleigh and the Earl of Essex vie for the favors of Queen Elizabeth I. The concept of "Merrie England" (or "Merry England") traditionally relates to Elizabethan times, when all was agreeable and pleasant. ("Merry" later became associated with the modern meaning "jolly," "lively," as if the time were one of revelry and merriment.)

Merry Mount   Howard Hanson, 1933.

The opera in three acts is set to a libretto by Richard Stokes based on Nathaniel Hawthorne's story *The May-Pole of Merry Mount* (1836), itself based on the Anglican settlement in 1625 of the site that became known as Merry Mount, now Quincy, Massachusetts. The story tells of the attempts of a Puritan pastor, Wrestling Bradford, to save the soul of Lady Marigold.

The Merry Widow (1) Franz Lehár, arr. John Lanchbery, 1975; (2) *see* Die **Lustige Witwe.**

The ballet in three acts, choreographed by Ronald Hynd, is set to the music and plot of (2).

The Merry Wives of Windsor (1) (Russian, *Vindzorskiye prokaznitsy*)   V.A. Oransky, 1942; (2) *see* Die **Lustigen Weiber von Windsor.**

The ballet in three acts (seven scenes), with a libretto and choreography by Vladimir Burmeyster, closely follows Shakespeare's comedy of the same name (1599).

Messages of the Late Miss R.V. Troussova   György Kurtág, 1976–80.

The song cycle for soprano and chamber ensemble, Op. 17, has 21 songs divided into three sections entitled (in translation) *Loneliness, A Little Erotic,* and *Bitter Experience–Delight and Grief.* The songs, with words by the Russian poet Rimma Dalos, are written from the viewpoint of the lady of the title, who looks back on a life of love, frustration, and despair.

Messe pour le temps présent *see* **Mass for Our Time.**

Messiah   George Frideric Handel, 1741.

The oratorio, set to a text compiled by Charles Jennens from the Bible and Prayer Book Psalter, is named with the Hebrew title of Christ, meaning "Anointed One." (The work is often popularly called *The Messiah*, but is properly simply *Messiah*.)

Métaboles ("Metaboles")   Henri Dutilleux, 1965.

The work for large orchestra consists of five pieces, each of which "metabolizes" into the following one. The individual titles of the pieces are: *Incantatoire, Linéaire, Obsessional, Torpide,* and *Flamboyant*. The nature of each is reflected in its title, so that *Linéaire*, for example, for solo strings, has a rich polyphony with a strict division of lines.

Metamorphic Variations   Arthur Bliss, 1972.

The variations for orchestra are based not on a single theme, as is usual, but on three themes, and these undergo a fairly complex series of transformations as the work progresses, more than the term "variation" normally implies. Hence the qualification in the title. The variations themselves have titles that range from the abstract, such as *Elements, Assertion,* and *Interjections,* to the concrete, such as *Polonaise* and *Funeral Processions*.

Metamorphosen ("Metamorphoses") Richard Strauss, 1945.

The study in C minor for 23 solo strings was composed as a lament for the destruction of the German cultural world in which the composer had lived. The title alludes to the radical changes that had taken place.

Metamorphoses   Paul Hindemith, 1952.

The ballet in four parts, choreographed by George Balanchine, is set to the composer's **Symphonic Metamorphoses on Themes of Carl Maria Weber**. Balanchine himself described the work as "a musical ballet with costumes and settings that change from one part of the ballet to the next. The costumes do not represent any particular type of people, or even a particular type of animal. They are merely intended ... to symbolize the metamorphoses of the different parts of the score. The ballet has nothing to do with Kafka's short story 'Metamorphosis'" (quoted in Koegler, pp. 281–2).

Michelangelo Sonnets *see* **Seven Sonnets of Michelangelo**.

The Midday Witch *see* The **Noon Witch**.

Le Midi ("Noon")   Joseph Haydn, 1761.

The Symphony No. 7 in C major follows No. 6, Le **Matin** ("Morning"), and precedes No. 8, Le **Soir** ("Evening").

The Midsummer Marriage   Michael Tippett, 1946–52.

The opera in three acts, to a libretto by the composer, concerns the quest of two young people for each other in marriage, their story being acted out against the background of a timeless English midsummer. *See also* **Ritual Dances**.

A Midsummer Night's Dream   (1) (German, *Ein Sommernachtstraum*) Felix Mendelssohn, 1826; (2) Benjamin Britten, 1960.

Mendelssohn's overture in E major, Op. 26, was inspired by Shakespeare's comedy of the same name (1595). He later added additional items of incidental music for a performance of the play in Potsdam (1843). (*See also* **Wedding March**.) Britten's opera in three acts is set to a libretto that he and Peter Pears based closely on the same play. The 1962 ballet in two acts (six scenes) of the same name, choreographed by George Balanchine, is set to Mendelssohn's music (plus some other pieces) and has a plot that roughly follows Shakespeare's play.

Mignon   Ambroise Thomas, 1866.

The opera in three acts is set to a libretto by Jules Barbier and Michel Carré based on Goethe's novel *Wilhelm Meisters Lehrjahre* ("Wilhelm Meister's Apprentice Years") (1797), in which Wilhelm Meister purchases Mignon from the gypsy band that had abducted her as a child in order to save her from ill treatment.

The Mikado   Arthur Sullivan, 1885.

The comic opera in two acts to a libretto by W.S. Gilbert is set in Japan and tells what happens when Nanki-Poo, son of the Mikado, disguises himself as a wandering minstrel to avoid the attentions of the elderly Katisha. The opera's subtitle is *The Town of Titipu*.

Mikrokosmos ("Microcosm")   Béla Bartók, 1926–39.

The 153 small pieces for piano, arranged in progressive order, from beginners' pieces to concert works, were written so the composer could follow his younger son Péter's progress on the piano. The title implies that the set is a "world in miniature." *Cf.* **Makrokosmos**.

Mikrophonie ("Microphony")   Karlheinz Stockhausen, 1964–5.

The title is that of two related works. *Mikrophonie I* (1964) is for six performers causing, picking up, and electronically controlling resonances from a tamtam. *Mikrophonie II* (1965) is for 12 singers ring-modulated against an electric organ. The title alludes to the use of electronics in both works.

Milana   Georgy Mayboroda, 1957.

The opera in four acts is set to a libretto by A. Turchinskaya based on her own dramatic poem about the activities of partisans in the Caucasus in World War II. The story centers on the Ukrainian girl, Milana, who guides Red Army soldiers through the mountains but who meets a tragic end at the hands of a traitor.

Military Symphony   Joseph Haydn, 1793–4.

The Symphony No. 100 in G major is so called because of its use of "military" instruments, with a trumpet call in the second movement. "The military music in it is that of the barracks and parade-ground rather than that of warfare" (Blom, p. 368).

The Miller-Magician, Fraud, and Matchmaker (Russian, *Mel'nik-koldun, obmanshchik i svat*)   Mikhail Sokolovsky, 1779.

The comic opera in three acts is set to a libretto by Alexander Ablesimov based on Russian folk motifs. The music itself draws on a number of folk tunes.

The Miller's Dance   Manuel de Falla, 1919.

The dance of the jealous miller in El **Sombrero de Tres Picos**.

Les Millions d'Arlequin ("Harlequin's Millions")   Riccardo Drigo, 1900.

The ballet in two acts, choreographed by Marius Petipa, is a fairy tale, telling how a good fairy helps Harlequin get hold of big sums of money so he can marry his beloved Columbine.

Mina   Edward Elgar, 1933.

The short, wistful piece for small orchestra is named for the composer's cairn terrier, whom he adored.

The Mines of Sulphur   Richard Rodney Bennett, 1963.

The opera in three acts is set to a libretto by Beverley Cross telling of the murder by a deserter and his gypsy girlfriend of the owner of an 18th-century English house. The arrival of a group of strolling players serves as a catalyst to the (figurative) "mines of sulphur" that finally ignite in the killing.

Minuet (French *menu*, "small").

The dance in triple time of this name, originally a French rustic dance adapted by the court in the 17th century, became the standard third symphony movement (together with a contrasting trio) in the 18th century. As such, or independently composed, it is found as the title of such popular pieces as Boccherini's *Minuet* from the String Quintet in E major, Op. 13 No. 5 (*c.*1775) or Paderewski's *Minuet* in G as No. 1 of the six *Humoresques de Concert* for piano.

Minute Waltz   Fryderyk Chopin, 1847.

The Waltz in D flat major, Op. 64 No. 1, for piano is so popularly named because it can be played in one minute (but only if taken at a faster tempo than it should be). It is also known as the *Dog Waltz*, because it is said to have been written when the dog of the composer's mistress, George Sand, ran round in circles after its own tail. *Cf.* **Cat Waltz**.

"Il Mio tesoro" ("My treasure").

Don Ottavio's love song to Donna Anna in Act 2 of Mozart's **Don Giovanni**

"Mir ist so wunderbar" ("It is so wonderful to me").

The quartet in Act 1 of Beethoven's **Fidelio**, in which Leonore, Marzelline, Jacquino, and Rocco express outwardly similar emotions of wonder for inwardly different reasons. The traditional English equivalent is "My heart and hand are thine"

"Mira, O Norma" ("See, O Norma").

The duet in Act 2 of Bellini's **Norma**, in which Adalgisa pleads with Norma not to give up her children.

Miracle in the Gorbals   Arthur Bliss, 1944.

The ballet in one act, with a libretto by Michael Bentall and choreography by Robert Helpmann, is a morality play set in the Gorbals, then a notorious slum district of Glasgow. The "miracle" is the rebirth of Christ in the modern world.

Miracle Symphony   Joseph Haydn, 1791.

The Symphony No. 96 in D major is so called because it is said that at its first performance in London the audience rushed forward to congratulate the composer, thereby miraculously escaping being crushed by a chandelier that fell on their seats. However, this incident actually occurred in 1795 after a performance of the Symphony No. 102 in B flat major (1794), so the nickname really belongs to that work.

The Miraculous Mandarin (Hungarian, *A csodálatos mandarin*)   Béla Bartók, 1918–19.

The pantomime in one act, Op. 19, to a scenario by Menyhért Lengyel, is a lurid melodrama about three pimps who force a prostitute to rob her customers. When a rich Chinese mandarin appears, they try to kill him, but he cannot die until the woman yields to his wish.

Mirandolina   Sergei Vasilenko, 1949.

The ballet in three acts (six scenes), with a libretto by P. Abolimov and V.A. Varkovitsky and choreography by Vasily Vainonen, is based on Carlo Goldoni's comedy of the same name, telling how Mirandolina, the young hostess of a country inn, dupes her three aristocratic suitors.

Mireille   Charles Gounod, 1864.

The opera in three (originally five) acts is set to a libretto by Michel Carré based on Frédéric Mistral's poem *Mirèio* (*Mireille*) (1859). The plot is set in 19th-century Arles and tells of the love between Mireille and Vincent. (*Mirèio* is the Occitan equivalent of French *Mireille*.)

Mirette   André Charles Messager, 1894.

The operetta in three acts, to a libretto by Michel Carré and lyrics by Frederic Weatherly and Adrian Ross, tells of a gypsy girl, Mirette, who finally marries another gypsy, Picoret, despite being courted by a gentleman landowner, Gérard de Montigny, engaged to Bianca.

Miroirs ("Mirrors")   Maurice Ravel, 1904–5.

The five piano pieces are musical "reflections" with individual titles as follows: *Noctuelles* ("Moths"), *Oiseaux tristes* ("Sad Birds"), *Une barque sur l'océan* ("A Boat on the Ocean"), *Alborada del gracioso* ("Aubade of the Clown"), *La Vallée des cloches* ("The Valley of the Bells").

A Mirror for Witches   Denis ApIvor, 1952.

The ballet in a prologue and five scenes, with a libretto and choreography by Andrée Howard, is based on Esther Forbes's novel of the same name (1928), recreating the trial of a 17th-century New England "witch woman," Dolly Bilby, as a rebellious outsider seeking escape from the tyranny of New England divines such as Cotton Mather.

A Mirror on which to Dwell   Elliott Carter, 1975.

The song cycle for soprano and ensemble is set to six poems by Elizabeth Bishop with individual titles as follows: (1) *Anaphora*, (2) *Argument*, (3) *Sandpiper,* (4) *Insomnia,* (5) *View of the Capitol from the Library of Congress,* (6) *O Breath.*

The Mirror Walkers   Pyotr Tchaikovsky, 1963.

The ballet in one act, with a libretto and choreography by Peter Wright, is set to the composer's Suite for Orchestra No. 1 in D major, Op. 43 (1878–9), and depicts two dancers who, working in their studio, pass through the mirror (like Alice) into a dream world of ideal perfection (unlike Alice).

Miserere ("Have Mercy")   (1) Gregorio Allegri, *c.* 1629; (2) Giuseppe Verdi, 1853.

Allegri's motet, for nine voices and two choirs, has the full title *Miserere mei, Deus* ("Have mercy upon me, O God"), as a setting of Psalm 90 in the Roman Catholic enumeration (Psalm 51 in the Prayer Book). In opera, the name is often used for the scene in Act 4 of Il **Trovatore** in which a chorus of monks prays for the soul soon to depart as Leonora wanders beneath the tower in which her doomed lover Manrico is held. Here the words are different, with opening lines: *"Miserere d'un' alma già vicina / Alla partenza che non ha ritorno"* ("Have mercy on a soul already close to the departing from which there is no return").

The Miserly Knight (Russian, *Skupoy rytsar'*)   Sergey Rachmaninov, 1903–5.

The opera in three acts, Op. 24, is set to a libretto based on Alexander Pushkin's poem of the same name (1830), telling of a knight's provocations at the hands of a greedy son and a dishonest usurer. An alternate English title is *The Covetous Knight.*

Miss Hellyett   Edmond Audran, 1890.

The operetta in three acts, to a libretto by Maxine Boucheron, is set in a Pyrenean resort in 1890 and tells of the search by Hellyett Smithson, daughter of a puritanical American clergyman, for the "Man of the Mountain," a young man who had rescued her when she had become entangled in a bush while out walking. She discovers that he is Paul Landrin, a painter staying at the hotel and the leader of its social life. (Her unusual first name may be a French version of "Eliot.")

Miss Julie (1) (Swedish, *Fröken Julie*) Ture Rangström, 1950; (2) William Alwyn, 1961–70; (3) Ned Rorem, 1965.

Rangström's ballet in one act and four scenes, with a libretto and choreography by Birgit Cullberg, Alwyn's opera in two acts to his own libretto, and Rorem's opera in two acts to a libretto by Kenward Elmslie are all based on August Strindberg's play of the same name (1888) telling of the self-centered, wilful daughter of a count who likes to humiliate the men who are attracted to her.

Missa Brevis Zoltán Kodály, 1958.

The ballet in 11 parts, choreographed by José Limón, is set to the composer's *Missa Brevis in Tempore Belli* ("Short Mass in Time of War") (1944) and depicts a man's lone struggle to survive the chaos and despair around him.

Missa del Cid Judith Weir, 1988.

The work for ten unaccompanied singers juxtaposes the Latin **Mass** with a 13th-century account of the exploits of the Spanish hero El Cid (*see* Le **Cid**).

Missa in angustiis *see* **Nelson Mass.**

Missa Papae Marcelli ("Mass of Pope Marcellus") Giovanni Palestrina, 1567.

The **Mass** for six voices was written for Pope Marcellus II (1501–1555), either for the commission he set up (the Council of Trent) to encourage the composition of sacred music with intelligible words, or more likely for his election in 1555. *See also* **Palestrina.**

Missa Solemnis ("Solemn Mass") Ludwig van Beethoven, 1819–22.

The title was originally used of any **Mass** in which all sections, apart from the readings of the Epistle and Gospel, were sung in polyphony or plainchant. In modern times it has become almost exclusively associated with the composer's Mass in D major, Op. 123, a grand and solemnly festive work that took four years to write.

Missa super "L'homme armé" ("Mass on 'The Armed Man'") Peter Maxwell Davies, 1971.

The work for speaker or singer and chamber ensemble is set to Latin passages from Luke 22, and is a revision of an earlier work, *L'homme armé* (1968), based on an old French folksong used by various composers as a basic melody in Masses from the 15th century. The song is itself perhaps named for a popular tavern.

Mitridate Eupatore ("Mithridates Eupator") Alessandro Scarlatti, 1707.

The opera in five acts, to a libretto by Girolamo Roberti, tells what happens when the king of Pontus so named, who succeeded to the throne in 120 BC, takes refuge in the court of King Ptolemy after being banished following the murder of his father by his mother, Stratonice, and her lover, Farnace. *Cf.* **Mitridate, rè di Ponto**.

Mitridate, rè di Ponto ("Mithridates, King of Pontus") W.A. Mozart, 1770.

The opera in three acts, K 87, is set to a libretto by Vittorio Amadeo Cigna-Santi based on Jean Racine's tragedy *Mithridate* (1673), telling how Mithridate VI, king of Pontus, vies with his sons, Xiphares and Pharnace, for the affections of the Greek princess, Monime (in the opera, Aspasia). *Cf.* **Mitridate Eupatore**.

Mlada Nikolai Rimsky-Korsakov, 1889–90.

The opera in four acts is set to the composer's own libretto based on the libretto for an earlier plan for an opera-ballet to be written in collaboration with Alexander Borodin, César Cui, and Modest Mussorgsky, with ballet music by Léon Minkus. The plot is set in 10th-century Pomerania and tells what happens when Voyslava poisons Mlada in order to replace her in the affections of Yaromir.

Mládi ("Youth") Leoš Janáček, 1924.

The suite in four movements for wind sextet is a musical interpretation of the title.

Moby Dick (1) Douglas Moore, 1927; (2) Bernard Herrmann, 1937–8; (3) Peter Mennin, 1952.

Moore's symphonic poem, Herrmann's cantata, with text selected by W. Clark Harrington, and Mennin's "concertato" for orchestra are all based on, or inspired by, Hermann Melville's novel of the same title (1851) about the great white whale that is the object of Captain Ahab's obsessive hunt.

Mode de valeurs et d'intensités ("Mode of Values and Intensities") Olivier Messiaen, 1949.

The title of the short piano piece should be understood in strictly musical terms, since the "values" are the lengths of the notes, and the "intensities" are their dynamics, or gradations of volume. The piece is a study in both, since it employs 12 note lengths, from 16th notes to dotted whole notes, and seven dynamic markings, from *ppp* (very soft) to *fff* (very loud).

Le Molière imaginaire ("The Imaginary Molière") Nino Rota, 1976.

The ballet comedy by Maurice Béjart is effectively a revue about the fortunes and misfortunes in the life of the French playwright, Molière (1622–1673), identifying some of the key characters in his plays with real life events. The title clearly puns on that of his last play, *Le Malade imaginaire* ("The Imaginary Invalid") (1673), in which the dramatist himself was acting the leading role when he collapsed on stage and died soon after.

La Molinara ("The Maid of the Mill") Giovanni Paisiello, 1789.

The opera in three acts, to a libretto by Giovanni Palomba, tells what happens when the lawyer, Pistofolo, the jilted lover, Caloandro, and the elderly governor, Rospolone, all write letters proposing marriage to Rachelina, a beautiful mill owner. The opera's subtitle is *L'amor contrastato* ("Lovers' Rivalry").

Moments musicals *see* **Moments musicaux**.

Moments musicaux ("Musical Moments") Franz Schubert, 1828.

The title is that of the six piano pieces in Op. 94. *Moment musical* was a term popular in the 19th century for a short piano piece of a romantic nature. The plural form is sometimes found in the (incorrect) form *Moments musicals*.

"Mon cœur s'ouvre à ta voix" ("My heart opens to thy voice").

Dalila's aria in Act 2 of Saint-Saëns's **Samson et Dalila**, in which she almost overcomes Samson's resolve not to reveal the secret of his strength. The traditional English title is "Softly awakes my heart."

Mona Lisa Max von Schillings, 1915.

The opera in a prologue, two acts, and an epilogue, to a libretto by Beatrice Dovsky, tells how a honeymooning couple visit a Carthusian monastery in Florence and are told the tale of Mona Lisa, whose elderly husband, Giacomo, shut her lover, Giovanni, into a cupboard to suffocate.

Der Mond ("The Moon") Carl Orff, 1937–8.

The opera in one act is set to the composer's own libretto based on the Grimm brothers' *Fairy Tales* (1812). The story tells what happens when how four boys steal the moon and

each takes a quarter to his grave. The subtitle is *Ein kleines Welttheater* ("A Little World Theater").

Il Mondo della luna ("The World on the Moon") Joseph Haydn, 1777.

The opera in three acts is set to an adaptation by P.F. Pastor of Carlo Goldoni's libretto originally written for Baldassare's opera of the same name (1750). The story tells what happens when the wealthy merchant, Buonafede, opposes the wishes of his daughters, Clarice and Flaminia, to marry Ecclitico and Ernesto, but is told by Ecclitico that he has been invited to visit the moon and begs to go with him.

Monna Vanna Henry Février, 1909.

The opera in four acts is a word-for-word setting of Maurice Maeterlinck's play of the same name (1902). The story is set as Florentine forces besiege Pisa in the late 15th century and tells what happens when the Florentine commander, Prinzivalle, offers to lift the siege if his childhood friend, Monna Vanna, now married to the Pisan leader, Colonno, will go to him.

Monotones Erik Satie, 1965.

The ballet in three movements, choreographed by Frederick Ashton, is set to the composer's **Gymnopédies** (orchestrated by Claude Debussy and Roland-Manuel) and is a pas de trois (dance for three). The title seems to imply a repetitive or subdued performance. It is hardly monotonous in the literal sense of a single tone or note.

Monsieur Beaucaire André Charles Messager, 1919.

The operetta in a prologue and three acts is set to a libretto by Frederick Lonsdale and Adrian Ross based on Booth Tarkington's novel of the same name (1900) telling of the adventures in 18th-century England of the Duke of Orleans, disguised as a barber (Monsieur Beaucaire).

Monsters of Grace Philip Glass, 1998.

The "digital opera in three dimensions" (audiovisual work mixing live action with 3-D movie projections) is set to a libretto based on the love poetry of the Persian mystic Jalal ad-Din ar-Rumi (1207–1273). Its title derives from the phrase "ministers of grace" in Shakespeare's *Hamlet*, as if spoken "monsters of grace." The composer explains: "It occurred to me that human love is a doorway into the divine. So grace refers to a divine activity which is given as a gift to human beings. A state of grace elevates you out of the human. The monsters are us: the 'defective souls' Aquinas refers to. Thus the piece is about the transformation of the ordinary world through the divine" (*The Times*, May 16, 1998).

Mont Juic Lennox Berkeley and Benjamin Britten, 1937.

The orchestral suite of Catalan dances in four movements derives its title from a hill in the southern suburbs of Barcelona. Berkeley wrote the first and second movements as his Op. 9, Britten the third and fourth as his Op. 12. The third movement is a lament entitled *Barcelona, July 1936*.

A Month in the Country Fryderyk Chopin arr. John Lanchbery, 1976.

The ballet in one act, choreographed by Frederick Ashton, is set to the composer's *Variations on "Là ci darem la mano"*, Op. 2 (1827), *Grande Fantaisie on Polish Airs*, Op. 13 (1828), **Andante Spianato**, and *Grande Polonaise brillante* in E flat major, Op. 22 (1830–1). The plot is based on that of Ivan Turgenev's play of the same name (1872), and concentrates on the love triangle between Natalia Petrovna, her ward, Vera, and her new tutor, Beliaev.

Monument for a Dead Boy (Dutch, *Monument voor een gestorven Jongen*) Jan Boerman, 1965.

The ballet in one act, with a libretto and choreography by Rudi van Dantzig, depicts in flashback the isolated life of a homosexual boy, a life that finally destroys him.

Monumentum pro Gesualdo ("Memorial for Gesualdo") Igor Stravinsky, 1960.

The plotless ballet in three parts, choreographed by George Balanchine, is set to the composer's work of the same name, in full *Monumentum pro Gesualdo di Venosa ad CD annum* ("Memorial for the 400th Anniversary of Gesualdo of Venosa") (1960), itself an instrumental recomposition of three madrigals by the Italian composer, Don Carlo Gesualdo, Prince of Venosa (c.1560–1613).

Mood Pictures *see* (1) **On Hearing the First Cuckoo in Spring**, (2) **Summer Night on the River**.

Moon Reindeer (Danish, *Maanerenen*) Knudåge Riisager, 1957.

The ballet in one act, with a libretto and choreography by Birgit Cullberg, tells what happens when a magician turns a Lapp girl into a white reindeer that lures young men to their death.

Moonlight Sonata (German, *Mondscheinsonate*) Ludwig van Beethoven, 1801.

The Piano Sonata No. 14 in C sharp minor, Op. 27 No. 2, was first so nicknamed in a review by the poet Heinrich Rellstab (1799–1860), who wrote that the first movement reminded him of moonlight on Lake Lucerne. The sonata is dedicated to the Countess Giulietta Guicciardi, leading some to assume that the title hints at the composer's affection for her, moonlight being a stock ingredient of a romance. ("But while there's moonlight and music and love and romance, / Let's face the music and dance." Irving Berlin, 1936.) The title may be apt for the opening movement but "it does not fit the other two movements in the least" (Blom, p. 376).

The Moor of Venice (German, *Der Mohr von Venedig*) Boris Blacher, 1955.

The ballet in a prologue, eight scenes, and an epilogue, with a libretto and choreography by Erika Hanka, essentially tells the story of Shakespeare's tragedy *Othello* (1605) (*see* **Otello**), but opens with Othello killing Desdemona. The story of their love, leading up to this event, then follows. *Cf.* The **Moor's Pavane**.

The Moor's Pavane Henry Purcell, 1949.

The ballet in one act, choreographed by José Limón, is a stylized account of the plot of Shakespeare's tragedy *Othello* (1605) (*see* **Otello**). *Cf.* The **Moor of Venice**.

Morgenblätter ("Morning Leaves") Johann Strauss II, 1864.

The waltz, Op. 279, was dedicated to the Vienna Journalists' Association. Hence the title, which is thus more appropriately rendered "Morning Papers." (German *Blatt* means not only "leaf" but also "sheet," "page," "paper.")

"Morgenlich leuchtend" *see* **Prize Song**.

Mörike-Lieder ("Songs of Mörike") Hugo Wolf, 1888.

The 53 songs for voice and piano are all settings of poems by Eduard Mörike (1804–1875), including *Elfenlied* ("Elf's Song"), *Gesang Weylas* ("Weyla's Song"), *Der Feuerreiter* ("The Fire Rider"), and *An die Geliebte* ("To the Beloved"). *Elfenlied* is a humorous poem about an elf who hears the night watchman call the hour (*Elfe!* "Eleven!") and thinks he is being summoned. Weyla is the goddess of an imaginary land called Orplid. The *Feuerreiter* is a figure of German folklore in the form of a man on a lean horse riding towards a building in which fire is about to break out. *An die Geliebte* expresses Mörike's love for Luise Rau.

Morning Heroes   Arthur Bliss, 1930.

The symphony for orator, chorus, and orchestra was written in memory of the composer's brother, killed in World War 1 (in which he himself also served). The texts are based on Homer (*Iliad*), Walt Whitman, Li-Tai-Po, Wilfred Owen (*Spring Offensive*), and Robert Nichols. "Morning heroes" are those in the morning of their lives.

Morning Song   *see* **Lieder ohne Worte**.

La Mort d'Adam   ("The Death of Adam") Jean-François Le Sueur, 1809.

The opera in three acts is set to a libretto by Nicolas Guillard based on Friedrich Gottlieb Klopstock's drama *Der Tod Adams* ("The Death of Adam") (1757), with added material from the Book of Genesis and John Milton's *Paradise Lost* (1667). The story tells how Adam, approaching death, is concerned because his sons, including Seth and Cain, will have to pay for his sins.

La Mort du cygne   *see* The **Dying Swan**.

Mosaic Quartet   Henry Cowell, 1935.

The composer prescribed that his String Quartet No. 2 be played "alternating the movements at the desire of the performers, treating each movement as a unit to build the mosaic pattern of the form" (quoted in Sadie, p. 464). Hence the title.

Mosè in Egitto   ("Moses in Egypt") Gioacchino Rossini, 1818.

The opera in four (originally three) acts is set to a libretto by Andrea Leone Tottola based on Francesco Ringhieri's tragedy *Sara in Egitto* ("Sarah in Egypt") (1747). The plot centers on the Old Testament story of the deliverance of the Hebrews from Egypt, led by Moses, but add a love interest in the involvement between Moses' sister, Elcia, and Pharaoh's son, Osiride. For the 1822 London production the opera was renamed *Pietro l'Eremita* ("Peter the Hermit"), and for the 1827 Paris revised version it became *Moïse et Pharaon* ("Moses and Pharaoh"). For the 1833 London production, with additions from Handel's **Israel in Egypt**, it was *The Israelites in Egypt*.

Moses und Aron   ("Moses and Aaron") Arnold Schoenberg, 1932.

The opera in two acts (the third unfinished) is set to the composer's own libretto based on the Old Testament story of Moses, his brother Aaron, and the Golden Calf, as told in Exodus. *See also* **Dance before the Golden Calf**.

The Mother   (1) (Czech, *Matka*) Alois Hába, 1931; (2) (Russian, *Mat*) Tikhon Khrennikov, 1957.

Hába's opera in ten scenes, Op. 35, to his own libretto, tells what happens when the smallholder, Kren, takes a new wife, Marusa, to help with the five children from his first marriage. Khrennikov's opera in four acts is set to a libretto by Aleksei Fayko based on Maxim Gorky's novel of the same name (1907) about the efforts of a mother and her son to support the struggle of the workers against oppression and exploitation by their bosses.

Mother Goose Suite   *see* **Ma mère l'Oye**.

The Mother of Us All   Virgil Thomson, 1947.

The opera in three acts, set to a libretto by Gertrude Stein, centers on the American women's rights champion, Susan B. Anthony (1820–1906).

Moto Perpetuo   ("Perpetual Motion")   Niccolò Paganini, *c.* 1830.

The work for violin and orchestra, Op. 11, is a pauseless piece with many rapid and repetitive note patterns, evoking perpetual motion. The Italian title has its Latin equivalent in **Perpetuum mobile**.

The Mountain Thrall   (Norwegian, *Den Bergtekne*)   Edvard Grieg, 1877–8.

The work for solo baritone, two horns, and strings, Op. 32, is based on an old Scandinavian folk tale, which tells what happens when a young man wandering in the woods near an enchanted "rune-stone" is bewitched by a giant's daughter and forgets his way home again.

Mourning Becomes Electra   Marvin Levy, 1967.

The opera in three acts is set to a libretto by Henry Butler based on Eugene O'Neill's dramatic trilogy of the same name (1931), itself a modern version of Aeschylus's *Oresteia* (458 BC) transferred to New England at the time of the Civil War. Thus Agamemnon is represented by Ezra Mannon, a general returning from the war, while Electra is his daughter, Lavinia. The modern Clytemnestra is Mannon's wife, Christine, and her lover, Aegisthus, is Adam Brant.

Movements for Piano and Orchestra
Igor Stravinsky, 1963.

The plotless ballet in five parts, choreographed by George Balanchine, is set to the composer's work of the same title (1959), as a "double concerto" for male and female dancers, both identified with the piano solo, their "movements" being literal dance steps.

Moves none, 1959.

The ballet without music by Jerome Robbins is "a ballet in silence about relationships ... between people" (Robbins, quoted in Koegler, p. 292). The title thus alludes to the work's sole active ingredient.

Mozart and Salieri (Russian, *Motsart i Sal'yeri*) Nikolai Rimsky-Korsakov, 1898.

The opera in one act is based on Alexander Pushkin's "little tragedy" of the same title (1830), telling how the Italian composer Salieri poisons Mozart out of jealousy. It was at one time believed that this was the actual cause of Mozart's early death.

Mozartiana (Russian, *Motsartiana*) Pyotr Tchaikovsky, 1887.

The Suite No. 4 for Orchestra in G major in four movements comprises arrangement of works by Mozart, as follows: (1) Gigue for piano, K 574, (2) Minuet for piano, K 355, (3) *Ave verum corpus* ("Hail, True Body"), K 618, in Liszt's orchestral arrangement, (4) Variations for piano on *Unser dummer Pöbel meint* ("Our Stupid Rabble Thinks"), K 455, itself based on an aria in Gluck's comic opera *La Rencontre imprévue* ("The Unforeseen Meeting") (1764). The 1933 plotless ballet in one act of the same name, choreographed by George Balanchine, is set to this same work.

Mr. Brouček's Excursion to the 15th Century *see* The Excursions of Mr. Brouček.

Mr. Brouček's Excursion to the Moon *see* The Excursions of Mr. Brouček.

Much Ado About Nothing Charles Villiers Stanford, 1901.

The opera in four acts is set to a libretto by Julian Russell as a simplified version of Shakespeare's comedy of the same name (1598), telling of the love of Claudio and Hero and of Benedick and Beatrice, together with the usual machinations and misunderstandings.

La Muette de Portici ("The Dumb Girl of Portici") Daniel Auber, 1828.

The opera in five acts is set to a libretto by Eugène Scribe and Germain Delavigne based on the historical Neapolitan uprising against their Spanish oppressors led by Masaniello (1847). The story tells how he raises the revolt when the viceroy, Alfonso, betrays his sister, Fenella, the "dumb girl of Portici." The opera is usually known to English speakers as *Masaniello*.

Murder in the Cathedral *see* Assassinio nella cattedrale.

Musa Djalil Nazib Zhiganov, 1957.

The operatic poem in seven scenes, to a libretto by Akhmed Fayzi, is based on the life of the Tatar poet, Musa Djalil (1906–1944), captured by the Germans in 1942 and executed in Spandau prison, Berlin.

La Muse ménagère ("The Household Muse") Darius Milhaud, 1944.

The piano work, Op. 245, consists of 15 pieces evoking family life. Individual titles include *Poetry, Music Together, Evening Quietude, Reading at Night, Fortune Teller, The Kitchen,* and *Doing the Washing.* The work was first published in the USA under its English title.

Musetta's Waltz Song Giacomo Puccini, 1896.

Musetta's aria in Act 2 of La **Bohème,** in which she hopes to recover Marcello's love as they meet in crowd outside the Café Momus. She sings it while dancing a slow waltz. It is also known by its leading words, "*Quando men vo*" ("When I am out walking").

Music for Strings, Percussion, and Celesta Béla Bartók, 1936.

The work has a factual title that baldly gives the rather unusual combination of instruments for which it is scored. Besides the celesta, the percussion includes piano, harp, xylophone, timpani, and noise instruments. The elements of the title are properly in the order stated, not *Music for Percussion, Strings, and Celesta* (Nicholas, p. 66).

Music for the Royal Fireworks *see* Fireworks Music.

Music in London William Boyce, *c.* 1750.

The Symphony No. 1 in B flat major has three movements, each devoted to an aspect of life in London. The first is lively, the second slow, and the third a jaunty jig.

The Music Makers Edward Elgar, 1911–12.

The ode, Op.69, for contralto or mezzosoprano, chorus, and orchestra is set to Arthur O'Shaughnessy's *Ode* (1874), beginning: "We are the music makers, / We are the dreamers of dreams." The work, originally entitled *The Dreamers*, contains a number of musical quotations from earlier compositions, including the **Enigma** theme and The **Dream of Gerontius**.

La Musica notturna delle strade di Madrid ("Night Music in the Streets of Madrid")   Luigi Boccherini, 1780.

The String Quintet in C major, Op. 30 No. 6, is a blatantly descriptive piece that includes impressions of a prayer bell, street singers, blind beggars, and a military retreat. The title gives some hint of the fun to come.

A Musical Joke *see* Ein **Musikalischer Spass**.

The Musical Offering *see* Das **Musikalische Opfer**.

Das Musikalische Opfer ("The Musical Offering")   J.S. Bach, 1747.

The collection of 13 pieces in various contrapuntal forms, BWV 1079, for keyboard and other instruments, all use a theme given the composer for extemporization by King Frederick the Great of Prussia. The "musical offering" is thus to him.

Ein Musikalischer Spass ("A Musical Joke")   W.A. Mozart, 1787.

The divertimento in F major, K 522, for two horns and string quartet, is a satire on contemporary composers and performers of popular music. The work contains wrong harmonies, wrongly distributed chords, and trills on wrong notes, among other intentional infelicities. "It is sometimes called by some such name as 'The Village Band,' etc., but Mozart's jest is not written at the expense of rustic musicians, but at that of incompetence in professional musical circles" (Blom, p. 386).

Musique pour célébrer des grands hommes ("Music to Celebrate Great Men")   Antonín Reicha, *c.*1803.

The full title of the four-movement symphony is *Musique pour célébrer des grands hommes qui se sont illustrés dans le service de la nation* ("Music to Celebrate Great Men Who Gained Fame in the Service of the Nation"). The work is designed to be performed in the open air, with cannon and an infantry march past, and is scored for two orchestras.

Mutations   Karlheinz Stockhausen, 1970.

The ballet with choreography by Glen Tetley and film choreography by Hans van Manen has a title that alludes to the way the two kinds of dance, live and on film, mutate from one to the other in a unified performance. The concept of change is also present in that some parts of the ballet are performed in the nude, with the dancers thus in an altered state.

My Brother, My Sisters (German, *Mein Bruder, meine Schwestern*)   Arnold Schoenberg and Anton von Webern, 1978.

The ballet in one act, choreographed by Kenneth Macmillan, is set to Schoenberg's Op. 16 and Webern's *Fünf Stücke* ("Five Pieces") for orchestra, Op. 10 (1911–13), plus his *Sechs Stücke* ("Six Pieces"), Op. 6 (1909–10), and depicts the half playful, half deadly relationships between a brother and his five sisters who live entirely isolated from society and who act out their fantasies.

My Heart Is Inditing *see* Coronation Anthem.

My Home (Czech, *Domov můj*)   Antonín Dvořák, 1882.

The orchestral work, Op. 62a, served as an overture to the composer's incidental music, Op. 62, to F.F. Šamberk's play *Josef Kajetán Tyl*, based on the life of the dramatist of this name (1808–1856), a pioneer of the Czech national theater. The overture title reflects that of the Czech national anthem, written by Tyl (music by František Škroup), *Where Is My Home?* (Czech *Kde domov můj?*).

The Mystic Trumpeter   Gustav Holst, 1904.

The scena, Op.18, for soprano and orchestra is set to words from Walt Whitman's poem of the same name (1872), in which the poet urges the trumpeter not to "conjure war's alarums" but to sound a last call for joy, freedom, worship, and love.

Mythical Hunters   Ödön Partos, 1965.

The ballet in one act, choreographed by Glen Tetley, portrays the stock situation in which the hunter becomes the hunted.

N

Nabucco ("Nebuchadnezzar")   Giuseppe Verdi, 1841.

The opera in four acts is set to a libretto by Temistocle Solera based on Eugène Anicet-Bourgeois and Francis Cornue's play *Nabucodonosor* (1836). The plot centers on the biblical king of Babylon and tells of his madness, recovery, and conversion to the faith of Jehovah. The opera's original title, *Nabucodonosor*, has been abbreviated as here since 1844.

Eine Nacht in Venedig ("A Night in Venice")   Johann Strauss II, 1883.

The operetta in three acts, to a libretto by F. Zell (pen name of Camillo Walzel) and Richard Genée, is set in 18th-century Venice and tells of a series of amorous disguises and delusions when the Duke of Urbino holds a ball at his palace during the carnival.

Nacht und Träume ("Night and Dreams") Franz Schubert, 1825.

The song for voice and piano, D 827, is set to a poem by Matthäus von Collin.

Das Nachtlager von Granada ("The Night Camp in Granada")   Conradin Kreutzer, 1834.

The opera in two acts is set to a libretto by Karl Johann Braun von Braunthal based on Friedrich Kind's play of the same name. The story is set in Spain in the mid–16th century and tells what happens when the Crown Prince of Spain, disguised as a hunter, is granted a night's shelter by shepherds.

Nachtstücke ("Night Pieces")   Robert Schumann, 1839.

The four pieces for solo piano, Op. 23, are effectively nocturnes. They have no individual titles, although the composer had originally planned to call them respectively (in translation) *Funeral March*, *Strange Company*, *Nocturnal Feast*, and *Round with Solo Voices*.

"Nacqui all'affanno" ("I was born in trouble").

Cenerentola's aria in Act 2 of Rossini's La **Cenerentola**, rejoicing at the change in her fortunes. A longer form of the words is "*Nacqui all'affanno e al pianto*" ("I was born in trouble and tears").

Namensfeier Overture ("Name Day") Ludwig van Beethoven, 1814.

The overture, Op. 115, was composed for the nameday festivities of Emperor Francis II of Austria (1768–1835).

Namouna   Édouard Lalo, 1882.

The ballet in two acts, with a libretto by Charles-Louis-Étienne Nuittier and Lucien Petipa and choreography by the latter, is set on Corfu and tells what happens when the Lord Adriani stakes all he has, including his favorite slave, Namouna, in a wager with Count Ollario.

Nana   Marius Constant, 1976.

The ballet in one act (nine scenes), with a Libretto by Edmonde Charles-Roux and choreography by Roland Petit, summarizes various scenes from Émile Zola's novel of the same name (1879), about the beautiful but ignorant courtesan, Nana, and her many lovers.

Nänic   Johannes Brahms, 1880–1.

The work, Op. 82, for chorus and orchestra, is a setting of the poem of the same name by Friedrich von Schiller (1800), a lament for the passing of beauty. The title is the German form of Latin *naenia* or *nenia*, "funeral dirge."

Napoli ("Naples")   various (see below), 1842.

The ballet in three acts, with a libretto and choreography by August Bournonville, is set to music by Holger Simon Paulli, E. Helsted, Niels Gade, and Hans Christian Mumbye. The story tells how Teresina, bride of the fisherman, Gennaro, is swept over board in a storm but is saved by the sea sprite, Golfo, who takes her to his blue grotto on the island of Capri, where Gennaro eventually finds her and marries her. The subtitle is *The Fisherman and His Bride* (Danish, *Fiskeren og hans Brud*).

Natalka Poltavka ("Natalia from Poltava") Nikolai Lysenko, 1889.

The opera in three acts is based on Ivan Kotlyarevsky's sentimental play of the same name (1819) about the love between the Ukrainian peasant girl, Natalka, and the young Petro.

Nathalie (German, *Das schweize Milchmädchen*, "The Swiss Milkmaid")   Adalbert Gyrowetz, 1821.

The ballet in two acts, subtitled *La Laitière suisse* ("The Swiss Milkmaid"), with a libretto and choreography by Filippo Taglioni, tells of the confusion that ensues when the peasant girl of the title is abducted by Oswald, brother of the lord of the manor, and wakes up in a castle where there is a lifesize statue of Oswald.

La Nativité du Seigneur ("The Birth of the Savior")   Olivier Messiaen, 1935.

The nine pieces (meditations) for organ center on the birth of Christ and have individual titles as follows: (1) *La Vierge et l'Enfant* ("The Virgin and Child"), (2) *Les Bergers* ("The Shepherds"), (3) *Desseins éternels* ("Eternal Designs"), (4) *Le Verbe* ("The Word"), (5) *Les Enfants de Dieu* ("The Children of God"), (6) *Les Anges* ("The Angels"), (7) *Jésus accepte la souffrance* ("Jesus Accepts Suffering"), (8) *Les Mages* ("The Wise Men"), (9) *Dieu parmi nous* ("God Among Us").

Nature, Life, and Love (Czech, *Příroda, Život, a Láska*)   Antonín Dvořák, 1891–2.

The three overtures that make up the cycle, also known as the *Triple Overture*, have individual titles *Amid Nature* (*V přírode*), Op. 91, *Carneval* (*Karneval*), Op. 92, and *Othello* (*Otello*), Op. 93. *Amid Nature* is also sometimes known in English as *In Nature's Realm*. *Carneval* is usually known by this (old-fashioned) German version of the name (modern German *Karneval*) rather than English *Carnival*. As their titles imply, the three overtures "present three aspects of the divine life-giving force's manifestations, a force which the composer designated as 'Nature'" (John Clapham, *Dvořák*, 1979). Dvořák originally considered calling *Amid Nature* "In Solitude" or "Summer Night." *Carneval* represents the pleasures of life, and *Othello*, inspired by Shakespeare's play, the desire and jealousy of love.

La Navarraise ("The Girl from Navarre")   Jules Massenet, 1893.

The opera in two acts is set to a libretto by Jules Claretie and Henri Cain based on the former's story *La Cigarette* ("The Cigarette"). The story tells what happens when the orphan girl, Anita (the "girl from Navarre" of the title), is in love with the sergeant, Araquil, but his father opposes the match because she has no dowry.

Negro Quartet *see* **American Quartet**.

Nelson   Lennox Berkeley, 1953.

The opera in three acts is set to a libretto by Alan Pryce-Jones about the English admiral, Horatio Nelson (1758–1805), treating his life from his meeting with Lady Hamilton until his death at Trafalgar.

Nelson Mass (German, *Nelsonmesse*)   Joseph Haydn, 1798.

The Mass No. 9 in D minor was headed by the composer *Missa in angustiis* ("Mass in time of peril"). The reason for the present name is uncertain. According to one theory, the mass was composed to celebrate Nelson's victory over the French at Aboukir Bay (1798). According to another, Nelson heard the mass performed at Eisenstadt in 1800. The latter theory has also been tied to a more specific event: "Nelson visited Eisenstadt in 1800, when he seems to have asked Haydn for his pen and presented him with his gold watch in return. The Mass may have been called Nelson Mass after this incident" (Blom, p. 396). It is also known as the *Imperial Mass* or *Coronation Mass*.

Nerone ("Nero") (1) Arrigo Boito, 1924; (2) Pietro Mascagni, 1934.

Boito's (incomplete) opera in four acts, to his own libretto, and Mascagni's opera in three acts, to a libretto by Giovanni Targioni-Tozzetti based on Pietro Cossa's comedy of the same name (1872), are both based on the life of the Roman emperor, Nero (AD 37–68).

"Nessun dorma" ("None shall sleep").

Calaf's aria in Act 3 of Puccini's **Turandot**, in which he reflects that he alone can reveal his name, while imperial heralds search Peking all night for someone who knows the secret. A fuller form is: "*Nessun dorma questa notte in Pekino*" ("None shall sleep tonight in Peking").

Neues vom Tage ("News of the Day")   Paul Hindemith, 1928–9.

The comic opera in three acts is set to a libretto by Marchellus Schiffer telling how the gutter press sets about getting its stories. The overture contains parts for typewriters, and the actual plot deals with the advantages of electricity in the home.

New England Holidays   Charles Ives, 1904–13.

The four movements of the (unnumbered) symphony, also known as the *Holidays Symphony*, comprise four pieces published previously: (1) *Washington's Birthday* (1909), (2) *Decoration Day* (1912), (3) *Fourth of July* (1911–13), and (4) *Thanksgiving and/or Forefathers' Day* (1904). These are the four major American holidays, here presented in calendar order (respectively in February, May, July, and November).

New World Symphony (Czech, *Z nového světa*, "From the New World")   Antonín Dvořák, 1893.

The Symphony No. 9 (formerly No. 5) in

E minor, Op. 95, is so named for the suggestion of American Negro folktunes in some of its themes, and especially of *Swing Low, Sweet Chariot*. The largo main theme of the second movement has actually been made into a Negro spiritual, *Goin' Home*. The symphony has long been a popular favorite: "The imaginative title 'From the New World' gives the work an initial advantage, but it is the quality of the colourful music itself that has set the seal on its widespread acceptance" (John Clapham, *Dvořák*, 1979).

Nigger Quartet *see* **American Quartet**.

The Night and Silence J.S. Bach arr. Charles Mackerras, 1958.

The "ballet of jealousy" in one act, choreographed by Walter Gore, is set to various orchestrated pieces by the composer and tells how the girl who is the central character "stole happily away from a Ball at the Castle to meet her true love" (program note, quoted in Koegler, p. 302). Hence the title, alluding to that quiet escape into the night. The words may have been suggested by Puck's line in Shakespeare's *A Midsummer Night's Dream* (1595): "Night and silence! Who is here?" (II, ii).

A Night at the Chinese Opera Judith Weir, 1986–7.

The opera in three acts is set to the composer's own libretto based partly on Chi Chun-Hsiang's 13th-century play *The Chao Family Orphan*, about a collaborator with the Mongolian regime. The title may owe something to the Marx Brothers' famous movie *A Night at the Opera* (1935).

A Night in Venice *see* Eine **Nacht in Venedig**.

Night Island (Dutch, *Nachteiland*) Claude Debussy, 1955.

The ballet in one act, with a libretto and choreography by Rudi van Dantzig, tells of the "fight of man with the powers of his ego for the purity, the ideals and the dreams, which are escaping with his youth" (program note, quoted in Koegler, p. 302). The title presumably refers to the individual's dark isolation in his struggle.

Night Journey William Schuman, 1947.
The ballet in one act, choreographed by Martha Graham, is a version of the Oedipus myth with Jocasta as the protagonist. The title alludes to the moment of her death when she relives her past, seeing how her years with Oedipus "were darkly crossed by the blind seer Tire-

sias until at last the truth burst from him" (program note, quoted in Koegler, p. 302).

Night on the Bare Mountain (Russian, *Noch' na Lysoy gore*) Modest Mussorgsky, 1867.

The orchestral work was inspired by the witches' sabbath in Nikolai Gogol's story *St. John's Eve* in the first part of his collection of stories *Evenings on a Farm near Dikanka* (1831–2). The work's full Russian title is *Ivanova noch' na Lysoy gore* ("St. John's Night on Bare Mountain"). St. John's Night (or St. John's Eve) is Midsummer Night (June 24).

Night Ride and Sunrise (Finnish, *Öinen ratsastus ja auringonnousu*) Jean Sibelius, 1907.

The tone poem, Op. 55, is musically descriptive of the events given in the title.

Night Shadow Vincenzo Bellini arr. Vittorio Rieti, 1946.

The ballet in one act, with a libretto by Rieti and choreography by George Balanchine, tells what happens when a poet and a sleepwalker meet at a masked ball in the garden of a manor. The music is partly from the composer's La **Sonnambula** and partly from other operas of his, but the plot is quite distinct from that of the named work, even though the ballet is also known as *La Somnambule* or *La Sonnambula*. *Cf.* La **Somnambule**.

The Nightingale (Russian, *Solovey*; French, *Le Rossignol*) Igor Stravinsky, 1914.

The opera (musical fairy tale) in three acts is set to a libretto by the composer and Stepan Nikolayevich Mitusov based on Hans Christian Andersen's tale of the same name (1845). The story, set in ancient China, tells how the Nightingale normally sings in the forest for the Fisherman but agrees to sing in the palace for the Emperor instead.

Nights in the Gardens of Spain *see* **Noches en los jardines de España**.

Nikita Vershinin Dmitry Kabalevsky, 1955.

The opera in four acts is set to a libretto by S. Tsenin based on Vsevolod Ivanov's graphic story of the Russian Civil War, *Armored Train 14–69* (1922), in which the hero is the partisan, Nikita Vershinin, his wife and child being killed by counterrevolutionaries.

Nile Scene Giuseppe Verdi, 1871.
The name generally given to Act 3 of **Aida**,

which takes place by moonlight on the banks of the Nile.

Nimrod   Edward Elgar, 1899.

The ninth of the **Enigma Variations** is a portrait of the composer's friend August Johannes Jaeger (1860–1909), a German musician who had settled in England and who was head of the publishing office at Novello, the music publishers that brought out Elgar's works. German *Jäger* (*Jaeger*) means "hunter," and Nimrod is the "mighty hunter" of the Old Testament (Genesis 10:9). (One could even take "August" as the equivalent of "mighty.") The piece commemorates an occasion when the two men discussed Beethoven's slow movements.

Nina   Louis Persuis, 1813.

The ballet in two acts, subtitled *La Folle par amour* ("Made Mad by Love"), with a libretto and choreography by Louis-Jacques Milon, is based on the comedy of the same name (1786) by Benoit Joseph Marsollier des Vivetières and Nicolas Dalayrac, itself providing the libretto for Giovanni Paisiello's eponymous opera (1789). The plot tells how Nina goes mad when her father tells her she must marry someone other than Germeuil, whom she loves.

1933 Symphony *see* **Symphony 1933**.

1912 Symphony   Hubert Parry, 1912.

The Symphony No. 5 in B minor, originally called *Symphonic Fantasia*, was in the end named for the year of its composition. The first three of its four linked movements are entitled respectively *Work*, *Love*, and *Play*, while the finale is an optimistic *Now*.

Ninth Symphony   Ludwig van Beethoven, 1822–4.

Although several composers wrote nine symphonies, Bruckner, Dvořák, Mahler, Schubert, and Vaughan Williams among them, the title is traditionally associated with Beethoven's **Choral Symphony**. The 1964 ballet of the same name (French, *Neuvième Symphonie*), choreographed by Maurice Béjart, is based on this work.

"Niun me tima" ("None shall fear me").

Otello's death scene in Act 4 of Verdi's **Otello**, in which he says that no one need fear him if they see him armed, for he is embarking on his last journey, his death.

Nixon in China   John Adams, 1984–7.

The opera in two acts is set to a libretto by Alice Goodman with a plot based on the visit of President Richard M. Nixon to China in 1972. Characters in the work include Nixon's wife, Pat, Henry Kissinger, Mao Tse-tung and Madame Mao, and Chou en Lai.

Nobilissima Visione ("Most Noble Vision") Paul Hindemith, 1938.

The choreographic legend in one act and five scenes, to the composer's own libretto, is based on the life of St. Francis of Assisi (1181–1226), whose "most noble vision" was that of Christ while he prayed in a grotto near Assisi.

Les Noces (Russian, *Svadebka*, "The Wedding")   Igor Stravinsky, 1914–17.

The cantata-ballet ("choreographic scenes with song and music") is set to words adapted by the composer from traditional Russian sources and centers on a wedding, as the title implies. The four scenes have individual titles: (1) *The Blessing of the Bride*, (2) *The Blessing of the Bridegroom*, (3) *The Bride's Departure from her Parents' Home*, (4) *The Wedding Feast*. English speakers generally refer to the work thus, but it is in no way French and "there is no justification for this title outside France" (Blom, p. 660).

Noches en los jardines de España ("Nights in the Gardens of Spain")   Manuel de Falla, 1911–15.

The symphonic impressions for piano and orchestra comprise three movements individually titled *En la Generalife* ("In the Generalife") (the summer palace and gardens of the Moorish kings near the Alhambra, Granada), *Danza lejana* ("Distant Dance"), and *En los jardines de la Sierra de Córdoba* ("In the gardens of the Sierra de Córdoba") (the mountain range west of Córdoba).

Noctambules ("Sleepwalkers")   Humphrey Searle, 1956.

The ballet in one act (two scenes), with a libretto and choreography by Kenneth MacMillan, tells what happens to the subjects of a demonic hypnotist when he "puts them to sleep."

Nocturne   Benjamin Britten, 1958.

The song cycle, Op. 60, for tenor, seven obbligato instruments, and strings, is a setting of eight poems about night (hence the title) by P.B. Shelley, Lord Alfred Tennyson, Samuel Taylor Coleridge, Thomas Middleton, William Wordsworth, Wilfred Owen, John Keats, and William Shakespeare. The word itself eventually goes back to Latin *nocturnus*, "of the night," and in musical terms applies to a composition that evokes a nocturnal atmosphere. More specifically, a nocturne is a piano piece of romantic character. This sense of the word was introduced by John Field, who published the first such piece in 1814. The genre was then taken up by Chopin.

Nocturnes   Claude Debussy, 1897–9.

The orchestral triptych comprises three movements: *Nuages* ("Clouds"), *Fêtes* ("Festivals"), and *Sirènes* ("Sirens"). The title pays homage to the American artist, James McNeill Whistler (1834–1903), who used the musical term for the titles of some of his paintings, such as *Nocturne in Blue and Silver* (1871–2). Debussy sought to re-create in music Whistler's coloring of grays and highlights.

"Non mi dir" ("Tell me not").

Donna Anna's aria in Act 2 of Mozart's **Don Giovanni**, in which she bids Don Ottavio speak no more of his hopes of marriage so soon after his father's death.

"Non più andrai" ("No more shalt thou go").

Figaro's aria in Act 1 of Mozart's Le **Nozze di Figaro**, in which he describes to Cherubino the different kind of life he will have as a soldier instead of a civilian.

"Non so più" ("I no longer know").

Cherubino's aria in Act 1 of Mozart's Le **Nozze di Figaro**, in which he pours out his youthful romantic confusion to Susanna. A longer form is: *"Non so più cosa son, cosa faccio"* ("I no longer know what I am, what I do").

Nones   Luciano Berio, 1954–5.

The orchestral work takes its title from the composer's projected cantata on W.H. Auden's poem of the same name (1951), itself named for the church service held at the ninth hour.

The Noon Witch (Czech, *Polednice*)   Antonín Dvořák, 1896.

The symphonic poem, Op. 108, is based on a ballad of the same name by Karel Jaromír Erben telling how a mother threatens to call the "noon witch" to her disobedient child. The witch calls (at midday, when her power is at its peak) and chases the mother as she clasps the child to her. The work is also known in English as *The Noonday Witch* or *The Midday Witch*.

The Noonday Witch *see* The **Noon Witch**.

Nordic Symphony   Howard Hanson, 1921.

The Symphony No. 1 in E minor, Op. 21, expresses the spirit of the composer's Swedish ancestors, settlers in the American Midwest. The four movements are entitled: (1) *Morning in the Hills*, (2) *Camp Meeting*, (3) *Lazy Afternoon*, (4) *Saturday Night*.

Norfolk Rhapsody   Ralph Vaughan Williams, 1906.

The orchestral work in E minor is based on three folksongs that the composer collected in 1905 in Norfolk, eastern England.

Norma   Vicenzo Bellini, 1831.

The opera in two acts is set to a libretto by Felice Romani based on Louis Alexandre Soumet's tragedy of the same name (1831). The story is set in 1st-century Gaul and centers on Norma, daughter of Oroveso, high priest of the Druids and herself their high priestess.

Norse Sonata   Edward MacDowell, 1900.

The Piano Sonata in D minor, Op. 57 No. 3, has Norse legend as its theme. The following lines appear at the head of the score: "Night had fallen on a day of deed. / The great rafters in the red-ribbed hall / Flashed crimson in the fitful flame / Of smoldering logs; / And from the stealthy shadows / That crept round Harold's throne / Rang out a Skald's strong voice / With tales of battles won, / Of Gudrun's loves and Sigurd, Siegmund's son."

North, East, South, West   Henry Hadley, 1910.

The Symphony No. 4 in D minor, Op. 64, devotes each of its four movements to a different point of the compass. *North* begins with a Lento grave and proceed to an Allegro energico. *East* is an Andante dolorosamente. *South* is a Scherzo with a ragtime character. *West* is a final Allegro.

North Country Sketches   Frederick Delius, 1913–14.

The orchestral work in four movements is a musical recollection of the composer's youth in Yorkshire, northern England. The first movement is entitled *Autumn*, evoking the spirit of the wind and mourning the fall of the year. The second is *Winter Landscape*, depicting the hard, bare countryside. The third is *Dance*, and the fourth, which was to have been called *Spring's Awakening*, is *The March of Spring*. (The former title would have been more appropriate, since the movement's marching rhythms are sporadic, not sustained.)

Northern Ballad   Arnold Bax, 1927.

The orchestral work was inspired by Sibelius's **Tapiola** and in its turn took northern Finland as its subject. There are two works so named, this being No. 1 and the other No. 2 (1934).

The Nose (Russian, *Nos*)   Dmitry Shostakovich, 1930.

The opera in three acts, Op. 15, is set to a libretto by the composer, Alexander Preys, Georgy Ionin, and Evgeny Zamyatin based on Nikolai Gogol's story of the same name (1851), with extracts from other works by Gogol. The story tells what happens when the civil servant Kovalyov wakes up one morning to discover his nose is missing.

"Nothung! Nothung!" ("Needful! Needful!").

Siegfried's song in Act 1 of Wagner's *Siegfried* in Der **Ring des Nibelungen**, forging the sword (named "Needful") which he knows his father, Wotan, has promised him in his hour of need. Its name is ambiguous, since German *Noth* (now *Not*) can mean both "need" and "affliction."

Notre Dame ("Our Lady")   Franz Schmidt, 1902–4, 1904–6.

The romantic opera in two acts is set to a libretto by the composer and Leopold Wilk based on Victor Hugo's novel *Notre-Dame de Paris*, usually known in English as *The Hunchback of Notre Dame* (1831). The story is set in medieval Paris and tells of the hopeless love of Quasimodo, the deaf and hunchbacked bell-ringer of Notre-Dame Cathedral, for the gypsy girl, Esmeralda. *Cf.* La **Esmeralda**, **Notre-Dame de Paris**.

Notre-Dame de Paris   Maurice Jarre, 1965.

The ballet in two acts, with a libretto and choreography by Roland Petit, is based on Victor Hugo's novel of the same name (1831) (*see* **Notre Dame**).

Notre Faust ("Our Faust")   various (see below), 1975.

The ballet (spectacle) in two parts, with a libretto and choreography by Maurice Béjart, is set to various sections of J.S. Bach's Mass in B minor, BWV 232 (1724–49), interpolated with tangos, and treats Goethe's poem of the same name (*see* **Faust**) as a black mass, presided over by the three archangels, Lucifer, Satan, and Beelzebub.

La Notte ("The Night")   Antonio Vivaldi, 1730.

The Concerto for Flute and Strings in G minor, Op. 10 No. 2, RV 439, is a musical representation of a night with its associated sleep, ghosts, and dreams. The presto second movement, with its eerie atmosphere, is thus separately titled *Fantasmi* ("Phantoms"), while the largo fifth movement, evoking a lethargic mood, is called *Il Sonno* ("Sleep").

Notturni ed Alba ("Nocturnes and Dawn") John McCabe, 1970.

The song cycle for soprano and orchestra in five movements is set to words from medieval Latin texts on the general theme of "light out of darkness."

Novae de Infinito Laudes ("New Praises of the Infinite")   Hans Werner Henze, 1962.

The cantata for four solo voices, chorus, and small orchestra is set to texts by the Italian philosopher Giordano Bruno (1548–1600), martyred by the Inquisition.

Novelletten   Robert Schumann, 1838.

The eight pieces for piano, Op. 21, are so named, although not having individual titles. The composer explained to his future wife, Clara Wieck, that he had wanted to include her name in the overall title, but since "*Wiecketten* would not sound well" he had chosen the name of another Clara, that of the British singer, Clara Novello (1818–1908), and had used her name instead. Piece No. 9 of **Bunte Blätter** is also *Novellette*. The title further plays on German *Novelle*, "short novel," so that *Novelletten* can be understood as "short stories," in this case romantic ones.

Noyes Fludde   Benjamin Britten, 1958.

The church opera in one act, Op.59, is a setting of a Chester miracle play for adults' and children's voices, chamber ensemble, and children's chorus and orchestra. "Noyes fludde" is Noah's flood, and the story is that of the biblical Flood, as told in Genesis 6–8. The Chester miracle plays date from medieval times. Hence the old spelling.

Le Nozze di Figaro ("The Marriage of Figaro")   W.A. Mozart, 1786.

The opera in four acts, K 492, is set to a libretto by Lorenzo da Ponte based on Beaumarchais's comedy *Le Mariage de Figaro, ou La Folle Journée* ("The Marriage of Figaro, or the Mad Day") (1784). The story takes place in 18th-century Spain and concerns the forthcoming marriage of Count Almaviva's valet, Figaro, to the Countess's maid, Susanna. The characters are largely those of Il **Barbiere di Siviglia**.

Les Nuits d'été ("Summer Nights")   Hector Berlioz, 1840–1.

The song cycle for soprano and orchestra, Op. 7, contains six songs set to early poems by Théophile Gautier. The individual titles are: (1) *Villanelle* ("Villanelle"), (2) *Le Spectre de la rose* ("The Specter of the Rose"), (3) *Sur les lagunes* ("On the Lagoons"), (4) *Absence* ("Absence"), (5) *Au cimetière* ("At the Cemetery"), and (6) *L'Île inconnue* ("The Unknown Island").

Nunc Dimittis ("Now lettest thou go").

The title of the Song of Simeon as the opening words of the Vulgate verse: "*Nunc dimittis servum tuum, Domine, secundum verbum tuum in pace,*" "Lord, now lettest thou thy servant depart in peace, according to thy word" (Luke 2:29). The passage has been set by many church composers, usually together with a **Magnificat**.

Die Nullte *see* **Symphony No. 0**.

The Nursery (Russian, *Detskaya*)   Modest Mussorgsky, 1868–72.

The song cycle, to the composer's own words, consists of seven pieces, with titles translating as follows: (1) *With Nurse*, (2) *In the Corner*, (3) *The Cockchafer*, (4) *With the Doll*, (5) *Going to Sleep*, (6) *On the Hobby-Horse*, (7) *The "Sailor" Cat*.

Nursery Suite   Edward Elgar, 1931.

The orchestral suite in seven movements was dedicated to the Duchess of York (later Queen Elizabeth, the Queen Mother) and her young daughters Princess Elizabeth (later Queen Elizabeth II), then aged five, and one-year-old Princess Margaret Rose. The "nursery" was thus theirs. The movements have individual titles as follows: (1) *Aubade*, (2) *The Serious Doll*, (3) *Busy-ness*, (4) *The Sad Doll*, (5) *The Wagon Passes*, (6) *The Merry Doll*, (7) *Dreaming—Envoy*.

Das Nusch-Nuschi ("The Nusch-Nuschi") Paul Hindemith, 1920.

The opera in one act, Op. 20, is set to a libretto by Franz Biel and according to the composer was written "for Burmese marionettes."

Nutcracker (Russian, *Shchelkunchik*; French, *Casse-noisette*)   Pyotr Tchaikovsky, 1892.

The ballet in two acts (three scenes), with a libretto by Marius Petipa and choreography by Lev Ivanov, is based on Alexandre Dumas's version of E.T.A. Hoffmann's tale *Der Nußknacker und der Mäusekönig* ("The Nutcracker and the Mouse King") (1816). The story centers on the little girl, Klara, who is given a nutcracker doll by her godfather, Drosselmeyer, for Christmas. It changes into a handsome prince and takes her on a fabulous journey. The music is familiar from the suite, Op.71a, arranged from eight of the ballet's numbers (1892): *Miniature Overture, March, Dance of the Sugar Plum Fairy, Russian Dance, Arab Dance, Chinese Dance, Dance of the Flutes,* and *Waltz of the Flowers*.

Nymphes des bois ("Nymphs of the Wood") Josquin Desprez, 1497.

The *chanson* is a lament on the death of the composer Johannes Ockeghem (*c*.1410–1497), opening with the words of the title: "*Nymphes des bois, déesses des fontaines, / Chantres expers de toutes nations, / Changez voz voix fort clères et haultaines / En cris tranchantz et lamentations*" ("Nymphs of the woods, goddesses of the fountains, fine singers of all the nations, change your strong, clear, high voices into searing cries and lamentations").

Nympholept   Arnold Bax, 1912–5.

The "nature poem for orchestra" was inspired by A.C. Swinburne's poem of the same name in his *Astrophel and Other Poems* (1894). A nympholept (literally "one caught by nymphs") is a person inspired with violent enthusiasm for the unattainable. In the composer's case, this was the pagan, pantheistic force of nature.

Nymphs and Shepherds   Henry Purcell, 1692.

The song is from the incidental music for Thomas Shadwell's play *The Libertine* (1692), a comic version of the **Don Juan** story. Nymphs and shepherds are romantically linked in pastoral poetry (or pastorally linked in romantic poetry). A classic example is John Milton's *Arcades* (1633), with its opening line: "Look, Nymphs and Shepherds, look!"

O

"O don fatale" ("O fatal gift").

Eboli's aria in Act 4 of Verdi's **Don Carlos**, in which she curses the fatal beauty that has been her downfall.

"O du, mein holder Abendstern" ("O thou, my fair evening star").

Wolfram's aria to the evening star in Act 3 of Wagner's **Tannhäuser**.

"O for the wings of a dove" *see* **Hear my Prayer**.

"O Isis und Osiris" ("O Isis and Osiris").

Sarastro's prayer to the two Egyptian gods in Act 2 of Mozart's Die **Zauberflöte**.

O King   Luciano Berio, 1967.

The work for mezzosoprano solo and five instruments is a tribute to the civil rights campaigner Martin Luther King (1929–1968) in which the words "O Martin Luther King" gradually evolve from vowel sounds. The biblical-seeming title alludes to the full form.

"O luce di quest'anima" ("O light of this soul").

Linda's aria in Act 1 of Donizetti's **Linda di Chamounix**, in which she sings of her love for Arthur.

O magnum mysterium ("O Great Mystery")   Peter Maxwell Davies, 1960.

The four carols for mixed chorus with instrumental sonatas and a fantasia for organ are set to Latin and medieval English texts. The title, alluding to the divine mystery of God, is that of a motet by the Spanish composer Tomás Luis de Victoria (1548–1611).

"O mio babbino caro" ("O my beloved father").

Lauretta's aria in Puccini's **Gianni Schicci**, in which she begs her father to let her marry Rinuccio. The aria is probably more familiar by its English title.

"O my beloved father" *see* **"O mio babbino caro."**

"O namenlose Freude" ("O unutterable joy").

The duet of reunion for Leonore and Florestan in Act 2 of Beethoven's **Fidelio**.

"O patria mia" ("O my native land").

Aida's aria in Act 3 of Verdi's **Aida**, in which she mourns that she will never again see her beloved homeland.

"O soave fanciulla" ("O gentle maiden").

The love duet between Rodolfo and Mimì ending Act 1 of Puccini's La **Bohème**.

"O terra, addio" ("O earth, farewell").

The closing duet between Aida and Radamès in Act 4 of Verdi's **Aida**, in which they bid farewell to life on earth before being entombed alive.

"O welche Lust" ("O what joy").

The prisoners' chorus in Act 1 of Beethoven's **Fidelio**, in which they praise the sun and freedom as they are released from their cells for exercise.

"O, wie ängstlich" ("O, how anxious").

Belmonte's aria in Act 1 of Mozart's Die **Entführung aus dem serail**, in which he expresses the anxiety in his heart as he once again hopes to find Constanze.

"O zitt're nicht" ("O tremble not").

The Queen of the Night's aria in Act 1 of Mozart's Die **Zauberflöte**, charging Tamino to rescue her daughter, Pamina, from Sarastro.

Oberon   Carl Maria von Weber, 1826.

The opera in three acts is set to an English libretto by James Robinson Planché based on William Sotheby's translation of Christoph Martin Wieland's epic poem of the same title (1780), itself based on *Huon de Bordeaux*, a French *chanson de geste* that forms part of the *Geste du roi* (early 13th century). In this, Huon's chief companion is Aubéron, king of the elfs, later to become the Oberon of Shakespeare's *A Midsummer Night's Dream* (1595). The story tells what happens when Oberon vows not to meet Titania again until he has found a faithful pair of lovers. The opera's subtitle is *The Elf King's Oath*.

Oberto   Giuseppe Verdi, 1835–9.

The opera in two acts, to a libretto by Antonio Piazza and Temistocle Solera, is set in Bassano in 1228 and tells what happens when Riccardo, Count of Salinguerra, who has seduced Leonora, the daughter of Oberto, Count of San Bonifacio, intends to marry Cuniza. The full title is *Oberto, conte di San Bonifacio*.

L'Oca del Cairo ("The Goose of Cairo")   W.A. Mozart, 1783.

The (unfinished) comic opera in two acts, K 422, is set to a libretto by Giovanni Battista Varesco telling of a series of amorous intrigues. The title refers to the mechanical toy goose in which one of the lovers was to hide while rescuing his beloved from a castle in Act II.

Occasional Oratorio   George Frideric Handel, 1746.

The oratorio, set to a libretto from Milton's *Psalms*, was composed to celebrate the suppression of the Jacobite rebellion. It was thus written for that particular occasion.

Ocean Symphony   Anton Rubinstein, 1851.

The Symphony No. 2 in C major in seven movements is a varying depiction of the ocean, much in the same way that Beethoven's **Pastoral Symphony** is a depiction of the country. It contains a *Sailor's Dance* but, unlike the other work, leaves the storm largely to the imagination of the listener. Its original alternate title was the *Ramsgate Symphony*, for the English seaside resort where the composer conceived it.

The Oceanides (Finnish, *Aallottaret*)   Jean Sibelius, 1914.

The symphonic poem for orchestra, Op. 73, is a musical description of the Oceanides, the daughters of Oceanus and Tethys in Greek mythology.

Octandre ("Octandrous")   Edgard Varèse, 1923.

The work for seven wind instruments and double bass takes its name from the botanical term for a plant that has eight stamens.

Octet   Franz Schubert, 1824.

The octet in F major for strings and wind instruments, D 803, is modeled on Beethoven's *Septet*, Op. 20 (1802). It contains the same instruments, but with two violins instead of one, and has six movements with analogous structures. It is almost twice as long as the original, however, and is more innovative. In short, it is "one up." Perhaps its title, also modeled on that of the original, was intended to suggest its superiority over the earlier work.

October Symphony (Russian, *Oktyabryu*, "To October")   Dmitri Shostakovich, 1927.

The Symphony No. 2 in B major for Chorus and Orchestra, with a text by Alexander Bezymensky, was inspired by the month in which the Bolshevik revolution occurred, October 1917. The title page of the score reads (in translation): "Dm. Shostakovich Op. 14. To October, A symphonic dedication with a closing story written to the words of A. Bezymensky for large orchestra and mixed chorus." The work received its première on November 6, 1927, on the eve of the tenth anniversary of the Revolution. (The calendar had changed in the meantime, with 13 days dropped in 1918.)

Ode   Nicolai Nabokov, 1928.

The ballet-oratorio in two acts, with a libretto by Boris Kochno and choreography by Léonide Massine, is based on Mikhail Lomonosov's *Ode* (1741) dedicated to the Russian Empress Elizabeth, itself a meditation on the beauty and harmony of nature.

Ode for St. Cecilia's Day   (1) Henry Purcell, 1683–92; 2) George Frideric Handel, 1739; (3) Hubert Parry, 1889.

Purcell composed four choral works of this title, three with English texts and one in Latin. Handel's choral work is a setting of John Dryden's poem *Alexander's Feast; or, The Power of Musique. An Ode in Honour of St. Cecilia's Day* (1697). *Cf.* **Alexander's Feast.** Parry's cantata, for soprano, baritone, chorus, and orchestra, is set to words from Alexander Pope's poem *Ode on St. Cecilia's Day* (1708). St. Cecilia is the patron saint of music.

Ode to Napoleon Buonaparte   Arnold Schoenberg, 1942.

The work, Op. 41, for reciter, piano, and string quartet, is a setting of Byron's poem of the same title (1814), written following Napoleon's abdication and banishment to Elba.

Odyssey   Nicholas Maw, 1972–87.

The lengthy orchestral work (lasting 90 minutes) aims to depict the composer's musical journey through life (he began writing it at 37, completed it at 52) and is named after Homer's epic poem describing the adventures of Odysseus on his voyage home from Troy.

Oedipe ("Oedipus")   Georges Enesco, 1921.

The opera in a prologue, four acts, and an epilogue is set to a libretto by Edmund Fleg based on Sophocles's tragedy *Oedipus Rex* (*c.*430 BC), telling how Oedipus, king of Thebes, was doomed from birth to kill his father, Laius, and marry his mother, Jocasta. *Cf.* **Oedipus Rex.**

Oedipus Rex   Igor Stravinsky, 1927.

The opera-oratorio in two acts is set to a libretto by Jean Cocteau based on Sophocles's tragedy *Oedipus the King* (*c.*430 BC), telling how Oedipus was doomed from birth to kill his father and marry his mother. *Cf.* **Oedipe.**

Of Mice and Men   Carlisle Floyd, 1970.

The opera in three acts, to the composer's own libretto, is based on John Steinbeck's novel of the same title (1937), telling of the two farm workers, George and Lennie, who hope to acquire a ranch of their own.

Offenbach in the Underworld Jacques Offenbach arr. George Crumb, 1955.

The ballet in one act, with a libretto and choreography by Antony Tudor, portrays the flirtations between the customers of a fashionable café in the 1870s: a famous operetta singer, a grand duke, a penniless painter, a dashing officer, and a débutante, all the kinds of characters that people the composer's operettas. The title puns on Offenbach's well known **Orpheus in the Underworld**.

Offertorium Sofia Gubaidulina, 1980–6.

The violin concerto is based on the theme from Bach's Das **Musikalische Opfer** ("The Musical Offering"). Hence the title. It was written in three versions: 1980, 1982, and 1986,

Les Offrandes oubliées ("The Forgotten Offerings") Olivier Messiaen, 1930.

The orchestral work (a "*méditation symphonique*") is in three parts, respectively entitled *The Cross*, *The Sin*, and *The Eucharist*. The "forgotten offerings" are those that have been made by Christ for the unworthy or negligent Christian.

L'Oiseau bleu ("The Blue Bird") Albert Wolff, 1919.

The opera has a libretto based on Maurice Maeterlink's fairy-tale play of the same name (1908), in which the Blue Bird is the spirit of happiness sought by children. When found, it always flies off to be pursued again.

L'Oiseau de feu *see* The **Firebird**.

Oiseaux exotiques ("Exotic Birds") Olivier Messiaen, 1955–6.

The work for piano, 11 wind instruments, and percussion aims to evoke the sight and sound of the birds of the title. The progression of the work depends on an arbitrary arrangement of 48 bird songs from different parts of the world, mainly North America, but also India, South America, China, Malaysia, and the Canary Islands. Their names alone are exotic, and include the red cardinal of Virginia, the liothrix of China, the shama of India, and the white-crested garulaxe of the Himalayas. *Cf.* **Catalogue d'oiseaux**, **Réveil des oiseaux**.

Ojos criollos: danse cubaine ("Creole Eyes: Cuban Dance") Louis Moreau Gottschalk, 1860.

The orchestral piece, based on the polka and the tango, reflects the composer's Creole background and Latin American influence.

Olav Trygvason Edvard Grieg, 1873.

The unfinished opera, Op. 70, is set to a libretto by Bjørnsterne Bjørnson telling of the return of King Olav Trygvason (*c.*964–1000) to Norway to claim his throne and establish the Christian faith. *Cf.* **Haakon Jarl**.

Old King Cole Ralph Vaughan Williams, 1923.

The ballet for orchestra and chorus is set to a libretto by Eileen Vulliamy and is based on English folk dances, the score incorporating some folksongs. *Old King Cole* is the well known nursery rhyme.

The Old Maid and the Thief Gian-Carlo Menotti, 1939.

The opera in one act, to the composer's own libretto, tells of a young man who steals everything from the three women who befriend him.

L'Olimpiade ("The Olympic Games") Antonio Vivaldi, 1734.

The opera in three acts, to a libretto by Pietro Metastasio, is set in Greece in mythological times and tells what happens when Lycidas asks his friend, Megacles, to represent him in the Olympic Games, the champion of which will win the hand of Aristea, daughter of King Clysthenes of Sicyon.

Olympiad Igor Stravinsky, 1968.

The plotless ballet in three movements, choreographed by Kenneth MacMillan, is set to the composer's **Symphony in Three Movements** and is essentially an athletic display. It was originally produced in Berlin under the equivalent German title, *Olympiade*.

The Olympians Arthur Bliss, 1949.

The opera in three acts is set to a libretto by J.B. Priestley telling how the ancient gods, now reduced to becoming a troupe of strolling players, regain their former power on one night every year.

Olympics Toshiro Mayuzumi, 1966.

The ballet in one act, choreographed by Gerald Arpino, is an abstract work inspired by the classical Olympic Games and danced by an all-male cast.

Olympie Gasparo Spontini, 1819.

The opera in three acts is set to a libretto by Michel Dieulafoy and Charles Brifaut based on Voltaire's tragedy of the same name (1762). The story tells what happens when Alexander the Great's successors, Cassandre and Antigone, vie for the hand of his daughter, Olympie.

Omar Khayyám   Granville Bantock, 1906–9.

The work for contralto, tenor, and bass soloists, chorus, and orchestra is set to text drawn from Edward FitzGerald's *Rubaiyát of Omar Khayyám* (1859).

"Ombra leggiera" *see* **Shadow Song.**

"Ombra mai fù" ("Shade never was").

Serse's aria in Act 1 of Handel's **Serse**, praising the tree in his garden that gives him shade. It has become popularly known as **Handel's Largo.**

L'Ombre ("The Shade")   L. Wilhelm Maurer, 1839.

The ballet in three acts, with a libretto and choreography by Filippo Taglioni, centers on the ghost of a murdered woman (the "shade" of the title) who returns to dance with her lover.

"Ombre légère" *see* **Shadow Song.**

On Hearing the First Cuckoo in Spring Frederick Delius, 1912.

The orchestral work, a musical evocation of the title, is the first of the *Mood Pictures* for small orchestra, the second being **Summer Night on the River.** The poetically descriptive nature of such titles is typical of the composer: "Intensely susceptible to the beauties of nature and to the emotions, joys, and sorrows of life, Delius made these the inspiration of all his most lovely works, the titles of which usually indicate the character of each one" (*Dictionary of National Biography*). The cuckoo call is heard unobtrusively on the clarinet.

On Sjølund's Fair Plains (Danish, *På Sjølunds fagre sletter*)   Niels Gade, 1842.

The Symphony No. 1 in C minor, Op. 5, has a first movement based on the melody that the composer had used in his 1840 setting of Bernhard Ingemann's song of the title.

On the Shore *see* **Lieder ohne Worte.**

On This Island   Benjamin Britten, 1937.

The five songs for high voice and piano. Op. 11, are set to poems by W.H. Auden. "This island" is Britain, as referred to in the poem *Look, Stranger!* (1936), which has the opening line, "Look, stranger, at this island now."

On Wenlock Edge   Ralph Vaughan Williams, 1908–9.

The song cycle for tenor, string quartet, and piano is set to six poems from A.E.Housman's *A Shropshire Lad* (1896). The first song is that of the title, as the opening words of poem No. 31: "On Wenlock Edge the wood's in trouble." (Wenlock Edge is a hill ridge in Shropshire.)

Ondine   Hans Werner Henze, 1958.

The ballet in three acts (five scenes), with a libretto and choreography by Frederick Ashton, is a Mediterranean version of Friedrich de la Motte Fouqué's fairy tale *Undine* (1811) about the water sprite of this name. *See* **Undine.**

"One fine day" *see* **"Un bel dì vedremo."**

One in Five   Joseph Strauss and Johann Strauss II, 1960.

The ballet in one act, choreographed by Ray Powell, centers on five clowns, one of them female, who give an impromptu entertainment.

Onegin   Pyotr Tchaikovsky arr. K.H. Stolze, 1965.

The ballet in three acts (six scenes), with a libretto and choreography by John Cranko, is based on the plot of Alexander Pushkin's verse novel *Eugene Onegin* (1831) but, somewhat perversely, does not use any of Tchaikovsky's music from his opera **Eugene Onegin.**

Opera   Luciano Berio, 1960–70.

As the bald title implies, the work is an "opera" in three acts, to a libretto by the composer and Umberto Eco, that interweaves three distinct narratives drawn from the sinking of the *Titanic*, Monteverdi's **Orfeo**, and a contemporary American drama about the care of the dying.

Der Opernball ("The Opera Ball") Richard Heuberger, 1898.

The operetta in three acts is set to a libretto by Victor Léon and Heinrich von Waldberg based on Alfred Delacour and Maurice Hennequin's farce *Les Dominos roses* ("The Pink Dominos"). The story tells how two young wives put the fidelity of their husbands to the test by hatching a plot that involves the disguise of a pink domino (cloak with mask) at the annual Opera Ball at the Paris Opéra.

The Oprichnik   Pyotr Tchaikovsky, 1874.

The opera in four acts, to the composer's own libretto, is based on Ivan Lazhechnikov's tragedy (or melodrama) of the same name

(1843). This is set in the reign of Ivan the Terrible (1533–84) and tells how Andrei, son of the boyar Morozov, whose family has been ruined by Prince Zhemchuzhny, loves the prince's daughter, Natalia, and becomes an oprichnik (member of the czar's private guard) with the aim of avenging his enemy. The opera is sometimes known in English as *The Life Guardsman*.

Opus 1   Anton von Webern, 1965.

The ballet in one act, choreographed by John Cranko, is set to the composer's Passacaglia, Op. 1 (1908) (hence the title), and tells the life story of a man striving in vain to attain the ideal. *Cf.* **Opus V**.

Opus V   Anton von Webern, 1966.

The plotless ballet in five movements, choreographed by Maurice Béjart, is set to the composer's String Quartet, Op. 5 (1909). Hence the title. *Cf.* **Opus 1**.

Opus 34   Arnold Schoenberg, 1954.

The ballet in two parts, choreographed by George Balanchine, is set to the composer's **Accompaniment to a Film Scene**, played twice. (The title is its opus number.) The first part of the ballet has no story. The second part suggests what the music might be accompanying on the screen.

Opus '65   T. Macero, 1965.

The ballet in one act, choreographed by Anna Sokolow, is a portrait of the younger generation of 1965 (hence the title) and the mid-1960s generally.

Opus clavicembalisticum ("Clavicembalistic Work")   Kaikhosru Shapurji Sorabji, 1930.

Despite its title, the long and complex work is for piano, not clavicembalo (the Italian word for the harpsichord).

"Or sai chi l'onore" ("Now know who my honor").

Donna Anna's aria in Act 1 of Mozart's **Don Giovanni**, in which she reveals to Don Ottavio that it was Giovanni who tried to seduce her.

"Ora e per sempre addio" ("Now and for ever farewell").

Otello's farewell to his past glories in Act 2 of Verdi's **Otello**.

L'Oracolo ("The Oracle")   Franco Leoni, 1905.

The opera in one act is set to a libretto by Camille Zanoni based on Chester Bailey Fer-

nald's story *The Cat and the Cherub* (1896). The story is one of murder, madness, and mayhem in San Francisco's Chinatown and tells how the evil opium dealer, Chim-Fen, abducts the child of the rich merchant, Hu-Tsin, and offers to "find" him in return for marriage to Ah-Yoe. The "oracle" of the title is Uin-Sci, father of Ah-Yoe's beloved, San-Lui.

Orb and Sceptre   William Walton, 1953.

The orchestral march was composed for the coronation of Queen Elizabeth II. Hence its title, referring to the two symbols of sovereignty carried by a monarch at his or her coronation. (The orb is a globe surmounted by a cross, the scepter a staff.)

Orbs   Ludwig van Beethoven, 1966.

The ballet in six parts, choreographed by Paul Taylor, is set to movements from the composer's last three string quartets and depicts the revolution of the planets around the sun. The title uses "orb" in its poetic sense as word for a heavenly body.

Oresteia (Russian, *Oresteya*)   Sergey Taneyev, 1895.

The operatic trilogy, in effect more like a three-act opera, is set to a libretto by Alexei Alexeevich Venkstern based on Aeschylus's trilogy of the same name (458 BC) (*Agamemnon, Choephori*, and *Eumenides*), telling the respective stories of the killing of Agamemnon by his wife, Clytemnestra, and her lover, Aegisthus, of the revenge killing by Orestes of his mother, Clytemnestra, and of Aegisthus, and of Athene's and Apollo's pleas on behalf of Orestes.

L'Orfeide ("The Orpheid")   Gian Francesco Malipiero, 1925.

The operatic triptych, to the composer's own text, is in three independent parts: (1) *La morte delle maschere* ("The Death of the Masques"), in which masked *commedia dell'arte* characters are replaced by real people, (2) *Sette canzoni* ("Seven Songs"), comprising seven distinct dramatic scenes, each expanding on a brief moment from life, and (3) *Orfeo, ovvero L'ottava canzone* ("Orpheus, or The Eighth Song"), in which Orfeo sings a song that lulls everyone to sleep except the Queen.

Orfeo ("Orpheus")   Claudio Monteverdi, 1607.

The opera in a prologue and five acts is set to a libretto by Alessandro Striggio based on the classical story of the journey of Orpheus to the underworld to rescue his wife, Eurydice. *Cf.* **Orfeo ed Euridice.**

Orfeo ed Euridice ("Orpheus and Eurydice")   Christoph Gluck, 1762.

The opera in three acts is set to a libretto by Ranieri de' Calzabigi based on the classical story about the great poet and musician, Orpheus, who followed his wife, Eurydice, to the underworld after her death to get her back. *Cf.* **Orfeo.**

Organ Solo Mass, W.A. Mozart, 1776.

The Mass in C major, K 259, is so called with reference to the important organ solo in the **Benedictus.**

Organ Symphony (French, *Symphonie avec orgue*)   Camille Saint-Saëns, 1886.

The composer had held several important posts as organist, and included the instrument in his Symphony No. 3 in C minor, Op. 78. It is generally regarded as the best of the three.

Orgelbüchlein ("Little Organ Book")   J.S. Bach, 1714–16.

The collection of chorale preludes for organ is so named because it contains only 46 brief pieces instead of the planned 164.

Orlando   George Frideric Handel, 1733.

The opera in three acts is set to an anonymous adaptation of Carlo Sigismondo Capece's libretto based on Lodovico Ariosto's poem *Orlando Furioso* ("Mad Orlando") (1516–32). This tells of the knight, Orlando, who is driven mad with love by the Chinese princess, Angelica. *Cf.* **Orlando Paladino.**

Orlando Paladino ("Orlando the Paladin")   Joseph Haydn, 1782.

The opera in three acts is set to a libretto by Nunziato Porta based on Lodovico Ariosto's poem *Orlando Furioso* ("Mad Orlando") (1516–32). *See* **Orlando.**

Ormindo   Francesco Cavalli, 1644.

The opera in three acts, to a libretto by Giovanni Faustini, is set in North Africa and tells what happens when Erisbe, queen of Morocco and Fez, elopes with the Tunisian prince, Ormindo.

Orphée aux enfers *see* **Orpheus in the Underworld.**

Orpheus   (1) Franz Liszt, 1853–4; (2) Igor Stravinsky, 1947.

Liszt's symphonic poem was composed as an introduction to his production of Gluck's *Orphée et Euridice* ("Orpheus and Eurydice") at Weimar. *Cf.* **Orfeo ed Euridice.** Stravinsky's ballet in three scenes was described by its choreographer, George Balanchine, as "A contemporary treatment of the ancient myth of Orpheus, the Greek musician who descended into Hades in search of his dead wife, Eurydice" (quoted in Koegler, p. 312).

Orpheus and Eurydice *see* **Orfeo ed Euridice.**

Orpheus in the Underworld (French, *Orphée aux enfers*)   Jacques Offenbach, 1858.

The operetta in four (originally two) acts is set to a libretto by Hector Crémieux and Ludovic Halévy that is a parody of the classical story of the musician, Orpheus, who seeks his dead wife, Eurydice, in the underworld. *Cf.* **Orfeo ed Euridice.**

Ossian   Jean-François Le Sueur, 1804.

The opera in five acts, to a libretto by Palat-Dercy and Jacques Marie Deschamps, is set in Scotland in mythical times and tells of the love of Rosmala for the Caledonian warlord, Ossian. The subtitle is *Les Bardes* ("The Bards"), referring to Ossian's dreams of the bards and heroes of the past.

Ossian's Song *see* **"Pourquoi me réveiller?"**

Osud *see* **Fate.**

Otello ("Othello")   (1) Gioacchino Rossini, 1816; (2) Giuseppe Verdi, 1887.

Rossini's opera in three acts is set to a libretto by Marchese Francesco Beria di Salsa loosely based on Shakspeare's tragedy *Othello* (1605), telling of the Moor and general of Venice who is destroyed by his jealousy of his wife, Desdemona. Verdi's opera in four acts is set to a libretto by Arrigo Boito that follows the original more closely.

Othello *see* **Nature, Life, and Love.**

Our Hunting Fathers   Benjamin Britten, 1936.

The symphonic song cycle, Op. 8, for soprano or tenor solo and orchestra is a setting of a text compiled and partly written by W.H. Auden centering on the inherent cruelty present in man.

Our Man in Havana   Malcolm Williamson, 1963.

The opera in three acts is set to a libretto by Sidney Gilliat based on Graham Greene's novel of the same title (1958) about a British intelligence agent in Cuba.

L'Ours *see* The **Bear Symphony**.

Overture (French *ouverture*, "opening").

Properly speaking this is the term for a piece of instrumental music which precedes an opera, an oratorio, or a play, if only to stop the audience chattering, but it is also sometimes used as an equivalent of a **Suite** (by Handel or Bach, for example). Some overtures are complete in themselves, or were written to precede some unknown or unrealized work, such as Bizet's *Overture* in A (*c.* 1855) or Witold Lutosławski's *Overture* for strings (1949).

Owen Wingrave   Benjamin Britten, 1971.

The opera in two acts, Op. 85, is set to a libretto by Myfanwy Piper based on the story of the same name by Henry James (1892) telling what happens when Owen Wingrave, the last of a military family, refuses to join the army because of his pacifist convictions.

The Owl and the Pussy-Cat   Humphrey Searle, 1951.

The work for speaker, flute, cello, and guitar is a setting of Edward Lear's humorous poem of the same name (1870) about the owl and the cat who "sailed away for a year and a day" and were married.

Ox Minuet (German, *Ochsenmenuette*) Ignaz Seyfried, 1823.

The minuet was formerly attributed to Haydn, who was said to have written it for a butcher who gave him an ox in return. Seyfried, who was Haydn's pupil, introduced it into his light opera *Die Ochsenmenuette* ("The Ox Minuet") (1823), based mainly on Haydn's works.

Oxana's Caprices *see* **Vakula the Smith**.

An Oxford Elegy   Ralph Vaughan Williams, 1949.

The work for speaker, mixed chorus, and small orchestra is set to a text adapted from Matthew Arnold's poems *The Scholar Gipsy* (1853) and *Thyrsis* (1867), both of which are set in and around Oxford. (The latter poem directly invokes the former.)

Oxford Symphony   Joseph Haydn, 1789.

The Symphony No. 92 in G major is so named because it was performed when the composer received an honorary doctorate at Oxford University in 1791. He did not have Oxford in mind at the time of its composition, however.

Ozaï   Casimir Gide, 1847.

The ballet in two acts (six scenes), with a libretto and choreography by Jean Coralli, is a variant on the once popular theory of the "noble savage." The plot is based on the adventures of the French navigator, Louis Antoine de Bougainville (1729–1811), whose *Voyage autour du monde* ("Voyage Around the World") (1771) helped popularize a belief in the moral worth of man in his natural state. Ozaï is thus the name of the "noble savage." The subtitle is *L'Insulaire* ("The Islander").

P

"Pace, pace mio Dio" ("Peace, peace my God").

Leonora's aria in Act 4 of Verdi's La **Forza del destino**, in which she prays for peace of mind.

Pacem in terris ("Peace on Earth")   Darius Milhaud, 1963.

The work for chorus and orchestra, Op. 404, was written in response to Pope John XXIII's encyclical of the same title, issued on April 2, 1963, in which he prescribed the ecumenism of the Christian Church, freedom of thought, abolition of racial discrimination, and the protection of the poor and oppressed.

Pacific 231   Arthur Honegger, 1923.

The work for orchestra is a musical impression of the starting up and running of a steam locomotive. The composer explained: "I have always had a passionate love of locomotives. What I have sought to accomplish ... is not to imitate the noises of a railway engine, but rather to translate into music a visual impression and a physical sensation" (quoted in Nicholas, p. 164). The title describes the type of locomotive and its wheel arrangement, the figure indicating the number of axles from front to back, *viz.* two pairs of leading uncoupled wheels, three pairs of coupled driving wheels, and one pair of trailing uncoupled wheels. (In the British notation this corresponds to 4-6-2, giving the number of wheels, not axles.) The *Pacific* was used for high speed passenger trains, and was itself so named as it first ran on the Missouri-Pacific Railroad.

Padmâvatî   Albert Roussel, 1914–18.

The opera-ballet in two acts, to a libretto by Louis Laroy, is set in Tchitor, India, in 1303. The story tells what happens when Ratan-sen, king of Tchitor, is offered an alliance by the Mogul sultan, Alaouddin, on condition he take Ratan-sen's wife, Padmâvâti, as a pledge.

Paganini   Franz Lehár, 1925.

The opera in three acts, to a libretto by Paul Knepler and Béla Jenbach, is loosely based on the life of the Italian violinist and composer, Niccolò Paganini (1782–1840).

Paganini Rhapsody *see* **Rhapsody on a Theme of Paganini**.

Paganiniana   Alfredo Casella, 1942.

The Divertimento for Orchestra, Op. 65, is based on themes by Paganini (*see* **Paganini**). Hence the name.

Pageant of Empire   Edward Elgar, 1924.

The work, a celebration of the British Empire, was first performed during the British Empire Exhibition at Wembley, London, and consists of eight songs for solo voice or chorus and orchestra set to texts by Alfred Noyes. The individual titles are: (1) *Shakespeare's England*, (2) *The Islands*, (3) *The Blue Mountains*, (4) *The Heart of Canada*, (5) *Sailing Westward*, (6) *Merchant Adventurers*, (7) *The Immortal Legions*, (8) *A Song of Union*.

I Pagliacci ("The Clowns")   Ruggero Leoncavallo, 1892.

The opera in a prologue and two acts is set in Calabria, southern Italy, in 1865 and is based on a true incident in which the visit of a troupe of traveling players ends tragically. In the play they put on, the troupe's leader, Canio, takes the part of the clown, Pagliaccio. (The clown's name means literally "Palliasse," from Italian *paglia*, "straw," since the sackcloth suit he wore made him look like a straw mattress.) *See also* **Cavalleria rusticana**.

Palestrina   Hans Pfitzner, 1911–15.

The opera in three acts, to the composer's own libretto, is based on the (false) legend that Giovanni Palestrina composed his **Missa Papae Marcelli** with the aim of persuading the Council of Trent not to ban polyphonic church music, in which the words were unintelligible.

Palindrome Symphony   Joseph Haydn, 1772.

The Symphony No. 42 in G major is sometimes known by this name. The reference is to the minuet in the third movement, which is marked "al rovescio" ("in reverse," since the second half of the minuet is obtained by playing the first half backwards. A palindrome (literally, "running back") is more commonly a word that reads the same backwards as it does forwards, such as *reviver*.

I Palpiti ("The Beats")   Niccolò Paganini, 1819.

The work for violin and orchestra, Op. 13, is a set of variations on the love song "**Di tanti palpiti**" from Rossini's opera **Tancredi**.

Pan Twardowski   Ludomir Różycki, 1921.

The ballet-pantomime in three acts (eight scenes), with a libretto by the composer and choreography by Piotr Zajlich, is based on a Polish variant of the **Faust** legend (*see* **Faust**), with Pan Twardowski ("Mr. Twardowski") in the place of Faust.

Pantoum   Maurice Ravel, 1914.

The second movement of the trio for violin, cello, and piano is so titled. Its form is based on the type of repetitive Malay verse known as a *pantoum* (properly, *pantun*), consisting of quatrains rhyming *ab ab, bc bc*, etc., and returning to rhyme *a* at the end.

Paolo e Virginia   Pietro Alessandro Guglielmi, 1817.

The opera is set to a libretto by Giuseppe Maria Diodati based on Jacques-Henri Bernadin de Saint-Pierre's novel *Paul et Virginie* (1788). *See* **Paul et Virginie**.

Le Papillon ("The Butterfly")   Jacques Offenbach, 1860.

The ballet in two acts (four scenes), with a libretto by Jules-Henri Verdoy de Saint-Georges and choreography by Marie Taglioni, has a plot that centers on Farfalla, a beautiful young girl who falls into the hands of the Bad Fairy, Hamza, and is turned into a butterfly.

Papillons ("Butterflies")   Robert Schumann, 1829–31.

The work for solo piano, Op. 2, comprises 12 short dance pieces partly suggested by the masked ball scene at the end of Jean-Paul Richter's *Flegeljahre* ("Years of Discretion") (1804). "The title *Papillons* could not have been better chosen, since nearly all of the twelve pieces underwent an elaborate metamorphosis, like larvae, before emerging in their full butterfly grace and charm" (Joan Chissell, *Schumann*, 1977).

But perhaps the composer had something more subtle in mind. "By 'Papillons', I suggest, he means motifs that can appear or disappear, fly forward or backward, and assume an infinite variety of shapes and colours" (Eric Sams in *Robert Schumann: The Man and His Music*, ed. Alan Walker, 1972.) The composer also used the title for piece No. 10 in **Carnaval**. *Cf.* Les **Papillons**.

Les Papillons ("The Butterflies")   Robert Schumann arr. Nicolai Tcherepnin, 1913.

The ballet in one act, choreographed by Michel Fokine, is set to the composer's **Papillons** and tells how Pierrot, strolling in a park at night during carnival time, meets a group of young girls, whom he takes for butterflies. The ballet was called *Papillon* at its first performance.

Pâquerette   François Benoist, 1851.

The ballet in three acts (five scenes), with a libretto by Théophile Gautier and choreography by Arthur Saint-Léon, tells what happens when Pâquerette ("Daisy"), a Flemish girl, accompanies her lover, François, when he has to join the army.

Paquita   Édouard Deldevez, 1846.

The ballet in two acts (three scenes), with a libretto by Paul Foucher and choreography by Joseph Mazilier, is set in Spain under Napoleonic occupation and tells how Paquita, a Spanish gypsy, saves the life of the French officer, Lucien, who falls in love with her.

Parade   Erik Satie, 1917.

The "*ballet réaliste*" ("realistic ballet") in one act, with a libretto by Jean Cocteau and choreography by Léonide Massine, centers on a group of French music hall artists who give a performance on a Sunday afternoon in the street outside their theater to attract an audience.

Paradise and the Peri (German, *Das Paradies und die Peri*)   Robert Schumann, 1843.

The cantata for soloists, chorus, and orchestra, Op. 50, is set to a text based on a translation and adaptation of Thomas Moore's oriental romance, *Lalla Rookh* (1817), which tells how the Peri, a fallen angel in Persian mythology, seeks readmission to Paradise.

Paradise Lost   Krzysztof Penderecki, 1976–8.

The opera in two acts is set to a libretto by Christopher Fry based on John Milton's poem (1667), centering on "Man's first disobedience" in the Garden of Eden.

Parergon zur Symphonia Domestica ("Parergon to the **Symphonia Domestica**")   Richard Strauss, 1925.

A parergon is a supplementary work (from Greek *para*, "beside," and *ergon*, "work"), and the composer adopted the term for this piano concerto, Op. 73, which uses the theme from his earlier **Symphonia Domestica**.

"Pari siamo" ("Alike are we").

Rigoletto's monologue in Act 1 of Verdi's **Rigoletto**, in which he reflects on the corrupt courtiers and the curse that he has brought on himself.

Paride ed Elena ("Paris and Helen")   Christoph Gluck, 1770.

The opera in five acts is set to a libretto by Ranieri de' Calzabigi based on the classical story telling how the Trojan prince, Paris, abducts the beautiful Helen from her husband, Menelaus, and so sparks off the Trojan War.

"Parigi, o cara" ("Paris, O dear one").

The duet in Act 3 of Verdi's La **Traviata**, in which Alfredo proposes to Violetta that they resume their life together far from the bustle of Paris. The words make more sense in their fuller version: "*Parigi, o cara, noi lasceremo*" ("We shall leave Paris, O dear one").

Paris   Darius Milhaud, 1948.

The suite of six pieces for four pianos, Op. 284, celebrates the recovery of Paris after World War II. The pieces evoke familiar features of the French capital: *Montmartre, L'Île Saint-Louis, Montparnasse, Bateaux-mouches, Longchamp*, and *La Tour Eiffel*. The *bateaux-mouches* (pleasure boats for sightseers on the Seine) run to the rhythm of a **Barcarolle**.

Paris Symphonies   Joseph Haydn, 1785–6.

The name is that of six symphonies: No. 82 in C major (the **Bear Symphony**), No. 83 in G minor (the **Hen Symphony**), No. 84 in E flat major, No. 85 in B flat major (the **Queen Symphony**), No. 86 in D major, and No. 87 in A major. These were all composed for the Comte d'Ogny and were first performed in Paris.

Paris Symphony   W.A. Mozart, 1778.

The Symphony No. 31 in D major, K 297, is so called because it was written in Paris and first performed there at the Concert Spirituel on the Feast of Corpus Christi, June 18, 1778.

Paris: The Song of a Great City   Frederick Delius, 1899.

The nocturne for orchestra, said the composer, "describes my impressions of night and early dawn with its peculiar street cries and Pan's goatherd. These cries are very characteristic of Paris and the piece begins and closes with them" (quoted in Berkowitz, p. 145).

Parisina   (1) Gaetano Donizetti, 1833; (2) Pietro Mascagni, 1913.

Donizetti's opera in three acts, to a libretto by Felice Romani, and Mascagni's opera in three (originally four) acts, to a libretto by Gabriele d'Annunzio, are both based on Byron's verse tale of the same name (1816), itself "grounded on a circumstance mentioned in Gibbon's 'Antiquities of the House of Brunswick'," and telling what happens when Prince Azo hears his wife, Parisina Malatesta, murmur the name of Hugo in her sleep, and so learns of her incestuous love for his bastard son. ("Prince Azo" was historically Niccolò III d'Este, duke of Ferrara from 1393 to 1441, but Byron changed his name to Azo, that of an earlier duke, "as more metrical.")

"Parmi veder le lagrime" ("For me to see the tears").

The Duke of Mantua's aria in Act 2 of Verdi's **Rigoletto**, in which he bemoans the abduction of Rigoletto's daughter, Gilda.

Le Parnasse, ou l'Apothéose de Corelli ("Parnassus, or the Apotheosis of Corelli") François Couperin, 1724.

The "grand trio sonata" is in the style of the Italian composer Arcangelo Corelli (1653–1713) and is a tribute to him. Corelli greatly influenced Couperin, who introduced his trio-sonata form into France.

Paroles tissées ("Woven Words")   Witold Lutosławski, 1965.

The work for tenor and 20 solo instruments, to words by Jean-François Chabrun, has a title that refers to the "interweaving" of the text and the instrumental parts to form an integrated musical texture.

La Part du diable ("The Devil's Share") Daniel Auber, 1843.

The opera, set to a libretto by Eugène Scribe, is based on the life of the Italian castrato Farinelli (1705–1782). The title refers to his voice and art, his part being sung by a soprano. The opera's alternate title is *Carlo Broschi*, his original name.

Parsifal   Richard Wagner, 1882.

The opera in three acts is set to the com-poser's own libretto based mainly on Wolfram von Eschenbach's poem *Parzival* (early 13th century), telling of the innocent young knight (Percival in the Arthurian romances) who sets out in search of the Holy Grail.

Partenope ("Parthenope")   George Frideric Handel, 1729–30.

The opera in three acts is set to a libretto adapted from Silvio Stampiglia's play of the same name (1699).

Partisans' Days (Russian, *Partizanskiye dni*) Boris Asafiev, 1937.

The ballet in four acts (six scenes), with a libretto by Vasily Vainonen and V. Dmitriev and choreography by Vainonen, depicts an episode in the Russian Civil War, when the partisans in the North Caucasus are fighting the White Guard Cossacks. The story tells how the beautiful but poor peasant girl, Nastya, is forced to marry a rich Cossack.

Partita (Italian, "Divided").

The word is most commonly used for a group of court dance forms, although it was originally used for a set of variations on a theme, in which the notes were "divided" into shorter notes, so forming embellishments. In the general sense, the best known examples are the six *Partitas* or **German Suites** (1731) in Bach's **Klavierübung**. William Walton also has a *Partita* for orchestra (1957). Bach's three *Partitas* for solo violin, BWV 1002, 1003, 1005, are actually marked *Partia* on the autograph score.

Le Pas d'acier ("The Steel Step"; Russian, *Stal'noy skok*, "The Steel Leap")   Sergei Prokofiev, 1925.

The ballet in two scenes, with a libretto by G.B. Yakulov and choreography by Léonide Massine, has no continuous plot, but shows scenes from Soviet life and ends with machines dancing in a factory. It was intended as a tribute to the early Soviet Constructivist artists.

Pas de dix ("Dance For Ten")   Alexander Glazunov, 1955.

The ballet in one act, choreographed by George Balanchine, is set to music from the last act of the composer's **Raymonda**. There is no actual story, and the ballet is simply an entertaining spectacle for ten dancers, as the title indicates.

Pas de Duke   Duke Ellington, 1976.

The dance for two, choreographed by Alvin Ailey, is a divertissement that contrasts modern and classical styles of dance. The title puns on *pas de deux* (dance for two).

Pas de quatre ("Dance For Four")   Cesare Pugni, 1845.

The plotless ballet divertissement, choreographed by Jules Joseph Perrot, is a dance for four epitomizing the romantic cult of the ballerina.

Passacaglia.

An instrumental piece with a ground bass, virtually indistinguishable from a **Chaconne**. The Italian word comes from Spanish *pasacalle*, from *pasar*, "to pass," and *calle*, "street." It was thus originally played in the streets. Apart from Bach's organ work entered below, it is found in an orchestral form as Webern's *Passacaglia*, Op. 1 (1908), among others.

Passacaglia in C Minor   J.S. Bach, 1938.

The ballet in one act, choreographed by Doris Humphrey, is set to the first part of the composer's *Passacaglia and Fugue* for organ, BWV 582, and is "an abstraction with dramatic overtones ... inspired by the need for love, tolerance, and nobility in a world given more and more to the denial of these things" (Doris Humphrey, quoted in Koegler, p. 319).

Passion *see* **Lieder ohne Worte**.

La Passione ("The Passion")   Joseph Haydn, 1768.

The Symphony No. 49 in F minor is so named because the adagio with which it opens suggests Passion music.

Il Pastor fido ("The Faithful Shepherd") George Frideric Handel, 1712.

The opera in three acts is set to a libretto by Giacomo Rossi based on Giovanni Battista Guarini's play of the same title (1585), itself based on Torquato Tasso's pastoral play *Aminta* (1573). The story is set in Arcadia and centers on Silvio, the "faithful shepherd" of the title, betrothed to Amarilli, and Dorinda, who loves him although he cares only for hunting.

Pastoral   Arthur Bliss, 1929.

The work for mezzosoprano, chorus, and orchestra, also known as *Lie Strewn the White Flocks*, aims to depict a Sicilian day from dawn to dusk, and is set to "pastoral" poems by Theocritus, Politian (Poliziano), Ben Jonson, John Fletcher, and Robert Nichols.

Pastoral Sonata   Ludwig van Beethoven, 1801.

The Piano Sonata No. 15 in D major, Op. 28, was so named by its publisher, presumably because of the "rustic" rhythm in the finale.

Pastoral Symphony   (1) George Frideric Handel, 1742; (2) (German, *Pastoral-Sinfonie*) Ludwig van Beethoven, 1809, (3) Ralph Vaughan Williams, 1916–21; (4) Alan Rawsthorne, 1959.

The short orchestral movement in Handel's **Messiah** depicts the calm of the first Christmas Eve, when the shepherds were told of Christ's birth. Beethoven's Symphony No. 6 in F major was inspired by the composer's love of nature and includes imitations of birdsong and a storm. Each of its five movements has a descriptive title: (1) *Erwachen heiterer Empfindungen bei der Ankunft auf dem Lande* ("Awakening of Joyful Feelings upon Arrival in the Country"), (2) *Szene am Bach* ("Scene by the Brook"), (3) *Lustiges Zusammensein der Landleute* ("Joyous Gathering of Country Folk"), (4) *Gewitter, Storm* ("Tempest, Storm"), (5) *Hirtengesang: Frohe unde dankbare Gefühle nach dem Sturm* ("Shepherd's Song: Happy and Thankful Feelings after the Storm"). The title page of the original score had the composer's own (French) heading *Symphonie pastorale*, and the first violin part had the inscription: "*Pastoral-Sinfonie oder Erinnerung an das Landleben* (*mehr Ausdruck der Empfindung als Mahlerey*)" ("Pastoral Symphony or Recollection of Country Life (more expression of emotion than painting)").

Vaughan Williams's Symphony No. 3 is not an evocation of the English countryside, as might be expected. It was begun in World War I when the composer was serving in the medical corps in France, and was a response to his experiences there: "A great deal of it incubated when I used to go up night after night with the ambulance waggon at Écoivres ... and there was a wonderful Corot-like landscape in the sunset — it's not really lambkins frisking at all as most people take for granted" (quoted in Staines and Buckley, p. 446). Rawsthorne's Symphony No. 2 is more conventional, and was written when he was living in a fairly remote village in Essex.

Pastorale d'été ("Summer Pastoral") Arthur Honegger, 1920.

The symphonic poem for small orchestra is a musical depiction of the title.

The Path of Thunder (Russian, *Tropoyu groma*)   Kara Karaev, 1958.

The ballet in three acts, with a libretto by

Yuri Slonimsky and choreographey by Konstantin Sergeyev, is based on Peter Abrahams' novel of the same name (1948), telling how the love of the South African black, Lenny, for the white girl, Sari, leads to the death of both of them.

Pathetic Sonata *see* **Pathétique Sonata**.

Pathetic Symphony (Russian, *Pateticheskaya simfoniya*)   Pyotr Tchaikovsky, 1893.

The Symphony No. 6 in B minor, Op. 74, has a title suggested by the composer's brother, Modest Tchaikovsky, the day after its first performance. (He had originally suggested "Tragic," but the composer rejected this, preferring "Pathetic.") The Russian word means more "passionate" (in the sense "emotionally charged") than "pathetic" in its usual English sense of "arousing pity." The work is sometimes known as the *Symphonie pathétique*, the French equivalent. *Cf.* **Pathétique Sonata**.

Pathétique Sonata ("Pathetic Sonata") Ludwig van Beethoven, 1797–8.

The Piano Sonata No. 8 in C minor, Op. 13, was originally named by the composer (in French) *Grande sonate pathétique*, "Great Pathetic Sonata." The title is believed to be connected in some way with the composer's growing deafness, which he first recognized at about this time.

Pathétique Symphony *see* **Pathetic Symphony**.

Patience   Arthur Sullivan, 1881.

The comic opera in two acts to a libretto by W.S. Gilbert is a satire on the contemporary cult of "aestheticism." Patience is a village milkmaid loved by the "fleshly" poet Reginald Bunthorne. Hence the work's subtitle, *Bunthorne's Bride* (although he does not marry her).

Les Patineurs ("The Skaters")   Giacomo Meyerbeer arr. Constant Lambert, 1937.

The ballet in one act, choreographed by Frederick Ashton, is set to music from the composer's operas Le **Prophète** and L'**Étoile du nord** and is essentially a divertissement, with the steps of the dancers simulating the movements of ice skaters.

Patrie ("Fatherland")   Georges Bizet, 1873.

The orchestral overture was inspired by the recent Franco-Prussian War (1870–1). "There is some mystery about the title. It has nothing to do with [Victorien] Sardou's play *Patrie*, then being converted into an opera by [Émile] Pala-

dilhe. [Charles] Pigot says that this rumour was put about by malignant persons who wished to suggest that Bizet wanted to set Sardou's work, but had been rejected in favour of Paladilhe" (Winton Dean, *Bizet*, 1975). It has been suggested that the "fatherland" Bizet had in mind was actually Poland, not France, although there is no hint of anything Polish in the score, which was originally entitled *Patrie!*

Paukenmesse ("Kettledrum Mass")   Joseph Haydn, 1796.

The Mass No. 7 in C major was named by the composer *Missa in tempore belli* ("Mass in Time of War"). Its military nature is reflected in the persistent use of the kettledrums that give the English title. (They even feature in the **Agnus Dei**, where one would normally expect them to be silent.) The work is also sometimes known as the *Kriegsmesse* ("War Mass").

Paukenwirbel Symphony *see* **Drumroll Symphony**.

Paul Bunyan   Benjamin Britten, 1941.

The opera in a prologue and two acts, Op. 17, to a libretto by W.H. Auden, is based on American folk legend. The story is set in pioneer days and centers on the lumberjack, Paul Bunyan, who never ages but grows taller every day, so that he is as big as the Empire State Building.

Paul et Virginie ("Paul and Virginia") Jean-François Le Sueur, 1794.

The opera in three acts is set to a libretto by Alphonse du Congé Debreuil based on Jacques-Henri Bernadin de Saint-Pierre's novel of the same name (1788). The story tells what happens when Virginie is forced to leave the island paradise (Mauritius) she shares with Paul in oder to go to France to be educated by a rich aunt.

Le Pauvre matelot ("The Poor Sailor") Darius Milhaud, 1927.

The opera in three acts, Op. 92, to a libretto by Jean Cocteau, tells what happens when a sailor returns home after a long absence, is not recognized by his wife, and tests her fidelity by pretending to be her husband's rich friend. The story was based on a newspaper report of an actual event.

Pavane.

The word was first applied to a dance of Italian origin, and as its name sometimes appears as *Padovana* it is usually assumed that it originated in Padua. However, it is a stately dance, so the actual source may be in an Italian or Spanish word deriving from Latin *pavo, pavonis,* "peacock." The name has been adopted in modern times for various compositions of a gentle nature, such as Fauré's *Pavane* for orchestra with optional mixed chorus, Op. 50 (1887).

Pavane pour une infante défunte

("Pavane for a Dead Infanta")   Maurice Ravel, 1899.

The work for solo piano evokes the Spanish court custom of performing a solemn ceremonial dance at a time of royal mourning. One can thus imagine the pavane being danced around the infanta's bier as it stood before the altar. "The 'infante défunte' in the title is not a defunct female infant, as is still sometimes supposed, and even stated in print, but a Spanish princess (infanta) of the royal house" (Blom, p. 430). The composer is said to have chosen the title simply for the alluring sound of the words, and it is essentially a one-line poem.

Le Pavillon d'Armide ("The Pavilion of Armida")   Nicolai Tcherepnin, 1907.

The ballet in one act (three scenes), with a libretto by Alexandre Benois and choreography by Michel Fokine, is vased on Théophile Gautier's story *Omphale* ("Omphalos"), telling how the Vicomte de Beaugency looks at the tapestry of Armida and her court and dreams that he is her Rinaldo. (*See* **Armida**.)

The Peacock Variations   Zoltán Kodály, 1938–9.

The orchestral work is a set of variations on the Hungarian folksong *Felszállott a páva* ("The Peacock Flies Up"). Hence the title.

The Pearl Fishers *see* Les **Pêcheurs de perles**.

Peasant Cantata (German, *Bauernkantate*) J.S. Bach, 1742.

The Cantata No. 212, *Mer hahn en neue Oberkeet* ("We Have a New Magistracy"), to a Saxon dialect libretto by Picander, is "noticeably rustic and comes as near to the manner of folksong as anything Bach ever wrote" (Blom, p. 431).

Les Pêcheurs de perles ("The Pearl Fishers")   Georges Bizet, 1863.

The opera in three acts, to a libretto by Eugène Cormon and Michel Carré, is set in Ceylon and tells what happens when Zurga, leader of the local fishermen, and Nadir, his friend, both love the same woman, the priestess Leïla, whose name gave the work's original title.

Peer Gynt   Edvard Grieg, 1874–5.

The 23 items of incidental music, Op. 23, were written for Henrik Ibsen's play of the same name (1867), which tells the story of the young idler and braggart, Peer Gynt, and his ever faithful sweetheart, Solveig. The work was then arranged as two orchestral suites with individually titled items. No. 1, Op. 46 (1888), comprises: (1) *Morning* (Norwegian, *Morgenstemning*, "Morning Mood"), (2) *Death of Aase* (Norwegian, *Åses død*), (3) *Anitra's Dance* (Norwegian, *Anitras dans*), (4) *In the Hall of the Mountain King* (Norwegian, *I Dovregubbens hall*). No. 2, Op. 55 (1891), comprises: (1) *Abduction of the Bride: Ingrid's Lament* (Norwegian, *Bruderovet: Ingrids klage*), (2) *Arabian Dance* (Norwegian, *Arabisk dans*), (3) *Peer Gynt's Homecoming* (Norwegian, *Peer Gynts hjemfart*), (4) *Solveig's Song* (Norwegian, *Solveigs sang*). Additional items sometimes performed are *Wedding March, Solveig's Cradle Song, Prelude,* and *Dance of the Mountain King's Daughter.*

Pelléas et Mélisande   Claude Debussy, 1893–5, 1901–2.

The opera in five acts is set to an almost verbatim version of Maurice Maeterlinck's tragedy of the same name (1892), telling how Mélisande, a mysterious girl discovered beside a stream, falls in love with her husband's brother, Pelléas, a young hunter.

Penelope   Rolf Liebermann, 1954.

The opera in two parts, to a libretto by Heinrich Strobel, is an updated version of the classical legend of Penelope, told in Homer's *Odyssey,* as the wife who waits faithfully for her husband, Odysseus, to return after the Trojan War. The story is based on an actual incident in World War II.

Pénélope ("Penelope")   Gabriel Fauré, 1907–12.

The opera in three acts is set to a libretto by René Fauchon based on Homer's *Odyssey,* in which Penelope is the wife besieged by suitors while her husband, Odysseus, is away during the Trojan War.

El Penitente ("The Penitent")   Louis Horst, 1940.

The ballet in one act, choreographed by Martha Graham, depicts three strolling players enacting a primitive morality play. At the first performance, Martha Graham took the part of the Virgin Mary and Mary Magdalene, Erick Hawkins was the Penitent, and Merce Cunningham was Christ.

A Penny for a Song   Richard Rodney Bennett, 1967.

The opera in two acts is set to a libretto by Colin Graham based on John Whiting's play of the same name (1951), a light historical drama set against a military background on the south coast of England in 1804, the time of the Napoleonic wars.

Penthesilea   (1) Hugo Wolf, 1883–5; (2) Othmar Schoeck, 1927.

Wolf's symphonic poem and Schoeck's opera are both based on Heinrich von Kleist's tragedy of the same name (1808), based on the classical legend of the slaying of the Amazon Penthesilea by Achilles during the Trojan War. (Kleist reverses the plot, so that Penthesilea kills Achilles.)

Pepita Jiménez   Isaac Albéniz, 1896.

The Spanish opera, set to an English libretto by Francis Burdett Money-Coutts, is based on Juan Valera's story of the same name (1874), telling what happens when a seminarist falls in love with the young widow named in the title.

"Per pietà"   ("For pity").

Fiordiligi's aria in Act 2 of Mozart's **Così fan tutte**, in which she begins to weaken before the advances of Ferrando, her sister Dorabella's disguised lover. A fuller version of the words is: *"Per pietà, ben mio, perdona"* ("For pity, my dear, pardon").

The Perfect Fool   Gustav Holst, 1923.

The comic opera in one act, Op. 39, is set to the composer's own libretto as an Elizabethan-style allegory that tells of a Princess wooed by a (Wagnerian) Traveler and a (Verdian) Troubador. She prefers the Perfect Fool, but he is not interested in her and refuses her.

La Péri   ("The Peri")   Friedrich Burgmüller, 1843.

The ballet in two acts (three scenes), with a libretto by Théophile Gautier and choreography by Jean Coralli, has a plot in which the poet, Sultan Achmet, meets the Queen of the Fairies (the "peri" of the title) in one of his opium dreams and is taken to her kingdom.

La Périchole   ("Périchole")   Jacques Offenbach, 1868.

The operetta in three (originally two) acts is set to a libretto by Henri Meilhac and Ludovic Halévy based on Prosper Mérimée's comedy *Le Carrosse du Saint-Sacrement* ("The Carriage of the Holy Sacrament") (1830). The plot is set in Peru in the mid–18th century and tells what happens when the street singer, Périchole, and her lover, Piquillo, are so poor they cannot even afford a wedding service.

Perpetuum mobile   ("Perpetual Motion")   Johann Strauss II, 1862.

The orchestral piece, Op. 257, subtitled *Musikalischer Scherz* ("Musical Joke"), is so named for its nonstop stream of rapid notes and repeated phrases, evoking perpetual motion. *Cf.* **Moto perpetuo.**

Perséphone   ("Persephone")   Igor Stravinsky, 1933–4.

The melodrama in three scenes, for narrator, tenor, chorus, children's chorus, and orchestra, is set to a libretto by André Gide based on the classical story of Persephone (Proserpine), daughter of Zeus (Jupiter) and Ceres (Demeter), who was abducted by Pluto, god of the underworld, to become his wife and rule over the shades.

Peter and the Wolf   (Russian, *Petya i volk*)   Sergey Prokofiev, 1936.

The symphonic fairy tale for narrator and orchestra, Op. 67, to the composer's own libretto, tells how the young boy, Peter, dupes a wily wolf. (The Russian form of the boy's name is a diminutive, so a closer English equivalent might be "Peterkin.")

Peter Grimes   Benjamin Britten, 1944–5.

The opera in a prologue and three acts, Op. 33, is set to a libretto by Montagu Slater based on George Crabbe's poem *The Borough* (1810). The story is set in a small Suffolk coastal town, The Borough, in about 1830, and opens with an inquest into the death of the apprentice of the fisherman, Peter Grimes. A verdict of accidental death is recorded, but Grimes is warned not to take on any more boy apprentices. "The Borough" is in fact Aldeburgh, the composer's hometown.

Peter Ibbetson   Deems Taylor, 1931.

The opera in three acts, to a libretto by the composer and Constance Collier, is based on the latter's play, itself founded on George du Maurier's novel of the same name (1891). The story is set in England and France over the period

1855–87 and tells what happens when Peter Ibbetson murders his tyrannical uncle, Colonel Ibbetson, and is sentenced to life imprisonment.

Peter Schmoll und seine Nachbarn
("Peter Schmoll and His Neighbors") Carl Maria von Weber, 1801–2.

The opera in two acts is set to a libretto by Joseph Türk based on Karl Gottlob Cramer's 'Gothic' novel of the same name (1798–9), in which Peter Schmoll is the central character.

Peter the First (Russian, *Pyotr pervyy*)
Andrei Petrov, 1975.

The opera in three acts, to a libretto by N. Kasatkina and Vladimir Vasilyov, centers on the Russian czar, Peter I (1672–1725), better known as Peter the Great. The opera was premièred in Leningrad (St. Petersburg), the city founded by Peter in 1703.

Le Petit Duc ("The Little Duke") Charles Lecocq, 1878.

The comic opera in three acts, to a libretto by Henri Meilhac and Ludovic Halévy, tells of the youthful marriage and lasting love, despite diversions and disguises, of the Duc de Parthenay (the "little duke" of the title) and his bride and wife, Blanche de Cambry, "the little duchess."

Petit Faust Hervé, 1869.

The operetta, set to a libretto by Hector Crémieux and Adolphe Jaime, is a parody of Goethe's verse tragedy *Faust* (1808) and in particular of Gounod's opera **Faust** based on it.

Petite messe solennelle ("Little Solemn Mass") Gioacchino Rossini, 1863.

The choral work, for soprano, contralto, tenor, and baritone soloists, chorus, two pianos, and harmonium, is a setting of the **Mass**. Its title does not relate to its brevity or the small number of instruments, but to the composer's unnecessarily modest assessment of its importance.

Petite Suite ("Little Suite") (1) Georges Bizet, 1871; (2) Claude Debussy, 1886–9.

Bizet's work is an orchestral version of Nos. 2, 3, 6, 11, and 12 from **Jeux d'enfants**. Debussy's composition for piano duet is original but modest in length and content, as its title suggests. Its four movements are individually named as follows: *En bateau* ("In a Boat"), *Cortège* ("Funeral Procession"), *Menuet* ("Minuet"), and *Ballet* ("Ballet").

Petite Symphonie ("Little Symphony")
Charles Gounod, 1885.

The work in four movements for nine wind instruments is effectively a "minisymphony." Hence the title.

Petite Symphonie Concertante ("Little Sinfonia Concertante") Frank Martin, 1946.

The work for harp, harpsichord, piano, and two string orchestras is a type of modest **Sinfonia Concertante**. Hence its title.

Les Petits riens ("The Little Nobodies")
W.A. Mozart, 1778.

The music so titled, K Anhang 10, was composed for a ballet-divertissement of the same name in three scenes with libretto and choreography by the Parisian ballet-master Jean Noverre. The original libretto has been lost, but according to a review in the *Journal de Paris* (June 12, 1778), the first scene has Amor captured by a shepherdess and imprisoned in a cage, the second has a shepherdess and a shepherd playing blind man's buff, and the third has Amor acting as matchmaker. The shepherdess and shepherd are thus presumably the "little nobodies" of the title. The music manuscript was rediscovered only in 1872.

Petrouchka *see* Petrushka.

Petrushka Igor Stravinsky, 1910–11.

The ballet (burlesque) in four scenes, with a libretto by Alexander Benois and choreography by Mikhail Fokine, is set in Admiralty Square, St. Petersburg, during the Shrovetide Fair, 1830, and tells what happens when the owner of a puppet fair brings Petrushka (the Russian Harlequin), the Ballerina, and the Moor, to life. The ballet is sometimes known as *Pétrouchka*, the French form of the name.

Phaedra (1) George Rochberg, 1973–4; (3) Benjamin Britten, 1975.

Rochberg's monodrama for mezzosoprano and orchestra and Britten's dramatic cantata, Op. 93, for mezzosoprano and small orchestra are both settings of extracts from Robert Lowell's English translation (1963) of Jean Racine's verse tragedy *Phèdre* ("Phaedra") (1677), about the sister of Ariadne and wife of Theseus who falls in love with her stepson, Hippolytus, and hangs herself when he rejects her advances. Rochberg's text was drawn from Lowell by Gene Rochberg. *Cf.* **Phèdre**.

Phèdre ("Phaedra") Georges Auric, 1950.

The ballet ("tragedy in choreography"), with a libretto by Jean Cocteau and choreography by Serge Lifar, is based on Jean Racine's verse tragedy *Phèdre* ("Phaedra") (1677), about the sister of Ariadne and wife of Theseus who falls in love with her stepson, Hippolytus. *See also* **Phaedra.**

Philémon et Baucis   Charles Gounod, 1860.

The opera in three acts is set to a libretto by Jules Barbier and Michel Carré based on Ovid's *Metamorphoses* (1st century AD). The story tells how Jupiter and Vulcan, gods traveling in disguise, are shown great hospitality by the poor elderly couple, Philemon and Baucis.

Philomel   Milton Babbitt, 1964.

The work for soprano, recorded soprano, and tapes of synthesized sound explores the moment of transformation of Philomel into a nightingale as told in Ovid's *Metamorphoses.*

Philosopher Symphony (German, *Philosoph-Symphonie*)   Joseph Haydn, 1764.

The Symphony No. 22 in E flat major is so called with reference to the "reflective" opening Adagio. The composer said he had once written a symphony in which God speaks to an unrepentant sinner. This could be it.

Phoebus and Pan (German, *Der Streit zwischen Phöbus und Pan*, "The Strife between Phoebus and Pan")   J.S. Bach, 1729.

The Cantata No. 201, *Geschwinde, ihr Wirbeln den Winde* ("Swift, Ye Whirlings of the Winds"), is set to a libretto by Picander based on the classical story of the musical contest between Phoebus (Apollo), playing the lyre, and Pan, playing the pipes. (Pan lost.) The work was written with the aim of satirizing a hostile music critic, said to be Johann Adolf Scheibe, editor of *Der critische Musikus*, who is represented by the character of Midas.

Piacevolezza ("Pleasantry")   Carl Nielsen, 1906–19.

The String Quartet No. 4 in F, Op. 44, was originally so called by the composer but he discarded the title on eventually completing the work.

Il Piccolo Marat ("Little Marat")   Pietro Mascagni, 1921.

The opera in three acts is set to a libretto by Giovacchino Forzano and Giovanni Targioni-Tozzetti based on Victor Martin's story *Sous la terreur* ("Under the Terror"). The story tells of the Terror in Paris that followed the murder of the revolutionary leader Jean-Paul Marat (1743–1793). "Little Marat" is the nickname of the Prince Jean-Charles de Fleury, who insinuates himself into the favor of the President of the Revolutionary Council to secure the release of his mother, condemned to death by the Jacobins.

Picnic at Tintagel   Arnold Bax, 1952.

The ballet in one act (three scenes), with a libretto and choreography by Frederick Ashton, is set to the composer's The **Garden of Fand** and tells the story of Tristan and Isolde (*see* **Tristan und Isolde**), setting it in 1916, the year Bax completed this work, at Tintagel, Cornwall, the coastal village associated with King Arthur.

Pictures at an Exhibition (Russian, *Kartinki s vystavki*)   Modest Mussorgsky, 1874.

The suite for solo piano is a musical representation of ten pictures and designs at a memorial exhibition for the composer's friend, the Russian artist Viktor Gartman (Victor Hartmann) (1834–1873). The individual titles of the pieces, with brief descriptions of the original depictions, are as follows: (1) *The Gnome* (a clumsy dwarf), (2) *The Old Castle* (a medieval castle before which a troubadour sings), (3) *Tuileries* (children and nurses in the Paris gardens so named), (4) *Bydlo* (Polish for "cattle": an ox-drawn wagon), (5) *Unhatched Chicks* (chicks battling in their shells), (6) *Samuel Goldenberg and Shmuyle* (two Polish Jews, one rich, one poor), (7) *Market Place at Limoges* (women arguing), (8) *Catacombs* (those in Paris), (9) *Baba-Yaga*, or *The Hut on Fowl's Legs* (a witch's dwelling), (10) *The Great Gate of Kiev* (the artist's design for a massive gate to that city). The Russian title literally translates as *Pictures from an Exhibition*, "but there is no harm in using a better English one" (Blom, p. 442).

Pièces pittoresques ("Picturesque Pieces")   Emmanuel Chabrier, 1889–91.

The work for piano consists of 10 allusively evocative pieces, titled respectively *Paysage* ("Landscape"), *Mélancolie* ("Melancholy"), *Tourbillon* ("Whirlwind"), *Sous-bois* ("Undergrowth"), *Mauresque* ("Moor"), *Idylle* ("Idyll"), *Danse villageoise* ("Village Dance"), *Improvisation* ("Improvization"), *Menuet pompeux* ("Pompous Minuet"), and *Scherzo-Valse* ("Scherzo-Waltz").

The Pied Piper   Aaron Copland, 1951.

The ballet in two parts, choreographed by Jerome Robbins, is set to the composer's Concerto for Clarinet and String Orchestra (1947–8). It "has nothing to do with the famous Pied

Piper of Hamelin and refers instead to the clarinet soloist" (program note, quoted in Koegler, p. 327). However, since the dancers fall under the clarinetist's spell one after another, and become his puppets, the notion of the piper of folklore, who lured first the rats, then the children, out of the town by playing his pipe, is not too remote.

Piège de lumière ("Light Trap")   Jean-Michel Damase, 1952.

The ballet in one act, with a libretto by Philippe Hériat and choreography by John Taras, depicts a group of escaped prisoners living in a tropical forest, where they catch butterflies. The story tells what happens when one of them catches the Queen of the Morphides, which poisons him.

Pierrot lunaire ("Moonstruck Pierrot") Arnold Schoenberg, 1912.

The melodrama, Op. 21, for female voice and chamber orchestra, is a cycle in three parts. Each part contains seven songs which are settings of poems of the same title (1884) by the Belgian poet Albert Giraud (real name Marie-Émile Albert) translated from French into German by Otto Erich Hartleben. The individual titles in each of the cycles are as follows: I (1) *Mondestrunken* ("Moondrunk"), (2) *Colombine*, (3) *Der Dandy* ("The Dandy"), (4) *Eine blaße Wäscherin* ("A Pale Washerwoman"), (5) *Valse de Chopin* ("Chopin Waltz"), (6) *Madonna*, (7) *Der kranke Mond* ("The Sick Moon"); II (1) *Die Nacht* ("The Night"), (2) *Gebet an Pierrot* ("Prayer to Pierrot"), (3) *Raub* ("Robbery"), (4) *Rote Messe* ("Red Mass"), (5) *Galgenlied* ("Gallows Song"), (6) *Enthauptung* ("Beheading"), (7) *Die Kreuze* ("The Crosses"); III (1) *Heimweh* ("Homesickness"), (2) *Gemeinheit* ("Meanness"), (3) *Parodie* ("Parody"), (4) *Der Mondfleck* ("The Moonstain"), (5) *Serenade*, (6) *Heimfahrt* ("Return Journey"), (7) *O alter Duft* ("O Ancient Scent"). Pierrot, the mournful, white-faced, white-dressed French buffoon, is here a *"pâle dandy bergamasque"* ("pale Bergomask dandy"), in a plot that involves the black mass and descriptions of depravity and sadomasochism (as may be gathered from some of the song titles).

La Pietra del Paragone ("The Touchstone") Gioacchino Rossini, 1812.

The comic opera in two acts, to a libretto by Luigi Rommanelli, tells how Count Asdrubale tests the genuineness of the affections of the three young widows who want to marry him by disguising himself as a Turk claiming that Asdrubale owes him a large sum of money.

The Pilgrims *see* **Lieder ohne Worte**.

The Pilgrims' Chorus   Richard Wagner, 1845.

The chorus of pilgrims in Act 1 and Act 3 of **Tannhäuser**. In Act 1 they sing *"Zur dir wall' ich"* ("To thee I go"), and in Act 3 *"Beglückt darf nun dich"* ("I may now thee in joy").

The Pilgrim's Progress   Ralph Vaughan Williams, 1925–51.

The opera ("morality") in four acts is set to the composer's own libretto based on John Bunyan's allegory of the same title (1674–9, 1684), about the journey of Christian (whose name is changed here to Pilgrim) to the Celestial City.

Pillar of Fire   Arnold Schoenberg, 1942.

The ballet in one act (two scenes), with a libretto and choreography by Antony Tudor, is based on the composer's **Verklärte Nacht** and tells what happens when the young woman, Hagar, fears that she will lose the man she loves to her flirtatious younger sister. The imagery of the title is ultimately biblical: "And I saw another mighty angel come down from heaven, clothed with a cloud: and a rainbow was upon his head, and his face was as it were the sun, and his feet as pillars of fire" (Revelation 10:1).

Pimmalione ("Pygmalion")   Luigi Cherubini, 1809.

The opera in one act is set to a libretto by Stefano Vestris based on Antonio Sografi's Italian version of Jean-Jacques Rousseau's monodrama *Pygmalion* (1770), itself drawing on the classical legend of the sculptor who falls in love with the statue of a woman that he creates and that comes alive as Galatea.

Pineapple Poll   Arthur Sullivan, arr. Charles Mackerras, 1951.

The ballet in one act (three scenes), with a libretto and choreography by John Cranko, is based on W.S. Gilbert's "Bab Ballad" *The Bumboat Woman's Story* (1869) in which Poll Pineapple is the old bumboat woman who ferried goods to the ships: "Ah! I've been young in my time, and I've played the deuce with men! / I'm speaking of ten years past — I was barely sixty then: / My cheeks were mellow and soft, and my eyes were large and sweet, / Poll Pineapple's eyes were the standing toast of the Royal Fleet!" The story tells how the young women of Portsmouth are so drawn to Captain Belaye that they disguise themselves as sailors to get on board his ship, H.M.S. *Hot Cross Bun*.

Pines of Rome *see* **Pini di Roma**.

Pini di Roma ("Pines of Rome")   Ottorino Respighi, 1923–4.

The symphonic poem is an evocation of Rome in four sections, individually titled *Villa Borghese*, *A Catacomb*, *Janiculum* (a ridge on the west bank of the Tiber), and *Appian Way*.

The Pipe of Desire   Frederick Converse, 1906.

The opera in one act, to a libretto by George Edward Burton, tells how Iola selfishly uses a magic pipe belonging to the Elf King and brings disaster to himself and to his lover, Naoia.

Pique Dame *see* The **Queen of Spades**.

Il Pirata ("The Pirate")   Vicenzo Bellini, 1827.

The opera in two acts is set to a libretto by Felice Romani based on the play *Bertram, ou Le Pirate* ("Bertram, or The Pirate") (1826) by Raimond (pen name of Isidore J.S. Taylor), in turn based on Charles Maturin's tragedy *Bertram, or the Castle of St. Aldobrand* (1816). The story is set in 13th-century Sicily and tells what happens when Gualtiero, formerly Count of Montalto but now an exile and pirate leader, returns to find that his beloved, Imogene, has married his enemy, Ernesto, Duke of Caldora.

The Pirates of Penzance   Arthur Sullivan, 1879.

The comic opera in two acts, to a libretto by W.S. Gilbert, is set in 19th-century Cornwall (where Penzance is a port) and tells what happens when Frederic, formerly apprenticed to a pirate crew, is now at 21 freed from his indentures. The subtitle is *The Slave of Duty*. The opera was originally to be about the relations between a group of burglars and a group of policemen, and was thus provisionally titled *The Robbers*. When in the United States, Gilbert decided to recast the burglars as pirates, and the work was renamed accordingly.

Pithoprakta   Iannis Xenakis, 1955–6.

The work has a Greek title meaning "action caused by probabilities." Each of its 50 instruments plays a different part, producing a range of sound amalgams categorized by the composer as a "cloud," "mass," "block," or "nebula" of sound. Each amalgam transforms into or blends with one or more of the others, an "action caused by probabilities" that finally produces a determinate end.

The Planets   Gustav Holst, 1914–16.

The orchestral suite, Op.32, is in seven movements. Each reflects the astrological association of a particular planet, and is titled accordingly: (1) *Mars, the Bringer of War*, (2) *Venus, the Bringer of Peace*, (3) *Mercury, the Winged Messenger*, (4) *Jupiter, the Bringer of Jollity*, (5) *Saturn, the Bringer of Old Age*, (6) *Uranus, the Magician*, (7) *Neptune, the Mystic*.

Platée ("Plataea")   Jean-Philippe Rameau, 1745.

The opera in a prologue and three acts is set to a text by Adrien-Joseph le Valois d'Orville based on a libretto by Jacques Autreau that itself draws on Book 9 of Pausanias's *Description of Greece* (*c*.AD 176). The story tells how Jupiter feigns love for the grotesque nymph, Plataea, in order to arouse the anger of his wife, Juno.

Playground   Gordon Crosse, 1979.

The ballet in one act, with a libretto and choreography by Kenneth MacMillan, centers on a young man who is attracted by children's games in a playground. He involves himself, only to be taken captive.

The Pleasure Dome of Kubla Khan
Charles Tomlinson Griffes, 1912.

The piece for piano, later orchestrated as a symphonic poem (1917), is based on Samuel Taylor Coleridge's poem *Kubla Khan* (1816), beginning "In Xanadu did Kubla Khan / A stately pleasure-dome decree."

Pli selon pli ("Fold Upon Fold")   Pierre Boulez, 1957–62.

The work for soprano and orchestra in five sections, some involving choice of order by the conductor, is subtitled *Portrait de Mallarmé* ("Portrait of Mallarmé"), for the French symbolist poet, Stéphane Mallarmé (1842–1898), and can be seen as a representation of his intricate, multitextured writing. The five sections have individual titles. The first is *Don* ("Gift"), the middle three, all using Mallarmé's poems, are all called *Improvisation*, and the fifth is *Tombeau* ("Tomb").

Poem of Ecstasy (Russian, *Poema ekstaza*; French *Poème d'extase*)   Alexander Skryabin, 1905–8.

The orchestral work, Op. 54, was based on the composer's own philosophical poem expressing his theosophical ideas on love and art. Hence the title.

Poème de l'amour et de la mer ("Poem of Love and the Sea")   Ernest Chausson, 1882.

The work for voice and orchestra (or piano) in three parts is set to a poem by Maurice Bouchor (1855–1929).

Poème de l'extase ("Poem of Ecstasy") Alexander Skryabin and Wolfgang Fortner, 1970.

The ballet in two parts, with a libretto and choreography by John Cranko, was suggested by Colette's novel *La Naissance du jour* ("The Birth of the Day") (1928) and portraits of women by the Austrian artist, Gustav Klimt (1862–1918), and tells the story of a young man who falls in love with a prima donna at a party. Fortner orchestrated the composer's Piano Sonata No. 9 in F (1913) as a prologue.

Poèmes pour Mi ("Poems for Mi") Olivier Messiaen, 1936.

The song cycle for soprano and piano is set to the composer's own poems and is dedicated to his first wife, violinist Claire Deslos, whom he nicknamed "Mi."

Poet and Peasant (German, *Dichter und Bauer*) Franz von Suppé, 1846.

The overture and incidental music were written for K. Elmar's play in three acts of the same name (1846).

The Poet's Echo Benjamin Britten, 1965.

The work for high voice and piano, Op. 76, comprises settings of six poems by Alexander Pushkin (1799–1837) in the original Russian and was composed for the Russian soprano, Galina Vishnevskaya, and Russian cellist and pianist, Mstislav Rostropovich, who gave its first performance in Moscow in December 1965.

Pohjola's Daughter Jean Sibelius, 1906.

The symphonic fantasia, Op. 49, is based on a legend from the Finnish epic, *Kalevala*, in which Pohjola ("the North") is a land ruled by an old witch, Louhi, whose beautiful daughter is wooed by the adventurer and charmer of women, Lemminkäinen. *See also* **Lemminkäinen Legends**, The **Swan of Tuonela**.

The Poisoned Kiss Ralph Vaughan Williams, 1927–9.

The opera in three acts, subtitled *The Empress and the Necromancer*, is set to a libretto by Evelyn Sharp based on Richard Garnett's story *The Poison Maid* in the collection *The Twilight of the Gods* (1888). The plot centers on the rivalry between a sorcerer and an empress, and tells how the sorcerer's daughter, Tormentilla, has been raised on poisons, so that when she meets the empress's son, Amaryllus, she will kill him if she kisses him.

Polish Symphony (Russian, *Pol'skaya simfoniya*) Pyotr Tchaikovsky, 1875.

The Symphony No. 3 in D major, Op. 29, is so called because the finale has the rhythm of a **Polonaise**.

Poliuto ("Polyeuctos") Gaetano Donizetti, 1838.

The opera in three acts is set to a libretto by Salvatore Cammarano based on Pierre Corneille's tragedy *Polyeucte* (1641) about the 3d-century Roman convert to Christianity of this name who is arrested and condemned to death. The opera was banned by the censor and revised in four acts with a libretto by Eugène Scribe under the title *Les Martyrs* ("The Martyrs") (1840). The plural refers to the shared martyrdom of Polyeuctos and his wife, Paulina.

Polly attr. Johann Christoph Pepusch, 1729.

The ballad opera in three acts is set to a libretto by John Gay with extra songs by Samuel Arnold. The work is a sequel to The **Beggar's Opera**, in which Polly Peachum is Lucy Lockit's rival for Macheath's love.

Polonia Edward Elgar, 1915.

The symphonic prelude for orchestra, Op. 76, was written for a concert given for the Polish Relief Fund. It was dedicated to Paderewski, a champion of the Polish cause in World War I, and contains a quotation from his *Polish Fantasy* for piano and orchestra (1893), one from Chopin, and also the Polish national anthem. The title is the medieval Latin name of Poland.

Polonaise (French, "Polish").

The name of the Polish national dance in triple time was made famous in the world of classical music by Chopin, who expressed his patriotic feeling in 13 of them, written between 1817 (when he was seven) and 1845. Other composers to write polonaises include Bach, Handel, Mozart, Beethoven, and Schubert.

Polovtsian Dances (Russian, *Polovetskiye plyaski*) Alexander Borodin, 1890.

The sequence of choral and orchestral pieces in Act 2 of **Prince Igor** is named for the Polovtsians (Polovtsy), the nomadic invaders of Russia who (in the opera) capture Igor.

Il Pomo d'oro ("The Golden Apple") Pietro Cesti, 1668.

The opera in five acts, to a libretto by

Francesco Sbarra, is based on the classical legend telling how Paris awarded a golden apple to Aphrodite as the most beautiful of the goddesses.

Pomona   Constant Lambert, 1926.

The ballet in one act, choreographed by Frederick Ashton, takes its title from the Roman goddess of fruit.

Pomp and Circumstance   Edward Elgar, 1901–30.

The title is that of a set of five marches for orchestra, Op. 39. No. 1 in A major and No. 2 in A minor were first performed in 1901, No. 3 in C minor in 1903, No. 4 in G major in 1907, and No. 5 in C major in 1930. The trio section of No. 1 became the finale of the **Coronation Ode**, itself separately titled by the opening words of its song, **Land of Hope and Glory**. The overall title was given by the composer and comes from Shakespeare: "Pride, pomp, and circumstance of glorious war" (*Othello*, III, iii).

"Porgi amor" ("Give love").

The Countess's aria in Act 2 of Mozart's Le **Nozze di Figaro**, in which she expresses her longing for her husband's love.

Porgy and Bess   George Gershwin, 1935.

The opera in three acts is set to a libretto by Du Bose Heyward and Ira Gershwin based on Du Bose and Dorothy Heward's novel *Porgy* (1925) about the rivalry between the cripple, Porgy, and the stevedore, Crown, for the affections of Bess.

Portrait Aria *see* **"Dies Bildnis ist bezaubernd schön."**

Portsmouth Point   William Walton, 1925.

The concert overture was inspired by Thomas Rowlandson's etching of the same title depicting a bustling 18th-century dockside scene at Portsmouth, Hampshire.

Posthorn Serenade   W.A. Mozart, 1779.

The Serenade No. 9 in D major, K 320, is so named for the prominent passage for posthorn, playing its four natural notes, in the second trio of the sixth movement.

Le Postillon de Longjumeau ("The Postilion of Longjumeau")   Adolphe Adam, 1836.

The opera in three acts, to a libretto by Adolphe de Leuven and Léon Lévy Brunswick, tells what happens when the postilion, Chapelou, the owner of a fine voice, is engaged by the Marquis de Courcy, manager of the royal amusements, to sing at Fontainebleau.

La Poule ("The Hen")   (1) Jean-Philippe Rameau, 1741; (2) *see* The **Hen Symphony**.

Piece No. 46 in Book 3 of the composer's harpsichord works is based on a musical imitation of a clucking hen. Hence the title.

La Poupée ("The Doll")   Edmond Audran, 1896.

The operetta in a prologue and three acts is set to a libretto by Maurice Ordonneau based on E.T.A. Hoffmann's story *Der Sandmann* ("The Sandman") (1816). (*See also* **Coppélia**.) The story tells how a young monk, Lancelot, wishing to help his impoverished monastery, learns that a rich uncle will give him a fortune if he marries. Faithful to his monastic vows, he buys what he takes to be a lifesize doll from the toymaker, Hilarius, with the aim of introducing it to his uncle as his bride. The "doll," however, turns out to be Hilarius's daughter, Alesia.

"Pourquoi me réveiller?" ("Why wake me?").

Werther's aria in Act 3 of Massenet's **Werther**, in which he sings a song of tragic love from the verses of Ossian, which in happier days he had translated with Charlotte. The aria is also known as *Ossian's Song*.

"Povere fiori" ("Poor flowers").

Adriana's aria in Act 4 of Cilea's **Adriana Lecouvreur**, in which she contemplates the faded bunch of violets (now poisoned by her rival, the Princesse de Bouillon) that she had given Maurizio.

The Power of Evil (Russian, *Vrazh'ya sila*) Alexander Serov, 1871.

The opera in five acts, completed after the composer's death by his wife and Nikolai Solovyov, is set to a libretto by Alexander Ostrovsky based on his play *Live Not As You Wish* (1855), with contributions by other writers. The story tells what happens when the young merchant, Pyotr, married to Dasha but obsessed with lust for the beautiful Grunya, is egged on by his drinking crony, Yeremka, to kill Dasha.

Practical Cats   Alan Rawsthorne, 1954.

The work for speaker and orchestra is a setting of six poems from T.S. Eliot's collection *Old Possum's Book of Practical Cats* (1939).

Prague Symphony   W.A. Mozart, 1786.

The Symphony No. 38 in D major, K 504, is so named because it was first performed during the composer's visit to Prague in 1787.

Le Pré aux clercs ("The Clerks' Meadow")
Ferdinand Hérold, 1832.

The opera in three acts is set to a libretto by François-Antine-Eugène de Planard based on Prosper Mérimée's novel *Chronique du règne de Charles IX* ("Chronicle of the Reign of Charles IX") (1829). This tells how the Baron de Mergy and the Comte de Comminges, rivals for the love of Isabelle de Béarn, fight a duel at the field known as the Pré aux clercs. The once popular opera was also known to English speakers by various other titles, including *The Challenge* and *The Field of Honor*.

Preciosa   Carl Maria Weber, 1820.

The overture, four choruses, song, three melodramas, and dances so titled were composed for Pius Alexander Wolff's German play of the same name about a gypsy, itself based on Cervantes's *La Gitanilla* ("The Gypsy Girl") (1613). This tells what happens when the 15-year-old gypsy girl Preciosa ("Beautiful") falls in love with a wealthy and handsome young man but tells him he can marry her only if he joins the gypsies for two years. *Cf.* The **Bohemian Girl**.

Prelude (Latin *praeludium*, "playing before").

A composition that precedes some other work, such as an opera, or that forms the first movement of a suite. There are also self-contained preludes, as those by Chopin, Rachmaninov, Debussy, and Shostakovich, among others. *See also* Das **Wohltemperierte Klavier.**

Prélude à l'après-midi d'un faune ("Prelude to *The Afternoon of a Faun*")   Claude Debussy, 1894.

The tone poem was inspired by Stéphane Mallarmé's long poem of the same name (1865), originally entitled *Monologue du faune* ("Monologue of the Faun"), telling how a faun, in a state between sleeping and waking in the afternoon, imagines he has seen a nymph. The work, as a **Prelude**, sets the mood for this reverie. *See also* L'**Après-midi d'un faune.**

Prelude and Fugue on the Name B.A.C.H.   Franz Liszt, 1850.

The organ work pays tribute to J.S. Bach by using the letters of his name in the German nomenclature as the notes for its theme, corresponding to English B flat, A, C, and B natural. Many other composers have done the same, such as Max Reger in his *Fantasia and Fugue on BACH* for organ (1900). The tribute is often simply in a passage, however, so that no reference is made in the title. Bach himself used the notes as one of the subjects in the final (unfinished) figure of Die **Kunst der Fuge.**

Préludes ("Preludes")   Claude Debussy, 1910–13.

The work comprises two sets of 12 piano pieces, as follows: I (1910) (1) *Danseuses de Delphes* ("Dancers of Delphi") (suggested by a pillar in the Louvre on which are sculpted three Bacchantes), (2) *Voiles* ("Sails"), (3) *Le Vent dans la plaine* ("The wind on the plain"), (4) *Les Sons et les parfums tournent dans l'air du soit* ("Sounds and scents whirl in the evening air"), (5) *Les Collines d'Anacapri* ("The hills of Anacapri"), (6) *Des Pas sur la neige* ("Footprints in the snow"), (7) *Ce qu'a vu le vent d'Ouest* ("What the West Wind saw"), (8) La **Fille aux cheveux de lin,** (9) *La Sérénade interrompue* ("The interrupted serenade"), (10) La **Cathédrale engloutie,** (11) *La Danse de Puck* ("Puck's dance"); (12) *Minstrels* ("Music hall artists"); II (1912–13) (1) **Brouillards,** (2) *Feuilles mortes* ("Dead leaves"), (3) *La Puerta del Vino* ("The Wine Gate") (a famous gate of the Alhambra, Granada), (4) *Les Fées sont d'exquises danseuses* ("Fairies are exquisite dancers"), (5) *Bruyères* ("Heaths"), (6) *General Lavine — eccentric* (a Paris music hall performer), (7) *La Terrasse des audiences du clair de lune* ("The terrace of the moonlight audiences"), (8) *Ondine,* (9) *Hommage à S. Pickwick, Esq., P.P.M.P.C.* ("Homage to S. Pickwick, Esq., P.P.M.P.C.") (suggested by the Dickens character), (10) *Canope* ("Canopus") (an ancient Egyptian jar holding the entrails taken from a body during the embalming process), (11) *Les Tierces alternées* ("Alternating thirds"), (12) **Feux d'artifice.** The title of No.4 in Book I is a quotation from Baudelaire. No. 11 is based on Shakespeare's *A Midsummer Night's Dream* (1595). The title of No. 7 in Book II is a phrase from Pierre Loti's *L'Inde* (*sans les Anglais*) ("The Indies (without the English))" (1903), and the piece quotes from the folksong *Au clair de la lune* ("By Moonlight"). No. 9 was suggested by Charles Dickens' *Pickwick Papers* (1837), which has Samuel Pickwick as its main character. The composer seems to have confused Pickwick's abbreviated title, correctly G.C.M.P.C., "General Chairman, Member Pickwick Club," with that of another character in the novel, Joseph Smiggers, who was P.V.P.M.P.C., "Perpetual Vice President, Member Pickwick Club."

Les Préludes ("The Preludes")   Franz Liszt, 1848.

The symphonic poem takes its title from

one of Alphonse de Lamartine's *Nouvelles Médi-tations poétiques* ("New Poetic Meditations") (1823), but the music was originally composed as the overture to *Les Quatre Éléments* ("The Four Elements"), four choruses for male voices with words by Joseph Autran and orchestration by August Conradi. The composer's preface to the revised score of the work (1854) states that life is treated as a series of preludes to the unknown afterlife.

"Prendi, l'anel ti dono" ("Take, I give thee the ring").

Elvino's aria as he places a ring on Amina's finger in Act 1 of Bellini's La **Sonnambula.**

"Près des remparts de Seville" ("Near the ramparts of Seville").

Carmen's aria in Act 1 of Bizet's **Carmen,** in which she tempts Don José to untie her hands and release her from arrest because, she says, he is in love with her.

Les Présages ("The Omens") Pyotr Tchaikovsky, 1933.

The ballet in four movements, with a libretto and choreography by Léonide Massine, is set to the composer's Symphony No. 5 in E minor, Op. 64 (1888), and depicts man's struggle with his destiny. The four parts have titles: (1) *Action,* (2) *Passion,* (3) *Frivolity,* (4) *War.*

Présence ("Presence") Bernd Zimmermann, 1968.

The ballet in one act, with a libretto and choreography by John Cranko, is set to the composer's *Concerto scénique* for violin, cello, and piano and centers on three literary characters regarded as respective symbols of sex, power, and idealism: Molly (Molly Bloom, from James Joyce's *Ulysses,* 1922), Roy (Ubu, from Alfred Jarry's *Ubu Roi,* 1896), and Don (Don Quixote, from Miguel Cervantes' *Don Quijote de la Mancha,* 1605–15).

Pribaoutki ("Song Games") Igor Stravinsky, 1918.

The work, for male voice, wind ensemble, and string quartet, comprises four settings of Russian popular texts. They are individually named as follows: (1) *L'Oncle Armand* ("Uncle Armand"), or *Kornillo,* (2) *Le Four* ("The Oven"), or *Natashka,* (3) *Le Colonel* ("The Colonel"), and (4) *Le Vieux et le Lièvre* ("The Old Man and the Hare"). The overall title is a French spelling of Russian *pribautki,* the plural of *pribautka,* a term for a type of humorous say-ing or witty anecdote, itself based on the verb *bayat',* "to say."

Il Prigioniero ("The Prisoner") Luigi Dallapiccola, 1944–8.

The opera in a prologue and one act is set to the composer's own libretto based on Villiers de l'Isle Adam's *La Torture par l'espérance* ("Torture by Hope") (1883) and the Belgian writer Charles Coster's nationalistic masterpiece, *La Légende d'Ulenspiegel et de Lamme Goedzak* ("The Legend of Eulenspiegel and Lamme Goedzak") (1866). The story is set in late 16th-century Saragossa and tells how a prisoner of the Inquisition is led to believe he can escape but falls victim to the worst torture of all, that of hope.

Prima Donna Arthur Benjamin, 1933.

The comic opera in one act is set to a libretto by Cedric Cliffe and is a satire on the rivalry between two prima donnas, "La Filomela" and Olimpia, in 18th-century Venice.

Prima la musica e poi le parole ("First the Music and Then the Words") Antonio Salieri, 1785.

The opera in one act is set to a libretto by Giovanni Battista Casti in the form of a discussion between a poet and a composer about the importance of their respective contributions to an opera. *See also* **Capriccio.**

Primitive Mysteries Louis Horst, 1931.

The ballet in three sections, choreographed by Martha Graham, is a work dealing with religious feelings in their most basic form. The three parts have titles: (1) *Hymn to the Virgin,* (2) *Crucifixus,* and (3) *Hosannah.*

Prince Igor (Russian, *Knyaz' Igor*) Alexander Borodin, 1869–87.

The opera in a prologue and four acts is set to the composer's own libretto based on a scenario by Vladimir Stasov that tells what happens when Prince Igor Svyatoslavich (1150–1202) is captured by the Polovtsy. *See also* **Polovtsian Dances, Yaroslavna.**

The Prince of the Pagodas Benjamin Britten, 1956.

The ballet in three acts, Op. 57, with a libretto and choreography by John Cranko, was inspired by the composer's visit to the Far East. It is a fairy tale about the Emperor of the Middle Kingdom and his two daughters, one of whom meets the Green Salamander in the Kingdom of the Pagodas and helps him regain his original form as a handsome prince.

The Princess and the Seven Knights
(Russian, *Skazka o myortvoy tsarevne i semi bogatyryakh*, "Tale of the Dead Czarevna and the Seven Knights") Anatol Lyadov arr. V.M. Deshevov, 1949.

The ballet in three acts (ten scenes), with a libretto by G. Jagdfeld and choreography by A.L. Andreiev and Boris Fenster, is an adaptation of the Snow White story, as retold by Alexander Pushkin in his fairy tale of the same name (1833). The Evil Queen becomes the vain Czarevna (czar's daughter) and the seven dwarfs are the seven knights.

Princess Ida   Arthur Sullivan, 1883.
The operetta in three acts, to a libretto by W.S. Gilbert, was originally billed as "A Respectful Operatic Per-Version of Tennyson's 'Princess'." The plot in fact follows *The Princess* (1847) fairly closely. The poem tells what happens when Princess Ida, to whom a prince was betrothed in childhood, becomes a devotee of women's rights, abjures marriage, and founds an all-female university. The opera's subtitle is *Castle Adamant*.

A Princess of Kensington   Edward German, 1903.
The comic opera in two acts, to a libretto by Basil Hood, opens on Midsummer Day in Kensington Gardens, London, a time when fairies can disguise themselves as mortals. The story tells how the Mountain Spirit, Azuriel, orders his betrothed, Kenna, the Princess of Kensington, daughter of Oberon, King of the Fairies, to produce her former mortal lover, Prince Albion, and prove that he is married to another mortal.

Printemps ("Spring")   Claude Debussy, 1887.
The symphonic suite for orchestra and female chorus is a depiction of the named season.

Der Prinz von Homburg ("The Prince of Homburg")   Hans Werner Henze, 1957–8.
The opera in three acts is set to a libretto by Ingeborg Bachmann based on Heinrich von Kleist's play *Prinz Friedrich von Homburg* (1821). The plot is set in the 17th century, and tells what happens when Prince Friedrich von Homburg, a poet and a dreamer, leads a disastrous charge in battle and is court-martialed.

Prize Song   Richard Wagner, 1868.
The song with which Walther wins the fair Eva in Act 3 of Die **Meistersinger von Nürn-**berg. It is also known by its opening words, "*Morgenlich leuchtend*" ("In the morning shining").

La Procesión del Rocío ("The Procession of the Rocío")   Joaquín Turina, 1913.
The symphonic poem in two parts is a musical depiction of the Rocío, a place of pilgrimage near Seville, Spain.

The Prodigal Son   (1) Arthur Sullivan, 1869; (2) (Russian, *Bludnyy syn*) Sergey Prokofiev, 1928; (3) Benjamin Britten, 1968; (4) *see* L'**Enfant prodigue**.
Sullivan's oratorio, Prokofiev's ballet, and Britten's church parable are all based on the biblical parable of the Prodigal Son (Luke 15), the young man who wasted his wealth on riotous living but was given a generous welcome by his father when he returned in poverty. Prokofiev's ballet in one act, with a libretto by Boris Kochno and choreography by George Balanchine, is sometimes known by the French title *Le fils prodigue*. The title is also occasionally applied to his Symphony No. 4 in C, Op. 47 (1929–30), as it is partly based on the ballet music. Britten's work is set to a text by William Plomer.

I Promessi Sposi ("The Betrothed")
(1) Enrico Petrella, 1869; (2) Amilcare Ponchielli, 1872.
Petrella's opera is set to a libretto by Antonio Ghislanzoni based on Alessandro Manzoni's romantic historical novel of the same name (1827), telling of the attempts of two peasants, Renzo and Lucia, to marry, despite the threats of a local grandee, Don Rodrigo. The opera's first performance was at Lecco, Lombardy, the scene of the story. Ponchielli's opera is based on the same book. The plural in the Italian title is not reflected in the English equivalent.

Prométhée ("Prometheus")   Gabriel Fauré, 1900.
The lyric tragedy, an open-air spectacle, is set to a libretto by Jean Lorrain and André Ferdinand Hérold based on Aeschylus' tragedy *Prometheus Bound* (after 467 BC), telling what happens when Prometheus, who has stolen fire from heaven for mankind, is punished by Zeus by being chained to a Scythian mountain.

Prometheus   Franz Liszt, 1850.
The symphonic poem was originally composed as the prelude to a setting of choruses from Johann Gottfried Herder's play *Prometheus Unbound* (1802), based on Aeschylus's tragedy

Prometheus Bound (*see* **Prométhée**). *Cf.* **Prometheus Unbound**.

Prometheus, the Poem of Fire (Russian, *Prometey, poema ognya*)   Alexander Skryabin, 1908–10.

The symphonic poem in F sharp major, Op. 60, for orchestra with piano, optional chorus, and "keyboard of light" (projecting colors on a screen), is loosely based on the Greek myth of Prometheus (*see* **Prométhée**). The work is also known by its equivalent French title, *Prométhée, le poème du feu*.

Prometheus Unbound   Hubert Parry, 1880.

The work is a setting for soloists, chorus, and orchestra of texts from P.B. Shelley's lyrical drama of the same name (1820), based on the Greek myth of Prometheus (*see* **Prométhée**), but with Prometheus finally released by Hercules (Heracles). The full title of Parry's work is *Scenes from Shelley's Prometheus Unbound*.

Le Prophète ("The Prophet")   Giacomo Meyerbeer, 1836–40.

The opera in five acts is set to a libretto by Eugène Scribe based on a historical incident in the 16th-century Anabaptist uprising when Jan Neuckelzoon (1309–1336) (Jean de Leyden in the opera, and the prophet of the title) has himself crowned in Münster in 1535.

The Prophets   Mario Castelnuovo-Tedesco, 1939.

The composer has explained his choice of title for the Violin Concerto No. 2: "'The Prophets' was supposed to be the title (and subtitle) of my second Violin Concerto; my first Violin Concerto had (as a title) 'Concerto Italiano' because it expressed the lyrical, Italian (almost post Vivaldi) side of my nature; and when Heifetz asked me to write another one I told him that I would like this time to express 'the other side' of my nature and my education — the Jewish one — so I called it 'The Prophets' and I even gave subtitles to the three individual movements, Isaiah, Jeremiah, and Elijah, but Heifetz wanted something more 'generic' so 'The Prophets' became the subtitle and the piece was known as 'Concerto No. 2'" (quoted in Berkowitz, p. 123). *See also* **Concerto Italiano**.

Proses lyriques ("Lyrics in Prose")   Claude Debussy, 1892–3.

The four songs for voice and piano, set to the composer's own text, have titles: *De rêve* ("Of a Dream"), *De grève* ("Of a Shore"), *De fleurs* ("Of Flowers"), and *De soir* ("Of Evening").

The Prospect Before Us   William Boyce arr. Constant Lambert, 1940.

The ballet in seven scenes, with a libretto and choreography by Ninette de Valois, is based on John Ebers's *Seven Years of the King's Theatre* (1828), telling of two rival London theater managers, Mr. Taylor of the King's Theatre, and Mr. O'Reilly of the Pantheon. The title comes from Thomas Rowlandson's engraving of the same name

The Protecting Veil   John Tavener, 1987.

The work in ten sections for cello and strings takes its inspiration from the Russian Orthodox feast of the Protecting Veil of the Mother of God (Russian, *Pokrov Bogoroditsy*), commemorating the alleged appearance of the Virgin Mary in a Constantinople church in 910. She is said to have spread a white veil over worshipers there and prayed for the world to be saved from its woes and suffering.

Der Prozess ("The Trial")   Gottfried von Einem, 1950–2.

The opera in nine scenes is set to a libretto by Boris Blacher and Heinz von Kramer based on Franz Kafka's novel of the same title (1925), telling of the arrest and trial of the bank official, Joseph K., for an unnamed crime.

Prozession ("Procession")   Karlheinz Stockhausen, 1967.

The work for various instruments contains no new music but simply instructions for playing "events" from other works by the composer. These all thus proceed in a "procession."

Prussian Quartets *see* King of Prussia Quartets.

Prussian Sonatas   C.P.E. Bach, 1742.

The six keyboard sonatas, W 48, are so called as they were produced under the patronage of Frederick the Great of Prussia. The composer had been appointed court cembalist in 1738.

Psalmus Hungaricus ("Hungarian Psalm") Zoltán Kodály, 1923.

The work, Op. 15, for tenor solo, chorus, children's chorus, orchestra, and organ, was written to celebrate the 50th anniversary of the union of the cities of Buda and Pest and is based on the text of Psalm 55 as paraphrased by the 16th-century Hungarian poet Mihály Végh.

Psyché ("Psyche") (1) Jean-Baptiste Lully, 1678; (2) Ambroise Thomas, 1857; (3) César Franck, 1888.

All three works are based on the classical story of Psyche, the beautiful Greek princess loved and abandoned by Cupid when she insisted on seeing his face. Lully's opera is set to a libretto by Thomas Corneille and Bernard de Fontenelle, Thomas' to one by Jules Barbier and Michel Carré. Franck's work is a suite for orchestra with choral interpolations.

Les P'tites Michu ("The Little Michus") André Charles Messager, 1897.

The operetta in three acts, to a libretto by Albert van Loo and Georges Duval, is set in Paris in 1810 and centers on the loves and eventual double marriage of two girls raised as twin sisters, Marie-Blanche Michu and Blanche-Marie Michu.

Pulcinella Giovanni Battista Pergolesi arr. Igor Stravinsky, 1919–20.

The ballet with song in one act, for soprano, tenor, bass, and chamber orchestra, with a libretto and choreography by Léonide Massine, has music adapted from various works by Pergolesi. The libretto is based on the Neapolitan play *The Four Pulcinellas* (*c*. 1700), itself centering on Pulcinella, the popular Italian figure corresponding to the French Polichinelle and the English Punch, although not humpbacked like these last two.

Punch and Judy Harrison Birtwistle, 1966–7.

The opera in one act is set to a libretto by Stephen Pruslin based loosely on the puppet play of the same name and having violence in the form of murder as its theme.

I Puritani ("The Puritans") Vincenzo Bellini, 1834.

The opera in three acts is set to a libretto by Carlo Pepoli based on Jacques Andot and Xavier Boniface Saintine's play *Têtes rondes et Cavaliers* ("Roundheads and Cavaliers") (1833), itself loosely based on Sir Walter Scott's novel *Old Mortality* (1816). The story tells what happens when the Cavalier, Lord Arthur Talbot, and the Puritan, Sir Richard Forth, both love Elvira, daughter of the Puritan prison warden, Lord Walton. The opera's full formal title is *I Puritani di Scozia* ("The Puritans of Scotland")

Push Comes to Shove Joseph Haydn and Joseph Lamb arr. David E. Bourne, 1976.

The ballet in one act, choreographed by Twyla Tharp, is "a mix of old and new music, time past and time present," with the dancers "in rare and droll combinations" (George Balanchine, quoted in Koegler, p. 337). The title quotes the colloquial phrase "when push comes to shove," meaning "if the worst comes to the worst."

Putnam's Camp *see* **Three Places in New England**.

Pygmalion Jean-Philippe Rameau, 1748.

The opera ballet in one act is set to a libretto by Ballot de Savor based on Antoine Houdart de la Motte's *Le Triomphe des arts* ("The Triumph of the Arts"). The classical story tells what happens when the sculptor, Pygmalion, falls in love with the female statue he has created.

Q

Qarrtsiluni Knudåge Riisager, 1942.

The ballet in one act, with a libretto by the composer and Harald Lander and choreography by the latter, has a title that is the Inuit (Eskimo) word for the transition between winter and spring. The ballet itself thus depicts a "rite of spring."

"Qual cor tradisti" ("What heart hast thou betrayed").

The duet in Act 2 of Bellini's **Norma**, in which Norma reproaches the guilty Pollione for having betrayed her.

"Quand'ero paggio" ("When I was a page").

Falstaff's aria in Act 2 of Verdi's **Falstaff**, in which he recalls the days when he was a slender and comely page to the Duke of Norfolk.

"Quando m'en vo'" *see* **Musetta's Waltz Song**.

"Quanto è bella!" ("How beautiful she is!").

Nemorino's aria in Act 1 of Donizetti's **L'Elisir d'amore**, in which he gazes at the beautiful young Adina.

Quartettsatz ("Quartet Movement") Franz Schubert, 1820.

The title is that of the first movement of the composer's unfinished string quartet in C minor,

D 703. Only 41 bars of the second movement remain. "The German word *Quartettsatz* is still frequently used as a title in English, although it might describe any separate quartet movement" (Blom, p. 464).

Les Quatre saisons ("The Four Seasons") Cesare Pugni, 1848.

The ballet divertissement in one act, choreographed by Jules Joseph Perrot, is a depiction of the changing seasons. *Cf.* The **Four Seasons**.

I Quattro rusteghi ("The Four Boors") Ermanno Wolf-Ferrari, 1906.

The opera in three acts is set to a libretto by Giuseppe Pizzolato based on Carlo Goldoni's comedy *I rusteghi* ("The Rustics") (1760). The story is set in 18th-century Venice and tells how four boorish fathers vainly attempt to control their wives' excesses. The opera is often known in English as *The School for Fathers*.

Quatuor pour la fin du temps ("Quartet for the End of Time") Olivier Messiaen, 1940.

The work for violin, clarinet, cello, and piano was written when the composer was interned in the prisoner-of-war camp Stalag 8A at Görlitz, Silesia, and was first performed there. World War II had then reached a stage that to many seemed like "the end of time," otherwise an apocalypse. There are eight movements based on imagery from the biblical Apocalypse with titles as follows: (1) *Liturgie de cristal* ("Crystal liturgy"), (2) *Vocalise pour l'ange qui annonce la fin du temps* ("Vocalise, for the angel who announces the end of time"), (3) *Abîme des oiseaux* ("Abyss of the Birds"), (4) *Intermède* ("Interlude"), (5) *Louange à l'éternité de Jésus* ("Praise to the eternity of Jesus"), (6) *Danse de la fureur, pour les sept trompettes* ("Dance of fury, for the seven trumpets"), (7) *Fouillis d'arcs-en-ciel, pour l'ange qui annonce la fin du temps* ("Tangles of rainbows, for the angel who announces the end of time"), (9) *Louange à l'immortalité de Jésus* ("Praise to the immortality of Jesus").

Queen Mary's Funeral Music Henry Purcell, 1695.

The music was composed for the funeral in Westminster Abbey, London, of Queen Mary II (1662–1694), wife of William III.

The Queen of Sheba *see* Die **Königin von Saba**.

The Queen of Spades (Russian, *Pikovaya dama*) Pyotr Tchaikovsky, 1890.

The opera in three acts is set to a libretto by the composer's brother, Modest Tchaikovsky, with contributions from himself, based on Alexander Pushkin's story of the same title (1834). It tells the story of the young officer, Hermann, who loves Lisa, granddaughter of the old Countess, a former gambler known as the Queen of Spades because she possessed the secret of the "three cards." The opera is still sometimes known in English as *Pique Dame*, with a French pronunciation. This is actually the German title, not the French, which is *La Dame de pique*. *See also* La **Dame de Pique**.

Queen Symphony Joseph Haydn, 1785.

The Symphony No. 85 in B flat major, the fourth of the **Paris Symphonies**, is so named because it was much admired by Marie Antoinette, queen of France. Its alternate title is *La Reine*, the French equivalent.

The Quest William Walton, 1943.

The ballet in five scenes, with a libretto by Doris Langley Moore and choreography by Frederick Ashton, was inspired by Edmund Spenser's poem *The Faerie Queene* (1591–6), and depicts the victory of St. George over the forces of evil.

"Questa o quella" ("This one or that one")

The Duke of Mantua's aria at the beginning of Act 1 of Verdi's **Rigoletto**, in which he declares that all women ("this one or that one") attract him.

"Qui la voce" ("Here the voice").

Elvira's **Mad Scene** in Act 2 of Bellini's I **Puritani**, following her derangement caused by her belief that Arthur has betrayed her.

Quiet City Aaron Copland, 1939.

The work for trumpet, English horn, and strings was originally the incidental music to Irwin Shaw's play of the same name (1939).

Quiet Flows the Don (Russian, *Tikhiy Don*, 'The Quiet Don") Ivan Dzerzhinsky, 1935.

The opera in four acts is set to a libretto by the composer's brother, Leonid Dzerzhinsky, based on the first two volumes (1928) of Mikhail Sholokhov's four-volume novel of the same name (1928–40), a story of love and war set at the time of the Russian Revolution.

A Quiet Place Leonard Bernstein, 1983.

The opera in one act, to a libretto by Stephen Wadsworth, was originally written as a sequel to **Trouble in Tahiti**, but the earlier opera was subsequently incorporated as two flashbacks.

Quintet   Jacques Ibert, 1963.

The ballet in one act, choreographed by Peter Wright, is set to the composer's Quintet for Woodwind (hence the title) and is in the style of a divertissement, based on the interplay between the dancers and the musicians, who are placed on the stage.

R

Rach 3   Sergey Rachmaninov, 1909.

A musician's nickname for the Piano Concerto No. 3 in D minor, Op. 30, brought before the public in the movie *Shine* (1996) about the pianist David Helfgott. This type of name is not unique, and any numbered work can be similarly dubbed, whether the composer's name is abbreviated or not. One can thus talk of "Beethoven 4" or "Brahms 2," although one will often need to know whether symphony or concerto is meant. Even a titled work can be referred to in this way, so that Beethoven's **Eroica Symphony** is equally "Beethoven 3."

"Rachel, quand du Seigneur" ("Rachel, when of the Lord").

Éléazar's aria in Act 4 of Halévy's La **Juive**, in which he wrestles with the dilemma whether to let Rachel die at the hands of the Christians or save her life by revealing to Cardinal Brogni that she is the latter's daughter.

Radamisto   George Frideric Handel, 1720.

The opera in three acts is set to a libretto by Nicola Francesco Haym adapted from Domenico Lalli's play *L'amour tirannico, o Zenobia* ("Tyrannous Love, or Zenobia") (1710), telling of the love of Rhadamistus and Zenobia, in turn from Tacitus, who tells what happens when Rhadamistus married Zenobia but murdered her at her own request when she became pregnant and unable to follow him into banishment.

Radetzky March   Johann Strauss I, 1848.

The march, Op. 228, is dedicated to the Austrian field marshal, Joseph Radetzky (1766–1858).

The Rage Over the Lost Penny (German, *Die Wut über den verlor'nen Groschen*)   Ludwig van Beethoven, 1825–6.

The Rondo a Capriccio for Piano in G major, Op. 129, was titled by the composer as *Leichte Kaprice alla ungharese quasi un capriccio* ("Light Caprice in the Hungarian Style Like a Capriccio"). The popular title above appears on the autograph in an unidentified hand. It matches the music, which is almost an intentional "much ado about nothing."

Rainbow 'Round My Shoulder   various (see below), 1959.

The ballet, choreographed by Donald McKayle, is set to traditional prison songs and deals with the experiences of a Southern chain gang. The title comes from the Al Jolson hit, *There's a Rainbow 'Round My Shoulder* (1928).

Raindrop Prelude *see* **Twenty-Four Preludes**.

The Rajah's Diamond   Alun Hoddinott, 1979.

The opera for television is set to a libretto by Myfanwy Piper based on a story in Robert Louis Stevenson's *New Arabian Nights* (1882).

Rakastava ("Loving One")   Jean Sibelius, 1911.

The work, Op. 14, originated (1893) as three songs for unaccompanied male chorus with a text from Book 1 of the *Kantelekar*. Their titles, in translation, are: (1) *Where is my Beloved?*, (2) *My Beloved's Path*, and (3) *Good Evening, My Little Bird*. The composition was then rewritten for string orchestra, triangle, and timpani in three movements with titles as follows: (1) *The Loving One*, (2) *The Path of the Beloved*, and (3) *Goodnight: Farewell*.

The Rake's Progress   Igor Stravinsky, 1947–51.

The opera in three acts and an epilogue is set to a libretto by W.H. Auden and Chester Kallman based on William Hogarth's series of engravings of the same title (1735). The story tells what happens when Tom Rakewell (the "rake" of the title) inherits a fortune and goes to London to enjoy the pleasures of life.

Rákóczy March   Hector Berlioz, 1846.

The Hungarian march tune, popularized by Liszt, is quoted in scene 3 of La **Damnation de Faust** although actually written earlier in around 1809 by an unknown composer (possibly János Bihari, a gypsy violinist). It is named in honor of Prince Ferenc Rákóczy (1676–1735), leader of the Hungarian revolt against Austria (1703–11). Berlioz's own name for the piece was *Marche hongroise* ("Hungarian March").

Ramifications György Ligeti, 1968–9.

The work for string orchestra or 12 solo strings is so named for its complex and highly active texture.

The Rape of Lucretia Benjamin Britten, 1946.

The opera in two acts is set to a libretto by Ronald Duncan based on André Obey's play *Le Viol de Lucrèce* ("The Rape of Lucretia") (1931), in turn based on Shakespeare's poem *The Rape of Lucrece* (1594), itself going back to Livy's history of Rome, begun in 25 BC, which tells among other events how Lucretia, wife of Tarquinius Collatinus, was raped by Sextus, son of Tarquinius Superbus, and subsequently committed suicide (in 509 BC) from shame.

Raphael (Russian, *Rafael'*) Anton Arensky, 1894.

The opera in one act, to a libretto by A. Kryukov, takes the Italian painter, Raphael (1483–1520), as its subject and recounts the story that the model for the *Sistine Madonna* (*c.*1512) was the artist's mistress, Margherita, nicknamed *La Fornarina* ("the baker's daughter").

La Rappresentatione di anima e di corpo ("The Representation of the Soul and the Body") Emilio de' Cavalieri, 1600.

The sacred dramatic oratorio, to a text by Agostino Manni, is an allegorical work in which the characters represent the various human attributes as well as the soul and the body.

Rapsodie espagnole ("Spanish Rhapsody") (1) Maurice Ravel, 1907–8; (2) Franz Liszt, 1863.

Ravel's orchestral work is written in the Spanish idiom cultivated by an otherwise typically French composer, as can be seen in the individual titles of its four sections: (1) *Prélude à la nuit* ("Prelude to Night"), (2) *Malagueña* ("Woman of Málaga"), (3) **Habanera**, (4) *Feria* ("Fair"). Liszt's work for solo piano is similarly Spanish in nature. *Cf.* **Rhapsody**.

Raymond Ambroise Thomas, 1851.

The opera is set to a libretto by Adolphe de Leuven and Joseph Bernard Rosier based on Alexandre Dumas' romantic novel *L'Homme au masque de fer* ("The Man in the Iron Mask") (1847), in which Raymond is one of the main characters. The opera's subtitle is *Le Secret de la Reine* ("The Queen's Secret").

Raymonda Alexander Glazunov, 1898.

The ballet in three acts (four scenes), with a libretto by Lydia Pashkova and Marius Petipa and choreography by the latter, tells what happens when Raymonda is due to marry Jean de Brienne but has the attentions of the Saracen knight, Abderakhman, forced on her while de Brienne is away on a crusade.

Razor Quartet (German, *Rasiermesserquartett*) Joseph Haydn, 1787.

The String Quartet in F minor, Op. 55 No. 2, is said to be so named because the composer exclaimed, when shaving, "I'd give my best quartet for a new razor," and was taken at his word by a visitor, the London music publisher, John Bland. The quartet was thus Haydn's side of the bargain.

Razumovsky Quartets Ludwig van Beethoven, 1805–6.

The String Quartets Nos. 1 in F major, 2 in E minor, and 3 in C major, Op. 59, are so called because they were dedicated to the Russian ambassador in Vienna, Count Andrey Razumovsky (1752–1836), a keen quartet player. *See also* **Hero Quartet**.

Il Rè cervo *see* **König Hirsch**.

"Re dell'abisso" ("King of the abyss").

Mlle Arvidson's aria in Act 1 of Verdi's **Un Ballo in maschera**, in which she conjures a spell for the crowd.

Un Re in ascolto ("A Listening King") Luciano Berio, 1979–84.

The opera in two acts is set to the composer's own libretto based on works by Italo Calvino, W.H. Auden, Friedrich Gotter, and Shakespeare. Calvino originally proposed a modern parable about a king who hears of his kingdom's collapse and his queen's infidelity through court gossip. Berio turned the king into a dying impresario named Prospero after the central figure in Shakespeare's *The Tempest* (1611). Prospero "listens" in the sense that he auditions three singers in the search for three female protagonists for his new production.

Il Rè pastore ("The Shepherd King") W.A. Mozart, 1775.

The opera in two acts, K 208, to a libretto by Pietro Metastasio, is based on the story that a poor shepherd, Amintas, was really the rightful heir to the throne of Alexander the Great. He is thus the "shepherd king" of the title.

Recital I (for Cathy) Luciano Berio, 1972.

The work for mezzosoprano and chamber

orchestra was written for the composer's former wife, the American singer Cathy Berberian, to whom he was married from 1950 to 1966.

"Recondita armonia" ("Hidden harmony").

Cavaradossi's aria in Act 1 of Puccini's **Tosca**, in which he contrasts the dark beauty of his beloved Tosca with the fair charms of the Marchesa Attavanti, the model for his painting of Mary Magdalene. A fuller version of the words is: "*Recondita armonia di bellezze diverse*" ("Hidden harmony of different beauties").

The Red Line (Finnish, *Punainen viiva*) Aulis Sallinen, 1976–8.

The opera in two acts, set to a libretto by the composer based on Ilmari Kianto's novel of the same name (1909), tells of a poor peasant family's struggle for survival in northern Finland. The "red line" of the title is two things: first a line that villagers must draw on a voting slip in order for things to change, and finally the slit throat of one of the main characters.

The Red Pony Aaron Copland, 1948.

The orchestral children's suite consists of six movements taken from the composer's music for the film (1949) based on John Steinbeck's story of the same name (1945), recounting episodes in the life of a boy on a Californian ranch.

The Red Poppy (Russian, *Krasnyy mak*) Reinhold Glière, 1926–7.

The ballet in three acts (eight scenes), with a libretto by M. Kurilko and choreography by Lev Lashchilin and Vassili Tikhomirov, is set in a port in Kuomingtang China in the 1920s and tells how the dancer, Tao-Hoa, is exploited by the capitalist, Li Shan-fu, and gives her life to save that of the leader of the revolutionary crowd of coolies. From 1957 the title was changed in the USSR to *The Red Flower* (Russian, *Krasnyy tsvetok*) to avoid associations with opium.

The Red Whirlwind (Russian, *Krasnyy vikhr'*) V. Deshevov, 1924.

The ballet in an epilogue, two "processes," and an epilogue, with a libretto and choreography by Fyodor Lopokov, was subtitled *The Bolsheviks* (Russian, *Bol'sheviki*) and intended as an allegory of the events of the Russian Revolution (1917). It was attacked as a prime example of the Proletkult (proletarian culture) and was performed only twice.

Reformation Symphony Felix Mendelssohn, 1830.

The Symphony No. 5 in D minor, Op. 107, was written for the tercentennial of the Augsburg Confession (1530), the Lutheran confession of faith presented to the Emperor Charles V as one of the key events in the Reformation. The symphony quotes the "Dresden Amen" and the Lutheran chorale *Ein' feste Burg* ("A Safe Stronghold").

Refrain Karlheinz Stockhausen, 1959.

The work for piano, celesta, and percussion has a score that prints its "refrain" on a transparent strip in such a way that it interferes with the music at different points in different performances. Hence the title, alluding to this distinctive feature.

Regina Marc Blitzstein, 1949.

The opera in three acts, to the composer's own libretto, is based on Lilian Hellman's play *The Little Foxes* (1939), telling of the machinations of the domineering Regina Giddens as she attempts to control the family business in a small town in the southern USA.

"Regnava nel silenzio" ("Silence was reigning").

Lucia's aria in Act 1 of Donizetti's **Lucia di Lammermoor**, in which she recounts to Alisa the legend of the fountain. The words make more sense if continued: "*Regnava nel silenzio / Alta la notte bruna*" ("The deep, dark night reigned in the silence").

Regrets *see* **Lieder ohne Worte**.

La Reine *see* The **Queen Symphony**.

La Reine de Saba ("The Queen of Sheba") Charles Gounod, 1862.

The opera in four acts is set to a libretto by Jules Barbier and Michel Carré based on Gérard de Nerval's poem *Les Nuits de Ramazan* ("The Nights of Ramazan") in his *Le Voyage en Orient* ("Journey to the Orient") (1851), in turn based on the old Arab legend telling of the love of King Soliman's master architect, Adoniram, for Balkis, Queen of Sheba. *Cf.* Die **Königin von Saba**.

Relâche Erik Satie, 1924.

The ballet in two acts, with a cinematographic entr'acte by René Clair, has a libretto by Francis Picabia and choreography by Jean Börlin. The title is the French theatrical term meaning "no show," "theater closed," and the ballet itself a Dadaist fantasy. Picabia described it as "life as I like it; life without a morrow, the life of today, everything for to-day, nothing for yesterday, nothing for to-morrow. Motor headlights, pearl necklaces, the rounded and slender forms of women, publicity, music, motor-cars, men in evening dress, movement, noise, play, clear and transparent water, the pleasure of laughter, that is Relâche" (quoted in Koegler, p. 344).

Reliquie ("Relic")   Franz Schubert, 1825.
The Piano Sonata No. 13 in C, D 840, is sometimes so called because only the first two movements were completed.

Le Renard ("The Fox"; Russian, *Bayka*, "A Story")   Igor Stravinsky, 1922.
The burlesque in song and dance, with a libretto by the composer and choreography by Bronislava Nijinska, is based on Charles-Ferdinand Ramuz's French translation of Alexander Afanasyev's Russian folk tales (1855–64). The story tells how the fox persuades the cock down from his perch by preaching to him, but the cat and the goat rescue him. The full original Russian title is *Bayka pro lisu, petukha, kotu du barana* ("The Story of the Fox, the Cock, the Cat, and the Goat").

La Rencontre ("The Encounter")   Henri Sauguet, 1948.
The ballet in one act, with a libretto by Boris Kochno and choreography by David Lichine, sets Oedipus's encounter with the Sphinx in a circus, with the Sphinx on a high platform. The subtitle is thus *Édipe et le Sphinx* ("Oedipus and the Sphinx").

Rendering   Luciano Berio, 1989.
The orchestral work is a "rendering" or realization in the style of Schubert of Schubert's late sketches for a tenth symphony, a process that the composer compared to restoring an old fresco to revive the colors but without disguising the damage that time has caused.

Le Rendezvous ("The Meeting")   J. Kosma, 1945.
The ballet by Roland Petit, with a libretto by Marcel Prévost, is an atmospheric drama set in the streets of Paris.

Les Rendezvous ("The Meetings")   Daniel Auber, 1933.
The ballet in one act, choreographed by Frederick Ashton, is set to music from the composer's opera *L'Enfant prodigue* ("The Prodigal Son") (1850) and is a suite of dances for young people in a park.

Répons ("Responses")   Pierre Boulez, 1981.
The work for chamber ensemble, soloists, and electro-acoustic devices aims to create "responses" from one soloist to another by various techniques, transforming the sounds they produce in the process.

Requiem   (1) Giuseppe Verdi, 1873–4; (2) Gabriel Fauré, 1887–8.
A *Requiem* is a setting of the Roman Catholic **Mass** for the Dead, which follows the text of the normal Mass but omits the **Gloria** and **Credo** and adds the **Dies Irae**. (The word itself is the first word of the text.) Verdi's *Requiem* is a setting of this Mass for concert performance arranged in nine sections: (1) *Requiem aeternam* ("Rest eternal") and *Kyrie eleison* ("Lord have mercy"), (2) *Dies Irae* ("Day of Wrath"), divided into *Tuba mirum* ("Hark, the trumpet"), *Liber scriptus* ("A book is written"), *Quid sum miser* ("How wretched am I"), *Rex tremendae* ("King of glory"), *Recordare* ("Remember"), *In gemisco* ("Sadly groaning"), *Confutatis* ("From the accursed"), and *Lacrimosa* ("Lamentation"), (3) *Domine Jesu Christe* ("Lord Jesus Christ"), (4) *Sanctus* ("Holy"), (5) *Agnus Dei* ("Lamb of God"), (6) *Lux eterna* ("Light eternal"), and (9) *Libera me* ("Deliver me"). This is a typical disposition, with a Latin text, although many variations are possible. The requiem itself was composed for the anniversary of the death of the Italian poet and novelist Alessandro Manzoni (1785–1873). Hence its alternate title of *Manzoni Requiem*. Fauré's *Requiem* for soprano, baritone, chorus, orchestra and organ is in seven movements: (1) *Introit and Kyrie*, (2) *Offertory*, (3) *Sanctus*, (4) *Pie Jesu* ("Piously, Jesus") (5) *Agnus Dei*, (6) *Libera me*, and (7) *In Paradisum* ("In paradise"). The 1977 ballet in one act of the same name, choreographed by Kenneth MacMillan, was set to Fauré's music and dedicated to the memory of the dancer, choreographer, and ballet director, John Cranko (1927–1973).

Requiem Canticles, Igor Stravinsky, 1972.
The ballet in six movements, choreographed by Jerome Robbins, is an abstract setting of the composer's choral work of the same title for alto, bass, chorus, and orchestra (1966). The canticles are the religious text to which the work is set.

Requiem for Those We Love *see* **When Lilacs Last in the Dooryard Bloom'd**.

Requiem Symphony   (1) (Russian, *Rekviyem pamyati V.I. Lenina*, "Requiem In Memory of V.I. Lenin") Dmitri Kabalevsky, 1933; (2) Howard Hanson, 1943.

Kabalevsky's Symphony No. 3 in B flat minor for Chorus and Orchestra was written in memory of Lenin (1870–1924), as the full Russian title indicates. Hanson's Symphony No. 4 was written in memory of his father, with the four movements named for the main parts of the **Requiem**: (1) *Kyrie*, (2) *Requiescat*, (3) *Dies Irae*, (4) *Lux Aeterna*.

Restlessness *see* **Lieder ohne Worte**.

Resurrection   Peter Maxwell Davies, 1987.

The opera, a satire on authoritarian figures and consumer society, is set to the composer's own libretto and centers on a (non-singing) dummy whose head explodes, following which he is "morally dissected" and operated on by surgeons who "resurrect" him as what appears to be a hero but is actually an Antichrist.

Resurrection Symphony   Gustav Mahler, 1888–94.

The Symphony No. 2 in C minor is so called because the finale is a setting for soprano and alto soloists, chorus, and orchestra of Friedrich Gottlieb Klopstock's *Resurrection Ode* (1771), beginning "*Aufersteh'n, ja aufersteh'n wirst du, / Mein Staub, nach kurzer Ruh!*" ("Rise again, yea, rise again shalt thou, / My dust, after brief rest!").

El Retablo de Maese Pedro ("Master Peter's Puppet Show")   Manuel de Falla, 1923.

The opera in one act for singers, puppets, and chamber orchestra is set to the composer's own libretto based on an incident in Miguel Cervantes's novel *Don Quixote* (1605–15). A boy narrator introduces the show by Peter's puppets to an audience that includes Don Quixote and Sancho Panza. The story they act tells how the fair Melisendra is rescued from the Moors by Don Gayferos. The piece was originally intended for performance with puppets taking all the parts, "puppet-size" for Peter's show and double the size for the human beings.

Retrospection *see* **Lieder ohne Worte**.

The Return *see* **Lieder ohne Worte**.

The Return of Don Juan   Kim Helweg, 1998.

The ballet, choreographed by Kim Brandstrup, partly bases its story on the Swedish film *The Devil's Eye* (1960), but like the movie ultimately goes back to a Danish radio play by Oluf Bang, *The Return of Don Juan*. This tells how

Don Juan is condemned to Hell not because he has seduced so many women, but "because he felt so little while doing so." His punishment is to undergo a series of sexually unfulfilled liaisons with beautiful women.

The Return to Paris   Jan Ladislav Dušek, 1807.

The Piano Sonata No. 13 in A flat, Op. 70, was written following the collapse of the composer's publishing firm in London and his return to Paris.

Le Rêve ("The Dream")   Alfred Bruneau, 1890.

The opera is set to a libretto by Louis Gallet, based on Émile Zola's novel of the same title (1888), telling how a foundling is brought up by a childless couple and dreams of saints and legends and of a rich lover who will come to her from the past. She weaves her dreams into the embroideries that her guardians teach her to make.

Le Réveil des oiseaux ("The Awakening of the Birds")   Olivier Messiaen, 1953.

The work for piano and orchestra incorporates notations of birdsong and was followed by similar works in **Oiseaux exotiques** and **Catalogue d'oiseaux**.

Revelation and Fall, Peter Maxwell Davies, 1965.

The work for soprano and 16 instruments is set to a text from Georg Trakl's collection of lyric poems *Offenbarung und Untergang* ("Revelation and Fall") (1912–14).

Revelations   various (see below), 1960.

The ballet in three sections, choreographed by Alvin Ailey, is set to music from traditional Negro folklore, and explores the many different forms of American Negro religious music. The titles of the three sections are *Pilgrims of Sorrow*, *Take Me to the Water*, and *Move, Members, Move*.

The Revenge   Charles Villiers Stanford, 1886.

The choral ballad, Op. 24, is a setting of Lord Alfred Tennyson's poem of the same name (1880) about Sir Richard Grenville's fight with the Spanish fleet at Flores in the Azores (1591), the *Revenge* being the name of his ship.

Reverie *see* **Lieder ohne Worte**.

Der Revisor ("The Inspector")   Werner Egk, 1957.

The opera in five acts is set to the composer's own libretto based on Nikolai Gogol's play *The Government Inspector* (also known in English as *The Inspector General*) (1836). This tells how the destitute civil servant, Khlestakov, is mistaken for the Government Inspector and lavishly entertained by the Mayor, his wife, and daughter.

Revolutionary Study   Fryderyk Chopin, 1831.

The Étude in C minor for piano, Op. 10, No. 12, is so called because it allegedly expresses the composer's fury on hearing that Warsaw had been captured by the Russians.

Rhapsody   Sergey Rachmaninov,1980.

The plotless ballet in one act, choreographed by Frederick Ashton, is set to the composer's **Rhapsody on a Theme of Paganini** and is simply a display of virtuoso dancing. In general terms, a rhapsody is a composition in one movement usually based on popular, national, or folk melodies. The term is frequently qualified in a title, as Liszt's **Hungarian Rhapsodies**, Stanford's **Irish Rhapsodies**, Ravel's **Rapsodie espagnole**, and Vaughan Williams's **Norfolk Rhapsody**. *Cf.* **Brigg Fair**. The word originally applied in ancient Greek to the recitation of parts of an epic poem. Hence its literal meaning of "stitched song."

Rhapsody in Blue   George Gershwin, 1924.

The work for piano and orchestra presents jazz music in a blues-type idiom within the structure of a classical symphony.

Rhapsody on a Theme of Paganini (Russian, *Rapsodiya na temu Paganini*)   Sergey Rachmaninov, 1934.

The work, Op. 43, for piano and orchestra contains 24 variations on Paganini's Caprice No. 24 in A minor for violin.

Das Rheingold   *see* Der **Ring des Nibelungen**.

Rhenish Symphony   Robert Schumann, 1850.

The Symphony No. 3 in E flat major, Op.97, was written following the composer's move to Düsseldorf, on the Rhine, and is so named because it expresses "all his feelings about about the Rhine, its scenery, its atmosphere, its legends, and the pageant of German history that had been played out on the river's banks and reflected in its waters" (Brian Schlotel in *Robert*

Schumann: The Man and His Music, ed. Alan Walker, 1972). The fourth of its five movements, the so called "cathedral" movement, was inspired by the installation of Archbishop von Geissel as cardinal at Cologne, also on the Rhine.

Rhodanienne Symphony (French, *Symphonie rhodanienne*)   Darius Milhaud, 1957.

The Symphony No. 8 in D major, Op. 362, is so named because it describes the course of the Rhône River from source to sea, French *rhodanienne* being the (feminine) adjectival form of its name. The first movement, subtitled *Avec mystère et violence* ("With mystery and violence"), describes the birth of the river in the Rhône Glacier in Switzerland. The second movement, subtitled *Avec sérénité et nonchalance* ("With serenity and nonchalance"), shows it crossing Lake Geneva. In the third movement, subtitled *Avec emportement* ("With feeling"), it flows to southern France. The last movement, subtitled *Rapide et majestueux* ("Rapid and majestic"), depicts it debouching into the Mediterranean.

Rice Aria   *see* "**Di tanti palpiti.**"

Ricercare   Mordecai Seter, 1966.

The ballet in one act, choreographed by Glen Tetley, is a duo ballet about a woman and a man after an emotional and sexual relationship. A ricercare (Italian for "to seek out," related to *recherché* and *research*) is technically an elaborate contrapuntal composition, but here the word is perhaps meant generally, for a dance in which the couple "seek out" the way ahead.

Richard Cœur-de-Lion ("Richard Lionheart")   André Grétry, 1784.

The comic opera in three acts is set to a libretto by Jean-Marie Sedaine based on a 13th-century fable telling how Blondel, the minstrel of Richard I of England (nicknamed Richard Lionheart for his bravery), disguises himself as a blind troubadour to search for his imprisoned master.

Ride of the Valkyries   Richard Wagner, 1876.

The name generally given to the choral scene that opens Act 3 of *Die Walküre* in Der **Ring des Nibelungen**, in which the Valkyries gather on a rocky peak.

Riders to the Sea   Ralph Vaughan Williams, 1925–32.

The opera in one act is set to a virtual verbatim version of John Millington Synge's play of the same title (1904), telling how the lives of Maurya's husband and all of her sons are lost to the sea off the west coast of Ireland, the last son as he is taking horses to a fair.

Rienzi   Richard Wagner, 1838–40.

The opera in five acts is set to the composer's own libretto based on Edward Bulwer Lytton's novel (1835) and Mary Russell Mitford's play (1828) of the same name. The full title is *Cola Rienzi: der Letzte der Tribunen* ("Cola Rienzi: the Last of the Tribunes"). The plot centers on the struggle in 14th-century Rome between the Orsinis and the Colonnas and tells what happens when Paolo Orsini attempts to abduct Irene, sister of the papal legate, Cola Rienzi.

Rigoletto   Giuseppe Verdi, 1850–1.

The opera in three acts is set to a libretto by Francesco Maria Pieve based on Victor Hugo's drama *Le Roi s'amuse* ("The King is Entertained") (1832). The story is set in 16th-century Mantua and centers on Rigoletto, the court jester, and the young woman, Gilda, who is believed by the courtiers to be his mistress but who is really his daughter. The opera's original title was *La maledizione* ("The Curse").

Rinaldo   George Frideric Handel, 1711.

The opera in three acts is set to a libretto by Giacomo Rossi based on Torquato Tasso's epic poem *La Gerusalemme liberata* ("Jerusalem Delivered") (1574). This centers on the capture of Jerusalem in 1099 by Godfrey of Bouillon but at the same time tells of the love between the crusader knight, Rinaldo, and the magician and seductress, Armida. *See also* **Armide**, Le **Pavillon d'Armide**, **Rinaldo and Armida**.

Rinaldo and Armida   Malcolm Arnold, 1955.

The ballet in one act, choreographed by Frederick Ashton, is one of the many accounts of the encounter between the warrior, Rinaldo, and the enchantress, Armida, from Torquato Tasso's epic poem *La Gerusalemme liberata* ("Jerusalem Delivered") (1574).

Der Ring des Nibelungen ("The Ring of the Nibelung")   Richard Wagner, 1876.

The operatic tetralogy, a "stage festival play for three days and a preliminary evening," is set to the composer's own libretto based on the *Nibelungenlied* ("Nibelung Song"), an allegory telling of the struggle for power between the Nibelung dwarfs, the Giants, and the Gods. The

tetralogy comprises four operas: (1) *Das Rheingold* ("The Rhine Gold"), (2) *Die Walküre* ("The Valkyrie"), (3) *Siegfried* ("Siegfried"), (4) *Götterdämmerung* ("Twilight of the Gods"). The "ring" of the title does not refer to the cycle but to the ring that the Nibelung dwarf, Alberich, must forge from the Rhine Gold to become master of the world. The Valkyries are the warrior daughters who bear the bodies of dead heroes to Valhalla. Siegfried is the hero who finds the treasure of the Nibelung. The saga ends with the destruction of Valhalla and the old order of the kingdom of the gods and the dawning of a new age of love. The overall English title is sometimes given in plural form as *The Ring of the Nibelungs*, and its colloquial short form is invariably *The Ring*.

The Ring of the Nibelung *see* Der **Ring des Nibelungen**.

Ringed by the Flat Horizon   George Benjamin, 1979–80.

The abstract tone poem takes its title from a line in T.S. Eliot's *The Waste Land* (1922): "Ringed by the flat horizon only." The work evokes a similar brooding landscape.

The Rio Grande   Constant Lambert, 1927.

The work for solo piano, chorus, and orchestra is a setting of Sacheverell Sitwell's exotic poem of the same name about sailors and their South America girls. The 1931 ballet in one act of the same name, choreographed by Frederick Ashton, is set to this work and based on the same poem, but originally had the title *A Day in a Southern Port*.

Rip van Winkle   George Frederick Bristow, 1855.

The "grand romantic opera" in three acts is set to a libretto by Johnathan Howard Wainwright based on Washington Irving's story of the same name (1819), telling of the henpecked husband, Rip van Winkle, who escapes from his wife by wandering off with his dog to the Catskill Mountains, just before the US War of Independence (American Revolution).

The Rising of the Moon   Nicholas Maw, 1967–70.

The comic opera in three acts is set to a libretto by Beverley Cross involving a romance, as the title suggests.

Risurrezione ("Resurrection")   Franco Alfano, 1904.

The opera in four acts is set to a libretto by

Cesare Hanau based on Leo Tolstoy's novel *Resurrection* (1900). The scene is set in Russian at the turn of the 20th century and the story tells what happens when Prince Dimitri seduces and then abandons his childhood friend, Katusha.

Rita   Gaetano Donizetti, 1860.

The comic opera in one act, subtitled *Le Mari battu* ("The Beaten Husband"), is set to a libretto by Gustave Vaëz and tells the story of Rita, a Swiss inn proprietress, and her henpecked husband, Gasparo.

The Rite of Spring (Russian, *Vesna svyashchennaya*, "Spring the Sacred"; French, *Le Sacre du printemps*, "The Sacring of Spring")   Igor Stravinsky, 1911–13.

The ballet, subtitled *Scenes of Pagan Russia*, is set to a libretto by Nikolay Roerich with choreography by Vaslav Nijinsky and centers on a young girl who dances herself to death in a sacrificial pagan rite. The French title is almost as common as the English. "There is no reason why in English-speaking countries a French title should be used for a work by a Russian composer and produced by the Russian Ballet. It was so called merely because it happened to be brought out in Paris" (Blom, p. 509).

"Ritorna vincitor" ("Return victorious").

Aida's aria in Act 1 of Verdi's **Aida**, expressing her longing for Radamès to return victorious from a war against her own father and country.

Il Ritorno d'Ulisse in patria ("The Return of Ulysses to his Homeland")   Claudio Monteverdi, 1640.

The opera in a prologue and five acts is set to a libretto by Giacomo Badoara based on the closing books of Homer's *Odyssey*, telling of the dangers encountered by Odysseus (Ulysses) in the ten years that it took him to make his journey home after the Trojan War.

Ritterballet ("Knightly Ballet")   Ludwig van Beethoven, 1791.

The ballet was conceived by Count Ferdinand von Waldstein (*see* **Waldstein Sonata**) and was clearly intended as a portrait of aristocrats taking part in a ball. It may have been accompanied by a text (libretto), but none survives. The eight parts are: (1) *March*, (2) *German Song*, (3) *Hunting Song*, (4) *Love Song*, (5) *War Dance*, (6) *Drinking Song*, (7) *German Dance*, and (8) *Coda*. The music itself, originally attributed to Waldstein, is usually known as *Musik zu einem Ritterballet* ("Music for a Knightly Ballet").

Ritual Dances   Michael Tippett, 1953.

The orchestral work comprises four dances from the opera The **Midsummer Marriage**, the first three from Act 2, the fourth from Act 3. Their individual titles and subtitles are: (1) *The Earth in Autumn* ("The Hound Chases the Hare"), (2) *The Waters in Winter* ("The Otter Pursues the Fish"), (3) *The Air in Spring* ("The Hawk Swoops on the Bird"), and (4) *Fire in Summer* (a celebration of carnal love).

Ritual Fire Dance   Manuel de Falla, 1915.

The title, in full *Ritual Fire Dance to Drive Off Evil Spirits*, is that of the 8th of the 13 connected sections in the ballet El **Amor brujo**, which features the danced exorcism (rite of purification) of the gypsy girl Candélas.

Rituals   Béla Bartók, 1975.

The ballet in three movements, choreographed by Kenneth MacMillan, was inspired by Japanese rituals and set to the composer's Sonata for Two Pianos and Percussion (1940). The three movements have titles as follows: (1) *Preparation for Combat and Self Defense*, (2) *Puppets* (in a wedding ceremony), and (3) *Celebration and Prayer* (after giving birth).

Rituel in memoriam Bruno Maderna   Pierre Boulez, 1974–5.

The orchestral work is Boulez's memorial to his friend and colleague, the Italian avant-garde composer and conductor Bruno Maderna (1920–1973).

A Rivulet *see* **Lieder ohne Worte**.

The Road of the Phoebe Snow   Duke Ellington and Billy Strayhorn, 1959.

The ballet in one act, choreographed by Talley Beatty, has a story as follows: "The Phoebe Snow is a train of the Lackawanna Railroad Line which still passes through the mid-western section of the United States. Legend has it that its name came from a meticulous lady named Phoebe Snow who traveled this line dressed in white satin and lace and looked out on the surrounding countryside with high disdain…. This ballet deals, first abstractly, then dramatically, with some incidents that may have happened on or near these railroad tracks" (program note, quoted in Koegler, p. 348).

Roaratorio   John Cage, 1979.

The work is an electronic composition incorporating thousands of words found in James Joyce's novel *Finnegans Wake* (1939). The punning title is worthy of James himself.

Robert le Diable ("Robert the Devil")
Giacomo Meyerbeer, 1831.

The opera in five acts, to a libretto by Eugène Scribe and Germain Delavigne, is set in 13th-century Sicily and tells the story of Robert, Duke of Normandy, the son of a mortal and the Devil, the latter masquerading as Bertram. The legendary duke has been identified with Robert the Magnificent, father of William the Conqueror, who was Duke of Normandy from 1027 to 1035.

Roberto Devereux ("Robert Devereux")
Gaetano Donizetti, 1837.

The opera in three acts, subtitled *Il Conte di Essex* ("The Earl of Essex"), is set to a libretto by Salvatore Cammarano based on François Ancelot's tragedy *Élisabeth d'Angleterre* ("Elizabeth of England") (1829). The plot is an embellished version of the love of Queen Elizabeth I (1533–1603) and her favorite, Robert Devereux, 2d Earl of Essex (1567–1601).

Robin Hood   George Macfarren, 1860.

The opera in three acts, to a libretto by John Oxenford, tells the story of the legendary outlaw of Sherwood Forest who "robbed from the rich to give to the poor."

Robinson Crusoé ("Robinson Crusoe")
Jacques Offenbach, 1867.

The opera is set to a libretto by Eugène Cormon and Hector Crémieux only remotely based on Daniel Defoe's novel of the same name (1719), in which Robinson Crusoe is an Englishman shipwrecked on a desert island.

Rodelinda   George Frideric Handel, 1725.

The opera in three acts, subtitled *Regina de' Longobardi* ("Queen of the Lombards"), is set to a libretto by Antonio Salvi and Francesco Haym based on Pierre Corneille's play *Pertharite, roi des Lombards* ("Pertharite, King of the Lombards") (1651). The plot is set in Milan and tells what happens when Bertarido (Pertharite), king of Lombardy, returns home to find that Grimoaldo has usurped his throne and is trying to force his wife, Rodelinda, to marry him.

Rodeo   Aaron Copland, 1942.

The ballet in one act, with a libretto and choreography by Agnes de Mille, is set in the Wild West and based on traditional songs. It is subtitled *The Courting at Burnt Ranch* and tells what happens when the cowboys on a Texas ranch chase all the women in sight but are unaware of the charms of a cowgirl working there.

The composer extracted four dance episodes from this work and used them for a suite of the same name (1943) with individual movements titled *Coralle Nocturne, Buckaroo Holiday, Saturday Night Waltz,* and *Hoedown.*

Rogneda   Alexander Serov, 1865.

The opera in five acts, to a libretto by Dmitri Averkiyev, is based on an episode in the history of Kievan Russia in *c.* 980 in which Prince Vladimir of Kiev captures Polotsk, abducts Rogneda, daughter of Prince Rogvolod, murders her father and two brothers, and forcibly makes her his wife.

Le Roi Arthus ("King Arthur")   Ernest Chausson, 1885–95.

The opera in three acts, Op. 23, is set to the composer's own libretto based on various episodes in the Arthurian cycle.

Le Roi Candaule ("King Candaule")   Cesare Pugni, 1868.

The ballet in four acts, with a libretto by Jules-Henri Versoy de Saint-Georges and Marius Petipa and choreography by the latter, tells how King Candaule of Lydia and his wife, Nisia, both fall victims to their own pride.

Le Roi David ("King David")   Arthur Honegger, 1921.

The *"psaume dramatique"* ("dramatic psalm") in five parts (28 numbers) for narrator, soprano, mezzosoprano, tenor, chorus, and orchestra is set to a text by René Morax based on the Old Testament story of David, king of Israel, as told in Samuel 1 and 2.

Le Roi de Lahore ("The King of Lahore")
Jules Massenet, 1875–6.

The opera in five acts is set to a libretto by Louis Gallet based on the Comte de Beauvoir's *Voyage autour du monde* ("Journey Around the World"), itself based on the Hindu epic, the *Mahabharata.* The story is set in 11th-century India and tells what happens when Alim, king of Lahore, and his minister, Scindia, both love the priestess, Sita.

Le Roi d'Ys ("The King of Ys")   Édouard Lalo, 1875–87.

The opera in three acts is set to a libretto by Édouard Blau based on a Breton legend. The story tells what happens when the king of Ys, in order to be reconciled to Karnac, offers him the hand of his daughter, Margared, who herself loves Mylio (who in turn loves the king's other daughter, Rozenn). The legendary city of Ys is said to be submerged beneath the sea off the Breton coast. *Cf.* La **Cathédrale englouti**.

Le Roi l'a dit ("The King Said So")   Léo Delibes, 1873.

The comic opera in three acts is set to a libretto by Edmond Gondinet telling what happens when the marquis de Montecontour falsely claims that he has fathered a son and is obliged to take on a peasant lad to act the part. All that ensues is because "the king said so."

Le Roi malgré lui ("The King Despite Himself")   Emmanuel Chabrier, 1887.

The comic opera in three acts is set to a libretto by Émile de Najac and Paul Burani based on Jacques Ancelot's 19th-century play of the same name. The story is set in France in 1574 and tells what happens when Henri de Valois, about to be crowned king of France, learns that there is a plot to assassinate him and disguises himself to join the conspirators.

Le Roi nu ("The Naked King")   Jean Françaix, 1936.

The ballet in one act (four scenes), with a libretto and choreography by Serge Lifar, is a version of Hans Christian Andersen's fairy tale *The Emperor's New Clothes* (1836), telling how the emperor parades in his "new clothes" which, as a young child innocently points out, turn out to be no clothes at all.

Roma   Georges Bizet, 1860–8.

The orchestral work that took the composer much of his short life was conceived in 1860: "I have in mind a symphony which I should like to call *Rome, Venice, Florence* and *Naples*. That works out wonderfully: Venice will be my andante, Rome my first movement, Florence my scherzo and Naples my finale. It's a new idea, I think" (quoted in Winton Dean, *Bizet*, 1975). Its history is checkered. Bizet made several alterations, and it was first performed, omitting the scherzo, in 1869 under the title *Fantaisie symphonique: Souvenirs de Rome*. The three movements were now individually entitled: *Une Chasse dans la forêt d'Ostie* ("A Hunt in the Forest of Ostia"), *Une Procession* ("A Procession"), and *Carnaval à Rome* ("Carnival in Rome"). These titles may have not have been Bizet's. The symphony was first performed complete in 1880, when it was called *Roma: Symphonie en quatre parties* ("Rome: Symphony in Four Parts"). That same year it was published as *Roma: Troisième suite de concert* ("Rome: Third Concert Suite"). The individual descriptive titles were then

dropped except for the finale, which became simply *Carnaval*.

The Roman Carnival *see* Le **Carnaval romain**.

Romance.

The word can be variable in its musical application, but it often applies to a composition of a specially personal or tender quality. Schumann wrote *Drei Romanzen* ("Three Romances") for oboe and piano, Op. 94 (1849), and Vaughan Williams has a *Romance* for harmonica, strings, and orchestra (1951). Arnold Bax's *Romance* for piano (1918) is marked with the English direction "Dreamy and passionate."

Romantic Symphony   (1) Anton Bruckner, 1874; (2) Howard Hanson, 1930.

Bruckner's Symphony No. 4 in E flat major was so named by the composer. The music was at least partly inspired by the location where it was written, in the village of Mondsee in the Austrian Alps, although the composer's notes indicate that he had medieval romanticism in mind as well as the "magic of nature." Hanson explains how he came to name his Symphony No. 2: "Concerning my Second Symphony, as the subtitle implies, it represents for me definite and acknowledged embracing of the romantic phrase. I recognize, of course, that romanticism is at the present time the poor stepchild, within the social standing of her older sister, neoclassicism.... My aim, in this symphony, has been to create a work young in spirit, romantic in temperament, and simple and direct in expression" (quoted in Berkowitz, p. 134). *Cf.* **Sinfonia Romantica**.

Romeo and Juliet (Russian, *Romeo i Dzhul'yetta*)   (1) Pyotr Tchaikovsky, 1869; (2) Sergey Prokofiev, 1938.

Tchaikovsky's fantasy overture for orchestra is based on Shakespeare's tragedy of the same name (1594), in which the young man, Romeo, falls desperately in love with Juliet, the daughter of a family feuding with his own. Prokofiev's ballet in a prologue, three acts, and an epilogue, with a libretto by Leonid Lavrovsky, Sergey Radlov, and the composer and choreographed by Ivo Psota, is closely based on the same play. *See also* I **Capuleti e i Montecchi**, **Giulietta e Romeo**.

Roméo et Juliette ("Romeo and Juliet") (1) Hector Berlioz, 1839; (2) Charles Gounod, 1867.

Berlioz's dramatic symphony, Op. 17, is set

to a text by Émile Deschamps based on Shakespeare's tragedy (*see* **Romeo and Juliet**), as is Gounod's opera in five acts, set to a libretto by Jules Barbier and Michel Carré.

Romeo und Julia ("Romeo and Juliet") Heinrich Sutermeister, 1940.

The opera in two acts is set to the composer's own libretto based on Shakespeare's tragedy (*see* **Romeo and Juliet**) but concentrating almost exclusively on the two lovers.

Romerzählung ("Rome Tale") Richard Wagner, 1845.

This is the name usually given to Tannhäuser's long narration of his pilgrimage to Rome in Act 3 of **Tannhäuser**.

La Rondine ("The Swallow") Giacomo Puccini, 1917.

The opera in three acts is set to a libretto by Giuseppe Adami translated from a German libretto by Alfred Maria Willner and Heinrich Reichert. The plot is set in Paris and Nice in the mid–19th century and tells what happens when the poet-philosopher, Prunier, reads the palm of Magda de Civry, mistress of the banker, Rambaldo, and predicts that, like the swallow, she will fly away from Paris, perhaps to find true love.

Rondo alla turca ("Rondo in the Turkish style") W.A. Mozart, 1778.

The composer gave this title to the third movement of his Piano Sonata No. 11 in A major, K 331. It evokes the music of a Turkish military band, with its typical cymbals, triangle, and bass drum. *Cf.* **Turkish Concerto**. A *rondo* ("round") is a type of composition in which the principal tune occurs at least three times in the same key, and by Mozart's time it had become the usual form for the last movement of a concerto or sonata.

Rooms K. Hopkins, 1955.

The ballet in one act, choreographed by Anna Sokolow, deals with loneliness in a big city. Its nine sections have the following titles: (1) *Alone*, (2) *Dream*, (3) *Escape*, (4) *Going*, (5) *Desire*, (6) *Panic*, (7) *Daydream*, (8) *The End?*, (9) *Alone*.

The Ropes of Time Jan Boerman, 1970.

The ballet in one act, choreographed by Rudi van Dantzig, sees life as the passage of time guided by ropes but of uncertain destination or destiny: "Every journey we make is an adventure into the unknown; each arrival a birth and each

departure a death" (Richard Buckle, program note, quoted in Koegler, p. 352).

Rosamunde ("Rosamund") Franz Schubert, 1823.

The original work of this name, D 797, comprised an overture, three entr'actes, two ballet pieces, and some vocal numbers written for Helmina von Chézy's play *Rosamunde, Fürstin von Cypern* ("Rosamund, Princess of Cyprus") (1823). However, the overture played at the first performance of this was the one already composed for **Alfonso und Estrelle** and published under that title as Op. 69, D 732. What is now generally known as the *Rosamunde* overture, D 644, was written in 1820 for Die **Zauberharfe**.

Rosc Catha Arnold Bax, 1910.

The orchestral tone poem has an Irish title meaning "battle hymn," otherwise an exhortative speech before battle.

Rose Latulipe H. Freeman, 1966.

The ballet in three acts, with a libretto by W. Solly and Brian Macdonald and choreography by the latter, is based on an old French-Canadian legend published in 1837 with a story similar to that of **Giselle**, but with Rose Latulippe in place of Giselle.

La Rose malade ("The Sick Rose") Gustav Mahler, 1973.

The ballet in three parts, choreographed by Roland Petit, is a duo for two lovers based on William Blake's mystical work *The Marriage of Heaven and Hell* (1791) and set to the Adagietto from the composer's Symphony No. 5 in C sharp minor (1901–2). The English form of the title is the same as the poem of this name (beginning "O Rose, thou art sick!") in Blake's *Songs of Experience* (1794).

The Rose of Castille Michael Balfe, 1857.

The opera in three acts is set to a libretto by Augustus Harris and Edmund Falconer based on Adolphe Adam's opera *Le Muletier de Tolède* ("The Muleteer of Toledo") (1854), itself set to a libretto by Louis François Clairville and Adolphe Philippe d'Ennery. The plot centers on a romantic attachment between the two characters named in the respective titles. Toledo is a city in the historic Spanish kingdom of Castille.

Rosen aus dem Süden ("Roses from the South") Johann Strauss II, 1880.

The waltz, Op. 388, is from the score of the three-act operetta *Das Spitzentuch der Königin* ("The Queen's Lace Handkerchief") (1880), set in Lisbon in 1580 and centering on the Spanish poet Miguel de Cervantes.

Der Rosenkavalier ("The Knight of the Rose")   Richard Strauss, 1911.

The opera in three acts, to a libretto by Hugo von Hofmannsthal, is set in Vienna in the 1740s and tells the story of the love between the Princess von Werdenberg (known in the opera as the Marschallin), her young suitor, Count Octavian, and his beloved Sophie, betrothed to the Marschallin's cousin, Baron Ochs. The Baron asks for a young knight to take the traditional Silver Rose to his bride, and Octavian is selected as the "Knight of the Rose" of the title.

Roses from the South *see* **Rosen aus dem Süden.**

Le Rossignol *see* The **Nightingale.**

The Rothko Chapel   Morton Feldman, 1971–2.

The composer attended the opening of the Rothko Chapel in Houston, Texas, in 1971 and was asked to write a piece of music both for the building and as a tribute to the painter Mark Rothko (1903–1970), 14 of whose canvases were hung there. This choral work was the result.

Le Rouet d'Omphale ("Omphale's Spinning Wheel")   Camille Saint-Saëns, 1871–2.

The symphonic poem, Op. 31, is based on the story about the mythical queen, Omphale, to whom Hercules, dressed as a woman, was a slave for three years, spinning wool for her.

Rout   Arthur Bliss, 1920.

The work for soprano and chamber orchestra aims to evoke the sound of a carnival heard from a distance, "rout" here being used in its old sense of "revelry."

Roxana's Song   Karol Szymanowski, 1918–24.

The song of Roxana, King Roger's wife, in honor of the Shepherd in Act 2 of **King Roger**. The music is well known from Pawel Kochánski's transcription for violin and piano.

Roxolane Symphony   Joseph Haydn, 1780.

The Symphony No. 63 in C major is apparently so called because the second movement uses material either from the incidental music for a play in which the heroine was Roxolane, or from an old French song or melody of this name. The title also has the form *La Roxelane*. The name is that of Roxolane (Roxelane) (*c*.1505–*c*.1559), wife of the Turkish sultan Soliman (Süleyman) the Magnificent (1494–1566).

Royal Fireworks Music *see* **Fireworks Music.**

The Royal Hunt of the Sun   Iain Hamilton, 1967–9.

The opera in two acts is set to the composer's own libretto based on Peter Shaffer's play of the same title (1964). This tells of the clash of cultures during the Spanish conquest of the Inca empire in Peru that led to the execution in 1833 of the last Inca emperor, Atahualpa.

Ruddigore   Arthur Sullivan, 1886–7.

The comic opera in two acts, to a libretto by W.S. Gilbert, centers on the curse hanging over the Murgatroyd family so that their heirs are doomed either to commit a crime a day or else die in agony. The subtitle is *The Witch's Curse*. The main title was originally *Ruddygore*, but following complaints of coarseness was altered by the composer to a less offensive spelling.

Rugby   Arthur Honegger, 1928.

The *mouvement symphonique* (symphonic movement) for orchestra is a musical impression of a game of rugby football.

Die Ruinen von Athen ("The Ruins of Athens")   Ludwig van Beethoven, 1811.

The overture and incidental music, Op. 113, was written for August von Kotzebue's play of the same name staged as an epilogue at the first night of the German theater in Budapest (1812).

Ruins and Visions   Benjamin Britten, 1953.

The ballet in one act, choreographed by Doris Humphrey, is set to the composer's String Quartet in D major (1931) and takes its title from Stephen Spender's book of poems of the same name (1942). "From the shelter of a garden we move into the extravagant atmosphere of the actor's stage, on into the raucousness of the street, then into the hideousness of a war-shattered place. As the action closes, the Actor leads a Litany of Survival" (program note, quoted in Koegler, p. 358).

The Ruins of Athens *see* Die **Ruinen von Athen.**

Rule, Britannia!   Thomas Arne, 1740.

The song, to words by James Thomson and

David Mallett, was written for inclusion in the masque **Alfred**, itself written to commemorate the succession of the House of Hanover to the British throne in 1701. The song famously urges the British to "rule the waves."

The Running Set　Ralph Vaughan Williams, 1933.

The work for orchestra is based on traditional tunes associated with the folkdance named in the title, itself originating in England but still found in the Appalachian Mountains, USA.

Rusalka　(1) Alexander Dargomyzhsky, 1856; (2) Antonín Dvořák, 1900.

Both works are also known in English as *The Water Sprite*. (*Rusalka*, now a Russian word for a water sprite or mermaid, derives from *Rusalia*, the name of both a pagan spring festival and Whitsuntide, in turn either from medieval Greek *Rousalia* or medieval Latin *Rosalia*, "Trinity," originally "festival of roses.") Dargomyzhsky's opera in four acts is set to his own libretto based on Alexander Pushkin's dramatic poem of the same name (1832), telling how the Prince seduces the Miller's daughter, Natasha, who becomes the water sprite when he abandons her. *See also* Das **Donauweibchen**. Dvořák's opera in three acts, Op. 114, is set to a libretto by Jaroslav Kvapil based on Friedrich de la Motte Fouqué's fairy romance *Undine* ("Ondine") (1811) (*see* **Undine**) and also drawing on Hans Christian Andersen's fairy tale *The Little Mermaid* (1836) and Gerhart Hauptmann's *Die versunkene Glocke* ("The Sunken Bell") (1896). Here, Rusalka wishes to become human so as to win the love of the Prince, and a witch agrees to arrange this so long as the sprite remains dumb and the Prince faithful. The two stories thus overlap. *Cf.* The **Fair Melusina**.

Les Ruses d'amour ("The Wiles of Love"; Russian, *Baryshnya-sluzhanka, ili Ispytaniye Damisa*, "Lady as Maid, or the Trial of Damis")　Alexander Glazunov, 1900.

The ballet in one act, with a libretto and choreography by Marius Petipa, animates a typical Watteau *fête champêtre*, in which Isabella, a duchess's daughter, dresses as a chambermaid to test the love of her betrothed, the Marquis Damis. An alternate title is *The Trial of Damis*, from the Russian original.

Ruslan and Ludmila (Russian, *Ruslan i Lyudmila*)　Mikhail Glinka, 1837–42.

The opera in five acts is set to a libretto by Valerian Fyodorovich Shirkov, Nestor Vasilye-

vich Kukolnik, and others based on Alexander Pushkin's poem of the same name (1820). The story tells what happens when Ludmila disappears from a feast for her three suitors, the poet-prince, Ratmir, the cowardly warrior, Farlaf, and the knight, Ruslan, and her father promises her to the one who can find her.

Russian Easter Festival Overture (Russian, *Svetlyy prazdnik*, "Bright Festival")　Nikolai Rimsky-Korsakov, 1888.

The overture is based on Russian Orthodox Church melodies, with a second half described by the composer as "expressing the transition from the solemnities of Passiontide to the vociferous communal rejoicings of Easter" (quoted in Nicholas, p. 243).

Russian Quartets (German, *Die russischen Quartette*)　Joseph Haydn, 1781.

The six string quartets, Op. 33 Nos. 38–43, are so named because they are dedicated to Grand Duke (later Emperor) Paul of Russia (1754–1801). They are also known as *Gli scherzi* ("The Scherzos"), for the character of their minuets, and as *Jungfernquartette* ("Maiden Quartets"). Three of the quartets have their individual names or nicknames: No. 38 is the **Joke Quartet**, No. 39 the **Bird Quartet**, and No. 42 **How do you do?**

Russian Soldier　Sergey Prokofiev, 1942.

The ballet in four scenes, with a libretto and choreography by Michel Fokine, is set to the composer's Suite from **Lieutenant Kijé** and was dedicated by Fokine to the Russian soldiers of World War II. The plot tells how a soldier, dying on the battlefield, recalls some of the events of his home and his life.

Russian Symphony (Russian, *Russkaya simfoniya*)　Anton Rubinstein, 1880.

The Symphony No. 5 in G minor is based almost entirely on Russian melodies. Hence its name.

Rustic Wedding (German, *Ländliche Hochzeit*)　Karl Goldmark, 1876.

The symphonic poem, Op. 26 No. 1, is so named for the individual titles of its five movements, as follows: (1) *Wedding March*, (2) *Bridal Song*, (3) *Scherzo*, (4) *In the Garden*, (5) *Finale*. The title of the fourth movement suggests that the wedding depicted was more rural than rustic, however.

Rustle of Spring (German, *Frühlingsrauschen*)　Christian Sinding, 1896.

The piano piece, No. 3 of six, Op. 32, evokes (or is intended to evoke) the rustling of leaves on trees when stirred by a spring breeze.

Ruth   Lennox Berkeley, 1956.

The opera in one act is set to a libretto by Eric Crozier based on the Old Testament Book of Ruth, telling of the woman who, when her husband died, left her homeland to return to the home of her mother-in-law, Naomi, where she eked out an existence in the fields of Boaz.

Ruy Blas   Felix Mendelssohn, 1839.

The overture, Op. 95, was written for a German performance of Victor Hugo's verse drama of the same name (1838), set in 17th-century Spain. Ruy Blas is a commoner and poet who is in love with the queen, Mary of Neuburg, and who temporarily becomes prime minister.

S

Sabbath Morning Service   Darius Milhaus, 1947.

The religious work for baritone solo, chorus, and orchestra, Op. 279, was written for the Temple Emanu-El in San Francisco, where the composer conducted the first performance. The original French title was *Service sacré* ("Sacred Service"), but the work is usually known by the above title in English to indicate its Jewish origin and content.

Saber Dance   (Russian, *Tanets s sablyami*) Aram Khachaturian, 1942.

The dance in Act 4 of **Gayané**, during the celebration of Gayaneh's marriage to Kasakov.

Sacountala   Ernest Reyer, 1858.

The ballet in two acts, with a libretto by Théophile Gautier and choreography by Lucien Petipa, is based on Kalidasa's 5th-century Sanskrit drama *Abhijnanasakuntala* ("The Recognition of Sakuntala"), telling of the seduction of the nymph, Sakuntala, by King Dushyanta. The title spells her name in the French fashion.

Le Sacre du printemps   *see*   The **Rite of Spring**.

Sacred and Profane   Benjamin Britten, 1975.

The eight songs for five unaccompanied voices are settings of medieval lyrics with individual titles as follows: (1) *St. Godric's Hymn*, (2) *I Mon Waxe Wod*, (3) *Lenten Is Come*, (4) *The Long Night*, (5) *Yif Ic Of Luve Can*, (6) *Carol*, (7) *Ye That Pasen By*, and (8) *A Death*. These alternate between "sacred" and "profane."

Sadko   Nikolai Rimsky-Korsakov, 1894–6.

The opera in five acts (seven scenes) is set to a libretto by the composer, Vladimir Belsky, and others based on the Russian fairy tale about the minstrel, Sadko, whose wanderings bring him to the sea princess, Volkhova, who promises that his net will be filled with golden fish.

Saffo   ("Sappho")   Giovanni Pacini, 1840.

The opera in three acts is set to a libretto by Salvatore Cammarano based partly on Franz Grillparzer's play *Sapho* (1818) but ultimately on the life and loves of the Greek poetess, Sappho (7th century BC). *Cf.* **Sapho**.

En Saga   ("A Saga")   Jean Sibelius, 1892.

The symphonic poem, Op. 9, depicts no particular incident but has a distinctive "narrative" tone. The work is invariably billed thus in English-speaking countries, with "En" sometimes wrongly taken to mean "in." "The word 'saga' being accepted as English, there is no good reason for persisting in the use of the Swedish form of the title of this work" (Blom, p. 156).

La Sagesse   ("Wisdom")   Darius Milhaud, 1945.

The staged cantata in four scenes, Op. 141, is set to Paul Claudel's play of the same name (1935) based on the parable of Wisdom's feast.

The Sailor's Return   Arthur Oldham, 1947.

The ballet in two acts (six scenes), with a libretto and choreography by Andrée Howard, is based on David Garnett's novel of the same name (1924), telling what happens when a sailor returns to his native village with his African bride.

Sails in St. Magnus I: Fifteen Keels Laid in Norway for Jerusalem-Farers   Peter Maxwell Davies, 1997.

The orchestral work is a tribute to the Scottish poet George Mackay Brown (1921–1996), a native of Orkney, the composer's own adopted home. The second part of the title quotes one of Brown's 14 epigrammatic "captions" from his Viking tale, *Crusader*, originally displayed under 14 sail-like banners in the nave of St. Magnus's Cathedral, Kirkwall, Orkney, in 1993. The work is the first of 14 projected compositions. Hence the serial number I.

St. Anne Fugue   J.S. Bach, 1739.

The Fugue in E flat for organ, BWV 552, the last item in Book 3 of the **Klavierübung**, is so called because it begins with the same notes as the hymn tune of this name (ascribed to William Croft and usually sung to the words "O God, our help in ages past").

St. Anthony Variations *see* **Variations on a Theme by Haydn.**

Saint François d'Assise ("St. Francis of Assisi")   Olivier Messiaen, 1975–83.

The opera in three acts and eight tableaux is set to the composer's own libretto and charts the progress of grace in St. Francis's soul. The eight tableaux or "Franciscan scenes" have titles translating as follows: (1) "Francis explains the necessity to endure suffering," (2) "Francis asks God to make him capable of loving a leper," (3) "Francis kisses the leper, who is cured," (4) "The angel discusses predestination with the monks," (5) "The angel gives Francis a foretaste of heavenly bliss," (6) "Francis preaches his sermon to the birds," (7) "Francis receives the stigmata," (8) "Francis dies and enters a new life."

St. John Passion (Latin, *Passio secundum Johannem*; German, *Johannespassion*)   J.S. Bach, 1724.

The work for soloists, chorus, and orchestra, is a setting of the Passion of Christ as narrated in St. John's Gospel, with interpolations based on a poem by Barthold Hinrich Brockes. The full English title is properly *The Passion According to St.John. Cf.* **St. Matthew Passion.**

St. Ludmila   Antonín Dvořák, 1885–6.

The oratorio, Op. 71, to a libretto by the poet Jaroslav Vrchlický, is based on the life of the Slavic saint, martyr, and patron of Bohemia, St. Ludmila (*c.*860–921), and her conversion of her people to the Christian faith.

St. Matthew Passion (Latin, *Passio secundum Matthaeum*; German, *Matthäuspassion*)   J.S. Bach, 1724.

The work for soloists, chorus, and orchestra, is a setting of the Passion of Christ as narrated in St. Matthew's Gospel, with interpolations by Picander (real name Christian Friedrich Henrici). The full English title is properly *The Passion According to St.Matthew. Cf.* **St. John Passion.**

The Saint of Bleecker Street   Gian-Carlo Menotti, 1953–4.

The opera in three acts, to the composer's own libretto, is set in New York's "Little Italy" and tells what happens when the religious mystic, Annina, the "saint" of the title, receives the stigmata on her palms.

St. Patrick's Breastplate   Arnold Bax, 1923.

The work for chorus and orchestra is a setting of words from the old Irish hymn *"Luireach naoimh Padraig"* ("Breastplate of St. Patrick"), familiar in Mrs. C.F. Alexander's modern translation (1889), beginning: "I bind unto myself today / The strong Name of the Trinity." (Bax's version has a different text, beginning: "I bind to myself in Tara today.")

St. Paul   Felix Mendelssohn, 1836.

The oratorio, Op. 36, for soloists, chorus, and orchestra, is set to a text by Julius Schubring based on the Acts of the Apostles, which tell of the conversion of Paul to Christianity and his important missionary work.

St. Paul's Suite   Gustav Holst, 1912–13.

The suite for string orchestra, Op. 29 No. 2, was written for the school orchestra of St. Paul's Girls' School, London, where the composer was director of music from 1905 to his death in 1934. Hence the name.

St. Petersburg Market (Russian, *Sankt-peterburgskiy Gostinyy dvor*)   Mikhail Matinsky, 1782.

The comic opera in three acts, to the composer's own libretto, is a satire on the unscrupulous merchants and traders of the day. The original music has not survived, and the opera is now known in its revised, 1792 version, with a score by Vasily Pashkevich, under the title *As You Live, So Shall Your Repute Be* (Russian, *Kak pozhivyosh', tak i proslyvyosh'*).

St. Thomas Wake   Peter Maxwell Davies, 1969.

The foxtrot for orchestra, contrasting the melody of a 17th-century **Pavane** by John Bull with a 20th-century danceband foxtrot, arose from the composer's memories of an air raid on Manchester in 1940 in which the cathedral, formerly St. Thomas's Parish Church, was damaged. A wake is both a vigil commemorating the dedication of a church and a celebration on such an occasion.

St. Vardan   Alan Hovhaness, 1950.

The Symphony No. 9, Op. 80, was written to commemorate the 1500th anniversary of the death in battle in 451 AD of the Armenian warrior St. Vardan Mamikonian.

Saints in Glory   J.S. Bach, 1744.

This nickname for the Prelude and Fugue No. 9 in E major in Book II of Das **Wohltemperierte Klavier** was bestowed on it by the English organist and composer, Samuel Wesley, for its "dignity and triumphant feeling" (Scholes, p. 677).

Les Saisons *see* The **Seasons** (2).

Sakuntala   Felix Weingartner, 1884.

The opera is set to the composer's own libretto based on Kalidasa's Sanskrit play of the same name (5th century AD) telling the story of Sakuntala, in Hindu mythology the daughter of Vismatritra and Menaka.

Salade ("Salad")   Darius Milhaud, 1924.

The *ballet chanté* ("sung ballet"), Op. 83, with a text by Albert Flamand and choreography by Léonide Massine, portrays the most familiar characters from the Italian *commedia dell'arte* in their usual complicated plots. The title comes from a 16th-century Spanish collection, *Libro de Cifra* ("Book of Cipher"), by the lutenist Luys Venegas de Henestrosa, that contained *ensaladas*, literally "salads," or mixtures of popular tunes.

Salammbô   Ernest Reyer, 1890.

The opera in five acts is set to a libretto by Camille du Locle based on Gustabe Flaubert's novel of the same name (1862), telling of the Carthaginian princess so named, the daughter of Hamilcar, who sacrifices her virginity to protect the sacred relics, then realizes she loves her violator, Mâtho, leader of the besiegers of Carthage.

Salavat Yulayev   Zagir Ismailov, 1955.

The opera in four acts, to a libretto by Bayazit Bikbay, centers on the Bashkir national hero and poet, Salavat Yulayev (1752–1800), an ally of the Cossack leader, Yemelyan Pugachov.

"Salce, salce" *see* **Willow Song**.

Salome   (1) Richard Strauss, 1903–5; (2) Peter Maxwell Davies, 1978.

Strauss's opera in one act is based on Hedwig Lachmann's German translation of Oscar Wilde's tragedy of the same name (1893), telling of the daughter of Herodias who so pleased King Herod that he offered her anything she desired. Her wish was for the head of St. John the Baptist (Mark 6:21–28). Davies's ballet in two acts, with a libretto and choreography by Flemming

Flindt, takes its plot direct from the biblical account. *See also* **Dance of the Seven Veils**.

Salomon Symphonies *see* **London Symphonies**.

El Salón México ("The Mexico Saloon")   Aaron Copland, 1936.

The orchestral work is based on popular Mexican themes. Its music was used for the 1943 ballet in one act of the same name, choreographed by Doris Humphrey, as a sequence of short sketches about a Mexican peasant who dreams of his encounters with various women.

Les Saltimbanques ("The Acrobats")   Louis Ganne, 1899.

The comic opera in three acts (four scenes), to a libretto by Maurice Ordonneau, is a story of circus life and circus folk, as the title implies.

Salut d'amour ("Love's Greeting")   Edward Elgar, 1888.

The short piece for piano, Op. 12, is a typical Victorian romantic work. An orchestral version appeared in 1889. The piece is sometimes known by the equivalent German title, *Liebesgruß*. Elgar composed the piece in response to a poem entitled "Love's Grace" given him by Alice Roberts, a friend who the following year would become his wife.

"Salut! demeure chaste et pure" ("Hail! dwelling chaste and pure").

Faust's rapturous address to Marguerite's house in Act 3 of Gounod's **Faust**.

Salve Regina ("Hail, Queen").

The title of a hymn of praise to the Virgin Mary, popular in medieval times, with the first two lines: "*Salve, regina, mater misericordiae, / Vita, dulcedo et spes nostra, salve!*" ("Hail, queen, mother of mercy, hail, our life, our sweetness, and our hope!"). Handel has a *Salve Regina* for soprano and strings (1707) and Poulenc one for unaccompanied chorus (1941).

Samson   George Frideric Handel, 1743.

The oratorio is set to a libretto by Newburgh Hamilton based on John Milton's verse tragedy *Samson Agonistes* (1617), dealing with the captivity of the blinded biblical hero Samson among the Philistines, and also on his poems "On the Morning of Christ's Nativity" (1629) and "At a Solemn Musick" (1645).

Samson et Dalila ("Samson and Delilah")   Camille Saint-Saëns, 1867–8, 1873–7.

The opera in three acts is set to a libretto by Ferdinand Lemaire based on the biblical story of the Hebrew warrior, Samson, and the Philistine temptress, Delilah, told in Judges 13–16.

Samstag aus Licht *see* **Licht.**

Sancta Civitas ("Holy City")   Ralph Vaughan Williams, 1923–5.

The oratorio for baritone, tenor, chorus, boys' chorus, and orchestra takes its text from the Book of Revelation, with additions from Taverner's Bible (1539). "And I John saw the holy city, new Jerusalem, coming down from God out of heaven" (Revelation 21:2).

Sanctus (Latin, "Holy").

One of the five main sections of the Roman Catholic **Mass**, with settings by a large number of composers. The opening words are: "*Sanctus, sanctus, sanctus, Dominus Deus Sabaoth*" ("Holy, holy, holy, Lord God of Hosts"). It is followed by the **Benedictus.**

The Sanguine Fan   Edward Elgar, 1976.

The ballet in one act, choreographed by Ronald Hynd, originated in 1917 as a mimed play set to a scenario by Ina Lowther based on a fan design drawn in sanguine (bloodred crayon) showing Pan and Echo with classical figures in the background. The plot revolves around a mislaid fan in the manner of a comedy by Oscar Wilde (although avoiding any direct reference to *Lady Windermere's Fan*). The present ballet was first produced under the equivalent French title *L'Éventail*, although the English title is now normally used in Britain.

Il Sant'Alessio ("St. Alexis")   Stefano Landi, 1632.

The opera in a prologue and three acts, to a libretto by Giulio Rospigliosi, tells what happens when Alessio renounces his wife and the world for the religious life.

"Saper vorreste" ("You would like to know").

Oscar's aria in Act 3 of Verdi's Un **Ballo in maschera**, in reply to Anckarstroem's question about the disguise of King Gustavus.

Sapho ("Sappho")   Jules Massenet, 1897.

The opera in five acts is set to a libretto by Henri Cain and Arthur Bernède based on Alphonse Daudet's novel of the same name (1884). This story tells of the unhappy love of Fanny Legrand, an artist's model who has been posing as Sappho for the sculptor, Caoudal, for an unsophisticated country youth, Jean Gaussin. *Cf.* **Saffo.**

Sarabande.

The 16th-century Spanish dance so named was introduced to France and England in the 17th century in a stately version, in slow triple time. It became a standard movement in orchestral suites by Purcell, Bach, and Handel, and was revived in the 20th century, for example in Satie's three *Sarabandes* for piano (1887–8) and as part of Debussy's *Suite pour le piano* (1896–1901).

Sardanapal ("Sardanapalus")   Peter Ludwig Hertel, 1865.

The ballet in four acts (six scenes), with a libretto and choreography by Paul Taglioni, centers on the legendary king of Assyria of this name, famous (or infamous) for his sybaritic way of life. (He adopted female dress and mannerisms and spent his days spinning and making clothes.)

Šárka   (1) Leoš Janáček, 1887; (2) Zdeněk Fibich, 1897.

Janáček's opera in three acts is set to a libretto by Julius Zeyer based on his play of the same name (1887) about the legendary Czech heroine who leads the revolt of the former queen's council of women and falls in love with the warrior-hero, Ctirad. Fibich's opera in three acts, to a libretto by Anežka Schulzová, is based on the same legend.

Sarnia   John Ireland, 1940–1.

The "island sequence" of three pieces for piano solo describes Guernsey in the Channel Islands, whose Roman name is said to have been *Sarnia* (although modern toponymists now assign this name to the much smaller island of Herm). The individual titles of the pieces are: (1) *Le Catioroc*, for the place of this name with its prehistoric remains, (2) *In a May Morning*, a tribute to Victor Hugo, who lived on Guernsey from 1855 through 1870, and (3) *Song of the Springtides*, for Algernon Charles Swinburne's poem of this name.

Satanella, oder Metamorphosen ("Satanella, or Metamorphoses") Peter Ludwig Hertel, 1852.

The ballet in one act, with a libretto and choreography by Paul Taglioni, is based on Jacques Cazotte's allegorical novel *Le Diable amoureux* ("The Amorous Devil") (1772). The story tells how the Heidelberg student, Karl, becomes ensnared by the she-devil, Satanella, who causes him to leave his betrothed.

Satyagraha   Philip Glass, 1978–80.

The opera in three acts is set to a libretto by the composer and Constance DeJong loosely based on the Hindu religious text known as the *Bhagavadgita*, and centers on the philosophy of *satyagraha*, or passive political resistance (in Sanskrit literally "truth obstinacy"), as advocated by Gandhi against British rule in India. Ghandi used the *Bhagavadgita* as his "dictionary of daily reference" and he is the work's central character.

Satyricon   John Ireland, 1946.

The comedy overture is based on Petronius's pornographic novel of low life (1st century AD), a quotation from which heads the work.

Saudades do Brazil ("Saudades of Brazil")
Darius Milhaud, 1921.

The set of piano pieces, Op. 67, later orchestrated, takes its title from Portuguese *saudade*, "longing," "nostalgia," this being a supposed feature of the Portuguese and Brazilian temperament.

Saul   George Frideric Handel, 1739.

The oratorio in three parts is set to a libretto by Charles Jennens based on Abraham Cowley's epic poem *Davideis* (1656), recounting the biblical history of David, and on the Old Testament Book of Samuel, where it is told how Saul, the first king of Israel, was deserted by God in favor of David. *Cf.* **Saul and David**.

Saul and David (Danish, *Saul og David*)
Carl Nielsen, 1902.

The opera in four acts is set to a libretto by Einar Christiansen based on the biblical Book of Samuel, where it is told how Saul, the first king of Israel, was deserted by God in favor of David. The elements of the account appearing in the opera include the summoning of the ghost of Samuel by the Witch of Endor, David's love for Saul's daughter, Mikal, Saul's persecution of David, and David's accession to the throne after Saul's death. *Cf.* **Saul**.

Savitri   Gustav Holst, 1916.

The chamber opera in one act is set to the composer's own libretto based on the Hindu epic, the *Mahabharata*. The plot is set in India and tells what happens when Savitri hears the voice of Death, who has come for her husband, Satyavan.

La Scala di seta ("The Silken Ladder")
Gioacchino Rossini, 1812.

The opera in one act is set to a libretto by Giuseppe Maria Foppa based on François-Antoine-Eugène de Planard's play *L'Échelle de soie* ("The Silken Ladder") and possibly a libretto made from it for Pierre Gaveaux's opera of the same name (1808). The silken ladder of the title is the one used nightly by Dorvil to rejoin his wife, Giulia, whom he has secretly married but who is living in the house of her tutor, Dormont.

Scapino   William Walton, 1941.

The score of the comedy overture is subtitled "after an etching from Jacques Callot's *Balli di Sfessania*, 1622." Scapino was a comic valet in the *commedia dell'arte* and the central character of Molière's comedy *Les Fourberies de Scapin* ("The Tricks of Scapin") (1671).

Scaramouche   (1) Jean Sibelius, 1922;
(2) Darius Milhaud, 1939.

Sibelius's ballet in three scenes, with a libretto by Paul Knudsen and choreography by Emilie Walborn, tells of a demonic fiddler who seduces an aristocratic lady. Milhaud's suite for two pianos, Op. 165b, is based on the incidental music for a production of Molière's play *Le médecin volant* ("The Flying Doctor") at the Théâtre Scaramouche, Paris. Hence the title. Scaramouche (Scaramuccia) himself was a stock character in the Italian theater, a wily soldier dressed in black. His name was adopted by the Italian comic actor, Tiberio Fiorilli (1608–1694), who settled in Paris and who almost certainly influenced Molière's acting style.

Scenes and Arias   Nicholas Maw, 1961–2.

The work for soprano, mezzosoprano, contralto, and orchestra is a setting of medieval love letters.

Scènes de ballet ("Ballet Scenes")   Igor Stravinsky, 1944.

The ballet divertissement, choreographed by Anton Dolin, comprises 11 dance numbers, which the composer prescribed should be performed by two soloists and a corps of four male dancers and 12 female.

Scenes from Childhood *see* **Kinderszenen**.

Scenes from Goethe's Faust (German, *Szenen aus Goethes "Faust"*)   Robert Schumann, 1843–53.

The overture and six other movements for soloists, chorus, and orchestra are settings of different scenes from Goethe's dramatic poem *Faust* (1808, 1832) about the philosopher who sells his soul to Mephistopheles (the Devil) in return for power. *See also* **Faust**.

Scenes from the Bavarian Highlands
Edward Elgar, 1895.

The six choral songs to piano accompaniment are set to texts adapted by the composer's wife from Bavarian folksongs. The individual titles are: (1) *The Dance*, (2) *False Love*, (3) *Lullaby*, (4) *Aspiration*, (5) *On the Alm*, (6) *The Marksman*.

Scenes from the Saga of King Olaf   Edward Elgar, 1894–5.

The cantata for soprano, tenor, and bass soloists, chorus, and orchestra is set to words from H.W. Longfellow's *The Saga of King Olaf* in *Tales of a Wayside Inn* (1863) with additions by Harry Acworth. Longfellow's own tale is based on Snorri Sturluson's account of the 11th-century king of Norway who championed Christianity among his heathen countrymen.

Scènes historiques ("Historical Scenes")
Jean Sibelius, 1899, 1912.

The composer gave the French title to two suites of orchestral pieces. No. 1 (1899), Op. 25, comprises *All'Overtura*, *Scène*, and *Festivo*. No. 2 (1912), Op. 66, comprises *The Chase*, *Love Song*, and *At the Drawbridge*. The depictions are only generally historical.

Scènes pittoresques ("Picturesque Scenes")
Jules Massenet, 1874.

The orchestral work is one of several sets of "scenes" descriptive of the title. Others include *Scènes hongroises* ("Hungarian Scenes") (1871), *Scènes napolitaines* ("Neapolitan Scenes") (1876), and *Scènes alsaciennes* ("Alsatian Scenes") (1881).

Der Schauspieldirektor ("The Impresario")
W.A. Mozart, 1786.

The opera in one act, K 486, is set to a libretto by Gottlieb Stephanie about a long-suffering impresario who has to cope with the rivalry between two prima donnas.

Schelomo ("Solomon")   Ernest Bloch, 1915–16.

The rhapsody for cello and orchestra is based on the Book of Ecclesiastes in the Apocrypha, the authorship of which is attributed to Solomon. The English version of the German name, *Shelomo*, is still sometimes used.

Gli Scherzi *see* Russian Quartets.

Scherzo (Italian, "Jest").

The term originally applied to vocal music, but in its present orchestral form the scherzo is really the creation of Beethoven, who developed it as the third movement of a symphony from the earlier minuet and trio of Haydn and Mozart. It is in 3/4 time and usually skittish or humorous in nature, as its name implies. Chopin called four of his piano works *Scherzi* (although they are more vigorous than jovial) and there is a popular *Scherzo* in Henry Charles Litolff's *Concert symphonique* No. 4 for piano and orchestra (*c*.1852).

Scherzo fantastique ("Fantastic Scherzo")
Igor Stravinsky, 1972.

The ballet in one act, choreographed by Jerome Robbins, is a display piece for two soloists and three accompanying male dancers.

Schicksalslied ("Song of Destiny")
Johannes Brahms, 1868–71.

The work for chorus and orchestra, Op. 54, is a setting of part of Friedrich Hölderlin's poem *Hyperions Schicksalslied* ("Hyperion's Song of Destiny") in Book 2 of his novel *Hyperion* (1799). The Hyperion here is not the figure of classical mythology but a Greek youth of the author's time who longs to free his country from Turkish occupation. The *Schicksalslied* is addressed by Hyperion to the "blessed genii," cosmic spirits in communion with the gods.

Schlagobers ("Whipped Cream")   Richard Strauss, 1921–2.

The "gay Viennese ballet" in two acts, with a libretto by the composer and choreography by Heinrich Kröller, has a title that refers to the dreams of a little boy who has eaten too much pastry at his confirmation party.

Die Schöne Galatea ("The Fair Galatea")
Franz von Suppé, 1865.

The operetta in one act, to a libretto by Poly Henrion (pen name of Leopold K. Dittmar and Kohl von Kohlenegg), is loosely based on the classical story of the sculptor, Pygmalion, and his statue of a beautiful woman who comes to life, Galatea, but adding Ganymede as Pygmalion's manservant and Midas as an art dealer.

Die Schöne Magelone ("The Fair Magelone")   Johannes Brahms, 1861.

The cycle of 15 songs or romances for solo violin and piano, Op. 33, consists of settings of extracts from Ludwig Tieck's novel *Die wunder-same Liebesgeschichte der schönen Magelone und des Grafen Peter aus der Provence* ("The Wonderful Love Story of the Fair Magelone and Count Peter of Provence") (1797). This is based on an old legend telling what happens when Magelone, daughter of a king of Naples and already promised in marriage, meets Count Peter of Provence and falls instantly in love with him. The musical work is often known in English as *The Magelone Romances*.

Die Schöne Melusine *see* The **Fair Melusina**.

Die Schöne Müllerin ("The Fair Maid of the Mill")   Franz Schubert, 1823.

The song cycle for male voice and piano, D 795, comprises settings of 20 poems from Wilhelm Müller's collection of folk lyrics, *Gedichte aus den hinterlassenen Papieren eines reisenden Walhornisten* ("Poems from the Posthumous Papers of a Traveling Bugler") (1821–4). The songs are about a miller's love for a girl (the "fair maid" of the title) who has been spirited away by a mysterious huntsman. Their titles are as follows: *Das Wandern* ("Wandering"), *Wohin?* ("Whither?"), *Halt!* ("Stop!"), *Danksagung an den Bach* ("Grateful Address to the Stream"), *Am Feierabend* ("After the Day's Work"), *Der Neugierige* ("The Curious One"), *Ungeduld* ("Impatience"), *Morgengruß* ("Morning Greeting"), *Des Müllers Blumen* ("The Miller's Flowers"), *Tränenregen* ("Rain of Tears"), *Mein!* ("Mine!"), *Pause* ("Pause"), *Mit dem grünen Lautenbande* ("With the Lute's Green Ribbon"), *Der Jäger* ("The Huntsman"), *Eifersucht und Stolz* ("Jealousy and Pride"), *Die liebe Farbe* ("The Beloved Color"), *Die böse Farbe* ("The Hated Color"), *Trockne Blumen* ("Dry Flowers"), *Der Müller und der Bach* ("The Miller and the Stream"), *Des Baches Wiegenlied* ("The Stream's Lullaby"). (The "stream" in all these is the millstream.) The songs are also known collectively as the *Müllerlieder* ("Miller Songs"), at least partly for the name of the poet. Their English title is sometimes given as *The Maid of the Mill*.

The School for Fathers *see* I **Quattro Rusteghi**.

School of Ballet   various (see below), 1961.

The ballet in one act, originally titled *Leçon de danse* ("Dance Lesson"), was choreographed by Asaf Messerer and set to music by Anatol Lyadov, Alexander Glazunov, Anton Rubinstein, Sergei Lyapunov, and Dmitri Shostakovich,

arranged by A. Zeitlin. The ballet opens with children at a dance class and progresses through the classwork of the company members until it reaches the climax, when the soloists display their techniques.

Schoolmaster Symphony (German, *Der Schulmeister*)   Joseph Haydn, 1774.

The Symphony No. 55 in E flat major is so named because the dotted figure in the slow movement suggests the admonishing finger of a schoolmaster. The composer is believed to have approved the title.

Die Schöpfung *see* The **Creation**.

Der Schulmeister *see* **Schoolmaster Symphony**.

Schumann Concerto   Robert Schumann, 1951.

The ballet in three movements, choreographed by Bronislava Nijinska, is an abstract setting of the composer's Piano Concerto in A minor, Op. 54 (1845), with the dancers following the romantic moods of the music.

Schwanda the Bagpiper *see* **Shvanda the Bagpiper**.

Der Schwanendreher ("The Hurdy-Gurdy Man")   Paul Hindemith, 1935.

The concerto for viola and small orchestra is based on German folksongs, with the individual titles of the three movements as follows: (1) *Zwischen Berg und tiefem Tal* ("Between mountain and deep valley"), (2) *Nun laube, Lindlein, laube* ("Now shed thy leaves, little linden"), (3) *Seid ihr nicht der Schwanendreher?* ("Are you not the hurdy-gurdy man?"). This last gives the title of the work as a whole, and is itself the title of a 17th-century song. According to the composer, the soloist "comes among merry company and performs the music he has brought from afar; songs grave and gay and, to conclude, a dance."

Schwanengesang ("Swan Song")   Franz Schubert, 1828.

The collection of 14 songs for voice and piano, D 957, was published as a "cycle" after the composer's death. Hence the name, as that of his "swan song." In published order, the titles are: *Liebesbotschaft* ("Love Message"), *Kriegers Ahnung* ("Warrior's Presentiment"), *Frühlingssehnsucht* ("Longing for Spring"), *Ständchen* ("Serenade"), *Aufenthalt* ("Staging Post"), *In der Ferne* ("In the Distance"), *Abschied* ("Farewell"),

Der Atlas ("Atlas"), *Ihr Bild* ("Her Portrait"), *Das Fischermädchen* ("The Fisher Girl"), *Die Stadt* ("The Town"), *Am Meer* ("By the Sea"), *Der Doppelgänger* ("The Ghostly Double"), *Die Taubenpost* ("The Pigeon Post"). Wilhelm Rellstab wrote the poems that gave the first seven songs, Heinrich Heine wrote those for the next six, and Johann Gabriel Seidl provided the words for the last.

Die Schwarze Maske ("The Black Mask") Krzysztof Penderecki, 1984–6.

The opera in three acts is set to a libretto by Harry Kupfer based on Georg Hauptmann's short play of the same name (1929).

Die Schweigsame Frau ("The Silent Women") Richard Strauss, 1935.

The opera in three acts is set to a libretto by Stefan Zweig based on Ben Jonson's play *Epicoene, or The Silent Woman* (1609). The plot centers on a retired English admiral who cannot stand noise of any kind and who is offered a "silent woman" as a bride.

Scipione ("Scipio") George Frideric Handel, 1726.

The opera in three acts is set to a libretto by Paolo Antonio Rolli based on Apostolo Zeno's play *Scipione nelle Spagne* ("Scipio in Spain") (1710) about the Roman general, Publius Cornelius Scipio (236–*c*.183 BC), who defeated the Carthaginians in Spain, invaded Africa, and defeated Hannibal.

Scotch Symphony (1) Felix Mendelssohn, 1952; (2) *see* **Scottish Symphony**.

The ballet in three movements, choreographed by George Balanchine, is set to all but the first movement of the composer's **Scottish Symphony**, which was formerly known in English as the *Scotch Symphony*. The ballet has a slightly Scottish atmosphere, particularly in the second movement, with its references to La **Sylphide**.

Scottish Fantasy (German, *Schottische Fantasie*) Max Bruch, 1879–80.

The fantasia on Scottish folk tunes for violin and orchestra features a particular such tune in each of its four movements, as follows: (1) *Auld Rob Morris*, (2) *The Dusty Miller*, (3) *I'm a Doun for Lack of Johnnie*, (4) *Scots Wha Hae wi' Wallace Bled*.

Scottish Symphony Felix Mendelssohn, 1830–42.

The Symphony No. 3 in A minor, Op. 56, was inspired by a visit to the royal residence at Holyrood, Edinburgh, and dedicated to Queen Victoria, who sometimes lived there. The work was formerly familiar in English as the *Scotch Symphony*. See also **Scotch Symphony**.

Scuola di ballo ("Dance School") Luigi Boccherini arr. Jean Françaix, 1924.

The ballet in one act, with a libretto and choreography by Léonide Massine, is based on Carlo Goldoni's comedy of the same name, telling what happens when an impresario visits a ballet school in his search for a new prima ballerina.

"Scuoti quella fronda di ciliego" *see* **Flower Duet** (2).

Scythian Suite (Russian, *Skifskaya syuita*) Sergey Prokofiev, 1914–15.

The work for orchestra in four movements, Op. 20, subtitled *Ala and Lolly*, is based on a subject from Scythian mythology, telling of the rivalry between the sun god, Veles, and the wooden idol, Ala. The work was originally commissioned for a ballet, but was rejected and became a concert piece. The Scythians were the ancient people of Iranian stock who migrated from Central Asia to southern Russia in the 8th and 7th centuries BC.

"Se il padre perdrei" ("If I should lose my father").

Ilia's aria in Act 2 of Mozart's **Idomeneo**, in which she reflects that if she had lost her father in Troy, Idomeneo would now be a father to her and Crete the place of her happiness.

"Se vuol ballare" ("If he wants to dance").

Figaro's aria in Act 1 of Mozart's Le **Nozze di Figaro**, in which he determines to make Count Almaviva dance to his tune.

The Sea Frank Bridge, 1910–11.

The orchestral suite in four movements is a musical depiction of the sea, as the title indicates. The individual movements have titles: (1) *Seascape*, (2) *Sea-foam*, (3) *Moonlight*, (4) *Storm*.

Sea Drift Frederick Delius, 1903–4.

The work for baritone, chorus, and orchestra is a setting of an extract from Walt Whitman's poem *Out of the Cradle Endlessly Rocking* (1871), the first of 11 in the cycle *Sea-Drift*. It tells of a boy who listens to the calls of a pair of mockingbirds by the sea. When the female leaves, the call of the male is interpreted by the whispering sea current (sea drift) as "Death."

Sea Fever   John Ireland, 1913.

The song for voice and piano is a setting of John Masefield's poem of the same name (1902), beginning "I must go down to the sea again."

Sea Interludes   Benjamin Britten, 1944–5.

The title is generally given to the orchestral interludes in **Peter Grimes**. Four are usually selected for concert performance, but there are actually six: *Dawn* opening Act 1, *Storm* between scenes 1 and 2 of Act 1, *Sunday Morning* opening Act 2, a passacaglia between scenes 1 and 2 of Act 2, *Moonlight* opening Act 3, and a final interlude between scenes 1 and 2 of Act 3.

Sea Pictures   Edward Elgar, 1897–9.

The song cycle for mezzo-soprano and orchestra, Op. 37, comprises settings of five poems about the sea, as follows: (1) *Sea-Slumber Song* by Roden Noel, (2) *In Haven* (*Capri*) by Caroline Alice Elgar (the composer's wife), (3) *Sabbath Morning at Sea* by Elizabeth Barrett Browning, (4) *Where Corals Lie* by Richard Garnett, (5) *The Swimmer* by Adam Lindsay Gordon.

Sea Piece with Birds   Virgil Thomson, 1952.

The orchestral work was inspired by a visit to the fishing town of Southwest Harbor, Maine, where the composer watched fishermen unloading codfish. He had originally gone there to pick up atmosphere for music for a proposed ballet with a plot about a lonely fisherman and a sea gull that becomes a ballerina, but this was never realized.

A Sea Symphony   Ralph Vaughan Williams, 1903–9.

The Symphony No. 1 in C for soprano and baritone soloists, chorus, and orchestra, is set to a text from poems by Walt Whitman about the sea. Its four movements have subtitles as follows: (1) *A Song for All Seas, All Ships* (1873), (2) *On the Beach at Night Alone* (1871), (3) *The Waves*, (4) *The Explorers*. (The first two subtitles are the titles of the original poems.)

The Seal Woman   Granville Bantock, 1924.

The opera is set to a libretto by Marjorie Kennedy Fraser based on a figure of Celtic folklore, the seal woman, a sea-fairy who turns into a seal and comes ashore to look for a human mate.

The Seasons   (1) (German, *Die Jahreszeiten*) Joseph Haydn, 1798; (2) Ludwig Spohr, 1850; (3) (Russian, *Vremena goda*) Alexander Glazunov, 1900.

Haydn's oratorio, for soprano, tenor, and bass soloists, chorus, and orchestra, is set to a text by Baron Gottfried van Swieten based Barthold Hinrich Brockes's German translation of James Thomson's poem of the same name (1726–30) in four books (one for each season) and a final hymn. Spohr's Symphony No. 9 in B minor, Op. 143, is in two main parts, each divided into three, as follows: I: *Winter, Transition to Spring, Spring*; II: *Summer, Transition to Autumn, Autumn*. Glazunov's ballet in one act and four scenes, with libretto and choreography by Marius Petipa, is a grand divertissement presenting each of the four seasons, beginning with winter. It is often known by its French title, *Les Saisons*.

Sebastian   Gian-Carlo Menotti, 1944.

The ballet in one act (three scenes), with a libretto by the composer and choreography by Edward Caton, is set in Venice at the close of the 17th century and tells how a Moorish slave substitutes himself for a wax figure and dies from the arrows shot into it, like the martyr, St. Sebastian.

Sechs Monologe aus "Jedermann" ("Six Monologues from 'Everyman'")   Frank Martin, 1943.

The song cycle is based on Hugo von Hofmannsthal's play *Jedermann* ("Everyman") (1911), based on the traditional religious parable of the rich man who is unexpectedly faced with death and who is brought for the first time to reflect on the salvation of his soul.

The Secret (Czech, *Tajemství*)   Bedřich Smetana, 1877–8.

The opera in three acts, to a libretto by Eliška Krásnohorská, is set in 18th-century Bohemia and tells how the rivalry between the two men Kalina and Malina has prevented their children, Vítek and Blaženka, from marrying and also Malina's sister, Roza, from marrying Kalina himself. A deceased friar has promised Kalina a secret which would enable him to marry Roza. The story tells what this is.

The Secret Marriage *see* Il **Matrimonio segreto**.

The Secret of Susanna *see* Il **Segreto di Susanna**.

Secular Games   R. Starer, 1962.

The ballet in three movements, choreographed by Martha Graham, is set to the composer's Concerto a Tre with titles for the movements as follows: (1) *Play With Thought: On a*

Socratic Island, (2) *Play With Dream: On a Utopian Island*, (3) *Play: On Any Island*.

"Il Segreto" ("The secret").

The drinking song sung by Maffeo in Act 2 of Donizetti's **Lucrezia Borgia** as the banqueters drink the wine poisoned by Lucrezia. A fuller form of the words is: *"Il segreto per esser felici"* ("The secret of being happy").

Il Segreto di Susanna ("Susanna's Secret") Ermanno Wolf-Ferrari, 1909.

The opera in one act, to a libretto by Enrico Golisciani, is set in Piedmont in 1840 and tells of the secret that Susannah finally reveals to her husband, Count Gil, who has grounds for suspecting she has been entertaining a lover.

Sehnsucht (German, "Longing").

This title is found for a number of romantic songs, one of the best known being Schubert's *Sehnsucht*, D 52 (1813), based on Schiller's poem of the same name.

"Selig wie di Sonne" ("Holy as the sun").

The quintet in Act 3 of Wagner's Doe **Meistersinger von Nürnberg**, in which Eva and Walther muse in delight on the song that they hope will win the prize in the coming contest, Magdalene and David reflect on the good fortune this could bring them, and Hans Sachs considers the loss of Eva.

Selina Gioacchino Rossini arr. Guy Warrack, 1948.

The ballet in one act, with a libretto by Andrée Howard and Peter Williams and choreography by Howard, is a "satire on the absurdities of the romantic convention" (Koegler, p. 374) centering on a woman named Selina.

Sellinger's Round various (see below), 1953.

The composite work for string orchestra, with full title *Sellinger's Round, Variations on an Elizabethan Theme*, consists of six variations on the Elizabethan tune of this name, composed to celebrate the Coronation of Elizabeth II in 1953 and first performed at the Aldeburgh Festival that year. The composers were Arthur Oldham, Michael Tippett, Lennox Berkeley, Benjamin Britten, Humphrey Searle, and William Walton. A round is properly an unaccompanied vocal "perpetual canon" at the unison or octave in which the voices enter in turn. It is not certain who Sellinger was. He may have been Sir Thomas Sellynger, buried in St. George's Chapel, Windsor, in *c.*1470, or else Sir Anthony

Saint-Leger, Lord Deputy of Ireland (*c.*1496–1559).

Semele George Frideric Handel, 1744.

The secular oratorio (masque) in three acts is set to an anonymous adaptation of William Congreve's libretto (1706) for an opera by John Eccles (first performed only in 1964), itself based on Book 3 of Ovid's *Metamorphoses* (1st century AD). This tells the story of Semele, daughter of Cadmos and Harmonia, who was loved by Zeus (Jupiter) and destroyed by him when he showed himself to her in his full glory.

Semiramide ("Semiramis") Gioacchino Rossini, 1822.

The opera in two acts is set to a libretto by Gaetano Rossi based on Voltaire's tragedy *Sémiramis* (1748), about the legendary queen of Assyria and Babylon, who with her lover, Assur, murders the king, Ninos.

"Sempre libera" ("Ever free").

The section of Violetta's aria "**Ah! fors' è lui**" in Act 1 of Verdi's La **Traviata** in which she declares she intends to abandon Alfredo's love and return to her former life of pleasure.

Semyon Kotko Sergey Prokofiev, 1940.

The opera in five acts is set to a libretto by the composer and Valentin Katayev based on the latter's story *I am the Son of Working People* (1937). The story tells what happens when Semyon Kotko returns to Ukraine after World War I and is caught up in the Civil War.

Sentimental Colloquy Paul Bowles, 1944.

The ballet in one act, choreographed by George Balanchine, is based on a poem by Paul Verlaine.

"Senza mamma, o bimbo" ("Without momma, O my baby").

Angelica's aria in Puccini's **Suor Angelica**, in which she grieves over the death of her illegitimate baby son and longs to join him in heaven.

Septet Extra Camille Saint-Saëns, 1973.

The ballet in five movements, choreographed by Hans van Manen, is set to the composer's Septet for Strings, Piano, and Trumpet (1881) and his Étude in Waltz Form, Op. 52 No. 6 (1877). The work is a humorous composition for ten dancers. The title refers primarily to the Septet, while the "extra" alludes both to the added Étude and to movements which the choreographer could not use in his previous ballets.

The Seraglio *see* Die **Entführung aus dem Serail**.

Seraphic Dialogue   Norman Dello Joio, 1955.

The ballet in one act, choreographed by Martha Graham, is centered on Joan of Arc, the "seraphic dialogue" being her communication with the "voices" of St. Michael, St. Catherine, and St. Margaret.

Serenade   (1) Pyotr Tchaikovsky, 1934; (2) *see* **Lieder ohne Worte**.

The ballet in four parts, choreographed by George Balanchine, is set to the composer's Serenade in C major for String Orchestra, Op. 48 (1880), and in the words of Balanchine, "tells its story musically and choreographically, without any extraneous narrative" (quoted in Koegler, p. 375). A serenade (from Italian *sereno*, "serene," but associated with *sera*, "evening") is properly openair evening music, typically sung by a lover below his beloved's bedroom window, but the term has been extended to other meanings.

Serenade for Tenor, Horn, and Strings   Benjamin Britten, 1943.

The song cycle, Op. 31, comprises a prologue and epilogue for solo horn enclosing settings of six poems on the theme of evening (hence "serenade") by six different poets: (1) Charles Cotton's *Pastoral*, (2) Lord Alfred Tennyson's *Nocturne*, (3) William Blake's *Elegy*, (4) the anonymous *Lyke-Wake Dirge*, (5) Ben Jonson's *Hymn*, and (6) John Keats's *Sonnet*. It was written for the tenor, Peter Pears, and horn player, Dennis Brain, who thus give a personal significance to the two parts named in the title.

Serenade Quartet   Joseph Haydn, 1768.

The string quartet in F major, Op. 3 No. 17, is so named from its second movement, which has a tune for the first violin over a pizzicato accompaniment for the other instruments.

Serenade to Music   Ralph Vaughan Williams, 1938.

The work for 16 solo voices and orchestra is a setting of Lorenzo's words from the last act of Shakespeare's *The Merchant of Venice* (1596), beginning, "How sweet the moonlight sleeps upon this bank! / Here will we sit, and let the sounds of music / Creep into our ears" (V.i.). The work was composed for Sir Henry Wood's golden jubilee concert at the Royal Albert Hall, London, and was dedicated to him "in grateful memory of his services to music."

Serenata notturna ("Nocturnal Serenade")   W.A. Mozart, 1776.

The Serenade No. 6 in D, K 239, for two small string orchestras, has a tautological title, since a **Serenade** is usually regarded as a piece to be played or sung in the evening anyway.

Serse ("Xerxes")   George Frideric Handel, 1737–8.

The opera in three acts is set to an anonymous text adapted from Silvio Stampiglia's libretto for Giovanni Battista Bononcini's opera *Il Xerse* ("Xerxes") (1694), itself based on Niccolò Minato's libretto for Pier Francesco Cavalli's opera of the same name (1654). The plot centers on the Persian king, Xerxes (*c*.519–465 BC), and embroils him in a number of fictitious amorous escapades.

La Serva padrona ("The Maid as Mistress")   Giovanni Pergolesi, 1733.

The intermezzo (to the opera *Il Prigioniero superbo*, "The Proud Prisoner") in two parts is set to a libretto by Gennaro Antonio Federico telling how the maid, Serpina, tricks her master, Uberto, into marrying her.

Servant of Two Masters (Czech, *Sluha dvou pánu*)   J. Burghauser, 1958.

The ballet in a prologue and three acts (four scenes), with a libretto by J. Rey and choreography by Jiří Němeček, is based on Carlo Goldoni's popular comedy of the same name (Italian, *Il servitore di due padroni*) (1745).

Service sacré *see* **Sabbath Morning Service**.

Seven American Poems   Arthur Bliss, 1940.

The seven songs for low voice and piano are set to poems by Edna St. Vincent Millay and Elinor Wylie, "each of which carries the burden of some vanished joy or beauty" (Christopher Palmer, *Bliss*, 1976).

The Seven Deadly Sins (German, *Die sieben Todsünden der Kleinbürger*, "The Seven Deadly Sins of the Petty Bourgeois")   Kurt Weill, 1933.

The ballet in a prologue, seven scenes, and an epilogue, with a libretto by Bertolt Brecht, was choreographed by George Balanchine, who recounts: "The ballet is the story of two Annas, a singing Anna who narrates the progress of a silent dancing Anna in her search for enough money to build a home for her family back in

Louisiana. Anna travels to seven American cities, in each of which she encounters a sin" (quoted in Koegler, p. 376). The ballet originally had a French title equivalent to the English, *Les sept péchés capitaux*.

The Seven Last Words (German, *Die sieben letzten Worte*)   Joseph Haydn, *c*.1796.

The cantata for soloists and chorus has the full title *The Seven Last Words of Our Savior on the Cross* (German, *Die sieben letzten Worte unseres Erlösers am Kreuz*). The work was originally commissioned by Cadiz Cathedral in 1785 as a set of seven orchestral interludes to separate the sermons on Good Friday. It was published in Vienna under the title *7 sonate, con un' introduzione, ed al fine un terremoto* ("7 Sonatas, with an Introduction, and at the End an Earthquake"). The "words" are those of Christ on the Cross, as quoted in the New Testament: (1) "Father, forgive them; for they know not what they do" (Luke 23:34), (2) "Today shalt thou be with me in paradise" (Luke 23:43), (3) "Woman behold thy son! ... Behold thy mother" (John 19:26, 27), (4) "Eli, Eli, lama sabachthani? [that is to say] My God, My God, why hast thou forsaken me?" (Matthew 27:46), (5) "I thirst" (John 19:28), (6) "It is finished" (John 19:30), (7) "Father, into thy hands I commend my spirit" (Luke 23:46).

Seven Rituals of Music   Henry Cowell, 1953.

The Symphony No. 11, in seven movements, aims to depict the seven different rituals of human life, from birth to death. Thus, the first movement depicts a child asleep, the second describes the ritual of work, the third is a song for the ritual of love, the fourth is a ritual of dance and play, the fifth is a ritual of magic, the sixth is a ritual of dance, and the seventh summarizes the previous themes and leads to music for the ritual of death.

Seven Sonnets of Michelangelo   Benjamin Britten, 1939–40.

The song cycle, Op. 22, for tenor and piano comprises Italian settings of Michelangelo's sonnets Nos. 16, 31, 30, 55, 38, 32, and 24 (*c*.1545). The work is sometimes known as just the *Michelangelo Sonnets*.

Seven Stars Symphony   Charles Koechlin, 1933.

The seven movements of the symphony, Op. 132, are each named for a different movie star, respectively Douglas Fairbanks, Lilian Har- vey, Greta Garbo, Clara Bow, Marlene Dietrich, Emil Jannings, and Charlie Chaplin. Astronomically, the "seven stars" are those of the Pleiades in the constellation Taurus. Koechlin's pleiad is purely cinematic.

Seventh Symphony (French, *La septième symphonie*)   Ludwig van Beethoven, 1938.

The ballet in four movements, choreographed by Léonide Massine, is set to the composer's Symphony No. 7 in A major, Op. 92 (1811–12), as the title indicates, with its movements titled as follows: (1) *The Creation*, (2) *The Earth*, (3) *The Sky*, (4) *Bacchanalia*. The symphony, described by Wagner as "the apotheosis of the dance," readily lends itself to a balletic interpretation.

Severn Suite   Edward Elgar, 1930.

The suite in five movements for brass band, Op. 87, takes its name from the river on which the composer's native city of Worcester stands. The work was given its first performance in that city and its movements have titles as follows: (1) *Introduction* (*Worcester Castle*), (2) *Toccata* (*Tournament*), (3) *Fugue* (*Cathedral*), (4) *Minuet* (*Commandery*), (5) *Coda*.

The Shades of Time (French, *Les Ombres du temps*)   Henri Dutilleux, 1997.

The "shades" of the orchestral work's title are the allusions, in the words of the composer, to the "timeless images of distant events whose intensity, in spite of the imprint of time, has never ceased to haunt me." The work, a meditation on World War II, has five movements with individual titles as follows: (1) *Les Heures* ("The Hours"), (2) *Ariel maléfique* ("Malefic Ariel"), (3) *Mémoire des ombres* ("Memory of the Shades"), (4) *Vagues de lumière* ("Waves of Light"), (5) *Dominante bleue?* ("Dominant Blue?"). The third movement, which has a treble solo, is dedicated to the German Jewish diarist Anne Frank (1929–1945), who perished in a concentration camp.

Shadow of the Wind   Gustav Mahler, 1948.

The ballet in six movements, choreographed by Anthony Tudor, is based on the composer's Das **Lied von der Erde**.

Shadow Song   Giacomo Meyerbeer, 1859.

Dinorah's aria in Act 2 of **Dinorah**, set in a birch wood by moonlight, beginning with the words: "*Ombre légère qui suit mes pas*" ("Light shade that follows my steps"). (The Italian equivalent is "*Ombra leggiera*.")

Shadowplay   Charles Koechlin, 1967.

The ballet in one act, with a libretto and choreography by Anthony Tudor, is based on the composer's orchestral work *Les Bandar-Log* ("The Bandar-Log") (1939–40), itself inspired by Rudyard Kipling's *The Jungle Book* (1894), in which the Bandar-Log are the Monkey-People. The ballet plot tells of the adventures and encounters of the Boy with Matted Hair (the equivalent of Mowgli) in the jungle

Shaker Loops   John Adams, 1983.

The work for string orchestra evolved from the composer's string septet of the same title (1978) that was inspired by the Minimalist tape-loop works of the 1960s. The first word of the title puns on both the musical word for a rapid tremolo and on the state of religious ecstasy attained by members of the Shaker sect. (*Cf.* The **Shakers**.)

The Shakers   Pauline Lawrence, 1930.

The ballet in one act, with a libretto and choreography by Doris Humphrey, was originally entitled *Dance of the Chosen* and evokes a religious meeting of the Shaker sect in the pioneer days of American history. (The Shakers were so named for their habit of trembling violently in a trancelike state during worship.)

Shakh-Senem, Reinhold Glière, 1927.

The opera in four acts is set to a libretto by Jafar Jabarly and M. Halperin based on Azerbaijani folklore. The story tells what happens when the beautiful Shakh-Senem, daughter of Bakhram-bek, loves the young poet, Harib, although her father wishes her to marry Veled, a powerful but despotic local ruler.

Sheep may safely graze (German, *Schafe können sicher weiden*)   J.S. Bach, *c.*1713.

The recitative and aria comes from the composer's secular cantata *Was mir behagt ist nur die munter Jagd!* ("What I enjoy is only the merry chase!"), BWV 208. The original connotation of the words was thus bucolic or at best pastoral, not religious.

Sheherazade (Russian, *Shekherazada*) Nikolai Rimsky-Korsakov, 1888.

The symphonic suite, Op. 35, is based on the *Thousand and One Nights* (*Arabian Nights*), in which Sheherazade (Scheherazade) is the bride of the emperor who marries and executes a new woman each day. She saves herself by telling him a new story each evening. The 1910 ballet in one act of the same name, with a libretto by Alexan-

dre Benois and choreography by Michel Fokine, is set to this work and is based on the first story, telling what happens when Zobeide, the favorite concubine and leader of the harem of Shariar, betrays him with the Golden Slave when she thinks he is away hunting.

Shéhérazade ("Sheherazade")   Maurice Ravel, 1898, 1903.

The overture for orchestra was followed five years later by the song cycle set to poems by Tristan Klingsor (real name Léon Leclère) based on the *Thousand and One Night* (*Arabian Nights*). (*See* **Sheherazade**.) The three songs have individual titles: *Asie* ("Asia"), *La Flûte enchantée* ("The Magic Flute"), and *L'Indifférent* ("The Indifferent One"). The first sings the glories of Asia, and begins (in translation): "Asia! Land of wonderful tales / Renowned in ancient lore."

Shepherd Fennel's Dance   Balfour Gardiner, 1910.

The orchestral piece is based on Thomas Hardy's story *The Three Strangers* in his *Wessex Tales* (1888). Shepherd Fennel is a minor character in this.

The Shepherd on the Rock *see* Der **Hirt auf dem Felsen**

The Shepherd's Complaint *see* **Lieder ohne Worte**.

The Shepherds of the Delectable Mountains   Ralph Vaughan Williams, 1921–2.

The pastoral episode in one act is set to the composer's own libretto based on John Bunyan's *The Pilgrim's Progress* (1674–9, 1684), in which the Delectable Mountains are the place whence the Celestial City may be seen and where Christian (the "Pilgrim") and his companion, Hopeful, talk with the shepherds Knowledge, Experience, Watchful, and Sincere.

Shirah   Alan Hovhaness, 1960.

The ballet in one act, choreographed by Pearl Lang, is "an ecstatic essay on the theme of mortality" (Koegler, p. 380) dedicated to the memory of the American critic and writer on ballet, Margaret Lloyd (1887–1960), represented here by the central character, Shirah.

Short Symphony   Aaron Copland, 1932–3.

The Symphony No 2 is succinctly named for its austerity and brevity.

A Shropshire Lad   George Butterworth, 1913.

The orchestral rhapsody is based on the theme from the song *Loveliest of Trees* in the song cycle (1912) of the same title comprising settings of poems from A.E. Housman's collection of verses so named (1896). The song took its text from No. 2 of the collection, beginning: "Loveliest of trees, the cherry now / Is hung with bloom along the bough."

Shuraleh Farid Yarullin, 1945.

The ballet in three acts (four scenes), with a libretto by Fayzi (pen name of the Tatar writer Akhmed Fayzullin) and Leonid Jacobson and choreography by the latter, tells the story of Shuraleh, a wood demon of Tatar folklore, and his influence on a pair of lovers.

Shvanda the Bagpiper (Czech, *Švanda dudák*) Jaromír Weinberger, 1927.

The opera in two acts is set to a libretto by Milos Kares and Max Brod based on Josef Kajetán Tyl's fairy-tale comedy *Strakonicky dudák* ("The Strakonice Piper") (1847). The story tells of the adventures that befall the bagpiper, Shvanda, after he falls in with the robber, Babinsky. The German form of the name, *Schwanda*, was formerly used in the English title.

Shylock Gabriel Fauré, 1889.

The work comprises six items of incidental music, Op. 57, for Edmund Haraucourt's verse-drama of this name based on Shakespeare's play *The Merchant of Venice* (1596), in which the Jewish moneylender Shylock is one of the main characters.

"Si colmi la calice" ("Let the cup be filled").

Lady Macbeth's drinking song in Act 2 of Verdi's **Macbeth**.

"Sì, fui soldato" ("Yes, I was a soldier").

Chénier's defense of his actions in the revolutionary tribunal in Act 3 of Giordano's **Andrea Chénier**.

Si j'étais roi ("If I Were King") Adolphe Adam, 1852.

The opera in three acts, to a libretto by Adolphe Philippe d'Ennery and Jules Brésil, is set in a kingdom by the sea in the 16th century and tells what happens when the fisherman, Zephoris, who longs to marry the Princess Nemea, rescues her from drowning and is invited as a joke by the King, her father, to lead a courtly life at his castle.

"Sì, mi chiamano Mimì" ("Yes, they call me Mimì").

Mimì's aria in Act 1 of Puccini's La **Bohème**, in which she describes herself to Rodolfo.

"Si può" ("If I may").

The prologue to Leoncavallo's I **Pagliacci**, in which the singer, usually Tonio, pokes his head through the curtains and asks the audience to listen to his account of the situation before the curtain goes up.

Siberia Umberto Giordano, 1903.

The opera in three acts, to a libretto by Luigi Illica, is set in Russian and tells what happens when Vassili, in love with Stephana, mistress of Prince Alexis, wounds him in a duel and is exiled to Siberia.

The Sicilian Vespers *see* Les **Vêpres Siciliennes**.

Le Siège de Corinthe ("The Siege of Corinth") Gioacchino Rossini, 1826.

The opera in three acts, to a libretto by Luigi Balocchi and Alexandre Soumet, is a revision of the earlier two-act opera **Maometto II**.

Das Siegeslied ("The Song of Victory") Havergal Brian, 1932–3.

The Symphony No. 4 for soprano, chorus, and orchestra is based on a German translation of Psalm 68, which begins: "Let God arise, let his enemies be scattered."

Siegfried *see* Der **Ring des Nibelungen**.

Siegfried Idyll Richard Wagner, 1870.

The work for small orchestra, written as a gift for the 33rd birthday (December 25, 1870) of the composer's wife, Cosima, incorporates material based on themes from an unfinished string quartet (1864), motifs from the opera *Siegfried* (*see* Der **Ring des Nibelungen**), on which Wagner was working when their son, Siegfried, was born (1869), and a lullaby (1869). The manuscript had the dedication: "Triebschen Idyll, with Fidi's Bird-Song and Orange Sunrise, presented as a Symphonic Birthday Greeting to his Cosima by her Richard, 1870." Triebschen was the name of their villa on Lake Lucerne; Fidi was the pet name of Siegfried; the "orange sunrise" was the orange wallpaper lit up by the sun on the morning of his birth. The birthday piece was performed on the staircase of the villa. Hence its nickname of *Treppenmusik* ("Stair Music") within the family circle. The predominantly lyrical and tranquil nature of the piece echoes Siegfried's own name, literally meaning "victory peace."

Siegfried's Journey to the Rhine
Richard Wagner, 1876.

The title is generally given to the orchestral interlude between the Prologue and Act 1 of *Götterdämmerung* in Der **Ring des Nibelungen**. It describes Siegfried's journey from Brünnhilde's rock to the castle of the Gibichungs.

The Sighing Wind *see* **Lieder ohne Worte**.

Signor Bruschino ("Signor Bruschino")
Gioacchino Rossini, 1812.

The opera in one act is set to a libretto by Giuseppe Maria Foppa based on the French comedy *Le Fils par hasard* ("The Son By Accident") by Alisan de Chazet and Maurice Ourry. The story is set in 18th-century Italy and tells how Florville, in order to marry Sofia, impersonates the young man, the son of Bruschino, to whom she has been betrothed but has never seen. The subtitle is the Italian equivalent of the French original, *Il figlio per azzardo*.

Il Signor di Pourceaugnac   Alberto
Franchetti, 1897.

The opera is set to a libretto by Ferdinando Fontana based on Molière's comedy *Monsieur de Pourceaugnac* (1669), in which the title character is a grotesque provincial from Limoges who is cruelly humiliated to prevent his marriage to Julie, daughter of Orgon.

"Signore, ascolta" ("Listen, Sire").

Liù's appeal to Calaf to abandon his attempt to woo Turandot in Act 1 of Puccini's **Turandot**.

Sigurd   Ernest Reyer, 1884.

The opera in five acts is set to a libretto by Camille du Locle and Alfred Blau based on the Siegfried episode in the Nibelung legend (*see* Der **Ring des Nibelungen**). The story tells what happens when Hilda, sister of King Gunther, asks Uta for magic aid to win the hero, Sigurd (the equivalent of Siegfried).

Sigurd Jorsalfar ("Sigurd the Crusader")
Edvard Grieg, 1872.

The five items of incidental music, Op. 22, were written for the play of this name by Bjørnstjerne Bjørnson as first staged in Oslo on the dramatist's 40th birthday.

The titles are as follows: (1) *Borghild's Dream* (Norwegian, *Borghilds drøm*), (2) *The Matching Game* (Norwegian, *Ved mandjævningen*), (3) *The Northland Folk* (Norwegian, *Nor-*

ronafolket), (4) *Homage March* (Norwegian, *Hyldningsmarsjen*), (5) *The King's Song* (Norwegian, *Kongekvadet*).

The Silken Ladder *see* La **Scala di seta**.

Simon Boccanegra   Giuseppe Verdi,
1856–7.

The opera in a prologue and three acts is set to a libretto by Francesco Maria Piave based on Antonio García Gutiérrez's play *Simón Boccanegra* (1843), about the first doge of Genoa, Simone Boccanegra (*c.*1301–1363), and the lost daughter, Amelia, born to him by Maria, daughter of the patrician leader, Jacopo Fiesco.

Simple Symphony   Benjamin Britten,
1933–4.

The work for string orchestra, Op. 4, is based on themes written when the composer was in his teens. It is thus relatively simple, as its name implies. Its four movements have individual (and analogously alliterative) titles: *Boisterous Bourrée*, *Playful Pizzicato*, *Sentimental Saraband*, and *Frolicsome Finale*.

Sinfonia *see* **Symphony**.

Sinfonia Antartica ("Antarctic Symphony")
Ralph Vaughan Williams, 1949–52.

The Symphony No. 7 for soprano solo, women's chorus, and orchestra, so named by the composer, is based on music he wrote for the film *Scott of the Antarctic* (1948). The second word of the title is often misspelled: "He [Peter Maxwell Davies] plans to write a homage to Vaughan Williams's *Sinfonia Antarctica*" (*The Times*, June 17, 1997).

Sinfonia Boreale ("Northern Symphony")
Vagn Holmboe, 1951–2.

The Symphony No. 8, Op. 56, was so named to indicate its Nordic character to the audience at its first performance, which was planned to take place in Vienna. In the event it was first performed in Copenhagen, the composer's native capital, so the title was otiose.

Sinfonia Concertante ("Concerto Symphony").

Any English translation of the Italian term is unsatisfactory and even misleading. It was used instead of **Concerto** by Haydn, Mozart, and others for a composition for more than one solo instrument and orchestra. An example is Mozart's *Sinfonia Concertante* for violin and viola in E flat major, K 364 (1779). The term has been used by modern composers for a work with only one solo instrument, implying that the the solo part is more closely bound in with that of the orchestra than in a conventional concerto. An example here is William Walton's *Sinfonia Concertante* for orchestra with piano (rather than for piano with orchestra) (1926–7).

Sinfonia da Requiem   Benjamin Britten, 1940.

The orchestral work, Op. 20, was written in memory of the composer's parents. It was commissioned by the Japanese government to celebrate the 2,600th anniversary of the founding of imperial Japan (traditionally 660 BC), but rejected because the titles of the three movements (*Lacrymosa, Dies irae, Requiem aeternam*) refer to the Roman Catholic liturgy.

Sinfonía de Antigona ("Antigone Symphony")   Carlos Chávez, 1933.

The Symphony No. 1 is based on the composer's earlier incidental music for a performance of Jean Cocteau's simplified version of Sophocles's tragedy *Antigone*. Hence the name.

Sinfonia espansiva ("Expansive Symphony")   Carl Nielsen, 1910–11.

The Symphony No. 3, Op. 27, has a title that relates to the expansion of the mind and spirit that it expresses, not to its length or scoring. "Its title, like all good titles, simply confirms what the work says in its own clear terms" (Robert Simpson, *Carl Nielsen*, 1952). The first movement is actually marked *Allegro espansivo*.

Sinfonía India ("Indian Symphony") Carlos Chávez, 1935.

The Symphony No. 2 quotes American Indian melodies. Hence its title (with "Indian" thus meaning "American Indian").

Sinfonia Romantica ("Romantic Symphony")   Carlos Chávez, 1953.

The Symphony No. 4 was originally titled *Short Symphony*. The composer then adopted the present title as an indication of the work's marked lyrical content. *Cf.* **Romantic Symphony**.

Sinfonia Sacra ("Sacred Symphony") Howard Hanson, 1955.

The composer explained that his Symphony No. 5 "does not attempt programmatically to tell the story of the first Easter but does attempt to evoke some of the atmosphere of tragedy and triumph, mysticism and affirmation of the story which is the essential symbol of the Christian faith" (quoted in Berkowitz, p. 143).

Sinfonia semplice ("Simple Symphony") Carl Nielsen, 1924–5.

The composer's Symphony No 6 was probably intended to complement the **Sinfonia espansiva** but in a mellower and more gently philosophical manner. "That this was indeed the case is shown by a letter he wrote to his daughter Anne Marie Telmányi in August 1924, where he said he was beginning a sixth Symphony, which was to be of 'completely idyllic character'; he remarked that he was going to write with the same simple enjoyment of the pure sound as the old *a capella* composers. This is clearly the origin of the title *Sinfonia semplice*" (Robert Simpson, *Carl Nielsen*, 1952). However, some of the work's passages appear to mock atonal modernity, and the title may well have been meant ironically.

Sinfonia tragica ("Tragic Symphony") Havergal Brian, 1948.

The Symphony No. 6 in D minor was originally written as the overture (or prelude) to a projected opera based on J.M. Synge's play *Deirdre of the Sorrows* (1910). Hence the title.

Sinfonietta   (1) Malcolm Williamson, 1967; (2) Leoš Janáček, 1978.

Williamson's plotless ballet in three movements, choreographed by Frederick Ashton, is set to the music he wrote for it. The three movements are named *Toccata, Elegy*, and *Tarantella*. Jánaček's ballet in five movements, choreographed by Jiří Kylián, is set to his orchestral work of the this name (1926) as an "ebullient hymn to life and the conquering of space" (Koegler, p. 381). The Italian word *sinfonietta* is properly the diminutive of *sinfonia*, so that the strict sense is "little symphony." In practice the term is used for a short and often light orchestral work, such as Erich Korngold's *Sinfonietta* (1912) or that by E.J. Moeran (1944).

Singulière Symphony ("Singular Symphony")   Franz Adolf Berwald, 1845.

The Symphony No.5 in C major is largely experimental in form and content. Hence the title.

Sir John in Love   Ralph Vaughan Williams, 1924–8.

The opera in four acts is set to the composer's own libretto based on Shakespeare's comedy *The Merry Wives of Windsor* (1599), in which Sir John Falstaff courts two women, Mistress Ford and Mistress Page, writing identical letters to each. *See also* **In Windsor Forest**.

Les Sirènes ("The Sirens")   Lord Berners, 1946.

The ballet in one act, choreographed by Frederick Ashton, is loosely based on Ouida's novel *Moths* (1880), with the heroine modeled on La Belle Otero. The setting is the beach of Trouville, France, at the height of the 1904 season, and the scene is peopled with a range of Edwardian eccentrics.

Six épigraphes antiques ("Six Ancient Inscriptions")   Claude Debussy, 1914.

The work for piano duet comprises six pieces with "ancient inscriptions" as individual titles: (1) *Pour invoquer Pan, dieu du vent d'été* ("To invoke Pan, god of the summer wind"), (2) *Pour un tombeau sans nom* ("For a nameless tomb"), (3) *Pour que la nuit soit propice* ("That night may be propitious"), (4) *Pour la danseuse aux crotales* ("For the dancing girl with castanets"), (5) *Pour l'Égyptienne* ("For the Egyptian girl"), (6) *Pour remercier la pluie du matin* ("To thank the morning rain").

Skating Rink   Arthur Honegger, 1922.

The ballet in one act, with a libretto by Riciotto Canudo and choreography by Jean Börlin, is a grotesque portrayal of people at a skating rink.

Slaughter on Tenth Avenue   Richard Rodgers, 1936.

The ballet from the composer's musical comedy *On Your Toes*, choreographed by George Balanchine, is the climax of the musical, which tells of the adventures of a young American member of a touring Russian company. The title refers to his fate.

Slavonic Dances   Antonín Dvořák, (1) 1878, (2) 1886.

The two sets of dances for piano duet (but often heard in the composer's orchestral version) are written in the style of Slavonic folk dances, but the melodies are original. (*Cf.* **Slavonic Rhapsodies**.) The first set comprises Nos. 1–8, Op. 46; the second Nos. 9–16, Op. 72.

Slavonic March (Russian, *Slavyanskiy marsh*)   Pyotry Tchaikovsky, 1876.

The orchestral march, Op. 31, is based on Slavic melodies and, like the **1812** overture, includes the old Russian national anthem. The work is also known by its equivalent French title, *Marche slave*.

Slavonic Rhapsodies   Antonín Dvořák, 1878.

The three orchestral works, Op. 45, are strongly suggestive of Slavonic folk music although the melodies are original. (*Cf.* **Slavonic Dances**.) No. 1 is in D major, No. 2 in G minor, and No. 3 in A flat major.

The Sleeping Beauty (Russian, *Spyashchaya krasavitsa*)   Pyotr Tchaikovsky, 1888.

The ballet in a prologue and three acts, with a libretto by Marius Petipa and choreography by Ivan Vsevolzhsky, is based on Charles Perrault's fairy tale *La Belle au bois dormant* ("Beauty Sleeping in the Wood") in his *Contes de ma mère l'Oye* ("Mother Goose Tales") (1697). This tells how a young princess has to wait a hundred years for the kiss of Prince Charming to free her from the deep sleep into which she has been placed by a wicked fairy. *See also* **Aurora's Wedding**, The **Sleeping Princess**.

The Sleeping Princess   Pyotr Tchaikovsky, 1921.

This is the English title of The **Sleeping Beauty** when it was premièred in London in the year stated by Sergei Diaghilev.

Sleepwalking Scene   Giuseppe Verdi, 1846–7.

The name is generally given to the scene in Act 4 of **Macbeth** in which a doctor and a gentlewoman observe Lady Macbeth walking and talking in her sleep.

Sly   Ermanno Wolf-Ferrari, 1927.

The opera in three acts is set to a libretto by Giovacchino Forzano based on the Induction to Shakespeare's play *The Taming of the Shrew* (1593), in which Christopher Sly is a drunken tinker. The story tells what happens when Sly antagonizes the Duke of Westmoreland at an inn and is taken to the Duke's castle.

"Smanie implacabili" ("Relentless longings").

Dorabella's aria in Act 1 of Mozart's **Così fan tutte**, in which she swears to give an example of doomed love to the Furies that torment her with longings.

The Snow Maiden (Russian, *Snegurochka*) (1) Nikolai Rimsky-Korsakov, 1880–1; (2) Pyotr Tchaikovsky, 1961.

Rimsky-Korsakov's opera in a prologue and four acts is set his own libretto based on Alexander Ostrovsky's play in verse of the same name (1873). This tells what happens when the Snow Maiden begs Spring to be allowed to remain, even though winter is ending. Tchaikovsky's

1961 ballet in three acts, with a libretto and choreography by Vladimir Burmeyster, is set to his incidental music for this play and to the first two movements of his Symphony No. 1 (**Winter Daydreams**).

"Soave sia il vento" ("May the wind be gentle").

The trio in Act 1 of Mozart's **Così fan tutte**, in which Fiordiligi, Dorabella and Don Alfonso wish for a calm sea as Ferrando and Guglielmo pretend to set off for the wars.

Sociable Songs   Peter Warlock, 1924–5.

The composer gave this title to three of his settings for male voices and piano of anonymous poems: *The Toper's Song*, *One More River*, and *The Lady's Birthday*. All three relate to sociable occasions.

Socrate ("Socrates")   Erik Satie, 1918.

The symphonic drama in three parts is set to Victor Cousin's French translation from the Greek of texts by Plato about the philosopher, Socrates (470–399 BC). The parts have individual titles as follows: *Portrait de Socrate* ("Portrait of Socrates"), *Les Bords de l'Ilissus* ("The Banks of the Ilissus"), and *Mort de Socrate* ("Death of Socrates").

"Softly awakes my heart" *see* "Mon cœur s'ouvre à ta voix."

Il Sogno di Scipione ("Scipio's Dream") W.A. Mozart, 1772.

The opera in one act, K 126, is set to a libretto by Pietro Metastasio based on Cicero's *Somnium Scipionis* ("Scipio's Dream") in *De Republica* ("On the Republic") (54–52 BC). The story is set in North Africa in the 2d century BC and tells what happens when the Roman general, Scipio, nephew of Scipio Africanus the Elder, is visited in his sleep by the Goddess of Fortune and the Goddess of Constancy, who ask him to choose one of them to guide him through life.

Le Soir ("Evening")   Joseph Haydn, 1761.

The Symphony No. 8 in G major follows on from Symphonies No. 6 and 7, Le **Matin** ("Morning") and Le **Midi** ("Noon"). The last movement is *La Tempête* ("The Storm").

Soir de fête ("Evening Celebration")   Léo Delibes arr. Henri Paul Busser, 1925.

The ballet divertissement, choreographed by Léo Staats, is set to an arrangement of the composer's La **Source**.

Soirées musicales ("Musical Evenings")   (1) Giaocchino Rossini, 1835; (2) Benjamin Britten, 1936.

Five of Rossini's collection of songs and duets of this name were orchestrated under the same title by Britten as his Op. 9. The rest were orchestrated by Resphigi for his ballet La **Boutique fantasque**. The name itself simply suggests an evening's musical entertainment.

"Sola, perduta, abbandonata" ("Alone, lost, abandoned").

Manon Lescaut's final aria in Act 4 of Puccini's **Manon Lescaut**, in which she awaits her death near New Orleans.

Die Soldaten ("The Soldiers")   Bernd Zimmermann, 1958–60.

The opera in four acts is set to the composer's own libretto based on Jakob Michael Reinhold Lenz's play of the same name (1776). The plot tells how Marie, engaged to Stolzius, is seduced by Baron Desportes, a high-ranking army officer. She subsequently takes a number of other lovers and ends up as a soldiers' prostitute.

Soldiers' Chorus   Charles Gounod, 1859.

The name is generally given to the chorus of soldiers in Act 4 of **Faust**, in which they vow to perpetuate the glory of their ancestors. The chorus begins: "*Gloire immortelle / De nos aieux, / Sois-nous fidèle, / Mourons comme eux!*" ("Immortal glory of our forefathers, be faithful to us, let us die as they did!").

The Soldier's Tale *see* L'**Histoire du soldat**.

Le Soleil de nuit ("The Night Sun") Nikolai Rimsky-Korsakov, 1915.

The ballet in one act, choreographed by Léonide Massine, is a series of Russian dances and scenes set to music from the composer's opera The **Snow Maiden**.

"Solenne in quest'ora" ("Solemn at this time").

The duet in Act 3 of Verdi's La **Forza del destino**, in which Alvaro and Carlo swear eternal friendship.

Solitaire   Malcolm Arnold, 1956.

The ballet in one act was choreographed by Kenneth MacMillan who described it as "a kind of game for one" (quoted in Koegler, p. 386). It is set to the composer's *English Dances*, Sets I, Op. 27 (1951), and II, Op. 33 (1955), and tells how a girl tries repeatedly to join in the activities of her friends but always finds herself alone.

Solomon   George Frideric Handel, 1749.

The oratorio is set to a biblical text by an unknown author about King Solomon, famous for his wisdom and justice. His story is told in 1 Kings and 1 and 2 Chronicles.

Solstice of Light   Peter Maxwell Davies, 1979.

The work in 14 movements for tenor solo, four-part chorus, and organ is set to a text by the Orkney poet, George Mackay Brown, and depicts the successive waves of "invaders" to Orkney from the earliest times to the present. The title evokes the light nights in Orkney at the time of the summer solstice.

Solveig   Edvard Grieg arr. Boris Asafiev and E. Kornblit, 1952.

The ballet suite in a prologue, three acts (five scenes), and an epilogue, choreographed by Leonid Jacobson, is set to music from the composer's **Peer Gynt** and centers on Solveig, Peer Gynt's faithful lover.

"Sombre forêt" ("Dark forest").

Mathilde's romance in Act 2 of Rossini's **Guillaume Tell**, in which she chooses the wild countryside over splendid palaces and sings of her love for Arnold.

El Sombrero de tres picos ("The Three-Cornered Hat")   Manuel de Falla, 1919.

The ballet in one act, with a libretto by Gregorio Martínez Sierra and choreography by Léonide Massine, is based on Pedro Antonio de Alarcón's story of the same title (1874). This tells of the ruses and disguises adopted for different purposes by a miller's wife, her jealous husband, and a senile mayor (the owner of the hat). The source of the plot is the same as for Wolf's opera Der **Corregidor**. The ballet is also known by the French title *Le Tricorne*.

La Somnambule ("The Sleepwalking Girl")   Ferdinand Hérold, 1827.

The pantomimic ballet in three acts, with a libretto by Eugène Scribe and Jean Aumer and choreography by the latter, is set in a village in Provence and tells what happens when Thérèse, betrothed to Edmond, walks in her sleep. The subtitle is *L'Arrivée d'un nouveau Seigneur* ("The Arrival of a New Lord"). It was this ballet that inspired Vincenzo Bellini's opera La **Sonnambula**. *Cf.* **Night Shadow**.

Somnambulism   Stan Kenton, 1953.

The ballet in one act, choreographed by Kenneth MacMillan, deals with the worries and anxieties of three dancers who eventually find, much to their relief, that they have been dreaming.

"Son lo spirito che nega" ("I am the spirit who denies").

Mefistofele's aria in Act 1 of Boito's **Mefistofele**, in which he declares himself to be the spirit of eternal denial.

Sonata (Italian, "Sounded").

The term was originally used in the 16th century for a musical work that was played rather than sung (as a **Cantata**). It later came to be used for a composition in several movements for piano or for one or more other instruments with a piano accompaniment, such as a violin sonata (violin and piano), flute sonata (flute and piano). A sonata by Haydn or Mozart typically has three movements, *Allegro* ("lively"), **Andante**, *Allegro*.

Sonata Fantasy (Russian, *Sonata-fantaziya*) Alexander Skryabin, 1892–7.

The Piano Sonata No. 2 in G sharp minor is a fantasy on the sea, with the first movement, for example, representing a warm night on the seashore and the second depicting a storm at sea.

Sonate à trois ("Sonata for Three")   Béla Bartók, 1957.

The ballet in one act, choreographed by Maurice Béjart, is set to the composer's Sonata for Two Pianos and Percussion (1937) and is based on Jean-Paul Sartre's play *Huis clos* ("In Camera") (1944). The story tells of two women and one man who are obliged to live together in a closed room from which there is no escape. The title relates both to the three dancers and to the three musicians who perform the sonata.

Song for Athene   John Tavener, 1993.

The choral work was written in memory of a young Greek actress of the title name, itself that of the Greek patron goddess of Athens and virgin goddess of arts, crafts, and war.

A Song for the Lord Mayor's Table William Walton, 1962.

The song cycle for soprano and piano comprises texts collected by Christopher Hassall from six poems: one each by William Blake, Thomas Jordan, Charles Morris, and William Wordsworth, and two by anonymous 18th-century poets. The work was written for the 1962 City of London Festival attended by the Lord Mayor of London. Hence the title.

Song of a Wayfarer (French, *Chant du compagnon errant*) Gustav Mahler, 1971.

The ballet in one act, choreographed by Maurice Béjart, is set to the composer's song cycle **Lieder eines fahrenden Gesellen** and tells of a romantic student who rages against himself until fate steps in to calm and comfort him.

Song of Destiny *see* **Schicksalslied**.

A Song of Summer Frederick Delius, 1930.

The orchestral work is an idealized evocation of summer, written when the composer was blind and paralyzed. He told his amanuensis, Eric Fenby, that "he must imagine sitting on heathery cliffs, looking out to sea: the sustained string chords had to suggest the stillness of sea and land, and the clear sky over all" (Burke, p. 117).

The Song of the Earth (1) Gustav Mahler, 1965; (2) *see* Das **Lied von der Erde**.

The ballet in six movements, choreographed by Kenneth MacMillan, is set to the composer's Das **Lied von der Erde** and loosely interprets the poems by Hans Bethge on which that work was based.

Song of the Flea (Russian, *Pesnya Mefistofelya o blokhe*, "Song of Mephistopheles about a Flea") Modest Mussorgsky, 1879.

The song for voice and piano is a setting of Mephistopheles's song in Goethe's *Faust* (1808, 1832).

Song of the High Hills Frederick Delius, 1911.

The work for wordless chorus and orchestra, although written in France, was inspired by a holiday visit to the mountains of Norway.

Song of the Night Karol Szymanowski, 1914–16.

The Symphony No. 3, Op. 27, for tenor (or soprano), male chorus, and orchestra, is set to a Czech translation of a poem of the same name by the 13th-century Persian mystic and poet, Jalal ad-Din ar-Rumi. An English translation of the tenor solo part reads: "Oh, do not sleep, friend, through the night. / You a soul, while we are suff'ring through this night. / Such quiet, such sleep… / I and God alone together in this night! / What a roar! / Joy arises, / Truth with gleaming wing is shining, in this night!" (program note, quoted in Berkowitz, pp. 145–6).

Song of the Traveler *see* **Lieder ohne Worte**.

Song of Triumph *see* **Triumphlied**.

Song to the Moon Antonín Dvořák, 1900.

This name is generally given to Rusalka's aria in Act 1 of **Rusalka**, in which she confides to the moon the secret of her longing (the handsome young prince she has fallen for).

Le Songe d'une nuit d'été ("The Midsummer Night's Dream") Ambroise Thomas, 1850.

The opera is set to a libretto by Joseph Bernard Rosier and Adolphe de Leuven *not* based on Shakespeare's play but Shakespeare, Queen Elizabeth, and Falstaff appear in it as characters.

Songs and Dances of Death (Russian, *Pesni i plyaski smerti*) Modest Mussorgsky, 1875–7.

The song cycle for voice and piano comprises settings of four poems by Arseny Golenishchev-Kutuzov (1848–1913). Each treats a different aspect of death. Their titles are: (1) *Trepak: Death and the Peasant*, (2) *Cradle Song: The Child Breathes Gently*, (3) *Death the Serenader: Soft is the Night*, (4) *Field Marshal Death: War Rumbles*.

Songs for Dov Michael Tippett, 1970.

The song cycle for tenor solo and small orchestra is set to the composer's own text for songs such as might have been sung by the itinerant musician Dov in his opera The **Knot Garden**.

Songs My Mother Taught Me (Czech, *Kdyz mne stará matka zpívat ucívala*) Antonín Dvořák, 1880.

The song for tenor and piano, to words by Adolf Heyduk, is No. 4 of the **Gypsy Melodies**.

Songs of a Wayfarer *see* **Lieder eines fahrenden Gesellen**.

Songs of Farewell (1) Hubert Parry, 1916–18; (2) Frederick Delius, 1930.

Parry's six unaccompanied secular motets are set to texts on the theme of parting by Henry Vaughan, John Davies, Thomas Campion, John Lockhart, John Donne, and from the Bible. Delius's five songs for double chorus and orchestra are settings on the same theme of poems by Walt Whitman.

Songs of Sunset Frederick Delius, 1906–8.

The work for mezzosoprano, baritone, chorus, and orchestra comprises settings of Ernest Dowson's poems of the same name.

Songs of the Fleet   Charles Villiers Stanford, 1910.

The five songs, Op. 117, for baritone, chorus, and orchestra are settings of poems about the sea and ships by Henry Newbolt (1862–1938). *Cf.* **Songs of the Sea.**

Songs of the Sea   Charles Villiers Stanford, 1904.

The five songs, Op. 91, for baritone, male chorus, and orchestra are settings of poems about the sea and ships by Henry Newbolt (1862–1938). The best known is *Drake's Drum* from *Admirals All* (1897). *Cf.* **Songs of the Fleet.**

Songs of Travel   Ralph Vaughan Williams, 1901–4.

The song cycle for voice and piano comprises settings of nine poems from Robert Louis Stevenson's collection of the same title (1896). Their theme is journeying, as is shown by the individual titles: (1) *The Vagabond*, (2) *Let Beauty Awake*, (3) *The Roadside Fire*, (4) *Youth and Love*, (5) *In Dreams*, (6) *The Infinite Shining Heavens*, (7) *Whither Must I Wander?*, (8) *Bright is the Ring of Words*, (9) *I Have Trod the Upward and the Downward Slope*.

Songs Without Words   *see* **Lieder ohne Worte.**

La Sonnambula ("The Sleepwalking Girl") Vicenzo Bellini, 1831.

The opera in two acts is set to a libretto by Felice Romani based on that by Eugène Scribe for Louis-Joseph-Ferdinand Hérold's ballet-pantomime La **Somnambule.** *Cf.* **Night Shadow.**

The Sorcerer   Arthur Sullivan, 1877.

The operetta in two acts, to a libretto by W.S. Gilbert, tells what happens when a sorcerer distributes a love potion that causes the drinker, if unmarried, to fall in love with the first person he sees.

The Sorcerer's Apprentice   *see* **L'Apprenti sorcier.**

Sorochintsy Fair (Russian, *Sorochinskaya yarmarka*)   Modest Mussorgsky, 1913.

The (unfinished) opera in three acts is set to the composer's own libretto based on Nikolai Gogol's story of the same name in his *Evenings on a Farm near Dikanka* (1831–2). The story is set in Sorochintsy, Ukraine, and tells what happens when Parasya meets her lover, Gritzko, at the fair (market), but is refused permission to marry him by her disapproving stepmother, Khivrya.

The Sorrowful Soul   *see* **Lieder ohne Worte.**

Sosarme, rè di Media ("Sosarme, King of Media")   George Frideric Handel, 1732.

The opera in three acts is set to an anonymous adaptation of Antonio Salvi's libretto for Giocomo Antonio Perti's opera *Dionisio, rè di Portogallo* ("Dionysius, King of Portugal") (1710). The story is set in Lydia and tells what happens when the Median king, Sosarme, attempts to mediate in the dispute for the throne between Haliates and his son, Argones, to whose sister, Elmira, he is engaged.

Sospiri ("Sighs")   Edward Elgar, 1914.

The work for strings, harp, and organ, Op. 70, was written after the death of the composer's friend, the American hostess Julia Worthington, whom he and his wife had first met in New York in 1905. "The brooding tragedy of the music, its Mahlerian intensity, suggest that these 'sighs' are for something known only to Elgar" (Michael Kennedy, *Portrait of Elgar*, 1982).

La Source ("The Spring")   Léo Delibes and Léon Minkus, 1866.

The ballet in three acts (four scenes), with a libretto by Charles-Louis-Étienne Nuittier and Arthur Saint-Léon and choreography by the latter, is set in a fictitious Persia and tells of Naïla, Spirit of the Spring, who helps Djemil, a hunter, to win his beloved, Nouredda. Delibes wrote the music for the second and third scenes, and Minkus for the first and fourth.

Souvenirs ("Memories")   Samuel Barber, 1953.

The ballet in one act, with a libretto and choreography by Todd Bolender, is set to an orchestrated version of the composer's original piano duet, Op. 28 (1951), and centers on the smart but eccentric clientele in a fashionable pre–World War I hotel.

Souvenirs de Bayreuth ("Memories of Bayreuth")   Gabriel Fauré and André Messager, 1888.

The work for piano duet is a "*fantaisie en forme de quadrille sur les thèmes favoris de l'Anneau du Nibelung de Richard Wagner*" ("fantasy in the form of a quadrille on favorite themes from Richard Wagner's *Ring of the Nibelung*"). *See* Der **Ring des Nibelungen.**

Spanisches Liederbuch ("Spanish Songbook")   Hugo Wolf, 1889–90.

The 44 songs for voice and piano are settings of ten sacred and 34 secular Spanish poems translated by Paul von Heyse and Emanuel Giebel and published collectively under the same title (1852).

Spanish Caprice *see* **Capriccio espagnol**.

Spanish Rhapsody *see* **Rapsodie espagnole**.

Spanish Symphony *see* **Symphonie espagnole**.

Spartacus (Russian, *Spartak*)   Aram Khachaturian, 1956.

The ballet in four acts (nine scenes), with a libretto by Nikolai Volkov and choreography by Leonid Jacobson, tells the story of the slave, Spartacus (died 71 BC), who leads a revolt against Roman oppression, is captured by the Roman general, Crassus, and is brought to Rome with his wife, Phrygia.

Spatzenmesse ("Sparrow Mass")   W.A. Mozart, 1775.

The Mass No. 10 in C major, K 225, is still sometimes so known from the "chirping" violin figures in the **Sanctus**.

The Specter's Bride (Czech, *Svatebni kosile*, "The Wedding Shift")   Antonín Dvořák, 1884.

The cantata for soprano, tenor, and bass solo, chorus, and orchestra, is based on a ballad by Karel Erben telling how a demon bridegroom woos and wins his bride.

Le Spectre de la rose ("The Spirit of the Rose"). Carl Maria Weber, 1911.

The ballet in one act, with a libretto by Jean-Louis Vaudoyer and choreography by Mikhail Fokine, is set to the composer's **Aufforderung zum Tanz** and tells of a girl who brings a rose home from a ball, falls asleep, and dreams that the spirit of the rose is dancing with her.

Spells   Richard Rodney Bennett, 1974.

The work for soprano, chorus, and orchestra consists of settings of Kathleen Raine's poems of the same name. The spells are love spells.

Spem in alium nunquam habui ("In no other is my hope")   Thomas Tallis, c.1573.

The motet in 40 parts for eight five-voice choruses was commissioned by Thomas Howard, 4th duke of Norfolk, as a rival to Alessandro Striggio's 40-part motet *Ecce beatem lucem* ("Behold the Blessed Light") (1561). The work is usually known by the short title *Spem in alium*.

Lo Speziale ("The Apothecary")   Joseph Haydn, 1768.

The opera in three acts, to the composer's own text based on a libretto by Carlo Goldoni, tells what happens when the old apothecary, Sempronio, wants to marry his ward, Grilletta, who is already loved by two others.

Spinnerlied *see* The **Bee's Wedding**.

Spinning Chorus   Richard Wagner, 1843.

The name is generally given to the chorus "*Summ' und brumm*" sung by the young women in Act 2 of Der **Fliegende Holländer**, expressing their wish that the spinning wheels could drive their lovers back from the sea.

Spinning Song *see* The **Bee's Wedding**..

"Spirito gentil" ("Gracious spirit").

Fernando's aria in Act 4 of Donizetti's La **Favorita**, in which he reflects on his love for Leonora as he is about to take his monastic vows.

The Spirit of England   Edward Elgar, 1915–17.

The three pieces, Op. 80, for soprano or tenor soloist, chorus, and orchestra, are settings of three poems by Laurence Binyon (1869–1943): *The Fourth of August, To Women*, and *For the Fallen*. The work was topical for World War I and the last poem (1914), though not the music, is still familiar from its recitation at memorial ceremonies for those killed in war. The date of the first poem, August 4, 1914, is that of Britain's declaration of war on Germany.

Spitfire Prelude and Fugue   William Walton, 1942.

The orchestral work comprises two items from the film music for *The First of the Few* (1942). The title refers to the Spitfire fighter aircraft used by the Royal Air Force in the Battle of Britain (1940). (The film told the story of its designer, R.J. Mitchell.)

Das Spitzentuch der Königin *see* **Rosen aus dem Süden**.

Lo Sposo deluso ("The Deluded Husband") W.A. Mozart, 1783.

The (unfinished) comic opera in two acts, K 430, to a libretto possibly by Lorenzo da Ponte, is subtitled *La rivalità di tre donne per un solo amante* ("The Rivalry of Three Women for a Single Lover") and tells what happens when the rich old bachelor, Bocconio, awaits his bride, Eugenia, a Roman noblewoman.

Spring Fire   Arnold Bax, 1913.

The orchestral work, effectively a symphony in four movements, took its inspiration from the first chorus of A.C. Swinburne's poetic drama *Atalanta in Calydon* (1865), beginning: "When the hounds of spring are on winter's traces." The title specifically relates to two lines of the third verse: "O that man's heart were as fire and could spring to her, / Fire, or the strength of the streams that spring!" The individual titles of the movements are: *Dawn and Sunrise, Full Day, Romance,* and *Maenads*.

Spring Sonata (German, *Frühlingssonate*) Ludwig van Beethoven, 1801.

The Violin Sonata in F major, Op. 24, is so called for its bright and cheerful character, as if "full of the joys of spring." The name is of German origin but was not given by Beethoven.

Spring Song (German, *Frühlingslied*) Felix Mendelssohn, 1842.

The piano piece Op. 62 No. 6 in A major in Book 5 of the **Lieder ohne Worte** is so named presumably because its light, upward arpeggios and rising opening phrase give a lyrical "uplift" like that of the season. The name is of German origin but was not given by the composer. This same piece was also formerly known as *Camberwell Green*, since at the time of its composition (June 1, 1842) Mendelssohn was staying with his wife's English relations, the Beneckes, at a house in Camberwell Green, in the former village of Camberwell, now absorbed into southeast London.

Spring Symphony   (1) Robert Schumann, 1841; (2) John Knowles Paine, 1880; (3) Benjamin Britten, 1948–9.

Schumann's Symphony No. 1 in B flat major, Op. 38, was so named by the composer, who in a letter of November 23, 1842 to Ludwig Spohr wrote: "It was inspired, if I may say so, by the spirit of spring which seems to possess us all anew every year, irrespective of age. The music is not intended to describe or paint anything definite, but I believe the season did much to shape the particular form it took" (quoted in Chissell, p. 50). He acknowledged that the initial inspiration for the work was a spring poem by Adolf Böttger, and had originally thought of giving individual titles to the four movements, as follows (in translation): (1) *Spring's Coming,* (2) *Evening,* (3) *Merry Playmates,* (4) *Full Spring.* "They are like the many titles for his piano pieces that Schumann thought

of *after* the music had been written in order to explain their moods" (Brian Schlotel, in *Robert Schumann: The Man and His Music,* ed. Alan Walker, 1972). At first the work was nameless, and the orchestral parts were published as *Symphony in B flat.* The title was presumably withheld from the public because it might be misunderstood. "Rather than have the general public expect a work of programmatic scene-painting, Schumann preferred to let the buoyant mood of the Symphony speak for itself" (*ibid.*). Paine's Symphony No. 2 in A major also celebrates the spring. Britten's choral work, Op. 44, for soprano, alto, and tenor soloists, boys' choir, chorus, and orchestra, is a setting of 14 poems by different English poets, past and present, evoking the progress of winter to spring and the arrival of summer. It was inspired by the countryside of the composer's native county of Suffolk.

Squares   Erik Satie, 1969.

The plotless ballet in two parts, choreographed by Hans van Manen, is a display in which five plus five dancers relate to the various square forms, such as a platform, that define the space. The work was originally set to the composer's **Gymnopédies**, played first on the piano, then in an orchestrated version, but for copyright reasons was subsequently replaced by a somewhat similar score specially composed by Zoltan Szilassy.

ST/10–1, 080262   Iannis Xenakis, 1962.

The work for ten instruments is one of several examples of the composer's so called "stochastic" music, from a mathematical term for a theory of probability (Greek *stokhos,* "aim"). He applied the term to musical procedures whereby the general sound contours are fixed but the inner details are either left to chance or calculated mathematically by computer. This particular title breaks down as follows: *ST* for "stochastic," *10–1* for the first stochastic piece for ten instruments, *080262* for the date of the computer calculations, February 8, 1962.

Stabat Mater ("The Mother Was Standing").

The opening words of a devotional poem about the Virgin Mary's vigil by Christ's Cross, originally ascribed to the 13th-century Franciscan monk Jacopone da Todi: "*Stabat Mater dolorosa, / Iuxta crucem lacrimosa, / Dum pendebat filius*" ("The mournful Mother stood weeping by the cross where her son hung"). There are settings by many composers, including Palestrina, Pergolesi, Haydn, Rossini, Verdi, and later musicians. Virgil Thomson, for example, has a

Stabat Mater (1931) for soprano solo and string quartet set to a French text by Max Jacob, and Lennox Berkeley has one for six solo voices and 12 instruments (1947).

Stadler Quintet (German, *Stadler-Quintett*) W.A. Mozart, 1789.

The Clarinet Quintet in A major, K 581, was written for the Austrian clarinetist Anton Stadler (1753–1812) and is named for him. Some programs have misattributed the dedication to the Benedictine abbot and musical theorist, Maximilian Stadler (1748–1833).

Stages   Arne Nordheim and Bob Downes, 1971.

The ballet, a mixed media production with films and projections, is in two stages. The first stage depicts the world as the underworld, while the second portrays the ways that humans have reacted to the events and stories of the past, which have now become the subjects of modern movies and comics. "We are left solely with our humanity at whatever stage it may be" (program note, quoted in Koegler, p. 392). Nordheim wrote the music for Stage 1 and Downes that for Stage 2.

Ständchen (German, "Serenade").

The term implies a serenade performed *standing*, and moreover a brief one, since the word has the German diminutive ending *-chen*. There are various romantic songs and pieces of this title, such as Schubert's **Hark, Hark the Lark** and Richard Strauss's *Ständchen*, Op. 17 No. 2 (1887).

Stanford in B flat   Charles Villiers Stanford, 1879.

This is the standard designation for the composer's Church Service, Op. 10, still regularly in use among British church and cathedral choirs and elsewhere in the English-speaking world.

Star Clusters, Nebulae, and Places in Devon   David Bedford, 1971.

In the work for mixed double chorus and brass band, one half of the chorus sings the names of clusters and nebulae while the other repeats the syllables of Devon placenames. "The awesome message is that light now reaching Devon from visible stars had begun its journey when the only human life in Devon was that of Bronze Age settlements" (Burke, p. 140).

The Starlight Express   Edward Elgar, 1915.

The incidental music, Op. 78, was composed for Violet Pearn's play based on Algernon Blackwood's children's story *A Prisoner in Fairyland* (1913). This tells how the children of an English family living in the Jura mountains form a secret society in which each member is a star. They believe that while they are asleep their spirits play among the stars and collect stardust, which they store in a cave. Their aim is to get their parents out of their bodies and into a star cave, and they are helped by Cousin Henry and figures from his own childhood, whom he brings in the Starlight Express, a train of thought.

Stars and Stripes   John Philip Sousa, 1958.

The ballet in five "campaigns," choreographed by George Balanchine and set to the composer's **Stars and Stripes Forever**, is "a kind of balletic parade led by four 'regiments.' The five campaigns or movements feature each regiment in turn and at the end they all combine" (Balanchine, quoted by Koegler, p. 393).

The Stars and Stripes Forever   John Philip Sousa, 1896.

The march is effectively a musical and also a military glorification of the Stars and Stripes, the flag of the United States.

The Stations of the Sun   Julian Anderson, 1998.

The orchestral work evokes the varying positions of the sun at different times and in different seasons. Hence the title, which perhaps intentionally suggests an allusion to the Stations of the Cross.

Stepan Razin   Alexander Kasyanov, 1939.

The opera in four acts, to a libretto by Nikolai Biryukov, centers on the Cossack hetman (head), Stepan (usually known as Stenka) Razin (*c*.1630–1671), leader of a rebellion on Russia's southeastern frontier in 1670–1.

Sternklang ("Starsound")   Karlheinz Stockhausen, 1971.

The work is for five electronic ensembles set up in a park at dusk and communicating with one another by means of musical messages sent through the air and by runner. The title evokes the time of day and the ethereal sound.

Stiffelio   Giuseppe Verdi, 1850.

The opera in three acts is set to a libretto by Francesco Maria Piave based on Émile Souvestre and Eugène Bourgeois's play *Le Pasteur, ou L'Évangile et le Foyer* ("The Pastor, or The Gospel and the Hearth") (1849). The story is set in early

19th-century Germany and tells what happens when the evangelical pastor, Stiffelio, returns home to discover that his wife, Lina, has been unfaithful. *See also* **Aroldo.**

The Still Point   Claude Debussy, 1955.

The ballet in one act, choreographed by Todd Bolender, is based on the first three movements of the composer's String Quartet (1893) and tells of the unhappiness of a young girl, who always feels rejected by her friends until she finds mutual love with a boy. She is then "at the still point of the turning world" (T.S. Eliot, *Four Quartets: East Coker*, 1940).

Stimmen... Verstummen... ("Voices... Fall Silent...")   Sofia Gubaidulina, 1986.

The symphony in 12 movements comprises a series of calm or silent episodes broken by restless chromatic passages. The ninth movement is also completely silent. Hence the title.

Stimmung ("Tuning," "Mood")   Karlheinz Stockhausen, 1968.

The work is for six unaccompanied singers who use Asian vocal techniques and electronic amplification to project the natural harmonics of a low B flat while chanting different "magic words," mainly the names of American and eastern divinities. This operation is the "tuning" and in turn creates an effect that is the "mood." A 1972 ballet in one act of the same name, choreographed by Maurice Béjart, is set to this work.

Stolen Happiness (Russian, *Ukradennoye schast'ye*)   Yuly Meytus, 1960.

The opera in three acts is set to a libretto by Maxim Rylsky based on Ivan Franko's play of the same name (1891). The story tells how Mikhaylo Gurman returns to his native village after a long absence only to find that the girl he loves, Anna, has married another. He accordingly determines to recover his "stolen happiness," her love.

Stone Angels   Paul Barker, 1998.

The children's opera, to the composer's own libretto, is written for a cast of 26 young girls and tells what happens when survivors of an air crash on an island off Greece encounter two groups of girls: the aggressive Stoners, who attack with stones, and the peaceful Glooks. The title reflects both groups and perhaps intentionally suggests "Stone Agers." It also evokes the "heavy-light," "earthbound-airborne" type of title, such as Led Zeppelin, Iron Butterfly, favored by rock groups. (Literally, of course, stone angels are angels carved in stone.)

The Stone Flower (Russian, *Kamennyy tsvetok*)   Sergey Prokofiev, 1948–53.

The ballet in a prologue and three acts, with a libretto by Mira Mendelson-Prokofieva and Leonid Lavrovsky and choreographed by the latter, is based on fairy tales from the Urals, collected by Pavel Petrovich Bazhov under the title of *The Malachite Casket* (1939). According to Yuri Grigorovich, who choreographed the 1957 production, it "tells of the fate of the stone carver Danila who wishes to see the full power of stone and show its beauty to the people. The creative urge which possesses Danila and the desire to create more perfect art is the leitmotif of the ballet" (quoted in Koegler, p. 394).

The Stone Guest (Russian, *Kamennyy gost'*)   Alexander Dargomyzhsky, 1872.

The opera in three acts is a setting of Alexander Pushkin's play of the same name (1830) based on the same story as **Don Giovanni.** The "stone guest" of the title is thus the statue of Donna Anna's dead father, the Commander (Commendatore), that is invited to dinner at Donna Anna's house by Don Juan and that drags him down to hell.

Stone Litany   Peter Maxwell Davies, 1973.

The work for mezzosoprano and orchestra was inspired by the Viking runes scratched in the walls of the prehistoric chieftain's grave of Maes Howe in Orkney, Scotland. The subtitle is accordingly *Runes for a House of the Dead.*

The Story of a Real Man (Russian, *Povest' o nastoyashchem cheloveke*)   Sergey Prokofiev, 1948.

The opera in four acts, Op. 117, is set to a libretto by the composer and Mira Mendelson-Prokofieva based on Boris Polevoy's novel of the same title (1946). This tells how the aviator, Aleksei, is shot down in a Russian forest in 1942 and wanders for 18 days before being found. He is taken to hospital, has both feet amputated, and is horrified to think he will never fly again. The Commandant tells him of another aviator who flew after similar injuries and Aleksei vows to do the same. He eventually does, as a "real man."

La Straniera ("The Foreign Woman")   Vicenzo Bellini, 1829.

The opera in two acts is set to a libretto by Felice Romani based on Victor-Charles Prévôt, Vicomte d'Arlincourt's novel *L'Étrangère* ("The Foreign Woman") (1825). The plot is set in 14th-century Brittany and tells how Arturo, engaged to Isoletta, falls in love with the stranger, Alaide, whom some believe to be a witch.

La Stravaganza ("The Extravagance") Antonio Vivaldi, *c.*1714.

The 12 violin concertos, Op. 4, are presumably so named because they were regarded as unusual or at any rate "different" in some way. Blom defines *stravaganza* as " a word sometimes used for a composition of a freakish nature" (p. 580).

Street Games Jacques Ibert, 1952.

The ballet in one act, with a libretto and choreography by Walter Gore, is set on a wharfside near Blackfriars Bridge, London, where children skip, play hopscotch, write on the wall, and generally enjoy the street games of the title.

Street Scene Kurt Weill, 1946.

The opera in two acts is set to a libretto by Elmer Rice based on his own play of the same name (1929) telling of everyday life in a New York tenement and what it leads to.

A Streetcar Named Desire Alex North arr. Rayburn Wright, 1952.

The ballet in one act, with a libretto and choreography by Valerie Bettis, is fairly closely based on the plot of Tennessee Williams's play of the same name (1947), centering on the faded Southern belle, Blanche DuBois, and her dreams of a life of romantic gentility.

"Stride la vampa" ("The blaze crackles").

Azucena's aria in Act 2 of Verdi's Il **Trovatore**, in which she stares at the fire and recalls her mother's death at the stake and cry for revenge.

The Stubborn Lovers (Czech, *Tvrdé palice*) Antonín Dvořák, 1874.

The comic opera in one act, Op. 17, to a libretto by Josef Štolba, tells the story of two lovers who marry despite the disapproval of their parents. The Czech title literally translates as "The Rigid Pigheaded Ones," and does not mention lovers as such.

Study Symphony Anton Bruckner, 1863.

The Symphony in F minor was intended by the composer to be a study in orchestration and composition. Hence its name. It is also known as *Symphony No. 00* as it precedes **Symphony No. 0**.

Der Sturm ("The Storm") Frank Martin, 1956.

The opera in three acts is a virtually verba-

tim setting of August von Schlegel's German translation of Shakespeare's romantic drama *The Tempest* (1611). *See* The **Tempest**.

Sudden Time George Benjamin, 1993.

The orchestral work takes its title from a line in a poem by Wallace Stevens: "It was like sudden time in a world without time." The work aims to represent a sense of time simultaneously condensed and extended.

"Suicidio!" ("Suicide!").

La Gioconda's dramatic monologue in Act 4 of Ponchielli's La **Gioconda**, in which she contemplates suicide.

Suite (French, "Following").

The term originally applied to a piece of instrumental music in several movements, usually in the style of a dance. It was superseded by the **Sonata** and the **Symphony**, and came to be used for works of a lighter type, such as Grieg's **Holberg Suite** and Elgar's two suites The **Wand of Youth**. Stravinsky revived the earlier sense in his *Suites* for small orchestra, No. 1 (1917–25) and No. 2 (1921).

Suite bergamasque ("Bergomask Suite") Claude Debussy, 1890.

The work for piano is in four movements: *Prélude*, *Menuet*, **Clair de lune**, and *Passepied*. The title appears to allude generally to the dances that form the basis of the second and fourth movements. A bergomask (French *bergamasque*, Italian *bergamasca*) is properly a peasant's dance from Bergamo, Italy. According to Kennedy (1996), Debussy used the term in the title "with little significance" (p. 68).

Suite en blanc ("Suite in White") Édouard Lalo, 1943.

The ballet in one act, choreographed by Serge Lifar, is a display piece set to a **Suite** from the composer's **Namouna**.

Suite No. 3 Pyotr Tchaikovsky, 1970.

The plotless ballet in four movements, choreographed by George Balanchine, adds the first three movements of the composer's Suite No. 3 in G, Op. 55 (1884), to the **Theme and Variations** (fourth movement) already choreographed by Balanchine for an earlier ballet.

Suite provençale ("Provençal Suite") Darius Milhaud, 1937.

The orchestral work, Op. 152b, is based on the composer's incidental music (Op. 152a) for Valmy's play *Bertrand de Born* (1936), on the

13th-century French troubadour of this name, and that (Op. 152c) for André Obey's play *Le Trompeur de Séville* ("The Rogue of Seville") (1937), a version of the **Don Juan** story. The title relates partly to these (Bertran de Born produced some of the best poems in Provençal literature) and partly to Milhaud's own native Provence. *Cf.* Le **Carnaval d'Aix**.

Summer Night on the River   Frederick Delius, 1911.

The orchestral work, the second of the composer's two *Mood Pictures* for small orchestra, has a generally evocative title designed to describe the particular "mood picture" depicted. The first of the two pieces is **On Hearing the First Cuckoo in Spring**.

Summer's Last Will and Testament
Constant Lambert, 1936.

The work for solo baritone, chorus, and orchestra, is a setting of five lyrics from Thomas Nashe's play of the same name (1600), an allegorical pageant in which Summer, personified as a dying man, decides to whom to leave his riches.

Summerspace   Morton Feldman, 1958.

The plotless ballet for six dancers, choreographed by Merce Cunningham, has a title that is simply evocative of warmth and freedom.

"Summertime."

Clara's lazy lullaby to her baby in Act 1 of Gershwin's **Porgy and Bess**. The opening words, "Summertime, and the living is easy," are as popularly known as the melody.

Sun Quartets (German, *Sonnenquartette*)
Joseph Haydn, 1772.

The six string quartets Op. 20, Nos. 31 in E flat major, 32 in C major, 33 in G minor, 34 in D major, 35 in F minor, and 36 in A major, were so nicknamed for the image of the sun engraved on the 1779 edition published by J.J. Hummel.

"Suoni la tromba" ("Sound the trumpet").

The duet between Riccardo (Sir Richard) and Giorgio (Sir George) in Act 2 of Bellini's I **Puritani**, in which they announce their readiness to meet Arthur in battle and avenge Elvira.

Suor Angelica ("Sister Angelica")   Giacomo Puccini, 1917.

The opera in one act, to a libretto by Giovacchino Forzano, is the second panel (part) of Il **Trittico**. It is set in a Tuscan convent in the late 17th century where Sister Angelica has been forced to take the veil after giving birth to a son out of wedlock.

Surprise Symphony (German, *Sinfonie mit dem Paukenschlag*, "Symphony with the Drumstroke")   Joseph Haydn, 1791.

The Symphony No. 94 in G major is so called because of the sudden loud chord, reinforced by a drumbeat, that comes in the slow movement. The composer is said to have commented, "That will make the ladies jump" (quoted in Blom, p. 585). The German title sometimes leads to confusion with the **Drumroll Symphony**, known in German as the *Paukenwirbel*.

A Survivor from Warsaw   Arnold Schoenberg, 1947.

The cantata for narrator, male chorus, and orchestra, Op. 46, with English text by the composer, was written in response to the testimonies of Jewish survivors of Nazi concentration camp atrocities.

Susannah   Carlisle Floyd, 1955.

The opera in two acts is set to the composer's own libretto based on the story in the Apocrypha of Susannah, a beautiful woman whose bath was observed by two lustful elders who accused her of adultery when she repelled their advances. The story is translated to Tennessee, and tells what happens when the local elders consider Susannah wanton for bathing in public and the itinerant evangelist, Blitch, tries to convert her.

Susanna's Secret *see* Il **Segreto di Susanna**.

Svetlana   Dmitry Klebanov, 1939.

The ballet in a prologue and three acts, choreographed by Alexander Radunsky, Lev Pospekhin, and Nikolai Popko, tells of Svetlana, a forester's daughter, who lives in the remote taiga and who sets her own house on fire in order to inform the frontier guards that a saboteur is active in the neighborhood.

Swan Lake (Russian, *Lebedinoye ozero*)
Pyotr Tchaikovsky, 1875–6.

The ballet in four acts, with a libretto by Vladimir Begichev and Vasily Geltser and choreography by Wenzel Reisinger, is based on motives from Johann Karl August Musäus's story *Der geraubte Schleier* ("The Stolen Veil") in his collection *Volksmärchen der Deutschen* ("Folktales of the Germans") (1782). The story centers on Princess Odette, who is turned into a swan by the magician, Robart, and who lives with her companions on the lake named for her. The ballet is also known by its equivalent French title, *Le Lac des cygnes*.

The Swan of Tuonela (Finnish, *Tuonelan joutsen*) Jean Sibelius, 1893.

The symphonic legend, Op. 22, No. 3, was composed as a prelude to an unfinished opera, *The Building of the Boat* (Finnish, *Veenen luominen*) (1893), but was published as the third movement of the **Lemminkäinen Legends**, itself based on the Finnish epic, *Kalevala*. Tuonela is the Finnish Hades, and the swan glides on the black river that surrounds it.

Sweeney Todd Malcolm Arnold, 1959.

The ballet in one act, with a libretto and choreography by John Cranko, is based on George Dubdin Pitt's melodrama *The Demon Barber of Fleet Street* (1847), about Sweeney Todd, a "demon barber" who slits his customers's throats and disposes of their bodies by having them made into meat pies.

Sweet Remembrance *see* Lieder ohne Worte.

La Sylphide ("The Sylph") Jean-Madeleine Schneitzhoeffer, 1832.

The ballet in two acts, with a libretto by Adolphe Nourrit and choreography by Filippo Taglioni, is based on Charles Nodier's story *Trilby, ou le Lutin d'Argail* ("Trilby, or The Imp of Argyll") (1822), set in Scotland. The plot tells what happens when the young farmer, James, is visited by the Sylph on the eve of his marriage to Effie and abandons his bride to follow her to the woods.

Les Sylphides ("The Sylphs") Fryderyk Chopin, 1907.

The ballet in one act was originally titled *Chopiniana*, for the composer of its music, and retains this name in Russia today (*Shopeniana*). It is choreographed by Mikhail Fokine and is a purely romantic work, with no actual plot. The "sylphs" are thus the dancers, so named for the spirits of the air in Germanic mythology.

Sylvia Léo Delibes, 1876.

The ballet in three acts, with a libretto by Jules Barbier and Baron de Reinach and choreography by Louis Mérante, is subtitled *La Nymphe de Diane* ("The Nymph of Diana") and tells of the love of the shepherd, Amyntas, for Sylvia, a nymph of Diana.

Symphonia armonie celestium revelationum ("Symphony of the harmony of heavenly revelations") Hildegard of Bingen, 1150s.

The choral work is a collection of the German abbess's 77 liturgical songs in the form of lyrical poems set to her own music. By "Symphony" she meant not only a harmonious combination of different sounds but also the divine harmony of the cosmos.

Symphonia domestica ("Domestic Symphony") Richard Strauss, 1902–3.

The orchestral work, Op.53, depicts a day in the life of the composer's family, with themes representing Strauss himself, his wife, Pauline, and their baby son. The title was given by the composer, and is thus not the Italian equivalent, *Sinfonia domestica*, as sometimes seen.

Symphonic Dances (Russian, *Simfonicheskiye tantsy*) Sergey Rachmaninov, 1940.

The orchestral work, Op. 45, consists of three movements inspired by the dance. Hence the title.

Symphonic Metamorphoses on Themes of Carl Maria von Weber Paul Hindemith, 1943.

The orchestral work originated in sketches (1940) for a ballet for Léonide Massine on themes from Weber, using the overture to **Turandot**. The final work in four movements uses themes as follows: (1) No. 4 of *Eight Pieces* for piano duet (1818–19), (2) (*Turandot Scherzo*) the theme from the overture mentioned (1809), (3) No. 2 of *Six Petites Pièces faciles* ("Six Easy Little Pieces") for piano duet (1801), (4) No. 7 of *Eight Pieces* for piano duet (1818–19).

Symphonic Variations César Franck, 1946.

The plotless ballet in one act, choreographed by Frederick Ashton, is set to the composer's *Variations symphoniques* for Piano and Orchestra (1885), with the six dancers reflecting the general flow and mood of the music.

Symphonie concertante ("Sinfonia Concertante") W.A. Mozart, 1947.

The plotless ballet in three movements, choreographed by George Balanchine, is set to the composer's **Sinfonia Concertante** in E flat major for Violin and Viola, K 364 (1779), with the dancers following the form and mood of the music.

Symphonie espagnole ("Spanish Symphony") Édouard Lalo, 1874.

The work for violin and orchestra, Op. 21, a violin concerto in all but name, contains Spanish themes and was composed for the Spanish violinist Pablo de Sarasate, who was the first to play it (1875).

Symphonie fantastique ("Fantastic Symphony") Hector Berlioz, 1830.

The Symphony No. 14 is subtitled *Épisode de la vie d'un artiste* ("Episode in the Life of an Artist") and was inspired by the composer's unrequited love for the Irish actress, Harriet Smithson. The background story concerns a young musician with a vivid imagination who has poisoned himself with opium in a fit of lovesick despair. The "fantastic" visions he has form the program of the symphony, with its five movements titled as follows: (1) *Rêveries, passions* ("Reveries, Passions"), (2) *Un bal* ("A Ball"), (3) *Scène aux champs* ("Scene in the Fields"), (4) *Marche au supplice* ("March to the Scaffold"), (5) *Songe d'une nuit du Sabbat* ("Dream of a Witches's Sabbath"). The 1936 ballet in five scenes of the same name has a libretto based on the original and is choreographed by Léonide Massine.

Symphonie funèbre et triomphale ("Funereal and Triumphal Symphony") Hector Berlioz, 1840.

The Symphony No. 2, Op. 15, sometimes known as *Grande Symphonie funèbre et triomphale* ("Grand Funereal and Triumphal Symphony"), was commissioned by the French government to mark the tenth anniversary of the 1830 July Revolution. It was originally scored for a large military band and played out of doors.

Symphonie gothique Charles-Marie Widor, 1895.

The Symphony No. 9 for Organ in C major, Op. 70, is intended as a musical depiction of the Gothic style of architecture. Hence the title.

Symphonie inachevée *see* **Unfinished Symphony**.

Symphonie pour un homme seul ("Symphony for a Lonely Man") Pierre Henry and Pierre Schaeffer, 1955.

The ballet in one act, choreographed by Maurice Béjart, centers on "a modern man trapped between technology and sex, manipulated by anonymous forces, and trying in vain to escape" (Koegler, p. 403).

Symphonie sur un chant montagnard français ("Symphony on a French Mountain Air") Vincent d'Indy, 1886.

The work for piano and orchestra, Op. 25, is subtitled *Symphonie cévenole* ("Cévennes Symphony"), indicating that the theme which inspired it came from these mountains in southern France.

Symphonies of Wind Instruments Igor Stravinsky, 1918–20.

The composer wrote the work for woodwind and brass as a memorial to Debussy and explained that the "symphonies" of the title was to be understood in its etymological sense of "soundings together." The composition is thus not at all symphonic in the modern sense but consists of a number of short "litanies" for different groups of instruments.

Symphony Dmitri Shostakovich, 1963.

The plotless ballet in four movements, choreographed by Kenneth MacMillan, is set to the composer's Symphony No. 1 in F minor, Op. 10 (1924–5), with the dancers reflecting the emotional tensions of the music. In the 17th and 18th centuries, a *symphony* (from the Greek meaning "sounding together"), now usually called a *sinfonia*, the equivalent Italian word, was what would now be known as an **Overture**, in other words a short piece introducing an opera. It was also an orchestral interlude, like Handel's **Pastoral Symphony** (1). As now used, a symphony is a large-scale orchestral work usually in four movements, otherwise effectively a **Sonata** for orchestra. Some of the works titled *Symphony* below, or *Symphonia* or *Symphonie* above, will not conform to any of these three types, however.

A Symphony for Fun Don Gillis, 1946–7.

The Symphony No. 5½ (*sic*) was so numbered because it was written while the composer was "marking time" between Symphonies No. 5 (1944–5) and No. 6 (1947). It was so named because it was a deliberate diversion. Its four movements have "fun" subtitles: *Perpetual Emotion*, *Spiritual?*, *Scherzofrenia*, and *Conclusion!*

Symphony in C (1) Igor Stravinsky, 1938–40; (2) Georges Bizet, 1947.

Stravinsky's Symphony in C major has a title that suggests a standard classical composition. But is it? "The title provokes two questions: 'symphony in what sense?' and 'in C in what sense?' As to the first, there are four separate movements ... which preserve much of the essential nature of traditional symphonic structure. The parallels between it and any symphony by Haydn, Beethoven or Tchaikovsky … are naturally not exact, but the differences are meaningful to no small degree because they are deviations from something approximating to a norm… As for the second question … the same kind of answer might suffice: not a classically functioning C major, but an unmistakable emphasis on a tonal and harmonic area associated with C as tonic. Here, too, there are 'deviations', however" (Whittall, pp. 60–1). There are no deviations from the classical norm in the symphony by Bizet (1855) that gave the title of George Balanchine's plotless ballet in four movements. A different team of dancers is used for each movement, with all teams finally combining in the fourth. The original title was *Le Palais de cristal* ("The Crystal Palace").

Symphony in Three Movements   Igor Stravinsky, 1942–5, 1972.

The work's title belies the varied nature of its three movements. The first movement incorporates the composer's sketches for an unfinished piano concerto, inspired by a film on China's "scorched earth" tactics. The second was written as film music to accompany the apparition of the Virgin Mary in the film *Song of Bernadette*. (This was not realized.) The third was the composer's response to wartime newsreels. George Balanchine's plotless ballet in three movements of the same name is set to this work, with the dancers interpreting the music in various asymmetrical patterns. *See also* **Symphony in C**.

Symphony 1933   Roy Harris, 1933.

The Symphony No. 1, as the composer's first, was named for the year of its composition. It was first performed on January 26, 1934.

Symphony No. 00 *see* **Study Symphony**.

Symphony No. 0 (German, *Die Nullte*) Anton Bruckner, 1863–4.

The Symphony in D minor was composed two years before the Symphony No. 1 in C minor (1865–6). Hence its unusual numeration, given by the composer. *Cf.* **Study Symphony**.

Symphony No. 5½ *see* **A Symphony for Fun**.

Symphony of a Thousand (German, *Sinfonie der Tausend*)   Gustav Mahler, 1907.

The Symphony No. 8 in E flat major is so named, somewhat misleadingly, for the vast vocal and instrumental forces needed to perform

it: three soprano soloists, two contralto, and one each tenor, baritone, and bass, double choir, boys' choir, orchestra, and organ. More than a thousand people did take part in the first performance (1910) but it is not necessary to use so many. The composer himself did not approve of the name.

A Symphony of Brotherhood   Jan Carlstedt, 1968–9.

The Symphony No. 2, Op. 25, was composed in homage to the U.S. clergyman and civil rights leader Martin Luther King, assassinated in 1968. Hence the title.

Symphony of Lamentation Songs   Henryk Górecki, 1976.

The Symphony No. 3 for soprano and orchestra, Op. 36, a vision of post–Holocaust humanity, bases its words on the Holy Cross lament and an inscription scratched on a cell wall by an 18-year-old girl imprisoned by the Nazis at Zakopane, in the Tatra Mountains. The work is also known as the *Symphony of Sorrowful Songs*.

Symphony of Psalms (French, *Symphonie des psaumes*)   Igor Stravinsky, 1930.

The work for chorus (and boy sopranos) and orchestra, in three movements, is set to a Latin text from Psalms 39, 40, and 150. The title is the composer's own. As he himself explained: "It is the singing of the Psalms that I am symphonizing" (quoted in Griffiths, p. 179). A 1978 ballet in one act of the same name, choreographed by Jiří Kylián, is a stark and formal interpretation of this work. It was originally produced in the Netherlands under the equivalent Dutch title, *Psalmensymfonie*.

Symphony of Sorrowful Songs *see* **Symphony of Lamentation Songs**.

Symphony on a French Mountain Air *see* **Symphonie sur un chant montagnard français**.

Symphony with a Bell (Russian, *Simfoniya s kolokolom*)   Aram Khachaturian, 1943.

The Symphony No. 2 in A minor is so named for the bell motif that runs through all its four movements, the bell here symbolizing patriotic fervor and victory in World War II.

Syrinx   Claude Debussy, 1913.

The work for solo flute (written for the French flutist, Louis Fleury, who gave its first performance) is named from the Greek word for the pan pipes, the instrument played by the mythical god Pan, half human, half goat.

T

Il Tabarro ("The Cloak")   Giacomo Puccini, 1913–16.

The opera in one act, to a libretto by Giuseppe Adami based on Didier Gold's tragedy *La Houppelande* ("The Cloak") (1910), is the first panel (part) of Il **Trittico**. The story tells how a Parisian bargee, Michele, discovering that a young stevedore, Luigi, is having an affair with his wife, Giorgetta, kills him and presents her with his body wrapped in his cloak.

"Tacea la notte placida" ("The calm night was still").

Leonora's aria in Act 1 of Verdi's Il **Trovatore**, in which she muses to Inez on the mysterious troubadour with whom she has fallen in love.

Tafelmusik ("Table Music")   Georg Philipp Telemann, 1733.

The work in three sections, each with six movements, for various groups of instruments, is "table music" in the sense that it is intended to be played at convivial gatherings at the table or after dinner. The term is generic for such music, whether sung or played. In Der **Rosenkavalier** the off-stage band in Act III is described to Baron Ochs as *Tafelmusik*.

The Tale of Czar Saltan (Russian, *Skazka o tsare Saltane*)   Nikolai Rimsky-Korsakov, 1900.

The opera in a prologue and four acts is set to a libretto by Vasily Ivanovich Belsky based on Alexander Pushkin's fairy-tale poem of the same title (1832) telling what happens when the sisters of Militrisa, wife of the Czar Saltan, cause her and her son, Prince Gvidon, to be set adrift in a cask. The full Russian title translates as *The Tale of Czar Saltan, of His Son, the Famous and Mighty Hero Prince Gvidon Saltanovich, and of the Beautiful Swan Princess. See also* The **Flight of the Bumble Bee**.

A Tale of Two Cities   Arthur Benjamin, 1949–50.

The opera in a prologue and three acts is set to a libretto by Cedric Cliffe based on Charles Dickens's novel (1859) of the same name about Paris and London (the "two cities" of the title) at the time of the French Revolution.

Tales from the Vienna Woods *see* **Geschichten aus dem Wienerwald**.

Tales of Hoffmann   (1) Jacques Offenbach, 1972; (2) *see* Les **Contes d'Hoffmann**.

The ballet in three acts, with a libretto and choreography by Peter Darrell, is set to the music of the composer's opera Les **Contes d'Hoffmann** and roughly follows its course.

Tallis Fantasia *see* **Fantasia on a Theme by Thomas Tallis**.

Tally-Ho!   Christoph Gluck arr. Mottl-Nordoff, 1944.

The ballet in one act, with a libretto and choreography by Agnes de Mille, is subtitled *The Frail Quarry* and is set in a French rococo park. The plot concerns a young wife who tries in vain to inspire the jealousy of her clever husband, who is absorbed in his books. The title alludes to the "chase" that she leads.

Tamara   Mily Balakirev, 1867–82.

The symphonic poem is based on Mikhail Lermontov's poem about the Georgian queen of this name who reigned from 1184 to 1207 and who is said to have disposed of her lovers by stabbing them and throwing their corpses from her turret into the waters below. *See also* **Thamar**.

Tamerlano ("Tamerlane")   George Frideric Handel, 1724.

The opera in three acts is set to a libretto by Nicola Francesco Haym adapted from the anonymous libretto *Bajazet* (1719), itself derived from Agostino Piovene's libretto *Tamerlano* (1711), with both based on Jacques Pradon's play *Tamerlan* (1695). The story is set in Bithinia in 1402 and tells what happens when the Tatar ruler, Tamerlano, has defeated and captured the Turkish emperor, Bajazet.

The Taming of the Shrew (1) Alessandro Scarlatti and Gerhard Stolze, 1969; (2) *see* Der **Widerspenstigen Zähmung**.

The ballet in two acts, with a libretto and choreography by John Cranko, roughly follows the plot of Shakespeare's play of the same name (1593), telling how Katharina (Kate), the "shrew" of the title, eventually becomes the submissive wife of the impoverished nobleman, Petruchio.

Tancredi ("Tancred")   Gioacchino Rossini, 1813.

The opera in two acts is set to a libretto by Gaetano Rossi based on Voltaire's tragedy *Tancrède* (1760) and Torquato Tasso's epic poem *Gerusalemme liberata* ("Jerusalem Delivered")

(1575). The plot is set in Syracuse and tells what happens when the Norman prince of Sicily, Tancred (died 1112), returns home from exile and prevents the marriage of his beloved, Amenaida, to his rival, Orbazzano.

Tannhäuser   Richard Wagner, 1845.

The opera in three acts is set to the composer's own libretto based on the German legend of the 13th-century minnesinger (minstrel-knight), Tannhäuser, who is torn between his all-consuming lust for Venus, queen of passion, and his aphysical love for the chaste virgin, Elisabeth, the Landgrave's daughter. The opera's full title is *Tannhäuser und der Sängerkrieg auf Wartburg* ("Tannhäuser and the Song Contest on the Wartburg"), the latter referring to the minstrels' contest for the hand of Elisabeth.

Der Tapfere Soldat *see* The **Chocolate Soldier**.

Tapiola   Jean Sibelius, 1925–6.

The title of the tone poem, Op. 112, is the old mythological name of Finland, deriving from the forest god, Tapio, who features in the Finnish epic, *Kalevala*.

Tarantella *see* **Lieder ohne Worte**.

Tarare   Antonio Salieri, 1787.

The opera in a prologue and five acts is set to a libretto by Pierre Augustin Caron de Beaumarchais based on a Persian tale. The story is set in Ormus, Persia, in 1680, and tells what happens when the popularity among his troops of the captain, Tarare, arouses the envy of King Atar.

Taras Bulba   (1) Leoš Janáček, 1915–18; (2) Nikolai Lysenko, 1924; (3) Vasily Soloviev-Sedoy, 1940.

Janáček's rhapsody for orchestra is based on Nikolay Gogol's story about the fictional Ukrainian Cossack leader of this name in his collection *Mirgorod* (1835). The work has three movements: (1) *Death of Andrea* (Czech, *Smrt Andrijova*), (2) *Death of Ostap* (Czech, *Smrt Ostapova*), (3) *Prophecy and Death of Taras Bulba* (Czech, *Proroctví a smrt Tarase Bulby*). Lysenko's opera in five acts, to a libretto by Mikhail Staritsky, and Soloviev-Sedoy's ballet in three acts, with a libretto by Semyon Kaplan and choreography by Fyodor Lopokov, are based on the same story.

The Taras Family (Russian, *Sem'ya Tarasa*) Dmitri Kabalevsky, 1947.

The opera in four acts, to a libretto by S. Tsenin, is based on Boris Gorbatov's novel *The Undefeated* (1943), about the fight against German occupying forces in Soviet Russia by the children of the worker, Taras, in World War II.

La Tarentule ("The Tarantula")   Casimir Gide, 1839.

The ballet in two acts (three scenes), with a libretto by Eugène Scribe and choreography by Jean Coralli, centers on the lovers, Luigi and Lauretta, and tells what happens when Luigi is bitten by a tarantula and Dr. Omeopatica says he will treat him only in return for Lauretta's hand.

Taverner   Peter Maxwell Davies, 1962–8.

The opera in two acts, to the composer's own libretto, is based on contemporary archive material regarding the life of the English composer, John Taverner (*c*.1490–1545).

Tel jour, telle nuit ("Such a Day, Such a Night")   Francis Poulenc, 1937.

The song cycle comprises settings of nine poems by Paul Éluard (1895–1952). Their titles are as follows: (1) *Bonne journée* ("Good day"), (2) *Une ruine coquille vide* ("The ruin of an empty shell"), (3) *Le Front comme un drapeau perdu* ("A brow like a lost flag"), (4) *Une roulotte couverte en tuiles* ("A caravan covered in tiles"), (5) *À toutes brides* ("Hell for leather"), (6) *Une herbe pauvre* ("A poor grass"), (7) *Je n'ai envie que de t'aimer* ("All I desire is to love thee"), (8) *Figure de force brûlante et farouche* ("Face of fiery and fierce strength"), (9) *Nous avons fait la nuit* ("We made the night").

Telemaco ("Telemachus")   Christoph Gluck, 1765.

The opera in two acts is set to a libretto by Marco Coltellini based on that for Alessandro Scarlatti's opera of the same name (1718), itself drawing on Homer's *Odyssey*. The story tells how Telemachus rescues his father, Ulysses (Odysseus), from his captivity on Circe's island.

Telemusik ("Telemusic")   Karlheinz Stockhausen, 1966.

The work is a tape piece that uses recordings of Japanese percussion instruments and snatches of music from around the world brought together by editing and intermodulation. "Tele-" here has its literal Greek sense of "far off," as in *telegraph* or *television*.

The Telephone   Gian-Carlo Menotti, 1947.

The opera in one act, to the composer's

own libretto, tells what happens when Ben visits Lucy on the eve of his departure to propose marriage but his attempts are constantly interrupted by the telephone ringing.

The Tempest   (1) Henry Purcell, 1695; (2) Ludwig van Beethoven, 1802; (3) (Russian, *Burya*) Pyotr Tchaikovsky, 1873; (4) Arthur Sullivan, 1862; (5) Arthur Bliss, 1920–1; (6) Jean Sibelius, 1925; (7) Arne Nordheim, 1979; (8) John C. Eaton, 1985.

Purcell's opera, to a libretto by Thomas Shadwell and John Dryden, Beethoven's Piano Sonata in D minor, Op. 31 No. 2, Tchaikovsky's symphonic fantasy, Op. 18, Sullivan's incidental music, Bliss's overture and interludes, Sibelius's incidental music, Op. 109, Nordheim's ballet in two parts, choreographed by Glen Tetley, and Eaton's opera, to a libretto by Andrew Porter, are all based on Shakespeare's play of the same name (1611), telling what happens when Prospero, duke of Milan, is ousted from his throne, turned adrift on the sea with his daughter, Miranda, and cast up on a lonely island. *See also* Der **Sturm**. (Beethoven's work is not officially so named, and there is even doubt regarding the statement by his biographer, Anton Schindler, that he said he took his inspiration from the play.)

Der Templer und die Jüdin ("The Templar and the Jewess")   Heinrich Marschner, 1829.

The opera in three acts is set to a libretto by Wilhelm August Wohlbrück based on Sir Walter Scott's novel *Ivanhoe* (1820) and Jakob Michael Reinhold Lenz's play *Das Gericht der Templer* ("The Court of the Templars") (1824). The story is set in York, England, in 1194 and tells what happens when the Norman Templars, De Bracy and Bois-Guilbert, meet in their pursuit of Rowena, ward of the Saxon, Cedric, and Rebecca, daughter of Isaac, the Jew of York. The "Templar and the Jewess" of the title are thus Bois-Guilbert and Rebecca.

Ten Days That Shook the World   Mark Karminsky, 1970.

The opera in a prologue and ten scenes is set to a libretto by V. Dubrovsky based on John Reed's book of the same name (1919), a graphic account of the Russian Revolution in Petrograd (St. Petersburg), with additions in the form of speeches and articles by Lenin. The ten scenes correspond to the ten days of the American writer's description, and have titles: (1) *Success!*, (2) *An End to War!*, (3) *Relentlessly On!*, (4) *Enemies*, (5) *Red Petrograd in Danger!*, (6) *Rebellion*, (7) *In the Smolny Institute* (the revolutionary headquarters), (8) *Funeral of the Reds*, (9) *Lenin's Sleepless Night*, (10) *The Revolution Continues!*

Ten Shulbrede Tunes   Hubert Parry, 1914.

The suite of ten pieces for piano is named for the family home, Shulbrede Priory, Sussex, of the composer's son-in-law, Arthur Ponsonby, who married his daughter, Dorothea, in 1898.

The Tender Land   Aaron Copland, 1952–4.

The opera in two acts, to a libretto by Horace Everett, is set in the American Midwest in the early 1950s. The story tells what happens when the farmer's daughter, Laurie Moss, graduates from high school and falls in love with the drifting farm hand, Martin.

The Tentacles of the Dark Nebula   David Bedford, 1969.

The work in three movements for tenor and instruments describes three stages in the life of a beach. In the first movement, a Neanderthal boy is the first human to set foot on a remote beach. In the second, a modern boy from a town plays on the beach in company with others. In the third, set in the future, a child visits the abandoned beach for the last time. The subject and title were inspired by Arthur C. Clarke's science fiction stories.

Teseo ("Theseus")   George Frideric Handel, 1713.

The opera in five acts is set to a libretto by Nicola Francesco Haym based on Philippe Quinault's libretto for Jean-Baptiste Lully's opera *Thésée* ("Theseus") (1675), centering on the exploits of the mythical Greek hero, Theseus.

Tess   Frédéric d'Erlanger, 1906.

The opera in four acts is set to a libretto by Luigi Illica based on Thomas Hardy's novel *Tess of the d'Urbervilles* (1891), telling of the tragic fate of the young country girl who is seduced and abandoned by d'Urberville.

Der Teufel ist Los ("The Devil to Pay")   Johann Standfuss, 1752.

The *Singspiel* (musical play) is set to a libretto by Christian Felix Weisse based on Charles Coffey's ballad opera of the same name (1731), itself adapted from Thomas Jevon's farce *The Devil of a Wife; or a Comical Transformation* (1686). The subtitle of Standfuss's work is *Die verwandelte Weiber* ("The Women Metamorphosed").

Thaïs   Jules Massenet, 1892–3.

The opera in three acts is set to a libretto by Louis Gallet based on Anatole France's novel of the same name (1890). The story is set in 4th-century Alexandria and tells what happens when the monk, Athanaël, resolves to rescue the beautiful courtesan, Thaïs, from her life of pleasure.

Thamar   Mily Balakirev, 1912.

The ballet in one act, with a libretto by Léon Bakst and choreography by Michel Fokine, is set to the composer's symphonic poem **Tamara** and tells the legendary story of this Georgian queen.

Thamos   W.A. Mozart, 1780.

The incidental music, K 345, was written for Tobias Philipp von Gebler's play of this name (1773), with full title *Thamos, König in Ägypten* ("Thamos, King of Egypt").

That Is the Show   Luciano Berio, 1971.

The ballet in five movements, choreographed by Norman Morrice, takes its title from the third movement of the composer's *Sinfonia* in four movements for eight voices and orchestra (1968–9). There is no continuous narrative, but the main theme, that of heroes and their womenfolk in fact and fiction, is suggested by the words and music of the score.

Theatre Piece   Wallingford Riegger, 1936.

The dance in eight parts, choreographed by Doris Humphrey, is the centerpiece of a trilogy, the others being *New Dance* and **With My Red Fires**. The group work for 19 dancers depicts the modern world as place of fierce competition. "Miss Humphrey has called it *Theatre Piece* to stress the fact that, even though this savage competition is dominant at the present time, it is far from being the whole of life. It distorts and kills too much of life that is good and erects symbols and numbers and figures in place of human values" (Doris Humphrey papers, quoted in Koegler, p. 414).

Theme and Variations   Pyotr Tchaikovsky, 1947.

The plotless ballet in one act, choreographed by George Balanchine, is set to the last movement of the composer's Suite for Orchestra No. 3 in G major, Op. 55 (1884), which bears this title and is frequently performed separately. Balanchine subsequently added the first three movements to create **Suite No. 3**.

Theodora   George Frideric Handel, 1750.

The oratorio is set to a text by Thomas Morell based on Roger Boyle's romance *The Martyrdom of Theodora and Didymus.*

There Is a Time   Norman Dello Joio, 1956.

The ballet in one act, choreographed by José Limón, bases its title on words from the Old Testament: "To every thing there is a season, and a time to every purpose under the heaven" (Ecclesiastes 3:1).

There Was a Time   Brian Hodgson, 1973.

The ballet in one act, choreographed by Christopher Bruce, takes its theme and title from Homer's *Iliad*: "There was a time when the countless tribes of men, though wide-dispersed, oppressed the surface of the deep-bosomed earth, and Zeus saw it and had pity and in his wise heart resolved to relieve the all-nurturing earth of men by causing the great struggle of the Ilian war, that the load of death might empty the world" (quoted in Koegler, p. 414).

Thérèse   Jules Massenet, 1907.

The opera in two acts, to a libretto by Jules Claretie, is set in Versailles and Paris in the late 18th century and tells what happens when the aristocratic soldier, Armand de Clerval, longs to return to his family home, owned by André Thorel, who hopes to return it to him one day but who is unaware that his wife, Thérèse, is Armand's former lover.

Theresienmesse ("Theresa Mass")   Joseph Haydn, 1799.

The Mass No. 10 in B flat major is said to be named for Maria Theresa (Marie-Thérèse) (1717–1780), wife of Francis II, emperor of Austria. This seems unlikely, however, as she had died almost 20 years earlier.

These Things Shall Be   John Ireland, 1936–7.

The cantata for baritone (or tenor) solo, chorus, and orchestra, is set to words from a hymn by John Addington Symonds (1840–1893) containing the lines: "These things shall be! A loftier race / Than e'er the world hath known shall rise."

Thesis   Henry Cowell, 1962.

The Symphony No. 15, more a suite of brief movements than a symphony proper, is presumably named for its "statement" of some kind, a thesis being a formal proposition.

Thespis   Arthur Sullivan, 1871.

The operetta, to a libretto by W.A. Gilbert,

has the subtitle *The Gods Grown Old* and tells of the mythical Greek actor Thespis (who gave the word *thespian*) and his troupe who take over the duties of the gods on Mount Olympus to enable them to have a holiday.

The Thieving Magpie *see* La **Gazza ladra**.

Third Symphony by Gustav Mahler (German, *Dritte Sinfonie von Gustav Mahler*) Gustav Mahler, 1975.

The ballet in six movements, choreographed by John Neumeier, has no actual plot but reflects the contents of the composer's Symphony No. 3 in D minor for contralto, women's and boys' choruses, and orchestra (1895–6). Neumeier retitled the six movements as follows: (1) *Yesterday*, (2) *Summer*, (3) *Autumn*, (4) *Night*, (5) *Angel*, and (6) *What Love Tells Me*. "It shows Man's inextinguishable desire for beauty and the ideal in a world falling to pieces" (Koegler, p. 414). *Cf.* **Ce que l'amour me dit**.

This Have I Done for my True Love Gustav Holst, 1916.

The work for unaccompanied chorus, Op. 34 No. 1, is a setting of a traditional carol.

Thomas and Sally Thomas Arne, 1760.

The opera in three acts, to a libretto by Isaac Bickerstaffe, tells what happens when Sally pines for her absent sailor husband, Thomas. The subtitle, *The Sailor's Return*, implies that all ends happily.

The Three-Cornered Hat *see* El **Sombrero de tres picos**.

3 Epitaphs Laneville-Johnson Union Brass Band, 1956.

The ballet for five dancers, choreographed by Paul Taylor, depicts the macabre antics of dancers in black costumes with tiny mirrors that cover their whole faces and bodies. The title is purely evocative. The work was originally created in 1953 with the title *Four Epitaphs*.

The Three Fat Men (Russian, *Tri tolstyaka*) V.A. Oransky, 1935.

The ballet in four acts (eight scenes), with a libretto by Yuri Olesha and choreography by Igor Moiseyev, centers on three capitalists. The story tells what happens when they throw the revolutionary, Prospero, into prison.

Three London Pieces John Ireland, 1917–20.

The three piano pieces depict different parts of London and are based on the composer's personal observation. The first is *Chelsea Reach*, evoking the slow tide of the Thames at this point. The second is *Ragamuffin*, written after hearing a scruffy young lad whistling as he walked down the street. The third is *Soho Forenoons*, suggesting the street buskers and gossiping shopkeepers of this district.

The Three Musketeers Georges Delerue, 1966.

The ballet in two acts, with a libretto and choreography by Flemming Flindt, is based on Alexandre Dumas's novel *Les Trois Mousquetaires* ("The Three Musketeers") (1844), telling of the adventures of the young Gascon, D'Artagnan, and his three comrades, Athos, Aramis, and Porthos. The ballet was originally produced in Copenhagen under the equivalent Danish title, *De tre Musketerer*.

The Three Mysteries Paul Creston, 1950.

The Symphony No. 3, Op. 48, is based on the life of Christ and has a title made explicit by the subtitles of the three movements: *The Nativity*, *The Crucifixion*, and *The Resurrection*.

Three Places in New England Charles Ives, 1908–14, orchestra

The orchestral work, also known as the *First Orchestral Set* or *A New England Symphony*, is in three movements. The first, *Boston Common*, with full title *The "Saint-Gaudens" on Boston Common: Colonel Shaw and His Colored Regiment*, is a slow meditation on the monument by Augustus Saint-Gaudens on Boston Common, Boston, Massachusetts, to Robert G. Shaw (1837–1863), colonel of the 54th Massachusetts Regiment, a regiment of colored troops, killed at Ft. Wagner, South Carolina, in the Revolutionary War. The second, *Putnam's Camp*, has a full title *Putnam's Camp, Redding, Connecticut*, the camp itself named for General Israel Putnam (1718–1790), the Revolutionary hero, who had his winter quarters here in 1778–9. The movement is an impression of a young boy leaving a Fourth of July picnic to have a vision of another incident from the Revoluionary War. The third, *The Housatonic at Stockbridge*, is named for the Housatonic River at Stockbridge, Massachusetts, where the composer walked with his wife, and is a slow winding of string music in dense harmony. These are thus the "three places in New England."

Three Screaming Popes Mark-Anthony Turnage, 1988–9.

The work for orchestra is based on Francis Bacon's series of paintings known as *The Screaming Popes* (1949–mid–1950s), one of which is based on Diego Velázquez's portrait of Pope Innocent X.

Three Virgins and a Devil   Ottorino Respighi, 1941.

The ballet in one act, with a libretto by Ramon Reed and choreography by Agnes de Mille, tells how the Devil tricks the Priggish One, the Greedy One, and the Lustful One (the "three virgins" of the title) into going into hell.

The Threepenny Opera *see* Die Dreigroschenoper.

Threni   Igor Stravinsky, 1957–8.

The choral work for soloists, chorus, and orchestra has the full Latin title *Threni: id est Lamentationes Jeremiae Prophetae* ("Threnodies: that is to say, the Lamentations of Jeremiah the Prophet"), and is set to a text from the Old Testament book so named, lamenting the destruction of Jerusalem. *Threni* itself is the Latin plural form of Greek *threnos*, "lament."

Threnody for the Victims of Hiroshima (Polish, *Tren pamieci ofiarom Hiroszimy*) Krzysztof Penderecki, 1960.

The work for 52 stringed instruments is a memorial to those who perished in Hiroshima, Japan, following the dropping of an atomic bomb on that city by the U.S. Army Air Forces on August 6, 1945. A threnody (Greek *threnos*, "wailing") is a song of lamentation.

Thus Spake Zarathustra *see* Also sprach Zarathustra.

Tiefland ("Lowland")   Eugen d'Albert, 1903.

The opera in a prologue and three acts is set to a libretto by Rudolf Lothar (pen name of Rudolph Spitzer) based on Ángel Guimerá's Catalan play *Terra baixa* ("Lowland") (1896). The story is set in the Pyrenees in the 19th century and tells what happens when the wealthy landowner, Sebastiano, marries off his mistress, Marta, to a young shepherd, Pedro, on condition he abandon his mountain life for the lowlands.

Tierkreis ("Zodiac")   Karlheinz Stockhausen, 1975–7.

The work is a set of 12 melodies, one for each sign of the zodiac. They were originally written for music boxes, but have also been published in various instrumental and vocal arrangements. The latter set the composer's own texts describing the attributes of each sign.

Till Eulenspiegel   Richard Strauss, 1894–5.

The tone poem, Op. 28, has the full title *Till Eulenspiegels lustige Streiche, nach alter Schelmenweise — in Rondeauform — für grosses Orchester gesetzt* ("Till Eulenspiegel's Merry Pranks, after an Old Rogue's Tune — in Rondo Form — Set for Full Orchestra"). The work was originally to have been an opera based on a 16th-century account of the German legend of the wily peasant, Till Eulenspiegel, who plays a number of tricks and vulgar practical jokes on tradespeople, priests, nobles, and in particular innkeepers. Till Eulenspiegel was usually known as Tyll Owlglass in English accounts of his capers.

Tilt   Igor Stravinsky,1971.

The ballet in two parts, choreographed by Hans van Manen, is set to the composer's Concerto in D for strings (1946) and is a purely formal work for three couples. It is performed twice, but the second time with the male and female dancers exchanging parts. Hence the title, alluding to a challenge or duel.

Time Off? Not a Ghost of a Chance! Elisabeth Lutyens, 1967–8.

The opera or "charade in four scenes with three interruptions," Op. 68, set to her own libretto, is the composer's tongue-in-cheek expression of her crowded creative life.

Time Out of Mind   Paul Creston, 1963.

The ballet in one act, choreographed by Brian MacDonald, portrays a modern fertility rite in which man's primitive instincts are released. The title takes the conventional sense of the phrase meaning "from time immemorial" and puns on it to allude to the expression of an latent force that normally remains hidden in the mind.

Tintagel   Arnold Bax, 1917–19.

The orchestral tone poem takes its name and inspiration from the coastal village of Tintagel, Cornwall, England, which has legendary connections with King Arthur. The composer explained: "The work is intended to evoke a tone-picture of the castle-crowned cliff of Tintagel, and more particularly, the wide distances of the Atlantic as seen from the cliffs of Cornwall on a sunny but not windless day" (quoted in Nicholas, p. 67).

Tiresias   Constant Lambert, 1950.

The ballet in three scenes, with a libretto by the composer and choreography by Frederick Ashton, depicts the double life of the mythical blind prophet as man and woman. He is struck blind by Hera when he proves her wrong in her argument with Zeus that a man's life is happier than a woman's, whereupon Zeus confers on him the gift of prophecy. *See also* Les **Mamelles de Tirésias**.

Titan Symphony (German, *Titan*)   Gustav Mahler, 1884–8.

The Symphony No. 1 in D major in four movements was originally so called by the composer after Jean Paul's four-volume, 35-chapter *Bildungsroman* of the same name (1800–3). (Jean Paul was the pseudonym of Johann Paul Friedrich Richter.) The symphony has little to do with the book, however, and the title was apparently chosen simply because it seemed apt. The two parts of the work, whose theme is "the sound of nature," were entitled *Aus den Tagen der Jugend: Blumen-, Frucht- und Dornenstücke* ("From the Days of Youth: Fruit, Flower, and Thorn Pieces") and *Ein Blumenkapitel* ("A Chapter of Flowers"). The first of these comes from Jean Paul's novel *Blumen-, Frucht- und Dornenstücke* (1796–7). The composer later disowned the titles, and today the symphony is billed by number, not name.

To a Nordic Princess   Percy Grainger, 1926.

The choral work, dedicated to the composer's Swedish-born wife, Ella Ström, was written for their wedding, held at the end of one of Grainger's concerts at the Hollywood Bowl.

To Be Sung of a Summer Night on the Water *see* **Aquarelles**.

To the Children (Russian, *K detyam*) Sergey Rachmaninov, 1906.

The song for voice and piano, Op. 26 No. 7, is a setting of the poem of the same name by Aleksei Khomyakov (1804–1860).

To the Memory of an Angel   Alban Berg, 1935.

The title of the Violin Concerto is properly a dedication. The work was impelled by the death of 18-year-old Manon Gropius, daughter of Gustav Mahler's widow by her second marriage. She is thus the "angel."

To the New Shores (Latvian, *Uz jauno krasto*)   Margers Zariņš, 1955.

The opera in four acts is set to a libretto by Fricis Rokpelnis based on Vilis Lācis's novel of the same name (1950–1). The story is set in Latvia in the years immediately after World War II and tells how rich peasants and collaborators, having gone to ground, attempt to undermine the country's reconstruction on Soviet lines.

Toccata (Italian, "Touched").

A term for a keyboard work in which the player displays a particular "touch," especially one that is rapid and delicate, as often required for a harpsichord or organ. Famous examples include Bach's **Dorian Toccata and Fugue**, Widor's *Toccata in F* as the fifth and final movement of his Organ Symphony in F minor, Op. 42 No. 1 (1878) (*see also* **Wedding March**), and Schumann's *Toccata in C*, Op. 7, for piano (1830).

Der Tod Jesu ("The Death of Jesus")   Karl Graun, 1755.

The passion cantata is set to a text by Karl Wilhelm Ramler based on the biblical story of the life and death of Christ.

Der Tod und das Mädchen ("Death and the Maiden")   Franz Schubert, 1817, 1824.

The song for voice and piano, D 531, is set to a poem by Matthias Claudius, with a four-line stanza spoken by the Maiden followed by a four line stanza spoken by Death, in which he gives a "quiet and reassuring answer to the maiden's agitated plea to be spared" (Blom, p. 130). The title is also that of the composer's String Quartet No. 14 in D minor, D 810, since the second part of the song is used as the theme for the variations in the second movement.

Der Tod und Verklärung ("Death and Transfiguration")   Richard Strauss, 1888–9.

The tone poem, Op. 24, is in four sections depicting a man's deathbed visions. The titles of the sections, which are played without a break, are: (1) *Sleep, Illness, Reverie*, (2) *Fever and Struggle with Death*, (3) *Dreams, Childhood Memories, and Death*, (4) *Transfiguration*.

Tom Jones   Edward German, 1907.

The comic opera in three acts is set to a libretto by Alexander M. Thompson, Robert Courtneidge, and Charles H. Taylor based on Henry Fielding's novel of the same name (1749) about the foundling, Tom Jones, who embarks on an adventurous journey to London and enjoys a number of colorful affairs.

Le Tombeau de Couperin ("The Tomb of Couperin")   Maurice Ravel, 1914–17.

The suite for solo piano, named for the French composer François Couperin (1688–1733), is written "in the form of a suite such as

Couperin might have written, but resembling him in spirit rather than in style" (Blom, p. 609). The "tomb" of the title is metaphorical, and the word is used for a work written in memory of someone, in this case not only Couperin but six of the composer's friends who died in World War I. They are commemorated in the work's six movements: (1) *Prélude*, (2) *Fugue*, (3) *Forlane*, (4) *Rigaudon*, (5), *Menuet*, (6) *Toccata*. The original planned title was simply *Suite française* ("French Suite").

Toreador Song   Georges Bizet, 1875.

The name is generally given to Escamillo's couplets in Act 2 of **Carmen**, in which he acknowledges the toasts to him and sings of the toreador's life. It opens with the words: "*Votre toast... je peux vous le rendre*" ("Your toast... I can return it to you").

Toreadoren ("Toreadors")   E. Helsted, 1840.

The idyllic ballet in two acts, with a libretto and choreography by August Bournonville, centers on Maria, the beautiful daughter of a Spanish innkeeper, and Alonzo, a handsome toreador, who love each other deeply but who are faced with a challenge on the appearance of the pretty French ballerina, Céleste.

Torquato Tasso   Gaetano Donizetti, 1833.

The opera in three acts is set to a libretto by Jacopo Ferretti based on Giovanni Rosini's play of the same name (1832), Carlo Goldoni's play *Tasso* (1755), Goethe's drama *Tasso* (1790), and Byron's poem *The Lament of Tasso* (1817), all of which are based on the life of the Italian poet, Torquato Tasso (1544–1595). The opera centers mainly on the love of Tasso for Eleonora, sister of the Duke of Ferrara.

Tosca   Giacomo Puccini, 1898–9.

The opera in three acts is set to a libretto by Giuseppe Giacosa and Luigi Illica based on Victorien Sardou's drama *La Tosca* (1887). The story is set in Rome in June 1800 and tells what happens when Baron Scarpia, chief of police, lusts after Tosca, the self-centered actress lover of the artist and republican loyalist, Mario Cavaradossi, who has aided the escape of Cesare Angelotti, former consul of the Roman Republic.

Tost Quartets   Joseph Haydn, 1788–90.

The 12 string quartets, Op. 54 Nos. 1–3, Op. 55 Nos. 1–3, and Op. 64 Nos. 1–6, are so called because they were dedicated to the Viennese violinist, Johann Tost.

Die Tote Stadt ("The Dead City")   Erich Korngold, 1920.

The opera in three acts is set to a libretto by Paul Schott (the joint pen name of the composer and his father) based on Siegfried Trebitsch's German translation of Georges Rodenbach's play *Le Mirage* ("The Mirage"), itself adapted from the latter's novella *Bruges-la-Morte* ("Bruges the Dead") (1892). The story is set in the Belgian city of Bruges in the late 19th century and tells what happens when Paul, in mourning for his wife, Marie, meets the dancer, Marietta, in whom he seems to see Marie. The title reflects the theme of death that runs through the plot.

Die Toten Augen ("The Blind Eyes")   Eugen d'Albert, 1916.

The opera in a prologue and one act is based on Hanns Heinz Ewers' German translation of Marc Henry's *Les Yeux morts* ("The Blind Eyes"). The story is set in Jerusalem on the first Palm Sunday and tells what happens when Myrtocle, the blind wife of the proconsul, Arcesius, has her sight restored by Jesus.

Totentanz ("Dance of Death")   Franz Liszt, 1849.

The work for piano and orchestra was inspired by Andrea Orcagna's attributed fresco *The Triumph of Death* (1360s), which the composer had seen in Pisa, Italy, in the late 1830s. In this, the figure of Death is a bat-winged woman. The work itself consists of variations on the **Dies Irae**.

Toward the Unknown Region   Ralph Vaughan Williams, 1905–7.

The song for mixed chorus and orchestra is set to words from Walt Whitman's *Whispers of Heavenly Death*, in which the poem *Darest Thou Now O Soul* (1868) begins: "Darest thou now O soul, / Walk out with me toward the unknown region."

Toy Symphony (German, *Kindersinfonie*, "Children's Symphony")   Leopold Mozart, 1788.

The freakish little symphony, at one time thought to be by Haydn, is scored for first and second violins, double bass, keyboard, and a range of toy instruments, including cuckoo, quail, nightingale, toy trumpet, toy drum, rattle, and triangle. It is said to have been composed for a set of toy instruments bought at a fair at Berchtesgaden. Hence its alternate title *Sinfonia Berchtoldsgadensis*. It is still played by school orchestras.

A Tragedy of Fashion   Eugene Goossens, 1926.

The ballet in one act, choreographed by Frederick Ashton, is set to the composer's *Kaleidoscope* and tells of a dressmaker who commits suicide when his dress is rejected by a wealthy customer. The subtitle is *The Scarlet Scissors*, alluding to his death.

Tragic Overture (German, *Tragische Ouvertüre*)   Johannes Brahms, 1880–1.

The concert overture, Op. 81, alludes to no particular tragedy and is presumably named for its "noble" and relatively serious nature by contrast with its companion piece, the **Academic Festival Overture**. It was written to commemorate the conferment on the composer of the honorary degree of doctor of philosophy by Breslau University in 1879.

Tragic Symphony   Franz Schubert, 1816.

The Symphony No. 4 in C minor, D 417, was so named by the composer, perhaps for the darkly introspective mood of the slow movement.

Tragica Sonata   Edward MacDowell, 1893.

The Piano Sonata No. 1 in G, Op. 45, is said to be so named for the composer's grief over the death of his teacher, Joachim Raff (1822–1882). The work has several somber passages.

Le Train Bleu ("The Blue Train")   Darius Milhaud, 1924.

The ballet in one act, Op. 84, with a libretto by Jean Cocteau and choreography by Bronislava Nijinska, is an *operetta dansée* concerning a smart but shallow society that pursues its pleasures and peccadilloes on a Mediterranean beach. The title refers to the express train of the name that runs (or ran) between Paris and the French Riviera. It does not actually appear.

The Traitor   Gunther Schuller, 1954.

The ballet in one act, with a libretto and choreography by José Limón, is a modern dance retelling of the biblical story of Christ and his betrayal by Judas.

Trans   Karlheinz Stockhausen, 1971.

The work is the transcription of a dream (hence the title), effected by a string orchestra bathed in magenta light that slowly bows sustained chords which change with the prerecorded shocks every few seconds of a weaving shuttle.

La Transfiguration de notre Seigneur Jésus-Christ ("The Transfiguration of Our Lord Jesus Christ")   Olivier Messiaen, 1965–9.

The work in 14 movements for tenor, baritone, chorus, piano, and orchestra is set to texts from the Bible, the Roman Catholic Missal, and St. Thomas Aquinas. The title indicates its specific devotional dedication and depiction.

Trauermusik ("Mourning Music")   Paul Hindemith, 1936.

The work in four short movements for viola (or violin or cello) and strings was written by the composer in a few hours, for performance the following day, on hearing of the death of George V (1865–1936), king of England.

Trauersymphonie ("Mourning Symphony")   Joseph Haydn, 1772.

The Symphony No. 44 in E minor is probably so nicknamed for its general suitability as "mourning music," especially the slow movement.

Trauerwalzer ("Mourning Waltz")   Franz Schubert, 1816.

The waltz for piano, Op. 9 No. 2, D 145, was so titled in 1821 by its publisher for its apparently contemplative nature. The composer himself disapproved of the title. In 1826 it was published by Schott of Mainz under the title *Sehnsuchtswalzer* ("Nostalgia Waltz") and attributed to Beethoven, but the piece, also known by the French title *Le Désir* ("The Desire"), was actually a blend of Schubert's original waltz and Friedrich Himmel's *Favoritwalzer* ("Favorite Waltz").

Träumerei *see* **Kinderszenen**.

The Travelling Companion   Charles Villiers Stanford, 1919.

The opera in four acts is set to a libretto by Henry Newbolt based on Hans Christian Andersen's fairy tale of the same title (1837).

La Traviata ("The Fallen Woman")   Giuseppe Verdi, 1853.

The opera in three acts is set to a libretto by Francesco Maria Piave based on Alexandre Dumas *fils*'s drama *La Dame aux camélias* ("The Lady of the Camelias") (1852), itself based on the novel of the same name (1848). The plot tells what happens when Alfredo Germont falls in love with the beautiful but consumptive courtesan (the "fallen woman" of the title), Violetta Valéry, known as the Lady of the Camelias. The opera is also known in English as *The Woman Gone Astray* or *The Fallen Woman*. (In the novel,

Alfredo is Armand, and Violetta Marguerite.) The Italian title word is grammatically the feminine singular past participle passive of the verb *traviare*, "to corrupt" (related to English *betray*), so literally means "she who has been corrupted."

Treemonisha   Scott Joplin, 1911.

The opera in three acts, to the composer's own libretto, is set in an Arkansas plantation in 1884 and tells what happens when the soothsayer, Zodzetrick, spreads superstition among the people and is reproached by Treemonisha.

Trend   Wallingford Riegger and Edgard Varèse, 1937.

The ballet in six parts, with a libretto and choreography by Hanya Holm, is set to music specially composed by Riegger and to Varèse's **Ionisation** and **Octandre**. It deals with the survival of society through decadence and collapse, the "trend" of the title.

Triad   Sergey Prokofiev, 1972.

The ballet in one act, choreographed by Kenneth MacMillan, is set to the composer's Violin Concerto No. 1 in D major, Op. 19 (1916–17), and is about a girl who intrudes on the close relationship between two brothers. Hence the title.

Trial by Jury   Arthur Sullivan, 1875.

The operetta ("dramatic cantata") in one act, to a libretto by W.S. Gilbert, is set in a court of justice and concerns the Learned Judge's hearing of a case for breach of promise (of marriage) between the Plaintiff, Angelina, and the Defendant, Edwin.

"Les Tringles des sistres tintaient" ("The rods of the sistrums jingled").

The trio sung by the gypsies Carmen, Frasquita, and Mercédès in Act 2 of Bizet's **Carmen**. It is also known as the *Chanson Bohémienne* ("Gypsy Song").

Le Triomphe de l'amour ("The Triumph of Love")   Jean-Baptiste Lully, 1681.

The *ballet de cour* in 20 entrées (numbers), to a text by Isaac de Benserade and Philippe Quinault, is a baroque spectacle which opens with Venus and Peace summoning the Graces, Dryads, and Naiads, and progresses to a climax in which all the participants pay homage to Love as the ruler of gods and men.

Trionfi ("Triumphs")   Carl Orff, 1953.

The theatrical triptych comprises **Carmina Burana**, **Catulli Carmina**, and **Trionfo di Afrodite**.

Trionfo di Afrodite ("Triumph of Aphrodite")   Carl Orff, 1950–1.

The scenic concerto for soloists, chorus, and orchestra, is a setting of Latin and Greek texts by Catullus, Sappho, and Euripides comprising various scenes in praise of love and marriage. Aphrodite is the Greek goddess of love, known to the Romans as Venus. The work is the third part of the trilogy **Trionfi**.

Triple Concerto   Ludwig van Beethoven, 1804.

The title is valid for any concerto for three solo instruments but is perhaps most readily associated with Beethoven's concerto in C major, Op. 56, for piano, violin, and cello.

Triple Overture *see* **Nature, Life, and Love**.

Tristan   Hans Werner Henze, 1974.

The ballet in one act, choreographed by Glen Tetley, is a semiabstract version of the legend of Tristan and Isolde (*see* **Tristan und Isolde**).

Tristan und Isolde ("Tristan and Isolde") Richard Wagner, 1865.

The opera in three acts is set to the composer's own libretto based on Godfrey of Strasbourg's *Tristan* (*c*.1210). The story, taken from Celtic (probably Breton) legend, tells what happens when Tristan, nephew of King Mark of Cornwall, is sent to fetch the Irish princess, Isolde, and bring her back as a wife for Mark. Tristan (Tristram) and Isolde (Yseult) are essentially the same as the characters of these names in Arthurian legend.

Tritsch-Tratsch Polka   Johann Strauss II, 1858.

The polka for orchestra, Op. 214, has a name amounting to "trish-trash," indicating something with a showy but superficial allure.

Il Trittico ("The Triptych")   Giacomo Puccini, 1913–18.

The composer gave this name to his set of three one-act operas, the tragedy Il **Tabarro**, the melodrama **Suor Angelica**, and the comedy **Gianni Schicchi**. They are not connected in subject matter, but were intended to be performed together as a single evening's entertainment.

Triumph of Death (Danish, *Dødens Triumf*) Thomas Koppel, 1971.

The television ballet by Flemming Flindt is based on Eugène Ionesco's play *Jeux de massacre*

("Killing Game") (1970) and is a lavish "dance of death" revue, depicting how modern humankind tries to escape the grim consequences of the plague.

The Triumph of Neptune   Lord Berners, 1926.

The pantomime in ten scenes to music, with a libretto by Sacheverell Sitwell and choreography by George Balanchine, is essentially a parodistic development, from a child's point of view, of the stories about Neptune, god of the sea.

The Triumph of Time   Harrison Birtwistle, 1972.

The orchestral work was inspired by Pieter Bruegel the Elder's painting *The Triumph of Death* (1562) and represents a time that triumphs by coexisting in past, present, and future.

Triumphal Symphony   Bedřich Smetana, 1854.

The composer's only symphony, in E major, also known as the *Festive*, has a finale that closes with a grand extended presentation of Haydn's *Emperor's Hymn* (see **Emperor Quartet**). The occasion of the actual "triumph" was the marriage of the Emperor Franz Josef to Elisabeth of Bavaria on April 24, 1854. (Smetana wished to dedicate the work to the Emperor but received no response to his request.)

Triumphlied   ("Song of Triumph") Johannes Brahms, 1870–1.

The work for baritone, chorus, and orchestra, Op. 55, is a setting of words from the Book of Revelation and was written to celebrate Prussia's defeat of France.

Troilus and Cressida   William Walton, 1947–54.

The opera in three acts is set to a libretto by Christopher Hassall based on Geoffrey Chaucer's poem *Troilus and Criseyde* (*c*.1383–5) and other sources, but not Shakespeare's *Troilus and Cressida* (*c*.1601). The story tells what happens when Cressida, daughter of the High Priest of Troy, Calkas, is turned from her intention of becoming a priestess by the love of Troilus.

Trois Chansons   ("Three Songs")   Maurice Ravel, 1916.

The three songs for voice (originally mixed chorus) and piano are settings of the composer's own poems, with individual titles: *Nicolette*, *Trois beaux oiseaux du paradis* ("Three beautiful birds of paradise"), and *Ronde* ("Round").

Trois Morceaux en forme de poire   ("Three Pear-Shaped Pieces")   Erik Satie, 1903.

The work for piano duet, which actually contains seven items, was written in response to a critic who commented that the composer's music had no form. Its title is typical of Satie's eccentric humor.

Trois Petites Liturgies de la présence divine   ("Three Little Liturgies of the Divine Presence")   Olivier Messiaen, 1944.

The work for women's chorus, piano, ondes Martenot, and orchestra is a setting of the composer's own words hymning the presence of God in the individual (*Antienne de la conversation intérieure*, "Antiphon of interior dialogue"), in himself (*Séquence du Verbe*, "Sequence of the Word"), and in all things (*Psalmodie de l'ubiquité par amour*, "Psalmody of love's omnipresence").

The Trojans   *see* Les **Troyens**.

Der Trompeter von Säckingen   ("The Trumpeter of Säckingen")   Victor Nessler, 1884.

The opera in four acts is set to a libretto by Rudolf Bunge based on Joseph Viktor von Scheffel's poem of the same name (1854). The scene is set in Säckingen just after the Thirty Years War and the story tells what happens when the trumpeter, Werner, falls in love with the high-born Maria, whose parents want her to marry the simpleton, Damian.

Trouble in Tahiti   Leonard Bernstein, 1952.

The opera in one act, to a libretto by the composer, is a domestic comedy about a quarreling suburban couple. It was later incorporated into a revised version of A **Quiet Place**.

The Trout   *see* Die **Forelle**.

Trout Quintet   (German, *Forellenquintett*) Franz Schubert, 1819.

The Piano Quintet in A major, D 667, is so named because the fourth of its five movements is a set of variations on the tune of the song Die **Forelle**.

Il Trovatore   ("The Troubadour")   Giuseppe Verdi, 1853.

The opera in four acts is set to a libretto by Salvatore Cammarano (completed by Leone Emanuele Bardare) based on García Guttiérrez's play *El trovador* (1836). The story is set in

15th-century Spain and centers on the troubadour, Manrico, leader of the rebel army, who is believed to be the son of the gypsy, Azucena. The plot reveals what happens when he loves Leonora, who is also loved by the Conte di Luna, head of the king's army.

Troy Game   Bob Downes, 1974.

The ballet in one act, choreographed by Robert North, is an all-male display "poking fun at muscle-flexing macho athleticism" (Koegler, p. 421). The title alludes to the Trojan War.

Les Troyens ("The Trojans")   Hector Berlioz, 1856–8.

The opera in five acts is set to the composer's own libretto based on Vergil's *Aeneid* (*c.* 27–19 BC), telling of the feats of the great warrior, Aeneas, in and following the Trojan War. In 1863, to achieve a performance in a single evening, the composer was obliged to divide the opera into two parts. Part 1, comprising the first two acts, became *La Prise de Troie* ("The Capture of Troy"). Part 2, comprising the remaining three acts, became *Les Troyens à Carthage* ("The Trojans at Carthage").

Trumpet Overture   Felix Mendelssohn, 1825.

The Overture for Orchestra in C major, Op. 101, is scored for two flutes, two oboes, two clarinets, two horns, two trumpets, two bassoons, three trombones, and strings. The title is something of a mystery, since the trumpets are in fact less prominent than the horns.

Trumpet Voluntary   Jeremiah Clarke, *c.*1700.

The name was given by Sir Henry Wood to his transcription of a keyboard piece for organ, brass, and kettledrums that was at first wrongly attributed to Purcell. The title denotes a musical piece which was not actually composed for the trumpet but which imitates its sound, as on a trumpet-like organ stop. (The word "voluntary" here is not the same as that used for an organ solo at the beginning or end of a church service.) Clarke's original title for the piece, which occurs in his *Choice lessons for the Harpsichord or Spinet*, published in 1700, was "The Prince of Denmark," referring to the consort of Queen Anne.

"Tu che di gel sei cinta" ("Thou who art girded in ice").

Liù's aria in Act 3 of Puccini's **Turandot**, in which she assures Turandot that one day she too will love the unknown prince (*i.e.* Calaf).

"Tu che le vanità" ("Thou who the vanities").

Elisabetta's aria in Act 5 of Verdi's **Don Carlos**, in which, kneeling before the tomb of Charles V, she bids farewell to her past. Her words are addressed to Don Carlos: "*Tu che le vanità conoscesti del mondo*" ("Thou who knewest the vanities of the world").

The Tulip of Harlem (Russian, *Garlemskiy tyul'pan*)   B.A. Fitingov-Shel, 1887.

The ballet in three acts (four scenes), choreographed by Lev Ivanov, is based on a Dutch legend.

Turandot   Giacomo Puccini, 1920–6.

The opera in three acts is set to a libretto by Renato Simone and Giuseppe Adami based on Carlo Gozzi's drama of the same name (1762), itself perhaps drawn from the *Thousand and One Nights* (*Arabian Nights*). The plot centers on Turandot, the cruel Princess of Peking, who poses three riddles for her suitors to answer. Whoever fails will die.

Turangalîla   Olivier Messiaen, 1947–8.

The symphony in ten movements was inspired by the Tristan and Isolde legend (*see* **Tristan und Isolde**) and has a title of Sanskrit origin, as the name of one of the rhythmic formulae of ancient Indian music. According to the composer, *turanga* means "time which runs" and *lîla* is "divine action in the cosmos, the play of creation, of destruction, of reconstruction, the play of life and death. Lîla is also love" (quoted in Griffiths, p. 185). The titles of the movements are: (1) *Introduction*, (2) *Chant d'amour I* ("Love Song I"), (3) *Turangalîla I*, (4) *Chant d'amour II* ("Love Song II"), (5) *Joie du sang des étoiles* ("Joy of the Blood of the Stars"), (6) *Jardin du sommeil d'amour* ("Garden of the Sleep of Love"), (7) *Turangalîla II*, (8) *Développement de l'amour* ("Development of Love"), (9) *Turangalîla III*, (10) *Final*.

Il Turco in Italia ("The Turk in Italy")   Gioacchino Rossini, 1814.

The opera in two acts is set to a libretto by Felice Romani based on Caterino Mazzolà's libretto for Franz Süssmayer's opera of the same name (1794). The story is set in 18th-century Naples and tells how the poet, Prosdocimo, seeks a plot for an opera. He devises a tale of intrigues and misunderstandings involving Fiorilla, her admirer, Don Narciso, her husband, Geronio, a visiting Turk (the one of the title), Selim, to whom she is attracted, and Selim's former beloved, Zaida.

Turkish Concerto   W.A. Mozart, 1775.

The Concerto for Violin No. 5 in A major, K 219, is so named for the "Turkish" style (that of a Turkish military band with its prominent percussion instruments) of the last movement. *Cf.* **Rondo alla turca.**

The Turn of the Screw   Benjamin Britten, 1954.

The opera in a prologue and two acts, Op. 54, is set to a libretto by Myfanwy Piper based on Henry James's story of the same name (1898), telling of the eventual death of the young orphan, Miles, from the pressure put on him by the conflicting demands of the Governess and the evil ghost of the former servant, Peter Quint. The "screw" of the title is represented by a theme that "turns" through 15 variations as interludes between the eight scenes of each act.

"Tutte le feste"   ("All the festivals").

Gilda's aria in Act 2 of Verdi's **Rigoletto,** in which she tells her father of the young man (the Duke of Mantua) who followed her from church. The full line is: "*Tutte le feste al tempio*" ("All the festivals at the church").

Twenty-Four Preludes   Fryderyk Chopin, 1836–9.

The 24 brief piano pieces, Op. 28, were individually named by the German conductor, pianist, and composer, Hans von Bülow. The titles are mostly romantically descriptive, but some have factual origins or personal references, real or imaginary: No. 1 in C major, *Reunion*; No. 2 in A minor, *Presentiment of Death*; No. 3 in G major, *Thou Art So Like a Flower* (from Heinrich Heine's poem beginning *Du bist wie eine Blume,* 1827); No. 4 in E minor, *Suffocation* (for the composer's consumptive attacks); No. 5 in D major, *Uncertainty*; No. 6 in B minor, *Tolling Bells*; No. 7 in A major, *The Polish Dance*; No. 8 in F sharp minor, *Desperation* (for his nervous agitation during the unexplained absence of his mistress, George Sand, and her son Maurice); No. 9 in E major, *Vision* (for his lack of inspiration, then its recovery); No. 10 in C sharp minor, *The Moth*; No. 11 in B major, *The Dragon Fly*; No. 12 in G sharp minor, *The Duel* (for his jealousy of rivals for the attention of George Sand); No. 13 in F sharp major, *Loss* (for his lost loved one); No. 14 in E flat minor, *Fear* (for his nervous hallucinations); No. 15 in D flat major, *Raindrop* (supposedly written while rain was pattering on the roof, the raindrops represented by the repeated note A flat); No. 16 in B flat minor,

Hades (for another hallucination); No. 17 in A flat major, *A Scene on the Place de Notre-Dame de Paris* (a moonlight tryst); No. 18 in F minor, *Suicide* (for the composer's desperation); No. 19 in E flat major, *Heartfelt Happiness* (for his recovered happiness); No. 20 in C minor, *Funeral March* (a premonition of the composer's death); No. 21 in B flat major, *Sunday* (worshipers arrive at church, attend Mass, then depart); No. 22 in G minor, *Impatience*; No. 23 in F major, *A Pleasure Boat*; No. 24 in D minor, *The Storm*. (For a translation of von Bülow's full interpretations, see "Chopin's Préludes, op. 28, analyzed," in *Musician*, No. 16, 1911, p. 88, pp. 137–8.)

Twilight   (1) (Georgian, *Daisi*) Zakhary Paliashvili, 1923; (2) (German, *Dämmern*) Alexander Skryabin, 1972; (3) John Cage, 1972.

Paliashvili's opera in three acts, to a libretto by Valerian Levanovich Gunia, tells what happens when Maro is engaged to the soldier, Kiazo, but actually loves Malkhaz. The title points to the relationship that is inevitably nearing its end. Skryabin's ballet, choreographed by John Neumeier, depicts a team of dancers who at the end of the day become united through their work. Cage's ballet in one act, choreographed by Hans van Manen, is set to the composer's suite for prepared piano, *Perilous Night* (1943–4), and depicts a woman and man aggressively fighting out their precarious relationship.

The Twilight of the Gods   *see* Der **Ring des Nibelungen.**

The Two Sisters   Cyril Rootham, 1922.

The opera, set to a libretto by Marjorie Fausset, is based on the Scottish ballad *The Twa Sisters of Binnorie.*

The Two Widows   (Czech, *Dvě vdovy*) Bedřich Smetana, 1873–4.

The comic opera in two acts is set to a libretto by Emanuel Züngl based on Pierre Jean Félicien Mallefille's comedy *Les deux veuves* ("The Two Widows") (1860). The story is set in a Bohemian castle in the 19th century and centers on the amatory intrigues of the two widows who live there, Karolina and Anezka.

Two Pictures   Béla Bartók, 1910.

The orchestral work, Op. 10, consists of two movements. The first, entitled *In Full Bloom,* is an evocation of nature and the countryside. The second, *Village Dance,* depicts a rollicking rustic festivity.

Tzigane ("Gypsy")   Maurice Ravel, 1924.

The concert rhapsody for violin and piano evokes the gypsy music of the bohemian world of Paris. The composer wrote the work for the Hungarian violinist Jelly d'Arányi (1893–1966).

U

"Udite, udite, o rustici" ("Hear, hear, O country folk").

Dulcamara's aria in Act 1 of Donizetti's L'**Elisir d'amore**, in which he advertises his quack wares.

Ugo conte di Parigi ("Hugo, Count of Paris")   Gaetano Donizetti, 1832.

The opera in two acts, to a libretto by Felice Romani, is set in 10th-century Paris and tells what happens when Falco, wishing the French crown to go to his own house of Anjou, plans to provoke rivalry between the famous soldier, Ugo, and the newly crowned king, Louis V.

L'Ultimo giorno di Pompei ("The Last Day of Pompeii")   Giovanni Pacini, 1825.

The opera, set to a libretto by Andrea Leone Tottola, is not based on Edward Bulwer-Lytton's historical novel *The Last Days of Pompeii* (1834), which was not then written, but it has the same event for its background: the destruction of the Roman town of Pompeii by Vesuvius in AD 79. It is possible that Bulwer-Lytton saw the opera when it was performed in London in 1831 and that it gave him the idea for his work.

Ultimos Ritos ("Last Rites")   John Tavener, 1972.

The oratorio, for soprano, alto, tenor, and bass soloists, five priests (speakers), chorus, organ, and large orchestra, is set to a text by St. John of the Cross (1542–1591) and the Crucifixus from the Nicene Creed. The "last rites" of the title are thus religious ones.

The Ulyanov Brothers (Russian, *Brat'ya Ul'yanovy*)   Yuly Meytus, 1967.

The opera in three acts, to a libretto by A. Vasilyeva and Dmitro Pavlychko, is set in Simbirsk, St. Petersburg, and Kazan over the two years 1886 and 1887 and tells of the young revolutionary, Alexander Ulyanov (1866–1887), executed for his participation in an assassination attempt on Alexander III, and his younger brother, Vladimir Ulyanov (1870–1924), better known as Lenin.

Ulysses   (1) Mátyás Seiber, 1946–7; (2) Luigi Dallapiccola, 1959–68.

Seiber's cantata is based on text from James Joyce's stream-of-consciousness novel of the same name (1922), in which the various chapters correspond approximately to the episodes of Homer's *Odyssey*, the Jewish businessman, Leopold Bloom, representing Odysseus (Ulysses). Dallapiccola's opera in a prologue, two acts, and an epilogue is set to his own libretto based on Homer's epic poem, describing the adventures of Odysseus during his return from the Trojan War to his kingdom of Ithaca.

Un (French, Italian, Spanish, "A").

For titles beginning with this word, see the next word, *e.g.* Un **Ballo in Maschera**. (Note that *un* can also mean "one," in which case it is the first word in the title, as below.)

"Un bel dì vedremo" ("One fine day we will see him").

Butterfly's aria in Act 2 of Puccini's **Madama Butterfly**, in which she sings of Pinkerton's hoped-for return. The aria was long familiar by the English title "One fine day," or alternately, "Some day he'll come."

"Un dì felice" ("One happy day").

The love duet between Violetta and Alfredo in Act 1 of Verdi's La **Traviata**.

Un jour ou deux ("One Day or Two")   John Cage, 1973.

The ballet in one act, choreographed by Merce Cunningham, lasts an evening and presents a variety of separate dance events, such as solos, duets, trios, and larger groups, performed either on their own or simultaneously. There is no actual story, except that of "the continuity of events as they succeed each other" (Cunningham, quoted in Koegler, p. 427).

Una (Italian, Spanish, "A").

For titles beginning with this word, see the next word, *e.g.* Una **Cosa rara**.

The Unanswered Question   Charles Ives, 1906.

The work for small orchestra, subtitled *A Contemplation of a Serious Matter*, is essentially a musical presentation of the title. The orchestra repeats simple harmonies as a "statement," while a trumpet set apart from the other players reiterates a question-like theme that is confusedly (and dissonantly) commented on by flutes. The question itself remains unidentified, as presumably the composer intended. *Cf.* **Central Park in the Dark**.

Undertow   William Schuman, 1945.

The ballet in a prologue, one act, and an epilogue, with a libretto and choreography by Antony Tudor, "attempts to show us why a young man, called the transgressor, commits murder" (George Balanchine, quoted in Koegler, p. 426).

Undine ("Ondine")   E.T.A. Hoffmann, 1816; (2) Albert Lortzing, 1845.

Hoffmann's opera in three acts and Lortzing's in four, each to the composer's own libretto, are both based on Friedrich de la Motte Fouqué's tale of the same name (1811) about the water sprite of central European legend who is the equivalent of the Slavonic **Rusalka**. (Her name is based on Latin *unda*, "wave.")

Une (French, "A").

For titles beginning with this word, see the next word, *e.g.* Une **Éducation manquée**.

Unfinished Symphony (German, *Unvollendete Sinfonie*)   Franz Schubert, 1822.

The Symphony No. 8 in B minor, D 759, contains only two movements of the expected four. The composer clearly intended to carry on, since he sketched a scherzo for the third movement and actually scored its first nine bars. It may be that he simply put it away and forgot it or, more likely, abandoned it because he lacked inspiration for the second half. There are unfinished symphonies by other composers, among them Tchaikovsky, Mahler, Elgar, and Shostakovich, but the title is generally taken to apply to Schubert's.

The Unicorn, the Gorgon, and the Manticore   Gian-Carlo Menotti, 1956.

The ballet, a "Madrigal Fable for Chorus, Dancers, and Nine Instruments," choreographed by John Butler, has the subtitle *The Three Sundays of a Poet* and depicts a poet strolling through the city with one of his favorite pets (named in the title) on three successive Sundays.

Union Jack   various (see below), 1976.

The ballet in three parts, choreographed by George Balanchine, is set to various folk, military, naval, and music hall themes arranged by Hershy Kay and takes its title from the British flag. "*Union Jack* acknowledges those ritual aspects of Britain as alive today in military ceremony and in theatrical vitality as they were in the 18th century" (information notice, quoted in Koegler, p. 426). The work was the New York City Ballet's contribution to the United States Bicentennial festivities.

United Quartet   Henry Cowell, 1936.

The String Quartet No. 4 is so named because it unites different musical cultures, in particular European and various kinds of folk music.

Universal Prayer   Andrzej Panufnik, 1968–9.

The cantata for soprano, contralto, tenor, and bass soloists, three harps, organ, and mixed chorus is set to Alexander Pope's poem *The Universal Prayer* (1738), beginning: "Father of all! in every age, / In every clime adored."

Universe Symphony   Charles Ives, 1911–16.

The (unfinished) symphony was conceived on a vast scale, as indicated in the composer's formula: "Plan for a Universe Symphony. 1. Formation of the countries and mountains. 2. Evolution in nature and humanity. 3. The rise of all to the spiritual" (quoted in Dearling, p. 183). The length of the work and number of performers are unlimited, and it has never been performed. (According to the composer's plan, several different orchestras, with huge choirs, were to be stationed on mountain tops and in valleys.) Its title indicates its infinite scope.

The Upsidedown Violin   Michael Nyman, 1992.

The orchestral work was written for the composer's band teamed with a Moroccan ensemble, the Orquestra Andaluzi de Telousan. The latter frequently altered or inverted Nyman's melodies in rehearsals, and he incorporated these into the final work, with the "upsidedown violins" playing alongside the conventional ones.

"Urna fatale" ("Fatal urn").

Carlo's aria in Act 3 of Verdi's La **Forza del destino**, in which he tries to resist the temptation to open the sealed casket containing the portrait of Leonora.

Utopia Limited   Arthur Sullivan, 1893.

The operetta in two acts, to a libretto by W.S. Gilbert, is subtitled *The Flowers of Progress* and is a satire on British colonialism and imperialism. The story is set in Utopia in the South Pacific. The title suggests a limited company. But as the King says just before the finale: "Henceforward Utopia will no longer be a Monarchy (Limited), but, what is a great deal better, a Limited Monarchy!".

Utrecht Te Deum and Jubilate   George Frideric Handel, 1712–3.

The liturgical settings were composed to

celebrate the Treaty of Utrecht (1713) that concluded the War of the Spanish Succession. Hence the name.

Utrenja   Krzysztof Penderecki, 1969–71.

The choral work derives its name from the Russian word for the Russian Orthodox service of morning prayer (matins). The work is in two parts, *The Entombment of Christ* and *The Resurrection of Christ*.

V

"Va, pensiero" *see* **Chorus of the Hebrew Slaves**.

Les Vainqueurs ("The Victors")   various (see below), 1969.

The ceremony in five scenes, choreographed by Maurice Béjart, is based on an idea by Richard Wagner and set to excerpts from his **Tristan und Isolde** with added classic Indian and Tibetan music. The work attempts to blend the ceremony of Indian initiation rites with the Tristan and Isolde story, the title coming from the *Tibetan Book of the Great Liberation*, which includes the words, "The victors are the Buddhas." The five scenes have titles: (1) *Mandala*, (2) *The Forest*, (3) *The Vessel*, (4) *On the Way to the Other Coast*, (5) *The Ocean*.

Le Vaisseau fantôme ("The Phantom Vessel")   Louis Dietsch, 1842.

The opera is set to a libretto by Bénédict Henri Révoil and Paul Henri Foucher based on Captain Frederick Marryat's novel *The Phantom Ship* (1839). Wagner accused Dietsch of basing it on his own scenario for *The Flying Dutchman* (*see* Der **Fliegende Holländer**).

Vakula the Smith (Russian, *Kuznets Vakula*) Pyotr Tchaikovsky, 1874.

The opera in three acts is set to a libretto by Yakov Polonsky based on Nikolai Gogol's story *Christmas Eve* (1823). The story is basically the same as that of Rimsky-Korsakov's **Christmas Eve**. The opera was revised in 1885 as *Cherevichki* ("Little Boots"), although often known in the West as *Oxana's Caprices*. The "little boots" are those that Oxana demands from Vakula if he is to claim her as his bride. Since these belong to the empress, another English title is *The Czarina's Shoes*. (The Russian word *chere-*

vichki is a diminutive form of *chereviki*, the name of the high-heeled leather boots worn by Ukrainian women.) The opera is also known in English as *Vakula the Blacksmith*.

The Valkyrie *see* Die **Walküre**.

Valkyrien ("Valkyries")   J.P.E. Hartmann, 1861.

The ballet in four acts, with a libretto and choreography by August Bournonville, interweaves the Valkyries theme (*see* Die **Walküre**) with the story of the death of Harald Hildetand, Odin taking the form of the king's counsellor to save him from the shame of dying in his bed.

Vallée d'Obermann ("Obermann Valley") Franz Liszt, 1848–54.

The work for solo piano is No. 6 of Book 1 of **Années de pèlerinage**. The Obermann Valley is in Switzerland.

La Valse ("The Waltz")   Maurice Ravel, 1920

The "*poème chorégraphique*" ("choreographic poem") for orchestra was defined by the composer as " a sort of apotheosis of the Viennese waltz" (quoted in Koegler, p. 430). The music itself imitates (or parodies) the style of Johann Strauss's waltzes. The original title was *Wien* ("Vienna"), as the composer intended the work to be a picture of the city as he saw it. When its character subsequently changed, the title changed with it. It was later produced as a ballet (1928).

Valse triste ("Sad Waltz")   Jean Sibelius, 1903.

The waltz for strings, Op. 44, was composed as part of the incidental music for a production of Arvid Järnefelt's play *Kuolema* ("Death"). Arvid Järnefelt (1861–1932) was the brother of the composer Armas Järnefelt (1869–1958), Sibelius's brother-in-law.

Valses nobles et sentimentales ("Noble and Sentimental Waltzes")   Maurice Ravel, 1911.

The eight short waltzes for solo piano were composed "after the example of Schubert" and the title was adopted as a combination of his *Valses Nobles*, D 969, Op. 77 (1827) and *Valses Sentimentales*, D 779, Op. 50 (1825). The composer himself pointed out: "The title, *Valses nobles et sentimentales*, shows clearly enough my intention to compose a chain of valses in the style of Schubert" (quoted in Norman Demuth, *Ravel*, 1947). The work was greeted with signs of disapproval at its first public performance, possibly because the title had led the audience to expect Viennese-style waltzes. See *also* **Adélaïde**.

Der Vampyr ("The Vampire")   Heinrich Marschner, 1827–8.

The opera in two acts is set to a libretto by Wilhelm August Wohlbrück based on John Polidori's story (formerly attributed to Byron) *The Vampyre* (1819). The plot tells what happens when the Scottish nobleman, Sir Ruthven, becomes a vampire.

Vanessa   Samuel Barber, 1956–7.

The opera in four acts, Op. 32, is set to a libretto by Gian-Carlo Menotti based on Isak Dinesen's *Seven Gothic Tales* (1934). The story is set in northern Europe in the opening years of the 20th century and tells what happens when Vanessa, having waited 20 years for her lover to return, is told by her son, Anatol, that he is dead.

Vanina Vanini   Nikolai Karetnikov, 1962.

The ballet in one act (seven scenes), with a libretto and choreography by the wife and husband team, Natalia Kasatkina and Vladimir Vasiliov, is based on Stendhal's story of the same name (1829), which tells what happens when an Italian princess, Vanina Vanini, hides a wounded Carbonaro in her father's house.

The Vanishing Bridegroom   Judith Weir, 1990.

The opera in three parts, to a libretto by the composer, is based on J.F. Campbell of Islay's edition of *Popular Tales of the West Highlands*, vol. 2 (1860), and Alexander Carmichael's edition of *Carmina Gadelica* ("Gaelic Songs"), vol. 2 (1900). The three separate stories from the former work, entitled respectively *The Inheritance*, *The Disappearance*, and *The Stranger*, worked here into a narrative about a particular marriage, tell what happens when, after the birth of his child, the Bridegroom is lured into a hillside and not seen again. The title thus refers to this central incident.

Vanna Lupa   Ildebrando Pizzetti, 1949.

The opera in three acts, to the composer's own libretto, contrasts the political ambition and thirst for revenge of a woman, nicknamed Lupa ("She-Wolf"), with her son's passion for freedom.

Variations   (1) John Cage, 1958–66; (2) Igor Stravinsky, 1966.

Cage's six works, for any number of players and any means of sound production, takes indeterminate music to extraordinary lengths. Some of the scores are simply transparent plastic sheets inscribed with lines and circles, with instructions how to "perform" them using any means. In *Variations V* (1965) the performer is simply given a description of previous performances, one of which included dance, film, television images, lighting effects, and scenery as well as sound. The very randomness of the works ensures that the title is an accurate description, since any one performance is bound to be a variation on any other. Stravinsky's plotless ballet in three parts, choreographed by George Balanchine, is set to his own *Variations* for orchestra (1964) played three times for a set of three dances. Each playing after the first will be a variation, albeit a slight one, on the one before.

Variations and Fugue on a Theme of Purcell *see* The **Young Person's Guide to the Orchestra**.

Variations for Four   Marguerite Keogh, 1957.

The divertissement, choreographed by Anton Dolin, is a display piece for four male dancers. The choreographer later added four female dancers, and adjusted the title accordingly to *Variations for Four plus Four*.

Variations on "America"   Charles Ives, 1891.

The work for organ comprises variations on the national hymn *America* ("My Country, 'tis of thee"), which has the same tune as *God Save the King*.

Variations on a Rococo Theme (Russian, *Variatsii na temu rokoko*)   Pyotr Tchaikovsky, 1876.

The work for cello and orchestra, Op. 33, is based on the composer's own theme that he regarded as being in a late baroque or early classical style.

Variations on a Theme by Handel Johannes Brahms, 1861.

The piano work, Op. 24, takes its theme from the air in Handel's harpsichord suite in B flat major, No. 1 of the second set of suites (1733).

Variations on a Theme by Haydn Johannes Brahms, 1873.

The orchestral work, Op. 56a, takes its theme from a suite in B flat major for military band by Haydn. It is now known that Haydn actually borrowed the theme, a fact that has led some purists to decry the title on the grounds of inaccuracy. However, since the composer gave it himself, "there seems no good reason to discard this title for a musicological nicety" (Kennedy, p. 759). The work is also popularly known as the *St. Anthony Variations*, because the theme itself is known as the *St. Anthony Chorale*.

Variations on a Theme of Frank Bridge
Benjamin Britten, 1937.
   The work for string orchestra, Op. 10, uses a theme from Bridge's *Idyll* No. 2 for string quartet (1906).

Variations on the name of Gabriel Fauré
Arnold Bax, 1949.
   The work for piano, later expanded into a suite for harp and orchestra, bases its theme on the musical letters in the name of the French composer Gabriel Fauré, with R as D, I as B, L as E, and U as G. These particular correspondences are reached by repeating the seven-note sequence A to G for the rest of the alphabet, so that H is A again, I is B, J is C, and so on. *Cf.* **Menuet sur le nom d'Haydn**.

"Le Veau d'or" ("The Golden Calf").
   Méphistophélès's mocking song to the crowd in Act 2 of Gounod's **Faust**, as an ironic celebration of man's worship of Mammon.

"Vedrai, carino" ("Thou shalt see, dear one").
   Zerlina's aria in Act 2 of Mozart's **Don Giovanni**, in which she comforts her lover, Masetto, after his beating by Giovanni. A fuller form of the words is: "*Vedrai, carino, se sei buonino*" ("Thou shalt see, dear one, if thou art kind").

Das Veilchen ("The Violet")   W.A. Mozart, 1785.
   The song for voice and piano, K 476, is based on Goethe's poem of this name written in 1773 or 1774, with a first line, "*Ein Veilchen auf der Wiese stand*" ("A violet stood in the meadow"). At the time of Mozart's composition the poem was still untitled and first received the name in 1800 when it appeared in Goethe's *Neue Schriften* ("New Works").

The Veiled Prophet of Khorassan
Charles Villiers Stanford, 1881.
   The opera is set to a libretto by William Barclay Squire based on Thomas Moore's set of four oriental tales in verse *Lalla Rookh* (1817). It takes its title from the first of these, which tells

of the prophet Hakem ben Haschem, who wears a silver veil "to dim the luster of his face," *i.e.* to hide its extreme ugliness.

Venetian Boat Song *see* **Venezianisches Gondellied**.

Venetian Games (Polish, *Gry weneckie*) Witold Lutosławski, 1960–1.
   The work for chamber orchestra, known also by its equivalent French title, *Jeux vénitiens*, uses limited aleatory (chance) procedures, and these represent the "games" of the title.

Veneziana ("Venetian")   Gaetano Donizetti arr. Denis ApIvor, 1953.
   The ballet in one act, choreographed by Andrée Howard, is set to music mainly from the composer's operas La **Favorite** and *Dom Sébastien* (1843). The theme suggests a masked ball in Venice during carnival time.

Venezianisches Gondellied ("Venetian Boat Song")   Felix Mendelssohn, 1829, 1835, 1845.
   The composer gave this title to three of the piano pieces in his **Lieder ohne Worte**: Op. 19 No. 6 in G minor in Book 1, Op. 30 No. 6 in F sharp minor in Book 2, and Op. 62 No. 5 in A minor in Book 5. Although usually translated in English as "Venetian Boat Song," the German literally means "Venetian Gondola Song," since the melody in each was thought of by the composer as the song of a Venetian gondolier.

Veni, Veni, Emmanuel ("O Come, O Come, Emmanuel")   James MacMillan, 1992.
   The percussion concerto bases its music on 15th-century French Advent plainchant, and is what the composer describes as "a musical exploration of the theology behind the Advent message" (quoted in Staines and Buckley, p. 233). The title is that of an Advent hymn based on the Latin antiphons which were sung in the early church in the week leading up to Christmas Day.

La Ventana ("The Window")   Hans Christian Lumbye, 1854.
   The ballet in one act, choreographed by August Bournonville, is a divertissement with a Spanish flavor centering on a window display. Hence the Spanish name, instead of the expected Danish one.

Venus   Othmar Schoeck, 1922.
   The opera, set to a libretto by Armin Rüeger, is based on Proper Mérimée's story *La*

Vénus d'Ille ("The Venus of Ille") (1837), telling what happens when a bridegroom takes off the diamond ring he is wearing to grip his tennis racket better and slips it on the finger of a bronze statue of Venus.

Venus and Adonis   John Blow, *c*.1684.
The opera (masque) in a prologue and three acts is set to a libretto by an unknown author based on the classical story of the love of Venus, goddess of love, for the handsome huntsman, Adonis.

Venusberg Music   Richard Wagner, 1845.
The name is generally given to the opening scene in Venus's realm in **Tannhäuser**.

Les Vêpres siciliennes ("The Sicilian Vespers")   Giuseppe Verdi, 1854.
The opera in five acts is set to a libretto by Eugène Scribe and Charles Duveyrier based on their earlier libretto for Gaetano Donizetti's opera Le **Duc d'Albe**. The plot is set in Sicily in 1282 and centers on the historical incident that year known as the Sicilian Vespers, when Sicilian patriots massacred the French in Palermo. (The riot began in a church at the hour of vespers on Easter Monday, March 30.) The opera is also known by its equivalent Italian title, *I vespri siciliani*. See also **Vespri**.

La Vera costanza ("True Constancy")   Joseph Haydn, 1777–8.
The opera in three acts is set to a libretto by Francesco Puttini that tells of the mutual loyalty of Rosina and Errico as husband and wife despite attempts by Errico's aunt, Irene, who is unaware they are married, to betroth Rosina to the fop, Villotto.

"Verdi prati" ("Green meadows").
Ruggiero's aria in Act 2 of Handel's **Alcina**, in which he says that the pleasant scene around him will soon revert to its former horror.

Verdi's Requiem *see* **Requiem** (1).

Vergebliches Ständchen ("Vain Serenade")   Johannes Brahms, 1882.
The song for voice and piano, the fourth of the set of five, Op.82, is set to traditional words.

"La Vergine degli angeli" ("The Virgin of the Angels").
Padre Guardiano's prayer in Act 2 of Verdi's La **Forza del destino**, asking that the Virgin may protect Leonora.

Das Verhör des Lukullus *see* **Die Verurteilung des Lukullus**.

Verklärte Nacht ("Transfigured Night")   Arnold Schoenberg, 1899.
The string sextet, Op. 4, is based on a poem in Richard Dehmel's *Weib und Welt* ("Wife and World") (1896) telling of a couple's walk through a moonlit grove. The woman confesses she is pregnant by another, there is a heartrending upheaval, the man forgives her, and the night is transfigured in a cloud of spiritual ecstasy.

Véronique ("Veronica")   André Charles Messager, 1898.
The operetta in three acts is set to a libretto by Albert van Loo and Georges Duval telling how Hélène de Solanges, about to be married to Florestan de Valaincourt, overhears him describing her unfavorably and so pretends to be a flower girl, Véronique, in order to teach him a lesson and win his love.

Das Verratene Meer ("The Sea Betrayed")   Hans Werner Henze, 1986–9.
The opera in two acts is set to a libretto by H.-U. Treichel of Yukio Mishima's novel *The Sailor Who Betrayed the Sea* (Japanese, *Gogo no eiko*) (1970).

Die Verschworenen *see* Der **Häusliche Krieg**.

Die Verurteilung des Lukullus ("The Condemnation of Lucullus")   Paul Dessau, 1950.
The opera in 12 scenes, to a libretto by Bertolt Brecht, is an antiwar protest telling what happens when the dead Roman general, Lucullus (*c*.106–before 56 BC), arrives in the underworld and must stand trial before he is allowed to enter the Elysian Fields. The opera has the alternate German title *Das Verhör des Lukullus* ("The Interrogation of Lucullus").

Vert-Vert   Jacques Offenbach, 1869.
The comic opera in three acts, to a libretto by Henri Meilhac and Charles Nuittier, opens in a French convent school with the burial of the school parrot, Vert-Vert ("Greenie"). The girls are so touched by the funeral oration given by the headmistress's young nephew, Monsieur Valentin, that they adopt him as the school pet, while he in turn assumes the name Vert-Vert.

Vesalii Icones ("Images of Vesalius")   Peter Maxwell Davies, 1969.
The theater piece for male dancer, solo cello, and ensemble comprises 14 dances based on the anatomical drawings by the Flemish

physician Andreas Vesalius in his *De humani corporis fabrica libri septem* ("The Seven Books on the Structure of the Human Body") (1543) with the 14 Stations of the Cross superimposed on the Vesalian images. Hence the title.

Vesperae solennes de confessore ("Solemn Vespers of the Confessor")   W.A. Mozart, 1780.

The work for four solo voices, chorus, orchestra, and organ, K 339, is a setting of the five psalms and **Magnificat** that comprise most of the Roman evening service of Vespers. *See also* **Laudate Dominum**.

Vespri ("Vespers")   Giuseppe Verdi, 1973.

The divertissement, choreographed by André Prokovsky, is a display piece set to the *Four Seasons* ballet music from the composer's Les **Vêpres siciliennes.**

I Vespri siciliani *see* Les **Vêpres siciliennes**.

La Vestale ("The Vestal Virgin")   Gasparo Spontini, 1805.

The opera in three acts is set to a libretto by Victor Joseph Étienne de Jouy (originally written for François Boieldieu and subsequently refused by Étienne-Nicolas Méhul) telling what happens when the vestal virgin, Giulia, who loves the general, Licinio, lets the sacred flame go out in the temple of Vesta when he visits her there during her vigil.

"Vesti la giubba" ("Put on the jacket").

Canio's aria in Act 1 of Leoncavallo's I **Pagliacci**, bemoaning his duty to don his clown's costume and make others laugh despite his own broken heart. The words are traditionally rendered in English as "On with the motley," a phrase that has entered the language to mean "On with the show," as a rallying call when one has to proceed in the face of difficulties. ("Motley" is properly the particolored costume worn by a fool or jester.)

Il Viaggio a Reims ("The Journey to Rheims")   Gioacchino Rossini, 1825.

The opera in one act is set to a libretto by Luigi Balocchi partly based on Madame de Staël's novel *Corinne, ou L'Italie* ("Corinne, or Italy") (1807). The story is set in Plombières, France, in 1825 and tells how a group of travelers to the coronation, finding no coach horses available at the inn, pass the time by telling stories and singing songs. The subtitle is *L'albergo del giglio d'oro* ("The Golden Lily Inn"). The

work was written for the coronation in Rheims of Charles X of France.

Victory   Richard Rodney Bennett, 1968–9.

The opera in three acts is set to a libretto by Beverley Cross based on Joseph Conrad's novel of the same name (1915) telling what happens when Axel Heyst, a reclusive wanderer, takes the English girl, Lena, to his island retreat in Indonesia. The novel is essentially a meditation on the biblical verse: "O death, where is thy sting? O grave, where is thy victory?" (1 Corinthians 15:57). Hence its title and that of the opera.

Victory Symphony   Ludwig van Beethoven, 1804–8.

The Symphony No. 5 in C minor, Op. 67, was so nicknamed in Britain during World War II from the rhythm of the four opening notes, like the letter "V" in Morse code ($\cdots$ –), used on the radio and elsewhere as a victory signal.

La Vida breve ("Brief Life")   Manuel de Falla, 1904–5.

The opera in two acts, to a libretto by Carlos Fernández Shaw, is set in Granada, Spain, at the turn of the 20th century and recounts the tragic outcome when the gypsy girl, Salud, who loves Paco, finds that he was only pretending to return her love and that in reality he plans to marry Carmela.

La Vie parisienne ("Parisian Life")   Jacques Offenbach, 1866.

The operetta in five (later four) acts, to a libretto by Henri Meilhac and Ludovic Halévy, is a satire on Second Empire morals (or lack of them) set in Paris in 1867. The story tells what happens when two penniless rakes, Raoul de Gardefeu and Bobinet, dupe two Swedish aristocrats into thinking they are tourist guides.

Vienna Waltzes   Johann Strauss II, Franz Lehár, and Richard Strauss, 1977.

The ballet in five parts, choreographed by George Balanchine, is set to Johann Strauss's **Tales from the Vienna Woods** and **Frühlingsstimmen,** Lehár's **Gold and Silver** concert waltz, and the waltzes from Richard Strauss's Der **Rosenkavalier.** The ballet follows these pieces in a revue of Vienna's 19th-century past.

Vier ernste Gesänge ("Five Serious Songs") Johannes Brahms, 1896.

The song cycle for voice and piano, Op.121, comprises four songs set to extracts from Luther's translation of the Bible. The individual titles are:

(1) *Denn es gehet dem Menschen* ("For it comes to man"), (2) *Ich wandte mich und sahe an alle* ("I turned and looked at all"), (3) *O Tod, O Tod, wie bitter bist du* ("O Death, O Death, how cruel thou art"), (4) *Wenn ich mit Engelszungen redete* ("Though I speak with the tongues of angels").

Vier letzte Lieder ("Four Last Songs") Richard Strauss, 1948.

The four songs for high voice and orchestra, set to poems by Joseph von Eichendorff and Hermann Hesse, were the composer's last works, and the title was given by the publisher after his death. (A fifth song remains unfinished.) In order of composition, the songs are: (1) *Im Abendrot* ("In the Sunset"), (2) *Frühling* ("Spring"), (3) *Beim Schlafengehen* ("Falling Asleep"), (4) *September* ("September"). The first of these is by Eichendorff, the others by Hesse. The composer himself is said to have favored the order (3), (4), (2), (1).

Vier Tondichtungen nach A. Böcklin ("Four Tone Poems after A. Böcklin") Max Reger, 1913.

The orchestral work comprises impressions of four paintings by Arnold Böcklin (1827–1901): *Island of the Dead* (*see* The **Isle of the Dead**), *Hermit with a Violin*, *Sport Among the Waves*, and *Bacchanal*.

Vigil Symphony James MacMillan, 1997.

The symphony in three movements celebrates the Easter Eve vigil of the Christian Church. The first and last movements are accordingly subtitled *Light* and *Water*, for the key elements in the Roman Catholic liturgy for this day.

The Village Band *see* Ein **Musikalischer Spass**.

The Village Coquettes John Pyke Hullah, 1836.

The opera in two acts is set to a libretto by Charles Dickens telling what happens when two village beauties, Rose Benson and her cousin Lucy, are courted by Squire Norton and his villainous friend, the Hon. Sparkins Flam.

A Village Romeo and Juliet Frederick Delius, 1899–1901.

The opera in a prologue and three acts is set to a German libretto by the composer based on Gottfried Keller's story *Romeo und Julia auf dem Dorfe* ("Romeo and Juliet from the Village") in his collection *Die Leute von Seldwyla* ("The People of Seldwyla") (1856, 1874). The plot is set in mid–19th-century Switzerland and tells of the doomed love between the girl Vrenchen and the boy Sali, the children of two quarreling farmers. The opera is also known by the German title of Keller's story. *See also* The **Walk to the Paradise Garden**.

Le Villi ("The Wili") Giacomo Puccini, 1883.

The opera in one act (later revised to two) is set to a libretto by Ferdinando Fontana based on Alphonse Karr's story *Les Wilis* ("The Wili") (1852). The story is set in the Black Forest in medieval times and tells how when Anna is abandoned by her fiancée, Roberto, and dies of grief, her spirit joins the wili, the ghosts of betrothed maidens deserted by their lovers. (*Cf.* **Giselle**.)

Le Vin herbé ("The Enchanted Wine") Frank Martin, 1938–41.

The secular oratorio is based on the legend of Tristan and Iseult. The title alludes to the love potion that the two accidentally drink and that binds them to each other in eternal love.

Vingt Regards sur l'Enfant Jésus ("Twenty Contemplations of the Child Jesus") Olivier Messiaen, 1944.

In the words of the composer, the set of 20 pieces for solo piano presents "the various contemplations of the child Jesus in the crib and the Adorations which are bestowed upon him" (quoted in Staines and Buckley, p. 259). Each piece has its own title: (1) *Regard du Père* ("Contemplation of the Father"), (2) *Regard de l'étoile* ("Contemplation of the Star"), (3) *L'échange* ("The Exchange"), (4) *Regard de la Vierge* ("Contemplation of the Virgin"), (5) *Regard du Fils sur le Fils* ("Contemplation of the Son over the Son"), (6) *Par lui tout a été fait* ("By him everything was made"), (7) *Regard de la Croix* ("Contemplation of the Cross"), (8) *Regard des hauteurs* ("Contemplation of the Heights"), (9) *Regard du temps* ("Contemplation of Time"), (10) *Regard de l'esprit de joie* ("Contemplation of the Joyful Spirit"), (11) *Première Communion de la Vierge* ("First Communion of the Virgin"), (12) *La Parole toute-puissante* ("The Omnipotent Word"), (13) *Noël* ("Christmas"), (14) *Regard des anges* ("Contemplation of the Angels"), (15) *Le Baiser de l'Enfant-Jésus* ("The Kiss of the Child Jesus"), (16) *Regard des prophètes, des bergers et des mages* ("Contemplation of the Prophets, Shepherds, and Magi"), (17) *Regard du silence* ("Contemplation of Silence"), (18) *Regard de l'onction terrible* ("Contemplation of the Dread Unction"), (19) *Je dors, mais mon cœur veille* ("I sleep, but my heart is awake"), (20) *Regard de l'église de l'amour* ("Contemplation of the Church of Love").

Viola Bedřich Smetana, 1884

The unfinished opera is set to a libretto by Eliška Krásnohorská based on Shakespeare's *Twelfth Night* (1601), in which Viola is a young woman who disguises herself as a man, falls in love with the duke Orsino, and is loved in turn (in her male disguise) by Olivia.

Violanta Erich Korngold, 1916.

The opera in one act, to a libretto by Hans Müller, is set in 15th-century Venice and tells what happens when Alfonso seduces Violanta's sister.

Violin Concerto Igor Stravinsky, 1972.

The plotless ballet in four movements, choreographed by George Balanchine, is set to the composer's Violin Concerto (1931), as the title states, and is danced by two couples and a corps of nine female dancers and seven male.

Violin Phase Steve Reich, 1967.

The piece for four violins has the first three violins all playing the same repeated phrases but spacing them out at time intervals of a half-note. The process is thus one of "phasing," or gradually separating parts from an initial unison. The fourth violin picks out the patterns that result at each stage of the phasing process.

The Violins of Saint-Jacques Malcolm Williamson, 1966.

The opera in three acts is set to a libretto by William Chappell based on Patrick Leigh Fermor's novel of the same title (1953). The story is set in the Caribbean shortly before a volcanic eruption.

Le Violon du Diable ("The Devil's Violin") Cesare Pugni, 1849.

The ballet in two acts, with a libretto and choreography by Arthur Saint-Léon, tells what happens when a sinister doctor bewitches the tone of the violin played by the young violinist, Urbain, when he falls in love with the beautiful Hélène.

The Vision *see* Lieder ohne Worte.

"Vision fugitive" ("Fleeting vision").

Hérode's aria in Act 2 of Massenet's **Hérodiade**, in which he sings of the vision of Salomé that haunts him day and night.

A Vision of Aeroplanes Ralph Vaughan Williams, 1956.

The motet for mixed chorus and organ is set to a biblical text from Ezekiel 1, in which the prophet describes his vision of "living creatures" and wheels in the air.

The Vision of Judgement Peter Racine Fricker, 1957–8.

The oratorio for soprano and tenor soloists, chorus, and orchestra, Op. 29, is set to a text compiled by the composer from the writings of the 8th-century Anglo-Saxon poet and scholar, Cynewulf.

The Vision of St. Augustine Michael Tippett, 1963–5.

The work for baritone, chorus, and orchestra is set to Latin texts from St. Augustine's *Confessions* (397–401) and from the Bible.

Visions de l'Amen ("Visions of the Amen") Olivier Messiaen, 1943.

The suite for two pianos has seven movements as seven images of concurrence, each with a title based on the prayer word *Amen*, as follows: (1) *Amen de la création* ("Amen of the Creation"), (2) *Amen des étoiles, de la planète à l'anneau* ("Amen of the Stars, of the Ringed Planet"), (3) *Amen de l'agonie de Jésus* ("Amen of the Agony of Jesus"), (4) *Amen du désir* ("Amen of Desire"), (5) *Amen des anges, des saints, du chant des oiseaux* ("Amen of the Angels, the Saints, the Song of Birds"), (6) *Amen du jugement* ("Amen of Judgement"), (7) *Amen de la consommation* ("Amen of Consummation").

Visions fugitives (Russian, *Mimolyotnosti*, "Fleeting Visions") Sergey Prokofiev, 1915–17.

The 20 pieces for piano, Op. 22, comprise miniature evocations of different kinds. The title quotes from Konstantin Balmont's poem "I do not know wisdom": "In every fugitive vision I see whole worlds. They change endlessly, flashing in playful rainbow colors."

The Visit of the Old Lady *see* Der Besuch der alten Dame.

"Vissi d'arte" ("I have lived for art").

Tosca's aria in Act 2 of Puccini's **Tosca**, in which she laments the unjustness of her fate (to surrender to Scarpia) and prays for strength to meet it. A fuller version is: "*Vissi d'arte, vissi d'amore*" ("I have lived for art, lived for love").

"Viva il vino" ("Long live wine").

Turiddu's drinking song in Mascagni's

Cavalleria rusticana. The words are more effective with their following adjective: "*Viva il vino spumeggiante*" ("Long live sparkling wine").

Viva Vivaldi! ("Long Live Vivaldi!") Antonio Vivaldi, 1965.

The plotless ballet in one act, choreographed by Gerald Arpino, is set to the composer's Violin Concerto in D major (*c.*1714) in an arrangement for orchestra with solo classic guitar. This gives the work a slight Spanish flavor. Hence the (euphonious) Spanish-style title.

La Vivandière ("The Vivandière") Cesare Pugni, 1844.

The ballet in one act, with a libretto and choreography by Arthur Saint-Léon, is set in a little village in Hungary and tells of the problems that beset Kathi, a vivandière, and Hans, an innkeeper's son, before they can get married. (A vivandière is a camp follower, a female attendant in a regiment who sells liquor and provisions.)

Vltava *see* **Má Vlast.**

Vocalise en forme d'habanera ("Vocalise in the Form of a Habanera") Maurice Ravel, 1907.

A vocalise (pronounced "vocaleez") is a wordless vocal piece sung to one or more vowels. Here, as one of the earliest examples of this type of music, it has piano accompaniment and takes the form of a **Habanera**. It was later transcribed for other instruments.

"Voce di donna" ("Voice of a woman").

La Cieca's aria in Act 1 of Puccini's La **Gioconda**, voicing her thanks to Laura for saving her from being condemned as a witch. A fuller form of the words is: "*Voce di donna o d'angelo*" ("Voice of a woman or angel").

Voces intimae ("Friendly Voices") Jean Sibelius, 1908–9.

The title is the composer's own for the String Quartet in D minor, Op. 56, with particular reference to the slow third movement.

Die Vögel ("The Birds") Walter Braunfels, 1920.

The opera is set to the composer's own libretto based on Aristophanes' comedy *The Birds* (414 BC), telling what happens when two fugitives from Athenian taxation and litigation, Euelpides and Pithetaurus, persuade the birds to found a city in the clouds (Nephelecoccygia, "Cloud-Cuckoo-Land").

"Der Vogelfänger bin ich, ja," ("Yes, I am the bird-catcher").

Papageno's aria introducing himself as the bird-catcher in Act 1 of Mozart's Die **Zauberflöte**.

"Voi che sapete" ("You who know").

Cherubino's song that he has just composed and that he sings to the Countess in Act 2 of Mozart's Le **Nozze di Figaro**.

"Voi lo sapete, o mamma" ("You know, O mother").

Santuzza's account to Mamma Lucia of her betrayal by Turiddu in Mascagni's **Cavalleria rusticana**.

The Voice of Ariadne Thea Musgrave, 1972–3.

The opera in three acts is set to a libretto by Amalia Elguera based on Henry James's story *The Last of the Valerii* (1874). The plot tells what happens when Count Valerio, fascinated by the legend of a statue buried in his garden, orders an excavation that produces a pedestal inscribed "Ariadne."

La Voix humaine ("The Human Voice") Francis Poulenc, 1958.

The opera ("*tragédie lyrique*") in one act, to a libretto by Jean Cocteau, represents one side of a telephone conversation between a young woman and her lover, who has jilted her.

Volkslied ("Folksong") Felix Mendelssohn, 1841.

The piano piece Op. 53 No. 5 in A minor in Book 4 of the **Lieder ohne Worte** was so named by the composer.

Volo di Notte ("Night Flight") Luigi Dallapiccola, 1940.

The opera in one act is set to the composer's own libretto based on Antoine de Saint-Exupéry's novel *Vol de nuit* ("Night Flight") (1931). The story is set in an airport control room and tells of the tensions that develop as the arrival of a pilot on a night flight is anxiously awaited.

Voluntaries Francis Poulenc, 1973.

The ballet in one act, choreographed by Glen Tetley, is set to the composer's Concerto in G minor for Organ, Strings, and Timpani (1938) and according to the choreographer, "is conceived as a linked series of voluntaries" (quoted in Koegler, p. 439), "voluntary" here in the sense of the organ improvisation played before or after a religious service. The title may also have been intended to suggest a free-ranging dance, one of the dancer's own "volition."

Von ewiger Liebe ("Eternal Love")
Johannes Brahms, 1868.

The song for voice and piano, the first of the set of four, Op. 43, is a setting of a poem by August Heinrich Hoffmann von Fallersleben (1798–1874).

Von Heute auf Morgen ("From Day to Day")   Arnold Schoenberg, 1928–9.

The comic opera in one act, to a libretto by Max Blonda (pen name of the composer's wife), recounts the ruses adopted by a wife to make her husband appreciate her. The work aims "to show, using everyday figures and goings-on, how … the merely modern, the fashionable, lives only 'from one day to the next,' from insecure hand to greedy mouth — in marriage, but at least equally in art, in politics, and in people's views about life" (Willi Reich, *Schoenberg: A Critical Biography*, translated by L. Black, 1971).

The Voyevoda   Pyotr Tchaikovsky, 1867–8.

The opera in three acts is set to a libretto by the composer and Alexander Ostrovsky loosely based on the latter's play of the same name (1864), about a military leader (voivode) and his dreams and fancies. The subtitle is *Dream on the Volga* (Russian, *Son na Volge*).

W

Wachet auf ("Awake")   J.S. Bach, 1731.

The church cantata No. 140 is based on a Lutheran chorale set to the words of a German hymn written by Philipp Nicolai in 1597. The English equivalent of the title is usually given as "Sleepers, wake" or "Wake, O wake." The full original title was "*Wachet auf, ruft uns die Stimme*" ("Awake, the voice calls us"). The prime religious imagery is of Christ as the bridegroom, as found in the parable of the wise and foolish virgins (Matthew 25:1–13). The title is also that of Bach's choral prelude for organ, BWV 645.

Der Waffenschmied ("The Armorer")
Albert Lortzing, 1846.

The opera in three acts is set to the composer's own libretto based on Friedrich Julius Wilhelm Ziegler's comedy *Liebhaber und Neben-*

buhler in einer Person ("Lover and Rival in One Person") (1790). The story is set in 16th-century Worms and tells of the love of Count Liebenau for Marie, daughter of the armorer, Stadinger, and of his wooing of her both as himself and in the guise of a young apprentice, Conrad.

Wagner Symphony   Anton Bruckner, 1873.

The Symphony No. 3 in D minor is so named because it was dedicated to Richard Wagner. The composer visited Wagner in Bayreuth and showed him several works, saying he would like to dedicate one to him. Wagner chose this symphony, with its bold trumpet theme.

"Wahn! Wahn!" ("Delusion! Delusion!").

Hans Sachs's monologue in Act 3 of Wagner's Die **Meistersinger von Nürnberg**, in which he meditates on the follies of the world.

Waisenhausmesse ("Orphanage Mass")
W.A. Mozart, 1768.

The Mass No. 4 in C minor, K 139, was composed for the dedication of the new Orphanage Church (German, *Waisenhauskirche*) at Salzburg. Hence the title.

Wait Till the Clouds Roll By   Joseph Haydn, *c.*1799.

The String Quartet in F major, Op. 77 No. 82, is (or was) so nicknamed because of the slight similarity between the opening phrase of the work and J.T. Wood's popular song of this name (1881) (music by H.J. Fulmer), with the lines: "Wait till the clouds roll by, Jenny, / Wait till the clouds roll by; / Jenny, my own true loved one, / Wait till the clouds roll by."

Waldszenen ("Woodland Scenes")   Robert Schumann, 1848–9.

The nine pieces for piano, Op. 82, with German forest romanticism as their general theme, have individual titles as follows: (1) *Eintritt* ("Entrance"), (2) *Jäger auf der Lauer* ("Huntsmen in Waiting"), (3) *Einsame Blumen* ("Lonely Blossoms"), (4) *Verrufene Stelle* ("Disreputable Place"), (5) *Freundliche Landschaft* ("Friendly Countryside"), (6) *Herberge* ("Inn"), (7) *Vogel als Prophet* ("Bird as Prophet"), (8) *Jagdlied* ("Hunting Song"), (9) *Abschied* ("Farewell").

Waldstein Sonata   Ludwig van Beethoven, 1804.

The Piano Sonata No. 21 in C major, Op. 53, was dedicated by the composer to his patron, Count Ferdinand von Waldstein (1762–1823). Hence the name.

Waldweben *see* **Forest Murmurs**.

The Walk to the Paradise Garden   Frederick Delius, 1907.

The intermezzo for orchestra before the last scene of A **Village Romeo and Juliet** takes its name from the village inn, the "Paradise Garden". (The evocative name is etymologically tautological, for *paradise* actually means "garden," as the Old Testament Garden of Eden.) The 1972 ballet in one act of the same name, choreographed by Frederick Ashton, is set to this work and depicts two ecstatic lovers who finally meet the Angel of Death.

Die Walküre *see* Der **Ring des Nibelungen**.

Wallenstein's Camp   Bedřich Smetana, 1858–9.

The symphonic poem was originally planned as an overture to Friedrich Schiller's play of the same name, *Wallensteins Lager* (1798), a prelude to his tragedy *Wallenstein*, centering on the Austrian general Albrecht Wallenstein (1583–1634), but finished as symphony-style work in four movements, with individual titles: *Crowd Scene, Dancing and Friar's Harangue, The Camp Asleep*, and *Reveille and March*.

La Wally ("Wally")   Alfredo Catalani, 1890–1.

The opera in four acts is set to a libretto by Luigi Illica based on Wilhelmine von Hillern's novel *Die Geyer-Wally* (1875). The story is set in the Tyrol at the turn of the 19th century and tells what happens when Hagenbach does not return the love of the hoyden girl, Wally. (The Italian conductor Arturo Toscanini liked the opera so much that he named his daughter Wally. The name itself is a pet form of Valerie.)

Walpurgis Night   Charles Gounod, 1869.

The ballet divertissement from the last act of the composer's opera **Faust** has often been performed as a separate ballet since this original production in Paris, choreographed by Henri Justament. The title refers to the witches' sabbath (held on St. Walpurgis' Night, the eve of May 1) to which Mephistopheles transports Faust with the aim of blotting out his memory of Marguerite.

Waltz (German *walzen*, "to revolve").

The well known dance in ¾ time, popularly associated with the ballroom, has been taken up by many composers, but especially the two Johann Strausses and Chopin. Beethoven and Schubert also wrote walzes, as did Tchaikovsky in his operas and ballets.

Ein Walzertraum ("A Waltz Dream") Oscar Straus, 1907.

The operetta in three acts is set to a libretto by Felix Dörmann and Leopold Jacobson based on a short story in Hans Müller's *Das Buch der Abenteuer* ("The Book of Adventures"). The story opens with the marriage of Princess Helene to the Viennese lieutenant, Niki, who is tempted away from his bride by a young girl, Franzi, and the romantic Dream Waltz that she sings. To win her new husband back, the Princess asks Franzi to teach her the words of the Waltz. Niki hears her singing it and gladly returns.

The Wand of Youth   Edward Elgar, 1907, 1908.

The two orchestral suites, Opp. 1a and 1b, were arranged and orchestrated from material the composer wrote for a family play in 1869, when he was 12. In this, the crossing of a stream in a woodland glade takes children, as if by the wave of a magic wand, into a realm remote from the unimaginative world of their parents. Suite No. 1 has seven parts: (1) *Overture*, (2) *Serenade*, (3) *Minuet*, (4) *Sun Dance*, (5) *Fairy Pipers*, (6) *Slumber Scene*, (7) *Fairies and Giants*. Suite No. 2 has six parts: (1) *March*, (2) *The Little Bells*, (3) *Moths and Butterflies*, (4) *Fountain Dance*, (5) *The Tame Bear*, (6) *Wild Bears*.

Der Wanderer ("The Wanderer")   Franz Schubert, 1816.

The song, D 493, takes its text from the poem of the same name by Georg Philipp Schmidt. The poet changed the original title of his poem, *Der Unglückliche* ("The Unhappy Man"), to *Der Fremdling* ("The Stranger"), leading Schubert to write on the frontispiece of a transposed version of the song (1818): "DER WANDERER: oder DER FREMDLING: oder DER UNGLÜCKLICHE." The wanderer himself is an unhappy lover roaming the earth in search of an unattainable ideal. The 1941 ballet in four scenes of the same name, with a libretto and choreography by Frederick Ashton, is set to the composer's **Wanderer Fantasy** and centers on a man who recapitulates in his imagination various episodes from his life.

The Wanderer *see* **Lieder ohne Worte**.

Wanderer Fantasy (German, *Wanderer-Fantasie*)   Franz Schubert, 1822.

The Fantasia in C major for piano, D 760,

is so called because the adagio section is a set of variations on a passage from the song Der **Wanderer**.

The Wandering Scholar   Gustav Holst, 1929–30.

The chamber opera in one act, Op. 50, is set to a libretto by Clifford Bax founded on an incident in Helen Waddell's study of the "vagrants" of the Middle Ages so titled (1927). The plot is set in 13th-century France and tells what happens when Alison receives the lecherous priest, Philippe, while her husband, Louis, is away at the market but is interrupted by the arrival of the scholar, Pierre.

War and Peace   (Russian, *Voyna i mir*) Sergey Prokofiev, 1941–3.

The opera in two parts (five acts) is set to a libretto by the composer and Mira Mendelson-Prokofieva based on Lev Tolstoy's novel of the same name (1869). The plot thus charts the tragic course of love of Natasha Rostova and Prince Andrey against the background of the Russian people's epic struggle against the forces of Napoleon. The work was composed and first performed in World War II, giving its plot (and title) a contemporary relevance.

War Requiem   Benjamin Britten, 1961.

The choral work, Op. 66, for soprano, tenor, and baritone soloists, boys' choir, chorus, organ, and orchestra, interpolates settings of poems by the war poet Wilfred Owen (1893–1918) in the composer's setting of the **Requiem** Mass. The first performance was in the new Coventry Cathedral, built after the historic one was destroyed by German air raids in World War II.

Warsaw Concerto   Richard Addinsell, 1941.

The pastiche of a romantic piano concerto in the style of Rachmaninov was specially composed for the British movie *Dangerous Moonlight* (US title, *Suicide Squadron*) (1941), in which it is played by the hero, a Polish bomber pilot and pianist who escapes from the Nazis and loses his memory after flying in the Battle of Britain.

The Wasps   Ralph Vaughan Williams, 1909.

The work for tenor and baritone soloists, male chorus, and orchestra was composed as incidental music for the 1909 Cambridge University production of Aristophanes' play of the same name (422 BC), satirizing the litigiousness of the Athenians in the person of the mean and waspish old man Philocleon.

Wat Tyler   Alan Bush, 1948–50.

The opera in a prologue and two acts is set to a libretto by Nancy Bush, the composer's wife, telling of events (from a left-wing viewpoint) surrounding the Peasants' Revolt of 1381 in which the rebels' leader, Wat Tyler, was killed.

Water Music   (1) George Frideric Handel, 1715; (2) John Cage, 1952; (3) (Japanese, *Mizu no kyoku*) Toru Takemitsu, 1960.

Handel's instrumental suite was probably written for a royal water party on the Thames River, although the story that he wrote it for such a party to restore himself to favor with George I is unsubstantiated. Cage's piano work requires the performer to provide a visual interest by pouring water from pots, blowing whistles under water, and the like. Takemitsu's electronic piece is made exclusively from the recorded sounds of water. The three identical titles thus conceal a totally disparate use of water for a musical end.

The Water Sprite   (1) (Czech, *Vodník*), Antonín Dvořák, 1896; (2) *see* **Rusalka**.

The symphonic poem, Op. 107, also known as *The Water Goblin*, is based on a ballad by K.J. Erben telling how a young girl overbalances into a lake while washing her clothes and falls prey to the water sprite in his underwater kingdom.

Water Study   none, 1928.

The ballet in one act, choreographed by Doris Humphrey, has no music but is set in silence for a group of 14 dancers. It is "a collection of images of water …, using movement that does not *describe* the movement of water but corresponds to its energies and spatial configurations" (Marcia B. Siegel, quoted in Koegler, p. 444).

Watermill   Teiji Ito, 1972.

The ballet in one act, choreographed by Jerome Robbins, is influence by Japanese *no* techniques and depicts a man summing up his life, which reflects the phases of the moon and the cycle of seasons. The title refers to the watermill that also symbolizes the flow of time.

Watts Symphony   Charles Villiers Stanford, 1905.

The Symphony No. 6 in E flat, with full title *In memoriam G.F. Watts*, is dedicated to the memory of the English artist George Frederic Watts (1817–1904).

Weber's Last Waltz   Karl Reissiger, 1826.

The piano piece was found among Weber's possessions at his death in 1826 and was long assumed to be by him. It is in fact by Reissiger, as No. 5 of his *Danses brillantes*, Op. 26. Its German title is *Webers letzter Gedanke* ("Weber's Last Thought").

We Come to the River (German, *Wir erreichen den Fluß*)   Hans Werner Henze, 1976.

The opera in two acts, to a libretto by Edward Bond, is an antiwar protest telling how a general who renounces violence is confined to a madhouse where he is smothered by the inmates under sheets they take for river water.

The Wedding *see* **Les Noces**.

A Wedding Bouquet   Lord Berners, 1937.

The ballet in one act, with a libretto by the composer and choreography by Frederick Ashton, is a comic work about a wedding, set in France at the turn of the 20th century. The story tells how the groom is embarrassed to find various former mistresses among the wedding guests, including Julia, who has gone mad with grief. Phrases from Gertrude Stein's play *They Must Be Wedded, To Their Wife* (1931) are spoken by a narrator seated at a table on the stage, and relate to the various incidents depicted.

Wedding Cake   Camille Saint-Saëns, 1886.

The Valse Caprice for Piano and Orchestra, Op. 76, is a series of sparkling waltzes. Hence the nickname, which conjures up the glitter of a wedding reception and the decorated cake itself.

Wedding Day at Troldhaugen (Norwegian, *Bryllupsdag på Troldhaugen*)   Edvard Grieg, 1897.

The piano piece, No. 6 of Book 8, Op. 65, of the *Lyric Pieces*, depicts the celebration of a wedding at Troldhaugen ("Troll Hill"), the composer's villa from 1885 outside Bergen, Norway. *See also* **Lyric Suite** (1).

Wedding March   (1) Richard Wagner, 1850; (2) Felix Mendelssohn, 1843.

There are two traditional marches for church weddings in the English-speaking world, both being organ arrangements of the original. The march for the entry of the bride, also known as *The Bridal Chorus* or *Here Comes the Bride*, comes from Act 3, Scene 1 of Wagner's opera **Lohengrin** as part of the wedding festivities of Elsa and Lohengrin. That for the exit of the married couple comes from the sixth number of Mendelssohn's incidental music to A **Midsummer Night's Dream**. The vogue for the Mendelssohn began in 1847 and was popularized in

1858 when Queen Victoria's daughter, Princess Victoria, the Princess Royal, used it for her wedding to Prince Friedrich Wilhelm of Prussia (the future German emperor, Friedrich III), at the Chapel Royal, St. James's Palace, London. The exit march is now also often the fifth movement (**Toccata**) of Charles-Marie Widor's Organ Symphony No. 5 (1878), a vogue begun by the Duchess of Kent, then Lady Katharine Worsley, on her marriage in 1961 to the Duke of Kent at York Minster. But the Widor is still more regarded as *a* wedding march than *the* Wedding March.

Wedding Scenes (Czech, *Svatební scény*) Bedřich Smetana, 1849.

The three pieces for piano, individually titled *Wedding Procession, Bride and Bridegroom*, and *Wedding Revels*, were written for the composer's pupil, Countess Marie F. Thun, at the time of her marriage to Baron L. Aerenthal.

Wedge Fugue   J.S. Bach, 1727–31.

The fugue in E minor for organ, BWV 548, is so called because of the "shape" of the subject, which proceeds in gradually widening intervals, like a wedge. This can be not only heard in the music but seen in its appearance in printed form.

Die Weihe des Hauses *see* **The Consecration of the House**.

Wein, Weib und Gesang *see* **Wine, Women, and Song**.

"Welche Wonne, welche Lust" ("What joy, what pleasure").

Blonde's aria in Act 2 of Mozart's Die **Entführung aus dem serail**, in which she delightedly receives the news of Belmonte's plans for escape.

The Well-Tempered Clavier *see* Das **Wohltemperierite Klavier**.

Welles Raises Kane   Bernard Herrmann, 1942.

The musical "portrait of Orson Welles" (1915–1985) is based on the music the composer wrote for the actor's films *Citizen Kane* (1940) and *The Magnificent Ambersons* (1942). Hence the punning title.

Werther   Jules Massenet, 1885–7.

The opera in four acts is set to a libretto by Édouard Blau, Paul Milliet, and Georges Hartmann based on Goethe's novel *Die Leiden des jungen Werthers* ("The Sorrows of Young

Werther") (1774), telling of the melancholy young poet, Werther, and his doomed love for the Bailie's daughter, Charlotte.

Wesendonck-Lieder *see* **Five Wesendonck Songs**.

West Side Story   Leonard Bernstein, 1956–7.

The musical in two acts, to a libretto by Arthur Laurents and choreography by Jerome Robbins, is based on Shakespeare's *Romeo and Juliet* (1594), but translates the rivalry between the Montagues and the Capulets into gang warfare terms, played out in New York's West Side.

Western Symphony   Hershy Kay, 1954.

The ballet in three movements was choreographed by George Balanchine, who wrote: "My idea in this ballet was to make a formal work that would derive its flavor from the informal American West.... I wanted to do a ballet without a story in an unmistakably native American idiom" (quoted in Koegler, p. 447). Hence the first word of the title.

The Whale   John Tavener, 1965–6.

The dramatic cantata for narrator, mezzosoprano, baritone, chorus, and orchestra is devoted to the whale in fact and fiction and is set to the composer's own text compiled from *Collins' Encyclopaedia* and the Vulgate (Latin version of the Bible).

"What is life without thee" *see* **"Che farò senza Euridice."**

"When I am laid in earth" *see* **Dido's Lament**.

When Lilacs Last in the Dooryard Bloom'd   Paul Hindemith, 1946.

The work for mezzosoprano, baritone, chorus, and orchestra, is set to the composer's German translation of Walt Whitman's poem of the same title (1865), itself an elegy on the death of Abraham Lincoln (1809–1865). The *Requiem for Those We Love*, as it is also known, was a lament for President F.D. Roosevelt (1882–1945) and the victims of World War II.

Where the Wild Things Are   Oliver Knussen, 1979–83.

The fantasy opera in one act (nine scenes), Op. 20, is set to a libretto by the composer and Maurice Sendak based on the latter's children's picture-book of the same title (1963), telling how Max, sent to his bedroom for causing chaos while wearing his wolf suit, imagines himself transported to the country of the Wild Things, who make him their king.

"Where'er you walk."

Jupiter's aria in Act 2 of Handel's **Semele**, in which he promises Semele shade over her head and springing flowers at her feet.

The Whims of Cupid and the Ballet Master (Danish, *Amors og Ballettmesterens Luner*)   Jens Lolle, 1786.

The ballet in one act, with a libretto and choreography by Vincenzo Galeotti, tells what happens when Cupid blindfolds the lovers that are brought to him from all over the world and mismatches the couples.

White Mass Sonata   Alexander Skryabin, 1911.

The Piano Sonata No. 7 in F sharp major, Op. 53, is so named for its "pure and saintly" style and content. *Cf.* **Black Mass Sonata**.

Who Cares?   George Gershwin arr. Hershy Kay, 1970.

The ballet in one act, choreographed by George Balanchine, is based on songs by the composer, and especially: "Who cares / If the sky cares to fall into the sea? / Who cares / What banks fail in Yonkers? / Long as you've got a kiss that conquers, / Why should I care? / Life is one long jubilee, / So long as I care for you / And you care for me" (1931).

Who Is Silvia? (German, *An Silvia*, "To Silvia")   Franz Schubert, 1826.

The song for voice and piano, D 891, was taken from Shakespeare's *The Two Gentlemen of Verona* (1594) (in which Silvia is the beloved of Proteus and a paragon of beauty) and translated into German by Eduard von Bauernfeld.

Der Widerspenstigen Zähmung ("The Taming of the Shrew")   Hermann Goetz, 1874.

The opera in four acts is set to a libretto by Joseph Viktor Widmann based on Shakespeare's comedy *The Taming of the Shrew* (1593), telling how Katharina (Kate), the "shrew" of the title, eventually becomes the submissive wife of the impoverished nobleman, Petruchio. (The play's German title literally translates as "The Taming of the Unruly One.")

Wiegenlied ("Cradle Song").

The title is used by several composers for a piece that is some form of lullaby, whether with or without words. The best known is probably Brahms's song *Wiegenlied*, Op. 49 No. 4 (1868), often known simply as *Brahms's Lullaby*. Schubert also has a *Wiegenlied*, D 498 (1815), set to words by an unknown writer, as has Richard Strauss, Op. 41 No. 1 (1899).

Wiener Blut ("Viennese Blood") Johann Strauss II, 1899.

The operetta in three acts, to a libretto by Viktor Léon and Leo Stein, is set in Vienna during the 1815 Congress. The story tells how the ambassador, Count Zedlau, although married to Gabriele, is having affairs with both the ballerina, Franzi, and the model, Pepi, who is engaged to his valet, Josef. The aged but amorous prime minister, Prince Ypsheim-Gindelbach, is equally besotted with Franzi. The rest of the plot adds to these entanglements with a mélange of intrigue and misunderstanding, all because "it's in the blood," Viennese blood. A famous number is the waltz, "*Wiener Blut, Wiener Blut, eigner Saft, voller Kraft, voller Gluht*" ("Vienna blood, Vienna blood, Flows its course, Full of force, Full in flood").

Wiener Frauen ("Viennese Women") Franz Lehár, 1902.

The operetta in three acts, to a libretto by Ottokar Tann-Bergler and Emil Norini, tells the story of the romantic entanglements of a Viennese piano tuner, Willibald Brandl. Of the various "Viennese women" available he eventually chooses Jeanette, maid to the bride, Claire, of Philip Rosner, whose piano he tuned at their wedding reception.

The Wild Dove *see* The **Wood Dove**.

Der Wildschütz ("The Poacher") Albert Lortzing, 1842.

The opera in three acts is set to the composer's own libretto based on August von Kotzebue's comedy *Der Rehbock* ("The Roebuck"). The story is set in a German village and castle in the early 19th century and tells what happens when Baculus, a schoolmaster on the estate of the Count of Eberbach, accidentally shoots a buck. The opera's subtitle is *Die Stimme der Natur* ("The Voice of Nature").

William Ratcliff (Russian, *Vil'yam Ratklif*) César Cui, 1869.

The opera in three acts is set to a libretto by Alexei Nikolaevich Pleshcheyev based on Heinrich Heine's play *Wilhelm Ratcliff* (1822). The story is set in northern Scotland in the 17th century and tells what happens when Maria marries Douglas who is then told by her father, MacGregor, that William Ratcliff, whom she had earlier rejected, had murdered her two subsequent fiancés. *See also* **Guglielmo Ratcliff**.

William Tell *see* **Guillaume Tell**.

Willow Song (1) Gioacchino Rossini, 1816; (2) Giuseppe Verdi, 1887.

The name is usually given to Desdemona's song "*Assisa al piè d'un salice*" ("Seated at the foot of a willow") in Act 3 of Rossini's **Otello** and to her song "*Salce, salce*" ("Willow, willow") in Act 4 of Verdi's opera of the same name.

The Wine of Summer Havergal Brian, 1937.

The Symphony No. 5 for baritone and orchestra is based on the poem of the same name by Lord Alfred Douglas.

Wine, Women, and Song ("Wein, Weib, und Gesang") Johann Strauss II, 1869.

The waltzes, Op. 333, evoke the more obvious pleasures of Viennese society. The English title is usually given as above, although properly it should be "Wine, Woman, and Song," in the singular. The phrase is not the composer's but dates back to the couplet attributed to Martin Luther (1483–1546): "*Wer nicht liebt Wein, Weib und Gesang, / Der bleibt ein Narr sein Leben lang*" ("Who loves not woman, wine, and song / Remains a fool his whole life long").

Wings Bob Downes, 1970.

The plotless ballet in one act, choreographed by Christopher Bruce, was inspired by birdlike movements. Hence the title.

Winter Daydreams (Russian, *Zimniye gryozy*) Pyotr Tchaikovsky, 1866.

The Symphony No. 1 in G minor, Op. 13, took its name from the title of its first movement, *Winter Reverie on a Journey*, on which the American critic, James G. Huneker, carpingly commented: "The slush must have been ankle deep."

Winter Legends Arnold Bax, 1929–30.

The work in three movements for piano and orchestra evokes the different moods and attributes of winter. "The title *Winter Legends* is appropriate, implying as it does both legendary and seasonal connotations" (Colin Scott-Sutherland, *Arnold Bax*, 1973).

Winter Words Benjamin Britten, 1953.

The song cycle for high voice and piano

comprises settings of eight poems by Thomas Hardy, as follows: (1) *At Day-Close in November*, (2) *Midnight on the Great Western, or The Journeying Boy*, (3) *Wagtail and Baby*, (4) *The Little Old Table*, (5) *The Choirmaster's Burial, or The Tenor Man's Story*, (6) *Proud Songsters, Thrushes, Finches, and Nightingales*, (7) *At the Railway Station, Upway, or The Convict and Boy with the Violin*, (8) *Before Life and After*. The overall title is taken from Hardy's last published volume of poetry (1928).

Winterbranch   LaMonte Young, 1964.

The plotless ballet for six dancers, choreographed by Merce Cunningham, is a creation in which "the dancers are alternately confined by deep darkness and exposed by glaring light coming from sharp angles" (Marcia B. Siegel, quoted in Koegler, p. 450). The title, alluding to a tree branch standing out starkly against a winter sky or winter snow, evokes this.

Winterreise ("Winter Journey")   Franz Schubert, 1827.

The song cycle for male voice and piano, D 911, comprises settings of 24 poems by Wilhelm Müller (1823–4). They are arranged in two books with individual titles as follows: I (1) *Gute Nacht* ("Good Night"), (2) *Die Wetterfahne* ("The Weather Vane"), (3) *Gefrorne Träne* ("Frozen Tears"), (4) *Erstarrung* ("Frozen Rigidity"), (5) *Der Lindenbaum* ("The Lime Tree"), (6) *Wasserflut* ("Flood"), (7) *Auf dem Fluße* ("On the River), (8) *Rückblick* ("Backward Glance"), (9) *Irrlicht* ("Will-o'-the-wisp"), (10) *Rast* ("Rest"), (11) *Frühlingstraum* ("Dream of Spring"), (12) *Einsamkeit* ("Loneliness"); II (13) *Die Post* ("The Post"), (14) *Der greise Kopf* ("The Hoary Head"), (15) *Die Krähe* ("The Crow"), (16) *Letzte Hoffnung* ("Last Hope"), (17) *Im Dorfe* ("In the Village"), (18) *Der stürmische Morgen* ("The Stormy Morning"), (19) *Täuschung* ("Delusion"), (20) *Der Wegweiser* ("The Waypost"), (21) *Das Wirtshaus* ("The Inn"), (22) *Mut* ("Courage"), (23) *Die Nebensonnen* ("Phantom Suns"), (24) *Der Leiermann* ("The Hurdy-Gurdy Man"). (These are in Schubert's chosen order, not Müller's.)

"Winterstürme" ("Winter storms").

Siegmund's song in Act 1 of Wagner's *Die Walküre* in Der **Ring des Nibelungen**, in which he describes the yielding of winter to spring.

The Wise Virgins   William Walton, 1940.

The ballet in one act, with choreography by Frederick Ashton, has a scenario based on the New Testament parable of the wise and foolish virgins (Matthew 25). The music is the composer's arrangement of nine items from the cantatas of J.S.Bach, one of them being **Sheep may safely graze**.

The Witch Boy   Leonard Salzedo, 1956.

The ballet in one act (three scenes), with a libretto and choreography by Jack Carter, is based on an American version of the Scottish ballad of Barbara Allen (whose lover dies of unrequited love, and who was then filled with remorse).

Witch Minuet *see* **Fifths Quartet**.

With My Red Fires   Wallingford Riegger, 1936.

The ballet in two parts, with a libretto and choreography by Doris Humphrey, is the final section of a trilogy, the first two being *New Dance* and **Theatre Piece**. The two parts are respectively titled *Ritual* and *Drama* and the plot tells how "two Lovers fight to maintain themselves against the oppressiveness of the Matriarch" (Koegler, p. 450). The title comes from a poem by William Blake: "For the Divine Appearance is Brotherhood, but I am love / Elevate into the Region of Brotherhood with my red fires" (*Jerusalem: Chapter 2*, 1815).

Without Response *see* **Lieder ohne Worte**.

Das Wohltemperierte Klavier ("The Well-Tempered Clavier")   J.S. Bach, 1722, 1744.

This was the composer's title for his collection of 48 preludes and fugues for keyboard in all the major and minor keys, BWV 846–93, the first 24 being written in 1722, the rest in 1744. The collection is often known colloquially as just *The 48*. "Well-tempered" means effectively "well adjusted in tuning," referring to the 12 equal semitones into which Bach divided the octave, making it possible to transpose and modulate into any key. Under this system, such pairs of notes as B sharp and C, or C sharp and D flat, are combined instead of being treated as two separate notes. This means that neither of them is "true" (B sharp has been "tempered" slightly up, C slightly down), but they are so close that the ear will accept them as identical. Such a system has many practical advantages, one being to reduce the number of finger keys needed on a keyboard. The work is sometimes known in English as *The Well-Tempered Clavichord*, since this is the instrument on which it has traditionally been played, and on which Bach would have played it. But it is clear that Bach meant the new "temperament" to apply to all keyboard instruments, even the organ, not just the clavichord. (There may also have been some uncertainly about the distinction between *clavier* and *clavichord*.)

Wolf's Glen Scene   Carl Maria von Weber, 1821.

The name is usually given to the scene ending Act 2 of Der **Freischütz**, in which seven magic bullets are molded. The Wolf's Glen is the haunt of Samiel, the wild huntsman.

The Wood Dove (Czech, *Holoubek*)   Antonín Dvořák, 1896.

The symphonic poem, Op. 110, is based on a ballad by Karel Jaromír Erben, telling how a young widow remarries but is reproached by the mournful cooing of a wood dove over the grave of her first husband, whom she had poisoned. Tormented by her conscience, she drowns herself. The work is also known in English as *The Wild Dove*.

The Wooden Prince (Hungarian, *A fából faragott királyfi*, "The Wood-Carved Prince") Béla Bartók, 1917.

The ballet in one act, with a libretto by Béla Balász and choreography by Otto Zöbisch, is a fairy tale that tells what happens when a prince's unrequited love for a princess prompts him to carve a wooden prince to win her admiration.

Worldes Blis   Peter Maxwell Davies, 1969.

The orchestral work was inspired by, and takes its title from, a sentence in a 13th-century monody: "worldes blis lasts no time at all"

Wotan's Farewell   Richard Wagner, 1876.

The name is usually given to the scene closing *Die Walküre* in Der **Ring des Nibelungen**, in which Wotan takes his leave of the sleeping Brünnhilde, whom he has laid on a fire-girt rock.

Wozzeck   Alban Berg, 1925.

The opera in three acts is set to the composer's own libretto based on Georg Büchner's drama of the same name (1836). The plot concerns the emotional and physical decline and suicide of the simple soldier named in the title. The story is based on a true incident, reported in contemporary newspaper accounts with the soldier's name spelled *Woyzeck*. The play's title is thus often quoted in this spelling, but not that of the opera.

The Wreckers   Ethel Smyth, 1903–4.

The opera in three acts is set to a French libretto by H.B. Laforestier (pen name of Harry Brewster) based on his own play. The story is set in 18th-century Cornwall and tells what happens when local folk pray for ships to be sent aground on the coast so they can wreck and despoil them. The opera was first performed in 1906 under the equivalent French title, *Les Naufrageurs*, and it was staged later that year in Leipzig under the German title *Strandrecht*. The first English performance was not until 1909.

Das Wunder der Heliane ("The Miracle of Heliane")   Erich Korngold, 1924–6.

The opera in five acts, with a libretto by Hans Kaltneker based on his own unpublished play *Die Heilige* ("The Saint"), is set in the kingdom of a harsh and despotic Ruler, where a Stranger has been imprisoned for bringing joy and hope to the people. The Ruler visits him in jail to tell him that the next day he will be executed. The plot tells what happens when he is later visited by the Ruler's pure and beautiful wife, Heliane, who wishes to comfort him.

Wuthering Heights   Bernard Herrmann, 1943–51.

The opera (lyric drama) in a prologue and four acts is set to a libretto by Lucille Fletcher adapted from Emily Brontë's novel of the same name (1847), telling of the passionate attachment between Cathy Earnshaw and the foundling her family had raised, Heathcliff.

X

Xerxes *see* **Serse**.

Y

Yan Tan Tethera   Harrison Birtwistle, 1983–4.

The "mechanical pastoral" is set to a libretto by Tony Harrison based on a north of England folk tale. The title represents the words of a children's counting-out rhyme, corresponding to "one, two, three". (A count from one to

five in this system goes: "yan, tan, tethera, peth-
era, pip." *Cf.* Welsh *un, dau, tri, pedwar, pump*.)

Yaroslav the Wise (Russian, *Yaroslav
Mudryy*)   Yuly Meytus, 1973.
The opera in three acts is set to a libretto
by A. Vasilyeva based on Ivan Kocherga's dramatic poem of the same name (1946), telling of
Yaroslav I (Yaroslav the Wise) (*c*.978–1054),
grand prince of Kiev (from 1019), who did much
to promote the spread of Christianity in ancient
Russia and who won several notable military victories. The opera includes the respective mar-
riages of Yaroslav's daughters, Elizabeth and
Anna, to Harald III, king of Norway, and Henry
I, king of France.

Yaroslavna   Boris Tishchenko, 1974.
The ballet in three acts, with a libretto and
choreography by Oleg Vinogradov, is based on
the medieval Russian epic *The Tale of Igor's Campaign*, an account of the unsuccessful campaign
of Prince Igor Svyatoslavich against the Polovtsy
in 1185. The story is presented from the angle of
the suffering women at home: Yaroslavna is
Igor's wife. *See also* **Prince Igor**.

The Year 1905 (Russian, *1905 god*)   Dmitry
Shostakovich, 1957.
The Symphony No. 11 in G minor, Op.
103, is a depiction of the 1905 Revolution and
contains many revolutionary songs.

The Yellow Cake Revue   Peter Maxwell
Davies, 1980.
The six cabaret songs for voice and piano
comment on the threat to the ecology and econ-
omy of the Orkney Islands, Scotland, caused by
the mining of uranium ore ("yellow cake").

Yemelyan Pugachov   Marian Koval, 1942.
The opera in five acts, to a libretto by Vasily
Kamensky, centers on the Cossack rebel leader so
named (*c*.1742–1775).

The Yeomen of the Guard   Arthur Sullivan, 1888.
The operetta in two acts, to a libretto by
W.S. Gilbert, tells how Colonel Fairfax, under
sentence of death at the Tower of London on a
trumped-up charge, marries a strolling player,
Elsie Maynard, to preserve his estate and escapes
with the help of Phoebe Meryll, daughter of one
of the Yeomen of the Guard, the warders (jail-
ers) at the Tower. The subtitle is *The Merryman
and His Maid*, meaning Fairfax and Elsie. The
operetta went though several changes of name.
It was originally called *The Tower of London*. This

became *The Tower Warder*, then *The Beefeaters*,
for the traditional nickname of the Yeomen. Sullivan thought this name rather coarse, however,
and *The Yeomen of the Guard* was adopted instead.

Yolanta *see* **Iolanta**.

The Young Guard (Russian, *Molodaya
gvardiya*)   Yuly Meytus, 1947.
The opera in four acts is set to a libretto by
Andrei Malyshko based on Alexander Fadeyev's
novel of the same name (1945) about the activities of the Young Guard (the underground
movement of the Komsomol, or Young Com-
munist League) in Krasnodon, eastern Ukraine,
in their resistance to the occupying German
forces in World War II.

**The Young Person's Guide to the
Orchestra**   Benjamin Britten, 1946.
The orchestral work with speaker, Op. 34,
was originally written for a documentary film,
The Instruments of the Orchestra (1946), in which
a narrator describes the different instruments and
sections of the orchestra and each plays a variation by the composer on a theme from Henry
Purcell's incidental music to the play *Abdelazer*
(1695). The new title was adopted for the work
played on its own, as a composition that could
still be used to introduce young people to the
makeup of an orchestra. It ends in a fugue, as
stated in the alternate title, not approved by the
composer, *Variations and Fugue on a Theme of
Purcell*. *See also* **Fanfare**.

Your Rockaby   Mark-Anthony Turnage,
1993.
The saxophone concerto was partly inspired by Samuel Beckett's female monologue
Rockaby (1982) and bases its title on it.

"Your tiny hand is frozen" *see* **"Che
gelida manina."**

Youth (Russian, *Yunost'*)   Mikhail Chulaki,
1949.
The ballet in four acts (six scenes), with a
libretto by Yuri Slonimsky and choreography by
Boris Fenster, is based on Nikolai Ostrovsky's
novel *How the Steel Was Tempered* (1934), set in
the Russian Civil War. The plot tells how the
children Petya, Dasha, and Dima join two rev-
olutionaries and help them accomplish heroic
deeds.

Z

Zadok the Priest   George Frideric Handel, 1727.

The anthem is the first of the four **Coronation Anthems**. It centers on the priest of the Old Testament who with Nathan the prophet played a decisive part in securing the throne for King Solomon after the death of David. The title represents the anthem's opening words: "Zadok the Priest and Nathan the prophet anointed Solomon King." The work is thus appropriate for a coronation, which involves the anointing of the monarch, and it has been played at almost every British coronation since its composition.

Zaïde   W.A. Mozart, 1779.

The (unfinished) opera in two acts, K 344, is set to a libretto by Johann Andreas Schachtner based on Franz Joseph Sebastiani's libretto *Das Serail* ("The Seraglio") (1779). The story is set in Turkey and tells what happens when Zaïde, the Sultan's favorite, takes pity on Gomatz, the Sultan's European captive, and provides him with money to escape.

Zampa   Ferdinand Hérold, 1831.

The opera in three acts, to a libretto by Anne-Honoré Joseph de Mélesville, is set in 17th-century Sicily and tells how the pirate chieftain, Zampa, attempts to abduct Camilla, the betrothed of Alfonso (who is actually Zampa's brother.) The subtitle is *La Fiancée de marbre* ("The Marble Betrothed"), referring to the marble statue which is inhabited by the spirit of Zampa's former wife, Alice, and which drowns him.

Der Zar läßt sich photographieren ("The czar has his photograph taken")   Kurt Weill, 1928.

The opera in one act, Op. 21, to a libretto by Georg Kaiser, is a satire on anarchist conspiracy and tells how the Czar unwittingly foils his would-be assassins during a trip to Paris.

Zar und Zimmermann ("Czar and Carpenter")   Albert Lortzing, 1837.

The comic opera in three acts is set to the composer's own libretto based on the play *Le Bourgmestre de Sardam* ("The Burgomaster of Saardam") (1818) by Anne-Honoré Joseph de Mélesville, Jean Toussaint Merle, and Eugène Centiran de Boirie. The plot is set in Saardam, Holland, in 1698, and tells how Peter the Great,

czar of Russia, disguised as Peter Michaelov, works in the shipyards to learn nautical trades and there befriends the deserter, Peter Ivanov, in love with the Burgomaster's daughter, Marie. The opera's subtitle is *Die zwei Peter* ("The Two Peters"), referring to the czar and the deserter, and it was first performed in London in 1871 under the title *Peter the Shipwright*.

Der Zarewitsch ("The Czarevich")   Franz Lehár, 1927.

The operetta in three acts is set to a libretto by Béla Jenbach and Heinrich Reichert based on Gabriela Zapolska-Scharlitt's play of the same name. The story is set in St. Petersburg and Naples at the end of the 19th century and tells what happens when, for political reasons, it is arranged for the Czarevich, the heir to the Russian throne, to marry the Princess Militza.

Die Zauberflöte ("The Magic Flute")   W.A. Mozart, 1791.

The opera in two acts, K 620, is set to a libretto by Emanuel Schikaneder based on various sources, including the story *Lulu* in Christoph Martin Wieland's collection of oriental fairy tales *Dschinnistan* ("Djinnistan") (1786) and the Abbé Jean Terrasson's novel *Sethos* (1731). The plot is set in ancient Egypt and centers on the prince, Tamino, who is provided with a magic flute and the birdcatcher, Papageno, as guide to help him rescue Pamina, daughter of the Queen of the Night, who has been abducted

Die Zauberharfe ("The Magic Harp")   Franz Schubert, 1820.

The music for the (unfinished) opera in three acts, D 644, to a libretto by Georg von Hoffmann, remains only as the overture (now known as **Rosamunde**) and one or two other items.

Zazà   Ruggero Leoncavallo, 1899–1900.

The opera in four acts is set to the composer's own libretto based on Pierre Simon and Charles Berton's play of the same name, telling of the affair between the Parisian music hall singer, Zazà, and Milio Dufresne, a married man-about-town.

"Zeffiretti lusinghieri" ("Little flattering breezes").

Ilia's aria in Act 3 of Mozart's **Idomeneo,** in which she bids the breezes fly to Idamante and tell him of her love.

Zeitmasze ("Tempi")   Karlheinz Stockhausen, 1955–6.

The work is for five woodwind instruments working as five tracks in independent or conjoined tempi. Hence the title.

Zémire et Azor ("Zemir and Azor")   André Grétry, 1771.

The comic opera in four acts is set to a libretto by Jean-François Marmontel based on Pierre Claude Nivelle de la Chaussée's comedy *Amour par amour* ("Love for Love") (1742), itself a version of the *Beauty and the Beast* fairy tale, as told by Charles Perrault in his *Contes de ma mère l'Oye* ("Mother Goose Tales") (1697). Zémire is the equivalent of Beauty, while Azor is the Beast who turns out to be a prince.

Zéphire et Flore ("Zephyr and Flora") Vladimir Dukelsky, 1925.

The ballet in one act, with a libretto by Boris Kochno and choreography by Léonide Massine, is an attempt to reconstruct Charles-Louis Didelot's 18th-century ballet **Flore et Zéphire**.

Der Zigeunerbaron ("The Gypsy Baron") Johann Strauss II, 1885.

The operetta in three acts is set to a libretto by Ignaz Schnitzer based on Maurus Jókai's libretto itself drawn from his own story *Saffi*. The plot is set in mid–18th-century Hungary and tells how Sándor Barinkay returns to claim his ancestral lands and marries a gypsy girl, Saffi, who turns out to be a princess. Barinkay thus becomes the "gypsy baron" of the title.

Zigeunerliebe ("Gypsy Love")   Franz Lehár, 1910.

The operetta in three acts, to a libretto by Robert Bondanzky and Alfred Maria Willner, tells of the love of Zorika, daughter of the landowner, Peter Dragotin, for the handsome young gypsy fiddler, Jozsi, whose tales of gypsy love fill her with romantic longing.

Zigeunerlieder ("Gypsy Songs")   Johannes Brahms, 1887.

The 11 songs for voices and piano, Op. 103, are set to texts adapted by Hugo Conrat from a prose version of Hungarian folk poems by one Fräulein Witzl.

Ziggurat   Karlheinz Stockhausen, 1967.

The ballet in one act, choreographed by Glen Tetley, is set to the composer's **Gesang der Jünglinge** and part of his **Kontakte**. "The *Ziggurat* was a mighty temple-tower of ascending rectilinear terraces built by the Assyrians and worshipped as the earth-soul. It is said to have been the Hanging Gardens of Babylon, perhaps the stairway of Jacob's dream, and the origin of the Tower of Babel" (program note, quoted in Koegler, p. 457).

The Zoo   Arthur Sullivan, 1875.

The operetta in one act, to a libretto by B.C. Stephenson, is set in Regent's Park Zoo, London, and tells what happens when Laetitia is forbidden by her father to marry the apothecary, Aesculapius, who thus plans to hang himself near the zoo's refreshment stall.

Der Zwerg ("The Dwarf")   Alexander Zemlinsky, 1920–1.

The opera in one act is set to a libretto by Georg Klaren based on Oscar Wilde's story *The Birthday of the Infanta* (1889). The story tells what happens when the spoilt Infanta, Donna Clara, is given an ugly dwarf as a birthday present. The opera is also known by the German title of the story, *Der Geburtstag der Infantin*, and this title was adopted in 1981 when the work was revived in Hamburg with a revised libretto closer to Wilde's original.

Gli Zingari ("The Gypsies")   Ruggero Leoncavallo, 1910.

The opera is set to a libretto by Enrico Cavacchioli and Giglielmo Emanuel based on Alexander Pushkin's narrative poem *The Gypsies* (1824), telling what happens when Aleko joins a band of gypsies (*see* **Aleko**).

Die Zwillingsbrüder ("The Twin Brothers") Franz Schubert, 1819.

The operetta in one act, D 647, is set to a libretto by Georg von Hoffmann based on the French vaudeville *Les deux Valentins* ("The Two Valentines"). The story tells how Lieschen, engaged to Anton, had earlier been promised to Franz Spiess if he returned in time from the Foreign Legion. He does, and claims her, but in the meantime his twin brother, Friedrich, long believed dead, arrives and blesses Lieschen's marriage with Anton.

Zyklus ("Cycle")   Karlheinz Stockhausen, 1959.

The work is for a solo percussionist who stands in the middle of his or her instruments and makes a circuit ("cycle") of them, beginning at any of various points.

BIBLIOGRAPHY

Anderson, James. *Bloomsbury Dictionary of Opera and Operetta*. London: Bloomsbury, 1989.

Arnold, Denis, gen. ed. *The New Oxford Companion to Music*. Oxford: Oxford University Press, 1983. 2 vols.

Barlow, Harold, and Sam Morgenstern, comps. *A Dictionary of Musical Themes*. London: Faber and Faber, 1983.

Berkowitz, Freda Pastor. *Popular Titles and Subtitles of Musical Compositions*. Metuchen, NJ: Scarecrow Press, 2d ed., 1975.

Blom, Eric, comp. *Everyman's Dictionary of Music*. With revisions and additions by Sir Jack Westrup. London: J.M. Dent, rev. ed., 1964.

Boyden, Matthew. *Opera: The Rough Guide*. London: Rough Guides, 1997.

Bowman, Walter P. "Musical Names: The Titles of Symphonies," in E. Wallace McMullen, ed., *Names New and Old: Papers of the Names Institute*. Madison, NJ: Penny Press, 1993.

Brewer, E. Cobham. *Authors and their Works with Dates: Being the Three Appendices to "The Reader's Handbook"*. London: Chatto and Windus, 1884. [Appendix III of this work is "Authors and Dates of Dramas and Operas"]

Brown, James D. *Biographical Dictionary of Musicians*. Paisley: Alexander Gardner, 1886.

Buluchevsky, Yury, and Vitaly Fomin. *Kratkiy muzykal'nyy slovar' dlya uchashchikhsya* [*Concise Musical Dictionary for Students*]. Leningrad: Muzyka, 5th ed., 1980.

Burke, John. *Musical Landscapes*. Exeter: Webb & Bower, 1983.

Cooper, Martin (ed.). *The Concise Encyclopedia of Music and Musicians*. London: Hutchinson, 4th (rev.) ed., 1978.

Dearling, Robert, and Celia Dearling, with Brian Rust. *The Guinness Book of Music Facts and Feats*. Enfield: Guinness Superlatives, 1976.

Downes, Edward. *Everyman's Guide to Orchestral Music*. London: J.M. Dent, 1978.

Harewood, The Earl of, and Antony Peattie, eds. *The New Kobbé's Opera Book*. London: Ebury Press, 11th ed., 1997.

Gammond, Peter. *The Oxford Companion to Popular Music*. Oxford: Oxford University Press, 1991.

Gilder, Eric. *Dictionary of Composers and Their Music*. London: Warner Books, 2d ed., 1993.

Glasser, Professor Stanley. *Classic fM A-Z of Classical Music*. London: Headline, 1994.

Gozenpud, Abram. *Kratkiy opernyy slovar'* [*Concise Dictionary of Opera*]. Kiev: Muzichna Ukraïna, 1986.

Griffiths, Paul. *A Concise History of Modern Music*. London: Thames and Hudson, 1978.

_____. *The Thames and Hudson Dictionary of 20th-Century Music*. London: Thames and Hudson, 1996.

Isaacs, Alan, and Elizabeth Martin, eds. *Dictionary of Music*. London: Hamlyn, 1982.

Jacobs, Arthur. *The Penguin Dictionary of Musical Performers*. London: Viking, 1990.

Kennedy, Michael. *The Concise Oxford Dictionary of Music*. Oxford: Oxford University Press, 4th ed., 1996.

_____. *The Oxford Dictionary of Music*. Oxford: Oxford University Press, 2d ed., 1994.

Koegler, Horst. *The Concise Oxford Dictionary of Ballet*. Oxford: Oxford University Press, 2d ed., 1987.

Kupferberg, Herbert. *The Book of Classical Music Lists*. New York: Facts On File, 1985.

Lubbock, Mark. *The Complete Book of Light Opera*. London: Putnam, 1962.

Nicholas, Jeremy. *The Classic fM Guide to Classical Music*. London: Pavilion Books, 1996.

The Opera Libretto Library: The Authentic Texts of the German, French, and Italian Operas with Music of the Principal Airs. New York: Avenel Books, 1980.

Osborne, Charles. *The Dictionary of Opera*. London: Macdonald, 1983.

Parsons, Denys, comp. *The Directory of Tunes and Musical Themes*. Cambridge: Spencer Brown, 1975.

Ranson, Phil. *By Any Other Name: A Guide to the Popular Names and Nicknames of Classical Music, and to Theme Music in Films, Radio, Television and Broadcast Advertisements*. Newcastle upon Tyne: Northern Regional Library System, 5th ed., 1984.

Sadie, Stanley, ed. *The New Grove Dictionary of Music and Musicians*. London: Macmillan, 1980. 20 vols.

_____, and Alison Latham, eds. *The Cambridge Music Guide*. Cambridge: Cambridge University Press, 1985.

Scholes, Percy A. *The Oxford Companion to Music*. Oxford: Oxford University Press, 10th ed., 1970. [Especially entry *Nicknamed Compositions*, pp. 677-83]

Soleil, Jean Jacques, and Guy Lelong. *Les œuvres-clés de la musique*. Paris: Bordas, 1988.

Staines, Joe, and Jonathan Buckley, eds. *The Rough Guide to Classical Music: An A-Z of Composers, Key Works and Top Recordings*. London: Rough Guides, 2d ed., 1998.

Vaynkop, Yulian, and Izrail Gusin. *Kratkiy biograficheskiy slovar' kompozitorov* [*Concise Biographical Dictionary of Composers*]. Leningrad: Muzyka, 4th ed., 1979.

Warrack, John, and Ewan West. *The Oxford Dictionary of Opera*. Oxford: Oxford University Press, 1992.

Whittall, Arnold. *Music since the First World War*. London: J.M. Dent, 1977.

INDEX OF COMPOSERS

This Index gives the page(s) where titles of works by individual or joint composers will be found. If more than one work appears on the page, the number of occurrences appears in parentheses, as for Alban Berg, the composer of two works on p. 160. Joint composers are individually listed only when their names appear in the entry's first paragraph (following the title), as for Niels Gade and J.P.E. Hartmann, both named as composers of A Folk Tale (p. 101). Composers described as "various" and mentioned in the second paragraph, as for La Marquise de Brinvillers (p. 166), are not included in the Index. Nor are arrangers, even if named in the first paragraph, as for the purpose of the titles in question they are not properly composers. They may, of course, appear elsewhere as composers in their own right. Thus George Crumb, arranger of Offenbach's music for Offenbach in the Underworld, is not indexed for that title (p. 190) but he is for his own works on pp. 18 and 163.